The War Was You and Me

The War Was You and Me

CIVILIANS IN THE AMERICAN CIVIL WAR

➤

Joan E. Cashin, Editor

PRINCETON UNIVERSITY PRESS

PRINCETON AND OXFORD

Library of Congress Cataloging-in-Publication Data

The war was you and me : civilians in the American Civil War / Joan E. Cashin, editor.
   p. cm.
  Includes bibliographical references and index.
  ISBN 0-691-09173-0 (alk. paper) — ISBN 0-691-09174-9 (pbk. : alk. paper)
   1. United States—History—Civil War, 1861–1865—Social aspects. 2. United
States—Social conditions—To 1865. 3. United States—History—Civil War,
1861–1865—Influence. I. Cashin, Joan E.

E468.9 .W28 2002
973.7'1—dc21   2001036869

British Library Cataloging-in-Publication Data is available

The war (that war so bloody and grim,

the war I will henceforth forget)

was you and me.

— WALT WHITMAN

Table of Contents

Editor's Acknowledgments   ix

Editor's Introduction   1
JOAN E. CASHIN

PART ONE ✦ *The South*

1. Of Bells, Booms, Sounds, and Silences: Listening to the Civil War South   9
   MARK M. SMITH

2. A Compound of Wonderful Potency: Women Teachers of the North in the Civil War South   35
   NINA SILBER

3. Slaves, Emancipation, and the Powers of War: Views from the Natchez District of Mississippi   60
   ANTHONY E. KAYE

4. Hearth, Home, and Family in the Fredericksburg Campaign   85
   GEORGE C. RABLE

5. The Uncertainty of Life: A Profile of Virginia's Civil War Widows   112
   ROBERT KENZER

6. Race, Memory, and Masculinity: Black Veterans Recall the Civil War   136
   W. FITZHUGH BRUNDAGE

PART TWO ✦ *The North*

7. An Inspiration to Work: Anna Elizabeth Dickinson, Public Orator   159
   J. MATTHEW GALLMAN

8. We Are Coming, Father Abraham—Eventually: The Problem of Northern Nationalism in the Pennsylvania Recruiting Drives of 1862   183
   WILLIAM BLAIR

9. Living on the Fault Line: African American Civilians and
    the Gettysburg Campaign   209
    MARGARET S. CREIGHTON

10. Cannonballs and Books: Reading and the Disruption of Social
    Ties on the New England Home Front   237
    RONALD J. ZBORAY AND MARY SARACINO ZBORAY

11. Deserters, Civilians, and Draft Resistance in the North   262
    JOAN E. CASHIN

12. Mary Surratt and the Plot to Assassinate Abraham Lincoln   286
    ELIZABETH D. LEONARD

PART THREE ✦ *The Border Regions*

13. On the Border: White Children and the Politics of War
    in Maryland   313
    PETER W. BARDAGLIO

14. Duty, Country, Race, and Party: The Evans Family of Ohio   332
    JOSEPH T. GLATTHAAR

15. Union Father, Rebel Son: Families and the Question of
    Civil War Loyalty   358
    AMY E. MURRELL

    About the Contributors   393

    Index   395

    ILLUSTRATIONS FOLLOW P. 208

Editor's Acknowledgments

✦ THIS BOOK is truly a collaborative effort, and I am delighted to thank the individuals who kindly helped me put it together. Gary Arnold of the Ohio Historical Society, Michael Meier of the National Archives, and Barbara DeWolfe and Don Wilcox of the William L. Clements Library at the University of Michigan generously assisted in locating documents and photographs. Megan Real was an unflagging research assistant, and Dave Johnson's computer wizardry was essential in preparing the volume for the publisher. Once again, I am grateful to Daniel Kornstein for his learned counsel and good advice.

Thomas LeBien, my superb editor at Princeton University Press, deserves special thanks. He shared our vision of the book, made astute editorial suggestions, and then steered it smoothly through production. I could not have asked for a better editor. I also appreciated the expertise of the capable staff at the Press, especially Linny Schenck and Maura Roessner. The contributors, all of them consummate professionals, were a pleasure to work with and talk to about history.

The War Was You and Me

Editor's Introduction

JOAN E. CASHIN

➤ WALT WHITMAN, a civilian who worked as a U.S. army nurse during the Civil War, wrote about the mighty conflict for the rest of his life, trying repeatedly in poetry and prose to fathom its impact on the country. Soon after the war closed, he penned the lines that form this book's epigraph while visiting Lake Ontario, far from the scene of any battle. The quote is truly Whitmanesque in its acuity. He understood that the war involved all of the American people in its historic sweep, in the suffering and hardship it caused, and the solemn issues at stake, and he anticipated the furious debate over how it would be remembered. The scholarship on the war is enormous, larger than any other period in the nation's history, and the literature includes many excellent titles on military history, biographies of famous politicians and generals, and work on soldiers in the ranks.[1] Some outstanding scholarship has appeared on what might be broadly described as the war's social history, regarding women's lives during the conflict, internal dissent within the South, and the Federal army's occupation of the Confederacy, while some biographies of prominent reformers include chapters on the war, and several community studies focus on the conflict.[2] But in the last dozen years only two volumes of essays have concentrated on civilians. In a collection edited by Maris Vinoskis in 1990, the authors skillfully examine the war's impact on the demography of the American population, the economy, and life in Northern communities. In a book edited by Catherine Clinton and Nina Silber in 1992, those authors analyze with equal skill how gender relations changed throughout the country. Both collections are filled with path-breaking work, highly accomplished essays that illuminate much about the civilian experience.[3]

Despite the multiple contributions of these books, there is still a great deal to discover about civilian life. Noncombatants constituted the majority of the nation's population, including the male population, and they provided much of the material supplies, financial resources, and information necessary to fight the war. Civilians also played a central role in the public discourse over the war's direction and larger meaning, debating each other and the men in the field. Furthermore, the unpredictable pace of battle sometimes blurred the line between soldier and noncombatant, as the fighting rolled across the Southern landscape (and in a few instances into the border states and the North) and uprooted thousands of people of both races. We do not know nearly enough about the people at the heart of the struggle, African Americans, most of whom were of course civilians.[4]

This scholarly neglect is all the more striking in light of the inherent drama of the civilian experience. Southerners black and white lived through the breakup of their basic social and economic institutions, while Northerners of both races witnessed the reorganization of much of civilian society to fight the war, even as citizens of the border regions grappled with elemental questions of loyalty that reached into the family itself. The war inspired a host of innovations in American culture, in everything from public oratory to mourning customs. These transformations worked themselves out in the destinies of thousands of civilians in ways that scholars have scarcely begun to explore.

Fortunately for historians, the archives are bursting with documentation on this subject. Many civilians were self-conscious about the war's significance and produced a tidal wave of letters and journals, even as soldiers described numerous interactions with civilians in their writings, while hundreds of people left memoirs, published and unpublished, after the war ended. The national, state, and local governments created a tremendous body of records on civilians, including but not restricted to the Southern Claims Commission, the Freedmen's Bureau Papers, pension files, the Dun and Bradstreet credit reports, the veterans' census of 1890, and the WPA Narratives. Scholars have yet to exploit fully the nation's newspapers or the massive photographic record for what they reveal civilians.[5]

The essays in this book, which are all based on original research, add abundantly to our knowledge of the war. They treat men, women, and children, blacks and whites, from working-class, middle-class, and affluent backgrounds; some articles examine specific events, some discuss particular communities, and others take a biographical approach. They do not concern the "home front" per se, since we focus not on one geographic place but on civilians all over the country, from California to New England. Two essays provide fresh perspectives on the war's premiere events, the Battle of Gettysburg and the Lincoln assassination, one by describing free blacks who were kidnapped into slavery during the famous battle, and the other by raising new questions about Mary Surratt's guilt. Despite the impressive variety of sources, methods, and arguments, some principal themes emerge.

Family and Community   The war threatened social bonds in the North and the border states, as well as the South. These disruptions are visible in the community resistance to the draft, bolstered by political opposition, in the North; in the white families from border regions who were divided by the war, literally father against son; in one white family's blunt exchanges about their son's service with a black army unit; and in the speed with which the war politicized teenagers and children, including very young children, in a border state. This conflict pitted siblings and generations against each other, and before it was done shook the family, the fundamental social unit, to its core.

Gender   The war unsettled, undermined, and sometimes destroyed traditional gender roles, in all regions, forcing people to reconsider their assumptions about appropriate behavior for men and women of both races. This is manifest in disputes between female teachers and army officials regarding the treatment of newly emancipated Southern blacks; the phenomenal career of the first professional fund-raiser in American history, a white woman affiliated with the Republican Party; and the desperate struggles of Confederate widows in the wartime and postwar South. Some people welcomed these changes, some deplored them, and many may have perceived them as another example of the war's unintended consequences.

Culture   In the North, the South, and the border states, the conflict changed the way people experienced the aesthetic, in the many new sounds generated by the war — the sounds of battle, preparation for battle, and the aftermath of battle — and the plethora of new things to read. At the same time, the war recast familiar cultural symbols, such as the images of home, idealized but all the more hypnotic, that figured in the minds of Union soldiers. After Appomattox, the war echoed in American culture for decades as civilians engaged in a fierce contest over what should be honored and what should be forgotten about the war narrative.

Race   Not everything changed during the war, however, and the ambivalence among white Northerners about abolition, and the countrywide opposition to racial equality, foreshadow the failure of Reconstruction. Warning signs abounded in the uneasy relations between escaped slaves and Yankee soldiers in Mississippi and elsewhere; in the white men who deserted the Union army rather than fight for Emancipation, and the white civilians who assisted them; and the great difficulty black Union veterans had in obtaining national recognition for their part in the war effort, recognition that was many years in the coming.

Family, community, gender, culture, and race represent important areas of historical inquiry, and as these fields evolve, we may pursue yet other inquiries. What about the ethnic Americans, the Irish and the Germans who arrived on these shores in the 1840s and 1850s? In both the Union and the Confederacy, they were suspected as disloyal, yet we do not know very much about their views of the fight. And what about émigrés from central and eastern Europe, such as the young Joseph Pulitzer, who arrived in the Union during the war and decided to join up? Second, let us ponder how the war modified the nature of fame, making individuals such as Frederick Douglass, already well known among activists, recognizable to a mass audience. What did celebrities who had hitherto lived in obscurity, such as Belle Boyd, make of their new-found fame? How do we account for the seemingly bottomless public demand for images of and information about these personalities? Finally, there is the matter of relations between veterans and civilians after the war. In many households, civilians could not always comprehend what soldiers had been through, and ex-soldiers could not grasp completely how much life at home had been transformed. How did civilian society change after 1865, when thousands of veterans came home?[6]

As Whitman suggested long ago, the Civil War changed almost every civilian who lived through it. This story, spellbinding in its drama and staggering in its complexity, has just begun to be told.

Notes

1. James E. Miller Jr., ed., *Complete Poetry and Selected Prose by Walt Whitman* (Boston, 1959), 250. Among many titles in this huge literature, see Brooks D. Simpson, *Ulysses S. Grant: Triumph Over Adversity* (Boston, 2000); Gary W. Gallagher, *Lee and His Generals in War and Memory* (Baton Rouge, 1998); David Herbert Donald, *Lincoln* (New York, 1995); Emory M. Thomas, *Robert E. Lee: A Biography* (New York, 1995); Joseph T. Glatthaar, *Forged in Battle: The Civil War Alliance of Black Soldiers and White Officers* (New York, 1990); Reid Mitchell, *Civil War Soldiers* (New York, 1988). James M. McPherson, *Battle Cry of Freedom: The Civil War Era* (New York, 1988), remains the best one-volume history of the entire war.

2. Drew Gilpin Faust, *Mothers of Invention: Women of the Slaveholding South in the American Civil War* (Chapel Hill, 1996); Noel C. Fisher, *War at Every Door: Partisan Politics and Guerilla Violence in East Tennessee, 1860–1869* (Chapel Hill, 1997); Stephen V. Ash, *When the Yankees Came: Conflict and Chaos in the Occupied South, 1861–1865* (Chapel Hill, 1995); Charles Royster, *The Destructive War: William Tecumseh Sherman, Stonewall Jackson, and the Americans* (New York, 1991); Thomas J. Brown, *Dorothea Dix: New England Reformer* (Cambridge, Mass., 1998); Wayne K. Durrill, *War of Another Kind: A Southern Community in the Great Rebellion* (New York, 1990). For a full discussion of the historiography, see James M. McPherson and William J. Cooper Jr., eds., *Writing the Civil War: The Quest to Understand* (Columbia, 1998).

3. Maris Vinovskis, ed., *Toward a Social History of the American Civil War:*

Exploratory Essays (Cambridge, 1990); Catherine Clinton and Nina Silber, eds., *Divided Houses: Gender and the Civil War* (New York, 1992).

4. Philip S. Paludan, *"A People's Contest": The Union and Civil War, 1861– 1865* (New York, 1988); Randall C. Jimerson, *The Private Civil War: Popular Thought during the Sectional Conflict* (Baton Rouge, 1988); Noralee Frankel, *Freedom's Women: Black Women and Families in Civil War Era Mississippi* (Bloomington, 1999); Leslie A. Schwalm, *A Hard Fight for We: Women's Transition from Slavery to Freedom in South Carolina* (Urbana, 1997).

5. For civilians in other wars, see Omer Bartov, *Mirrors of Destruction: War, Genocide, and Modern Identity* (New York, 2000); Cecil D. Eby, *Hungary at War: Civilians and Soldiers in World War II* (University Park, Pa., 1998); Peter Goldman and Tony Fuller, *Charlie Company: What Vietnam Did to Us* (New York, 1983).

6. For pioneering work on these topics, see Thomas H. O'Connor, *Civil War Boston: Home Front and Battlefield* (Boston, 1997); Mary Panzer, *Mathew Brady and the Image of History*, with an essay by Jeana K. Brady (Washington, D.C., 1997); Michael Fellman, *Citizen Sherman: A Life of William Tecumseh Sherman* (New York, 1995); Eric T. Dean Jr., *Shook Over Hell: Post-Traumatic Stress, Vietnam, and the Civil War* (Cambridge, Mass., 1997); Stuart McConnell, *Glorious Contentment: The Grand Army of the Republic, 1865–1900* (Chapel Hill, 1992).

PART ONE ✈ *The South*

Chapter 1

Of Bells, Booms, Sounds, and Silences: Listening to the Civil War South

MARK M. SMITH

Heard Pasts?

Whatever else it was, the American Civil War was noisy, cacophonous, and decidedly loud. Union and Confederate soldiers spoke endlessly about "the roar and din of the artillery" and confessed that shells "pass over us with a sound that makes our flesh crawl." Talk of "cannon balls whizzing & bursting over our heads" was common enough to have worked its way quietly into the titles of books on the military history of the war. For all of this implicit recognition of the noises of war, though, we know little about how soldiers perceived and reacted to battlefield soundscapes. Unsurprisingly, then, our knowledge of the perception of sounds and the ways that they affected and were comprehended by civilians on the Civil War home front is even less developed. It is, in fact, shockingly sparse.[1]

The relative absence of historical inquiry into Civil War soundscapes is quite in keeping with the vast majority of historical work on nineteenth-century America. Inclined to examine the past through the eyes rather than the ears of historical actors, historians have tended not to listen to (and, ergo, not hear) the heard worlds of the past. There is no compelling reason for this deafness. I suspect that the revolution in print in the eighteenth and nineteenth centuries, the assumed ascendancy of vision in the antebellum period, and our modern tendency to privilege sight over sound have inclined us to expect historical actors to appreciate and wring meaning from their worlds visually rather than aurally.[2]

This assumption is, of course, quite incorrect: elites and nonelites alike in the nineteenth century understood their worlds by hearing and listening as much as they did by seeing and looking.[3] Indeed, the heard world provided all nineteenth-century Americans with important metaphorical and literal information about the nature of their societies and themselves. Elites, for example, heard social order during the course of everyday interaction and, simultaneously, at an abstracted level. Ruling classes, North and South, agreed on much when it came to perceiving and shaping their heard environments. Both vested profound meaning in, for example, the ringing of bells to mark national and local celebrations, signal alarms, regulate labor, toll deaths, summon parishioners, and locate themselves and their societies in time and space. They also agreed that industrious activity hummed happily and that economic recession was disturbingly silent.[4]

There were, though, important differences separating how antebellum ruling classes in both sections constructed one another. Northern elites embraced the hum of industry and a qualified pulse of democracy while Southern masters countered with an acoustic construction that embraced the pulse of industriousness, not industrialism or the noise of wage labor; one that stressed the quietude of the Southern social order, an order that made tranquillity the proxy for a way of life. Slaveholders wanted quietude, not silence. Silence was, in fact, dangerous and closely associated with plotting bondpeople. Quietude was slaveholders' preferred register, for it provided a soundscape that was pastoral and connoted a particular set of social and economic relations in which slavery was literally and metaphorically in harmony with a rural, socially conservative soundscape. This was both an idealized and actual world where masters were determined to control the production and consumption of sounds and noises. Thus, slaveholders embraced the sounds of industriousness as an index of their society's economic productivity but rejected the noise of industrialism because it was a talisman for liberal, not conservative, capitalism.[5]

The argument that consciousness of place and identity were constructed and shaped through the heard world is perfectly consistent with the little theoretical work done on historical soundscape studies. R. Murray Schafer uses the term "keynote sounds" for those sounds that imprint "themselves so deeply on the people hearing them that life without them would be sensed as a distinct impoverishment." While these keynotes or soundmarks are created by, among other factors, "geography and climate," they are also produced by specific cultural, social, and economic relations. Slavery, as a mode of production, had a particular and meaningful keynote to antebellum slaveholders; for northern elites, the sound of democratic capitalism and industry had its own soundmark. "[O]nce a soundmark has been identified, it deserves," argues Schafer, "to be protected, for soundmarks make the acoustic life of the community unique." Sounds, then, serve as anchors to regions, as acoustic identifiers of community, and, as a result, if those soundscapes or soundmarks are threatened by other, alien sounds, communities interpret those sounds as noise and as threats to their identities and ways of life. This is precisely what happened in the years leading up to civil war.[6] The antebellum sectional and, in fact, intrasectional contest in preserving and shaping sectional keynotes continued during the war itself. One way to understand the unfolding and meaning of that contest is to listen to how Southerners on the home front heard the war and its meaning. All of this listening and hearing, of course, occurred in a context defined by the gravest Constitutional issues and many thousands of deaths at home and on field. These critically important matters were themselves inscribed with aural meanings and helped shaped how and which events were heard.

Listening to how various Southern constituencies heard the Civil War is important for (at least) three reasons. First, listening to the heard war muddies the tidy distinction some historians have made about the separateness of home and battlefield and contributes to a more recent emphasis stressing the conceptual necessity of blending of the two, particularly when trying to understand the Confederacy.[7] Second, particular Southern constituencies constructed the soundscapes of the Civil War differently. There were, in effect, multiple acoustic home fronts during the war, and they were contingent on time, place, and status. And, third, listening to actual and perceived soundscapes in the Civil War South suggests how, in addition to all the other well-known contradictions that wilted the Southern will to prosecute the war, the introduction of new noises and the muting of old sounds probably helped erode Confederates' long-term commitment and ability to resist their noisy Northern enemy.[8] Unlike Northerners, who found the fewer new noises generated by the war perfectly compatible with their imagined and preferred future, Southern elites experienced new and deeply troubling noises and silences. While mobilization in the North was, for the most part, in harmony with their idealized and actual industrial, free-labor soundscape, gearing up for war in the South quickly became too Northern for many white Southern tastes. Because the actual sounds of war were far fainter in the North, there was much less adjustment to make than in the South where noises of battle and strife increasingly encroached on the Southern, tranquil, idealized home front. In the end, such radical changes in the Southern soundscape, while inspiring feverish resistance and even a degree of accommodation in the first instance, probably had the effect of enervating the Southern will to win not just because of the new noises inaugurated by the war but also because this conflagration muted traditional Southern sounds. Although sometimes unintended, sound itself became part of psychological warfare on the Confederate home front. For other Southern constituencies, slaves in particular, the sounds of war were the welcomed notes of freedom.

An exploration of these three issues allows us not merely to appreciate a hitherto neglected dimension of the war but sharpens our understanding of how various Southern constituencies attached multiple meanings to the significance of the sectional conflict. To be sure, those fighting the war heard the tumult of battle, the noise of military loss, and the sound of victory. But, and as this essay is dedicated to demonstrating, we need to venture beyond the noise of war on the battlefield and examine the aural world of the Confederate home front in order to appreciate the full complexity of Southern understandings of the war. Sounds of war and noises of military encounter were not spatially delimited: noises, shrieks, cannonading, and a host of other sounds echoed, literally and figuratively, on the home front, thus joining southern home front and battlefield acoustically and metaphorically. The combined effects of the war generally created what white Southerners in part heard as the silence of economic, social, and political ruin in the South, a silence that gained literal and metaphorical power through the South's loss of bells during the conflict.

The essay concludes with an examination of the aural worlds of the enslaved during the war. Slaves, too, heard the noises and silences of the war. But, unlike their masters and mistresses, they used and understood these sounds differently and impregnated them with alternative meanings. For many ex-slaves interviewed in the 1930s, memories of the war were aural and what they heard at the time proved useful. Slaves during the Civil War listened hard to the blending of military and plantation soundscapes in order to ascertain the location of Union troops and flee to freedom. They also measured freedom itself in aural terms. While Confederates lamented the silence of defeat, the loss of many of their soundmarks, and what they perceived as the impending cacophony of black independence, ex-slaves, not unlike antebellum abolitionists, celebrated the sound of freedom's bell. Freedpeople made their freedom heard and they reconfigured the hated noise of the plantation bell into an icon that proclaimed the sound of Emancipation and the silencing of slavery.

Earwitnessing Home Front(s)

The greatest changes to the Northern soundscape inaugurated by the Civil War were more of degree and less of kind. Sounds of war and sounds of home mingled in cities where Union forces prepared for war, the cadence of accelerated industrialization feeding into a long-held respect for the sound of industrial capitalism. Home to the army's transportation bureau during the war, Washington, D.C., hummed with industrial life preparing for others' military deaths. By 1863 "the streets resound with the deafening rumble of heavy wagons." The "Horseshoeing [sic] Establishment" was loud but its timbre was reassuring to those anxious for both military and ideological victory: "Two hundred men . . . beating out an anvil chorus that rings in a deafening peal upon the ear, and dies away over the housetops and across the placid river in a soft, melodious chime, like the music of the bells . . . the roar of the bellows sounds like the rush of a tempest sweeping upon a forest." Whatever changes the war introduced to the Northern soundscape, it also left much of it intact. Preparations for battle and occasional Confederate advances notwithstanding, the Northern soundscape generally experienced an amplified continuity that most found acceptable.[9]

Unlike the majority of Northern civilians, most Southerners on the home front came to hear the war literally as well as metaphorically. For them, the Civil War was an acoustic hemorrhaging, the end of a way of life that had invested in social quietude and tranquility. The master class found it increasingly difficult to control and contain the soundscape of the Civil War South, especially as the war went on and Union forces invaded, bringing with them sounds of freedom and industrial might, noises planters had long loathed.

Confederate soundscapes obviously depended not just on how sounds from the past were remembered and conceptualized metaphorically but, in a more immediate sense, on the extent of Union advance in particular regions of the Confederacy. The coming of Union noises and the sounds of war was important for reaffirming the Confederate commitment to their heard pasts as well as for counterpointing how very new, different, and disruptive the present sounded or, in some instances, did not sound. For most Southerners, the initial phases of the war were quiet and more reminiscent of the Old South than of the new noisy one that was their future. Witness the early wartime correspondence of Savannah River rice planter Louis Manigault. In late March 1861, sounds usual prevailed. "Mr Capers tells me all things are going on well on the plantation," wrote Manigault to his father. "I find thus far all very quiet, and we will occupy ourselves in Threshing the Crop." In fact, the Confederate soundscape sounded utterly normal and peaceful, not warlike: "Macon," commented Manigault, "is quite a pretty Town, of about Ten Thousand inhabitants, and it is quiet there as if we were still a part of the United States." By November, strains of war were still distant and were nowhere near loud or alien enough to drown out the happy hum of Manigault's industrious plantation or disrupt the tranquility of slave labor. "[O]ur people are working well and Cheerfully," wrote Manigault, elaborating, "I yesterday rode over the entire plantation with Mr Capers, and I have no reason to complain of any thing. In every direction the steam of the various Threshers indicated that the usual plantation work was going on. . . . it is difficult to realize, in the midst of our quietude, that *nearly* within sight, on Daufuskie Island, the Yankees have entered Mr Stoddard's House."[10]

Little had changed by December. In fact, Manigault was more preoccupied with the customary disruptions to plantation life than he was with the possibility that new forces would interrupt his plantation serenity. At times, Manigault could hardly believe his ears: "Every thing on the plantation, and as far as the eye can reach, is going on in our usual quiet manner," he told his father on December 5, 1861, "and the News Paper . . . alone indicates that we are having troubles in our midst." Be that as it may, Manigault still felt on guard at this time of the year. He explained: "Christmas is always a very bad time for Negroes, and it is always a God-Send (any year, but far more so this) when that Holyday is over, and we all resume our quiet plantation work." But customary plantation quietude was profiled even more sharply in anticipation of the social noise of war and the impending disruption of tranquil plantation order. Extra precautions were therefore taken: "Mr Capers wishes me to mention that the three Negroes now Confined should by no means be allowed at any moment to Converse or see each other."[11]

Even when strains of war began to percolate their home fronts, a good deal of Confederate effort was dedicated to shaping the heard world of their homeland. Slaves, most obviously, continued to have what they said and were permitted to hear regulated and checked. So did suspect whites. A rightly skittish Northerner in Columbia, South Carolina, made both points in early 1861. As Johnson M. Mundy, who helped in the design and construction of Columbia's State House, explained to his sister: "It may . . . prove interesting to you, to have some account of what is said and done in the 'Palmetto State', from one who is an eye and ear witness. . . . Everything about me indicates Revolution. The people cry 'oppression', and 'give me liberty or give me death' is upon every tongue, excepting the *slaves*, who have been taught to fear, and submit to their rightful masters." Mundy felt peculiarly conscious of his own, enforced silence: "You may think that a person from the North would not find himself very much at home surrounded by such elements. And you think rightly. He is under great restraint, as his words and actions are closely watched, lest [he] conflict too strongly with Southern principles." Confederates generally attempted to control the political soundscape of the Confederacy and hoped that the noisy words of Southern Unionists would "be hushed in the din of the conflict and the shouts of a glorious victory."[12]

Yet, the very nature of this particular war meant that Southern soundscapes would change regardless of the immediate military outcome. Victory, for example, required gearing up the South's military might through rapid industrialization. This, in itself, threatened to make the

Confederate soundscape more Northern, more modern. Social quietude, it was hoped, would return with Confederate victory. Loss, though, promised to alter the Southern soundscape permanently, or so it seemed. For surely a defeated South would be remade in the image of a society that coveted the hum of industrialism and liberal democracy?[13]

The physical act of mobilizing for war meant that antebellum Southern metaphors of quietude and serenity came under strain. In some respects, the traditional Southern endorsement of the sound of industriousness proved sufficiently flexible to accommodate the upped volume that accompanied mobilization. Louis Manigault had suggested as much when he alluded to the comforting beat of his steam threshers in 1861. Likewise, Susan Bradford Eppes recalled that the beginning of the war on her Florida plantation sounded initially like a very protracted Sunday. So that the plantation's "white men . . . might enlist, Saturday the mills shut down — the mighty throb of the huge engine ceased — but then it always stopped for Sunday. Monday morning silence still reigned." But reinvention is the mother of necessity and the Union naval blockade and the demands of war generally encouraged planters to introduce "new industries" and accelerate old ones. As a result, "The whirr of the spinning-wheel, the clump, clump of the loom, and the shoe-maker hammering . . . grew to be familiar sounds" on some Civil War plantations. In this way, at home and on field, the Civil War increased in volume. Indeed, beyond Eppes's Pine Hill plantation, the sound of gearing up for war could be heard on neighboring plantations: "Carpenters were called in and new loom patterned. . . . Soon . . . the whirr of the wheel and the noise of the baton could be heard in almost every home."[14] These were satisfying cadences, infused with strains of patriotism, industriousness, and laden with the hope of victory.

Southern comfort with the sound of industriousness, though, was strained by the sheer scale of preparation necessary for the South's effective prosecution of the war. If the Union's long-term intent was in part to inscribe modernity onto the South, then it succeeded not least because the war altered the South's soundscape and enfranchised not only new sounds but upped the volume of old ones. Even at the beginning of the war, in Richmond correspondents noted how preparations for battle had increased noise levels literally and figuratively and altered social timbre by accelerating industrialization. Richmond was "amid all the tumult and bustle of war. . . . The clatter of military trappings, the rattle of heavy freight wagons and the measured tap of the drum constitute the music of our times," reported one observer. Even the Southern nocturnal soundscape, so long the idealized refuge of quietude, was disrupted: "At night most of our citizens retire into their dwellings. . . .

The shrill whistle of the locomotive during the still hours announces the arrival of more troops."[15]

An increase in social noise was also discernable. Although George Fitzhugh heard the strains of revolution in the North and chortled in 1862 that the "mob rules despotically among our enemies" he also heard "the senseless clamor of home-keeping people," slaves and women presumably, in the Confederacy itself. Voices of protest grew louder, especially from traditionally quieter Southern constituencies such as elite women. Northerners in the South at the beginning of the war confirmed the increased volume and shift in timbre. A *New York Herald* reporter noted on a trip from Richmond to Nashville in November 1861 the noisiness of the Southern people: "The contrast between the South and the North . . . is most remarkable. When I come into the Northern States I find the people pursuing their usual peaceful avocations, without any apparent disturbance or interruption, as if the blast of war had never sounded in their ears," which, of course, it had not, literally, for most. Go south, though, and "War is on every tongue. . . . Day and night you hear nothing but war shouts."[16] In some regions of the Confederacy, the pressures of war, even as early 1861, were beginning to alter a Southern soundscape that had invested profound meaning in the social and political value of quietude.

Cannon booms and blasts meant that sounds of war leaked physically and metaphorically into and onto the civilian home front. Initially, civilians listened actively for the new and novel strains of Mars in their own backyards. They were not disappointed. The roar of Union naval attacks on Port Royal in November 1861 spilled into listening ears in Charleston: "Yesterday evening the attack commenced at Port Royal and during the day there were numbers of persons gathered together on the battery listening to the booming of the cannon which tho' faint could be distinctly heard." To be sure, fancied some in early 1863, delicious bites of Confederate victory could be heard from field and sea. Charleston's harbor accentuated sounds of Confederate victory. Sounds of "firing rolled round the harbor in one incessant din." They could also be heard from land: "West, the fierce struggle for the Mississippi Valley is at last begun," reported the *Charleston Mercury* in 1863, "and, amidst the din and tumult of the unequal contest, we think we can distinguish the shouts of victory. Doubt and discord reign in the councils of our enemies. With us, all is confidence." Successful battles and, indeed, the winning of the war itself, would be heard, according to a Georgia volunteer in 1862. "[V]ictory," he maintained, "shall be resounded to all nations of the earth."[17]

As war progressed, choices narrowed and the liberty of selective listening gave way to enforced hearing. Without ear-lids, Southern civilians, at least those near enough to military action, found that they had no choice but to hear the sickening thud of Confederate defeat. Not only would they never hear the sweet strains of ultimate victory but the process of defeat altered in profound and meaningful ways the Southern soundscape. Sometimes, Southerners did not have to wait long for those changes. Sounds of war came quickly to Virginia, for example. As one correspondent for the *Charleston Mercury* wrote from Charlottesville in August 1861: "The dull rumble of the ambulances, bringing in the sick and wounded from the front, echoes on the hillside."[18]

Southerners on the home front, then, did not always have to see the war to know that it was happening or interpret its meaning. Plainly, sounds of the sick, the injured, and the dying — all intimately tied to the blasts of cannon — scared Southern civilians. Many of them heard these noises and came to resent the nervousness that booms and blasts caused them, not simply because such noises were the harbingers of physical pain but also because they disrupted social and aural registers. Union and Confederate forces alike generated new sounds and noises, and both came in for criticism from civilians upset with the disruption of their customary keynotes. Charlestonians were particularly resentful of Confederate officers testing the alertness of their troops. When in June 1861 the Confederate commander at Fort Moultrie started "a heavy cannonading, which continued for several hours, [and] was heard in the harbor to see whether our garrisons [at Forts Sumter and Beauregard] were mindful of their duties in the night as well as in the day time," Charlestonians became chagrined at what they considered unnecessary and nerve-wracking noise. As the *Charleston Mercury* commented: "[I]f Col. RIPLEY should continue the discipline, does he not bid fair to rival the fire alarm telegraph, with its ringing of bells, in alarming the community?"[19]

Military sounds threatened the function of civil ones and, in the process, tapped into Southerners' deepest fears. How were urban Confederates supposed to distinguish between sounds of martial war and sounds of civil war? How were they to know when bells signaled military invasion or servile insurrection? Bells, rattles, and miscellaneous aural cues had been used in the Old South to alert whites to slave insurrection. Now those cues were muddled and confused. As a hotel guest in Charleston remarked during a bombardment that "resembled the whirr of a phantom brigade of cavalry, galloping in mid air": "A watchman was running frantically down the street and, when he reached the corner just below me, commenced striking with his staff against the curb — a signal of alarm practiced among the Charleston police." The sounds of war made an already skittish Southern master class even more nervous.[20]

War's sounds could, of course, become incorporated relatively quickly into the evolving Confederate soundscape, even if this incorporation was grudging and temporary. How long, precisely, Confederates were willing to put up with these new noises for the cause of the South, no one quite knew. But put up with them they did, at least for some of the time. In 1864, the *Charleston Mercury* described retrospectively the aural novelty of the first bombardment of that city and, in effect, illustrated how quickly Charlestonians had become accustomed to the noises of war. At a "time when the bombardment was still a novelty to our people," Charlestonians sat awake in the early hours "listening to the monotonous sound of the cannonade kept up on the enemy position from the batteries on James Island." Now, in 1864, such sounds were hardly remarked upon in a dying Confederacy.[21]

The Silence and Noise of Confederate Defeat

Instances of accommodation to the new soundscapes notwithstanding, sounds of war grated against remembered sounds of the Old South. Some people never quite got used to the new timbre. The sounds of government, especially when it quashed sounds of Southern business and commerce, proved particularly aggravating. Late in the war, in Richmond the "rumbling of government wagons monopolized the privilege of making a noise during the day, nearly all other vehicles having been withdrawn from the thoroughfares of business and mercantile operations in a great measure suspended." As late as 1864, Charlestonians complained still of the "strange commingling of sounds," namely, "the soft, sweet tones of the church bells inviting the people to the house of prayer, and the boom of cannon and crash of shells summoning the unfortunate soldier to the dark abodes of eternity. The one was the gentle messenger of peace and life, the other the dread summoner of suffering and death!"[22]

Noisy though Old South cities could be, the sounds of war approached cacophony and offered sure aural testimony to the death of a constructed quiet and serene South and the invasion of a noisy, mobocratic, liberal capitalist North. Fleeing Atlantans in 1864 left behind what sounded like a Yankee Sodom: "Mingling in the air are sounds of the Sabbath bells, the shrieks of a score of locomotives, the rumbling of cars and carts, the shouts of drivers and unceasing hum of a modern Babel. The spectacle is more melancholy than interesting." Southern soundscapes past were drowned by Confederate soundmarks present thanks to the Union war machine. Christmas sounds in Charleston in 1862 were muffled by war's cacophony: "[H]ow the gladsome pealing of our ancient chimes, which were wont to usher in the morn of Nativity, are drowned today in the din of a ruthless war."[23]

Southerners knew that their loss would be heard as much as seen. In Charleston, by 1864 impending loss was heard "in the din of the bombardment." Loss meant noise for Confederate troops and civilians alike after the surrender. They encountered jubilant "drunk Yankees, and they were so noisy" and "drunken soldiers and Negroes carousing, shouting, embracing, and preaching." What they found after the war confirmed long-held fears: restless blacks, slave and free, "cracking whips, throwing stones, and yelling at the tops of their lungs." Captain Benjamin Wesley Justice of Lee's Army of Northern Virginia captured the essence of why Confederates came, by 1864, to loath the noise of war and why, in aural terms, they had fought it in the first place — to preserve their imagined quiet, peaceable, orderly South. As he wrote to his wife in May 1864: "I am heartily sick of blood & the sound of artillery & small arms & the ghastly, pale face of death and all the horrible sights & sounds of war. I long more intensely & earnestly for the sweet rest & quiet of home than ever before."[24]

Everything Confederates feared came true, though not all at once. Even though Northerners must have wondered if their impending victory would stimulate the South to the isms they had hoped, reports from 1865 suggested not. From Savannah, Georgia, little was heard: "In the city all is quiet and as calm as a Sunday morning in a country village," listened a correspondent from the *New York Herald*. Plainly, the "quiet streets," the "talk in low tones" by "Men in all colors" was indicative of an Old South marked by "idleness and a singular lethargy." Only "the resuscitating influences of a band of keen, sharp, wide-awake business men from the North . . . stir them up for a moment." A reporter for the *New York Herald* put his finger on the aural dimension of Union victory in October 1863, should it come to pass. "[I]n the future," he whimsied, "we may make further progress into the heart of the sacred soil, till our cars run into the streets of Richmond, and the dome of the rebel Capitol itself re-echoes the shrill whistles of our proud engines."[25]

Beyond the noise of Union victory, military loss also meant that a blanket of disconcerting silence enveloped the Southern home front. For some, this silence was reminiscent of past tranquilities, real or imagined. Although Charleston's residents had become "accustomed to the howl of rushing shell . . . , [n]ow that quiet and safety are insured they propose to repair and live comfortably once more." A return to the quiet life — and all the meaning that Southern masters attached to that term — was not easily achieved. Silence there was to be sure. Too much so, perhaps. War had destroyed Charleston's commerce so that "the silent streets" no longer hummed with the industriousness and economic vibrancy grounded in slavery. A *New York Herald* reporter, stationed in Port Royal, listened to Beaufort at the end of 1861 and heard only ruin: "The streets of the village were silent . . . The silence of death was over the deserted streets." "The whole country on both sides of the James, the Rappahannock, and the Potomac" by August 1862 "has been reduced to a desert . . . The houses along the road are as silent as death. The inhabitants have fled; the inclosures are all broken down; the windows and doors staved in; the very desolation sits brooding in silence over the land." In 1865, a Union sailor described his "first setting affoot in Charleston" and offered the following assessment of the city: "The lower portion of the city was entirely deserted long before our occupation and its warehouses, mansions, churches hotels &c abandoned to utter solitude and dilapidation. Shells from our Morris Island lodgment dropped almost daily into this part of the town committing havoc at pleasure with masonry & roofs. We see traces of them everywhere." But there were signs of life and confirmation of victory to Northern ears: "Further up, the hum of industry is now started."[26]

Among the most demoralizing losses for Confederate civilians and soldiers alike was their lessened ability to toll their few victories and many losses. Equally aggravating was the Union's continued ability to sound Southern losses for them as well as signal their own stunning victories. "Let us hope," opined the *Charleston Mercury* in July 1863, "that our enemies will never light bonfires, ring their bells, fire cannon and serenade President LINCOLN, at the fall of Charleston."[27] The hope was unrequited.

The importance of bells in shaping the meaning of the outcome of the Civil War may be gauged by looking at how those who retained them used them. Because the Union had less need to melt bell metal for cannon, their celebrations of victory were heard through both bell and cannon. Traditional Northern punctuations of the national year remained and, in fact, were augmented by the war. Having waxed lyrically about prewar Fourth of July celebrations, in 1863 a reporter for the *New York Herald* chortled: "[W]e shall have a new cause for celebrating the day if it is made the anniversary of the beginning of the regeneration as well as of the first establishment of the nation." He spoke of Gettysburg. That the Thirteenth Amendment was rung in was, of course, entirely fitting. Little wonder that Lee's surrender was heard in "the Northern air [which] stirred far and wide with the glad peels of thousands of church bells."[28]

Whatever small victories and whatever large losses the Confederacy experienced during and at the close of the Civil War, Southerners were less able than Northerners to use bell tolls and peals as aural signatures. The principal reason for the disintegration of this particular Southern soundmark had to do with the state of Southern industry, the Confederacy's limited access to raw materials, the Union blockade, and the South's need to procure metal for the successful prosecution of the war. In April 1862, the Confederate government solicited "bells as can be spared during the War, for the purpose of providing light artillery for the public defense." Public sounds now became part of the public defense in a corporeal manner. Liberty bells, then, took many guises and, as such, bell donation was cast as patriotic: "Those who are willing to devote their bells for this patriotic purpose will receive receipts for them, and the bells will be replaced, if required, at the close of the War, or they will be purchased at fair prices." Donors could send their bells to one of ten depots in the Confederacy.[29]

Not all Southern bells were melted. Some were protected and moved. William J. Grayson wrote in his diary on June 12, 1862, that "[t]he bells, today, were taken down from the steeple of St. Michael's Church to be sent to Columbia" because Charlestonians feared Union forces would steal them. Others remained, for example, in Petersburg by the end of war. Atlanta retained some too. The city's evacuation on September 18, 1864, was marked by "the Sabbath bells . . . tolling their solemn chimes." Some bells were deemed too important to the coordination of Confederate military and civil life to melt. In addition to "boatswains' whistles; the fife and rolling drum, . . . bells of . . . ships striking the passing hour — bell answering to bell and echo[ing] back again on the passing breeze" were critical for shipping, martial and merchant. Bells also remained important for alerting Richmond's denizens of immediate danger. The *New York Herald* reported in early 1864 that "the bells of the city were rung and men were rushing through the streets, crying, 'To arms! To arms! The Yankees are coming! The Yankees are coming!' "[30]

Moreover, God's men were sometimes reluctant to part with His sounds. When lobbied for his church's two bells in March 1862, Catholic bishop William Henry of Natchez, Mississippi, hesitated to deploy His bells for Mars's cannon. Confederate leaders, including P. G. T. Beauregard (who issued the call), countered by pointing to the loyalty of planters and stressing that the temporary disruption of Southern soundmarks through the appropriation of church bells would, in the long run, help preserve the integrity of future Southern soundscapes. While Beauregard agreed with Father Mullon of New Orleans that "[o]ur wives and children have been accustomed to the call, and would miss the tones of 'the church-going bell'," he argued: "[I]f there is no alternative we must make the sacrifice, and should I need it I will avail myself of your offer to contribute the bell of Saint Patrick's Church, that it may rebuke with a tongue of fire the vandals who in this war have polluted God's altar. . . . I can only hope that the day is not far distant when peace will once more bless our country and I shall visit again a quiet home." Father Mullon had a point, though. When church bells remained unmolested, the familiarity of their sound, their reassertion that the South was still the South, provided solace.[31]

When bells were donated, their absence could sometimes be a blessing in disguise. Confederates on the home front managed to do without, sometimes to the benefit of their nerves and, indeed, improved coordination. So common were bell alarms during the war that Southerners became insensible and deaf to their foreboding. Although in Petersburg by 1864 the ringing of "the Courthouse and engine bells" at the common sight of advancing Union troops prompted citizens to respond "with their usual alacrity," some civilians became inured to alarms. Richmond officials saw the problem and tried to overcome it. In May 1864, "the reserve forces of militia were called out—not by a repetition of the unearthly clangor of bells . . . but by the more quiet method of printed notices. . . . The difference in the effect of this mode of assembling the people was manifest in the calmer and less bustling, but equally prompt manner in which it was responded to." This new device, born partly of necessity, worked in instances not requiring immediate alarm and action: "The idea of alarm is so inseparably associated with the din of fire bells, that whenever they sound they invariably produce an undue excitement, and on such occasions especially produce unnecessary and painful agitation among those whose peace should be most particularly consulted."[32]

On the whole, though, Confederates donated bells to the cause, apparently in some numbers. Planters especially responded enthusiastically to the call. The war, then, divested the South of many of its bells and, in the process, deprived Southerners of their historical, civic, and community soundmarks, cues terribly important for identifying themselves and their space. The Union took all of this as good news. Melting of sacred bells must mean desperation, so Federals reasoned. The blockade was having desired effects, reported the *New York Herald* in April 1862, for "it is plain that the rebels are deficient both in cannon and small arms." Indeed, the "recent appeal, asking for the church bells and the bells used by the planters to be sent to the rebel foundries, to be cast into field pieces, is a palpable proof of their deep need of artillery." This, reckoned Federals, was surely the gasp of a dying cause. "This call upon the churches for their bells to be cast into cannon is not a new expedient of war," noted the *Herald*. Indeed, it "is an old device of the Mexicans." This was encouraging, for "we cannot perceive that they have derived any advantages from it in the way of independence." Anyway, "we are strong in the belief that within a few days we shall have such glorious tidings from the Southwest and from Virginia as will satisfy the Southern people of the folly of converting . . . their church-going bells into the horrid music of field artillery."[33]

Even better that such bells were captured. Sniffed a reporter for *Harper's Weekly* in 1862: "Four hundred and eighteen rebel church bells, which had been sent to New Orleans in response to the call of General Beauregard, and captured in that city, were sold in Boston on the 30th ult." This was some loss for the Confederacy and no little gain for the Union: "They weighed together upward of one hundred thousand pounds, and brought about twenty-four thousand dollars." That the Confederacy had to melt bells for cannon and run the risk of losing them in transit to the various depots only added to their cost of the war.[34]

The melting of bells for cannon and the attendant disappearance, even temporarily, of familiar Southern sounds is a good example of contemporaries hearing in the absence of the heard. "Keynote sounds," argues R. Murray Schafer, are "noticed when they change, and when they disappear altogether." In a South that looked to bells to govern myriad aspects of life, mundane and spiritual, the disappearance of familiar tones, tones anchored precisely in time and space, was psychologically devastating. St. Phillips of Charleston donated its bells for the Confederate cause. What followed was "almost 115 years of silence from our bell tower" until new ones were installed in the 1970s. So, too, in Columbia, South Carolina. Emma Le Conte lamented the silence of "the old town clock [she meant bell] whose familiar stroke we miss so much" following Sherman's razing of the city. By the spring of 1863, Union reports revealed the comparative quiet. In addition to the "very deplorable" appearance of the city, "there are but three bells of any size or consequence, the remainder having all been taken down and melted up for cannon." Sounds of God, of markets, of place were now muted and alien and the confident ringing of bells to announce secession was now replaced by meek silence.[35]

In addition to silencing some traditional Southern cues, the absence of bells meant that Confederates could not mark their wretched losses. When, early in the war, Southern cities still had bells in abundance, loss of life was signalled aurally. In July 1861, Charleston honored the dead at Manassas by suspending business for a day and issuing aural marks for the deceased: "The tolling bells, the heavy beat of the muffled drum, and the melancholy dirge for the departed soldier, resounded mournfully over the house tops and through the streets of our quiet city."[36] Such aural marking became increasingly difficult as the war progressed, precisely at the times when Confederates most needed the sounds.

Most galling, perhaps, was the Union's use of Southern bells. Confederates went to some lengths to prevent the Union from celebrating victory using their bells. "Two contrabands came in today from Charleston," wrote Percival Drayton to Gideon Welles in June 1862. "Like the rest I have seen, they represent the harbour as completely blocked up. . . . Another piece of information from our runaways was that the banks had been removed to Columbia as well as the Church bells, as he said to prevent our ringing them if we got into the city." If Confederates could not celebrate either precious wins or toll increasing losses with their ever fewer bells, they were damned if Yankees would appropriate Southern sounds for their celebrations.[37]

The Confederate soundscape of 1865, as heard in the ears of white Southerners, was radically different from that in 1860. The customary tolls of old and familiar bells were greatly diminished and far fainter than ever before; the tolerable register of Southern industry was drowned by the necessity of rapid mobilization and industrialization; and the quiet soundscape of a rural South had been muddied by military booms, whizzes, and Mars's alarm. More disturbing still, the idealized quietude of slavery—the serenity of organic social and economic relations—was now replaced first with a disturbing silence that Southerners had always feared from slaves and, second, by a full-throated cry of freedom—a sound that the master class had heard only in the antebellum North and in their wildest nightmares.

The Slave Home Front

Slaves mapped their own meanings onto—and derived their own advantages from—the sounds of the Civil War. The conflict brought new sounds to the plantation soundscape and slaves noticed. "I never had heard such noises in my life," recalled Easter Reed. "I hadn't never heard a fife or a drum." "I remember what a roar and din the guns made," recalled Susie King Taylor following the firing on Fort Pulaski. "I heard dem guns at Fort Sumter," said Hector Godbold of South Carolina. As a young slave in New Orleans, Dinah Watson heard the war and struggled for analogies: "The cannons was roaring like thunder."[38]

Novelty aside, bondpeople knew to listen to the Civil War soundscape, and for good reason. Slaves used the sounds of war to ascertain the location of Union troops and freedom's lines. "We heard the cannons shooting when they was fighting at Mansfield [Texas]," recalled Allen Williams. Of Sherman's crash through Georgia, Ella Johnson recalled, "We could see the sky all red and hear the distant roar of guns." Listening enabled a few to locate the rough direction of Union lines. For those who remained on plantations, old tactics of hard listening learned under bondage proved handy: "I . . . was awakened late in the night by the sound of a wagon, and hushed noises. I knew that the ex-slaves (as many as possible) were escaping."[39]

The aural world of slaves during the war was one of continuity and change. On the one hand, they listened closely, as they had always done, to glean information; on the other, news of impending victory loosened tight tongues, relaxed taut vocal cords, and allowed the slave community to shape more fully than ever before the soundscapes of the Southern plantation. As he did with many things, Booker T. Washington captured the essence of the process: "The news and mutterings of great events [during the war] were swiftly carried from one plantation to another. . . . As the great day drew nearer, there was more singing in the slave quarters than usual. It was bolder, had more ring, and lasted longer into the night." As they had before the onset of hostilities, slaves in wartime communicated important information to one another through song. They sang of God when they meant Union troops; they intoned slavery when they meant freedom. But veiled meanings did not escape slaveholders who sometimes jailed slaves for singing because they understood the communicative function of songs. Patrols during the war clamped down on slaves' religious gatherings and so essayed to stifle the mutterings of freedom.[40]

Such efforts, though, fell short not least because the serenity insisted upon by Old South masters had encouraged antebellum slaves to master the heard world. Acoustic skills developed under slavery proved handy during the war, especially the ability to control volume. "I also remember the whispering among the slaves—their talking of the possibility of freedom," recalled Mary Gladdy of wartime Georgia. Mary Barbour remembered the coming of Union forces and her father's admonitions for silence in an effort to reach the lines. Her father woke her at night, "all the time telling me to keep quiet. One of the twins hollered some, and Pappy put his hand over its mouth to keep it quiet." The strategy worked: the family reached Union lines in New Bern, North Carolina.[41]

Louis Hughes escaped from his master during the war first by remembering the importance of silent escape from antebellum days and, second, by recognizing that the new sounds of war gave him some acoustic room for manoeuver. With two companions, Hughes determined to escape from Tennessee and was guided by the wise head and ears of "Uncle Alfred," who "cautioned us not to speak above a whisper" so as not to alert "the rebel troops camped on both sides of us." Alfred scouted, returned, and reported, "I can not hear a sound . . . so let us go on." The small group ventured onward with cultivated stealth: "[T]here was no talking above a whisper, for fear of being heard by the soldiers." Vigilance reigned: "Alfred and I had made a turn around the place, listening to see if we could hear any noise, or see any trace of soldiers." Luck proved elusive: "[S]uddenly I heard the yelp of blood hounds in the distance. . . . the sound came nearer and nearer, and then we heard men yelling." Their defence was twofold, olfactory and aural. Alfred told Hughes, "[L]et me oil your feet." The reasoning? "He had with him a bottle of ointment made of turpentine and onions, a preparation used to throw hounds off a trail." Feet anointed, they ran, with Alfred's advice on the aural art of successful escape in their ears: "Don't let the brushes touch you." Had Alfred followed his own advice, escape would have been possible: "[Alfred] ran through the bushes with such a rattling noise one could have heard him a great distance. He wore one of those old fashioned oil coats made in Virginia; and, as he ran, the bushes, striking against the coat, made a noise like the beating of a tine board with sticks." Their pursuers soon caught up with them.[42]

Returned to his plantation, Hughes still listened for the chance to elope. The plantation was, by his account, a quiet place during the war, at least among the slave community. Even tepid news of freedom made slaves "unspeakably happy." And that was precisely the point: thoughts of freedom usually remained silent unless context (or mistake) dictated otherwise. "They were afraid to let the master know that they ever thought of such a thing," continued Hughes, "and they never dreamed of speaking about it except among themselves." Only distance from masters' ears provided safety: "They would laugh and chat about freedom in their cabins." Hughes kept ears pricked for clues of freedom's coming. "One winter night," he recalled, "I was awakened by a rumbling noise like that of heavy wagons, which continued steadily and so long a time that I finally concluded it must be an army passing." It was. And Yankees they were. So Hughes followed them to Union lines and ended up in Canada.[43]

Slaves' hearing and listening was heightened during the Civil War. Muttered news by careless whites could mean the difference between enduring slavery and enjoying freedom; keeping an ear out for cannon and loose words was just as effective as keeping an eye out. Whites knew as much. As war progressed, so white lips pursed tighter. Such self-imposed silence — distasteful though it was to a people used to sounding off — was necessary. Susan Bradford Eppes recalled that during the war her slaves "took to listening under the windows at night and 'Totin' news'." Such behavior put whites on aural alert. They were at once quieter — a delicious irony given their own admonitions to slaves — and sensitive to what they heard. Eppes conveyed some sense of skittishness, years after the war. "[S]creams and groans . . . were heard in the back-yard," she remembered, adding, "it is needless to say we were a nervous set in those days so we rushed in the direction of the out-cry." Mary Chesnut agreed. Not "by one word or look can we detect any change in the demeanour of these Negro servants," she remarked on war's eve. "Are they stolidly stupid, or wiser than we are, silent and strong, biding their time."⁴⁴ The war answered her question.

Sounding Freedom

Slaves celebrated the coming of freedom by reshaping the aural environment to their tastes: they sang loudly and, in effect, drowned out slavery. Sarah Louise Augustus remembered that slaves on her plantation "began to shout and pray" upon hearing of their freedom. "On de day dat de slaves wuz sot free in Texas," remembered Andy Williams, slaves marked the date aurally, just as had millions of white Americans before the war. "Den Mamy broke loose er shoutin' an' she sang an' hollered all day." Freedom meant that "De Lord has heard de groans of de people" and, as a result, the people asked, "haven't we a right to rejoice?" "Maw," told Harriette Benton, ex-slave from Georgia, "she says dat de Yankees done come pass our plantation and dat when dey come, de whole Jasper County started screaming and hollerin' like dey's all crazy." Emancipation upped the volume in the South. The announcement of freedom itself was sometimes a loud affair and introduced sounds alien to the region. "At every station from Lake City to Tallahassee," recalled James M. Dancy in 1933, "the train was stopped and an announcement made through a megaphone to the negroes living on the plantations which lined the road that President Lincoln had declared them free and equal citizens." News of nearby Union forces caused aural celebrations in slave cabins. "When word came dat dey was comin'," recalled Nettie Henry, "it soun' lak a moanin' win' in de quarter. Ever'body . . . march' 'roun' de room an' sorter sing-lak." The circular shuffle marked not the death of a loved one but, rather, the death of slavery.⁴⁵

Sometimes, freedom took on a new aural meaning even as it was announced with old sounds of enslavement. "I will never forget the day of freedom," said Lewis Williams. "All the hands was in field when old Marster come from Milam with the news. He blow the horn and everybody come to the house." James Bolton heard the doubleness of the plantation horn, which, with one blow, took on new meaning: "One mawnin' Marster blowed the bugle his own self, an' called us all up to the big 'ouse yahd. He tole us, 'You all jes' as free as Ah is.[']" Others marked freedom by redefining the meaning of the plantation bell, the old enforcer of work. Here, the bell was reconfigured to mark freedom so that many ex-slaves referred to "de day when freedom rung out." In other instances, the silencing of the bell marked freedom. When a company of African American federal troops arrived on the Ball family's plantation during the war, the first thing they did was find the work bell, pull it down, and smash it.[46]

For others, such as Mary Anderson, the coming of freedom was a crescendo of sorts with sound and silence counterpointing the gravity of emancipation. At the outbreak of war she heard cannon, "something that sounded like thunder." The effect on her owners was clear: "Missus and Marster began to walk around and act queer." Then the silence: "The grown slaves were whispering to each other." Thunder, again: "Next day I heard it again, boom, boom, boom." And then the news: "At nine o'clock, all the slaves gathered at the great house, and Marster and Missus come out on the porch and stood side by side. You could hear a pin drop, everything was so quiet." Freedom was greeted with "whooping and laughing."[47]

For elite Southern whites, the departure (albeit temporary) of labor from plantations left them without recognizable aural cues and bearings. Without slaves to ring house bells, for example, plantation mistresses and masters were strangely lost. Susan Bradford Eppes found the absence of familiar bells and the ensuing silence of freedom eerie and confusing. Testifying unwittingly just how dependent she had become on her slave's bell-summoning, she wrote: "The New Year dawned clear and cold. Snuggling down in our blankets we waited to hear the rising bell — it was getting late — could it be we had not heard the bell? Alack and alas, no bell had rung. The white folks were all alone on the hill — not a negro was there — one and all they had gone — stealing away in the night." So utterly dependent had the white household become on the sound of the slave-rung bell that they, in an act as pitiful as it is staggering, stayed in bed waiting for it to ring.[48]

More perturbing still for whites was the newness of the postbellum soundscape — one marked with the unchecked sounds of black folk. Freedpeople's protracted meetings after slavery lasted days, the participants "making noise enough to really distract every body in the vicinity." Freedom had made an idealized quiet class noisy because it had freed them to participate and express their religious and political convictions at an unprecedented volume. Antebellum hush arbors and quiet prayer meetings gave way to full-throated religious expression, and the pent-up sound of centuries of slavery finally found release. Emancipation for whites was the end of what they liked to imagine was a quiet, disciplined, orderly way of life. In its stead came a noisy black class and "political meetings of a very excitable character." "The turmoil and confusion of the times must have resembled, to a marked degree," wrote Eppes in 1925, "the Union-labor spirit of today."[49]

Accustomed to years of mastery, Southern whites did not relinquish their idealized soundscape without a fight, even in the face of freedom and Union military presence. Initial options were few, however. When thousands of African Americans celebrated the Fourth of July at the South Carolina College chapel in 1865, whites could hear only "strange Negro songs . . . a terrible noise" and had to "shut themselves within doors" to mute strains of black freedom. But when the din had died, opportunities to reassert control were found. Labor contracts with freed people, for example, included provisions that had very little to do with labor but far more to do with the reimposition of an acoustic order that echoed the old slave-master relationship. The first article of agreement between workers and Samuel G. Page of South Carolina, signed in 1866, required that laborers "in all cases to avoid curseing [sic] and swearing in his presence." It is hardly surprising that another planter, George Wise, apparently had few immediate takers on his plantation after the war. His proposed contract stated: "Impudence, swearing, or indecent and unseemly language to; or in the presence of the employer, or his Family, or agent; or quarelling or fighting; so as to disturb the peace; will [be] fined one dollar for the first offence; and if repeated; will be followed by dismissal." Article three was similarly revealing of Wise's wish to govern his plantation's soundscape: "No general conversation will [be] allowed during working hours." Wise and Page were not alone in their desire to reestablish control over plantation soundscapes, and they found some unlikely allies in men of Northern blood. While these men certainly did not want to resurrect the noises of slavery, they did want to exercise control over the sounds of free labor. Their rather rosy view of free wage labor from the antebellum period was beginning to dissipate during and after the war. Not only did Northern elites come to doubt some of their own earlier protestations about the reliability of the laboring classes (their reservations had in fact always existed) but they doubted that blacks would make the transition to a Northern vision of a disciplined market freedom quietly or peacefully. And more than that, they too were beginning to tire of Mars's war and Reconstruction's din and looked of all places southward for a place to relax and consume quietude away from their ever bustling and increasingly noisy, radically individualist Northern society.[50]

Just as the cadence of war, the shock of shelling, the deafening barrage of Union industrial might helped shaped the outcome of the war on the battlefield, so the changing soundscape of the Confederate South helped inspire or erode resistance to the Union advance. In addition to the devastating loss of loved ones, the war caused some profound changes in the South's soundscapes, at times making it sound as Northern as any industrial city. The deprivation of familiar sounds took its toll on Southern civilians and soldiers who, without their bells, found themselves impotent to toll even their defeats.

Conversely, the war was an acoustic victory for the enslaved, albeit temporarily. Not only did they use the sounds of war to help locate freedom's lines, but they marked their freedom by appropriating the sounds of slavery and injecting into the Confederate and post-emancipation South their own sounds in a manner far more vigorous and forceful than enslavement had ever allowed. Ultimately, this was a war that not only inaugurated profound debates about the nature of freedom and citizenship but also changed the soundscape of a region forever. The predominant soundmarks of slavery were replaced by the haltingly slow keynotes of free wage labor in a postwar South that proved reluctant to relinquish its Old South echoes.

Notes

Parts of this essay were delivered as "Hard Listening to the American Civil War" at a conference on "Listening to Archives," held at the University of Technology, Sydney, Australia, November 24, 2000. I remain grateful for the helpful comments offered on that occasion. Thanks also to Joan Cashin for her sage suggestions and editorial recommendations. This essay is drawn in part from chapters 8, 9, and 10 of my *Listening to Nineteenth-Century America*. Copyright © 2001 by the University of North Carolina Press. Used by permission of the publisher.

1. "Additional Details of the Battle of Pittsburgh," *New York Herald*, Apr. 9, 1862; *Charleston Mercury*, July 25, 1861; William L. Jones (48th Regt., N.C. Troops), Petersburg, Va., to "Dear Brother," June 19, 1862, p. 2, MSS 0-61, box 140, Civil War Papers, Special Collections, Robert Manning Strozier Library, Florida State University, Tallahassee, Fla. (hereafter FSU); Peter Cozzens, *This Terrible Sound: The Battle of Chickamauga* (Urbana and Chicago, 1996). For what we do know about aurality in the war, see Earl J. Hess, *The Union Soldier in Battle: Enduring the Ordeal of Combat* (Lawrence, Kans., 1997), 15–18, 28, 46, 112–13 esp.; Charles Ross, "Ssh! Battle in Progress!" *Civil War Times Illustrated* 35 (Dec. 1996): pp. 56–62. For the broader context, consult Mark M. Smith, *Listening to Nineteenth-Century America* (Chapel Hill, 2001).

2. Richard Rath, "Sounding the Chesapeake: Indian and English Soundways in the Settling of Jamestown" (paper presented to the Omohundro Institute of Early American History and Culture, Mar. 16, 2000), 3 (reference is to the on-line version of this paper available at http://way.net/rcr/chesapeake); Douglas Kahn, *Noise, Water, Meat: A History of Sound in the Arts* (Cambridge, Mass., 1999), 2–19 esp.

3. Bernard Hibbitts, "Making Sense of Metaphors: Visuality, Aurality and the Reconfiguration of American Legal Discourse," 16 *Cardozo Law Review* 229 (1994), pt. 1 esp. (reference is to the on-line version of this article available

at http://law.pitt.edu/hibbitts/meta_int.html); Bruce R. Smith, *The Acoustic World of Early Modern England* (Chicago, 1999); Alain Corbin, *Village Bells: Sound and Meaning in the Nineteenth-Century French Countryside*, trans. Martin Thom (New York, 1998); Leigh Eric Schmidt, *Hearing Things: Religion, Illusion, and the American Enlightenment* (Cambridge, Mass., 2000); R. Murray Schafer, *The Tuning of the World: Toward a Theory of Soundscape Design* (Philadelphia, 1980); Peter Bailey, *Popular Culture and Performance in the Victorian City* (Cambridge, 1998), chap. 9.

4. "Chime of Church Bells," *Harper's Weekly*, May 26, 1860, 324; "Amalgam Bells," ibid., Apr. 25, 1863, 272; ibid., Oct. 30, 1858, 691; Corbin, *Village Bells*; Mark M. Smith, "Listening to the Heard Worlds of Antebellum America," *Journal of The Historical Society* 1 (June 2000): 70–71.

5. Smith, "Listening to the Heard Worlds"; Mark M. Smith, *Mastered by the Clock: Time, Slavery, and Freedom in the American South* (Chapel Hill, 1997); Hibbitts, "Making Sense of Metaphors," pt. 1 esp.

6. Schafer, *Tuning*, 7–10, 152, 162; Barry Truax, ed., *The World Soundscape Project's Handbook for Acoustic Ecology* (Vancouver, B.C., 1978), 68 esp.; Smith, *Listening to Nineteenth-Century America*, 261–70.

7. James L. Roark, "Behind the Lines: Confederate Economy and Society," in *Writing the Civil War: The Quest to Understand*, ed. James M. McPherson and William J. Cooper Jr. (Columbia, S.C., 1998), 201–27; Drew Gilpin Faust, " 'Ours as Well as That of the Men': Women and Gender in the Civil War," ibid., 228–40; Peter Kolchin, "Slavery and Freedom in the Civil War South," ibid., 241–60.

8. Drew Gilpin Faust, *The Creation of Confederate Nationalism: Ideology and Identity in the Civil War South* (Baton Rouge, 1988). We know from the work of psychoacousticians that prolonged exposure to noises that threaten the customary soundmarks of a particular locale can inspire opposition to those noises (witness modern anti-noise legislation), sometimes encourage accommodation to those alien sounds that then become normalized, or often fatigue individuals and communities to the point of grudging acceptance and capitulation to those noises. See Stephen Handel, *Listening: An Introduction to the Perception of Auditory Events* (Cambridge, Mass., 1989), chap. 6 esp.; J. D. Miller, "Effects of Noise on People," "General Psychological and Sociological Effects of Noise," and "General Physiological Effects of Noise," in *Hearing*, vol. 4, *Handbook of Perception*, ed. Edward C. Carterette and Morton P. Friedman, (New York, 1978), 609–40, 641–75, 677–82; K. D. Kryter, *Effects of Noise on Man* (New York, 1970), 270–77 esp.

9. "The United States Army," *New York Herald*, Oct. 30, 1863. See, too, ibid., Apr. 11, 13, 15, 1861; S. M. Carpenter, "The Rebel Invasion," *New York Herald*, June 25, 1863; "For Our Country and For Glory," ibid., Apr. 22, 1861; Smith, *Listening to Nineteenth-Century America*, chaps. 8–9.

10. Louis Manigault, Gowrie (Savannah River), to "Mon Cher Pere" [Charles Manigault], Mar. 22, 1861, 1, 2; Nov. 24, 1861, 1, 4, South Caroliniana Library, University of South Carolina, Columbia, S.C. (hereafter SCL).

11. Louis Manigault, Gowrie (Argyle Island), to "Mon Cher Pere" [Charles Manigault], Dec. 5, 1861, 1–3, SCL.

12. David K. Puckett, "' . . . the chains which had bound us so long were well nigh broken': The Transition from Slavery to Freedom in Columbia, S.C., 1850–1865" (master's thesis, University of South Carolina, 1998), 9, 25; Johnson M. Mundy, Columbia [S.C.], to "My dear Sister" [Mary E. Mundy], Feb. 20, 1861, 2–3, SCL; "From Virginia," *Charleston Mercury*, Jan. 1, 1862.

13. On the Confederacy's rapid entry to industrial modernity, see Raimondo Luraghi, "The Civil War and the Modernization of American Society: Social Structure and Industrial Revolution in the Old South before and during the War," *Civil War History* 18 (Sept. 1972): 244 esp.; Mary A. DeCredico, *Patriotism for Profit: Georgia's Urban Entrepreneurs and the Confederate War Effort* (Chapel Hill, 1990); Charles B. Dew, *Ironmaker to the Confederacy: Joseph R. Anderson and the Tredegar Iron Works* (New Haven, 1966); Roark, "Behind the Lines," 210–11 esp.

14. "Negro of the Old South," by Susan Bradford Eppes, typed manuscript, pp. 76–77, Pine Hill Plantation Papers, folder 4, MSS 0-204, box 368, FSU; "Through Some Eventful Years," by Susan Bradford Eppes, typed manuscript, p. 156, Pine Hill Plantation Papers, box 368, FSU.

15. "Our Richmond Correspondence," *Charleston Mercury*, June 24, 1861.

16. George Fitzhugh, "Conduct of the War," *De Bow's Review* 32 (Jan./Feb. 1862): 139–46; Faust, *Creation of Confederate Nationalism*, 52–54; "Notes of a Recent Tour in the South," *New York Herald*, Nov. 12, 1861.

17. Anonymous [Charleston, S.C.?] to "Dearest Mattie," [Nov. 8?, 1861], SCL; "News of the Victory," *Charleston Mercury*, July 2, 1862; "Happy New Year!" *Charleston Mercury*, Jan. 1, 1863; W. T. J. [Company E, 20th Regt., Georgia Volunteer Infantry] to "Miss Jennie [Smith]," Feb. 21, 1862, p. 1, Letters of Confederate Soldiers, MSS 0-70, box 141, FSU. Whites also listened for Union troops. See George W. Yarbrough, *Boyhood and Other Days in Georgia* (Nashville, 1917), 43; Benjamin F. McPherson, "I Must Tell: An Autobiography," unedited manuscript, p. 78, Civil War Collection, Ralph B. Draughon Library, Archives and Special Collections, Auburn University, Auburn, Ala. (hereafter AU); Joan E. Cashin, "Into the Trackless Wilderness: The Refugee Experience in the Civil War," in *A Woman's War: Southern Women, Civil War, and the Confederate Legacy*, ed. Edward D. C. Campbell Jr. and Kym S. Rice (Richmond and Charlottesville, 1996), p. 35.

18. J. D. B., "Notes of the War," *Charleston Mercury*, Aug. 29, 1861.

19. "The Firing Yesterday Morning," *Charleston Mercury*, June 19, 1861.

20. "Siege Matters—Three Hundred and Eighty Eighth Day," *Charleston Mercury*, Aug. 1, 1864. On Southern skittishness, see Smith, *Listening to Nineteenth-Century America*, 68, 69, 88–91, 184–85; Winthrop D. Jordan, *Tumult and Silence at Second Creek: A Inquiry into a Civil War Slave Conspiracy* (Baton Rouge, 1993), 1, 26–27.

21. "Siege Matters—Three Hundred and Eighty Eighth Day," *Charleston Mercury*, Aug. 1, 1864.

22. "The News," *Richmond Enquirer*, May 13, 1864; "Army Correspondence," *Charleston Mercury*, June 28, 1864.

23. "From the Army at Atlanta," *Charleston Mercury*, July 20, 1864; "Merry Christmas," *Charleston Mercury*, Dec. 25, 1862.

24. "Siege Matters," *Charleston Mercury*, Mar. 10, 1864; McPherson, "I Must Tell," 114; Mrs. Sarah Campbell Bryce, *The Personal Experience of Mrs. Campbell Bryce during the Burning of Columbia, South Carolina, by General William T. Sherman's Army, February 17, 1865* (Philadelphia, 1899), 9; *Daily Southern Guardian*, Sept. 17, 1863; Capt. Benjamin Wesley Justice to his wife, May 20, 1864, quoted in J. Tracy Power, *Lee's Miserables: Life in the Army of Northern Virginia from the Wilderness to Appomattox* (Chapel Hill, 1998), 14.

25. "Savannah," *New York Herald*, Feb. 16, 1865; "Meade's Army," *New York Herald*, Oct. 9, 1863.

26. "Charleston," *New York Herald*, Feb. 28, 1865; "News from Port Royal," *New York Herald*, Dec. 20, 1861; "The Coming of Autumn and Winter," *Charleston Mercury*, Aug. 29, 1862; Anonymous, Charleston Harbour, to "Dear Parents & Sister," June 10, 1865, p. 1, SCL.

27. "The Lesson Taught by the Fall of Vicksburg and Port Hudson," *Charleston Mercury*, July 24, 1863.

28. "The Celebration of the Fourth of July," *New York Herald*, July 6, 1863; "The Situation," *New York Herald*, Feb. 3, Apr. 11, 1865.

29. "The Value of Church Bells," *Charleston Mercury*, Apr. 3, 1862.

30. Richard J. Calhoun, ed., *Witness to Sorrow: The Antebellum Autobiography of William J. Grayson* (Columbia, S.C., 1990), 226; "The Situation," *New York Herald*, Jan. 22, 1865, Sept. 29, 1864; "The Porter-Butler Expedition," *Charleston Mercury*, Jan. 3, 1865; "Important from Richmond," *New York Herald*, Feb. 10, 1864.

31. (Elder) William Henry, Bishop of Natchez (Mississippi), to Archbishop John Mary Odin, C.M., New Orleans, La., Mar. 16, 1862; Calendar: 1862, Notre Dame Archives Calendar (accessed at http://cawley.archives.nd.edu/calendar/cal1862c.html); P.G.T. Beauregard, Jackson, Tenn., to Father Mullon, Saint Patrick's Church, New Orleans, La., Mar. 20, 1862, Confederate correspondence, orders, and returns relating to operations in Kentucky, Tennessee, North Mississippi, North Alabama, and Southwest Virginia from March 4 to June 10, 1863 — #3, *Official Records of the Union and Confederate Armies*, ser. 1, vol. X/2 [S#11] (*Army Official Record Computer File* [CD-ROM, Wilmington, N.C., 1995]); Yarbrough, *Boyhood and Other Days*, 44.

32. "The News," *Richmond Enquirer*, May 13, 1864; "The Enemy's Dash on Petersburg," *Charleston Mercury*, June 13, 1864.

33. "Desperation of the Rebels — Their Deficiency in Arms," *New York Herald*, Apr. 20, 1862; "The New Defensive System of the Rebellion," *New York Herald*, Apr. 7, 1862; "The Mississippi," *New York Herald*, Sept. 17, 1863.

34. "Sale of Rebel Bells in Boston," *Harper's Weekly*, Aug. 16, 1862, 515.

35. Julia and Edward K. Pritchard, Charleston, S.C., to Harmannus H. Van Bergen, Atlanta, Ga., July 27, 1976, Samford Carillon Dedication folder, Miscellaneous Collections, ser. 1: Auburn University; Schafer, *Tuning*, 60; Le Conte, quoted in Smith, *Mastered by the Clock*, 45. "Important News," *New York Herald*, Apr. 7, 1863; Puckett, " . . . the chains which bound us," 26.

36. "Last Honors to the Heroes of Manassas," *Charleston Mercury*, July 27, 1861.

37. P[ercival] Drayton, Flag Officer of S[amuel] F[rancis] DuPont, to "My

dear Commodore" [Gideon Welles], U.S.S. Pawnee, Stono, June 19, 1862, pp. 1–2, SCL.

38. George P. Rawick, ed., *The American Slave: A Composite Autobiography*, 41 vols. (Westport, Conn., 1972–1979) supp. ser. 1, vol. 4, *Ga. Narrs.*, pt. 2, 508; Susie King Taylor, *Reminiscences of My Life in Camp* (New York, 1968), 33; Rawick, *American Slave*, supp. ser. 1, vol. 11, *N.C. and S.C. Narrs.*, 146; supp. ser. 1, vol. 3, *Ga. Narrs.*, pt. 1, 116; supp. ser. 2, vol. 10, *Tx. Narrs.*, pt. 9, 3996. See too ibid., supp. ser. 2, vol. 10, *Tx. Narrs.*, pt. 9, 4022.

39. Rawick, *American Slave*, supp. ser. 2, vol. 10, *Tx. Narrs.*, pt. 9, 4061; supp. ser. 1, vol. 4, *Ga. Narrs.*, pt. 2, 346–47.

40. Booker T. Washington, *Up from Slavery*, in *Three Negro Classics* (New York, 1965), 38–39; Lawrence W. Levine, *Black Culture and Black Consciousness: Afro-American Folk Thought from Slavery to Freedom* (New York, 1978), 51–52.

41. Rawick, *American Slave*, supp. ser. 1, vol. 3, *Ga. Narrs.*, pt. 1, 261; Belinda Hurmence, ed., *Before Freedom: Forty-Eight Oral Histories of Former North and South Carolina Slaves* (New York, 1990), 12–13.

42. Louis Hughes, *Thirty Years a Slave, from Bondage to Freedom: An Autobiography* (New York, 1969), 142–44.

43. Hughes, *Thirty Years a Slave*, 146, 150–51.

44. "Negro of the Old South," by Susan Bradford Eppes, typed manuscript, pp. 86, 87, Pine Hill Plantation Papers, folder 4, MSS 0-204, box 368, FSU; Ben Ames, ed., *A Diary from Dixie* (Boston, 1949), 38.

45. Rawick, *American Slave*, supp. ser. 2, vol. 10, *Tx. Narrs.*, pt. 9, 4046–47; Hurmence, *Before Freedom*, 24; Rawick, *American Slave*, supp. ser. 2, vol. 10, *Tx. Narrs.*, pt. 9, 4068; William Wells Brown, *The Negro in the American Rebellion, His Heroism and His Fidelity* (New York, 1968), 114; Rawick, *American Slave*, supp. ser. 1, vol. 3, *Ga. Narrs.*, pt. 1, 51; James M. Dancy, "Memoirs of the Civil War and Reconstruction," typescript, 1933, p. 12, Miscellaneous Manuscript Collection, box 27, Special Collections, Smathers Library, University of Florida, Gainesville, Fla.; Alan Brown and David Taylor, *Gabr'l Blow Sof': Sumter County, Alabama Slave Narratives* (Livingston, Ala., 1997), 57.

46. Rawick, *American Slave*, supp. ser. 2, vol. 10, *Tx. Narrs.*, pt. 9, 4095, 4101; supp. ser. 1, vol. 3, *Ga. Narrs.*, pt. 1, 87; supp. ser. 2, vol. 10, *Tx. Narrs.*, pt. 9, 4105; Edward Ball, *Slaves in the Family* (New York, 1999), 345.

47. Hurmence, *Before Freedom*, 40–41.

48. "Negro of the Old South," by Susan Bradford Eppes, typed manuscript, p. 91, Pine Hill Plantation Papers, folder 4, MSS 0-204, box 368, FSU.

49. Ibid., 115, 117, 132; Smith, "Listening to the Heard Worlds"; Mark M. Smith, "Time, Sound, and the Virginia Slave," in *Afro-Virginian History and Culture*, ed. John Saillant (New York, 1999), 47–49 esp.

50. Emma Le Conte, *When the World Ended*, ed. Earl Schenck Miers (New York, 1957), 113–14; Articles of agreement between Samuel G. Page and Freedpeople, Jan. 31, 1866, Marion District, S.C., SCL; Articles of agreement between George Wise and Freedpeople, Newberry District, 1866. Contract until "January 1867," SCL; Smith, *Listening to Nineteenth-Century America*, chap. 10.

Chapter 2

A Compound of Wonderful Potency: Women Teachers of the North in the Civil War South

NINA SILBER

✦ IN APRIL 1862, with the Civil War entering its second year, Harriet Ware joined a small band of missionaries who ventured from the relative tranquility of Boston, Philadelphia, and New York into the heart of the Southern Confederacy. Descended from a prominent Boston Unitarian family, Harriet Ware traded the security of her Northern home for a position as a teacher to "contraband" slaves in the Union-occupied Sea Islands off the South Carolina coast. Like many Yankee missionaries unaccustomed to Southern heat, Ware returned north during the summer and fall of 1862 but came back to the islands in December. Discovering that some of her charges—during the missionaries' absence—had seen fit to provision themselves with furnishings from a nearby home, Ware reflected on the morally tenuous condition of the island's black inhabitants and the need for missionary supervision. The incident showed, she remarked in a letter home, that these people "should have the care and oversight of white people in this transition state."[1]

Indeed, Harriet Ware believed this was her foremost purpose for being in the South: to influence the "transition state" for African Americans. And, in this regard, Harriet Ware's wartime work drew her into the most significant development of the Civil War era: the emancipation of four million black men and women from slavery. As one of hundreds of teachers who came in contact with the former slaves during the war years, Ware was much more than a simple instructor of letters, of Bible passages, or even, as her letter indicates, of moral propriety. She was, in effect, a civilian negotiator in the struggle for freedom. Participating in a subtle give-and-take with the former slaves, Ware, along with other Northern missionaries who lived among the black men and women in various parts of the occupied Confederacy, helped to define the possibilities, and the limits, of the freedpeoples' new emancipation. As a woman, Harriet Ware played an important part in casting the emancipation process in a gendered context. She, and others like her, provided the government with a female voice for directing the former slaves — a voice which federal officials no doubt hoped would convey a certain degree of sympathy for the slaves' plight and thus signal the U.S. government's intention to treat black men and women differently than their Confederate masters had. But the feminine perspective that Ware and other female teachers brought to their work could also, at times, push the emancipation process in directions that ran counter to Union military and political objectives.

Although most accounts refer to them as "teachers," this description can be somewhat misleading for this particular group of civilians in the South. Along with men, Northern women traveled to black communities in the wartime South, serving more as missionaries, with both a religious and secular focus. Their work included keeping house for their own colleagues, supervising black laborers on occupied plantations, providing medical aid and distributing clothes to the freedpeople, and offering instruction in reading, writing, religion, sewing, and "proper" habits of dress and punctuality. This field of labor became available to women in the months after November 1861 when the Union army took possession of the South Carolina Sea Islands and made themselves responsible for thousands of slaves who had been left in the wake of the slaveowners' desertion. With each advance of the Union army into the Confederacy, more of the region's slaves likewise came under federal oversight. Initially designated as "contraband," some of these black men and women gained their freedom when the Lincoln administration at last made emancipation a goal of the Union war effort. But even before the official dawn of freedom, various societies had sprung up throughout the North, committed to aiding the former slaves and recruiting Northern civilians who could offer direct and immediate assistance by living among those once in bondage. Organized by both religious and secular leaders in the North, and receiving various degrees of government assistance, these societies, by the end of the war, could count nine hundred teachers as their agents throughout the former Confederacy. During the war, as other portions of the Confederacy came under Union occupation and more black men and women entered a legal way station between slavery and freedom, the army and the federal government continued to make use of Northern men and women who could offer assistance to the former slaves. The work done by missionaries, and by their sponsoring societies, eventually paved the way for, and directly influenced the establishment of, the Freedmen's Bureau of the Reconstruction era.[2]

Scholars interested in Reconstruction and Northern abolitionists in the wartime and postwar years have not overlooked these dedicated Yankee missionaries and teachers. Yet, by and large, the literature which examines the specific work of Northern female teachers in the

South has focused on the postwar period, and thus slights the contributions these women made to the wartime agenda and to the shaping of the emancipation experience. Likewise, scant attention has been paid to the ways in which the emancipation experience prompted Northern women to reexamine their own concerns about gender, race, and class relations. This essay places the work of the female teachers in the context of emancipation—when different avenues and possibilities emerged for the former slaves, and when African-American men and women attempted to explore those possibilities in conjunction with, or often at odds with, Northern and Southern whites. While several scholars have recently focused attention on how the former slaves navigated this historical terrain, and especially on the slaves' role in bringing about their own liberation, my emphasis here is on Northern women and their participation in the slaves' liberation, how they were affected by the experience and how their presence shaped and influenced that historical moment when Northern whites and former slaves began to first grapple with the meaning of black freedom.[3]

Northern women who enlisted as teachers during the war were, no doubt, much like their Yankee sisters who undertook other forms of wartime service. They desired to do more than just wait and pray at home; like men, they wanted to act. Most women who became teachers would have also embraced the principles of those abolitionists, and sympathetic Republicans, who believed the time had come to do more than just criticize slavery, that it was time to hasten the demise of the "peculiar institution." As the advance of the Northern army drew more slaves into Union lines, one group of abolitionists, along with prominent members of the Lincoln Administration, hoped to see the people of the North guide black men and women across the threshold of emancipation, to teach them, in their own way, what freedom meant. Although a number of abolitionists objected to this work as meddling paternalism, and indeed it often was, the men and women who participated in the various freedmen's aid commissions saw this as an important humanitarian and educational opportunity.[4]

Aside from abolitionist sympathies, other factors also shaped the pool of those civilians who undertook this wartime missionary work. More than half of those going south hailed from New England and three-fourths were women. In addition, most of the women were unmarried, including both older women who had chosen not to marry and younger women in their premarital years. Most teachers were white, but a few black women served as well, including some who had been recently freed from slavery. In general, the black female teachers, more than the whites, came from less privileged economic circumstances and so were more dependent on the meager salaries that were provided.[5]

While most teachers, black and white, maintained a strong commitment to antislavery goals, many were also guided in their work by economic objectives. Certainly, an important motivation for many white participants in this emancipation experiment was ensuring the continued production of a lucrative cotton crop. But the leaders and missionaries in the freedmen's aid work also intended to initiate their own program of emancipation, one which blended (sometimes in contradictory ways) labor imperatives with middle-class ideals. They intended to ensure black productivity and demonstrate the advantages of free labor, while also introducing a program of educational, moral, and domestic uplift. Perhaps one of their overriding concerns, in this initial period, was to establish the idea that freedom from slavery did not mean license to live without constraints. Fearing the unruly nature of the former slaves on Craney Island in Virginia, Lucy Chase claimed that "they ought to enter freedom through the path of moral restraint." In this regard, teachers believed not only in lessons in reading and writing but also in punctuality, cleanliness, temperance, and hard work, values seen as sacrosanct by most white middle-class Northerners.[6]

In addition, teachers also offered specific instructions with respect to gender, emphasizing notions of "manly" self-reliance, female morality, and domestic order. Antislavery Northerners had frequently wielded their image of a clean and well-ordered household in their battle against slavery, and missionaries continued to promote the ideals of a well-kept home against the spectre of the abused home life of the "peculiar institution." Although they no doubt held differing opinions about the former slaves' domestic inclinations, missionaries would have agreed that slavery had had a debilitating effect on home and family life. Consequently, teachers hoped to instill among the former bondsmen a proper sense of familial relations by stressing the importance of marital bonds, men's economic responsibilities, and female housewifery. The domestic focus of this work seemed to offer a logical opening for female participation as wartime missionaries. Edward Pierce, appointed by Treasury Secretary Salmon P. Chase to oversee the conditions of the former slaves in the newly occupied Sea Islands, believed that considerable attention should be paid to the home conditions of the so-called "contrabands." "Whoever, under our new system, is charged with [the contrabands'] superintendence," he wrote to Chase in February 1862, "should see that they attend more to the cleanliness of their persons and houses, and that, as in families of white people, they take their meals together at a table."[7]

But despite his identification of this domestic component of the freedpeople's initiation into freedom, Pierce was initially reluctant to bring women into the field. After all, in the beginning of 1862, despite a foothold along the coast of South Carolina, the Union army was hardly an invincible military force, and whatever territory they occupied remained subject, at any time, to Confederate counterattack. Women, many believed, might not be safe and might in fact be a burden in such a setting. So when the first band of missionaries set sail for the Sea Islands, in March 1862, twelve women were included in this group known as "Gideon's Band" (a reference to the Old Testament hero who delivered the people of Israel from their warlike oppressors). Pierce, however, regarded their participation "as yet an experiment" and gave the Reverend Mansfield French, chief representative of the National Freedmen's Relief Association of New York, full responsibility for the ladies' care. Indeed, one of the women from that original voyage was advised a few months later to return north as the coming summer heat and threatening military situation would soon mean that the ladies "instead of doing anything will themselves be a care." As late as September 1862, Charlotte Forten, a young black New Englander hoping to sail south, was informed by the Boston commission in charge of freedmen's aid work that "they were not sending women at present."[8]

Although concerns persisted about the possible harm that might befall women in potentially dangerous Southern outposts, women soon joined the delegations arriving in the newly occupied areas. By March 1862, French's organization reported that they had enlisted the services of eight women, both married and unmarried, who would go south "as nurses and teachers, and while they consider themselves under the care of this Association, we have not asked them to sign the agreement [i.e., specifying salary and terms of employment] made with the men, nor have we agreed to pay them for their services." The societies, however, including the National Freedmen's Relief Association, soon did offer salaries even to female teachers. Nonetheless, the pay was never substantial (generally between twenty and thirty dollars per month) and was usually less than what male teachers or missionaries received.[9]

Aside from low pay, female teachers encountered other obstacles that discouraged them in their work. They faced numerous practical problems in locating schoolrooms, establishing routines and regular attendance on the part of their pupils, and securing books and supplies. In addition, like other women who embarked upon war work, especially on or near the battlefronts, they entered a male-dominated military world that was often hostile and suspicious of female participation. Recalling her trip to the Sea Islands in 1864, Elizabeth Botume reflected on the difficulties women faced just travelling to the war zones. "An unprotected woman without a military friend on one of these government boats," she wrote, "had a hard time, being often rudely treated, or entirely neglected." Once female teachers had arrived within some proximity of the military, the intimidation continued. Laura Towne, a

Philadelphia abolitionist who taught in the Sea Islands, heard rumors recounting how "the rebels had landed and carried away a lady" and concluded that Union soldiers were no doubt trying to frighten newly arrived females. Towne, like most of her female colleagues, remained.[10]

Despite this military intimidation, a number of Union officials, plantation supervisors, and other observers soon came to appreciate the work of female teachers, even, in fact, finding their contribution indispensible. Reverend French's second and third reports from the Sea Islands point to an increasing reliance on feminine input and express implicit faith that "the ladies will soon make a little change, at least" in the former slaves' conditions. But while there was increasing support for bringing female missionaries south, observers also maintained that such women had to be carefully selected, echoing some of the discussions which influenced the recruitment of nurses in the Northern states. Most believed this was a field for older and more practically oriented women, and took pains to discourage those who might be perceived as youthful romantics. They also stressed the need for women who could cooperate with, or perhaps not be cowed by, Union officials. Following her visit to Port Royal and the Sea Islands in March 1862, Mrs. James Harlan of New York responded to a very detailed set of questions put to her by the Reverend French's association, confirming that his "experiment" to bring ladies seemed to be successful, provided they were carefully selected. "Women of the right character," she wrote, "could and doubtless will be very useful to the poor people around Port Royal. . . . But they should be selected with care from those whose position and character would command the respect of the military and civil officers of the Government. . . . The preference should be given to ladies of maturity, of strong practical common sense, rather than exquisite literary tastes." Ultimately, Mrs. Harlan believed, the Port Royal experiment would greatly benefit from the presence of more ladies, although perhaps at a slightly later date, "after the work shall have been systematized." Apparently, by July 1862, General Rufus Saxton, the Union military commander in charge of the Sea Islands, believed that time had almost come. "Should our occupation of this country continue until Autumn," he wrote to the National Freedmen's Relief Association, "I think it is important to have some ladies here for teachers, they labor to better advantage in this field, than men particularly with the children."[11]

Occasionally, some of the sponsoring societies did try to recruit male teachers, often in settings where the conditions were more physically challenging or the students were especially unruly. But by 1863 and 1864, teachers and superintendents throughout the occupied South frequently asked for more women to join the ranks. Isaac Hubbs wrote to the American Missionary Association, also involved in the wartime recruitment of teachers, from Louisiana in March of 1864 requesting another fifty to one hundred teachers, "chiefly females." And Asa Fiske, the "superintendent of contrabands" in Memphis, Tennessee, made a similar appeal in March 1863, attempting to clarify his preference for women. "I think," he wrote to the readers of *American Missionary*, "we need women, rather than men, especially for the instruction of the children. And that not only on account of their peculiar adaptation to the work. . . . Every sensible, educated, good woman, among these people, is a fountain of immeasurable good. Combine the teacher, and the sensible, refined woman, and you get a compound of wonderful potency."[12]

But what was this "wonderful potency," and what, more specifically, could female teachers accomplish that men could not? In part, female teachers earned respect for their pedagogical abilities: for their patient skill in providing basic literacy skills to the former slaves, especially children. Most likely the increasing feminization of the teaching profession in the antebellum North predisposed government and aid society officials to favor women in these positions. Moreover, officials like Fiske, Hubbs, and Gen. Saxton also valued the unique lessons that women teachers could impart, especially to female ex-slaves and especially in regard to household matters. But, at a more subtle level, male administrators and superintendents in occupied areas came to appreciate a uniquely feminine presence in areas where black men and women had very recently been released from the shackles of slavery. Before long, they recognized the value in presenting the new, postslavery arrangements with a feminine face.

Indeed, the white women themselves believed they offered a unique perspective to these missionary efforts, sometimes defining their role in terms of calming and reassuring "confused" groups of contrabands. Laura Towne had been in the Sea Islands only a short time before she became a frequent visitor to the plantation cabins. "We ladies," she wrote in her diary in April 1862, "are borrowed, to go talk to the negroes, from one plantation to another." Susan Walker, who lived on the Sea Islands during this same period, also participated in these ladies' visits and remarked on how frequently the black inhabitants spoke of being " 'confused' . . . about themselves . . . whether they belong to themselves or somebody else." But, Walker found, they appeared grateful for their white female visitors. "Bless the Lord," said one black woman as she took Walker's hands, "we glad you come." Towne confirmed the positive effects their presence seemed to have, especially on "the negro women." "They think a white lady a great safeguard from danger," Towne wrote in a letter home, "and they say they are 'confused' if there are no ladies about."[13]

While such remarks reveal something of the teachers' perspective, they provide only a one-sided glance at the freedpeople's perceptions of the missionary presence. In some respects, the meeting of Northern missionaries with a black population struggling to end its ties to slavery brought together two contrasting visions of emancipation. Most notably, the missionaries' emphasis on cotton production frequently clashed with the former slaves' desire for increasing labor autonomy. Many former slaves preferred growing corn and other subsistence crops and were reluctant to cooperate with the missionaries' overriding focus on cotton. In general, though, conflicts flared more with male civilians, who tended to spend more time supervising the new labor arrangements than did Northern women. Yet, in a number of instances, male missionaries did ask their female companions to convince the former slaves to grow cotton and to comply with the somewhat mystical power of "the government." In such cases, women assumed the responsibility for explaining the limits and restrictions connected with the freedpeople's new status and urged them to recognize, in effect, that their freedom meant not independence so much as a new type of dependence. "Women gathered around me," Susan Walker wrote of one of her early visits, "and I tried to explain to them as simply as I could what government is; the power that I and they must obey." It is possible that, on a subtle level, the former slaves may have more readily accepted the message of compliance when voiced by women, given that the messengers were, like themselves, dependent beings in a universe dominated by white men. Perhaps, too, by having Northern white women state the arguments, the new economic and political compulsions would seem less like a continuation of the old system of patriarchal command and more like a new departure. In any case, it does seem that the missionaries and their societies sensed that they could, in certain situations, increase their effectiveness by voicing their authority through a female channel.[14]

Aside from labor autonomy, the former slaves, especially black women, made the safety and integrity of their families their chief concern in the transition to freedom. On this score, they were again often reluctant to accede to missionaries' demands to labor in white peoples' homes and give up precious time with their own families, and were especially alarmed when black men were taken to perform military or other forms of government service. Safety and security from reenslavement tended, understandably, to be a principal preoccupation for former slaves. Northern missionaries, such as Susan Walker and Laura Towne, may have read that anxiety about reenslavement as "confusion." And, although it may be possible that Towne and Walker exaggerated the positive influences that white ladies had in their contacts with the former slaves, their reports still suggest that, from the perspective of local blacks, especially black women, there was something reassuring about this Yankee female presence. Certainly it would be preferable to have such ladies about as opposed to the unsettling uncertainty of seeing only white men, whose presence suggested possible military turmoil or Confederate counterattack. The white female presence, too, likely calmed fears which many African-American women may have had about rape and sexual abuse. In other respects, too, Northern female civilians may have appeared to be more sympathetic with the concerns of former slaves, especially given the premium they, too, placed on family bonds and household stability. Although the white women often took a very different view than black women of the former slaves' domestic arrangements, at least they showed concern for the well-being of children and families.[15]

The presence of black female teachers, in contrast, often did not elicit the same responses among the freedpeople, nor did it reveal the same clashes in attitude. When Charlotte Forten arrived at last on St. Helena Island in the fall of 1862, she was the first and only black teacher there and received, at least initially, a decidedly mixed reception from the local contrabands, some of whom resented having to work for the young black woman. White missionaries, too, were sometimes distant and unfriendly towards Forten. Colonel Higginson, who was commanding black soldiers on the Sea Islands, believed freedpeople's attitudes toward Forten only began to change after they had heard her skillful piano playing. Perhaps, in the eyes of both black and white, this bourgeois accomplishment marked her with a distinctly elevated status that placed her closer to the white ladies. Indeed, the fact that many black teachers often received prejudicial treatment from their white colleagues certainly would have sent signals that may have influenced how freedpeople treated and perceived African-American missionaries. Arriving in Norfolk in 1864, Sarah Stanley found that the white missionary already stationed there revealed "an especial pleasure in advocating the inferiority of 'negroes' and the necessity of social distinction, with special application to colored missionary teachers." Such contempt may have encouraged certain sympathies between the former slaves and the black teachers, but also might have marked the black teachers as figures of less importance and authority when it came to aiding those who were newly freed. It also seems possible that white missionaries and Union officials may have assumed that black women would be less effective in influencing the gender and domestic arrangements of the former slaves, and so tried to channel their missionary efforts in different directions. Both Charlotte Forten and Susie King Taylor, a former slave turned teacher, were encouraged by Union officials to teach not the women and children (as most of the white teachers did) but newly recruited black soldiers instead.[16]

In any event, both white and black women would have won considerable respect from the freedpeople simply by offering their principal service: teaching. In this way, too, they sent out another signal that the Union intended to carry out a program of emancipation marked by more than just a transition to a new type of coercive labor. As a group, Northern female civilians in the South, black and white, likely gave more attention to various forms of "teaching" than men, who often split their time between teaching and plantation management. From the perspective of the ex-slaves, the teachers had the power to make them more than just "contraband," to bring them closer to a condition of freedom in which they could do more than just toil arduously for a new white man. As the former slaves saw it, one of the most important components of their newly freed status would be the opportunity to educate themselves, to attain the type of knowledge that had been forbidden them by their white slave masters and slave mistresses. Seventy-five years after the Union occupation of the Sea Islands, ex-slave Sam Mitchell retained this powerful memory that linked emancipation with schooling. "After Freedom come," Mitchell told an interviewer in the 1930s, "everybody do as he please. De Yankee open school for nigger and teacher lib in Maussa house." Maggie Black, also from South Carolina, recalled that after freedom, "uh lady from de north come dere en Miss Leggett send we chillun to school." Black remembered this female teacher as a person of considerable authority, noting how she had "uh big box fa her stand jes lak uh preacher." In the 1860s, teachers frequently remarked how education, and the promise of schooling, more than anything else, had the power to motivate and inspire the former slaves. And while the initial talk concerning the teachers' role had mainly focused on the domestic instruction they could impart, it soon became clear to all how valuable it would be if they also taught basic reading and writing. "Every step of his creeping progress into the mysteries of letters," wrote Lucy Chase from Craney Island in February 1863 regarding the typical former slave, "elevates his spirit like faith in a brilliant promise."[17]

What was at stake, explained William Gannett, a former labor superintendent on the Sea Islands, and Edward Hale, a leader of the Boston Freedmen's Aid Commission, was the ability of Northerners to bring the former slaves into their fold, to instruct them in their version of emancipation by gaining their trust and confidence, something which, apparently, could be done to greater effect with women as the instructors. Writing up their summary of freedmen's aid work at the end of the war, Gannett and Hale not only praised women's participation in this work, especially their "courage and endurance," but they also observed that "had the teachers sent from the North no use to make of the alphabet but as a talisman to win the confidence of a people whom the army was not using well, and whom their old masters had used so ill, for that use only would the machinery of the schools have been invaluable." In effect, the Northern female teacher could soften the severity of wartime occupation and provide proof that freedom could be secured if trust were placed in Yankee missionaries and Yankee ways.[18]

Most teachers embraced their role as freedom-givers in earnest. Laura Towne may have been more vociferous than others in promoting an abolitionist agenda, but she reflected a spirit that others also possessed. She was especially hostile to labor superintendents who were reluctant to tell the slaves they were free and who continued to hold out threats of returning recalcitrant workers to their masters. For her part, Towne preferred to be completely open about encouraging a program of total emancipation, before the Union government had taken steps in this direction. Austa French, the wife of the Reverend Mansfield French, likewise urged a more forthright path to emancipation in the murky pre-Proclamation period. "They are free," she wrote of the Sea Island inhabitants, "and must remain so, unless this government can kidnap, which cannot, of course, be thought of. Our Government will not defile itself with that villainous work."[19]

Yet, despite French's optimistic view of the government's position, and despite the growing emphasis on women's influence in these missionary endeavors, female teachers often disagreed with Union officials' emancipation policies, and especially their methods of dealing with the former slaves and their families. The demands of the war, and longstanding prejudices, influenced Union men who more often than not believed the former slaves would only respond to strict compulsions and arbitrary demands. Even more, the Union military frequently undermined the teachers' emphasis on an ordered and stable family life, most notably in the sexual abuse of African-American women and the seizure of black men to perform military and other government service. In this context, Northern female teachers, while hardly viewing the local blacks (including black women) as their social equals, nonetheless found themselves at odds with the army and the government, and tried to assert a stronger womanly, and often "maternal," perspective that focused on the needs and concerns of black women and the black family.

On one level, there was general agreement regarding one of the most important functions that female teachers had come to perform: to instruct former slave women in better methods of domestic care. In this

regard, missionaries occasionally upheld an image of female coopera-
tion that could even transcend racial divisions. In his original plan to
bring women, the Reverend French had explicitly defined the work of
female teachers in terms of these "counsels as women can best communicate to women." Harriet Ware visited the contraband dwellings on
her plantation where she helped mothers care for sick babies and even
showed some how to bake Yankee-style bread. Susan Walker likewise
"preached industry and cleanliness," and was especially pleased when
some African-American women began whitewashing their homes.[20]

Moreover, Northern female teachers seemed especially concerned to
establish a proper moral climate of familial relations and to help reunite
African-American families. As one teacher noted, this work of building
family ties offered a hopeful contrast to the sad destruction that many
Northern families had experienced as a result of the war. "While multi-
tudes at the North are lamenting the terrible war which has deprived
them of loved ones," wrote Harriet Taylor from Portsmouth, Virginia,
in 1863, "it is consoling to see its good effects in the reunion of husbands and wives, or parents and children, long separated by the power
of slavery." To further this process, Northern female teachers, along
with male missionaries, worked to encourage legal marriages among
African-American couples. "I urge upon them," wrote a teacher from
St. Helena Village in 1863, "the importance of legal marriage — as right,
and as a benefit to children." Seeking to ritualize and celebrate the marital experience, Yankee teachers and missionaries often organized multiple marriage ceremonies, sometimes uniting forty or more couples in a
single celebration. Northern women also felt the need to offer instruction in matters of chastity and sexual fidelity, often gaining sympathy
for the sexual degradation many black women suffered under slavery.
"Never, never!" explained Austa French, "did we realize the curse, as in
South Carolina, in the case of poor slave women."[21]

But, in undertaking this work, teachers found their efforts to create
an atmosphere of sexual propriety and family bonding constantly undermined by the Union administration and military. Writing from Portsmouth, Virginia, in 1863, where slaves had not yet been officially freed
by the Emancipation Proclamation, one female teacher urged the Lincoln administration to further its emancipation policies for the sake of
the family. "Instances innumerable are met," she remarked in a letter to
American Missionary, "where one part of the family do not know in
what part of the world the others are. It will be encouraging when our
Government will or can do something to make them secure against
being re-enslaved." Even more outrageous, though, were the innumerable instances of Union soldiers sexually abusing African-American
women. Mrs. Harlan, reporting to the Freedmen's Relief Association in

1862, condemned the shameful abuse of black women in and around Port Royal. And Esther Hawks, a white physician working with the Freedmen's Aid Society in the Sea Islands, believed sexual abuse was rampant. "No colored woman or girl," she wrote in 1862, "was safe from the brutal lusts of the [white] soldiers—and by soldiers I mean both officers and men."[22]

Men, both Union officials and civilian relief workers, tended to see the problem more in terms of black women's immorality than white men's abuse. A. S. Hitchcock, the acting superintendent of contrabands in the Department of the South, reported in 1864 on the problem of "dissolute persons hanging around the central Posts of the Department" and targeted, in particular, the "young women" who "flock back & forth by scores to Hilton Head, to Beaufort, to the country simply to while away their time . . . or what is worse to live by lasciviousness." Like many other Union officials, Hitchcock correlated black women's peddling and trading activites with a depraved sense of morality. Even more explicit in his denunciation of the former slave women's supposed impurity was General Rufus Saxton who, in 1863, told the American Freedmen's Inquiry Commission that "the colored women are proud to have illict intercourse with white men."[23]

In contrast, female teachers generally took a much dimmer view of the moral integrity of their male colleagues and male soldiers. Many saw themselves having a special role to play in safeguarding black women from male lust and protecting them from potentially abusive situations. Certainly Marcia Colton did when she came to Craney Island in 1864 to reform a group of black prostitutes. "The Military & Moral authorities," she wrote, "think it is a Military necessity to have a Magdalen Camp on Craney Island, a sort of out-door Prison Life where they can send these Women who having just emerged from Slavery, and beset by bad Men (& many of these are connected with the Federal Army), [are] led astray from the paths of virtue." Colton, like other female teachers, came to believe that women, much more so than men, could better negotiate the former slave women's journey from the morally depraved atmosphere of slavery to the morally upright climate of freedom. Thus Colton claimed that the officers in charge viewed the problem "with Man's judgement," while she saw it "from a Christian & moral standpoint, with Woman's Pity for the degraded and fallen of our own sex." Laura Towne likewise hoped to see more Northern women come to the Sea Islands in order to combat the potentially immoral climate that was fostered by the contact between white male superintendents and black women. Towne understood the problem when she realized that the former slave women avoided taking clothing from the young white men on the plantations, "thinking it will be taken as a

kind of advance for notice — such notice as the best of them have probably dreaded, but which the worst have sought." From the perspective of
black women, Northern female teachers probably did provide a more
secure avenue to a new, less abusive condition of freedom. As both the
white and black women suspected, with only white men present to negotiate the conditions, the emancipation process would certainly have
been even more morally compromised. "Women should be here — good
elderly women," Towne wrote regarding the need for a better moral
climate for female slaves.[24]

Regardless of the female teachers' presence, however, black families
continued to withstand various assaults from the Union regime. Soon
after the Port Royal experiment had begun, the Union military initiated
a policy, which would be in effect in parts of the occupied Confederacy
throughout the war, of continuously appropriating the labor of black
men for both military and agricultural duties. When General David
Hunter became military governor of the Union's Department of the
South in March of 1862, he quickly dispatched his troops to the Sea
Island plantations in order to remove able-bodied black men. Often
forcing black men to accompany them back to their camps, Hunter's
troops intimidated the local population with sometimes angry displays
of martial law and military weaponry. Hunter, for his part, saw this as a
necessary step in the push for an emancipation order. Many black families viewed this intrusion with considerable fear and occasional resistance, anxious that this would make those left behind more vulnerable
to Confederate assault. Black women, in particular, objected to this
threat to family security and integrity. "The womens all hold back der
husbands," explained one African-American soldier, "didn't want them
to go sogering, 'cause they get killed."[25]

To some extent, Northern female teachers responded to black women's
fears and expressed similar concerns with what seemed to be an ugly
reminder of the slave system's disregard for black family life. *American
Missionary* reported in 1863 that they had received numerous reports
from their various agents in the field that expressed alarm at the "indis-
criminate impressment" of black men into government service. Female
teachers worried, in particular, about black women's anxiety after the
departure of their husbands and menfolk. As the day approached when
Hunter's order would be implemented, Laura Towne dreaded seeing
how "the darkness was to close around them" and tried to assure "poor
Bess" that no harm would come to the women. As the military impressment of the former slaves continued, teachers continued to express concern about the seemingly arbitrary removal of black men from their
homes. "When will our Government learn," wrote one teacher in Au-

gust 1863, "to deal justly by this people? . . . they cannot but think that this is a queer way to treat *free* people."[26]

In general, the teachers did not oppose the idea of black men serving in the military, only the manner in which they were made to serve. Harriet Ware fumed when General Hunter initiated a draft among the former slave men, thus reversing an earlier pledge that black men would not be forced to join the army. She believed it only furthered mistrust and suspicion between the Yankees and the former slaves. Female teachers, in fact, sometimes made themselves the intermediaries in this tense situation, again offering a female voice to government directives by trying to present the military necessities with a more humane face. Thus when the Union captain arrived at her plantation in May of 1862 and ordered his soldiers to load their guns in the face of the negro men, Susan Walker could restrain herself no longer. "Stepping down from the porch to where the negroes stood," she wrote, "I assured them I knew no more than themselves . . . but believed [Hunter] to be their friend. . . . I promised to take good care of their families in their absence." She made a special promise to one man in particular whose wife, he explained, was "in family way." As the men departed, the women cried but were also "half assured by my presence in their midst, that nothing wrong would be done." It is, of course, hard to assess just how "assured" the women on this plantation were. But it is clear that female civilians, like Walker, intended to remind Union officials and the former slaves that the abolitionist commitment to family stability would not be completely disregarded, even in the face of military necessity. It even seems likely that female teachers gained an exaggerated sense of their womanly influence, believing that they alone could impart a proper vision of feminine behavior amidst the morally chaotic circumstances of the war. The enlistment of black men led one teacher on Roanoke Island to remind the local black women that they were not "at liberty to marry again" simply because their husbands were absent. To counteract this real, or, more likely, assumed, proclivity toward infidelity, she helped them compose letters in which they affirmed their marital commitments.[27]

The Thanksgiving celebrations that occurred on the Sea Islands in November 1862 suggest that some Union officials may have recognized the useful role that female teachers could play in establishing in the minds of the contrabands a distinction between the old regime and the new. As they had done in their initial visits to the plantations, and in their attempts to counsel former slave women, female teachers tried, in effect, to demarcate emancipation from slavery, in part by underscoring black women's role. The November holiday became the occasion for much singing, celebrating, and speech-making, especially on the part of Union officials who urged black men to enlist in the new regiment being formed by Colonel Higginson. Prominent among the speakers was Frances Gage, an experienced abolitionist and women's rights crusader, who had come to the Sea Islands the previous month with her daughter Mary. Having impressed the Union military governor with her organizing skills, she became one of the few women to run a wartime plantation. By November, she had earned a position of authority, which no doubt led Union officials to give her a place on the Thanksgiving speakers' platform. She delivered, observed Charlotte Forten, a "beautiful appeal to the mothers, urging them not to keep back their sons from the war . . . but to send them forth willingly and gladly as she had done hers, to fight for liberty." This, of course, was a much different approach to the enlistment problem than had previously been tried, especially in its incorporation of a uniquely feminine perspective. Forten, in fact, believed the slaves were greatly moved by Gage's words. Perhaps as proof of the success of the Thanksgiving speech, Gage repeated her arguments one month later at the New Year's celebration, ushering in the era of emancipation, on January 1, 1863.[28]

Of course arbitrary impressments continued, and white women often remained observers in the process. But, on numerous occasions, they tried to become more of a presence in the enlistment of African-American troops, recognizing that their encouragements often had important effects on the former slaves. Sometimes this took the form of displaying the flag near the school houses or holding mock drills with students and field hands. By the end of the war, some female teachers even initiated the type of gendered send-off rituals that white communities carried out during the war, rituals that underscored black women's and children's home-front support for the departing soldiers. Anna Gardner, a teacher in New Berne, North Carolina, organized one such ceremony in January 1865. The students in her school purchased a flag for the troops and "an interesting young lady of color" presented the flag to the men of the First North Carolina Heavy Artillery. Thus, Northern female teachers again made some attempts to elevate the status of black women, in part by bringing to the enlistment process a greater emphasis on feminine participation.[29]

In various ways, then, Northern female teachers managed to bring a gendered perspective to the emancipation process. True, male coworkers often echoed similar messages with respect to black families and the sexual abuse of black women. But, more so than male missionaries, female teachers had been called upon, often by the same Union officials whom they later challenged, to cast the emancipation process in gendered terms, to bring their unique values and perspectives, as well as domestic skill and talents, to the former slaves. A man who had recently traveled to occupied Tennessee told a women's seminary class in Illinois in 1863 that female civilians, specifically, were needed to help the sick and hungry contraband he had encountered. "What can a man do to help such a suffering mass of humanity?" he asked, and then went on to explain that "a woman is needed. Nothing else will do." Joanna Moore, a student at the seminary, responded to this appeal; so did numerous other female teachers who also went south during the Civil War years, hoping to bring their moral influence and feminine authority to bear upon the emancipation experience. Moreover, female teachers may have been better positioned than their male colleagues to carry out this program of protecting women and families, especially since some of the evidence suggests that the former slaves may have preferred the presence of Northern white women. And, to a great extent, it was the teachers' gendered message, despite an occasionally exaggerated sense of feminine influence, that could signal the difference between the old regime and the new. In protecting black women from the unwanted advances of Union soldiers, or emphasizing the protection of the black family in the face of military impressment, Northern female teachers attempted to put a stop to the continued sexual and familial abuse that black men and women had known as slaves.[30]

Yet, none of this is meant to suggest that the teachers fully embraced the former slaves, either women or men, as equals. While the wartime experience may have given women teachers an enhanced appreciation of "womanly" influence and "feminine" needs, they also, more often than not, came to associate true feminine values with women of a higher social status. Thus, at times, female teachers expressed sympathy and even affection for female former slaves, but they also seemed doubtful and generally pessimistic about slave women's femininity. Initial feelings of womanly compassion could often collapse as teachers became frustrated with their uplift efforts. Marcia Colton, for example, the teacher on Craney Island who viewed the problem of black female prostitution there with a "Woman's Pity," questioned if she would be able to overcome the "African heathenism" of her female charges. Many Northern teachers even came to sympathize with the former plantation mistresses and seemed to identify more strongly with slave-owning women's alleged attempts to gently guide and instruct their slaves than with the womanly sufferings of the ex-bondswomen. Many white teachers complained bitterly of the poor housekeeping skills shown by former slave women, especially the inefficient work they did for the teachers and missionaries themselves. The housecleaning and dishwashing chores seemed especially taxing to Harriet Ware and prompted one of her white female housemates to "pity the Southern housekeepers." Even Austa French, wife of Reverend Mansfield French and one who generally gushed with sympathy for her black sisters, felt some compassion for slave-owning women when she tried to get her Sea Island household in order. "If we never believed [the] assertion that 'it was the mistress that was the slave,'" she remarked, "we do now, most cordially, from some weeks' experience with their servants." For many teachers, then, an initial tendency to empathize with female black slaves evaporated and turned into feelings of white female superiority.[31]

The teachers' willingness to replace feminine compassion with race (and class) superiority is perhaps best illustrated by their position regarding the compensated labor of black women. Despite a continued desire to uplift former slave women into the realm of middle-class housewifery, to teach them the virtues of neatness and cleanliness in their homes, female teachers felt just as strongly, if not more so, that black women learn to be self-supporting individuals. In part, their views took shape amidst the unique circumstances of the wartime period, when black women often found themselves deprived of male economic support. But their attitude also reflected larger concerns about white charity and black dependence.

Like other Union officials and representatives of the aid societies, teachers believed in ending, as quickly as possible, the former slaves' reliance on charitable donations. Treasury agent Edward Pierce endorsed the missionaries' intent to make the freedpeople into self-supporting individuals. Teachers, who generally subscribed to the free labor ideals of Northern society, probably possessed strong cultural prejudices against economic dependence as well. Many, in fact, viewed self-support as a symbol of the slaves' new freedom, especially for black men, and would have no doubt endorsed Lucy Chase's view that paid work "would be a crown of manliness" for the former slave.[32]

Yet, while Chase's language reflected prevailing assumptions that linked manhood and economic independence, such language clouded the economic reality: Yankee instructors generally insisted on a program of regular wage-work for both men and women in the African-American community. Few teachers objected to keeping women, and even children, laboring in the fields for several hours each day, even though this reduced the time spent in their schoolrooms. Their objections, to the extent they raised any, had more to do with the failure of the government or the superintendents to distribute wages, not with the work itself. Austa French voiced one of the few objections heard amongst Northern missionaries to the continued field labor of black women. "If our government," she wrote after her trip to the Sea Islands, "cannot afford to let women confine their labors mostly to the house and garden, at least, it condemns four millions, still to live in a half-civilized manner." More typical was the attitude of Treasury agent Edward Pierce. "Field-work," wrote Pierce, " . . . may not be consistent with the finest feminine culture or the most complete womanliness; but it in no way conflicts with virtue, self-respect, and social development. Women work in the field in Switzerland . . . and we may look with pride on the triumphs of this generation, when the American negroes become the peers of the Swiss peasantry. Better a woman with a hoe than without it, when she is not yet fitted for the needle or the book."[33]

Pierce's remarks were not only obviously condescending, but remarkably evasive as well. On the one hand, his comments ignored those white women, in his own country, who also worked in the fields, perhaps because he assumed their work merely entailed "assistance" to male farmers. Moreover, by likening the field work of black women to the agricultural labors of the Swiss peasantry he obscured one of the crucial factors of the emancipation experience: that freedom, for women as well as for men, generally entailed a transition not to subsistence farming but to wage and contract labor. Yet, his comments on women's aptitude "for the needle or the book" point to a reality with which Americans in the 1860s were familiar. In certain trades and professions, women's wage-work was by no means unknown. Both the shoe and textile trades of New England, for example, had expanded and industrialized thanks largely to a feminized work force. Even more, the very women sent to counsel the former slaves were themselves receiving wages for their labors, although most of them were probably not dependent on the scant incomes they received.

But while not unknown, women's wage-work posed distinct problems for Northerners living in the middle years of the nineteenth century. As industrialization proceeded in the Northeast, most Americans affirmed the link between manhood and "breadwinning" and tended to view wage-earning women as symbolic threats to this new economic understanding of masculinity. Both middle- and working-class men thus frequently castigated women's wage-work as a threat to male authority. Middle-class women often concurred and felt called upon to intrude in working-class neighborhoods in cases where poor women were forced to labor outside the private confines of their own homes. Reformers assumed that working-class home-life, because it lacked a woman's maternal oversight, warranted middle-class domestication. And while some middle-class females did undertake wage-work, such as those who taught in both Northern and Southern schools, most did so as unmarried women who would not have to compromise their domestic and familial obligations. Others emphasized that the salaries they received as teachers were so low that the whole undertaking was more an exercise in feminine self-sacrifice than in professional advancement. Some no doubt justified their wage-earning activity as an extension of their feminine responsibility towards children.[34]

But unlike poor white women (who might be domesticated by middle-class reformers) or middle-class teachers (who remained unmarried but assumed maternal responsibility for their students), black women were assigned a more marginal position with respect to the ideals of the male breadwinner and female housewife. In other words, while Northern white women often managed to justify their wage-earning work as labor that furthered the predominant cult of domesticity, black women were offered no such justifications. True, female teachers spoke of making former slave women conscious of their domestic responsibilities, much as middle-class reformers did in Northern urban slums. But because they were determined to have all the former slaves — men and women — prove their ability to support themselves, Yankee instructors generally insisted that former slave women work for some type of compensation, and not always in feminized occupations. In part, their determination was shaped by some of the specific circumstances of the war period, when black men were often taken to perform military or other government service and black women were left on their own. The American Freedmen's Inquiry Commission addressed this problem in October 1863 when they expressed hope that women and children in the contraband camps might support themselves by providing laundry or other services for the troops. If those conditions proved "demoralizing," they suggested that women and children be moved to "abandoned plantations" that they would cultivate.[35]

Under these circumstances, as some missionary workers occasionally realized, teachers would ultimately fall short in their goal of instructing black women in middle-class housewifery, an obviously unattainable objective for women who had to labor arduously outside their homes, or for those left homeless in the war's aftermath. The National Freedmen's Relief Association of New York thus identified such housewife skills as part of their educational objectives for black women, but their inquiries revealed the practical limitations of this program. According to the organization's representative, Mrs. James Harlan, women's household labor proceeded "with as much skill and success as any one could reasonably expect of a poor, destitute, ignorant, oppressed people." Two years later, in 1864, Carolyn Jocelyn wrote from Hilton Head with a little more sensitivity as to the source of the housekeeping problem. The field work, she found, was "mostly performed by women and children, for all the men of a suitable age are in the army. But their outdoor employment has led them to neglect too much their houses; and few have any idea of making them comfortable and attractive." In many ways, then, black women became caught in an inescapable bind: viewed as lazy and dependent if they failed to earn wages, they could also never appear truly civilized, and thus truly feminine, if they continued to neglect their homes.[36]

As the war progressed, and more slaves came into Union lines, the pattern persisted in which black men left to perform military or government service while women and children stayed to fend for themselves. Such circumstances apparently made teachers increasingly wary of accepting too many charitable distributions and more determined to push for the further proletarianization of black women. Teachers moved quickly to establish various "industrial" schools, including numerous schools for training black women, especially in sewing. To many, this type of instruction seemed an ideal solution to the problem of black women's dependence on Northern charity. In learning to sew, not only could black women make their own clothes, they could also attain a useful skill that could earn them money. Lucy Chase, who hung an "A.B.C. card upon the walls," planned to teach sewing and literacy simultaneously. Some teachers, still hoping to raise up black women to middle-class standards of housewifery, believed they could teach sewing as well as good housekeeping. One Norfolk, Virginia, teacher claimed her sewing school could, in addition to lessons in needle work, "also teach these mothers and wives how to live good lives, and how to make a happy, social, virtuous home."[37]

Others, however, especially in the later years of the war, began to view the sewing schools as a route to paid employment. Lucy Chase hoped "to get an army contract for" her pupils' needles and in 1864 wrote of obtaining for her sewers "permanent situations in manufacturing establishments." In 1864, one man even hoped, as he explained in a letter to General Saxton, "to employ the negro women of Beaufort in the manufacture of Hoop Skirts." And Elizabeth Botume, although she did not make plans to place her female sewers in paid occupations, nonetheless intended to employ black women as household servants, even if this meant blurring the distinction between slavery and freedom. As Botume explained, she had not come to do laundry, but to teach, and so would "pay regular wages" for household service. "But," she added, "I should expect good work, and no make-believe." In this way, Botume, Chase, and others showed an increasing willingness to retreat from the middle-class standard regarding women's paid employment. Wages, they believed, more than domestic housewifery, would push black women towards a true state of emancipation.[38]

For all slaves, throughout the South, emancipation became the law of the land with the ratification of the Thirteenth Amendment in January 1865. This, of course, by no means ended the negotiations over the meaning of freedom for black Americans. Indeed, the battles intensified during the Reconstruction years as black labor, black education, and political equality became hotly contested terrains. In addition, the debate was joined, in the postwar years, by a new crop of female teachers—white and black—who came south to initiate thousands of new schools in which they continued to instruct the former slaves in housework, personal hygiene, economic self-sufficiency, as well as reading and writing. And, as they had done in the wartime years, these Yankee instructors, along with other Northern agents of Reconstruction, ultimately retreated from a program that might have allowed the former slaves to rise above an impoverished, proletarianized status and join the ranks of a middle class.

Still, there were moments, especially during the war years, when Northern female teachers found ways to exercise their own subtle influences on the emancipation process. In many instances, their presence and their actions signaled, both to themselves and to the former slaves, a departure from conditions of enslavement. Indeed, male officials and administrators often drew consciously on this female influence in order to reassure the former slaves that their freedom was something more than the life of labor and compulsion they had previously known. The teachers, to a great extent, drew on their own gendered perceptions of family and femininity in attempting to safeguard former slaves, especially black women, from Union policies that blurred the line between slavery and freedom. They hoped to protect black women from Union men's sexual abuse; and they tried, in various ways, to underscore the integrity of the black family when black men were ordered to undertake military and other government service. Ultimately, though, most female teachers continued to associate true womanliness with women of the middle and upper classes. Doubtful of black women's genuine femininity, the teachers actively promoted programs of wage labor outside the home for black women. Stymied by wartime circumstances, a general distrust of economic dependence, and especially by their own class and racial prejudices, Northern teachers furthered and promoted the practice that marginalized black women from Victorian America's cultural ideal of the female housewife.[39]

Notes

Thanks to Drew Faust, Eric Foner, Louis Hutchins, Irwin Silber, Daniel Stowell, and Elizabeth Varon for their insightful comments on an earlier draft of this essay.

1. Elizabeth Ware Pearson, ed., *Letters from Port Royal, 1862–1868* (New York, 1969), 126.

2. Willie Lee Rose, *Rehearsal for Reconstruction: The Port Royal Experiment* (New York, 1964); James McPherson, *The Struggle for Equality: Abolitionists and the Negro in the Civil War and Reconstruction* (Princeton, 1964); Leon Litwack, *Been in the Storm So Long: The Aftermath of Slavery* (New

York, 1979). At one point, General O. O. Howard estimated that over 200,000 freed people had received some amount of instruction during the war.

3. Jacqueline Jones, *Soldiers of Light and Love: Northern Teachers and Georgia Blacks, 1865–1873* (Chapel Hill, 1980); Ronald Butchart, *Northern Schools, Southern Blacks, and Reconstruction: Freedmen's Education, 1862–1875* (Westport, Conn., 1980); Henry Swint, *The Northern Teacher in the South, 1862–1870* (New York, 1967); Perry Chang, "'Angels of Peace in a Smitten Land': The Northern Teachers' Crusade in the Reconstruction South Reconsidered," *Southern Historian* 16 (1995): 26–45. Studies that examine the emancipation process include Litwack, *Been in the Storm So Long*; Ira Berlin, Barbara J. Fields, Thavolia Glymph, Joseph P. Reidy, and Leslie S. Rowland, eds., *Freedom: A Documentary History of Emancipation, 1861–1867*, ser. 1, vol. 1, *The Destruction of Slavery* (Cambridge, 1985); Leslie Schwalm, *A Hard Fight for We: Women's Transition from Slavery to Freedom in South Carolina* (Urbana, 1997).

4. McPherson, *Struggle for Equality.*

5. James McPherson, *The Abolitionist Legacy: From Reconstruction to the NAACP* (Princeton, 1975), 165; Julie Roy Jeffrey, *The Great Silent Army of Abolitionists: Ordinary Women in the Antislavery Movement* (Chapel Hill, 1998), 226–28.

6. Henry Swint, *Dear Ones at Home: Letters from Contraband Camps* (Nashville, 1966), 24.

7. Rose, *Rehearsal*; Amy Dru Stanley, *From Bondage to Contract: Wage Labor, Marriage, and the Market in the Age of Slave Emancipation* (Cambridge, 1998), 139; Edward Pierce, "The Negroes at Port Royal. Report of E. L. Pierce, Government Agent, to the Hon. Salmon P. Chase, Secretary of the Treasury" (Boston, 1862), 8.

8. Rose, *Rehearsal*, 44; Pierce, "Negroes at Port Royal," 33–34; Henry Noble Sherwood, ed., "The Journal of Miss Susan Walker, March 3rd to June 6th, 1862," *Quarterly Publication of the Historical and Philosophical Society of Ohio* 7 (January–March, 1912): 45; Brenda Stevenson, ed., *The Journals of Charlotte Forten Grimke* (New York, 1988), 381. It is, of course, quite possible that Charlotte Forten was discouraged by the Boston group not because of her sex but because of her race.

9. Rose, *Rehearsal*, 52–54; Pearson, *Letters from Port Royal*, 10–11; National Freedmen's Relief Association, By-Laws and Minutes, 1862–1868 (Boston Public Library Rare Books [hereafter BPL]), 42–43

10. Elizabeth Hyde Botume, *First Days amongst the Contrabands* (New York, 1968), 25; Rupert S. Holland, *Letters and Diary of Laura M. Towne* (New York, 1969), 11. See also Ruth Currie-McDaniel, "Northern Women in the South," *Georgia Historical Quarterly* 76 (1992): 284–312.

11. Second and Third Reports of Rev. Mr. French (March 15, 1862, and March 25, 1862); letter from Mrs. James Harlan, March 31, 1862, letter from General Rufus Saxton, July 9, 1862. All documents in National Freedmen's Relief Association, By-Laws and Minutes, 1862–1868 (BPL).

12. *American Missionary* (January 1864), 17, (May 1864), 128, (February 1864), 38; letter of Isaac Hubbs, Mar. 5, 1864, *American Missionary* (May

1864), 132; letter of Asa Fiske, March 13, 1863, *American Missionary* (May 1863).

13. Holland, *Letters and Diary of Laura Towne*, 16; Sherwood, "Journal of Susan Walker," 18, 29, 22; Holland, 21.

14. Holland, *Letters and Diary of Laura Towne*, 21; Sherwood, "Journal of Susan Walker," 21, 35.

15. Jacqueline Jones, *Labor of Love, Labor of Sorrow* (New York, 1985), 44–51; Schwalm, *A Hard Fight for We*, 97–104.

16. Stevenson, *Journals of Charlotte Forten Grimke*, 40–41; Jeffrey, *The Great Silent Army of Abolitionism*, 226–28; Susie King Taylor, *Reminiscences of My Life in Camp* (New York, 1968), 52.

17. Litwack, *Been in the Storm So Long*, 473–74; George P. Rawick, ed., *The American Slave: A Composite Autobiography* (Westport, Conn., 1972), vol. 3, *S.C. Narrs.*, 203, and vol. 2, *S.C. Narrs.*, 59–60. Other recollections by former slaves of Northern teachers can be found in Rawick, *American Slave*, vol. 16, *Tenn. Narrs.*, 72, and vol. 12, *Ga. Narrs.*, 219; Swint, *Dear Ones at Home*, 41.

18. William Gannett and Edward Hale, "The Freedmen at Port Royal," *North American Review* (July 1865): 4; Gannett and Hale, "The Education of the Freedmen," *North American Review* (October 1865), 533.

19. Holland, *Letters and Diary of Laura Towne*, 8; Mrs. A. M. French, *Slavery in South Carolina and the Ex-Slaves; or, The Port Royal Mission* (1862; reprint, New York, 1969), 19.

20. Pierce, "Negroes at Port Royal," 33–34; Pearson, *Letters from Port Royal*, 144–45; Sherwood, "Journal of Susan Walker," 20; Sylvia D. Hoffert, "Yankee Schoolmarms and the Domestication of the South," *Southern Studies* 24 (1985).

21. Letter of Harriet Taylor, March 30, 1863, *American Missionary* (May 1863), 107–8; letter of E. S. Williams, St. Helena Village, April 26, 1863, *American Missionary* (June 1863), 139–40; French, *Slavery in South Carolina*, 92–98.

22. Letter of Miss S. Drummond, July 29, 1863, *American Missionary* (September 1863), 201; letter from Mrs. James Harlan, March 31, 1862 in National Freedmen's Relief Association, By-Laws and Minutes, 1862–1868 (BPL); Hawks, quoted in Schwalm, *A Hard Fight for We*, 102–3.

23. Hitchcock report, quoted in Ira Berlin, Joseph P. Reidy, and Leslie S. Rowland, eds., *Freedom: A Documentary History of Emancipation 1861–1867*, ser. 1, vol. 3, *The Wartime Genesis of Free Labor: The Lower South* (Cambridge, 1990), 316–17; Saxton, quoted in Schwalm, *A Hard Fight for We*, 102–3.

24. Marcia Colton, quoted in Litwack, *Been in the Storm So Long*, 458; Holland, *Letters and Diary of Laura Towne*, 24.

25. Rose, *Rehearsal*, 144–46; Litwack, *Been in the Storm So Long*, 76.

26. *American Missionary* (August 1863), 179; Holland, *Letters and Diary of Laura Towne*, 43; *American Missionary* (August 1863), 180.

27. Pearson, *Letters from Port Royal*, 172; Sherwood, "Journal of Susan

Walker," 39; letter of Miss E. James, August 13, 1864, *American Missionary* (October 1864), 237.

28. Stevenson, *Journals of Charlotte Forten Grimke*, 405–6; Pearson, *Letters from Port Royal*, 132.

29. Rose, *Rehearsal*, 192; letter of Anna Gardner, January 1, 1865, *Freedmen's Record* (February 1865), 21.

30. Daniel Stowell, *Rebuilding Zion: The Religious Reconstruction of the South, 1863–1877* (New York, 1998), 52.

31. Litwack, *Been in the Storm So Long*, 458; Pearson *Letters from Port Royal*, 23; French, *Slavery in South Carolina*, 80.

32. Edward Pierce, "Freedmen at Port Royal," *Atlantic Monthly* 12 (September 1863), 297; Swint, *Dear Ones at Home*, 118.

33. French, *Slavery in South Carolina*, 105; Pierce, "Freedmen at Port Royal," 307.

34. Jeanne Boydston, *Home and Work: Housework, Wages, and the Ideology of Labor in the Early Republic* (New York, 1990), 150–59; letter, *American Missionary* (August 1863), 181.

35. "Condition of the Freedmen," Preliminary Report of the American Freedmen's Inquiry Commission, *American Missionary* (October 1863), 222–23.

36. National Freedmen's Relief Association, By-Laws and Minutes, 1862–1868 (BPL), 107–115; letter of Carolyn Jocelyn, July 20, 1864, *American Missionary* (October 1864), 239.

37. Swint, *Dear Ones at Home*, 29; letter of Mary Fletcher, December 6, 1864, *Freedmen's Record* (January 1865), 6.

38. Swint, *Dear Ones at Home*, 117; June 13, 1864, minutes, National Freedmen's Relief Association, By-Laws and Minutes, 1862–1868 (BPL); Botume, *First Days*, 128.

39. Eric Foner, *Reconstruction: America's Unfinished Revolution* (New York, 1988).

Chapter 3

Slaves, Emancipation, and the Powers of War: Views from the Natchez District of Mississippi

ANTHONY E. KAYE

✦ DURING the spring and summer of 1862, the lumberman Andrew Brown ran the Confederate flag over his mill up and down the pole as Federal boats came and went. Slaves in the town of Natchez learned a good deal about the Civil War by keeping an eye on Brown. Anderson Thomas's wife belonged to Brown, and Thomas noted that her owner was in a fighting mood when Union gunboats first appeared within sight of the town after the capture of New Orleans in April 1862. As Thomas made his way through the crowd on the bluffs overlooking the Mississippi River, he heard Brown upbraid an associate for making the leery prediction that the Confederates "would never catch Old Farragut asleep." Yet slaves in Natchez also saw the telltale signs of Brown's faltering resolve. Jacob Robinson, Brown's head sawyer during the war, observed that "whenever a Gun Boat made its appearance the flag would be hauled down and as Soon as the Gun Boat would be Out of sight the flag would be hoisted this was by Mr. Brown's Orders." During the siege of Vicksburg in the summer of 1863, Brown took the Confederate flag down for good.[1]

Such close scrutiny gave slaves in the Natchez District penetrating insights into the Civil War. A burgeoning literature has described the destruction of slavery across the South in rich detail. Numerous studies have mapped the subversion of plantation discipline, the exodus to Union lines, enlistment in the Union army, the origins of free labor, the reconstitution of freedpeoples' families, and transformations in relations of gender. The fine-grained analysis of emancipation, moreover, has revealed a great deal about how slaves understood slavery and freedom. Yet much work remains to plumb the depths of slaves' interpretations of the war and emancipation. During Reconstruction, thousands of former slaves testified before the Southern Claims Commission, created to compensate loyal Southerners for property the Union army had confiscated. The commission questioned freedpeople at length to probe their title to goods they had lost, the circumstances of confiscation, and claimants' wartime sympathies. Though the testimony dates from the 1870s, ex-slaves offered vivid accounts of their experiences during the war and, most important, what they saw, heard, and said about it in the event.[2] This evidence reveals that, in the Natchez District, many slaves came to terms with forms of power that were new in their experience, and had different, surprisingly nuanced, ideas about just when they gained their freedom.

Slaves' complex interpretations of the war offer new perspectives on a longstanding debate about who freed the slaves. Vincent Harding has popularized the conclusion that the slaves freed themselves.[3] Some historians have argued that Lincoln was indeed the Great Emancipator.[4] Others have contended that a broad coalition, beginning with the slaves and extending to abolitionists, Union soldiers, their commanders, Republicans in Congress, and finally Lincoln, transformed a war to preserve the Union into a war against slavery.[5] From the vantage point of the slaves themselves, the matter of who freed the slaves was inextricably tied to when they gained their freedom. Slaves in the Natchez District focused on three distinct moments of emancipation: Mr. Lincoln's proclamation, the siege of Vicksburg, and the end of the war. Moreover, when they looked behind the war to its main protagonists, they saw neither Lincoln nor a grand coalition but new forms of power, namely, the law, the state, and the nation. The slaves' grasp of this complicated, even chaotic political moment suggests how deeply the conflict transformed their understanding of power itself.

Before the Civil War, slaves in the Natchez District thought of power in fundamentally personal terms. In Mississippi, as elsewhere in the Old South, the state, the law, and the market impinged decisively on slavery.[6] Yet most slaves did not recognize the hand of these institutions at work on their own lives. Instead, the routines of their society made it plain as noonday that masters determined the rules of discipline and punishment, the fate of marriages, and the terms of trade. Slaves knew all too well that owners claimed the authority to join men and women together in marriage and to wrest them apart by sale. Slaves were also painfully aware that masters had the power to define rules of proper behavior and punish transgressions. Moreover, slaves understood that owners claimed the prerogative to pay customary prices for goods that slaves produced on their own account. Slaves in the Natchez District harbored no illusions that owners were the only people to wield power there and had to reckon with yeomen, overseers, drivers, and other slaves, too. Nonetheless, they took the broad powers that slaveholders appropriated to themselves as the archetype of power itself and reasonably concluded that, in their society, power was located in persons.[7]

In late 1860, the struggle over unionism and secession briefly split the slaveholders of the Natchez District. Wilkinson, Jefferson, and Claiborne counties went with the standard-bearer of Southern rights in the presidential election, John C. Breckinridge, while Adams and Warren counties voted Unionist and chose "cooperationist" delegates to the Secession Convention at Jackson. Secessionists rightly understood the cooperationist platform of a united Southern front to demand guarantees from the North as an attempt to forestall disunion. Yet cooperationists also urged the South to form a Confederacy if the North proved unforthcoming. On January 9, 1861, the convention voted to leave the Union by a margin of over five to one. Within little more than a month, Mississippi's representatives withdrew from the United States Congress, Jefferson Davis of Warren County ascended to the Confederate presidency, and planters convened a mass meeting at the Natchez courthouse to declare their resolve to stand by the decision to secede.[8] As slaveholders closed ranks, a wide-ranging and far-reaching debate among their slaves was just beginning.

In 1861 and 1862, slaves across the Natchez District watched and listened and pooled their intelligence on the aims and prospects of the Civil War. Slaves fashioned lines of communication within networks of kinship, work, trade, worship, and sociability. Owners unintentionally made themselves, and slaves who worked in close proximity to them, a critical nexus in these personal lines of communication. An owner's tirade, for example, against God-forsaken Yankees, rampaging over some distant corner of the Confederacy, hell-bent on destroying slavery, might speak volumes about what was at stake in the war to slaves who cooked, waited at table, tended the garden, or drove the carriage. Teamsters, artisans, free black people — anyone who was mobile or literate — also used the ability to reconnoiter over a broad terrain to make themselves authorities on military issues.[9] On Sophia Fox's plantation in Warren County, several lines of communication converged in the person of Samuel Chase. His mother had nursed their owner, who employed him as both a waiter and teamster. Chase proved a valuable source of information to fellow slaves like Lewis Jackson: "Sam being a favorite of Old Mistress and her family, Soon learned from them, after the beginning of the War, that if the Union army succeeded in whipping the South, that all the Slaves would most likely be set free."[10]

Preachers had singular opportunities to collect and purvey information, which they exploited to the full. Their calling moved some to learn to read, allowed them to minister to slaves on many plantations, and gave their interpretations of the war the weight of revelation and prophecy. Harrison Winfield, a preacher and blacksmith, spread the good word as far as the Fox plantation three miles distant from his owner's:

"It was generally believed by all the Slaves of my acquaintance, that if the federal army conquered the South, that the Slaves of the U.S. would be set free."[11] That consensus prevailed among slaves throughout the South.[12]

Many expected God to take a hand in such a prodigious conflict. Prayers for His intervention went up from the circle of men around Nelson Finley, a blacksmith in Woodville, who told them he "hoped to God that the Federals would whip the south." This fellowship did not take God's name in vain but in anguish, in gratitude, in awe, and in hope. "Whenever we heard that the Rebels had whipped the Union men," Mack Washington related, "we were down hearted & would almost cry & we prayed together that the Union troops would whip the Rebels & when we heard the Union troops would whip the Rebels we thanked God & prayed for them." And God's power was not the only one they saw at work in the struggle.

Like others in the Natchez District, they arrived at an understanding that the war had bound up the issue of slavery and freedom with a clash between states and nations. Many slaves became acutely aware that their owners' defense of slavery entailed the parallel project of building a new Confederate nation and a government to rule it. Finley sketched out the full dimensions of Southern nation-building to his comrades. He told Washington "that the Southern people wanted to do as they pleased & to keep the Colored people in Slavery & to keep the poor white Man down — & to have a Country of their own." Finley understood that it required some apparatus to accomplish the subordination of a strata of white people as well as slaves, and explained to William Harris that creating a new government went hand in hand with creating a new country. The "rebels wanted to keep the colored people in slavery forever & didnt want to allow any poor man a chance & wanted to have a government separate from the North — so that they could keep the yankees out of it."[13]

Some slaves first encountered the new powers that be in the public rituals in which slaveholders marked the organization of the Confederacy and cultivated nationalist sentiment. The South's mobilization for war entailed a fateful transfer of power from slaveholders to the local, state, and central arms of the Confederate government. On Washington's Birthday in February 1861, Natchez glowed and thundered as the town claimed the Founder's mantle for their own struggle for independence with a reading of his Farewell Address, a hundred-gun salute, and a torchlit procession through the streets. The rich symbolism of nation-building was meant for citizens, but the carpenter Richard Sullivan was one of the many slaves who crowded the sidewalks that evening, and took note of the float that Andrew Brown contributed to the parade.

The contraption gave Sullivan a powerful insight into the war through a vivid metaphor of government that stuck with him. Years later, he recalled the sight of "a large Pall . . . rigged up as a Ship and called the Ship of State."[14]

Attending the festivities on Washington's Birthday was one of many ways slaves learned about the new forms of power that the war had called into play. After the parade, Brown mounted the "Ship of State" atop his mill. That gave slaves who lived in Natchez or came into town from the hinterland over a year to mull over that symbol of statehood. Of course, there were easier ways to learn about the nation-state than interpreting its imagery. The transformation of towns into seats of Confederate government and fulcrums of nationalism gave slaves in Vicksburg, Natchez, and county seats like Woodville a better purchase on the politics of the war than slaves in the hinterlands. The latter were nonetheless well aware of the new relations of power. On the Green plantation in Warren County, Cato Rux gathered that the South was creating a new nation with its own body of law because his mistress said as much. "She told me that she was for the union and had been all her life. but now she had to obey the laws of the country in which she was then living."[15]

Confederate mobilization forcefully announced the presence of government to many slaves. As they conferred about the war, they often crossed paths with the revitalized slave patrol. A savage punishment administered to a carriage driver in Claiborne County put a fellow slave on notice. Edward Howard observed that Bailer's loose talk about the war brought down the wrath of "a lot of Confederates" who "whipped him nearly to death."[16] Impressment brought the magnitude of Confederate power home to slaves by the sea change it effected. When the army put men to work, it removed them from home, kin, the control of owners, and undermined the latter's authority. Slaveholders' objections to impressment, and the Confederate government's indifference to them, could reveal much to slaves about the limits of their masters' authority in this new state of affairs. Several men belonging to O. M. Blanton saw his personal authority go into eclipse when the army impressed them to build fortifications at Vicksburg. Owners generally did not take an imploring tone in matters of discipline, so Jeff Claiborne took note when Blanton "said he was sorry to see us go," and expressed his hope that they would not run away. Claiborne saw further evidence that power was no longer located in his owner when Blanton subsequently looked in on them. "He said he would do all he could to get us home, but it was not in his power to release us."[17]

The slaves' deliberations in 1861 and 1862 laid the groundwork for a range of views about when they gained their freedom. To be sure, no direct correlation existed between which new forms of power slaves discerned and the particular moment they subsequently claimed their freedom. The consensus that the destruction of slavery depended on the outcome of the fighting encouraged slaves to expect the end of the war to be the moment of emancipation. That selfsame notion only gained depth among civilians who also recognized the war as a struggle over law, government, and nationality, for they understood that making emancipation stick required uprooting these new forms of power, too. Yet the procedure of interpreting titanic changes from their subtle outward signs — an owner's solicitous demeanor, stray terms like "country" or "government" from the lexicon of the nation-state, and suggestive images in the iconography of nationalism such as the Ship of State — inevitably led to varied understandings of the powers of war and their potentialities.

As the war brought slaves in the Natchez District face-to-face with the Union army, they entered into unprecedented relationships with the nation-state through its military arm, and came to different conclusions about the precise moment when emancipation was at hand. Some slaves in the region took the Emancipation Proclamation as that moment. Early in the war, Lewis Jackson shared in the consensus around the Fox plantation that the Union would have to whip the South for slaves to gain their freedom. But the edict changed Jackson's mind, and he considered himself "freed by Abraham Lincoln's Proclamation." It carried particular force among slaves whose owners had abandoned their plantations. To those who reaped the fruits of their own labor, no longer worked under the supervision of owners, and were even in possession of the latter's property in some cases, the proclamation of emancipation gave new liberties an august imprimatur. In March 1862, Thomas C. Drummond's owner withdrew from Jefferson County across the Mississippi to Louisiana and sent his slaves east of the Natchez District. Drummond collected wages as a railroad brakeman, traded widely, accumulated livestock and other goods rapidly. Under those circumstances, the Emancipation Proclamation felt liberating to Drummond. Yet few slaves in the region were in such enviable circumstances in early 1863.[18]

The force of the Emancipation Proclamation was lost on the great mass of slaves in the region because it was, to their way of thinking, remote. First, word of the edict did not circulate widely among slaves in some areas far from Union lines, including the Natchez District. There, the personal networks of kinship, labor, trade, and worship in which slaves exchanged information about the war stopped well short of Washington, D.C. Second, the proclamation paled before the slaves' belief that they would gain their freedom if the Union won the war. Two men in Vicksburg took a dim view of the preliminary proclamation of emancipation when they scrutinized it from that vantage in the fall of 1862. What struck the carpenter George W. Walton and the drayman Ambrose Holmes was not the declaration that slaves in rebel states like Mississippi would be "thenceforward, and forever free" come New Year's Day but the offer to rejoin the Union before then and thereby evade emancipation. "We were afraid they would accept the terms offered & slavery would not be abolished. We wanted the rebels to be conquered," Walton recalled. He and Holmes had come to believe, like most slaves, that emancipation hung in the balance with the outcome of the war, and they saw nothing in the proclamation to alter that conviction. In both these ways, the edict was marginal in slaves' understanding of the war.[19]

Third, and most important, Lincoln's edict failed to measure up to slaves' conceptions of power, old as well as new. To those who had begun to apprehend the force of states and nations, Lincoln's declaration changed little. At first glance, the notion that Lincoln destroyed slavery at will seems well suited to slaves who located power in persons. Yet the myriad powers of slaveholders acquired much of their force in the ability to decide the fate of families, dictate the terms of labor, and impose discipline and punishment on the ground. As far as slaves in the Natchez District could see, Lincoln was in no position to exercise such broad authority. The president was far away, at a place called Washington. Lincoln, in short, did not cut much of a figure to slaves in southwestern Mississippi because he exercised none of the prerogatives that they identified with real power.

Civilians in the Natchez District encountered the Union army at close quarters during the siege of Vicksburg in the spring and summer of 1863. General U. S. Grant had tried to bring the war south to that vicinity since the Union victory at Shiloh, but his advance stalled at Holly Springs in northern Mississippi in October 1862. During the winter, all of Grant's effort and ingenuity brought Union forces no closer to the Natchez District than Chickasaw Bluffs, where troops under General William T. Sherman disembarked from boats on the Yazoo River and briefly menaced Confederate defenses north of Vicksburg. Then, on April 30, 1863, Grant's troops crossed the Mississippi River south of town, marched northeast to the state capital in Jackson, turned around to head due west toward Vicksburg. They drove twenty thousand Confederates off Champion's Hill on May 16 and finally crossed the Big Black River in Warren County the next day. Union troops dug entrenchments in a broad arc around Vicksburg to lay siege to the city in May and June and swept over nearby plantations in small detachments to seize cattle, sheep, chickens, wagons, fodder, fence rails, and whatever livestock, food crops, or movable property could feed, shelter, or otherwise provision the army. The confiscation and destruction of property was fearsome.[20]

In Warren County, many slaves who saw the Union army in the throes of impressment deemed this the moment of their emancipation. Edward Hicks watched squads of Union troops go relentlessly about their business on an adjoining plantation, emptying the smokehouse, leading away horses and mules, carrying off corn, killing scores of hogs for weeks on end. "I saw them at it every day until they got all he had." After Squire Myers watched two such expeditions drive off virtually all the stock on his owner's place, "I Knew that Mr Johnson was jist broke up." The Union army's ability to carry off livestock bodily, break open smokehouses with impunity, and literally disassemble property lines by taking fence rails vividly proved that slaveholders no longer commanded control over their property.[21] Many slaves left their owners shortly after witnessing such formidable displays of the Union army's power. Samuel Chase had long ago decided he had no intention of leaving his owner and agreed with other slaves on the Fox plantation that the Union army would have to win the war if they were to gain their freedom. But Union troops camped in the woods on the Fox place, foraged widely there and in the vicinity. Like other slaves, Chase concluded that "I became free about the time the Federals were besieging Vicksburg."[22]

The fall of Vicksburg, on Independence Day, resounded to slaves across the Natchez District as a clarion of freedom. The Union's victory appeared conclusive to slaves who, residing in town, saw it at close range. Albert Webster claimed to speak not only for himself but the hack-driver he worked for and every other slave they knew in the city: "[A]fter the surrender of Vicksburg he as well as all of us were positive that we were free." The import of the event issued forth into the countryside, dramatically on many plantations, as a moment of truth in Jefferson County on the McCoy place. There, the news circulated among the slaves while the overseer prepared to refugee them to Texas. At least eleven slaves decamped for Union lines before they were carried off, despite the wrenching separations that their bold step entailed. Judy and Nelson Davis left without Mrs. Davis's sister, Lucinda, while Emily and Harris Stewart were never to see their nineteen-year-old son again.[23]

Reunion with kin, payment of wages, or a new freedom of speech confirmed the liberating force of the taking of Vicksburg. Olive Lee had lived separately from her husband, and considered herself free when he left their owners' plantation in the hinterland and joined her in town. Peter Jackson, a slave on the Acuff place in Warren County, decided that he was free as soon as the siege ended and he went to work for himself. The fall of Vicksburg marked the collapse of Confederate police powers that had first alerted many slaves to the state-building dimension of the war. The danger that had hung over their war counsels suddenly lifted with the smoke of the siege. William Green, who had left his owner's place to wait on a Union colonel before the capture of the city, took the liberty to speak his mind only afterwards: "We talked secretly — That is among ourselves (the colored people) — We could not have expressed our opinions in public, before the yankees Came, after that we talked very openly."[24]

The reverberations from Vicksburg carried further into the district when the Union army captured Natchez, about sixty-five miles to the south, on July 13, 1863. The events came so hard on the heels of one another that it is unclear whether some slaves in Adams County acted on the consequence of the former, in anticipation or the aftermath of the latter. On York plantation, one hundred slaves finished working their potatoes and left the place on the Saturday after the taking of Vicksburg, two days before the fall of Natchez, and the rest followed suit two days afterwards. As in Vicksburg, the emancipatory effect of Union occupation was pervasive, and virtually instantaneous in the town proper. Thomas Turner, a mail and messenger servant for the Surget family, spread the word early in the war that his mistress had said the slaves would gain their freedom when the Yankees gained the day. When the Union army arrived in town, she made clear that day had come, and offered to pay wages or rent land to anyone who stayed on the place. But Turner concluded he did not need his owner's protection to have his freedom and went to Natchez instead. Turner's son Wallace went, too, and recalled that "I Knew that after the union soldiers Came here. that the war gave us our freedom."[25] Slaves made their way to town from plantations far and wide. Colonel Thomas E. G. Ransom reported on the third day of the occupation that they were arriving by the thousands. By the end of August, twenty thousand men, women, and children had gathered at Vicksburg as well.[26]

The siege of Vicksburg revealed itself to most slaves as the most critical moment of emancipation before the end of the war. Indeed, the siege was not one such moment but several. Slaves deemed freedom at hand when they took in the sight of the Union army in the act of confiscation, got wind of the surrender of Vicksburg, or heard tell of the capture of Natchez. The emancipating influence of the Union army spread as its occupation of the Natchez District took hold. General Ransom's report to his superiors betrayed some doubt about the status of the civilians who entered his lines when he requested "some instructions as to what policy I shall pursue with regard to the negroes." "With regard to the contrabands," replied General James B. McPherson, "you can say to them they are free." For many slaves, such assertions could literally go without saying as they took confiscation, enlistment, and other encounters with the Union army for the moment of emancipation in late 1863 and 1864.[27]

Yet most slaves in the Natchez District did not consider emancipation an accomplished fact in the summer of 1863. For one thing, the majority were still on their owners' plantations.[28] Among the thousands who made off for Natchez or Vicksburg, many did not equate leaving their owners with the destruction of slavery. Some did not consider themselves free because they had left family and friends behind who were not. Some drew a further distinction between their own freedom and the fate of slavery itself. Despite impressive Union victories in the vicinity, slaves had long recognized that the war was playing out in a larger theater. After the siege of Vicksburg, they held fast to their view that slavery would not be destroyed until the Union won the war. They rightly understood that the war was far from over. Thus, thousands of men in the Natchez District enlisted in the Union army in July and August on the conviction that the war between the Confederacy and the Union, between slavery and freedom, could still go either way.

Union occupation, and the multiple transformations it wrought in the daily lives of thousands of slaves, introduced many African Americans to the powers of the nation-state. Some had already discerned those forces behind the war and encountered them directly in the workings of Confederate policing and impressment. Yet the alliance between the Confederate government and slavery had concealed the state behind the personal exercise of power that continued to define slaves' daily routine in 1861 and 1862. The Union army's commitment to emancipation removed that cloak with verve. Enlisting in the army or marrying under its auspices engaged people in rites that explicitly invoked law, government, and nationality. Military service immersed men in those new forms of power by inducting soldiers into an institution where military law defined rules that were binding on officers and enlisted troops alike.[29] Encountering the nation-state in its military arm critically shaped the thinking of both soldiers and civilians. Confiscation and enlistment were, in many respects, poles apart as relations to the Union army. Yet both revealed how readily new forms of power coexisted with old ones.

It struck liberated slaves as a hard thing indeed that Federals, like slaveowners, appropriated the fruits of labor without payment. Their expectations of a liberating army had not prepared them for the confiscation of their property right along with slaveholders'. Surprise as well as anger put the edge on the protests that men and women registered with foraging soldiers. In Warren County, the scope of confiscation became increasingly clear over the summer of 1863, and the scarcity of food crops and draft animals made slaves anxious to hold onto some means of subsistence, even after the army began to distribute rations in Vicksburg. The practice seemed wrongheaded to Sabitha Walker, who watched Union squads strip the Hall plantation of poultry, hogs, cattle, horses, and mules in August: "[T]he United States took everything away from our place and then turned around and fed us—I thought that they had ought to leave us something." The army also failed to make good on promises to pay wages to hundreds of men it put to work. A foraging party took Daniel Murfee's corn and his horse before he went to work on fortifications around Vicksburg. After the town fell, he joined two hundred men at the courthouse to collect their pay, but they were promptly surrounded by troops and pressed into the army, except for thirty men, including Murfee, deemed unfit for duty. Neither confiscation nor unpaid labor altered his conviction that he became a free man when the siege began. Yet his indignation about his unpaid labor remained palpable ten years later. He was promised wages of twenty dollars per month, "but I never got a cent."[30]

In the rituals of enlistment, the Union army often imposed the mark of slavery upon soldiers. In regiments across the South, men enlisted under their father's surname as a mark of emancipation. But it is often overlooked that Union officers imposed an owner's name upon many soldiers who wanted to adopt their family's. Harrison Willis lived apart from his father, Mike Barnes, who belonged to another owner in Claiborne County. Willis went by his owner's name, but resolved to take his father's when he enlisted in the 66th United States Colored Infantry at Vicksburg in November 1863. He presented himself as Harrison Barnes to the enrolling officer, who promptly asked his master's name and enlisted him as Harrison Willis.[31]

Yet enlistment was, for all recruits, an initiation to national loyalty and the rule of law. Within six days, every soldier took an oath pledging their "true allegiance to the United States of America," to "serve them honestly and faithfully," to obey orders "according to the Rules and Articles for the government of the armies." To soldiers in the 52nd USCI, the army symbolized the rule of law in the spring of 1864 by swearing them in at the courthouse in Vicksburg. Enlistment routinely underscored the rule of law with a reading of the Articles of War, which required every regiment to read them out every six months. The latter requirement was only observed in the breach in many regiments, and the rule of law was imperfect at best. Still, soldiers understood military law as a critical break with the personal exercise of power that defined slavery. The army's requirement that punishments conform strictly to military law, for example, contrasted sharply with slaveholders' claim to dictate the terms of discipline.[32]

The Union army also imparted powerful lessons on the rule of law to civilians. Regimental chaplains recorded 4,627 marriages at Natchez, Vicksburg, and around Davis Bend in 1864–65. Matrimony took on an air of the command performance at several towns in the Mississippi Valley during the spring of 1864, where Union authorities, refusing to recognize marriages consecrated in slavery, urged couples to wed. In April, nuptials took on particular urgency at Natchez, where officials exempted soldiers' wives from an order requiring anyone without gainful employment to leave town. Yet liberated slaves also believed the ceremonies gave a new authority to the bond between husband and wife,[33] which they neatly evoked in the resonant phrase, marriage "under the flag."[34] The term referred, in part, to a location: a flag often hung nearby at the weddings regimental officers performed. More important, liberated slaves imbued the practice with meanings symbolic of a new bond between husband and wife wrought with stronger mettle than the personal authority of slaveholders. Patsy Clayborne resolved that she and her soldier had to have a military wedding after she heard the soldiers drumming women out of Natchez say that "those who had wifes must get married by the United States Laws." In short, couples were quick to marry "under the flag" because they wanted to appropriate the powers of law and nation to the bonds of marriage.[35]

The occupation cleared the ground for a revolution in relations of work in 1863 and 1864. When the Yankees took Natchez, the Reed clan left their owner's Jefferson County plantation and entered into a range of wage labor for the Union army. The brothers Reed, James and Daniel, enlisted with their two cousins in the 58th USCI, where they earned ten dollars per month (seven in cash and three in clothing). Meanwhile, their uncle, Moses Reed, drove a wagon at the regimental hospital. In early 1864, both the Reed brothers died there of small pox, and Daniel's widow, Phillis Reed, went to work as a nurse where she had tended her husband. Phillis and Moses Reed thus joined the ranks of military laborers, who also received ten dollars per month performing the heavy work of nurses, laundresses, and cooks, building fortifications, and teamstering. Others toiled for varied rates off the payroll as personal servants, washing clothes, cutting cordwood, barbering, and hack driving. Men and women who worked for the Union army in their different capacities understood the wage relation as a fundamental break with the personal exercises of power that defined the relations of work under slavery. For the change sheared away the many powers—from the crack of the whip to the breaking up of families—that slaveholders employed to put slaves to their labors.[36]

Army regulations for wage labor on plantations provided for that transformation, too. As men entered Union ranks as both soldiers and military laborers, women comprised a growing majority of workers in the fields of the Natchez District. In March 1864, Adjutant General Lorenzo Thomas's Order No. 9 prohibited flogging, set wages at seven dollars per month for women and ten dollars for men, and repeatedly cast the advent of free labor as a "revolution." Federal authorities extricated masters from the management of numerous plantations along the Mississippi River by requiring planters of "doubted loyalty" to take on a Union-minded partner, typically a Northerner. When Thomas's order went into effect, a Treasury Department official counted 244 plantations in the hinterlands of Natchez and Vicksburg operated by lessees. Many women as well as men secured better terms in practice than Thomas offered on paper. On the Hawkins place in Warren County, Julia Ann McCaskill rented a tract for a share of the cotton and corn she raised, while Philip Hart and Gabriel Boger paid five dollars per acre for two seventeen-acre plots that they worked together and gained use of a pasture in return for clearing land.[37]

Yet the terms of wage labor bore some resemblances to those of slave labor for those who worked under Order No. 9. Union commanders in Louisiana and Mississippi used the new work regime to cultivate the loyalty of local planters. In fact, Thomas assured the leading men of the Natchez District whom he consorted with that the conventions of slave labor would serve as the model for his regulations. A provision to withhold one-half of monthly wages until the end of the year immobilized laborers. In several particulars, the rules simply codified and regularized obligations that slaves and owners had contested before the war. Thus, free labor also obliged field hands to work from sunup to sundown, entitled them to Sunday as a day of rest, adequate rations of food, and each family to a separate dwelling and plot of land to cultivate on their own account. Even Yankee planters required laborers to continue to work in gangs supervised by overseers. The similarities to slavery that women and men saw in the wartime system of free labor was the source of a palpable consternation. John Eaton, General Superintendent of Freedmen, observed from his Vicksburg headquarters that laborers were reluctant to enter into wage relations with either "their old masters" or lessees because of "their terror of finding themselves tricked into some form of bondage."[38]

Even the Union army's most utopian enterprise exhibited continuites with slavery along with radical departures from it. The origins of the Yankees' experiment at Davis Bend dated back to 1825, when Joseph Davis crossed paths with the socialist Robert Owen in a stagecoach. Davis thought slavery was fertile ground for Owen's rationalist theories of cooperative labor, and organized his plantation and his brother Jefferson Davis's accordingly. Slaves traded extensively in poultry and garden truck and served as jurors on a court with jurisdiction over discipline and the Davises as judge. During the siege of Vicksburg, Grant resolved to make the bend the site of "'a Negro paradise.'" In 1864, about six hundred freedpeople combined under army regulations into "companies" to lease land. Each member covered part of the company's expenses, received a share of its profits, and had a say in choosing their representative to other companies, which combined to form "colonies." A union officer presided over each colony as superintendent with authority to subject every member to his orders, his notion of proper field work, and the punishment of work without pay. Another 110 people worked for a Northern lessee under the terms of Thomas's general regulations for wage labor. On the Home Farm, over one thousand worked merely for rations.

That the majority of freedpeople on Davis Bend received no wages cast no doubt over their certitude that they were slaves no more. At an Independence Day celebration, they sang,

De Lord he makes us free indeed
 In his own time an' way.
We plant de rice and cotton seed,
 And see de sprout some day:
We know it come, but not de why, —
 De Lord know more dan we.
We 'spected freedom by an' by;
 An' now we all are free.[39]

Union stewardship of Davis Bend reached its apogee in 1865. Authorities expanded the system of communal tenantry from 76 to 181 companies, paid some wages to laborers on the Home Farm, and invited freedpeople to elect their own judges and sheriffs to reconvene the court. Union regulations enjoined the judges to decide cases "according to their Ideas of justice." Yet one judge made clear that he did not weigh his views alone when he castigated two defendants as "the cause that respectable colored people are slandered, and called thieving and lazy." To thousands of civilians from across the Natchez District and distant parts who passed though the bend in 1865, the court was unprecedented.[40]

Throughout the district, some liberated slaves developed a keen understanding of market relations. On the plantations in the region, a market in free labor was still in the future in 1863 and 1864. The elements of the antebellum organization of field work reproduced in Order No. 9, the compulsory cast that the military occupation gave to the whole terrain of work, the enlistment of military laborers and soldiers in the overriding causes of winning the war and destroying slavery — all this gave liberated slaves little reason to mistake free labor for a market relation. Men and women who worked for wages, however, acquired the means to buy goods. Furthermore, many used wages earned in the army's employ to set themselves up as independent producers.[41] In contrast to towns like Charleston, Savannah, and New Orleans, where slave women were active traders, men largely controlled relations of exchange in the Natchez District until the war.[42] Sarah Burton cooked for a Union regiment, bought a mule and cart, peddled fruits and vegetables, "bought Sugar to Sell again," and, in collaboration with her new husband, earned enough to buy a sow and complete an incongruous team for their four-horse wagon with one horse and three mules. People who worked on their own hook embraced market notions of trade with particular alacrity as they sold their produce and bought means of subsistence and production.[43]

Many liberated slaves came alive to principles of the market and conducted trade along those lines. Some folks kept close tabs on fluctuations in the prices fetched by corn, cordwood, or mules of a particular grade. Gold, silver, and greenbacks all were common currency during the Union occupation, and some people kept track of prices in different mediums of exchange. Edward Hicks, for example, noted the price of horses in "U.S. money" ($125) and corn in gold ($1 per bushel).[44] In the sudden onrush of trade, the hack-driver Henry Banks took to a notion of market relations that objectified them and imbued money itself with all their ostensible power. To him, money's uncanny ability to gather men in commerce and move goods between them after the fall of Vicksburg verged on alchemy, as money seemed to take different physical forms, and even take flight, at least metaphorically: "The Cotton Buyers were thick and spent money like water and the soldiers had just got paid, and their money just flew around, especially the big officers who didn't appear to care anything about it." Banks and other hackmen in town were quick to charge whatever the traffic would bear: "They would pay anything you asked, and we asked all we thought we could get." Entering into market relations with strangers like soldiers and cotton buyers was a simpler affair than doing so with owners, whom liberated slaves were accustomed to trading with on the basis of customary prices. Henry Hunt had bought a fine sow pig before the war for two dollars but did not let customary prices dictate the terms of trade when he sold it to his wife's owner for a tidy profit at twelve dollars in silver.[45]

Some came to wonder whether the powers of war, formidable though they were, constituted a stable foundation for an enduring freedom. Henry Watson, like his fellow slave Samuel Chase, deemed himself a free man early in the siege of Vicksburg. Yet Watson considered his freedom a precarious thing, for during the summer and fall he often told his friend James Puckett that he aimed "to Keep free." And between the vagaries of wage labor and the heavy hand of the Union army, keeping free was a struggle. In October, foraging troops confiscated his livestock. After a month cooking for the company that took his property, he tried to enlist, was rejected as physically unfit, and joined the Pioneer Corps for a year instead. He was promised a soldier's pay, which was the going rate for military laborers in late 1863, but "I never got a cent of pay for what I done." We will never know whether Watson believed he was keeping free during that year of unpaid labor. When Puckett saw him then, Watson said, appropriately enough, "that he was a pioneer."[46] For others, the Yankees' uncertain hold on the Natchez District made freedom tenuous. Confederate scouts made forays into Warren County, the very heart of occupied territory, throughout 1864. In August, rebels captured Gabriel Boger on the Hawkins place just eleven miles outside Vicksburg and put two shots through his hat as he made his escape. Such perils gave many people good cause not to put too fine a point on just when they gained their freedom.[47]

Thus, many people took the end of the war as the moment of emancipation. Years later, Boger said, "I was made free by the war." Many others said much the same when the Southern Claims Commission asked when they had gained their freedom. Some elaborated and pinpointed the siege of Vicksburg. Others, however, made clear they had the end of the war in mind. Elvira Anderson, for example, said "[T]he war freed me." She lived on a plantation in Warren County, washed and ironed at a nearby army hospital during the summer of 1863, and left for Vicksburg in September after she married a soldier. "I was threatened because my husband belonged to the Union Army & was compelled to leave the Noland place." Finally, she "[b]ecame free at the close of the war."[48]

Anthony Lewis was typical of slaves who had resolved early on in the war that they would gain their freedom when the Union conquered the South. A teamster and gardener in Claiborne County, Lewis was in his fifties in 1861 and, in the words of his niece's husband, "a sort of a preacher among us and we looked up to him and advised with him." Lewis told the young men who gathered after nightfall "that the Yankees were fighting to free them, but if the Confederates were successful they would still be in slavery." Lewis and his comrades followed the war as best they could. They "rejoiced" at news of Northern victories, according to Clem Hardeman, and put "long faces on" upon hearing of setbacks. There is no evidence the Emancipation Proclamation came to their notice. When the Union army arrived in full force in the Natchez District in 1863, Lewis harbored no illusions that the war was over and urged his two sons to enlist. Like many others, Lewis considered himself "freed by the war," which was to say, "I became free when the war ended."[49]

The plural moments of emancipation offer an additional perspective to the debate over who freed the slaves. Slaves considered themselves free at different junctures because their understandings of power and the war were changing and, consequently, varied. Many people held fast to the consensus of 1861–62 that the Union would have to win the war to destroy slavery, and later said that the war freed them. Despite the interpretation of some historians, then, the freedpeople of the Natchez District did not believe that they freed themselves. What is just as surprising, only a few slaves who had already parted company with their owners took Mr. Lincoln's proclamation as the moment of their emancipation. A great many more resolved that they were free at some point during the siege of Vicksburg — the beginning of the bombardment, a foraging party's show of force, the surrender of the city, or the capture of Natchez. Lincoln, alone or in tandem with abolitionists, and Radical Republicans were not the prime movers behind emancipation to slaves in the Natchez District, who increasingly identified the war and its liberating tendencies with powers of law, state, and nation.

The perspectives of these slaves offer important insights into the meaning of freedom. A growing body of work is divided over whether emancipation represented continuity or change.[50] Arguments for continuity have acquired new luster from post-structuralist currents of thought that are skeptical of diametrical oppositions, like slavery and freedom. Some scholars have pointed to the persistence of compulsion in the transition to free labor and suggested that in practice the difference between slavery and freedom during the era of emancipation in the Americas was minimal.[51] That conclusion pays no mind to the freedpeople's point of view.[52] For they understood that they had ceased to be property and, therefore, could no longer be subject to the will of owners whose word was law, whipped, bought and sold with impunity, their families broken and scattered. They never faltered in their conviction that slavery would be destroyed when the Union whipped the South. Instead, they made their struggle against the strange, unprecedented collaborations between old and new forms of power the crux of an epoch-making transition from slavery to freedom.

Notes

I would like to thank Barbara J. Fields and Eric Foner as well as Elizabeth Blackmar, Drew Gilpin Faust, and Peter Kolchin for incisive criticism of an earlier version of this essay and Joan E. Cashin for astute editing of the present manuscript.

1. Testimony of Burr Lewis, Anderson Thomas, 21 July 1875, and Randall Pollard, 28 January 1874, and Jacob Robinson, 24 July 1875 and n.d., Andrew Brown claim, case 1233, Congressional Jurisdiction Case Files, Records of the United States Court of Claims, Record Group (hereafter RG) 123, National Archives (hereafter NA); Leon F. Litwack, *Been in the Storm So Long: The Aftermath of Slavery* (New York, 1980), 3–4, 8, 115–16.

2. Mississippi case files, ser. 732, Approved Claims, Southern Claims Commission (hereafter SCC), 3rd Auditor, Records of the United States General Accounting Office, RG 217, NA. See also Frank W. Klingberg, *The Southern Claims Commission* (Berkeley, 1955). Many claims disallowed by the commission were appealed to the United States Court of Claims. Records of those cases include the evidence taken by the Claims Commission as well as testimony submitted to the Court of Claims during the 1880s. See Congressional Jurisdiction Case Files, Records of the United States Court of Claims, RG 123, NA.

3. Vincent Harding, *There Is a River: The Black Struggle for Freedom in America* (New York, 1981), 225–26; Stephen V. Ash, *Middle Tennessee Society Transformed, 1860–1870: War and Peace in the Upper South* (Baton Rouge, 1988), 111–12, 114–15, 210; Michael Fellman, "Emancipation in Missouri," *Missouri Historical Review* 83 (1988): 36–56, esp. 36, 40–42; Leslie A. Schwalm, *A Hard Fight for We: Women's Transition from Slavery to Freedom in South Carolina* (Urbana, 1997), 117, 126.

4. LaWanda Cox, *Lincoln and Black Freedom: A Study in Presidential Leadership* (1981; reprint, Columbia, S.C., 1994); James M. McPherson, *Abraham Lincoln and the Second American Revolution* (New York, 1991), 23–42; idem, "Who Freed the Slaves?" *Reconstruction* 2, no. 3 (1994): 35–40, reprinted with slight modifications in idem, *Drawn with the Sword: Reflections on the American Civil War* (New York, 1996), 192–207.

5. W. E. B. Du Bois, *Black Reconstruction in America, 1860–1880* (1935; reprint, New York, 1962), 55–86; John W. Blassingame, "The Recruitment of Colored Troops in Kentucky, Maryland and Missouri, 1863–1865," *Historian* 29 (1967): 533–45; Ira Berlin, Barbara J. Fields, Thavolia Glymph, Joseph P. Reidy, and Leslie S. Rowland, eds., *Freedom: A Documentary History of Emancipation, 1861–1867*, ser. 1, vol. 1, *The Destruction of Slavery* (Cambridge, 1985), 1–56; Barbara J. Fields, "Who Freed the Slaves?" in *The Civil War: An Illustrated History*, ed. Geoffrey C. Ward with Ken Burns and Ric Burns (New York, 1990), 178–81; Ira Berlin, "Emancipation and Its Meaning in American Life," *Reconstruction* 2, no. 3 (1994): 41–44; Ira Berlin, "Who Freed the Slaves? Emancipation and Its Meaning," in *Union and Emancipation: Essays on Politics and Race in the Civil War Era*, ed. David W. Blight and Brooks D. Simpson (Kent, Ohio, 1997), 105–21; Joseph P. Reidy, *From Slavery to Agrarian Capitalism in the Cotton Plantation South: Central Georgia, 1800–1880* (Chapel Hill, 1992), 108–35; John Cimprich, *Slavery's End in Tennessee, 1861–1865* (University, 1985), 3–4, 21, 60, 98, 116–17.

6. Charles S. Sydnor, *Slavery in Mississippi* (1933; reprint, Baton Rouge, 1966), 63–64, 78–79; Eugene D. Genovese, *Roll, Jordan, Roll: The World the Slaves Made* (New York, 1974), 32, 37–70; Mark Tushnet, *The American Law of Slavery, 1810–1860: Considerations of Humanity and Interest* (Princeton, 1981); Willie Lee Rose, "The Domestication of Slavery," in *Slavery and Free-*

dom, expanded edition, ed. William W. Freehling (Oxford, 1982), 23– 25; Peter Kolchin, *American Slavery, 1619–1877* (New York, 1993), 127–32; Michael Tadman, *Speculators and Slaves: Masters, Traders, and Slaves in the Old South* (Madison, 1989).

7. Anthony E. Kaye, "The Personality of Power: The Ideology of Slaves in the Natchez District and the Delta of Mississippi, 1830–1865" (Ph.D. diss., Columbia University, 1999).

8. Percy L. Rainwater, *Mississippi: Storm Center of Secession, 1856–1861* (1938; reprint, New York, 1969), 196, 198–99; William L. Barney, *The Secessionist Impulse: Alabama and Mississippi in 1860* (Princeton, 1974), 132, 145–50, 197–99, 231–32, 237–38, 265–66, 272; John K. Bettersworth, *Confederate Mississippi: The People and Policies of a Cotton State in Wartime* (Baton Rouge, 1943), 7–9, 15.

9. Bell Irvin Wiley, *Southern Negroes, 1861–1865* (1938; reprint, Baton Rouge, 1965), 16–19; Benjamin Quarles, *The Negro in the Civil War* (Boston, 1953), 52–53; Paul D. Escott, "The Context of Freedom: Georgia's Slaves during the Civil War," *Georgia Historical Quarterly* 58 (Spring 1974): 81–83; Litwack, *Been in the Storm So Long*, 5, 21–27; Berlin et al., *Destruction of Slavery*, 8–9, 25; Schwalm, *Hard Fight for We*, 126; Lynda J. Morgan, *Emancipation in Virginia's Tobacco Belt, 1850–1870* (Athens, Ga., 1992), 106–8.

10. Testimony of Lewis Jackson, 23 September 1887, Samuel Chase claim, case 1990, Congressional Jurisdiction, RG 123, NA.

11. Testimony of Harrison Winfield, 23 September 1887, Samuel Chase claim, case 1990, Congressional Jurisdiction, RG 123, NA; Janet Duitsman Cornelius, *"When I Can Read My Title Clear": Literacy, Slavery, and Religion in the Antebellum South* (Columbia, S.C., 1991), 3, 59–60, 85–94.

12. Quarles, *Negro in the Civil War*, 51–52; Litwack, *Been in the Storm So Long*, 27; Berlin et al., *Destruction of Slavery*, 9–10; Barbara J. Fields, *Slavery and Freedom on the Middle Ground: Maryland during the Nineteenth Century* (New Haven, 1985), 92; Willie Lee Rose, *Rehearsal for Reconstruction: The Port Royal Experiment* (1964; reprint, London, 1976), 4, 12–13; Edmund L. Drago, "How Sherman's March through Georgia Affected the Slaves," *Georgia Historical Quarterly* 57 (Fall 1973): 362–63; Escott, "The Context of Freedom," 81–83; Carl Moneyhon, *The Impact of the Civil War and Reconstruction on Arkansas: Persistence in the Midst of Ruin* (Baton Rouge, 1994), 135–36.

13. Testimony of Nelson Finley, William Harris, Mack Washington, 30 January 1874, Nelson Finley claim, case 16219, Wilkinson County, Mississippi case files, Approved Claims, SCC, RG 217, NA; James M. McPherson, *The Negro's Civil War: How American Blacks Felt and Acted during the War for the Union* (1965; reprint, New York, 1991), 57–59, 62–63, 67–68, 210; Drago, "How Sherman's March through Georgia Affected the Slaves," 364–65; Litwack, *Been in the Storm So Long*, 24–25, 108–9, 121–22, 169–72, 217–18; Harding, *There Is a River*, 220, 226–28; Cimprich, *Slavery's End in Tennessee*, 21–22, 60, 84–85.

14. Testimony of Richard Sullivan, n.d., and Burr Lewis, Charles Henderson, Randall Thompson, Anderson Thomas, 21 July 1875, and Jacob Robinson,

David Young, 24 July 1875, Andrew Brown claim, case 1233, Congressional Jurisdiction, RG 123, NA; Drew Gilpin Faust, *The Creation of Confederate Nationalism: Ideology and Identity in the Civil War* (Baton Rouge, 1987), esp. 14–21; idem, "Altars of Sacrifice: Confederate Women and the Narratives of War," *Journal of American History* 76 (March 1990): 1200–1228; Reidy, *From Slavery to Agrarian Capitalism*, 109, 114.

15. Testimony of Cato Rux, 15 January 1873, claim of Hal W. Green estate, case 7864, Congressional Jurisdiction, RG 123, NA.

16. Testimony of Edward Howard, 1 June 1874, Martha Crane claim, case 8313, Congressional Jurisdiction, RG 123, NA; Testimony of George Braxton, 5 July 1873, Thomas Turner claim, case 4330, Adams County, Mississippi case files, Approved Claims, SCC, RG 217, NA.

17. Testimony of Jeff Claiborne, 2 November 1891, and London Mitchell, James Crawford, 11 May 1875, and H. F. Kriger, 29 October 1891, Martha R. Blanton claim, case 3307, Congressional Jurisdiction, RG 123, NA; James L. Roark, *Masters without Slaves: Southern Planters in the Civil War and Reconstruction* (New York, 1977), 80; Lawrence N. Powell and Michael Wayne, "Self-Interest and the Decline of Confederate Nationalism," in *The Old South in the Crucible of War*, ed. Harry Owens and James Cooke (Jackson, Miss., 1983), 31–32; Moneyhon, *Impact of the Civil War and Reconstruction on Arkansas*, 115–16; Schwalm, *Hard Fight for We*, 82–85; Berlin et al., *Destruction of Slavery*, 40–41.

18. Testimony of Lewis Jackson, 23 September 1887, Samuel Chase claim, case 1990, Congressional Jurisdiction, RG 123, NA; Testimony of Allen Harris, 10 March 1875, Allen Harris claim, case 16557; Testimony of Thomas C. Drummond, Martha Bradshaw, 28 May 1875, and Thomas Brown, 22 June 1875, and Alexander Brown, 2 July 1875, Thomas C. Drummond claim, case 16294, Warren County, Mississippi case files, Approved Claims, SCC, RG 217, NA; William Wells Brown, *The Negro in the American Rebellion: His Heroism and His Fidelity* (Boston, 1867), 308.

19. Testimony of George W. Walton, Ambrose Holmes, 4 October 1871, Ambrose Holmes claim, case 6971, Warren County, Mississippi case files, Approved Claims, SCC, RG 217, NA; Litwack, *Been in the Storm So Long*, 20; Clarence L. Mohr, *On the Threshold of Freedom: Masters and Slaves in Civil War Georgia* (Athens, Ga., 1986), 72; Reidy, *From Slavery to Agrarian Capitalism*, 133–34; Susan E. O'Donovan, "Transforming Work: Slavery, Free Labor, and the Household in Southwest Georgia, 1850–1880," (Ph.D. diss., University of California, San Diego, 1997), 164–65.

20. James M. McPherson, *Battle Cry of Freedom: The Civil War Era* (New York, 1988), 578–79, 581, 586–88, 626–32; Mark Grimsley, *The Hard Hand of War: Union Military Policy toward Southern Civilians, 1861–1865* (Cambridge, 1995), 151–57.

21. Testimony of Edward Hicks, 13 May 1875, Absalom Grant claim, case 5516, Congressional Jurisdiction, RG 123; Testimony of Squire Myers, 21 July 1873, John M. Johnson claim, case 18061, Warren County, Mississippi case files, Approved Claims, SCC, RG 217, NA; John Cimprich, "Slave Behavior during the Federal Occupation of Tennessee, 1862–1865," *Historian* 44 (1982):

335, 342; LeeAnn Whites, *The Civil War as a Crisis in Gender: Augusta, Georgia, 1860–1890* (Athens, Ga., 1995), 122–24.

22. Testimony of Henry A. Leach, 21 November 1874, Elisha Fox claim, case 3668; Testimony of William Green, 6 March 1875, and Mary G. Wright, 5 March 1875, William Green claim, case 6962, Warren County, Mississippi case files, Approved Claims, SCC, RG 217, NA; Testimony of Cyrus Lee, 6 November 1876, Mary A. Brooks claim, case 3480; Testimony of Charles Anderson, 15 January 1873, claim of Hal W. Green estate, case 7864; Testimony of Samuel Chase, Henry Watson, 14 September 1872, Samuel Chase claim, case 1990, Congressional Jurisdiction, RG 123, NA; James T. Currie, *Enclave: Vicksburg and Her Plantations, 1863–1870* (Jackson, Miss., 1980), xxi–xxiii.

23. Testimony of Henry Banks, Albert Webster, 24 June 1873, Henry Banks claim, case 14443; Testimony of John Cole, 20 May 1873, John Cole claim, case 16558, Warren County, Mississippi case files, Approved Claims, SCC, RG 217, NA; Mary Carter and Lucinda Braziel, Susan Swanson, [Exhibits], 12 February 1875, Nelson Davis file, Widow's Certificate 92460; Em[ily] Stewart, [Exhibit], 20 February 1875, and Thomas Swanson, [Exhibit], 1 March 1875, and Stephen Jones, [Exhibit], 2 March 1875, Harris Stewart file, Widow's Certificate 132717; Mary Carter, Affidavit, 8 March 1876, George Carter file, Widow's Certificate 173491, Civil War and Later Pension Files, 1861–1942, Records of the Veterans Administration, RG 15, NA.

24. Testimony of Olive Lee, 1 March 1875, Olive Lee claim, case 10664; Testimony of Peter Jackson, 15 October 1872, Peter Jackson claim, case 14295; Testimony of William Green, n.d. [1871], Dick Green claim, case 6963; Testimony of William Green, n.d., William Green claim, case 6962, Warren County, Mississippi case files, Approved Claims, SCC, RG 217, NA; Litwack, *Been in the Storm So Long*, 107.

25. 11 July 1863, York Plantation Journal, Metcalfe Family Papers, microfilm, Mississippi Department of Archives and History; Mahalia Dorris, General Affidavit, 25 February 1888, and Roley Washington, General Affidavit, 4 February 1889, Foster Dorris file, Mother's Certificate 271888, Civil War Pension Files, RG 15, NA; Testimony of Henry Anderson, 15 January 1873, Henry Anderson claim, case 17480; Testimony of Joseph Johnson, 4 January 1878, Alfred Swann claim, case 19740; Testimony of Wallace Turner, 5 July 1873, Thomas Turner claim, case 4330, Adams County, Mississippi case files, Approved Claims, SCC, RG 217, NA; Ira Berlin, Thavolia Glymph, Steven F. Miller, Joseph P. Reidy, Leslie S. Rowland, Julie Saville, eds., *Freedom*, ser. 1, vol. 3, *The Wartime Genesis of Free Labor: The Lower South* (Cambridge, 1990), doc. 174, pp. 628–29.

26. Mary Ann Madison, Deposition, 24 January 1887, and George Hamlin, Alexander White, Depositions, 12 February 1887, William Madison file, Widow's Certificate 232198; Frances Taylor, Deposition, 25 August 1893, Samuel McDowell file, Father's Certificate 384066, Civil War Pension Files, RG 15, NA; Ronald L. F. Davis, *The Black Experience in Natchez, 1720–1880* (Natchez Historical Park, Miss., 1994), 133–34; John Eaton, *Grant, Lincoln and the Freedmen: Reminiscences of the Civil War with Special Reference to the Work for the Contrabands and Freedmen of the Mississippi Valley* (New York,

1907), 105; Bell Irvin Wiley, *The Plain People of the Confederacy* (1943; reprint, Chicago, 1963), 70–72.

27. Testimony of Nelson Finley, 30 January 1874, Nelson Finley claim, case 16219, Wilkinson County; Testimony of Henry Hunt, 6 May 1873, Henry Hunt claim, case 10840, Warren County, Mississippi case files, Approved Claims, SCC, RG 217, NA; Davis, *Black Experience in Natchez*, 133–34; Berlin et al., *Destruction of Slavery*, 15–16, 33–34, 60–61.

28. Genovese, *Roll, Jordan, Roll*, 97; Litwack, *Been in the Storm So Long*, 154.

29. Ira Berlin, Joseph P. Reidy, Leslie S. Rowland, eds., *Freedom*, ser. 2, *The Black Military Experience* (Cambridge, 1982), 433–42, esp. 433–36.

30. Testimony of Sabitha Walker, 1 August 1873, Mary E. Hall claim, case 5119; Testimony of Lewis Baker, 7 March 1872, Lewis Baker claim, case 8475, Congressional Jurisdiction, RG 123, NA; Amos Wright, Deposition, 5 February 1912, William Wright file, Widow's Application 856421, Civil War Pension Files, RG 15, NA; Testimony of Daniel Murfee, 21 July 1873, Daniel Murfee claim, case 18062, Warren County, Mississippi case files, Approved Claims, SCC, RG 217, NA; Stephen V. Ash, *When the Yankees Came: Conflict and Chaos in the Occupied South, 1861–1865* (Chapel Hill, 1995), 82; Escott, "The Context of Freedom," 92–93; Drago, "How Sherman's March through Georgia Affected the Slaves," 371; Litwack, *Been in the Storm So Long*, 123–25; Schwalm, *Hard Fight for We*, 100–101.

31. Harrison Willis, Deposition, 23 July 1900, Harrison Barnes file, Invalid's Certificate 987018; Jesse Branson, Deposition, 22 March 1899, Jesse Branson file, Invalid's Certificate 766387; Lewis Griffin, Deposition, 20 February 1904, and Gabe Phillips, Deposition, 21 January 1904, Archie Coal file, Minor's Application 576366, Civil War Pension Files, RG 15, NA.

32. United States War Department, *Revised United States Army Regulations* (Philadelphia, 1863), 131, 486–87, 501–2; Caesar Gordon alias Kearney, Deposition, 28 January 1902, file of Caesar Kearney (alias Caesar Gordon), Invalid's Application 967953, Civil War Pension Files, RG 15, NA; Joseph T. Glatthaar, *Forged in Battle: The Civil War Alliance of Black Soldiers and White Officers* (New York, 1990), 111–20; Berlin et al., *Black Military Experience*, doc. 179, pp. 28–29, 433–36, 439–42.

33. Berlin et al., *Wartime Genesis*, docs. 188, 201, 202A–B, pp. 73, 649, 810; Berlin et al., *Black Military Experience*, docs. 276A, 286, 309, p. 660; Herbert G. Gutman, *The Black Family in Slavery and Freedom, 1750–1925* (New York, 1976), 18–19, 21–24, 412–18; Noralee Frankel, *Freedom's Women: Black Women and Families in Civil War Era Mississippi* (Bloomington, 1999), 40–45; C. Peter Ripley, "The Black Family in Transition: Louisiana, 1860–1865," *Journal of Southern History* 41 (August 1975): 379–80; Louis S. Gerteis, *From Contraband to Freedman: Federal Policy toward Southern Blacks, 1861–1865* (Westport, Conn., 1973), 85–86; Cimprich, *Slavery's End in Tennessee*, 74–75.

34. Harry Nichols, Deposition, 25 May 1918, and Adjutant General's Office to U.S. Bureau of Pensions, 9 July 1923, Harry Nichols file, Invalid's Certificate 1074493; Jennie Williams, Deposition, 5 October 1904, Daniel Robinson file,

Widow's Certificate 581335; Henry Brown, Deposition, 22 October 1917, Benjamin Fort file, Invalid's Certificate 989519; Elijah Hall to U.S. Bureau of Pensions, 8 September 1899, Invalid's Application 790901, Civil War Pension Files, RG 15, NA; Frankel, *Freedom's Women*, 41.

35. William Carter to U.S. Bureau of Pensions, 19 May 1899, and 6 April 1915, William Carter file, Invalid's Certificate 1005623; Patsy (Clayborne) Payton, [Exhibit], 19 January 1875, file of Beverly Payton (alias Dudley Payton), Widow's Certificate 168060, Civil War Pension Files, RG 15, NA.

36. Moses Reed, Joseph Thornton, Depositions, 9 January 1889, and Phillis Reed, Deposition, 12 January 1888, file of Daniel Doddin (alias Daniel Reed), Widow's Certificate 252874, Civil War Pension Files, RG 15, NA; Berlin et al., *Black Military Experience*, doc. 50, pp. 17–18, 20–22, 30, 362–68; Berlin et al., *Wartime Genesis*, 20–24, 40–41, 45–46, 50–51; Berlin et al., *Destruction of Slavery*, 32–34, 250, 254–56, 258.

37. Testimony of Philip Hart, 6 September 1871, Gabriel Boger claim, case 6940; Testimony of Philip Hart, Ellen Anderson, 9 May 1871, and Julia Ann McCaskill, 9 September 1871, Julia Ann McCaskill claim, case 1946, Warren County; Testimony of Wallace Turner, 5 July 1873, Thomas Turner claim, case 4330, Adams County, Mississippi case files, Approved Claims, SCC, RG 217, NA; Berlin et al., *Wartime Genesis*, docs. 198, 209, pp. 24, 41–42, 47, 64–65, 635–36, 643–46; Lawrence N. Powell, *New Masters: Northern Planters during the Civil War and Reconstruction* (New Haven, 1980), 45–48, 109; Frankel, *Freedom's Women*, 20–21, 28, 45–55.

38. Gerteis, *From Contraband to Freedman*, 85, 92–97, 102–6; C. Peter Ripley, *Slaves and Freedmen in Civil War Louisiana* (Baton Rouge, 1976), 44–49, 56–59, 74–75, 88–91; Powell, *New Masters*, 46–47, 82–86, 102; Powell and Wayne, "Self-Interest and the Decline of Confederate Nationalism," 34–37; Cimprich, *Slavery's End in Tennessee*, 68, 71–72; Berlin et al., *Wartime Genesis*, doc. 198, p. 49; Eaton, *Grant, Lincoln, and the Freedmen*, 116, 122, 207.

39. For Independence Day song, see Brown, *Negro in the American Revolution*, 306. Janet S. Hermann, *The Pursuit of a Dream* (New York, 1983), 3–9, 12–14, 37–60; Thavolia Glymph, "The Second Middle Passage: The Transition from Slavery to Freedom at Davis Bend, Mississippi" (Ph.D. diss., Purdue University, 1994), 17–24, 47–51, 102–5; Eaton, *Grant, Lincoln, and the Freedmen*, 85–86; Currie, *Enclave*, 83, 92–94; Quarles, *Negro in the Civil War*, 285–86; Steven J. Ross, "Freed Soil, Freed Labor, Freed Men: John Eaton and the Davis Bend Experiment," *Journal of Southern History* 44 (May 1978): 225–26.

40. Berlin et al., *Wartime Genesis*, doc. 220; Glymph, "Second Middle Passage," 117–23; Ross, "Freed Soil, Freed Labor, Freed Men," 222–26; Currie, *Enclave*, 101–7.

41. Eaton, *Grant, Lincoln, and the Freedmen*, 218–19; Michael Wayne, *The Reshaping of Plantation Society: The Natchez District, 1860–1880* (Baton Rouge, 1983), 42–46, 50–51, 200–202; Ripley, *Slaves and Freedmen in Civil War Louisiana*, 76–83, table 1; Berlin et al., *Wartime Genesis*, 24–26, 43–44, 70–72.

42. Robert Olwell, "'Loose and Disorderly': Slave Women in the Eighteenth-

Century Charleston Marketplace," in *More than Chattel: Black Women and Slavery in the Americas*, ed. David Barry Gaspar and Darlene Clark Hine (Bloomington, 1996), 97–110; Betty Wood, *Women's Work, Men's Work: The Informal Slave Economies of Lowcountry Georgia* (Athens, Ga., 1995), 84–87, 91–92, 142–45; Daniel H. Usner Jr., *Indians, Settlers, and Slaves in a Frontier Exchange Economy: The Lower Mississippi Valley before 1783* (Chapel Hill, 1992), 202; Lyle Saxon et al., comps., *Gumbo-Ya-Ya: A Collection of Louisiana Folk Tales* (New York, 1945), 30–36, 43–44; Kaye, "Personality of Power," 240–43.

43. Testimony of Sarah Burton, 24 March 1875, and Summary Report, 4 December 1876, Sarah Burton claim, case 8009, Congressional Jurisdiction, RG 123, NA; Testimony of Millie Washington, Morris Gearry, 26 July 1872, George Washington claim, case 13910; Testimony of Henry Watson, Emma Watson, 11 October 1863, Henry Watson claim, case 16555; Testimony of Allen Harris, 10 March 1875, and Lewis Johnson, 3 March 1875, Allen Harris claim, case 16557, Warren County; Testimony of Henry Anderson, Gallian Wickliff, 15 January 1873, Henry Anderson claim, case 17480, Adams County, Mississippi case files, Approved Claims, SCC, RG 217, NA; Vernon L. Wharton, *The Negro in Mississippi, 1865–1890* (1947; reprint, New York, 1965), 34–35; Schwalm, *Hard Fight for We*, 100–101.

44. Testimony of Henry Anderson, 15 January 1873, Henry Anderson claim, case 17480; Testimony of John Mann, 4 January 1878, Alfred Swan claim, case 19740, Adams County; Testimony of Thomas C. Drummond, 28 May 1875, Thomas C. Drummond claim, case 16294; Testimony of Russell Giles, 16 May 1877, Russell Giles claim, case 11583, Warren County, Mississippi case files, Approved Claims, SCC, RG 217, NA; Testimony of Edward Hicks, 13 May 1875, Absalom Grant claim, case 5516, Congressional Jurisdiction, RG 123, NA; Bettersworth, *Confederate Mississippi*, 104–6, 108–111; Ash, *When the Yankees Came*, 80.

45. Testimony of Henry Banks, 24 June 1873, Henry Banks claim, case 14443; Testimony of Henry Hunt, 6 May 1873, Henry Hunt claim, case 10840, Warren County, Mississippi case files, Approved Claims, SCC, RG 217, NA. On the concept of objectification, see Karl Marx, *Capital: A Critique of Political Economy*, vol. 1, (1887; reprint, New York, 1967), 76–89; Georg Lukacs, *History and Class Consciousness: Studies in Marxist Dialectics* (Cambridge, Mass., 1971), 83–87.

46. Testimony of Henry Watson, James Puckett, 11 October 1873, Henry Watson claim, case 16555, Warren County, Mississippi case files, Approved Claims, SCC, RG 217, NA; James E. Yeatman, *A Report on the Condition of the Freedmen of the Mississippi* (St. Louis, 1864), 8; Mohr, *On the Threshold of Freedom*, 90–91.

47. Testimony of Gabriel Boger, 9 September 1871, Philip Hart claim, case 1945, Warren County, Mississippi case files, Approved Claims, SCC, RG 217, NA; Caesar Gordon alias Kearney, Deposition, 28 January 1902, file of Caesar Kearney (alias Caesar Gordon), Invalid's Application 967953; Patsy Payton, [Exhibit], 19 January 1875, file of Beverly Payton (alias Dudley Payton), Widow's Certificate 168060, Civil War Pension Files, RG 15, NA; Eaton, *Grant,*

Lincoln, and the Freedmen, 157–58. Berlin et al., *Wartime Genesis,* docs. 137, 168, 209, 213, pp. 68, 642–44, 826, 876n3; Berlin et al., *Destruction of Slavery,* 35–36, 260; Ash, *When the Yankees Came,* 76–77, 99–107, 165–69; Gerteis, *From Contraband to Freedman,* 158–60; Currie, *Enclave,* 62–66; Litwack, *Been in the Storm So Long,* 173–76; Roark, *Masters without Slaves,* 118; Powell, *New Masters,* 45–46.

48. Testimony of Elvira Anderson, 5 May 1873, Elvira Anderson claim, case 14172; Testimony of William Green, 6 March 1875, William Green claim, case 6962; Testimony of Peter Jackson, n.d., Peter Jackson claim, case 14295; Testimony of Matilda Anderson, 20 May 1873, Matilda Anderson claim, case 6935, Warren County, Mississippi case files, Approved Claims, SCC, RG 217, NA; Testimony of Richard Eastman, 25 September 1873, Richard Eastman claim, case 8244, Congressional Jurisdiction, RG 123, NA. Litwack, *Been in the Storm So Long,* 177.

49. Testimony of Anthony Lewis, Clem Hardeman, Lloyd Wigenton, 20 July 1872, Anthony Lewis claim, case 15293, Claiborne County, Mississippi case files, Approved Claims, SCC, RG 217, NA.

50. Peter Kolchin, "Slavery and Freedom in the Civil War South," in *Writing the Civil War: The Quest to Understand,* ed. James M. McPherson and William J. Cooper Jr. (Columbia, S.C., 1998), 240–60, esp. 254–57.

51. Saidiya V. Hartman, *Scenes of Subjection: Terror, Slavery, and Self-Making in Nineteenth-Century America* (Oxford, 1997), esp. 6–7, 10, 116–19, 125–32, 139; Mary Turner, "Introduction," in *From Chattel Slaves to Wage Slaves: The Dynamics of Labour Bargaining in the Americas,* ed. Mary Turner (London, 1995), 1–30; Pieter C. Emmer, "The Price of Freedom: The Constraints of Change in Postemancipation America," in *The Meaning of Freedom: Economics, Politics, and Culture after Slavery,* ed. Frank McGlynn and Seymour Drescher (Pittsburgh, 1992), 23–47; Jay R. Mandle, *Not Slave, Not Free: The African-American Economic Experience since the Civil War* (Durham, 1992), a revised version of *The Roots of Black Poverty: The Southern Plantation Economy since the Civil War* (Durham, 1978).

52. Sidney W. Mintz, "Panglosses and Pollyannas; or, Whose Reality Are We Talking About?" in *Meaning of Freedom,* 245–56.

Chapter 4

Hearth, Home, and Family in the Fredericksburg Campaign

GEORGE C. RABLE

✦ "HOME, how well we know how to estimate the value of that little word," Lieutenant Edward Williams of the 114th Pennsylvania Infantry confessed to his wife shortly after the Battle of Fredericksburg. "It means all that men care for. Glory and honor sink into insignificance alongside . . . all its endearments."[1] Suitable enough sentiments given all the recent bloodletting, but also a remark that only hinted at the depth, complexity, and irony of a word fraught with multiple and deeply emotional meanings for his generation.

Civil wars by their very nature challenge, distend, and sometimes destroy notions of home, but the word "home" also evokes a host of vivid, often contradictory images. Soldiers and civilians shared common ideas about home even though their disparate experiences also created sometimes disparate thinking. Although writers have explored the cultural meaning of home in other societies, Civil War historians — despite the recent explosion of interest in the social history of the era — have done little work on this subject.[2] Given the myriad definitions and emotional connotations of home, context becomes critical.

The entire Fredericksburg campaign offers an excellent opportunity for exploring the subject of "home" in part because the battle was fought between Thanksgiving and Christmas in 1862 — two holidays laden with images of home. Shortly after the fall elections in 1862, President Abraham Lincoln had replaced General George B. McClellan as commander of the Army of the Potomac with General Ambrose E. Burnside. The army's rapid advance to the Rappahannock River had raised Northern hopes, but delays, followed by a bloody battle on December 13 during which the Confederates easily repulsed a serious of poorly planned Union assaults against well-defended positions, just as quickly dashed them. The engagement occurred in the midst of a civil war whose outcome remained uncertain but that had lasted long enough that both soldiers and civilians — Union and Confederate — were keenly feeling not only their separation but also a sense of what they were sacrificing in "home" life and perhaps "home" values. Ideas about home crossed sectional boundaries, yet the Union troops' sack of Fredericksburg—that had begun almost as soon as the first regiments of Burnside's army crossed the river and continued off and on until the army's withdrawal on the night of December 15—added several ironic twists to a war supposedly fought to preserve home and hearth.

For Northern soldiers, especially New Englanders who had grown up with stories about Pilgrims and Indians, Thanksgiving Day made absence from home all that more poignant.[3] In camp, holding religious services and other ceremonies and observing at least some Thanksgiving traditions helped sustain morale and connections to home. Men fell into formation for a reading of their governor's Thanksgiving proclamation, though to cynical veterans such activities seemed poor substitutes for a regular Thanksgiving dinner. After being asked by the chaplain to repeat, "God save the Commonwealth of Massachusetts," members of the 35th Massachusetts decided they needed more saving than their home state.[4]

But this was the middle of the nineteenth century, and such affairs could not be complete without some speechmaking, speechmaking that upheld home values. The Victorian middle class on both sides of the Atlantic had come to see the home as a center of moral virtue.[5] Many civilians worried about their loved ones far away in a cold army camp, no longer subject to the salutary influences of domestic life. Therefore officers not only waxed eloquent about the sacred Union cause but also warned men against various temptations. Chaplains urged the boys to stay sober and tried to focus their minds on gratitude and other elevated sentiments.

Yet for some Northern soldiers more than for Americans generally, the historical meaning of Thanksgiving also weighed on their minds. Even though tinged with a lingering Calvinistic fatalism, their reflections expressed appreciation for the preservation of their own lives and the continued health of their families. "We are to day an *unbroken* Circle upon probationary ground," a New Hampshire sergeant cautioned his wife.[6] How easy to envision the family gathering around the table for the traditional holiday feast or attending a Thanksgiving church service. Whatever the tensions and problems that his folks had faced, a soldier in camp remembered a room filled to overflowing with love and affection. The men regaled comrades with old stories, recalled holiday traditions, and described what they would be eating back home. A New York private jokingly commissioned an older brother to devour his share of the family dinner. The pleasant sketch appearing in some illustrated newspapers of an extended family crowded around a Thanksgiving table groaning with rich food contrasted starkly with the spartan realities of army life. Yet the troops also tried to imagine the war at an end, the family circle restored, and everyone grateful for the blessings of peace. Newspaper editors offered sentimental descriptions of empty chairs set around the Thanksgiving table.[7]

For the Northern public, Thanksgiving became a great celebration of American religious nationalism. "Christianity and civilization are engaged in deadly conflict with the paganism and barbarity of feudal ages," declared one small-town editor. Others agreed that the fate of republican liberty hung in the balance.[8] But, as in 1776, much would depend upon the endurance of the home folks. The more general hope was that the war would serve some larger purpose by stimulating public virtue. According to one Presbyterian divine, a righteous crusade brought out the best in human nature and so the domestic circle might remain upright and cheerful. As Governor Edwin Morgan of New York observed in his Thanksgiving proclamation, even war "does not shut out all sunshine from our homes." People continued to work and love, and the "storm without makes them gather closer together about the family hearth. With less of egotism and of worldly pride than before, chastened by adversity, they are happier than ever."[9]

Families with loved ones in the army therefore clung all that more fervently to holiday traditions. Attending church, gathering around the table, munching on the usual apples, candy, and nuts after dinner—but how hard it was to enter into the spirit of the occasion. Catherine Eaton told her husband how they had likely "thought of each other at the same moment many times" on Thanksgiving Day. The clergy thanked God for an abundant harvest, but the war had seriously disrupted the season's usual rhythms. If people would contrast the prosperity of New York with the desolation of Virginia, a Dutch Reformed minister suggested, they would count their many blessings. This surely belabored the obvious and offered cold comfort to civilians who had lost loved ones, feared they soon would, or struggled along without a breadwinner. Two Philadelphia ministers feebly advised their parishioners to be thankful that things were no worse.[10] Yet Thanksgiving had originated as a celebration of deliverance from hunger and despair, and many Americans must have wondered as the year 1862 neared its end when their deliverance from the horrors of civil war would come.

In the camps, many soldiers could easily imagine the hardships of their Pilgrim forbears. The standard Federal ration of a pound of meat and a pound of hard bread, though sufficient in quantity, fell short in variety and nutrition. The amenities of dining were ignored. "When we get home again," a New Hampshire recruit mused, "we will not any more sit at the table to eat, but will seize our grub in our fists, and eat it on the wood pile, or in the back yard like soldiers."[11] Such humor, however, hardly concealed how much men missed gathering about the family table, how separated they felt from civilians during a holiday.

The best medicine for homesickness became encouraging words from home, and a lot of this medicine got dispensed. Home news boosted morale every bit as much as victories or good rations. Writing and reading letters did far more than ease camp monotony: it allowed soldiers to convey some sense of their momentous experiences to family and friends.[12]

The soldiers' desire for letters easily surpassed the abilities of even conscientious civlians to supply them. Although the Federals delivered the mail more efficiently than the Confederates, General Ambrose E. Burnside's troops would never have believed it. It took sixteen days for his wife's letters to reach camp, one Michigan recruit groused. And of course on a day when your regiment received no mail, a neighboring one always seemed to be tearing through a large sack of letters. With units so often on the move, prompt delivery could hardly be guaranteed even for properly addressed letters, by no means a certainty itself. Most soldiers endured lengthy periods with nary a missive. "It does not suit a man with a family to be in the army," Colonel Robert McAllister sadly remarked after over six weeks with no word from home.[13]

For Confederates, too, the connection between soldier morale and home news became obvious when mail turned into the highlight of otherwise humdrum days. Soldiers would endure much for their country, but being cut off from word of family and friends seemed unbearable. Yet oftentimes the fault lay with the correspondents. Trying to prod his insecure wife to write more often, a lonely Georgian assured her that he would never exchange "affection, kindness, sympathy, constant love & greetings" for "eloquence." Nothing could so lower a man's spirits as the realization that family no longer cared enough to write regularly, though many soldiers proved equally neglectful, and in some cases both civilians and volunteers faltered. Like many Federals, Confederate soldiers kept a close count of letters received and often adopted a standard of strict reciprocity — news from camp depending on receiving news from home. Some even vowed to write no more letters until they received one in return.[14]

Irregular mail threatened relationships already strained by separation. "[I] do not know if i have Relatives or Friends yet on the Earth," a Michigan volunteer wrote in disgust. Regular correspondence became a test of love and devotion; no word from home drove some to the verge of a mental breakdown. A sudden halt in mail immediately betokened trouble at home, perhaps illness or death. Yet soldiers excused their own lapses, assuming civilians had more time for scribbling. Descriptions of awkwardly scratching out a note on a cracker-box desk in flickering light on a cold night with smoke blowing in the eyes were undoubtedly meant to make the home folks feel guilty and prod them into writing more often themselves.[15]

The men treasured the letters they did receive and read them until they nearly fell apart. "You do not know how consoling and comforting your letters are," a New York surgeon informed his wife. "As you say, 'it is almost like seeing you,' and they are the only things which reconcile me to my situation."[16]

The soldiers' letters ultimately revealed how torn they were between patriotic and family obligations. The men might speak of duty and honor, and women might even embrace those values, but that hardly lessened the trauma of separation. "The soldier when he enters the field, is presumed to sever all ties of home," mused a Wisconsin surgeon. But this was impossible because just as "a man cannot have a home without a country, but what is country without a home, that center of all his hopes and his affections!" The soldier enlisted to fight for his family, but soon realized how much he was expected to sacrifice for so little reward: "Strike from his affections that of home and family, and how much of country will be left? When I get back I'll ask some old bachelor to tell me." Company and regiment became a partial substitute for the soldiers' family and community, but the men's hopes and dreams remained at home. "Bless the dear children," Lieutenant Colonel Joshua Lawrence Chamberlain of the 20th Maine wrote with deep feeling. "I don't dare to think of them too much. It makes me rather sad, & then I do not forget that I am here in the face of death every day."[17]

Thoughts of home. They came rushing in unexpectedly and could not be controlled. Sitting in his cold tent with a fire going, an Indiana major imagined his wife and children attending church. The unforgiving Virginia mud and rain and snow only made the more familiar surroundings of home seem more attractive. "I have seen no state I like so well as I do Michigan," commented one lonesome Wolverine.[18]

Being away from home turned many a soldier into a hopeless romantic who stared at family pictures or penned ardent love letters. George W. Ballock, a member of General Winfield Scott Hancock's staff, told his wife how he longed for the day when "I can leave war . . . and bask once more in the sunshine of your love." At age thirty-seven, he admitted that the "stern realities of life may have somewhat tempered the vivacity of youth." Yet he loved her with all his heart, and his "only regret is, Jennie, that I have not been able to love you better." Tonight, he assured her, "you will be with me in dreams. I shall feel your loving arms around me. Your soft cheek will be pressed to mine." These conventional sentimental effusions—that might run for a page or more in letter after letter with these men seemingly never exhausting adjectives to describe their wives' perfection—did not disguise the erotic undertones. Although sexual desire was seldom expressed openly, a plain-speaking New Hampshire sergeant commented on the "hearty" appearance of a comrade recently returned to the regiment: "I reckon it didn't hurt him any to sleep with a woman a spel."[19]

In the midst of such swirling and conflicting emotions, love remained a powerful anchor. The gentle teasing of a soldier who joked with his wife about inviting a woman to warm up his tent; the sudden realization that a couple's deep affection for each other came without limits or conditions, unchangeable even in the face of war; a major who recalled the last night spent with his wife in the syrupy language of the era ("you never seemed lovelier to me than on that night") also noted how her "lips rival its [sic] purest carnation"; an Alabama lieutenant imagining his wife sitting before a fire in her dressing gown euphemistically claimed to be "homesick."[20] Impulses both carnal and tender filled and overflowed letters, but the real world of war and inescapable practicalities intruded on the most romantic reflections.

Playing with children, the simple pleasures of a walk or a game, all evoked fond memories. Adults still hoped that childhood could remain a period of security without the sort of nagging doubts that haunted adult minds.[21] Short notes and school compositions from their children helped men retain home ties. Although they could offer a few words of advice or some admonitions about the importance of good character, the war often intruded into efforts to maintain relationships. Dreaming about a frolic with his son and daughter, a New York engineer awoke in "desolate woods with my wearied and fatigued comrades sleeping around." In the "dead of night" he could only pray for a safe return home, while realizing how quickly his children would be grown. More ominously, a New York infantryman had a nightmare about Frankie, Charlie, and little Alta climbing a steep mountain. He at first saw a "vast army of soldiers in battle array" but this turned out to be an "army of angels making heavenly music and our children were hurrying to join them."[22]

Yet for most families keeping love alive and combating loneliness involved much less frightening and more mundane matters. From Lancaster, Wisconsin, Catharine Eaton begged her husband, Samuel, a chaplain in the famous Iron Brigade, to wangle a furlough. She filled her letters with news of their local church and their friends' problems. Struggling as a minister's wife in his absence but gaining confidence in "find[ing] my sphere," she prized his letters but also felt sad as the holiday season approached. Fearing that Samuel might shrink his new flannel shirt, she sent along detailed washing instructions. Their son, James, reported doing well in both Latin and Greek but doubted he could handle both during the next school term. Soldiers savored such homey details. Private James R. Woodworth of the 44th New York nearly cried when he received his wife Phoebe's letters, laughed at reports of their little sons' pranks, and wrote fervently of his undying love. He fussed over her recent ankle injury and advised her to relax with his old books. A pious man, Woodworth liked to imagine them both reading scripture at the same time and hoped their separation would bring them closer to God.[23] Nothing dramatic here, merely the struggles of ordinary families in an extraordinary time.

For, given all the problems plaguing both the army and individual soldiers, the pangs of loneliness hit men the hardest. To recall a loving wife or playful child added to the sense of dull dissatisfaction, if not outright despair, that hung over the army. Even sweet dreams of family suddenly became frightening. One night a New York sergeant dreamed of coming home, only to find his wife indifferent to him and ready to take the hand of a well-dressed gentleman riding in a fancy carriage. Although he claimed that the smoke hurt his eyes as he wrote about this nightmare, he could not help but cry.[24]

A vivid imagination could be a mixed blessing, but many men enjoyed picturing what their loved ones might be doing at home. After the battle, as the troops settled into winter quarters, they hoped their families remembered the poor soldiers in the chilly camps. The belief that people still cared and that there was still something to fight for helped soldiers go about their daily tasks, no matter how mundane. At the same time, a Massachusetts officer warmly praised his wife for becoming the mainstay of the local soldiers' aid society. Less-than-perfect husbands naturally claimed to be changed men, and whatever the truth of such statements, many had grown to appreciate domestic life.[25]

Yet home remained far away and that irreducible fact compounded the suffering of soldiers in camp. A dutiful son fussed over his mother's sprained ankle, wishing he were home so he could help out with the cooking. Soldiers naturally dreaded word of family illness, especially when misdirected letters held up news of recovery. Even at a distance, the men recognized obvious signs of anxiety among their home folks but felt powerless to help. Separation by itself created health problems, and a corporal in the Irish Brigade suggested that his wife visit the doctor to get some medicine for her nervousness. There was nothing he could do other than write because soldiers seldom received furloughs to care for ailing family members or even attend a mother's funeral.[26]

Financial woes heightened emotional strains. Husbands worried about all the neglected details relating to farms and business but also hesitated to burden their families with such responsibilities and perhaps doubted that anyone could manage their affairs properly. They of course knew that their simply leaving home would leave their families with much work to do and new tasks to assume, but they also hesitated either to give up control of family finances or to acknowledge the sacrifices that their own patriotism had imposed on their loved ones. How hard to think of families feeling the pinch of high prices and neglecting their own needs as even once comfortable households barely scraped by. A New York surgeon, who had not been paid for months and had to ask for a little cash and a few stamps from home, nevertheless wanted his wife to be "independent enough" to hire a servant girl.[27] Domestic economy remained precarious as men and women struggled with what often amounted to reversed roles — wives managing household business and husbands offering occasional advice.

Even for the Confederates after Fredericksburg and despite their victory, loneliness ate away at morale. Elan developed from shared sacrifices and glorious triumphs but also depended on individual dispositions and emotional health. Sometimes word from home only added to the sadness that afflicted so many soldiers in camp. "I read over your letter a moment ago," a young South Carolinian wrote to a favorite aunt, "but its contents were so tinctured with a feeling of melancholy, that it added very little to cheer me up." He longed to "meet again around the family fireside, and converse happily of the war as a thing that is past and gone forever." But escaping history would never be that easy. When families described the pain of separation, soldiers had to steel themselves to persevere while hoping against hope for a happy reunion in the not-too-distant future. Even vivid images of a wife and child at home became bittersweet as soldiers felt both a powerful sense of duty and a gnawing fear of dying far from home.[28]

Home troubles could not be put on hold for the war's duration, and separation may have healed some old wounds but surely exacerbated family tensions. Like the Federals, the poorly paid Confederates worried about their loved ones suffering from want of necessities, some coldly urging their wives to economize, others relying on their spouse's judgment to allocate the family's shrinking resources. Distance complicated marital problems and added to the likelihood of misunderstanding. The imperious General Dorsey Pender often hurt his long-suffering wife, Fanny, with some ill-chosen words, and neither of them ever quite forgave or forgot. The travails of childbirth in the midst of war caused great anxiety at home and in camp, but even simple stories of a youngster's latest antics sometimes proved more sad than comforting. In Lexington, Virginia, Margaret Junkin Preston noticed how children's games had turned warlike, filled with shooting Yankees, taking prisoners, hobbling about on crutches, and punctuated with military jargon.[29]

At least these mock battles were bloodless, though death and disease of course were no strangers to the home front. As families fretted about the safety of their soldier boys, so too the men in uniform grew anxious over health problems back home. Knowing that a parent or wife or child had fallen ill sent hearts racing with worry. Memories of children who had died before the war still devastated couples separated in their grief and no longer able to comfort each other. Knowing he would likely never see many of his relatives and friends again, an Alabama surgeon reverted to an all-too-true biblical cliché: "[M]an is a [sic] few days and full of trouble." Husbands and wives seemed worn down by care, and war made immediate relief from their troubles unlikely, as nightmares about the future offered a constant reminder of life's transitory nature. Loved ones hoped to meet again in the world to come, but many men doubted they would see home again.[30]

Soldiers could not help thinking about countless families desolated by the deaths of loved ones in hospitals and on battlefields. Yet many of these same men had to cope with the loss of friends and family at home. A Pennsylvanian advised his fiancée not to mourn her dead grandmother excessively or become "old maidish." Soldiers steeled themselves with that religious fatalism so pervasive among the Civil War generation. Noting the irony of his beloved wife dying quietly at home while he survived the hardships of war, a Massachusetts man reduced his grief to a familiar formula: "Such are the inscrutable decrees of providence." Nor, given the frequency of death at home and in the field, should it be surprising that between 1862 and 1863 sales of life insurance policies more than doubled.[31]

Discussion of possible death often filled letters written by soldiers on the eve of battle. A fastidious New Jersey colonel told his wife what to do should he be wounded or killed—including details on the recovery and burial of his body. With such matters arranged he could ready himself for the big fight. Other soldiers simply hoped to escape injury or death once again. "You must not worry about me, Libbie," a Massachusetts volunteer advised his wife. "For you know I have been, as you say, lucky, thus far and I feel I shall continue to be." Whether this sounded cheerful or fatalistic was uncertain, but other men sought more solid reassurance. In marked reversal from the prescribed pattern of virtue at home and vice in camp, one devout soldier—whose parents were reportedly notorious swearers and drinkers—gathered much of his company together for prayer. He was prepared to die and hoped that each fellow was ready to meet his Maker.[32]

Many of his comrades and a fair number of Confederates had that privilege because the casualties at Fredericksburg had been staggering: 1,284 dead, 9,600 wounded, 1,769 captured or missing, for a total of 12,653 on the Union side; 595 killed, 4,061 wounded, 653 captured or missing, for a total of 5,309 on the Confederate side.[33]

The sheer numbers went beyond most people's ability to grasp, but name after endless name in long printed columns drove home the costs of war. In Charleston, South Carolina, by December 20, the first meager reports from the battlefield appeared along with telegrams detailing the fate of particular soldiers. Young Emma Holmes found that her diary had become "nothing but a record of death." In New York City, that same day, Elizabeth Freeman, though grateful for the safety of her son, commented on how word of heavy casualties at Fredericksburg had depressed everyone. In Lancaster, Wisconsin, Catherine Eaton advised her husband that only God's "restraining power" had saved his life. News of a great battle always cast civilians into pits of helpless anxiety. There was no way, aside from prayer, for mothers or fathers or wives or siblings to prepare for the worst news if it came.[34]

After receiving the first accounts of a bloody battle in Virginia, a Michigan woman cried for three days before learning that her son had emerged unscathed. Many soldiers dispatched short notes to relieve the anxiety at home, but impatient families clamored for immediate news. All too often no word came at all, no name on a list, no account of a regiment's losses. Prayers and hopes became focused, selfish, and almost superstitious; a Maine volunteer perceptively remarked, "The peculiar feature of war is that each expect *someone else* to fall."[35]

As soldiers themselves recognized, rumors and false reports heightened civilian fears. On the one hand, men reported to have been badly wounded or even killed had come through the battle without a scratch. On the other hand, a soldier would be listed as slightly wounded or rapidly improving, and the next day he would be dead. In Madison Parish, Louisiana, Kate Stone learned that a Lieutenant Stone — not related to her family — had been killed at Fredericksburg. On Christmas morning, an elderly neighbor informed the family that the dead man was in fact Kate's brother. Her mother collapsed with grief, but one of the family rode off to find a newspaper that confirmed the earlier account. Despite their relief, the Christmas celebration was ruined, and they later learned that their boy had been slightly wounded after all.[36]

Yet sometimes the news was more disturbing. When Phillip Hacker of the 5th Michigan was hit in the right groin by a minié ball, his brother quickly informed their parents. On the last day of the year, Hacker was able to write but screamed in agony when anyone changed his bed. He fretted about the "coldness" of his spiritual life and longed for a purer love of God. Stoically thankful that his wound was not worse but admitting it was bad enough, he asked his mother to be brave. By the end of January, still in severe pain, he had submitted to God's will but bitterly complained that "this cursed war has blighted the hopes of being anybody." Less than a month latter, Hacker died of dysentery and complications from his wound.[37] For Hacker's parents back in Michigan, their son had slowly slipped away at a distance, and the very fact that he had not died at home in familiar surroundings only made his passing that much more painful for them.

Civilians cherished detailed accounts from anyone who had been with their boys to the last. Friends and chaplains would write reassuringly that soldiers killed in battle or who had died right after an amputation had not suffered long. Such letters typically portrayed the men as calm, prayerful, and resigned to their fate. One comrade even included Captain Washington Brown's dying words: "Oh Lord receive my spirit! Goodbye Eliza, dear mother and all the dear ones at home, I wish to meet you all in Heaven. I have prayed for you. Goodbye I am done." Piety, love of family, hopes for a reunion in the afterlife — Brown's painfully uttered sentences touched on many of the period's central images and values. Letters from superior officers usually described how such men had carried the colors, led the regiment, or succored the wounded. As in any war, death transformed nearly everyone into a brave hero who had spoken lovingly of home and family. To dismiss all this as pro forma or sentimental mush overlooks an idealism and loyalty that soldiers on both sides would not have found either unrealistic or unusual.[38]

Families therefore made herculean efforts to bring their loved ones home. A man detailed from the regiment sometimes accompanied an officer's corpse on a boat or train; more commonly a relative made the difficult journey to retrieve a body. What a religious periodical termed war's "melancholy harvest" soon reached the grieving families. By custom, on Nantucket Island a steamer arriving with such ghastly cargo flew its flag at half-mast — eight men from that small place had been killed at Fredericksburg.[39] Such losses — that would not have near the impact in some city — could overwhelm a small community.

On Christmas day, the corpse of Lieutenant Leander Alley (19th Massachusetts, killed in the street fighting on December 11) arrived on Nantucket Island. From the wharf, a flag-draped hearse topped by a gilt eagle wound through the streets to the family home where hundreds of people paid their respects. The next day schools and businesses were closed, and after what the local newspaper described as "impressive funeral services," scores of children followed a procession to the Unitarian cemetery. A few days latter, a three-mile-long cortege in Richmond accompanied the metallic caskets containing the bodies of Francis

Dunbar Ruggles and two other men from Louisiana's Washington Artillery, but in the beleaguered Confederacy even mourning cloth was in short supply, and more often than not, a brief prayer service at home (usually without the corpse) would have to suffice. Even though nineteenth-century Americans had considerable experience with premature death, great battles laid a simultaneous blanket of sorrow on thousands of households.[40]

Nor would the grieving end any time soon. Uncertainty wreaked emotional havoc, and horrific news threw civilians into despair. On December 20, in Greensboro, Alabama, Fannie Borden anxiously wrote to her husband for news about her brother Ruffin "Bud" Gray, serving in a brigade of Mississippi troops that had stoutly resisted attempts by Federal engineers to lay pontoons across the Rappahannock River. By Christmas, word had arrived that Bud had been mortally wounded by an artillery round. Fannie took some comfort in imagining a heavenly reunion but also uttered a common lament: "[H]ow horrible to think of dying among strangers with no dear friend or relative near." Fannie especially regretted that he had never made an "open profession of religion."[41]

More commonly, however, civilians wondered why God had allowed so many Christian soldiers to suffer and die? The men's piety—lovingly sketched in numerous Yankee and Rebel accounts—made the sacrifice of life all that more poignant. As products of Christian homes, some soldiers had professed their faith at a young age and even in the army had maintained close ties with their pastors and local churches. Their eulogists compiled long lists of virtues. Devout soldiers had overcome the temptations of vice; they had shunned swearing; they had dutifully observed the Sabbath. A Roxbury minister praised Lieutenant Edgar M. Newcomb of the 19th Massachusetts for avoiding the coarser features of camp life by exhibiting an almost "womanly purity and refinement."[42] Wartime rhetoric still associated supposedly feminine virtues—especially motherly ones—with home. And what often seemed most missing from camp was the influence of a mother or wife who had been in essence the spiritual leader of the household.

Civilians, North and South, reserved their greatest respect for dutiful young men who, as one Virginia woman put it, had taken up "carnal weapons" to fight in a noble cause. Dying men wished their families to know that they had died in full assurance of resurrection. Lieutenant Newcomb even suggested that he could better serve his country in the hereafter; in what may have been an out-of-body experience, he quietly stated, "It is all light ahead." For pious families, knowledge that loved ones had died with such spiritual confidence proved a great comfort. At

Lieutenant Newcomb's funeral back in Boston, a choir even sang, "I Would Not Live Always."[43]

Yet sometimes the Lord seemed so far away, and the war especially seemed to open a spiritual chasm between camp and home. It sorely tested civilians but threatened to consume the soldiers' faith. Notably pious people were naturally much concerned about the state of religion throughout the country, but they especially worried about the army. Would the men hold fast to their spiritual moorings or would military life destroy their moral character? The war, some hoped, would slow the onslaught of secular influences, especially the seemingly rampant materialism so evident during the 1850s boom, that had both fascinated and troubled many devout folks during the antebellum decades. Soldiers and civilians increasingly relied on religious language to describe their daily struggles with separation, danger, and death. Clergy and laity alike invoked God's will to restore order to increasingly chaotic lives.[44]

Nowhere was the gap between soldier and civilian experience more apparent than on the Sabbath. "There is no Sunday in the army" became a military cliché. The day seemed like any other, as routine camp duties and marching continued—and so did the card-playing. Simply to enjoy a quiet Sunday at home became a man's humble but profound wish. Devout soldiers missed hearing church bells, dressing up for services, and even listening to exhortatory sermons. The trouble was camp life hardly inspired spiritual discipline. "My experience goes to convince me that religion stands a poor show for increase in the Army," a Maine private lamented. A "true Christian," he admitted, could "grow in grace in the army as well as other places," but would receive little encouragement from his comrades. Men who had not heard a sermon in months talked of returning home to worship God—as if worship seemed hardly possible in camp. "I have gone entirely wild," a Georgia sergeant confessed to his wife, "and if I ever get back I shall have my name taken off the church book for it is a shame and disgrace to the cause of Christ for it to be there."[45]

All the more reason then to treasure a real worship service—even in cold weather. Despite a fierce wind blowing, a Pennsylvania captain described a particularly moving sermon as "quite a treat and . . . justly appreciated by all the men." Lively weekday prayer meetings helped devout young men ward off temptation, but Sunday services more effectively secured bonds between soldiers and their families worshiping back home. "Thank God for the Sabbath the day of rest when you lift our souls from the low groveling earth to the heavens above," a Hoosier exulted.[46]

Yet believers faced what Pennsylvania chaplain Alexander M. Stewart called an "uphill business to accomplish anything for Jesus in the camp."

The seeming indifference of the men and their commanders was a constant discouragement. Sermons, tracts, and many soldier letters were filled with complaints about drinking, profanity, gambling and what some observers politely termed "lasciviousness." "What are the abominations of savages and heathens compared with the wickedness of our army?" Stewart asked, a question that starkly expressed one of the more obvious contrasts between camp and home. The men and officers might seem receptive to the message but would still swear horribly on the slightest provocation.[47]

"He has become desperately wicked," a shocked Pennsylvanian wrote of one boy from his hometown and wondered what the lad's father would think if he could hear the "awful oaths" spewing from his son's mouth. In a letter to a religious newspaper, Chaplain Andrew Jackson Hartsock of the 133rd Pennsylvania admitted that "profanity abounds to a dreadful extent" and that "some things are considered right in the army that would be considered greatly out of place at home." Relatively minor vices of course often encouraged more dangerous practices, including brawling and dereliction of duty. Bad habits would likely follow soldiers back to civilian life. Hartsock managed to persuade his men to burn two decks of cards but recognized that soldiers without much reading matter easily got bored, quickly tired of the same old conversations around the camp fires, and gambled to "while the time the away." He formed a "Regimental Christian Union" by compiling a list of men who strove to live a purer life and "escape the wrath to come."[48] Not coincidentally, this organization clearly tried to create an atmosphere that more resembled a pious household.

During revival meetings held in winter camp, many men reflected on their misspent youth and fretted over their shortcomings before receiving assurance of salvation. The comfort of knowing that families prayed for their deliverance gave some soldiers a sense of genuine peace about their own fates. Young volunteers fondly recalled their home churches. Attending a Presbyterian service, a member of Barksdale's brigade listened to the "treble voice of the fair sex" and engaged in some pleasant reverie about "times of old."[49] Soldiers struggling to lead a Christian life especially relished letters that encouraged their walk with Jesus. The most devout men urged relatives to read the Bible regularly and accept Christ as their savior. "Life is short. Death is certain," Virgil Mattoon of the 24th New York warned his brother, and he could only pray for an "unbroken family circle in Heaven."[50]

Ironically, some of the same Federals who so treasured thoughts of heavenly reunion and memories of church services had themselves become the invaders and destroyers of homes.[51] Aggressive foraging in northern Virginia had partly set the stage for a loosening of restraints in protecting enemy property. Beginning on the night of December 11, intensifing the following day, and persisting until the Federal withdrawal from Fredericksburg on December 15, looting turned many houses in that poor town into veritable shambles. Once gracious parlors were "strewn with . . . dirt and filth," noted an observant Hoosier, "and even ladies' clothing thrown in confusion or torn to pieces." Rare books lay tattered and torn on the floors of despoiled libraries. Piles of miscellaneous trash littered the corners of various rooms. Some members of the 19th Massachusetts, who had done such hard fighting the day before, filled their canteens with molasses and poured the goo all over one house.[52]

The Federals had changed once sleepy Fredericksburg into a chaotic world where the functions of various private and public spaces seemed oddly if not obscenely confused. While the interiors of many homes became great trash heaps, expensive furniture was strewn in the streets. Looters lounged about on stuffed sofas or chairs, ate off fine china, drank from gold and silver cups, or even pounded on pianos al fresco. Other men hauled out featherbeds to sleep under the heavens. The destruction continued even on the streets of the town. Furniture was smashed— one mahogany bureau was used for kindling—old books became stepping-stones for muddy boots. All manner of household goods lay on sidewalks or in the streets. To the men of one New Hampshire regiment it seemed a "mighty whirlwind" had swept through Fredericksburg.[53]

Such actions confirmed Confederate images of remorseless Yankee invaders, and the sense of outrage shared by both civilians and Confederate soldiers was not entirely lost on the Federals. Union soldiers felt a need to somehow justify this invasion of private space. As a member of Burnside's headquarters guard put it, "The cursed Rebels brought it all on themselves by their own maddened folly." For those soldiers from godly homes whose families fretted about the effects of army life on their moral character, a spirit of righteous vengeance might cover the proverbial multitude of sins. "Men who at home were modest and unassuming now seemed to be possessed with an insatiate desire to destroy everything in sight," one artillery officer noticed. An undeniable callousness held sway among the troops who continued to loot even while under fire and then joke about it.[54] Their families might well have shuddered in disbelief to see and hear how military life had transformed these young men.

For folks back home who might question whether the bombardment and sack could possibly be justified, Private Roland E. Bowen had a terse response: "Mother you know but very little about War." But some civilians as well as many soldiers were by this time adjusting their beliefs about the nature of war. This increasingly callous attitude could rationalize nearly anything, but even the extensive damage did not satisfy the more bloodthirsty. "I wish that we had burnt the whole of it [Fredericksburg] over their heads," a Connecticut volunteer informed his father.[55]

Yet the sack of private homes also deeply disturbed some Federals. A fair number of soldiers, who could hardly believe that the fortunes of war now respected neither gender nor age, were appalled at what they had witnessed. For men who had grown up husbanding their resources and property, seeing the wanton destruction of valuables and ordinary household items, in clear violation of army regulations, was almost more than they could stand. Children's toys scattered about in the wreckage especially unnerved family men. When looters cleaned their guns with ladies' silken gowns, the domestic symbolism became equally disturbing. One volunteer sadly conceded that the sack of Fredericksburg had been "done in a manner worthy of the Gothic of the Goths or the hungrish of the Huns."[56]

Victims of the bombardment and sack neither philosophized nor analyzed the Federals' behavior: they inventoried their property. Estimates for household goods damaged or stolen ranged from a few dollars to several thousand per household. Citizens carefully listed missing furniture, crockery, silverware, clothing, sheets, books, and food. Nearly anything had attracted the Yankees' attention. Emilie Caldwell had lost paintings, carpet, wine glasses, sauce tureens, and a dressing gown; her list went on for two full pages. By contrast, Lucy Southard missed common items, including "every piece of clothing my [five] children had except what they had on." Several people claimed to have lost nearly everything. "I can tell you much better what they left, than what they destroyed," one man observed ruefully. Reports of the destruction plunged those civilians who had fled before the bombardment into even greater despair.[57]

Confederate soldiers already sympathetic to the refugees and civilians driven by bombardment from their homes grew livid at the sack of Fredericksburg. "A monument to the barbarity of the abolitionists," fumed one young staff officer.[58] These latest outrages only reconfirmed stock Confederate images of Federal malevolence. Gruesome tales of civilian suffering immediately became staples of unofficial propaganda. The dastardly Yankees had dared invade the sacred home — entering the most private recesses of domestic life. Newspapers ran long lists of items destroyed, giving special emphasis to vile bluecoats accoutered in pilfered women's clothing.[59]

At the time, it was easy to believe that the sack of Fredericksburg had pushed the war to a new level of destructiveness and cruelty. Even some

Federal marauders conceded that a fearful precedent had been set, throwing the meaning of noncombatant into flux. And however they might condemn their enemies' wanton disregard for civilian lives and property, the Confederates must also have wondered if this war would any longer be fought out solely between the contending armies. Would the "home front" literally become "the front"?

Not only had the sack of Fredericksburg and the battle itself occurred shortly after Thanksgiving—the most "homey" of holidays—but these events had transpired less than two weeks before Christmas, another holiday that evoked equally powerful domestic yearning. "My heart is filled with gratitude to Almighty God for his unspeakable mercies," Robert E. Lee wrote to his wife on Christmas Day. "I have seen His hand in all the events of the war. Oh if our people would recognize it & cease from vain self boasting & adulation." In a note to daughter Mildred, he recalled the joys of former Christmases now sadly contrasted to the sorry condition of "desecrated and pillaged" Virginia.[60]

Standing at his picket post jawing with some Yankees on the other side of the Rappahannock River, Virginian Henry Krebs considered December 25, 1862, the most "unpleasant Christmas" in his life. "Just another day in camp" became the lament of many forlorn soldiers. Another Virginian expressed his reaction in a series of negatives: "no egg nog, no turkey, no mince pie, nothing to eat or drink but our rations." A dull, cheerless time, and into the men's minds flooded warm memories of home that only added to the ennui. For the more spiritually minded there seemed to be no Christmas in the army, no recognition of Christ's birth. Secular traditions had already crowded out much of the day's religious meaning: cards, shopping, and presents had come to define the holiday, especially in cities but elsewhere as well. Christmas in America was a relatively new holiday, and some familiar traditions had only appeared in the 1850s, but already by the time of time of the Civil War its material trappings had sunk deep roots in American culture, making a Christmas spent in the army all that more miserable. A "festival that was formally devoted entirely to pleasure" nearly passed unnoticed in the camps, a Georgia lieutenant reflected.[61]

Paltry attempts at merrymaking and perhaps of bit of whiskey provided relief from the routine of winter camp but could never suppress thoughts of home. Recollections of Christmases past—the children with their stockings, a cozy fire, a plump turkey, or the traditional pound cake sitting on a table—all churned up emotions. A miserable Mississippian hoped that at least he and his wife might be gazing at the same stars in the heavens; an adjutant in General Jubal Early's division decided to spend the day writing a letter home even though he really wanted to hug his wife and romp with their dear boys. Melancholy reflections on families separated for the holidays, the inadequate consolation of imagining loved ones gathering for Christmas dinner, brave efforts to appear satisfied with sparse meals, cordial wishes for a good holiday at home only made the languorous camps more depressing.[62]

On one level, Christmas on the home front followed familiar patterns — newspaper advertisements for books or perfume or brandy, the anticipation of wide-eyed children, the bustle of holiday meals. In Richmond, young boys set off the usual firecrackers. Yet now women also had to think about the soldiers in the hospitals, and the demands on their charity occurred amidst shortages and inflation. If the holiday spirit seemed far away to the soldiers, many civilians also found it difficult to sustain Christmas traditions. For one Fredericksburg refugee, the day was especially sad because "Tommy's stocking . . . was the only relic of Xmas we had," and to make matters worse, some Confederate soldiers stole six turkeys on Christmas Eve. Everyone noticed and many remarked how the holiday seemed so "different." A foreboding gloom tempered innocent joy. To a staff officer on leave in North Carolina, the explanation seemed obvious: "All thoughts are absorbed in the war."[63]

The costs of the fighting kept mounting and peace seemed far away. With so many men away from home and prices so high, many people expected a "dull" Christmas, though one editor assured the children that Santa Claus would still come and printed the now-standard "Night before Christmas." War, however, predated the birth of Christ, and humans had never been able to escape its cruelties. Thinking back on Christmas just one year ago, South Carolina Private Tally Simpson found little to celebrate: "If all the dead . . . could be heaped in one pile and all the wounded be gathered together in one group, the pale faces of the dead and groans of the wounded would send such a thrill of horror through the hearts of the originators of this war that their very souls would rack with such pain that they would prefer being dead and in torment than to stand before God with such terrible crimes blackening their characters."[64]

For the Federals as well, fat pork and hardtack for two or even three meals made Christmas Day, 1862, especially hard to swallow. "A gay old Christmas dinner," a Massachusetts volunteer wrote his mother, but at least he had not found bugs and worms in his crackers like one disgusted Michigan recruit. Leftover vegetable soup or a tough piece of beef made for spartan dining, even for men who had grown up poor. "I use to think times was hard at home but this is out of my head," a disconsolate Pennsylvanian told his sister.[65]

But a family sending a box to camp could make all the difference in the world. To a Maine volunteer it made his bivouac seem just like home. The boys would go to sleep on Christmas Eve "with feelings akin to those of children expecting Santa Claus." He admitted that soldiers had grown rather "childish" when it came to "grub." On Christmas Day, however, when a long-expected box had still not appeared, his "mental thermometer not only plummeted to below zero, it got right down off the nail and lay on the floor."[66]

A gill or two of liquor might relieve the gloom, and some regiments did draw a Christmas Day whiskey ration — one Pennsylvania lieutenant even noted how men accustomed to voting as "repeaters" back home got into line more than once. It was an ordinary enough day except for the alcohol, and even then many camps remained quiet. An Indiana major told his wife that he did not drink nearly as much in army as he had at home, but he may have been dissembling, or the poor quality of the booze may have slaked his thirst.[67]

Although, the horrors of Fredericksburg still haunted men's minds, on Christmas Day, 1862, domestic concerns monopolized their thoughts. Like the Confederates, Federals simply wished they were home. How could a Christmas be merry when it was spent far away from loved ones? To be once again with one's wife or children — imagining it were so could relieve the oppressive dullness of camp. Men could envision the eager young folks hanging their stockings, the tree all decorated, families praying for their safety. Just as at Thanksgiving, the soldier boys could see and almost taste the food. They missed setting off firecrackers, they dreamed of the warm family hearth, they recalled the familiar church pew.[68]

In lonely camps, men prayed for their families and tried to rekindle the season's message of love and peace — no small task in 1862. Thankfulness for the year's blessings, especially for loved ones untouched by the painful losses so many others had suffered, offered hope, but a hope tinged with sadness. Not being able to exchange presents became both frustrating and depressing. One Michigan lieutenant briefly noted it was Christmas Day but then decided that he had better tell his wife of nine years how much he loved her and appreciated her as a Christian mother. No wonder a New Hampshire private cherished a *Harper's Weekly* drawing entitled "Christmas Eve" that showed a wife in one panel earnestly praying at home while in the other panel her soldier husband sat near a small sentry fire. Soldiers whose thoughts on the subject often verged toward maudlin sentimentality (by our standards) liked to imagine what their families might be doing on this most sacred (and domestic) of all holidays.[69]

For soldiers and civilians, Yank and Reb, home remained a sacred place.[70] The contrast between the celebration of holidays and sack of houses created serious tensions, and perhaps what a psychologist would even label cognitive dissonance, but the contradictions and complexities of "home" only heightened the intensity of the emotional turmoil. Death, sacrifice, and even the threat of spiritual apostasy further highlighted the stakes involved in a war that literally divided families in ways that went far beyond the stale cliché of a "brothers' war." An entire generation had to more consciously than ever think about home, the values and meanings of domestic life, and everything that a horrific war threatened to destroy. The gap between the experiences, thoughts, and emotions of civilians and soldiers remained all too real, yet the soldiers literally fought for homes, and civilians struggled to maintain home values in the midst of wrenching political, economic, and emotional change. Both groups experienced a kind of "nostalgia," in both the modern and contemporary sense of the word. They could look back on domestic life in an idealized way and at the same time feel a great sadness over what had been sacrificed and what more might still be lost. Loneliness and separation compounded the anguish of civil war as thousands of people came to agree with Lieutenant Williams about the priceless value of home.

Notes

1. Edward J. Hagerty, *Collis' Zouavesi: The 114th Pennsylvania in the Civil War.* (Baton Route, 1997), 131–32.
2. For an important exception, see Reid Mitchell, *The Vacant Chair: The Northern Soldier Leaves Home* (New York, 1993), esp. 19–37. For scattered comments and insights, Randall C. Jimerson, *The Private Civil War: Popular Thought during the Sectional Conflict* (Baton Rouge, 1988), 24–25; Joan E. Cashin, "Into the Trackless Wilderness: The Refugee Experience in the Civil War," in *A Woman's War: Southern Women, Civil War, and the Confederate Legacy* ed. Edward D. C. Campbell Jr. and Kym S. Rice (Richmond, 1996), 33; Catherine Clinton and Nina Silber, eds., *Divided Houses: Gender and the Civil War* (New York, 1992), passim; George C. Rable, *Civil Wars: Women and the Crisis of Southern Nationalism* (Urbana, 1989), 50–72.
3. Thanksgiving had not yet been recognized as an official holiday by either the president or Congress. Beginning in 1863 Lincoln would issue Thanksgiving proclamations, but it was not until 1941 that Congress made it a legal holiday.
4. *History of the Thirty-Fifth Regiment Massachusetts Volunteers, 1862–1865* (Boston, 1884), 73.
5. Walter Houghton, *The Victorian Frame of Mind* (New Haven, 1957), 342–43.
6. George E. Upton to his wife, December 2, 1862, Upton Papers, New Hampshire Historical Society (hereafter NHHS). Because virtually all the evidence on religious attitudes comes from Protestant soldiers, this essay does not take into account the somewhat different attitudes toward death and dying by Catholics.

7. Edward King Wightman, *From Antietam to Fort Fisher: The Civil War Letters of Edward King Wightman, 1862–1865*, ed. Edward G. Longacre (Rutherford, N.J., 1985), 82; *Hartford (Conn.) Daily Courant*, November 27, 1862.

8. *Yonkers (N.Y.) Examiner*, November 27, 1862; "Thanksgiving Day," *Christian Inquirer* 17 (December 6, 1862): n.p.; *Boston Daily Advertiser*, November 27, 1862; *Philadelphia Public Ledger*, November 27, 1862; *Indianapolis Daily State Sentinel*, November 27, 1862.

9. *Philadelphia Inquirer*, November 27, 1862; *New York Times*, November 28, 1862; *Albany (N.Y.) Atlas and Argus*, November 27, 1862; *Albany (N.Y.) Evening Journal*, November 26, 1862.

10. George W. Ballock to his wife, November 25, 1862, Ballock Papers, William R. Perkins Library, Duke University (hereafter Duke); Catherine Eaton to Samuel W. Eaton, November 28, 1862, Edward Dwight Eaton Papers, State Historical Society of Wisconsin (hereafter SHSW); *New York Tribune*, November 28, 1862: *Newark (N.J.) Daily Advertiser*, November 26, 1862; *Philadelphia Inquirer*, November 28, 1862.

11. S. Millett Thompson, *Thirteenth Regiment of New Hampshire Volunteer Infantry in the War of the Rebellion, 1861–1865* (Boston, 1888), 24.

12. The heavy reliance on letters as sources for this essay undoubtedly means that both the soldiers and civilians cited were more likely than others perhaps to place an emphasis on "home" themes in their correspondence. Yet the importance of home is overwhelming and reflects the beliefs of many soldiers and civilians.

13. John H. Pardington to Sarah Pardington, November 27, 1862, Pardington Papers, copies, Fredericksburg and Spotsylvania National Military Park (hereafter FSNMP); Robert McAllister, *The Civil War Letters of General Robert McAllister*, ed. James I. Robertson Jr. (New Brunswick, N.J., 1965), 235. For additional discussion of the connection between home news and morale, see Mitchell, *Vacant Chair*, 25–26.

14. Alfred E. Doby to his wife, January 15, 1863, Doby Letters, Museum of the Confederacy (hereafter MC); Francis Marion Coker to his wife, December 18, 1862, Coker Letters, Hodgson Heidler Collection, Special Collections, University of Georgia Library (hereafter UG); Dick Simpson and Tally Simpson, *Far, Far from Home: The Wartime Letters of Dick and Tally Simpson, 3rd South Carolina Volunteers*, ed. Guy R. Everson and Edward H. Simpson (New York, 1994), 167; Lucius S. J. Owen to his mother, January 5, 1863, Owen Letters, Civil War Times Illustrated Collection, United States Army Military History Institute (hereafter USAMHI); William Goodrich Morton to his mother, December 26, 1862, Morton Letters, copies, FSNMP.

15. Rohloff C. Hacker to William and Barbara Woll Hacker, November 23, 1862, Hacker Brothers Papers, Schoff Civil War Collection, Clements Library, University of Michigan (hereafter CL-UM); William Franklin Draper to his mother, November 30, 1862, Draper Papers, Library of Congress (hereafter LC); J. Frank Sterling to his father, November 7, 1862, Sterling Papers, Special Collections, Rutgers University; Samuel Morrow to his brother, November 26, 1862, Harrisburg Civil War Roundtable Collection, USAMHI. It is also fair to

say that at least some soldiers were more than happy to be away from less than desirable homes.

16. Daniel M. Holt, *A Surgeon's Civil War: The Letters and Diary of Daniel M. Holt*, ed. James M. Greiner, Janet L. Coryell, and James R. Smither (Kent, Ohio, 1994), 52.

17. Alfred Lewis Castleman, *The Army of the Potomac. Behind the Scenes. A Diary of Unwritten History, from Organization of the Army by General George McClellan, to the Close of the Campaign in Virginia, during the First Day of January, 1863* (Milwaukee, 1863), 216; Joshua Lawrence Chamberlain, *Through Blood and Fire: Selected Civil War Papers of Major General Joshua Lawrence Chamberlain* (Mechanicsburg, Pa., 1996), 34–35.

18. Elijah Henry Clay Cavins, *The Civil War Letters of Col. Elijah H. C. Cavins, 14th Indiana*, comp. Barbara A. Smith (Owensboro, Ky., 1981), 106; John H. Pardington to Sarah Pardington, November 12, 1862, Pardington Papers, copies, FSNMP.

19. George W. Ballock to his wife, November 10, 18, December 3, 1862, Ballock Papers, Duke; George E. Upton to his wife, December 2, 1862, Upton Papers, NHHS.

20. Jedediah Hotchkiss to Sara Ann Comfort Hotchkiss, January 11, 1863, Hotchkiss Papers, LC; Henry Dickerson McDaniel, *With Unabated Trust: Major Henry McDaniel's Love Letters from Confederate Battlefields as Treasured in Hester McDonald's Bonnet Box*, ed. Anita B. Sims (Monroe, Ga., 1977), 124; James M. Simpson to Addie Simpson, January 6, 1863, Allen and Simpson Family Papers, Southern Historical Collection, University of North Carolina (hereafter SHC-UNC).

21. Houghton, *Victorian Frame of Mind*, 344.

22. George W. Ballock to his sister, November 14, 1862, Ballock to his wife, November 25, 1862, Ballock Papers, Duke; James B. Post to his wife, November 27, 1862, Post Papers, Civil War Miscellaneous Collection (hereafter CWMC), USAMHI; John Smart to Ann Smart, November 26, 1862, Smart Letters, copies, FSNMP; Charles Barber, *The Civil War Letters of Charles Barber, Private, 104th New York Volunteer Infantry*, ed. Raymond G. Barber and Gary E. Swinson (Torrance, Calif., 1991), 102.

23. Catherine Eaton to Samuel W. Eaton, November 12, 22, December 3, 8, 15, 1862, James Eaton to Samuel W. Eaton, November 26, 1862, Edward Dwight Eaton Papers, SHSW; James R. Woodworth to Phoebe Woodworth, November 12, 13, 16, 30, December 8, 1862, Woodworth Papers, Lawrence Hotchkiss Collection, CL-UM.

24. Alexander Way to his wife, December 18, 1862, Way Letters, copies, FSNMP; John F. L. Hartwell, *To My Beloved Wife and Boy at Home: The Letters and Diaries of Orderly Sergeant John F. L. Hartwell*, ed. Ann Hartwell Britton and Thomas J. Reed (Madison, N.J., 1998), 36–38.

25. Henry Grimes Marshall to "Dear Hattie," December 28, 1862, Marshall Letters, Schoff Civil War Collection, CL-UM; Henry F. Young to "Dear Delia," January 25, 1863, Young Papers, SHSW; William Franklin Draper to his wife, January 18, 1863, Draper Papers, LC; John R. Coye to his wife, December 19,

1862, Coye Letters, copies, FSNMP; Jacob Bechtel to "Miss Cannie," January 15, 1863, Bechtel Letters, Gettysburg National Military Park.

26. James P. Coburn to his father, January 28, 1863, Coburn Papers, USAMHI; Peter Welsh, *Irish Green and Union Blue: The Civil War Letters of Peter Welsh, Color Sergeant, 28th Regiment Massachusetts Volunteers*, ed. Lawrence Frederick Kohl and Margaret Cosse Richard (New York, 1986). 60; Andrew Elmer Ford, *The Story of the Fifteenth Regiment Massachusetts Volunteer Infantry in the Civil War, 1861–1864* (Clinton, Mass., 1898), 233–34.

27. James R. Woodworth to Phoebe Woodworth, January 12, 1863, Woodworth Papers, Lawrence Hotchkiss Collection, CL-UM; Albert Foster to his family, January 18, 1863, Foster Letters, copies, FSNMP; George W. Barr to Vinnie Barr, December 23, 1862, Barr Papers, Schoff Civil War Collection, CL-UM.

28. Simpson and Simpson, *Far, Far from Home*, 167; Francis Marion Coker to his wife, Coker Letters, Hodgson Heidler Collection, UG; Alfred E. Doby to his wife, January 20, 25, 1863, Doby Letters, MC; Jedediah Hotchkiss to Sara Ann Comfort Hotchkiss, January 23, 1863, Hotchkiss Papers, LC.

29. Thomas Claybrook Elder to Anna Fitzhugh Elder, January 3, 1863, Elder Papers, Virginia Historical Society (hereafter VHS); S. G. Pryor, *A Post of Honor: The Pryor Letters, 1861–1863* (Fort Valley, Ga., 1989), 304; William Dorsey Pender, *The General to His Lady: The Civil War Letters of William Dorsey Pender to Fanny Pender*, ed. William W. Hassler (Chapel Hill, 1965), 195–96; William Ross Stillwell to "My Dear Mollie," December [n.d.], 1862, Stillwell Letters, Georgia Department of Archives and History (hereafter GDAH); Hester Reeve to Edward Payson Reeve, December 22, 1862, Reeve Papers, SHC-UNC; Elizabeth Preston Allan, *The Life and Letters of Margaret Junkin Preston* (Boston, 1903), 159–60.

30. William Ross Stillwell to "My dear Mollie," January 15, 1863, Stillwell Letters, GDAH; Samuel H. Walkup to his wife, January 1, 1863, Walkup Papers, SHC-UNC; Constantine Hege to his parents, December 21, 1862, Hege Letters, Louis Leigh Collection, USAMHI; Pryor, *Post of Honor*, 301–2; Jonathan Fuller Coghill to his home folks, January 25, 1863, Coghill Letters, Auburn University Archives; J. G. Montgomery to "Dear Bro Arthur and Sister Bettie," January 9, 1863, Montgomery Letter, copy, FSNMP; Jedediah Hotchkiss to Sara Ann Comfort Hotchkiss, December 17, 1862, Hotchkiss Papers, LC.

31. Abiel Hall Edwards *Dear Friend Anna: The Civil War Letters of a Common Soldier from Maine*, ed. Beverly Hayes Kallgres and James L. Crouthamel (Orono, Maine, 1992), 38; Zerah Coston Monks to Hannah T. Rohrer, December 4, 1862, Monks-Rohrer Letters, Special Collections, Robert W. Woodruff Library, Emory University; Warren Hapgood Freeman, *Letters from Two Brothers Serving in the War for the Union* (Cambridge, Mass., 1871), 57; United States Bureau of the Census, *Historical Statistics of the United States*, 2 vols. (Washington, 1975), 2:7057.

32. McAllister, *Civil War Letters of Robert McAllister*, 240; Charles H. Eagor to his wife, December 12, 1862, Eagor Letters, Lewis Leigh Collection,

USAMHI; Horatio Balch Hackett, *Christian Memorials of the War; or Scenes and Incidents Illustrative of Religious Faith and Principle, Patriotism, Bravery of Our Army*. (Boston, 1864), 79–81.

33. Thomas L. Livermore, *Numbers and Losses in the Civil War in America, 1861–1865* (Bloomington, 1957), 96; *The War of the Rebellion: A Compilation of the Official Records of the Union and Confederate Armies* (Washington, D.C., 1880–1901), ser. 1, vol. 21, 129–42, 558–62.

34. Emma Holmes, *The Diary of Miss Emma Holmes*, ed. John F. Marszalek (Baton Rouge, 1979), 218; William Thompson Lusk, *War Letters of William Thompson Lusk* (New York, 1911), 252–53; Catherine Eaton to Samuel W. Eaton, December 15, 1862, Edward Dwight Eaton Papers, SHSW; Anzolette E. Pendleton to William Nelson Pendleton, December 18, 1862, Pendleton Papers, SHC-UNC.

35. Orson Blair Curtis, *History of the Twenty-Fourth Michigan of the Iron Brigade, Known as the Detroit and Wayne County Regiment* (Detroit, 1891), 107; Robert Wentworth to his daughter, December 25, 1862, Edwin O. Wentworth Papers, LC; John Haley, *The Rebel Yell and the Yankee Hurrah: The Civil War Journal of a Maine Volunteer*, ed. Ruth L. Silliker (Camden, Maine, 1985), 60.

36. Henry Livermore Abbott, *Fallen Leaves: The Civil War Letters of Major Henry Livermore Abbott*, ed. Robert Garth Scott (Kent, Ohio, 1991), 160; Curtis, *History of Twenty-Fourth Michigan*, 82; Kate Stone, *Brokenburn: The Journal of Kate Stone, 1861–1868*, ed. John Q. Anderson (Baton Rouge, 1955), 164–65.

37. Rohloff C. Hacker to his parents, December 18, 1862, Philip Hacker to his parents, December 31, 1862, January 14, 1863, Philip Hacker to his father, January 5, 1863, Philip Hacker to his mother, January 18, February 1, 1863, Hacker Brothers Papers, CL-UM.

38. Abbott, *Fallen Leaves*, 150; J. C. Allen to "Cousin Sallie," December 18, 1862, Richard W. Milner Collection, GDAH; John H. Mitchell to Rebecca Mitchell, December 17, 1862, Mitchell Letter, copy, FSNMP; G. A. Evans, undated statement, Washington Brown Papers, Special Collections, Virginia Polytechnic Institute and State University; Hagerty, *Collis' Zouaves*, 133–34; Norman W. Camp to Amanda Wolcott, December 20, 1862, Wolcott Collection, copy, FSNMP. Captain Brown's words have a kind of "set piece" quality, but it is important to remember that people at the time often spoke in such language.

39. *Athens (Pa.) Gazette*, March 11, 1897; William Withington to his wife, December 18, 1862, Withington Papers, Michigan Historical Collection, Bentley Library, University of Michigan (hereafter MHC, BL-UM); *German Reformed Messenger* 28 (January 7, 1863): 2; Richard F. Miller and Robert F. Mooney, *The Civil War: The Nantucket Experience* (Nantucket, Mass., 1994), 24.

40. Miller and Mooney, *Civil War: Nantucket Experience*, 24, 137; Emmeline Ruggles, "A Soldier and a Letter," *Confederate Veteran* 38 (March 1930): 89.

41. Winifred Borden, ed., *The Legacy of Fannie and Joseph* (n.p., 1992), 130–31, 134–36, 139, 143.

42. *Christian Reformed Messenger* 28 (January 7, 1863): 2; *Raleigh (N.C.) Weekly Standard*, January 7, 1863; William Johnson Bacon, *Memorial of William Kirland Bacon, Late Adjutant of the Twenty-Sixth Regiment of New York State Volunteers* (Utica, 1863), 20–41 51–62, 78–81; John Oliver Means, *Waiting for Daybreak, A Discourse at the Funeral of the Lieut. Edgar M. Newcomb, of the Mass. 19th Reg't Who Died December 20, 1862, of Wounds Received at Fredericksburg, Preached in Park Street Church, December 27* (Boston, 1863), 6–9.

43. Judith Brockenbrough McGuire, *Diary of a Southern Refugee during the War* (New York, 1867), 179–80; David Beem to his wife, January 22, 1863, Beem Papers, Indiana Historical Society (hereafter IHS); Means, *Waiting for Daybreak*, 12–13; Albert Blodgett Weymouth, *Memorial Sketch of Lieut. Edgar M. Newcomb of the Nineteenth Mass. Vols.* (Malden, Mass., 1883), 111–21.

44. Anne C. Rose, *Victorian America and the Civil War* (Cambridge, 1992), 17–38, 59–67; Phillip Shaw Paludan, *"A People's Contest": The Union and the Civil War, 1861–1865* (New York, 1988), 363–65; Mitchell, *Vacant Chair*, 31–32.

45. Nathan B. Webb Diary, December 7, 1862, CL-UM; Marion Hill Fitzpatrick, *Letters to Amanda: The Civil War Letters of Marion Hill Fitzpatrick, Army of Northern Virginia*, ed. Jeffrey C. Lowe and Sam Hodges (Macon, Ga., 1998), 39.

46. Robert Taggart Diary, December 21, 1862, Jay Luvaas Collection, USAMHI; Henry Grimes Marshall to "Dear Hattie," January 25, 1863, Marshall Letters, Schoff Civil War Collection, CL-UM; Henry C. Marsh Diary, January 4, 1863, Indiana State Library.

47. A. M. Stewart, *Camp, March and Battle-field* (Philadelphia, 1865), 255–58; Samuel W. Eaton to Warner Eaton, December 1, 1862, Edward Dwight Eaton Papers, SHSW.

48. William Penn Oberlin to "Annie," January 13, 1863, Oberlin Papers, CWMC, USAMHI; Andrew Jackson Hartsock, *Soldier of the Cross: The Civil War Diary and Correspondence of Rev. Andrew Jackson Hartsock*, ed. James C. and Eleanor A. Duram (Manhattan, Kans., 1979), 26–28, 166.

49. David L. Bozeman to his family, December 27, 1862, Bozeman Letters, copies, FSNMP; Robert A. Moore, *A Life for the Confederacy as Recorded in the Pocket Diaries of Pvt. Robert A. Moore, Co. G, 17th Mississippi Regiment, Confederate Guards*, ed. James W. Silver (Jackson, Tenn., 1959), 129–30.

50. United States Christian Commission, *First Annual Report* (Philadelphia, 1863), 59–60; Virgil W. Mattoon to "Dear Brother John," December 28, 1862, Mattoon Papers, Connecticut Historical Society.

51. Reid Mitchell (*Vacant Chair*, 36–37) discusses this development with reference to Sherman's march but the assaults on Southern homes began earlier.

52. David Beem to his wife, December 18, 1862, Beem Papers, IHS; Milo Grow to his wife, December 18, 1862, Grow Letters, copies, FSNMP; Ernest Linden Waitt, *History of the Nineteenth Regiment Massachusetts Volunteer Infantry, 1861–1865* (Salem, Mass., 1906), 176.

53. O. Leland Barlow to his sister, December 16, 1862, Barlow Papers, Con-

necticut State Library (hereafter CSL); Charles J. Borden to "Dear Friend," December 18, 1862, Borden Papers, Duke; G. O. Bartlett to Ira Andrews, December 18, 1862, Bartlett Papers, Gilder Lehrman Collection, Pierpont Morgan Library, New York; *Lancaster (Pa.) Daily Evening Express*, December 23, 1862; *Philadelphia Inquirer*, January 2, 1863; Thompson, *Thirteenth New Hampshire*, 45.

54. *New York Tribune*, December 15, 1862; John S. Crocker to his wife, December 12, 1862, Crocker Papers, Brockett Collection, Department of Manuscripts and Archives, Cornell University; Thomas Rice, "All the Imps of Hell Let Loose," *Civil War Times Illustrated* 22 (June 1983): 14; Nathan B. Webb Diary, December 19, 1862, Schoff Collection, CL-UM.

55. Roland R. Bowen, *From Ball's Bluff to Gettysburg . . . and Beyond: The Civil War Letters of Private Roland E. Bowen, 15th Massachusetts Infantry, 1861–1864*, ed. Gregory A. Coco (Gettysburg, Pa., 1994), 141; Ellis M. Stevens to Daniel Stevens, December 12, 1862, Daniel Stevens Papers, CSL.

56. George L. Prescott to ?, December 11–12, 1862, Prescott Papers, Massachusetts Historical Society; *Rochester (N.Y.) Daily Democrat and American*, December 27, 1862; John Godfrey to Horace Godfrey, December 14, 1862, Godfrey Papers, NHHS; [an unidentified member of the 24th New York] to "Dear Jeemes," December 18, 1862, Lyons Family Papers, Special Collections, United States Military Academy.

57. Civil War Damage Inventories, Drawer 491, Office of the Clerk of the Circuit Court of Fredericksburg, Virginia; Lizzie Maxwell Alsop Diary, December 29, 1862, VHS; Jane Howison Beale, *The Journal of Jane Howison Beale of Fredericksburg Virginia, 1850–1862* (Fredericksburg, Va., 1995), 74–75.

58. Osmun Latrobe Diary, December 12, 1862, VHS.

59. *Augusta (Ga.) Daily Constitutionalist*, January 4, 1863; *Richmond Daily Dispatch*, December 18, 1862; *Richmond Daily Enquirer*, December 18, 22, 1862.

60. Robert E. Lee, *The Wartime Papers of R. E. Lee*. ed. Clifford Dowdey and Louis H. Manarin (New York, 1961), 379–81.

61. Henry Clay Krebs to Lizzie Beard, December 25, 1862, Krebs Papers, Duke; William D. Henderson, *12th Virginia Infantry* (Lynchburg, Va., 1984), 43; John Simmons Shipp Diary, December 25, 1862, VHS; J. F. Shaffner to "My dearest friend," December 26, 1862, Shaffner Papers, North Carolina Division of Archives and History; Alexander E. Pendleton to his sister, December 28, 1862, William Nelson Pendleton Papers, SHC-UNC.

62. Philip H. Powers to his wife, December 25, 1862, Powers Letters, Lewis Leigh Collection, USAMHI; Miles H. Hill to his sister, December 24, 1862, Morgan Hill Family Papers, Troup County Archives, LaGrange, Georgia; H. Waters Berryman to his mother, December 27, 1862, Berryman Letters, USAMHI; Austin C. Dobbins, *Grandfather's Journal: Company B, Sixteenth Mississippi Infantry Volunteers Harris' Brigade, Mahone's Division, A. N. V.* (Dayton, Oh., 1988), 116; Samuel J. C. Moore to his wife, December 25, 1862, Moore Papers, SHC-UNC.

63. *Charleston Daily Courier*, December 24, 1862; *Richard Daily Dispatch*, December 24, 1862; *Richmond Daily Dispatch*, December 25, 29, 1862; J. B.

Jones, *A Rebel War Clerk's Diary at the Confederate States Capital*, 2 vols. (Philadelphia, 1866), 1:224; Maria Hamilton Diary, December 25, 1862, copy, FSNMP; George H. T. Greer, "All Thoughts Are Absorbed in the War," *Civil War Times Illustrated* 17 (December 1978): 35.

64. *Richmond Daily Whig*, December 24, 1862; *Richmond Daily Dispatch*, December 25, 1862; *Richmond Daily Enquirer*, December 25, 1862; *Charleston Daily Courier*, December 25, 1862; Simpson and Simpson, *Far, Far from Home*, 168.

65. Cornelius Richmond to his wife, December 25, 1862, Richmond Papers, copies, FSNMP; George H. Patch to his mother, December 27, 1862, Patch Papers, Lewis Leigh Collection, USAMHI; *Wellsboro (Pa.) Agitator*, January 4, 1863; John D. Withrow to Sarah Withrow, December 28, 1862, Withrow Letters, FSNMP.

66. George H. Mellish to his mother, December 26, 1862, Mellish Papers, Henry E. Huntington Library, San Marino, California; William Hamilton to his mother, December 28, 1862, Hamilton Papers, LC; John W. Ames to his mother, January 4, 1863, Ames Papers, USAMHI; Haley, *Rebel Yell and Yankee Hurrah*, 63–64.

67. Henry C. Heisler to his sister, January 5, 1863, Heisler Papers, LC; Frederick Lyman Hitchcock, *War from the Inside: The Story of the 132nd. Regiment Pennsylvania Volunteer Infantry in the War for the Suppression of the Rebellion, 1862–1863* (Philadelphia, 1904), 148–49: *Rochester (N.Y.) Daily Union and Advertiser*, January 5, 1863; Cavins, *Civil War Letters of Cavins*, 130.

68. Robert Taggart Diary, December 25, 1862, Jay Luvaas Collection, USAMHI; George W. Ballock to Jenny Ballock, December 23, 25, 1862, Ballock Papers, Duke; Lewis Nettleton to "My own dear love," December 25, 1862, Nettleton-Baldwin Family Papers, Duke; George W. Barr to Vinnie Barr, December 25, 1862, Barr Papers, Schoff Collection, CL-UM; Cavins, *Civil War Letters of Cavins*, 126; John Claude Buchanan to Sophie Buchanan, Buchanan Papers, MHC, BL-UM; Hartsock, *Soldier of the Cross*, 47; David Beem to his wife, December 25, 1862, Beem Papers, IHS.

69. Cyrus Bacon Diary, December 25, 1862, copy, FSNMP; James R. Woodworth to Phoebe Woodworth, December 25, 1862, Woodworth Papers, Lawrence Hotchkiss Collection, CL-UM; John Claude Buchanan to Sophie Buchanan, December 24, 1862, Buchanan Family Papers, MHC, BL-UM; Edward Hutchinson to "Dear Emma," December 22, 1862, Hutchinson Letters, copies, FSNMP; John Harrison Foye to his sister, January 18, 1863, Foye Papers, NHHS; "Christmas Eve," *Harper's Weekly* 7 (January 3, 1863): 8; Lois Hill, ed. *Poems and Songs of the Civil War* (New York, 1990), 68.

70. Houghton, *Victorian Frame of Mind*, 346–47.

Chapter 5

The Uncertainty of Life: A Profile of Virginia's Civil War Widows

ROBERT KENZER

✦ SUSAN COGHILL undoubtedly was disappointed that she and her husband, Alexander, could not spend June 24, 1862, their first wedding anniversary, together. Three months before, Alexander had enlisted as a private in Company F of the 55th Virginia Infantry and was now stationed near Richmond with other Confederate forces facing invading Union troops under the command of General George B. McClellan. Susan would learn that the day after their anniversary Alexander was killed in action at Mechanicsville, just thirty miles southwest of the couple's Essex County home. When Susan received news of her loss, she must have wondered about her fate and that of her newborn son, Thomas.

The previous summer, at the time of his marriage to Susan, Alexander Coghill was not a wealthy man. Rather, he was a propertyless bricklayer residing in the home of his sixty-eight-year-old mother, Elizabeth, the owner of only $200 in real estate. Despite her emotional loss, Susan survived the death of her husband, as did young Thomas of the father he never really knew. They did this largely through the support of Susan's brother, Richard House. Over the next two to three decades Susan, who never remarried, and young Thomas lived in her brother Richard's home, along with his wife and their children. Susan appears never to have had a home of her own. By 1900 she lived on the farm owned by her then thirty-eight-year-old son Thomas, his wife, and her three grandchildren. Susan was never employed, but beginning in 1888 began to receive a thirty-dollar annual pension from Virginia as compensation for the loss of her husband. This essay examines whether in her reliance on relatives and her failure to remarry Susan Coghill represents a typical Civil War widow.

Despite the heightened interest in the social history of the Civil War during the last two decades, especially the impact of the conflict on women, no scholar has written even an article-length study on Confederate widows.[1] One of the things that makes the paucity of scholarship on these widows so striking is that Margaret Mitchell portrayed the most famous Southern fictional character of this era, Scarlett O'Hara, as a widow in *Gone with the Wind*. I have briefly discussed widows in one Southern community, discovering that a number of these women actually improved their financial status after the loss of their husband-soldiers. In *Mothers of Invention: Women of the Slaveholding South in the American Civil War*, Drew Gilpin Faust notes how during the war those few widows who were "actively seeking romance and remarriage" attracted considerable public attention.[2]

Like most upper South states, Virginia was slow to join the Confederacy. After the fall of Fort Sumter and two days after President Abraham Lincoln called on the states to raise 75,000 troops to put down the insurrection, however, Virginia quickly left the Union and began to raise soldiers for the Southern cause. With the largest white population of any Southern state (1,105,000), Virginia also had the largest number of men of military age (196,500). While Virginians and North Carolinians in later years would disagree which state contributed the largest number of men to the military, there is no question that many Virginia men paid the ultimate price, as somewhere between 20,000 and 30,000 died in the Confederate service. Since about one-fifth of these men were married, the war also produced about 4,000 to 6,000 Virginia Confederate widows.[3]

This essay, which examines nearly 3,000 of Virginia's Confederate widows, is based on Southern death claim records and the Virginia state pension files. The death claim records were compiled by the Office of the Second Auditor of the Confederate government in Richmond, Virginia.[4] In the fall of 1862 the Confederate Congress passed legislation that entitled the survivor of a Southern soldier or sailor to receive his back pay or other funds owed to him at the time of his death. The process of filing a death claim was very complicated and exhausting for the survivors of servicemen, many of whom lived hundreds and in some cases a thousand miles away from the battlefield where their loved ones fell. Nevertheless, within a year of the passage of the law more than 42,433 claims had been filed by families, and nearly 12,000 had been settled. Because the Second Auditor's Office carefully noted the relationship between the individual filing the death claim and the deceased soldier, it is possible to determine how many of these claimants were the widows of soldiers.

The Confederate death claims include the names of 1,297 Virginia widows. Besides listing the name of the widow and her place of residence, these records generally note the soldier's name, rank, military unit, his birthplace, date and place of death, and the amount to which the widow was entitled. Reflecting the fact that the vast majority of the deceased soldiers were privates, two-thirds of the death claimants received less than $100.[5] Most of this money represented how many months in arrears the Confederate government had fallen in paying its troops. The small handful of widows who received more than $400 were nearly always the survivors of officers, whose pay was considerably higher than privates and who often received additional compensation for bounties, horses, clothing, and other effects.

Another factor that lowered the amount widows received in death claims was that about one-third of claimants used the aid of a lawyer to file their claim. The staff in the Second Auditor's Office simply could not process and verify the hundreds of claims from across the Confederacy that it received each day. The slightest mistake or confusion on a form could cause a delay of up to a year—a period that could make the final payment in inflated Confederate currency virtually worthless. Hence, Richmond attorneys were invaluable representatives not just for claimants as far away as Texas, but even for Virginians. In addition, members of the Confederate Congress and the Virginia legislature also expedited the claims made by their Virginia constituents.

Once the war ended, of course, the widows of Virginia's soldiers could not look to a national Confederate government for assistance. Further, even though the Commonwealth of Virginia began to provide support for its disabled Confederate veterans in 1867, it was not until 1888 that the state legislature finally initiated appropriations for the widows of those soldiers who had died during the Civil War.[6] Even the 1888 law was not particularly generous to widows, for only those women whose husbands died during the conflict and who had never remarried could receive a pension. In order to receive the thirty-dollar annual income payment, a sum about one-third the amount received by the widows of Union soldiers from the federal government, Virginia widows could not have an annual income of more than $300 and could own no more than $1,000 in personal property.[7] So those widows who requested pensions generally were seriously in need of assistance. Despite these restrictions, 1,899 Virginia widows filed for these pensions between 1888 and 1899.

Clearly the death claims and pension records do not contain information on every Virginia woman who lost a husband during the Civil War.[8] While the death claims include fewer total names, they are more representative of widows than the pension records, which are heavily weighed towards poorer women and confined exclusively to widows who did not remarry. Therefore, this essay's statistical analysis is based largely on the widows who filed death claims. The pension records will be used as well to provide additional information on those pensioners who many years earlier filed death claims.

A statistical profile of Virginia women whose husbands died during the Civil War reveals that two-thirds of them had married during the 1850s, and the median length of their marriage was six years.[9] Reflective of the short duration of their antebellum marriages, these wives were still quite young before the war. More than half of them were still in their twenties, and their median age was only twenty-seven. Their husbands were only a bit older, half of them either in their late twenties or early thirties, and their median age was thirty years. While the number of children per couple ranged from none to as many as fourteen, the median number stood at only two.[10] Two-thirds of these couples lived in nuclear households containing only the wife, husband, and children. The small number of couples who lived in other people's homes generally were newlyweds residing with their parents.[11]

In those households that contained inhabitants beyond the children, perhaps two-thirds of these other residents were related to the couple.[12] The presence of these kinfolks would be critical for many of the wives whose husbands would die in the war. For example, on the eve of the war Mary and William T. Bailey as well as their two infants lived in the Mecklenburg County home of Mary's sixty-eight-year-old father, William Morton Sr. While Mary and William owned no property, Mary's father possessed $8,000 in real estate and $18,000 in personal estate. Seven years after William died at the Battle of Chancellorsville, Mary and her children were still residing with her father.

Relatives were not only important when they lived within the same household as the couple. In 1860 Joseph and Catherine Boss and their three small children lived on a farm next door to John's parents, John B. and Nancy Boss. Sometime during the war, perhaps after Joseph died of disease in November of 1862, Catherine moved into her in-laws' home. She and her children would still be residing there five years after the war.

Given antebellum Virginia's rural economy, it is not surprising that three-fifths of the husbands of these women worked in agricultural positions, primarily as farmers, overseers, or farm laborers. About another fifth of these husbands earned a living with their various skills and crafts, particularly as carpenters, bootmakers, and shoemakers. Only one in twenty of the husbands worked in professional or mercantile occupations.[13]

While the overwhelming majority of the wives were not gainfully employed, every day these women performed valuable labor in their households. Much of their time, of course, was spent fulfilling the many necessary tasks to meet the constant needs of their husbands and children.[14] Furthermore, clearly many of the wives assisted their husbands in their occupations and trades. Since the majority of these women were the wives of farmers, at key times of the year, especially during the planting and harvest, their labor would have been essential. Of course, many performed such critical daily tasks as milking cows and collecting eggs.

All thirteen of the wives who worked for a salary did what would have been considered traditional female tasks: one was a domestic, four were seamstresses, and eight were engaged in spinning. All of these women, whose ages ranged from twenty-one to forty-five years, had working husbands, and six of the couples owned real estate and all but one couple had some form of property. The wealthiest couple, Catherine and John Vermillion, owned $9,250 in property. While John ran his mercantile firm, Catherine was a spinner. One seamstress, Susannah Keith, a thirty-eight-year-old with three children ranging in age from ten to sixteen years, actually owned $200 in real estate in her own name. Indeed, of all the women who filed death claims Susannah was the only one who owned property in her name, while her husband, James, a farm laborer, only owned thirty dollars in personal estate. Finally, all but two of these wives performed their occupations despite having children living at home. Taken as a whole, before the war very few of the women who would become widows were gainfully employed in jobs that could sustain them and their children after the loss of their husbands.

Because so many of the couples were recently married, only one-third of them owned real estate on the eve of the war.[15] Still, there were some very substantial landowners in the group. The wealthiest couple, Angus and Cornelia McDonald, owned $60,000 worth of land. Significantly, Angus, who would serve as a colonel, at age sixty was the oldest husband to die during the war and leave a widow. Cornelia, his second wife, was only thirty-nine years old the year the war began. Nearly all the couples possessed some personal property, but the median value of all of these estates only totaled $150. Thus, it seems likely that only a small portion of these couples owned even one slave.[16]

Like the vast majority of Virginian men who answered their state's call, nearly all of the husbands who would leave their wives widows entered the military by choice. Less than 2 percent were conscripted. Further, the overwhelming majority who enlisted did so early in the war, half of them joining the army in 1861 and nearly all the rest in 1862.[17]

Since nine-tenths of the husband-soldiers who died in the war served their entire time as privates, few of these men earned more than the standard pay of eleven dollars per month.[18] Still, the pay was substantial enough to prompt middle-class and yeoman widows to file for death claims.

These claims generally were filed early in the war as half the husband-soldiers would die in 1862, and another fourth in 1863. The cause of death—known for about seven-tenths of the men—was slightly more likely to result from wounds than disease.[19] While those who died from disease perished throughout the year, the battle-related deaths were heavily concentrated during three points in time: the Seven Days' Battle from June 25 to July 1, 1862; the three weeks in August of 1862 between the Battles of Cedar Mountain and Second Manassas; and the two-month span in 1863 between the Battles of Chancellorsville and Gettysburg. The five days of fighting at Second Manassas and Gettysburg alone accounted for nearly one-fifth of all such battle-related fatalities, an extraordinary harvest of death that must have been especially shocking to the civilians at home.[20]

Given the fact that most Virginia troops served in the eastern theater, it is not surprising that most of these husband-soldiers died in battles in that area. Some Virginians also fell on such distant battlefields as Vicksburg (in Mississippi) and Chickamauga (in Georgia), and many also died in captivity in prison camps throughout the North.

Although it would provide only some consolation to their families, a modest share of the wounded and ill husband-soldiers died at home. Many stationed within Virginia's borders were sent home to be cared for by their families. For example, on May 15, 1862, John W. Jennings was admitted to Chimborazo Hospital in Richmond suffering from an unspecified fever, and the next day he was furloughed and sent home to Pittsylvania County, where his wife, Winnifred, could nurse him. Despite Winnifred's best efforts, John died within three months, leaving behind a widow and two infant daughters, Anne and Celester.

While the wartime experiences of these wives varied considerably, the story of one Civil War couple, Lorenzo and Barbara Hylton of Floyd County, is representative of what many Virginia couples experienced during the conflict. On July 23, 1857, Lorenzo Dow Hylton married Barbara Ellen Huff, when he was twenty-six years old, a year or two younger than his bride. About a year later, the couple's first child, a girl named Lutaro, was born. In 1860 Lorenzo, a machinist, and Barbara did not own any real estate, but possessed $484 in personal estate. Barbara's seventy-one-year-old mother, Margaret Huff, lived in their home, and next door resided Lorenzo's parents, Burwell and Mary, as well as Lorenzo's numerous brothers and sisters.

On March 24, 1862, Lorenzo enlisted in Company D of the 54th Virginia Infantry. Two months later he was elected a second lieutenant. Unlike most Virginia husband-soldiers, Lorenzo would travel a good deal out of his native state, as his unit served in Kentucky, Georgia, and Tennessee, so Lorenzo and Barbara probably wrote frequently to one another. In the first of their surviving letters, dated April 24, 1862, Barbara informed her husband that she had just given birth to their third child, another daughter.[21] She encouraged Lorenzo to "send the name that you choose that it should be called." Evidently Lorenzo selected the name "Raziner," or, as the daughter was more commonly called, "Rose." Besides this significant news, Barbara discussed the difficulties that many families were having with crops. As spring planting was progressing, she told Lorenzo that his father and brother were helping to plant their family's corn. Barbara stressed her desire that if possible Lorenzo should return home to help with the harvest. Before closing her letter, she inquired, "I want to know if you have received the coat and socks that I sent to you." Barbara ended her letter with a brief, but tender, poem:

Dear Husband thou art kind and true
And every day I think of you
So my dear husband think of me
While many mile apart we be.

Lorenzo wrote his wife again in October 1862 from Bath County, Kentucky, where his unit had just participated in General Braxton Bragg's invasion of the state.[22] He began by telling Barbara of his relief that the health of his wife and second daughter had improved and he then informed Barbara that his unit was about to leave Kentucky and return to "old Virginia." After warning his wife that the Confederate troops would find it difficult to dislodge themselves from Kentucky, as their daily rations were quite low, turning to domestic concerns Lorenzo stressed that he wanted his wife or his father to sell the family's cattle. Recognizing, as so many servicemen did, that his wife truly understood the condition of the local economy better than he did, Lorenzo instructed Barbara to try to get forty dollars for the cattle but, if she could not, to fatten and sell the hogs. In words which could not have been very comforting to Barbara, Lorenzo concluded that he would "try and come home . . . if I live. So you must do the best you can[.] Say nothing more at present."

By late 1862 Lorenzo had returned to Virginia and was encamped just south of Petersburg. Three days before the end of the year Lorenzo told Barbara that he hoped that the rumors were true that his unit would establish its winter quarters at its present location.[23] He went on to reveal to her, "So much I hop[e] and trust that this hor[r]ible war will be brought to an end before long. I am getting tired of it. I would like to get home once more to stay there." Perhaps as a Christmas present, Lorenzo next revealed that he had had his "likeness taken" in a photograph that he planned to send to her. A month later, on February 1,

1863, Lorenzo wrote his father that after a fellow soldier left the photo with his uncle his father should pick it up and deliver it to Barbara.[24]

Around the time Barbara received the photo of her husband she drafted the following poem for him:[25]

When I received your likeness
I was overfilled with joy
I looked upon your smiling face
And laid it in the drawer

I often look upon it
And shed a many tear
And think of you my husband
The one I love so dear

Although this may not be the most eloquent verse of the war, it does convey her loneliness very well. Barbara poignantly added that after the children recognized their father in the photo they wondered if turning the picture frame over would "let poor pap come out."

In his only surviving letter to Barbara from 1863, Lorenzo emphasized his "wish to God that this war would come to an end. So as we al[l] get to come home and enjoy the great Blessing that [we] once did enjoy."[26] He warned his wife, however, that the coming spring would witness severe fighting and that he doubted whether the "talk of compromise" would lead to anything. Again dependent on his wife, he noted that he had received the sewing thread that she had sent him.

Lorenzo was correct in believing that 1863 would be a year of great fighting. What he did not anticipate, however, was that he again would be sent out of Virginia. His unit went to Chattanooga, Tennessee, where he was wounded at Missionary Ridge on November 25. In early 1864 Lorenzo wrote Barbara from the hospital in Marietta, Georgia, beginning by noting how it "gave grate satisfaction to hear from you." He went on to add, "I will say to you that I am still improving[.] I can turn myself without help and can set up long enough to wash and comb my hair." He would apply for a furlough if his health continued to improve. Like so many husband-soldiers, he closed with the words, "So remains your husband untill de[a]th."[27]

Less than a month later Lorenzo's cousin, who was encamped near Dalton, Georgia, informed Barbara of the sad news of her husband's death.[28] While Lorenzo had appeared to be doing well, his condition abruptly declined and he died three weeks after he wrote his last letter to Barbara. Ira Hylton, Lorenzo's brother, sent Barbara a lock of her husband's hair, a common ritual in the nineteenth century.[29] Ira also encouraged her to authorize someone to bring Lorenzo's effects, which included his watch, overcoat, and thirty dollars, and also noted that at his death Lorenzo was due several months of pay. Barbara would file a death claim seven months later, well after Lorenzo was buried in a Confederate cemetery in Marietta.

"Knowing the uncertainty of life & the certainty of death," Private Edward Bates of the 57th Virginia Infantry wrote a will in the summer of 1861.[30] Composing this document, Edward believed, was "for the good of my beloved wife Sally," who he had recently married. While other soldiers wrote wills, what made Edward's decision to write one somewhat surprising was that the previous year he had only owned twenty-five dollars in personal property in Pittsylvania County. Nevertheless, Edward directed that his debts be paid and that his "will and desire" was that Sally receive his "perishable property" and be appointed the will's executrix.

In fact, Edward Bates's action was exceptional, since few of the Virginia husband-soldiers who died during the Civil War had enough property to be concerned about its disbursement. Instead, they simply let their estates go into probate. Common law dictated that in such cases their wives would receive their dower rights or one-third of the estate. The remaining two-thirds of the property would be divided equally among their children when they reached adulthood.[31]

An analysis of thirty-four wills written by Virginia husband-soldiers who would die in the conflict indicates that the act of writing these documents was prompted by the growing realization that death might be near. Half of these wills were written during 1862, the year by which the majority of soldier-husbands had entered the army. Many had already witnessed how quickly other men's lives could be terminated. The war surely prompted many soldiers to write these documents earlier in their lives than they would have done in the absence of the conflict. For example, on April 24, 1862, Captain Benjamin Walton, a resident of Bath County, stressed that he was writing his will after "being called out in defense of my country by the Governor of the State and being apprised of the dangers of a soldier's life." Walton's decision was a good one. Six weeks later he died of wounds in a Staunton hospital, leaving behind his widow Margaret and their seven children.

It seems to be the case that affluent husband-soldiers were more likely to write wills than poorer men.[32] Slightly more than three-fourths of these men owned some real estate, with a median value of $1,000. In fact, with their personal property included, one-fourth of these testators owned more than $5,000 in total property. Furthermore, most of these testators had been married for a number of years. Indeed, their median year of marriage was 1852 and three-tenths of them had been married as early as 1846. Fewer than one-fifth of them were under age thirty, and their median age was thirty-four.[33]

It is not surprising that a majority selected wives as their executors, a crucial decision for any testator.[34] As William S. Parran of Orange County emphasized, "Having full confidence in the judgment of my beloved wife, I appoint her executrix of my estate and she shall not be required to give security." In fact, exactly half of the thirty-four testators specified in their wills that their wives were to be the sole heir, although most of them also generally noted that when their wives died they expected that the estate would be divided among the surviving children on an equal basis. None of these men even suggested what might be the consequences if their wives remarried. About another two-fifths of those husbands raised the possibility that their wives might remarry, and they indicated that if the wives did so they then would be entitled to keep only the one-third dower of the estate.[35] The remaining two-thirds of the property thereafter would be divided equally among the children.

The fact that half of the men left all of their estate to their wives without mentioning remarriage does not necessarily mean that the soldier-husbands intended to allow their wives to keep all the estate if they did find another husband. Indeed, no husband went so far as to dictate that if his wife remarried that she would still be allowed to keep all of the estate. Clearly any man who wrote a will was as concerned about the welfare of his children as of his wife. If a wife was allowed to remarry and take her property into her new marriage, the property might not be used for the full benefit of his children. If, for example, in her subsequent marriage a wife had additional children, she might then allow her first husband's property to be conveyed to them and thus diminish the legacy to the children from her first marriage. Further, the evidence suggests that the husbands who left their wives their dower rights upon remarriage, and nothing more, owned twice as much property as other men.[36]

Though most Civil War widows did not remarry, it is difficult to determine exactly why. Perhaps some feared that they would lose much of their estate. We can surmise something, however, about the women who did remarry. Margaret Walton, who received dower from her husband's estate, not only remarried when her husband died in June of 1862, but she did so quickly, by the end of 1863. Perhaps the fact that even one-third of the couple's $9,000 of real estate represented a fairly substantial amount of money shaped her decision to remarry. Significantly, by 1870 Margaret still possessed $3,000 in real estate, or exactly one-third of the couple's prewar amount of land. Margaret's decision to marry Fleming Keyser, a man thirty-one years her senior, ironically meant that she soon would find herself a widow again. Likewise, when Lieutenant Rufus Turner wrote his will in March 1862 he specified that his wife Rachel would receive one-half of his Patrick County estate, which included $4,000 in real estate in 1860. He also required that the remainder of the property be sold to pay the family's debts and educate their children. Rufus died six months later, leaving Rachel with two infant daughters. When Rachel chose to remarry in 1867, she kept control of her inheritance. As a result, by 1870 she actually owned $100 more in land than did her new husband, James Hines.

Elizabeth Mitchell of Pittsylvania County represents one woman who remarried despite losing property, for her husband Moses specified in his will that if she did so she would be entitled to only one-third of the estate. Perhaps the fact that the couple owned only $725 in real estate in 1860 convinced Elizabeth that she did not have much to lose financially. In any case, she married Caleb Hundley in 1867. Elizabeth's choice did not seem to hurt her financially, because three years after their marriage the couple owned $1,000 in land. Mary Chambers of Franklin County was another widow who was undeterred by a similar clause in her husband's will. Again, the couple owned so little estate before the war — only $575 — that it may not have mattered to her. Less than one year after the end of the war, Mary agreed to marry James Durham, a man nine years her junior.

The wills of these men who died in the war suggest both that husbands were more conscious of their mortality and that they felt that by leaving a will they could help their wives. Like the vast majority of husband-soldiers they were farmers, but they clearly were more likely to own a significant amount of property than their peers who did not leave wills. Finally, given the economic ravages of the war, even fewer of these men could insure that their families would emerge from the conflict on a strong financial footing.

The plight of Civil War widows was intertwined with those women whose husbands would not die in military service, as their contermporaries realized. By 1863 the Virginia legislature, recognizing the increasing hardships of both widows and the wives of soldiers, authorized the county courts to create a system for providing food for these women and their children. While the counties had been trying to help these women for some time, the legislature now gave the local governments much greater authority to borrow money, impress foodstuffs, and establish a better process for gathering the names of needy families.[37]

How effectively the county governments responded to the needs of widows and their children is best demonstrated in Henry County, in southwestern Virginia, where the most extensive set of detailed public records have survived.[38] At its June term in 1863 the county court defined that the family of indigent soldiers "shall include only his wife or widow and his children." Further, only those children between the ages of one and ten years would be eligible, along with their mothers, to receive food. Each month wives and widows would be entitled to receive up to one bushel of grain or its equivalent in flour, and eight pounds of bacon. Children would be allotted up to half a bushel of grain and three pounds of bacon. The court specified that no widows or children were to receive supplies for more than one year after the husband's death and that childless wives and widows "who are young & healthy" were to receive only a half-portion of supplies. Over the last seven months of 1863, the county court dispersed supplies to 198 women, one third of whom were widows of soldiers. Probably a similar share of the 529 children who received aid were also the sons and daughters of deceased soldiers. The seven months of aid cost the county the staggering sum of nearly $29,000 (or about $5.50 per recipient per month), an amount more than three times greater than the county's antebellum annual budget.[39]

It appears that nearly every Henry County widow whose husband had died by 1863 received aid from the local government at some point during that year. All but two of the fifteen widows who filed death claims for their deceased husbands' pay arrears were given aid by the court sometime during 1863 and 1864. In fact, many of these women were already receiving some form of assistance even before the new guidelines were established in June of 1863. For example, Elizabeth Hopper, the mother of at least six young children, received three bushels of corn and ten pounds of bacon in early May 1863, five weeks before her husband William died of typhoid fever in a Lynchburg hospital. More typically, however, women began to receive aid after their husbands died. Elizabeth Cooper, the mother of two children under age five, received eight pounds of beef in November of 1863, four months after her husband Hailey died.

The poorest women were the most likely to request assistance. Only about one-fourth of widows who requested aid had owned land in 1860. By comparison, half of those who did not seek the county's assistance had owned land before the war.[40] Hence, despite the personal tragedy of losing her husband John while serving in Virginia's 24th Infantry, Elizabeth Reamey could rest assured that the couple's holdings — $16,000 in land and $10,000 in personal estate — would help her and her three children to avoid having to look to the local government for help. Likewise, for those women who had always lived on the edge of subsistence, the choice of requesting aid was virtually preordained. For example, Dolly Seay and spouse James had neither personal nor real estate in

1860. So it is not surprising that when James died of pneumonia in November 1862, Dolly asked the county court for help to feed herself and her three young sons, George, Charles, and William.

Given the rising prices and growing shortages that all Southerners were experiencing by 1863, even property-owning widows needed to ask the local government for help. Therefore, after her husband Josiah died from an acute infection in August of 1862, Louisa Doss, the owner of $600 in real estate two years before, turned to the county court in 1863 for herself and her four children. Even some relatively affluent women eventually needed the court's help. Nancy Philpott and her husband Edward owned $2,100 in real estate and $2,600 in personal estate when the war started, but in July of 1864, after Edward died, the widow immediately turned to the county court to feed herself and her six children. So many people were in need that there seemed to be no stigma attached to it.

Unfortunately for Nancy Philpott, by the time she turned to the county court in 1864 it was becoming increasingly harder for that body to assist the growing ranks of the needy. In the spring of that year, the court found it necessary to pay the wives, widows, and children of indigent soldiers five dollars apiece in Confederate money in lieu of meat. Providing them with depreciating paper money that few people with goods to sell were eager to accept was a poor substitute for dispensing actual food.

The difficulties encountered by local governments were particularly evident to P. P. Davis, the commissioner responsible for providing aid in the Oak Level District of Henry County, where Nancy Philpott lived. By the summer of 1864, Davis took care to eliminate assisting children over the age of nine, noting that he had just erased such a girl from the rolls, but he emphasized how families in his district were writing letters to him emphasizing that "they ought to have more if it could be done." In July, Davis, finding it impossible to aid the "increasing number" of families in his district with wheat, was unable to furnish two families with anything at all.

By the fall of 1864 conditions in Henry County had only worsened. Davis now reported that he could not "furnish anything" and feared that in his district grain could not be bought "at any price." Sympathetic to the plight of his neighbors, he stressed how many of them were "suffering for bread, as well as for meat." Those who looked towards him, he regretted, were "turned empty away." He finished his report by remarking that "there ought to be some arrangements made by which they could have bread at least." But local conditions only worsened with the passing months as more women and children were added to the rolls of the needy. Records of several county districts suggest how many more people were suffering. The number of civilians receiving assistance increased by one-third in one district in the 1864 calendar year and more than doubled in another district.[41] Ironically, only the Union army would rescue these hungry widows, wives, and their children. On May 15, 1865, a month after the war had ended, the Union army dispersed supplies to the court of Henry County that specifically were used to aid these women.[42]

How did these women and their children survive through the conflict as well as during the immediate postwar years? Whom did they turn to for help? Husband-soldiers who left wills mentioning the possibility of their wives remarrying after their death probably had little reason to be concerned. The terrible loss of so many unmarried men as well as husbands made it likely that even if they wished to remarry few widows would be able to find another spouse. It is virtually impossible to determine what share of Virginia's Civil War widows remarried, as the records simply do not lend themselves to calculating such an exact measurement. The records do suggest, however, the great difficulty that widows faced if they considered finding another husband.

Virginia's state marriage index allows us to determine that 156 widows who filed death claims later remarried. In addition, another 163 widows who filed death claims received pensions from Virginia after 1888, clear evidence exists that these women did not remarry.[43] Unfortunately, since no correspondence nor other materials survive to explain why some widows remarried and others did not, we must investigate some socioeconomic and demographic factors that may have shaped their decisions.

The first thing to note about those widows who remarried is that most of them wed either during the war or in its immediate aftermath (see Table 1). The most common year of remarriage was 1866, and slightly more than half of these women became brides again in either 1865, 1866, or 1867. Only about one-fifth of these women married after 1870. The widow's age seems to have had the greatest influence on whether she remarried. Those who remarried had a median age in 1860 of twenty-four years compared to twenty-nine years for those women who did not remarry.[44] Furthermore, there was a near-linear relationship between a woman's age and her likelihood of marrying. The majority of all women who had been under age twenty-five in 1860 remarried and slightly more than three-fourths of those who had been under twenty years of age found a second husband (see Table 2). Fewer than half of the women who were in their early thirties by the end of the war remarried. Among women who had reached their late thirties or early forties the likelihood of remarriage stood consistently at about only one in four. No woman who had reached her fifties remarried.

TABLE 1.
Year of Remarriage of Virginia Civil War Widows

Year Remarried	Number of Remarriages	Percentage of Remarriages
1863	8	5%
1864	5	3
1865	26	17
1866	39	25
1867	24	15
1868	14	9
1869	11	7
1870–74	21	13
1875–79	4	3
1880–85	4	3
Total	156	100%
Median Year 1866/67		

Source: Confederate Death Claim Records, vols. 13–20, 22, 34, Office of the Second Auditor, Record Group 109, National Archives, Washington, D.C.; Confederate Pension Rolls, 1888–1899, microfilm copy, Library of Virginia; Marriage Records, Virginia Vital Records, microfilm copy, Library of Virginia.

It may be that those women who were least likely to remarry may not have wanted to do so because many now had children old enough to help support them and their siblings. The median year of prewar marriage for those who did not remarry was 1854, versus 1857 for those who did remarry. Looked at another way, those women who did not

TABLE 2.
Percentage of Virginia Civil War Widows Who Remarried, Based on Age and Wealth

| Age in 1860 | Amount of Total Estate Value in 1860 | | | |
	$ 0–99	$100–999	$1,000 or More	Total
Under 20 Years	64%	100%	100%	78%
20–24	60	68	75	65
25–29	35	53	45	44
30–34	18	32	17	25
35–39	14	30	27	25
40–44	0	50	0	23
45 or More	0	0	0	0
Total	41%	50%	40%	44%

Source: Same as Table 1.

remarry were five times more likely to have been married before 1850. They were twice as likely to have at least one teenaged child and three times more likely to have a son or daughter at least the age of fifteen years than those women who remarried once their husband-soldiers died.[45]

We can see this dilemma in the case of Malinda Dodd. In 1860 forty-one-year-old Malinda and her husband, forty-two-year-old Samuel, resided on their Pittsylvania County farm. The couple owned $1,500 in real estate and $1,350 in personal estate. Malinda and Samuel had married in 1840 and twenty years later had eight children ranging in age from two months to seventeen years. Nine months after he enlisted in Virginia's 38th Infantry, Samuel died of pneumonia at Richmond's Chimborazo Hospital. Five years after the war Malinda and her children still resided on their farm, though its value had been greatly reduced to just $500. The census listed the widow as "keeping house," but her oldest remaining son, twenty-four-year-old James, appeared as a farmer, while twenty-two-year-old son Oliver, nineteen-year-old Samuel, and fifteen-year-old Benjamin worked as farm laborers. Significantly, by 1880 Malinda, now in her early sixties, still headed her household, but two of her sons remained with her to help manage the farm. Because her sons were old and responsible enough to replace the labor lost by the death of their father, Malinda simply had no pressing economic need to look for another husband.

It is also the case that mature daughters could be valuable financial assets for their widowed mothers. For example, in 1860 Catherine Rosenbalm, age thirty-six, resided in Washington County with her husband Isaac, age forty. After fifteen years of marriage the couple had five children. After Isaac died from wounds in 1862 received at Second Manassas, Catherine did not remarry. Instead, she relied on the labor of her son Aaron, age eighteen in 1870 and, equally important, on twenty-one-year-old daughter Ellen and fifteen-year-old daughter Rachel, both of whom brought in precious income by working as a weaver and spinner, respectively.

A widow's economic status, though secondary to her age, also played a role in her decision whether to remarry (see Table 2). Every widow who had been younger than age twenty and owned at least $100 of property in 1860 remarried, while only about three-fifths of those widows of a comparable age who owned smaller amounts or no property at all did so. Even women who wanted or needed to remarry would have found it difficult to do so because of the enormous loss of men. Hence, many of those women who remarried had to find a husband much younger or older than themselves, or, to phrase it another way, much younger or older than their previous husbands. The median differences between these women and their first and second husbands remained fairly constant at three years, but where less than than one-fifth of women had been married to a first husband either ten or more years their senior or five or more years their junior, in their second marriage nearly half of women selected such men.[46]

Mary Ingram exemplifies a widow who chose a second husband significantly older than her first. In 1859, when Mary and Thomas Ingram married, she was eighteen and he was twenty-four years old. Thomas was a mariner in Lancaster County, which is bordered by both the Rappahannock River and the Chesapeake Bay. After the wedding the couple lived in the household of an oysterman, J. T. Robertson. Ann, their only child, was born during the first year of the war. In 1863 Thomas, a member of the 55th Virginia Infantry, died from wounds sustained at Fredericksburg. Mary wed again in 1865. While her new husband, William B. Spillman, was also a Lancaster County resident, this fifty-five-year-old fisherman was twice Mary's age.

The widow Mary Jane Terry also remarried a man some years her senior. In 1860, her husband, William, a Patrick County farm laborer, owned no land but possessed $200 in personal property; he was twenty-five years old, Mary Jane was twenty-three. By the first year of the war they had a young son and daughter. The next year William died from disease while serving in the 12th Virginia Infantry, but the following year Mary Jane found a new husband, Jesse Pratt, of neighboring Floyd County. Jesse Pratt was a much more affluent husband than William Terry, the owner of $1,000 in real estate and $600 in personal estate in 1870, but was fifty years old, or twice the age of Mary Jane. Himself a widower, Jesse was the father of two sons.

As previously noted, a considerable number of widows also married significantly younger men. When Julia Ann Long married Alexander Wyant on the day after Christmas in 1854, the groom was twenty-three years old and the bride was twenty-one. Over the next six years the couple had three children. On the eve of the war Julia and Alexander owned a farm in Rockingham County with real estate worth $1,000 and personal property of $300. When Alexander, a corporal in the 10th Virginia Infantry, was killed in 1863 at the Battle of Chancellorsville, he left behind not only a widow and three fatherless children but also a fourth child, his namesake, born after his father's death. On January 29, 1867, Julia married Joseph M. Baugher, another Rockingham County farmer, who was eight years her junior. By 1870 the couple owned $1,000 in real estate, exactly the same amount Julia and Alexander had owned a decade before, perhaps from Julia's dowery.

Irene Webb also selected a second husband her junior. She married her first husband, Enoch, sometime during the mid-1850s. By 1860 the couple, both of whom were twenty-four years old, owned a Carroll County farm worth a bit more than $300 as well as nearly $200 in personal estate. By 1862 they were the parents of five young children. Enoch died while serving in the 45th Virginia Infantry. On November 1, 1866, thirty-one-year-old Irene married twenty-two-year-old David C. Rakes, another Carroll County farmer. It was his first marriage. David, in fact, was only ten years older than Irene's eldest son, Lafayette. Within three years the couple was living on a farm valued at $600, twice the value of the farm Irene and Enoch had owned in 1860.

Like Irene Webb Rakes, those widows who chose to remarry financially benefited by their decision. Whereas 46 percent of these women and their first husbands had owned land before the war, 57 percent of them owned land with their second husbands by 1870, a truly remarkable increase given the severe economic difficulties Virginians faced during the war and its aftermath.[47] It is impossible to determine, however, if this increase resulted from the combining of the widows' estates with those of their new husbands or from the fact that the second husbands were considerably older than their first husbands and therefore had substantially more time to acquire real estate. What is clear, however, is that while those widows who did not remarry and later filed for pensions did not fare nearly as well as these women, they too experienced some improvement in their financial status. Where one-fourth of them owned land in 1860, one-third did so by 1870.[48] Again, given the economic difficulties of the era, gains of any amount seem impressive.

Many of the widows who seem to have experienced a decline in economic status were in reality protected by the safety net of relatives. For example, in 1860, three years after their marriage, Mary and Albert Saunders owned $400 of real estate and $300 in personal estate in Goochland County. These parents of two children would have another baby within a year. Albert, a member of the 10th Virginia Infantry, died on August 4, 1863, from wounds received at Gettysburg. Seven years later Mary appears to have become an impoverished widow. Actually, she and her children now lived with her seventy-year-old father and fifty-four-year-old mother, Marshall and Ann Hicks, the owners of $2,131 in property.

This role of kinship ties as well as the increased likelihood of owning land in 1870 meant that few of these women needed to take gainful employment. Indeed, in 1860, when all of them were married, only 2.4 percent of these women had paid occupations outside of the home. In 1870, even when three-fourths of them no longer had a husband, only 1.8 percent were gainfully employed.[49] Just as before the war, those women who worked found employment in traditionally female occupations; they made dresses, weaved, and spun cloth.

Raising three daughters without a husband could not have been an easy task for Barbara Hylton who, like the vast majority of Civil War widows, appears never to have been gainfully employed outside the home. Barbara also was responsible for providing for her elderly mother, Margaret, who continued to reside in the family's house years after the war's conclusion. Barbara and her husband, Lorenzo, had owned little property before the war, and five years after the conflict her personal estate had fallen to only one-fifth its antebellum value. The one thing that Barbara had plenty of was other Hylton neighbors, including Lorenzo's aging father, who owned a moderate amount of land and who surely would have aided his daughter-in-law and grandchildren through the war and postwar years. In addition, to help remember her husband and their father, Barbara and her three daughters also had Lorenzo's Civil War photograph as well as the lock of his hair. Despite her close ties to her relatives, Barbara decided to remarry. In 1875 she wed James Dillion, a farmer from neighboring Patrick County who, at age sixty-seven, was twenty years Barbara's senior. This marriage would not last long, as James lived only seven more years. After his death Barbara would remain on the couple's farm nearly thirty more years until her death in 1911.

These Southern women, like the millions of other civilians throughout both the North and South, were not prepared to lose their loved ones in the war. Given the fact that most of them had recently married and just started their families, few had the financial resources to provide for themselves once their husbands died. Even the few who owned property faced financial difficulties when their husbands either wrote no will or crafted one that limited their wives to their dower rights whether they remained widows or remarried. Further, given the tremendous shortage of men after the conflict, the opportunity to remarry was quite restricted except for the youngest and wealthiest Southern women. Unlike the colorful, fictitious widow Scarlett O'Hara, these women were not still dreaming of the never-attainable Ashley Wilkes. Further, if any of them had been fortunate enough to capture a Rhett Butler, there is every reason to believe they would have done their very best to keep him. Instead, even those widows like Barbara Hylton who were able to remarry often were restricted to much older or younger husbands. Still, like Scarlett O'Hara, these were tough and resilient women, but they also were realists. Despite their difficult circumstances, they did not face the war and postwar years completely on their own. During the war their local governments tried, though with limited success, to provide for them. Further, during the postwar years their now-adult children as well as nearby kin also helped them survive the emotional and economic catastrophe of losing their spouses in the nation's bloodiest war.

Notes

1. On Union widows, see Amy E. Holmes, "'Such Is the Price We Pay': American Widows and the Civil War Pension System," in *Toward a Social History of the Civil War* ed. Maris A. Vinovskis (Cambridge, 1990), 171–95; Megan J. McClintock, "Civil War Pensions and the Reconstruction of Union Families," *Journal of American History* 66 (1996): 456–80.

2. Robert C. Kenzer, *Kinship and Neighborhood in a Southern Community: Orange County, North Carolina, 1849–1881* (Knoxville, 1987), 97–99; Drew Gilpin Faust, *Mothers of Invention: Women of the Slaveholding South in the American Civil War* (Chapel Hill, 1996), 149–50. Though she focuses on a single community, Jennifer Lynn Gross provides the most thorough study of Confederate widows in "'You All Must Do the Best You Can': The Civil War Widows of Brunswick County, Virginia, 1860–1920" (master's thesis, University of Richmond, 1995). While he does not frequently refer specifically to the situation of widows, in *Civil Wars: Women and the Crisis of Southern Nationalism* (Urbana, 1989) George Rable describes the forces which shaped the lives of Southern women throughout the war.

3. James I. Robertson, *Civil War Virginia: Battleground for a Nation* (Charlottesville, 1991), 15, 175, provides the number of Virginia men of military age and estimates for wartime fatalities.

4. Henry Putney Beers, *The Confederacy: A Guide to the Archives of the Government of the Confederate States of America*, rev. ed. (Washington, D.C., 1986) 111–12, enumerates the number of claims and settlements through the program's first year.

5. The distribution of funds that 833 Virginia widows received in death claims was as follows: less than $25 (7%), $25–$49 (20%), $50–$99 (39%), $100–$199 (27%), $200–$299 (4%), $300–$399 (1%), $400–$900 (2%). See Confederate Death Claim Records, vols. 13–20, 22, 34, Office of the Second Auditor, Record Group 109, National Archives.

6. Mark E. Rodgers, *Tracing the Civil War Veterans Pension System in the State of Virginia: Entitlement or Privilege* (Lewiston, N.Y., 1999); W. Jackson Dickens Jr., "An Arm and a Leg for the Confederacy: Virginia's Disabled Veteran Legislation, 1865 to 1888" (master's thesis, University of Richmond, 1997); Jeffrey R. Morrison, "'Increasing the Pensions of These Worthy Heroes': Virginia's Confederate Pensions, 1888 to 1927" (master's thesis, University of Richmond, 1996).

7. In "Widows and Civil War Pension System," 173, Holmes notes that under the 1890 federal pension system widows who married Union soldiers before June 27, 1890, were entitled to $8 per month.

8. Each volume of the Virginia Regimental Histories Series contains a roster of all of the soldiers who served in every unit. In the one volume of this series that uses both the death claim and pensions records (the 56th Virginia Infantry) in compiling its roster, 21.8% of the soldiers who died were found to have left widows. Therefore, if the rate for this unit was typical, given Robertson's estimate of 20,000 to 30,000 Virginia fatalities, there would have been about 4,360 to 6,540 Virginia widows. As noted, 1,297 Virginia women filed death claims and 1,899 Virginia women filed for pensions. A total of 296 filed for both. Hence, my research has identified 2,900 total widows.

9. The following statistical profile is based on a smaller sample of the 541 widows who could be found in the 1860 federal manuscript census residing in those counties of Virginia that did not form the new state of West Virginia and who already were married to the husbands who would die in the war. The year of marriage was determined by tracing the 541 widows sample in Virginia's State Vital Records, microfilm copy, Library of Virginia, Richmond (hereafter LV). In addition, all those women who filed a death claim and later for a pension were also included since the pension records note the year of marriage of nearly every applicant. Further, a variety of transcribed and printed county records reveal the year of those marriages that preceded 1853, the first year when Virginia began to require that all counties record marriages for the state. The year of first marriage could be determined for 480 widows: the majority, 325 (68%), wed during the 1850s and the median year of marriage was 1856.

10. Only those children were included who clearly belonged to both the husband and wife, had the same surname as the father, were not less than fifteen years younger than the mother, and who would not have been born before the year of marriage. The number of couples with no children was 78 (14%), 96 (18%) with one child, 123 (23%) with two children, 91 (17%) with three children, 153 (28%) with four or more children.

11. Only 7% of these couples resided in someone else's home. A total of twenty-one of the thirty-nine (54%) can be determined as living in the household of either the husband or bride's parents — eleven in the husband's and ten in the bride's.

12. The 182 households contained 222 inhabitants besides the husband, wife, and their common children, sixteen of whom were either free black or mulatto domestic servants or farm laborers; sixteen were the parents of either the wife or husband; twenty-six were children under twenty-one years with the same surname as the husband or of the wife's maiden name (very likely children from a husband's previous marriage or younger siblings of the wife), forty-eight were children under twenty-one years with different surnames than either the father or the wife's maiden name but who likely were still related to either the husband or the wife. Therefore, at least 137 of the 206 (67%) whites likely were related to either the husband or wife.

13. Of the 515 husbands who were listed with an occupation, 307 (57%) could be classified as working in agriculture; 67 (13%) as various types of laborers; 113 (22%) in skills/crafts, or services; and 28 (5%) held white collar, professional, or mercantile positions.

14. On women's contribution to the household economy, see Bill Cecil-

Fronsman, *Common Whites: Class and Culture in Antebellum North Carolina* (Lexington, Ky., 1992), 134, 143–45, 212.

15. Since 66% of the couples owned no real estate in 1860, their median real estate value was zero. Only 15% owned more than $1,000 in real estate.

16. While 85% of the couples owned some total estate, only 21% owned more than $1,000 worth.

17. Only 8 of 412 (2%) husbands for whom service records are found in the various Virginia Regimental History Series volumes are noted as being conscripts. The 404 husbands who enlisted did so during the following years: 203 (50%) in 1861, 178 (44%) in 1862, 22 (5%) in 1863, and 1 (.2%) in 1864.

18. In addition to the 484 of the 541 (90%) husbands who served as privates, another 57 achieved higher rank: corporal (7), sergeant (18), lieutenant (10), captain (15), major (4), and colonel (3).

19. Of the 978 husband-soldiers, 311 died of disease or illness, 382 were killed in action or died of wounds, and 285 died from other or nonspecified causes.

20. The 75 husbands killed as a result of Second Manassas (36) and Gettysburg (39) compose 20% of the 382 total.

21. Barbara E. Hylton to Lorenzo D. Hylton, April 24, 1862, Huff-Hylton Families Papers (Ms98-001), Special Collections, Digital Library and Archives, University Libraries, Virginia Polytechnic Institute and State University.

22. Lorenzo D. Hylton to Barbara E. Hylton, October 18, 1862, Huff-Hylton Families Papers.

23. Lorenzo D. Hylton to Barbara E. Hylton, December 28, 1862, Huff-Hylton Families Papers.

24. Lorenzo D. Hylton to Burwell Hylton, February 1, 1863, Huff-Hylton Families Papers.

25. Undated poem, Huff-Hylton Families Papers.

26. Lorenzo D. Hylton to Barbara E. Hylton, March 12, 1863, Huff-Hylton Families Papers.

27. Lorenzo D. Hylton to Barbara E. Hylton, January 20, 1864, Huff-Hylton Families Papers.

28. Samuel Slusher to Barbara E. Hylton, February 15, 1864, Huff-Hylton Families Papers.

29. Ira S. Hylton to Barbara E. Hylton, February 18, 1864, Huff-Hylton Families Papers.

30. The following analysis of thirty-four wills is based on an examination of the will books of the ten counties (Bedford, Caroline, Charlotte, Franklin, Grayson, Halifax, Henry, Patrick, Pittsylvania, and Pulaski) that contained the largest number of women who filed death claims as well as of three other counties (Bath, Orange, and Princess Anne) that have printed will-indexes for the war years, all located in LV. Joan E. Cashin ("According to His Wish and Desire: Female Kin and Female Slaves in Planter Wills," in *Women of the American South: A Multicultural Reader* Christie Anne Farnham, ed. [New York, 1997], 90–119) provides the best analysis of antebellum wills of planters. Though considerably less affluent than the planters in Cashin's study, the husbands of these Virginia widows appear to have been much more fair-minded toward their wives.

31. For a thorough discussion of the scholarship on Southern inheritance in this era, see Gross, "'You All Must Do the Best You Can,'" 55–71.

32. The real estate value in 1860 could be determined for twenty-seven testators. A total of twenty-one (78%) of them owned some real estate. Of the twenty-eight men whose total estate can be determined, seven (25%) owned at least $5,000 of property.

33. The year of marriage can be determined for twenty-nine of these testators. A total of nine (31%) were married as early as 1846.

34. In twelve of the twenty-one (57%) cases in which the testator specified his executor, he selected his wife.

35. A total of fourteen of the thirty-four (41%) testators noted the possibility of their wives remarrying.

36. The testators who specified that their widows would receive only the dower had a median real estate value of $1,000–$1,200, compared to only $400 for those testators who left all of their property to their widows without any mention of potential remarriage. The median total estate value of each group was $1,450 versus $600.

37. William Frank Zornow, "Aid for the Indigent Families of Soldiers in Virginia, 1861–1865," *Virginia Magazine of History and Biography* 66 (1958): 454–58; William Blair, *Virginia's Private War: Feeding Body and Soul in the Confederacy, 1861–1865* (New York, 1998).

38. The following discussion of Henry County's aid to soldiers' families is based on Record of Indigent Soldiers' Families as well as Provisions for Soldiers' Families, Henry County, LV.

39. One-third of the 198 women who received supplies in Henry County during the last seven months of 1863 were soldiers' widows. The total annual expenditure of Henry's County Court on June 11, 1861 was only $7,870; Henry County Court Minutes, bk. 6, 1859–1864, microfilm copy, LV.

40. Six out of thirteen widows who did not request aid had owned land in 1860, compared to seven of twenty-seven who requested aid.

41. While at the outset of 1864 the Court House District provided twenty-one widows and wives with provisions, by the beginning of 1865 the number rose to thirty. The comparable rise in the Irisburg District was from twenty-five to fifty-three.

42. The aforementioned Dolly Seay, along with her children, was listed as one of the women who received aid from the Union army.

43. One hundred twenty-eight of the 156 widows who remarried consisted of women who filed a death claim, were found married in the 1860 manuscript census, and whose year of remarriage could be determined. Another 28 of the 156 were women who filed a death claim but could not be found in the 1860 census, but whose year of remarriage could be determined. The 163 widows who received pensions only include pensioners who were found in the 1860 manuscript census.

44. All subsequent discussion of remarriage is based only on those 130 widows who remarried and who could be found in the 1860 manuscript census.

45. Twenty-four percent of women who remarried had been married before 1850, compared to only 5% of those who did not remarry. Only 19.4% of the

women who remarried had at least one child as old as eight years old in 1860 and therefore at least thirteen years old by 1865. Among women who did not remarry the comparable measurement was 41%.

46. No first husbands were twenty or more years older then their wives, but 11% of second husbands were. Only 12% of first husbands were ten or more years older than their wives, but 28% of second husbands were. While only 6% of first husbands were five or more years younger than their wives, 19% of second husbands were. Hence, nearly half (47%) of these women married a man somewhat younger or older than their age.

47. It was possible to find sixty-three of the widows who had remarried in the 1860 and 1870 manuscript censuses.

48. It was possible to find eighty-one of the widows who would file for pensions in the 1870 manuscript census. The widows who did not remarry appear to have been far less financially deprived or desperate than the Richmond women described in Elna Green, "Infanticide and Infant Abandonment in the New South: Richmond, Virginia, 1865–1915," *Journal of Family History* 24 (1999): 187–211.

49. The 226 Civil War widows who could be found in the 1870 manuscript were composed of sixty-three women who had remarried by 1870, fifteen who would marry later, eighty-one who would not remarry since they later filed for pensions, and sixty-seven whose postwar marital status cannot be determined with certainty.

Chapter 6

Race, Memory, and Masculinity:
Black Veterans Recall the Civil War

W. FITZHUGH BRUNDAGE

◆ To THE BLACK correspondent of the *New Orleans Tribune*, the close formations and military bearing of several hundred black veterans marching through the streets of New Orleans on October 29, 1865, was as "noble" a demonstration of the "manhood of the colored race" as he had ever witnessed. In February 1866, Col. Charles T. Trowbridge, a white officer in the 33rd U.S. Colored Infantry, prophesied an enduring legacy for his troops when they were mustered out on Morris Island, South Carolina. He praised his audience, "whose valor and heroism has won for your race a name which will live as long as the undying pages of history shall endure." And Colonel Thomas Morgan, another white officer of black troops, recalled the performance of black troops in the Battle of Nashville and their exceptional "record of coolness, bravery [and] manliness." "A new chapter in the history of liberty," he predicted, "had been written. It had been shown that marching under the flag of freedom, animated by a love of liberty, even the slave becomes a man and a hero."[1]

These three appraisals of black veterans attest to the sense of accomplishment and anticipation that surrounded black soldiers at the conclusion of the Civil War. Blacks, of course, had fought in previous American conflicts (excluding the Mexican War) and in each instance had harbored hopes that their service would secure their equality and rights as citizens. These aspirations, however, had remained unfulfilled. But the accolades in New Orleans, South Carolina, and elsewhere hinted that black Civil War veterans would enjoy unprecedented respect and long-sought rights in the restored Union. Like the image of the noble black amputee presented to the nation by the goddess Columbia in Thomas Nast's cartoon "Franchise, and Not This Man?" black veterans stood before the nation with their claims for honor and justice. The demeanor of black veterans themselves revealed that many would settle for nothing less. Brimming with confidence and determination, few seemed inclined to submit quietly to oppression at the hands of former slaveholders and other whites. As a Freedmen's Bureau official in Mississippi observed, "No negro who has ever been a soldier can be again imposed upon; they have learnt what it is to be free and they will infuse their feelings into others."[2]

If black veterans were determined to fulfill their long-repressed aspirations for freedom and equality, many Southern whites were equally intent on frustrating their hopes. Black veterans were an intolerable affront and bitter reminder of defeat for many whites. Shortly after the war, a white doctor in Brentsville, Virginia, vented commonplace sentiments when he raged, "[W]e will not allow niggers to come among us and brag about having been in the yankee army. It is as much as we can do to tolerate it in white men." He and similarly aroused whites cultivated, according to the local Freedmen's Bureau agent, "an insane malice" against black veterans. Such animus sometimes erupted in vicious violence, as when a party of Confederate veterans in Georgia raped a black soldier's wife, after which they ranted that they ought to have shot her because her husband had been in "the God damned Yankee army" and vowed "to kill every black son-of-a-bitch that they could ever find that fought against them."[3]

From the earliest days of Reconstruction, then, black veterans emerged as both participants and symbols in the struggle to determine the meaning and legacy of the Civil War. During the late nineteenth and early twentieth centuries, Southerners, white and black, evinced an acute concern about the past. The conditions in the New South — wrenching economic transformation, political turmoil, and chronic racial tensions — seemed to demand new means to create social cohesion, express identity, and structure social relations. The past offered a framework of sorts and an inspiration for contending groups of Southerners as they sought to secure new sources of cultural authority. This contest to define the historical memory of the Civil War and of black veterans in particular was bound up in a far larger struggle over the cultural authority — the power — to define the future of the region. Southerners, like groups in other societies and ages, sought to sort the past in particular ways in order to legitimize their current power or aspirations. Representations of history in the South were instruments of, and even constituted, power. The struggle to define particular memories about the Civil War as authoritative and others as illegitimate fictions was a contest over who exercised the power to make some historical narratives possible and to silence others. That the struggle to forge historical memory in the postbellum South was a contest over discourse did not diminish its gravity.[4]

In the competition over the meaning of the past in the postbellum South, the crafters of historical memory — black and white — did not haphazardly inscribe meaning onto some preordained cultural tradition or representation of the past. Instead they devised ceremonies and formalized expressions, ranging from public monuments to civic rituals, specific to their own times, needs, and possibilities. White Southerners, who were anxious to secure their unchallenged power, labored to establish new bonds of loyalty among themselves and with those they sought to rule. Some white Southerners were intent on subduing blacks, but others envisioned restoring the bonds of loyalty that they believed had once existed between slaves and their masters. White Union veterans in the South, whether native to or immigrants in the region, were eager to enjoy all of the privileges accorded to whites there, and consequently they avoided public gestures, such as flaunting their status as victors, that were likely to alienate white Southerners. Meanwhile, African Americans, including black veterans, struggled to extend the boundaries of their freedom in the face of white hostility, in part by building up community institutions and recounting their own version of history.

Black veterans in the half-century after the Civil War were vigilant defenders of the memory of their military service and valor. Although hampered by limited resources and white opposition, blacks adopted parades, commemorative celebrations, and other spectacles of memory to disseminate and perpetuate a recalled past in which black veterans occupied a conspicuous place. They understood the importance of interrupting their individual, day-to-day routines in order to enter into public space and perform coordinated roles in pageants of representation. By insinuating celebrations of black veterans and history into the region's routine of civic life, Southern blacks strove to break down their historical exclusion from the "ceremonial citizenship" that was central to community pride and self-definition. By providing blacks in general and veterans in particular with an opportunity to recall and honor their military service, commemorative celebrations represented unmistakable cultural resistance to both the cult of the Lost Cause and the ascendant national culture of sectional reconciliation.[5]

The intensity of the contest over the historical memory of black veterans in part reflected the simple fact that the states of the former Confederacy were home not only to former secessionists but also to nearly one hundred thousand black men who fought for the Union. More than half of all black Union troops had been recruited in the slave South. In the decades after the war, as death and illness took their toll, the proportion of black Civil War veterans who lived in the South actually increased. By 1890, almost three-quarters (or 39,000) of the approximately 54,000 surviving black veterans lived below the Mason-Dixon line.[6] Wherever black veterans resided in the South, some rose to positions of prominence. For many, their veterans' pensions provided an invaluable source of capital that enabled them to establish themselves as successful tradesmen in the region's burgeoning urban centers. Drawing upon the prestige attached to their military service and their comparative affluence, some took the lead in organizing the array of social, educational, and religious institutions that freedom demanded. In Louisiana, for instance, veterans of the Native Guards led the early political mobilization of the freedpeople and the campaign for civil rights there. And once Southern blacks secured the right to vote, veterans, including Robert Smalls of South Carolina, Pinckney B. S. Pinchback of Louisiana, and Josiah Walls of Florida, emerged as formidable political leaders. Throughout the South as a whole, at least eighty-seven black veterans served in state legislatures during Reconstruction.[7]

But even as black veterans joined with other blacks to seize the promise of freedom in the Reconstruction South, the early forecasts of the acceptance of black veterans proved to be wildly optimistic. Indeed, precisely because black veterans often performed visible roles within black communities, they were particular targets of white Southerners who keenly resented them as both symbols of black pride and vivid reminders of the destruction of slavery. As the rape of the soldier's wife in Georgia demonstrated, white vigilantes and rioters alike apparently singled out black veterans and their families, and the toll of murdered black veterans mounted in proportion to the urgency of the campaigns to reestablish white rule in the South.[8]

However much black veterans premised their claims to civil rights on the basis of their military service, they, like their white counterparts, initially displayed little enthusiasm for the organized remembrance of their wartime experiences. An early attempt to organize black veterans, the Colored Soldiers and Sailor League, failed to survive its infancy. Founded in 1866, the league single-mindedly promoted voting rights for black veterans by extolling their demonstrated patriotism. The organization held a well-attended meeting in Philadelphia in 1867 and generated enough enthusiasm to establish chapters as far away as Wilmington, North Carolina, eight months after the meeting. But the league remained a skeletal organization whose mission was fulfilled by Reconstruction legislation and the Fifteenth Amendment. Moreover, black veterans, who enthusiastically embraced the message of equality, shunned black veterans' organizations in preference for racially inclusive groups.[9]

African American veterans looked to the Grand Army of the Republic (GAR), the preeminent veterans' group, as the proper body to defend their interests and to champion their memory. Founded in 1866, the GAR initially grew and prospered as a de facto political arm of the Republican Party during the heated political contests of Reconstruction. The commemoration of Union veterans, black and white, immediately became entwined with partisan politics. But when the Republican Party's commitment to reform in the South waned, the GAR's mission became ill-defined and the organization floundered. Only in the 1880s, when the organization advocated federal pensions for veterans, did it revive and subsequently expand on a large scale into the South. Although the Department of Virginia and North Carolina had been established in 1871, not until 1883 was the next Southern department — Arkansas — founded. Within the next six years, six more departments were established. By 1891 every former state of the Confederacy was represented within the organization, and the number of Southern posts totaled 313, with a combined membership of nearly 11,000.[10]

As the organization reestablished itself in the South, black veterans there for the first time joined in significant numbers and organized local posts. The expansion of the GAR consequently posed the question of whether black veterans would be gathered in integrated or segregated posts within departments and in turn whether Southern departments would be segregated within the national organization. The question generated particular controversy wherever blacks comprised a large percentage of the veterans. In 1890, for instance, blacks accounted for more than half of all surviving Union veterans in Memphis and Nashville. In Charleston and Norfolk, blacks constituted three-quarters of the potential GAR members. On the state level, black veterans outnumbered white Union veterans by as many as three to one in South Carolina, Mississippi, and Louisiana.[11]

In these states and wherever black veterans predominated, integrated GAR posts presumably would have been governed by black members. Many white veterans in the South, who complained of the certain ostracism they would endure if they joined biracial posts, endorsed the segregation of black veterans into separate posts. Some white veterans went further and refused to remain members of departments in which black posts outnumbered white posts. Not to do so, one white Southern GAR member complained, "would place us directly under them. That we will not stand."[12] Moreover, according to other white veterans, blacks were too incompetent to organize or to run posts. Prompted by these prejudices, white officers of the Louisiana and Mississippi Department during the early 1890s resolutely refused to recognize black posts, thereby precipitating a contentious debate within the national organization over the merits of segregation. Whether motivated by pragmatism or separatist leanings, some black posts, including six of the nine posts in Louisiana and Mississippi, accepted the proposal for segregated departments. But many more flatly rejected it.[13]

Eventually, by the mid-1890s, the national organization resolved to accept the tacit segregation of posts even while it explicitly refused to segregate departments. De facto segregation prevailed in virtually all public functions conducted by most GAR posts. Not only were meetings conducted separately, but white and black posts even organized separate Memorial Day exercises. So complete was the segregation that the *Richmond Dispatch* and the *Savannah Morning News*, two representative voices of white Southern opinion, noted approvingly that "the color-line was strictly drawn" during the Memorial Day ceremonies from Richmond to Mobile in 1895.[14]

The debate over segregation within the GAR during the early 1890s attracted national attention because it was symptomatic of an ongoing revision of the meaning attached to the Civil War and to the role of blacks in their own liberation. Simultaneous with the GAR's revival in the South and the controversy over segregation within the organization, more and more white GAR members embraced the ascendant culture of sectional reconciliation. Some white veterans used Memorial Day exercises in the South as a pretext to repudiate such Reconstruction measures as the Fifteenth Amendment and to endorse the enduring superiority of Anglo-Saxons, Northern and Southern. In other instances, white GAR posts conducted ceremonies that offended black sensibilities. For example, 1892 Memorial Day ceremonies at Andersonville National Cemetery were not only segregated with separate ceremonies for whites and blacks, but also the white GAR organizers invited Atlanta newspaper editor John Temple Graves to give the day's oration. Graves, a militant white supremacist, used the occasion to lambast blacks for their alleged intellectual and moral shortcomings and to urge their emigration to a black homeland or Africa. While a familiar topic for Graves's oratory, the proposal was a calculated insult to both the memory of black veterans who had fought to preserve the union and to the accomplishments of African Americans since Emancipation. Other white veterans joined with their former enemies in the most conspicuous rituals of national harmony, the recurrent and highly sentimentalized Blue and Gray reunions that brought together elderly "Johnny Rebs" and "Billy Yanks." Black veterans were pointedly excluded from these carefully staged celebrations of military valor.

The unmistakable implication of the culture of reconciliation and the omission of black veterans from it was that neither they nor their cause merited incorporation into the emerging consensus over the war and its origins. And at a time when many white veterans seemed impatient to forget that emancipation was one of the war's legacies and that blacks had a hand in the Union victory, Confederate veterans strained to celebrate blacks who "served" in the Confederacy. Reports of ceremonies, hosted by members of the United Confederate Veterans (UCV), to honor aged blacks who had purportedly worn Confederate grey and had adopted the southern cause as their own filled the columns of white newspapers and the *Confederate Veteran* at the century's close. Finally, popular lecturers fanned out across the South and the nation during the 1890s disseminating heroic accounts of the Confederate cause and nostalgic portraits of the Old South and the bonds between slaves and masters. By 1914, when Washington Gardner, the GAR commander, proclaimed that "there is military glory enough in the past to cause Americans for all time to point with pride to the fact that actors of both sides were their countrymen," the process of rapprochement was virtually complete.[15]

The evolving representations of the Civil War almost certainly left black veterans more cynical than confident about the commitment of the GAR or any whites to defend either the rights or the memory of black veterans. It was small comfort that the prediction of Comrade Richey, a black veteran of Kentucky, that blacks would "be ostracized and put out of the Grand Army of the Republic" was not fulfilled. That white Union veterans enthusiastically embraced their former foes and that a policy of segregation emerged within the GAR was a severe blow to the expectations of black veterans. As one black GAR member queried at the 1891 national encampment, "If you turn your back upon us, whom shall we look to, where shall we go?"[16]

The implications of these trends for the memory of black military valor were made manifest by the profusion of monuments that celebrated the common (white) soldier. The proliferation of soldier monuments during the late nineteenth century "militarized the landscape of civic patriotism" in the United States for the first time. Black soldiers, however, were virtually invisible in the commemoration of war and soldiering; they won no place on the pedestal of civic recognition. In the North the typical common soldier monument reasserted the primacy of the white male citizen by depicting the face of the nation as white. In the South the black soldier could not be represented without acknowledging the Union cause or its identification with the abolition of slavery. As early as 1888, George Washington Williams, the pioneering black historian, drew attention to this symbolic lacuna. "The deathless deeds of the white soldier's valor," he observed, "are not only embalmed in song and story, but are carved in marble and bronze. But nowhere in all this free land in there a monument to brave Negro soldiers." The *New York Age* agreed, noting that "white people build monuments to white people" while blacks remained idle. Prompted by such concerns, aroused blacks made several unsuccessful attempts to erect monuments to black soldiers in the late nineteenth century. But at century's end only three monuments depicted blacks in military service, and none of them were located in the South.[17]

By the 1890s, then, black veterans confronted unmistakable evidence of advancing amnesia regarding their participation in the most important event in the nation's history. The white leadership of the GAR was little inclined to promote the historical memory of black veterans at a time when it tolerated systematic, if informal discrimination. Some former officers, including Col. Trowbridge of the 33rd U. S. Colored Infantry, protested the abuse and discrimination that black veterans endured. But most of the Union war heroes remained either unconcerned or expressed no opinion on the matter. Black veterans themselves had only limited means with which to counter the prevailing narratives of white sacrifice and black invisibility. They lacked both the political power and the financial resources to erect monuments to black military prowess in the civic spaces of the South. And despite the seemingly insatiable appetite for the published recollections of white Civil War soldiers, black veterans who published their memoirs attracted only tiny audiences.[18]

Black veterans and communities, however, were not idle in the face of the advancing culture of reconciliation. Black veterans had practical reasons to insist that their service be acknowledged. Veteran Henry F. Downing explained in his application for a veteran's pension, "I served America faithfully and it seems hard that my wife and I in our old age should be allowed to want for the common necessities of life."[19] As Downing's application suggests, the pension application process often precipitated, in a very tangible fashion, acts of private and collective memory. Name changes, illiteracy, poverty, and the absence of personal records — the legacies of slavery — made the application process especially daunting for black veterans. In order to provide the copious documentation that pension administrators demanded, black veterans often had to collect testimonials from fellow soldiers and neighbors. Individual application files consequently often prompted collective acts of testimony that demonstrated that blacks felt entitled to recognition for their service to the Union cause.

Public celebrations, to an even greater degree, provided blacks with highly visible platforms for both the expression of black collective memory in general and the commemoration of black veterans in particular. The robust celebratory culture of black memory that flourished during the late-nineteenth century ensured that the black sense of the past was something more than a rhetorical discourse accessible principally to literate, elite African Americans. Instead, black memory existed as recurring events that could be joined in and appreciated collectively. Such celebrations had a unique capacity to celebrate the battle-scarred black veteran before an audience that incorporated the breadth of the black community, from the college-trained preacher to the illiterate day laborer and the impressionable school child.

Within a decade of the Civil War's end, Southern African Americans had adopted at least a half-dozen major holidays and countless lesser occasions during which they staged elaborate processions and ceremonies. New Year's Day, previously "the most bitter day of the year" because of its associations with slave auctions, now provided an occasion to commemorate, "with acclamations of the wildest joy and expressions of ecstacy," Lincoln's 1863 Emancipation Proclamation and the abolition of slavery. Southern blacks joined in the February commemoration of Washington's birthday, using it to highlight the cruel irony that their ancestors had fought beside Washington to found a nation that subsequently had rejected them. To the extent that Lincoln's birthday was celebrated in the South it was by African Americans, who understandably were eager to link closely their history with that of their martyred liberator. They added February 18, Frederick Douglass's purported birthday, to their calendar of holidays after the beloved abolitionist's death in 1895. The eager participation of blacks in Charleston, South Carolina, in 1865 and elsewhere helped to establish Memorial Day in late May as the fitting commemoration of military valor and sacrifice. They also gave new meaning to Independence Day. Only at the end of the nineteenth century when the patriotic fervor sparked by the Spanish-American War swept the region, did most white Southerners resume celebrating publicly the nation's founding. Blacks understood that if the Declaration of Independence was to be a resounding appeal to liberty and equality, the Fourth of July, its anniversary, was the appropriate occasion to present their unfulfilled claims to freedom. By the end of the nineteenth century, then, the calendar was virtually packed with public festivities during which Southern African Americans recalled their heroes and celebrated their history.[20]

The size and spectacle of black ceremonies testified to the significance that blacks attached to them. In Norfolk, Virginia, for instance, Emancipation Day on each January 1 routinely attracted tens of thousands of onlookers eager to watch parades that stretched for miles through the principal streets of the city. In Beaufort, South Carolina, Memorial Day evolved into a similar region-wide celebration that enticed visitors and black military units from the Carolinas and Georgia. In Vicksburg, Mississippi, Fourth of July festivities included "grand parades" of several hundred marchers and brass bands through the main thoroughfares of the city before gathering before the city's imposing court house and listening to long slates of speakers. Similarly, the combination of pageantry and festive atmosphere in Charleston, South Carolina, each Independence Day drew black excursionists from as far away as Columbia, Savannah, and Augusta.[21]

Black veterans assumed prominent roles in these celebrations as both organizers and participants. They asserted their capacity for civic leadership by arranging the commemorative celebrations that were the particular focus of racial pride. GAR posts in Elizabeth City, North Carolina, and Nashville, for instance, staged the local Emancipation Day ceremonies. Likewise, black GAR members often took the lead in organizing Lincoln and Douglass Day celebrations as well as the Fourth of July. And wherever GAR posts existed, they typically oversaw Memorial Day festivities, ranging from parades to the decoration of veterans' graves.[22]

Whether black veterans organized the ceremonies or not, they often enjoyed the privilege and prestige of occupying the front ranks of the processions that were the climax of most commemorative celebrations. The social and political symbolism of black military service suffused black commemorative celebrations and dictated the ordering of the parades in even the smallest black communities. During the celebration of Evacuation Day (the anniversary of the fall of Richmond), in tiny Oak Union, Virginia, on April 3, 1906, for example, festivities began at dawn when a cavalcade of thirty-odd horseback riders, escorted by elderly Civil War veterans and two standard bearers, one flying the United States flag and the other the local Emancipation Day association flag, set out on a twelve-mile ride through small settlements scattered across the surrounding Albemarle County countryside.[23] In the larger cities of the region, black GAR posts often turned out en masse to participate in parades on virtually all of the important holidays. Until at least 1915, black GAR members led the Memorial Day processions in Richmond. Likewise, black Civil War veterans still chaperoned the Lincoln Day parade through the streets of Savannah as late as 1917.[24]

The veterans served as role models for the companies of black militia and fraternal society members who marched beside them during commemorative parades. Marching veterans reminded black and white spectators that battlefield heroics knew no color line at a time when the legitimacy of black military service was in question. Although the tradition of militia duty extended back to the republic's founding, black militias were recent innovations that arose during Reconstruction when Republican governments welcomed black veterans and others into the formerly all-white state militias. Intent on demonstrating civic responsibility and dissuading white extralegal violence, black men eagerly joined the militias. At best, Southern whites grudgingly tolerated the black militias. Eventually, at the turn of the century, white lawmakers succeeded in using the rallying cry of white supremacy to abolish them, thereby threatening to deprive black men of the opportunity to perpetuate the tradition of military and civic service exemplified by Civil War veterans.

Long-established black secret orders, however, quickly transformed themselves into quasi-military organizations, complete with precision drill squads and elaborate faux-military uniforms, and took their place with black veterans in commemorative exercises. Angered by the disbandment of black militia in 1905, blacks in Savannah, for example, displayed renewed determination to stage holidays with appropriate fanfare. On Emancipation Day in 1906, the "uniform ranks" of the Knights of Pythias escorted a mile-long parade through the principal streets of the city. The men in uniform may not have been in the militia, but the local black newspaper nevertheless reported their maneuvers as though they were. "The men in the entire line," the newspaper crowed, "presented an excellent appearance. They were a fine body of men and that showed the great possibility of the race." Similarly, readers of news accounts of the Richmond Knights of Pythias Emancipation Day parade in 1898 might be excused for having presumed they were reading about a military drill. The description of the brigadier general's "glittering, heavily gold-plated uniform," complete with a "silk-folding chapeau, heavily gold-plated epaulets, gold plated belt and sword, a 14 foot long imported silk sash as per regulations, gauntlets, and a suit of dark blue cloth," warranted the same extended notice that had previously been devoted to the attire of militiamen.[25]

Because blacks were excluded from monumental representations of military valor and their record of soldiering was disparaged by many whites, any recognition of their military service during commemorative pageants was charged with symbolic significance. Through the immediacy of commemorative celebrations, parading veterans helped audiences to transcend time and to reconnect themselves with the historical and legendary events experienced by the veterans. Lines of black veterans were a reminder of the blacks who, by fighting at Port Hudson, Milliken's Bend, Fort Wagner, and Nashville had connected the agency of ordinary men with great deeds, including the destruction of slavery and the eventual achievement of political rights. By associating themselves with the central events in their race's history, by promoting themselves as exemplary patriots, and by adopting the names of esteemed Union officers and slain black war heroes, GAR posts, such as the Robert G. Shaw post in Savannah, the David M. Hunter post in Beaufort, South Carolina, and the André Caillous and the Anselmas Planciancois posts in Louisiana, joined the front ranks of the custodians of black memory.[26]

Black veterans represented an explicit refutation of racist interpretations of the Civil War's legacy not only by their presence in the commemorative ceremonies but also as symbols invoked by black orators during celebrations. Black speakers pointedly rejected the prevailing

Southern white interpretation of the causes and meaning of the Civil War. Southern whites, of course, strenuously defended secession and were acutely sensitive to any suggestion that the defense of slavery had motivated their failed rebellion. The black counternarrative was equally unambiguous. Over and over again, black orators insisted that the Civil War had been God's punishment for slavery, that the plight of African Americans had been the catalyst for the nation's Armageddon, and that black soldiers had played a decisive role in the conflict's outcome.

Emancipation, orators emphasized, endured as the most hallowed accomplishment of the war and of black veterans. Rather than a tactical sleight of hand dictated by wartime exigencies (as many white Southerners claimed and more and more white Northerners agreed), the Emancipation Proclamation was a redemptive act through which God wrought national regeneration. A banner that hung from the speaker's platform during the January 1, 1866, Emancipation celebration in Richmond made this point by proclaiming that "this is the Lord's work, it is marvelous in our sight." For Rev. L. B. Maxwell, the Civil War was the moment when "the prayers of our ancestors came up before God for recognition." Then, like the Jehovah of the Old Testament, "God by the blood of a million people . . . [had] avenged the wrongs of our people, wiped out slavery forever." Divine will, announced Rev. W. H. Dixon of Norfolk's First Baptist Church, had operated through human agency during the Civil War: "God in answer to our fathers' and mothers' prayers seemed to have whispered to Lincoln in Psalms telling him that the Negro's emancipation was the country's only redemption." Two decades later, a Lincoln Day orator in Savannah detected the same divine purpose. "The hand of Providence was in this movement," he contended, and "the time had come for doing away with an iniquitous system that was bound, if continued, to work the ruin of both races." "God," he concluded, "did thus use men and measures to execute his purpose in the ripeness of time."[27]

If black orators stressed the role of providential design in the war's outcome and the elimination of slavery, they nevertheless insisted that human agency had played a crucial role as well. Against the backdrop of the heightened patriotism of the late nineteenth century, African American orators retold the nation's recent history so as to establish their claim that they had made signal contributions to the preservation of the Union. Black speakers boasted that the black veterans gathered before them indeed had been authors of history who deserved the nation's unstinting respect for their deeds. In 1867 Aaron Bradley, a former slave and a Republican firebrand, informed Savannah blacks that recent black heroism was only the latest evidence of black valor: "Hannibal was a Negro; . . . the first martyr of the Revolution was a

Negro; the French Revolution was caused by a Negro insurrection in Santo Domingo, and in the recent war [the Civil War] the colored troops fought nobly." Two decades later, George Arnold insisted that it had been black soldiers who had "washed the blood scars of slavery out of the American flag." Speaking to an Emancipation Day audience in 1889, Rev. L. B. Maxwell proclaimed, "There has not been a great movement in this country since the Negro has been on American soil — political or social — upon which he has had no influence." He substantiated his claim with a litany of black Civil War soldiers who "fought like men, like freemen and not like slaves." Likewise, in 1902 Rev. C. L. Bonner traced the record of black heroism "from the blood of [Crispus] Attucks" before the American Revolution to "the blood stained walls of Fort Wagner" during the Civil War.[28]

The emphasis that black orators placed on black military valor underscored the connections that whites and blacks alike drew between manhood, patriotism, and military service. At century's close, when American imperialism and militarism crested, the contributions of black women to the Civil War, such as those made by Harriet Tubman, Susie King Taylor, and the dozens of black women who fought in disguise as men, seemingly merited no mention in the celebrations of black wartime valor. Instead, black men anxious to defend the historical and contemporary record of black soldiers were keen on encouraging, as Theophilus G. Stewart, a journalist, educator, and member of the A.M.E. Church, put it, "the production of a robust and chivalric manhood." Lurking behind Stewart's appeal was anxiety about the prognosis for black manhood. A preoccupation of late-nineteenth-century American culture, ideas of masculinity seemed in flux at a time when headlong economic and social transformations eroded older notions of manhood. By no means was this uncertainty about manhood confined to black men. Yet the issue may have had special significance for black men, who bore the stigma both of violated manhood during slavery and of the continuing reality of the sexual exploitation of black women by white men. Moreover, American popular culture generated seemingly limitless emasculating stereotypes of black men. Reflecting diffuse concerns about black masculinity, commemorative orators, in conjunction with commemorative processions, affirmed the capacity of black men to shoulder the obligations of citizenship and to exhibit military prowess. That many blacks during the late nineteenth century began to reinterpret the whole history of the race in an effort to compile a cavalcade of heroic black manhood testified to the precariousness of the freedmen's and the black soldiers' hold on manhood.[29]

If the commemorative spectacles and oratory exposed the embattled sensibilities of veterans and other Southern blacks, they nonetheless posed an unmistakable challenge to white understandings of the past. White Southerners understood that the contest over the meaning of southern history was not just between Northerners and Southerners, but also between white and black Southerners. White Southerners had argued with their Northern counterparts for decades and could find a measure of satisfaction in the acquiescence of many Northern whites to much of white Southern interpretation of the past. But when white Southerners systematically set about codifying their heroic narrative and filling the civic landscape with monuments to it, they also were conscious of the challenge from Southern black counternarratives (and to a lesser degree the dissenting voices of some white Union veterans in the South). The mocking derision that whites showered on black veterans and on commemorative spectacles leaves little doubt that whites understood that these rituals of black memory represented a form of cultural resistance. For all of the efforts of Southern whites to enshrine their historical understanding of slavery, the Civil War, and black capacities, the processions of black veterans, the paeans to black valor, and the solemn decoration of soldiers' graves made manifest an alternative historical memory.

The prestige and importance accorded black Civil War veterans within the black community, however, could not assuage the veterans' anxieties that the inexorable passage of time, the dispiriting apathy of some blacks, and the hostility of whites eventually would expunge their record of service from collective memory. At the turn of the twentieth century, the complaints of black veterans about the waning recognition of their sacrifice grew frequent and urgent. In 1895, Christan A. Fleetwood, a recipient of the Congressional Medal of Honor, lamented the "absolute effacement of remembrance of the gallant deeds done for the country by its brave black soldiers." By the second decade of the twentieth century, black veterans especially deplored the apparent declining popular interest in Memorial Day. In 1915 Cosby Washington, the commander of the Custer Post of the GAR in Richmond, Virginia, asked, "Why is it that the great bulk of colored people who want to be called our race leaders from another standpoint and along other lines seem to take such little interest in the work of decorating graves at the National Cemetery once a year?" A year later, the *Richmond Planet* made a similar appeal: "We feel sure if the colored youth were taught patriotism the condition of the race would be better from every standpoint. The future is so difficult to understand, it is very essential that the colored man be taught this great principle." Such despair was animated by the black veterans' sense of their impending mortality. Like the Confederate veterans who comprised what historian David Herbert Donald has called the "generation of defeat," black veterans at the dawn of the new century could not escape the evidence of their shrinking numbers and waning influence. After the 1913 Memorial Day ceremonies at Beaufort National Cemetery the *Savannah Tribune*, a black weekly, acknowledged as much when it observed: "There was an appreciable diminution in the ranks of the veterans this year as compared to last year, caused by the ravaging work of 'Father Time.' "[30]

The laments about obliteration of the memory of black military service acquired urgency at a time of unmistakable white efforts to marginalize all expressions of black historical memory. Throughout the late nineteenth century, black veterans had risked persecution whenever they donned their uniforms and GAR regalia. Even an official history of the GAR laconically conceded that Southern posts had confronted an "intense feeling of opposition then manifested to any meeting of Union soldiers."[31] Although whites in some communities tolerated black commemorative celebrations, in other places they systematically set out to suppress them. In Mobile in 1898, for instance, white newspapers crowed that "for the first time in local history there was a general public participation" in Memorial Day celebrations. In fact, what the news accounts actually meant was that "hitherto the services were almost wholly in charge of the colored militia" and beginning in that year white members of the GAR and United Confederate Veterans jointly staged the ceremonies.[32]

A similar process of exclusion took place in Atlanta during the Fourth of July. Since the Civil War, white Atlantans, like most white Southerners, had refrained from or openly repudiated any observation of the Fourth of July. But after the Spanish American War, which prompted frenetic nationalism even among former Confederates, Southern white enthusiasm for the anniversary of national independence reawakened. Leading the efforts to revive white celebration of the Fourth in Atlanta and many other parts of the South were the Daughters of the American Revolution and other patriotic societies. In Atlanta, they prodded public officials to stage large patriotic festivities, including parades of white veterans and troops, which monopolized public spaces that blacks had previously used without challenge. As a consequence, black veterans and other groups who had celebrated the holiday for decades without any competition found themselves and their festivities pushed to the margins of the city landscape.[33]

An even more glaring example of the campaign by whites to suppress black memory occurred in Andersonville, Georgia. The annual Memorial Day ceremonies at the site of the notorious Confederate prisoner-of-war camp and a national cemetery attracted thousands of black excursionists from across Georgia and Alabama. Crowds, estimated at more than ten thousand in number, gathered to picnic, listen to speeches, and decorate cemetery graves. The festivities at this particularly problematic reminder of the Confederacy proved especially obnoxious to white Georgians. They claimed to be offended by the lawlessness that accompanied the holiday, but even law-abiding black celebrants provoked hostility. Beginning in 1899, local authorities, bolstered by "a posse of hand picked men" and state militia, intervened and stifled the celebrations altogether. Opponents of the black festivities, supported by the governor, pressured the railroads to stop running excursion trains with reduced fares for visitors attending the Andersonville ceremonies. The cessation of excursion fares and the presence of white police and troops had an immediate effect: within two years white news accounts praised the military for simultaneously keeping away "the disorderly colored element" while attracting "the increased attendance of the white people." By 1905 blacks were virtually excluded from the Memorial Day exercises at Andersonville, which now became pretexts for celebrations of national reconciliation and of (white) Union and Confederate valor. Neither slavery nor black gallantry merited even cursory mention in these and subsequent ceremonies. In Andersonville and elsewhere, the reassertion of white cultural authority over patriotic celebrations understandably exacerbated the anxieties of black veterans that the near hegemony of white memory in the public spaces of the South threatened to eradicate any enduring recognition of their singular patriotic service.[34]

With time the struggles of the black Civil War veterans seemed increasingly distant from and tangential to the concerns of twentieth-century blacks. Author Richard Wright, for example, recalled his grandfather, a Union veteran who boasted of having killed "mo'n mah fair share of them damn rebels," as a man gripped by hate and fantasies of renewed war. Bereft of empathy for him, Wright voiced the impatience and cynicism of youth.[35] That Wright, who was born in 1908, was oblivious to the historical memory that his grandfather cultivated was evidence of the ephemeral quality of all historical memory. But even more than that, Wright's perception of his grandfather bespoke the inability of black veterans to perpetuate public recognition of their sense of their wartime deeds.

To a degree, the receding recollection of the role of blacks in the Civil War was inescapable. The fleeting character of memory demands the continuous creation and re-creation of a sense of the past; no enduring social memory can be entirely static. For black historical memory to retain its capacity to speak to and mobilize its intended audience, it necessarily had to address contemporary concerns about the past. Consequently, although veterans and other crafters of black historical memory may have resolved to create a version of the past that was impervious to change, their very success was dependent on the ongoing evolution of the memory they propagated. The memory of black Civil

War veterans inevitably, then, was altered by the subsequent experiences of blacks. At the beginning of the twentieth century, the shrinking ranks of black Civil War veterans perhaps enjoyed their greatest symbolic standing in the black community. They contradicted the dominant white narrative of the Civil War as well as the ascendant white representations of black masculinity in an age when ideas of masculinity, civilization, and nationalism were inextricably fused. They reminded blacks of their patriotic sacrifices at a time when whites impeded, whether by disbanding black militias or by discriminating against black soldiers, black military participation. But with World War I, a new generation of black veterans returned and took precedence in the celebration of black citizenship and service. As the number of Civil War veterans rapidly shrunk, the veterans themselves increasingly became curiosities or, as in the case of Richard Wright's grandfather, objects of pity. Civil War veterans lingered on for years to come and eventually in 1951 the last black Civil War veteran, Joseph Clovese, died.[36]

If the erosion of the memory of black veterans was fated, it was also the consequence of design. Because memories are transitory, blacks yearned to make them permanent by fashioning physical testaments of memory and to mark off sacred places.[37] For at least a half century following the Civil War, blacks labored to give their recalled past fulsome public expression. As Memorial Day ceremonies vividly demonstrated, blacks endowed cemeteries with enduring commemorative significance when they decorated the graves of veterans. And wherever a tradition of commemorative processions of veterans and others existed, urban streetscapes, if only temporarily, also became sites of memory. Yet, blacks could never anchor their memory of the Civil War in the public spaces of the South in the same manner that whites could. White Southerners, after all, had the power and resources required to create a landscape dense with totemic relics. They simultaneously enjoyed the authority to remember the past by forgetting parts of it. They chose to recall an antebellum past of loyal and frolicking "servants" when they erected monuments to "faithful" slaves. The black aspirations for freedom that sustained the freedmen who joined the Union army had no place in that memory, and hence whites raised no statues of black soldiers in the South. Over the course of decades Southern whites, with the complicity of white Northerners, seized the cultural power necessary to make their memories about the Civil War authoritative while rendering those of blacks illegitimate or imperceptible. The resulting silences in the historical narrative of the South — silences about the moral dilemmas of slavery and about the black struggle for freedom — relegated the experience and memory of black veterans to the obscure shadows of the past from which they would be retrieved only recently.[38]

Notes

1. *New Orleans Tribune*, October 31, 1865; Ira Berlin, Joseph P. Reidy, and Leslie S. Rowland, eds., *Freedom: A Documentary History of Emancipation, 1861–1867*, ser. 2, *The Black Military Experience* (Cambridge, 1982), 786; Thomas J. Morgan, "*Reminiscences of Services with Colored Troops in the Army of the Cumberland, 1863–1865*," in *Personal Narratives of Events in the War of the Rebellion, Being Papers Read before the Rhode Island Soldiers and Sailors Historical Society* (Providence, 1885), 44–45.

2. Donald R. Shaffer, "Marching On: African-American Civil War Veterans in Postbellum America, 1865–1951" (Ph.D. diss., University of Maryland, 1996), 67.

3. Berlin, Reidy, and Rowland, *Black Military Experience*, 800; Joseph T. Glatthaar, *Forged in Battle: The Civil War Alliance of Black Soldiers and White Officers* (New York, 1990), 253.

4. Works that analyze how memories reinforce collective identity include John Bodnar, *Remaking America: Public Memory, Commemoration, and Patriotism in the Twentieth Century* (Princeton, 1992); W. Fitzhugh Brundage, ed., *Where These Memories Grow: History, Memory, and Southern Identity* (Chapel Hill, 2000); Marie-Noelle Bourguet, Lucette Valensi, and Nathan Wachtel, *Between Memory and History* (New York, 1990); James Fentress and Chris Wickham, *Social Memory* (London, 1992); Eric Hobsbawm and Terence Ranger, eds., *The Invention of Tradition* (Cambridge, 1983); George Lipsitz, *Time Passages: Collective Memory and American Popular Culture* (Minneapolis, 1990); David Thelen, ed., "Introduction" to *Memory and American History* (Bloomington, 1990), vii–xix; and Michel-Rolph Trouillot, *Silencing the Past: Power and the Production of History* (Boston, 1995).

5. See Mary P. Ryan, *Civic Wars: Democracy and Public Life in the American City during the Nineteenth Century* (Berkeley, 1997), esp. chap. 2.

6. The distribution of black veterans varied from place to place in roughly the same pattern as the extent of black participation in the Union army had varied. Just as the largest number of black soldiers had been recruited in the border states, so too did residents of the upper South comprise the largest proportion of veterans. In contrast, where the Union army arrived late in the war— Alabama and Texas, for instance—the number of both black recruits and subsequent resident veterans was small. See Berlin, Reidy, and Rowland, *Black Military Experience*, 12; Shaffer, "Marching On," chap. 4.

7. Eric Foner, *Freedom's Lawmakers: A Directory of Black Officeholders During Reconstruction* (Baton Rouge, 1996), 292–95; Luther P. Jackson, *Negro Office-Holders in Virginia, 1865–1895* (Norfolk, 1945); Schaffer, "Marching On," chap. 6.

8. Glatthaar, *Forged in Battle*, 252–53; Shaffer, "Marching On," 67–68.

9. Philip S. Foner and George E. Walker, eds., *Proceedings of the Black National and State Conventions, 1865–1900* (Philadelphia, 1986), 289–97; Shaffer, "Marching On," 246–48; Glatthaar, *Forged in Battle*, 250.

10. *Journal of the Fiftieth National Encampment, Grand Army of the Republic, Kansas City, Mo., Aug. 28 to Sept. 2, 1916* (Washington, D.C., 1917), 50;

Wallace E. Davies, "The Problem of Race Segregation in the Grand Army of the Republic," *Journal of Southern History* 13 (August 1947): 355. On the revival of the GAR in general, see Mary R. Dearing, *Veterans in Politics: The Story of the G. A. R.* (Baton Rouge, 1952), and Stuart McConnell, *Glorious Contentment: The Grand Army of the Republic, 1865–1900* (Chapel Hill, 1992).

11. Blacks, for instance, accounted for three-quarters of the 1,033 members in the Department of Louisiana and Mississippi in 1897 (Federal Census of 1890, 803, 815–16; Shaffer, "Marching On," 258).

12. Davies, "Problem of Race Segregation," 358.

13. On the debate, see Davies, "Problem of Race Segregation," 354–72; Dearing, *Veterans in Politics*, 411–21; McConnell, *Glorious Contentment*, 213–18; Shaffer, "Marching On," 250–75.

14. *Savannah Morning News*, May 31, 1892, May 30, 1895; *Richmond Dispatch*, May 31, 1895; Davies, "Problem of Race Segregation," 358.

15. *Atlanta Constitution*, May 31, 1892; Vance Robert Skarstedt, "The Confederate Veteran Movement and National Reconciliation" (Ph.D. diss., Florida State University, 1993), 90–92; *Confederate Veteran* 22 (February 1914), 65. For a curiously positive assessment of UCV celebrations of black "Confederates," see Skarstedt, "Confederate Veteran Movement," 250–51.

16. Quoted in *Public Opinion* 11 (1891): 452.

17. The monuments were in Brooklyn, Cleveland, and Boston. Kirk Savage, *Standing Soldier, Kneeling Slaves: Race, War, and Monument in Nineteenth-Century America* (Princeton, 1997), 178; George Washington Williams, *A History of the Negro Troops in the War of the Rebellion, 1861–1865* (1888; reprint, New York, 1968), 328; *New York Age*, January 2, 1889.

18. David W. Blight, *Race and Reunion: The Civil War in American Memory, 1863–1915* (Cambridge, Mass., 2000), chaps. 4–5.

19. Quoted in Shaffer, "Marching On," 216. Shaffer estimates that more than 72,000 African American veterans secured pensions perhaps as many as 100,000 applied for pensions. Shaffer, "Marching On," 237–38.

20. *Augusta (Ga.) Colored American*, January 13, 1866; Benjamin Quarles, "Historic Afro-American Holidays," *Negro Digest* 16 (February 1967): 18; Blight, *Race and Reunion*, chap. 9.

21. *New York Age*, January 19, 1889; *Indianapolis Freeman*, July 19, 1890; George Brown Tindall, *South Carolina Negroes, 1877–1900* (Columbia, S.C., 1970), 288–90.

22. *Nashville Banner*, January 2, 1891; *Elizabeth City (N.C.) Carolinian*, January 6, 1892, January 4, 1893, January 5, 1895; *Savannah Tribune*, February 6, 1892, February 15, 1908, January 9, 1909, February 3, 1912; *Richmond Planet*, January 23, December 25, 1897, May 27, 1915, January 16, 1917, February 24, 1917; *Indianapolis Freeman*, January 14, 1893; *Petersburg Index*, July 7, 1874, July 6, 1877; Atlanta *Constitution*, July 1–4, 1891.

23. *Washington Bee*, September 21, 1901; H. W. Clark to Mary Church Terrell, August 1, September 11, 1922, Mary Church Terrell Papers, Library of Congress; *Richmond Planet*, April 14, 1906.

24. *Richmond Planet*, June 2, 1906, May 27, 1915; *Savannah Tribune*, February 13, 1909, May 31, June 7, 1913, May 30, June 6, 1914, February 17, 1917, May 24, 1919.

25. See Donald L. Grant, *The Way It Was in the South: The Black Experience in Georgia* (New York, 1993), 299–300; Bobby L. Lovett, *The African-American History of Nashville, Tennessee, 1780–1930* (Fayetteville, 1999), 101; Howard N. Rabinowitz, *Race Relations in the Urban South 1865–1890* (New York, 1978), 227–30; Lawrence D. Rice, *The Negro in Texas, 1874–1900* (Baton Rouge, 1971), 270–71; Otis A. Singletary, *Negro Militia and Reconstruction* (New York, 1963); Tindall, *South Carolina Negroes*, 286–88. *Savannah Tribune*, January 6, 1906; *Richmond Planet*, January 8, 1898.

26. Joseph T. Wilson, *The Black Phalanx: A History of the Negro Soldiers of the United States in the Wars of 1775–1812, 1861–65* [sic] (Hartford, 1887), 527–28.

27. *Richmond Dispatch*, January 2, 1866; *Savannah Tribune*, January 5, 1889; *Columbia State*, January 1, 1892; *Richmond Planet*, December 11, 1897; *Savannah Tribune*, February 24, 1917. See also *New Orleans Louisianian*, July 9, 1881; *Petersburg Lancet*, January 13, 1883, January 17, 1885; *Nashville Banner*, January 2, 1891; *Ocala Evening Star*, January 2, 1901; Emancipation Day Resolutions, p. 2, January 2, 1899, Charles N. Hunter Papers, Rare Book, Manuscript, and Special Collections Library, Duke University. On black millennialism, see Timothy E. Fulop, " 'The Future Golden Day of the Race': Millennialism and Black Americans in the Nadir, 1877–1901," *Harvard Theological Review* 84 (1991): 75–99.

28. *Savannah Daily Republican*, July 6, 1867; Laura F. Edwards, *Gendered Strife and Confusion: The Political Culture of Reconstruction* (Urbana, 1997), 194; *Savannah Tribune*, January 5, 1889, January 7, 1893, March 14, 1896, January 4, 1902. For other representative accounts of black heroism, see *Indianapolis Freeman*, January 13, 1894; *Savannah Tribune*, January 9, 1904, January 5, 1907, January 10, 1914, *Ocala Evening Star*, January 2, 1906; *Richmond Planet*, January 9, 1915.

29. Theophilus G. Stewart, "The Army as a Trained Force," in *Masterpieces of Negro Eloquence: The Best Speeches by the Negro from the Days of Slavery to the Present Time*, ed. Alice Moore Dunbar (1914; reprint, New York, 1970), 278. On masculinity and black military service, see Jim Cullen, " 'I's a Man Now' ": Gender and African American Men," in *Divided Houses: Gender and the Civil War*, ed. Catherine Clinton and Nina Silber (New York, 1992), 76–91. See also Hazel Carby, *Race Men* (Cambridge, Mass., 1998), chap. 1; Kevin K. Gaines, *Uplifting the Race: Black Leadership, Politics, and Culture in the Twentieth Century* (Chapel Hill, 1996), esp. chap. 4; and Darlene Clark Hine and Earnestine Jenkins, "Black Men's History: Toward a Gendered Perspective," in *A Question of Manhood: "Manhood Rights": The Construction of Black Male History and Manhood, 1750–1870* (Bloomington, 1999): 46–56.

30. Christian A. Fleetwood, *The Negro as Soldier* (Washington D.C., 1895), 18; *Richmond Planet*, May 27, 1915, May 20, 1916, April 21, 1917; *Savannah Tribune*, June 7, 1913. See also *ibid*, June 6, 1914.

31. Robert B. Beath, *History of the Grand Army of the Republic* (New York, 1889), 639.

32. *Atlanta Constitution*, May 31, 1898. For a similar reassertion of control over Memorial Day by whites in Florence, South Carolina, see *Atlanta Constitution*, May 31, 1899.

33. *Atlanta Constitution,* July 4–5, 1902, July 4–5, 1903, July 4–5, 1904.

34. *Albany (Ga.) Weekly Herald,* June 1, 1895, June 6, 1896; *Americus (Ga.) Times-Recorder,* May 29–31, 1895, May 30–31, 1896, May 28–31, 1897, May 29–31, 1898, May 30–31, 1899, May 30–June 1, 1900, May 29–June 1, 1901, May 29–May 31, 1902, May 29–May 31, 1903, May 28–May 31, 1905; *Atlanta Constitution,* May 30, 31, 1890, May 31, 1891, May 31, 1892, May 31, 1893, May 31, 1894, May 30, 1895, May 30, 1896, May 29, 1897, May 31, 1898, May 29, 31, 1899, May 30, 31, June 1, 1900, May 31, 1901, May 26, 31, 1902; *Macon Telegraph,* May 30–31, 1895, May 29, 1897, May 31, 1898, June 1, 1900, May 30, 1901, May 30, 1902, May 31, 1902; *Savannah Morning News,* May 31, 1892, May 31, 1893, May 29, 1895, May 30, 1897, May 31, 1898, May 30, 1901, May 31, 1902, May 31, 1903, May 31, 1904, May 31, 1905, May 30, 31, 1907, May 30, 1908.

35. Richard Wright, *Black Boy* (New York, 1966), 155.

36. Shaffer, "Marching On," 317–18.

37. Pierre Nora, "Between Memory and History: *Les Lieux de Memoire,*" *Representations* 26 (Spring 1989): 13. See also Nathan Wachtel, "Memory and History: Introduction," *History and Anthropology* 12 (October 1986): 212; and L. S. Vygotsky, *Mind in Society: The Development of Higher Psychological Processes* (Cambridge, Mass., 1978), 51.

38. This process is traced in Catherine W. Bishir, "Landmarks of Power: Building a Southern Past, 1855–1915," *Southern Cultures,* inaugural issue (1994): 5–46; Gaines Foster, *Ghosts of the Confederacy: Defeat, the Lost Cause, and the Emergence of the New South, 1865 to 1913* (New York, 1987); and Savage, *Standing Soldiers, Kneeling Slaves,* chap. 5.

PART TWO ➤ *The North*

Chapter 7

An Inspiration to Work:
Anna Elizabeth Dickinson, Public Orator

J. MATTHEW GALLMAN

✤ In 1869, S. M. Betts and Company of Hartford, Connecticut, published *Eminent Women of the Age; Being Narratives of the Lives and Deeds of the Most Prominent Women of the Present Generation*. It was indeed an impressive volume, featuring biographical sketches of forty-nine leading activists, authors, educators, actresses and physicians, illustrated with fourteen engraved portraits of the collection's most celebrated women. Among the longest entries was Elizabeth Cady Stanton's thirty-four-page life of Anna Elizabeth Dickinson, who was — at twenty-six — also among the youngest women in the volume.[1]

Born in 1842, Anna Dickinson was the youngest of five children of Philadelphia Quakers. Her father, John, died when Dickinson was two, only hours after speaking at an antislavery meeting. Following in her father's abolitionist footsteps, Dickinson published an essay on "Slavery" in William Lloyd Garrison's *The Liberator* when she was only fourteen. According to Stanton, the defining moment for Dickinson came in January 1860 when she attended two public meetings on "women's rights and wrongs." Long bothered by gender inequities, the seventeen-year-old rose to speak at the first meeting and then returned the following Sunday when she delivered a withering attack on a man who had presumed to discuss women's inherent limitations. "Never," according to Stanton, "was an audience more electrified and amazed than they were with the eloquence and power of the young girl."[2]

During the next year, as the nation was absorbed in sectional crisis, Dickinson developed a reputation in the Philadelphia area as a fiery young orator, speaking largely on abolitionism and women's rights. With the outbreak of war, Dickinson took a position at the United States Mint, but she was fired shortly after accusing Union General George McClellan of treason for his failures at the Battle of Ball's Bluff. In 1862 Garrison arranged for Dickinson to deliver a series of lectures on "The National Crisis" to New England audiences. By this point Dickinson had dreams of supporting herself, and aiding her family, through lecture fees. The crucial step came early the following year when New Hampshire Republicans invited her to stump in the 1863 campaign.

Dickinson spent much of 1863 traveling across New Hampshire, Maine, Connecticut, Pennsylvania, and New York, attacking Democrats and supporting Republican candidates. She proved an extremely effective partisan speaker, attracting large audiences — sometimes several thousand paying customers — and earning the praise of party loyalists, who were happy to pay $100 or more, a remarkable fee for the day, for a single campaign appearance. One of Dickinson's most celebrated moments came on April 4 when she delivered the Connecticut Republican Party's election eve address at Hartford's Allyn Hall. Between campaign appearances, Dickinson made high profile — and well paid — appearances in New York City, Philadelphia, and Chicago. Her unusually high six-hundred-dollar fee for two lectures at the Northwestern Sanitary Fair in Chicago raised some eyebrows, particularly since the event was a patriotic fund-raiser, but the feisty Dickinson answered her critics by pointing out that in making the trip she had sacrificed nearly twice that amount in lost speaking fees in the East while the paying audiences in Chicago had netted the fair a healthy profit.[3] Stanton, who was present when Dickinson spoke at New York's Cooper Institute, recalled that "on no two occasions of my life have I been so deeply moved, so exalted, so lost in overflowing gratitude, that woman had revealed her power in oratory." In January 1864 Dickinson accepted an invitation from more than a hundred senators and representatives to speak before them in the nation's capital. Stanton recalled the moment with deep satisfaction, declaring that Dickinson "was honored as no man in the nation ever had been." In the weeks to come she repeated the address to audiences in Philadelphia, New York, and Boston. During the 1864 campaign, Dickinson spoke out against George McClellan and the Democrats, while having little direct praise for Abraham Lincoln and his cautious policies towards reconstruction. Anna Dickinson, Stanton concluded, was no mere parrot of radical male ideas; rather, "[h]er heroic courage, indomitable will, brilliant imagination, religious earnestness, and prophetic forecast, gave her an utterance that no man's thought could paint or inspire."[4]

Dickinson's prominent treatment in *Eminent Women of the Age* is an indication of her fame in the immediate postwar years. The following year *Harper's Bazar* republished eight of the volume's etchings in a composite image honoring "The Champions of Woman's Suffrage," with Dickinson's image appearing in a place of prominence at the bottom center, balanced by portraits of Stanton and Susan B. Anthony on the top row. Still shy of her twenty-seventh birthday, Dickinson was truly one of the nation's most famed public women.

The public praise and private emotions that Anna Dickinson inspired in 1868 must have been heady stuff for the young Philadelphian, but by then she had established herself as a national celebrity. This essay will examine Dickinson's experiences during the war years, when she first emerged as a national sensation. Her fame presented fascinating challenges to a society that had little experience with women speaking in public before mixed audiences and almost no familiarity with partisan politicking by those generally consigned to "the weaker sex." The handful of mid-century women who appeared on public platforms commonly spoke on the reforms of the day, specifically women's rights and abolitionism, and only rarely had access to more explicitly partisan stages.[5] Dickinson, a strong advocate of both reform causes, stretched the received gender boundaries both by her excursions into an explicitly political arena and by her powerful, dynamic mode of speech. A small woman with striking dark eyes and short-cropped hair, Dickinson captivated — and enraged — civilian audiences across the wartime North with a combination of eloquence, sarcastic wit, and bold, occasionally outrageous statements. Although physically frail, and periodically silenced by throat problems or other ailments, Dickinson spoke with a powerful voice that managed to fill large halls. Contemporary accounts describe her pacing up and down platforms before packed houses of men and women, delivering prepared remarks without notes and often spiced with clever barbs aimed at local Copperhead editors or unruly hecklers.[6]

The published responses to Dickinson's wartime appearances fell along a political spectrum. Northern Democrats were quick to dismiss both the message and the messenger, assailing Dickinson as a "sexless" gender transgressor, an attractive sideshow, or a mouthpiece for radical men. Republican newspapers embraced Anna as an eloquent, charismatic advocate, even while some editors exhibited discomfort with her fame, often selecting language that stressed her distinctive — even otherworldly — persona, thus differentiating her from the rank and file of American womankind. Whatever their political perspective or their opinions about the propriety of Dickinson's public appearances, Northern observers agreed that Anna Dickinson was one of America's most celebrated women.[7]

Before long, this celebrity took on a life of its own, delivering to Dickinson a fame that few Civil War–era Americans could duplicate. She was, in a sense, the equal of the nation's most famed actresses. Like famed actress Fanny Kemble before her, Anna Dickinson became a popular commodity, featured in newspaper stories, engravings, and the various trappings of national celebrity.[8] Like the Civil War's greatest military heroes, Dickinson became a popular subject of the latest in photographic technology: the commercially distributed *cartes de visite*.[9] Dickinson sat for numerous portaits, both during and after the war, including at least one visit to Mathew Brady's New York studio. These reproduced images became a major contributor to Dickinson's burgeoning fame, as Northerners placed her carte de visite in their personal albums alongside pictures of Lincoln, Grant, and the nation's leading political and military figures.

How did Dickinson deal with both her wartime celebrity and the trappings of life as an unmarried woman on the road? As her fame grew, she constructed a complex, messy web of intimate friends, political advisors, casual acquaintances, and adoring strangers. It was in a sense a private life almost completely defined by her public fame, even while her family ostensibly tried to separate the two. At the center of that world were the members of her immediate family. Dickinson's relationships with her mother, her sister Susan, and her three older brothers were all shaped by her wartime fame and fortune. Long before Dickinson's trip to Boston, Anna and Susan shared thoughts and schemes about how they would support themselves and their widowed mother.[10] Things changed for the sisters when Dickinson went north in 1862. On April 20 an ailing Wendell Phillips invited her to speak in his stead at Boston's Music. "Think of *that* mum," an enthusiastic Dickinson wrote home, "this small snip, — acting as Wendall Philllipses substitute & at his own request at that." The crowd was large and distinguished, and Dickinson was thrilled to report that her performance had been a smashing success, earning special praise from both Phillips and the revered William Lloyd Garrison, who suggested that more lectures should follow. "I do not expect to be very rich" just yet, she reported, but clearly the future looked bright, and soon new offers would indeed follow.[11]

Before long Dickinson was traveling from town to town throughout New England, giving lectures for modest fees to enthusiastic audiences. Susan and her mother tracked Dickinson's progress through her periodic letters and reports in local newspapers. In the process, their relationships became curiously recast. Letters from home inquired about Dickinson's new friends and her sometimes precarious health, but those sisterly and maternal concerns were interspersed with increasingly urgent reports on overdue bills and other house expenses. As winter fell in 1862, and Dickinson's lecturing pace slowed, Susan told her younger sister that "I hope . . . both for thy sake and ours that thee will be pretty well paid for what thee gets to do, both for thy sake and ours. What a weight would be taken off if we were only fairly out of debt."[12] Such was the pressure on the twenty-year-old orator.

The invitation to campaign in New Hampshire the following year was a crucial step for Dickinson's speaking career, but it was also an important boon to the Dickinson family finances. Throughout 1863 Susan kept up a regular correspondence with her campaigning sister, peppered with references to new bills and other fiscal woes. In July, when ill health and physical exhaustion forced Dickinson to postpone several Connecticut lectures, Susan responded with characteristic mixed messages, urging her sister to rest up and protect her health, while dropping hints about the financial strains that she and her mother faced when Anna's checks failed to arrive.[13] This confusion of roles was typical of Dickinson's family correspondence. Although the youngest child, her successes had placed her in the peculiar position as family provider, leading to an unusual recasting of traditional roles.

Susan and Anna were clearly close, frequently exchanging gossip about friends or potential love interests, but one wonders how they navigated this new relationship. While Anna was off basking in the adoration of crowds, Susan—nine years her senior—was at home in Philadelphia taking care of their mother, running the household, and—increasingly—attending to Anna's correspondence and other bureaucratic needs. As Christmas 1863 approached, Susan responded to a note from Anna with these words: "Thank thee for the money and for what thee so kindly says about money matters in general. Thee's a dear, good, kind sister—and thee knows I think it none the less that I don't often put my feelings into words."[14] Dickinson's prior note does not survive, but it appears that she had tried to set Susan's mind at ease about the family's dependence on her earnings. On the one hand, this exchange shows the bond between the two sisters, but on the other hand the very need for such a discussion points to the awkwardness of their evolving roles.

Dickinson's relationship with her mother was perhaps even more challenging. The Quaker widow worried about her youngest daughter's physical and spiritual health, while also expressing some discomfort with Dickinson's public life and even greater anxiety at rumors that she might turn to a career on the stage. Still, Mrs. Dickinson appeared proud of her daughter's patriotic contributions, and she realized that her household depended on Anna's earnings. A month after Dickinson's triumphant appearance in Washington, Mrs. Dickinson sent her a wistful note regretting that her peripatetic daughter had "no home of thy own to rest at," while also declaring that "my own precious child . . . thou art the chief burden bearer for us all and nobly have thou born it." The letter was full of motherly concern for daughter's well-being, but it closed with a familiar reminder: "When thee [send] funds for home expenses please send $11.75 to pay the bill for the blankets."[15]

Dickinson was in less regular contact with her three brothers. The two eldest, John and Edwin, each spent part of the war years living in California. Both suffered from poor health and apparently provided little if any financial support to their mother and sisters. Samuel, two years Anna's senior, began the war as a clerk in a store until he eventually won a position in Washington with his sister's assistance. Samuel was drafted in 1863 but was able to secure an exemption, probably on medical grounds. Although her three brothers ranged from two to seven years older than she, Dickinson ended up providing each with some form of professional or financial assistance during the 1860s, even footing the bill for Samuel's funeral when he died of tuberculosis late in the decade.[16]

As her family's chief "burden bearer," Anna Dickinson was hardly living out the roles typically defined by her age and gender. Her hectic speaking and travel schedule could have posed further challenges to Dickinson's gender identity, but at least for the war years she mediated the public character of her itinerant status by playing the role as perpetual house guest: wherever she traveled local residents were happy to take her in, sometimes competing for the honor of having Anna Dickinson under their roof.[17] When she first went to Boston in 1862 Dickinson stayed with William Lloyd Garrison and his family, reporting that "Mr Garrison has treated me like a father since I came — his family are delightful." Later that year she moved from the Garrisons' to the Sargents', a transition that she hoped had been achieved without undue tensions.[18]

Wherever she journeyed in the wartime North, Dickinson became almost the adopted daughter of one or more host families. Subsequent letters revealed a growing list of correspondents who shared an intense affection for the young orator. When she visited New Bedford, Massachusetts, in the spring of 1862, Dickinson stayed at the home of Joseph Ricketson. Shortly after her brief visit, Ricketson sent Dickinson a long letter declaring that words could not properly express the impact that she had had on him and his family. Months later, frustrated by his inability to secure her a return invitation, Ricketson declared: "I want not only to hear you lecture but I want to see you 'dreadfully' — & so do Fanny & Ruth who send their best love."[19] Connecticut minister Nathaniel Burton hosted Dickinson when she passed through Hartford in 1863, and later introduced her to an audience at Allyn Hall. Two years later the overwrought (and married) minister declared, "I yearn for you like a thirsty ox for the brookside. I do Anna, I solemnly do."[20] During her wartime visits to both Boston and Hartford's Nook Farm, Dickinson split her time between several families, rapidly becoming the center of an exciting social whirl, with residents competing for the privilege of hosting the young orator.

When she traveled further from home, Dickinson was more likely to be taken in by a single family. Shortly after the election of 1864, she accepted an invitation to deliver her "Plea for Woman" in Pittsburgh. Dickinson stayed for just a few days with the Irish family there, but long enough to make a large impact on the entire family while winning the heart of Elias Irish. Less than a week after her lecture, Irish wrote Dickinson a touching, flirtatious letter declaring that "there has been a world of sighing about this house since you went away. Have the goodness when next thee comest to Pittsburgh, to leave the quiver of arrows at home." In Milwaukee she stayed with R. N. and Sallie Austin, who both corresponded with Dickinson into the postwar years. In response to an unexpected note after a lengthy silence, Sallie Austin wrote asking if Dickinson had found peace and wisdom in her hectic life "or if you still give some people who love you heartaches on your account because of your recklessness."[21] In quite different ways these letters suggest the immediate — and ongoing — intimacy that so often characterized Dickinson's relations with her numerous hosts. Anna Dickinson was simultaneously both a powerful heroine who drew those around her into her orbit and a fragile young woman whom many sought to protect from the world's ills. Hers was a charisma shared by only a handful of public figures.

In her travels Dickinson befriended quite a few younger women who saw in her a role model and an inspiration. The patterns in these relationships suggest something about Dickinson's own personal experiences and the chord that she struck in others of her sex. Long before she became famous, Dickinson was close friends with Lillie Atkinson, a young Quaker from Cherry Lawn, New Jersey. Atkinson, a year younger than Dickinson, filled her letters with personal news and commentary on abolitionist doctrine, occasionally expressing frustration when older men failed to take her opinions seriously. In preparation for a debate on women's rights in early 1861, Lillie wrote to Anna — already a veteran of several such platforms — for a few pointers, vowing to take her older friend's ideas and "clothe them in my own language." Two years later, when Dickinson had become a national celebrity and their correspondence had waned, Atkinson went to hear her old friend speak but had no opportunity to shake her hand after the performance. Instead, she sent a teasing, slightly melancholy, note. "Please, dear Anna," she wrote, "I dont know how to write properly to persons who have become so great and famous, and find myself looking back with a sigh at those dear old days of years agone, when I could talk to thee without fear of thy *greatness*." Following the lecture Lillie had spent her evening reading their old letters and remembering their past friendship with teary eyes about what had once been. But beyond the sadness of friends who had drifted apart, Atkinson seemed particularly pained by measuring herself against Dickinson's achievements and worried that her old friend would conclude that she had been "standing still" rather than developing her own skills and commitment. From Lillie's perspective the relationship with Anna had evolved from one of personal intimacy and shared political passion to an unequal relationship in which she followed Dickinson's success from a distance while finding her own public activism diminished in comparison. Meanwhile, by the middle of 1863 Dickinson was receiving stacks of mail from across the country, generally arriving in packets forwarded to her by her sister in Philadelphia. Whatever her thoughts about Lillie Atkinson, it is a safe bet that they no longer consumed much of her attention.[22]

Even the most loyal companion would have found old relationships crowded out by the new attachments that Anna Dickinson developed on the road. In her first trip to Boston Dickinson became fast friends with young Fanny Garrison, who shared her bed with the visiting abolitionist. Soon after Dickinson left, Garrison wrote declaring that "I missed my soft pillow so many times, and have wished some how or other I might wake up and find a pair of some body's dear arms around me." The intimacy of their nights together clearly had an important impact on Fanny Garrison, elevating Dickinson to a special place in her consciousness. "Remember Fanny longs to hug and kiss you & tell you how much she loves you," she declared at the close of one letter. And with Dickinson's November 1862 return to Boston only a month away Fanny was thrilled that "soon I will hug and kiss you really."

What did the two talk about in their nights together? Judging from the subsequent letters they shared an expected amount of personal gossip (Dickinson had developed a particular interest in Garrison's brother Wendall), but their correspondence was really much more about abolitionism, party politics, and women's rights. With her school's graduation just around the corner, Garrison revealed ambivalence about her approaching independence and the challenges that awaited. After sketching her recent visit to Cambridge for Harvard's "Class day," Garrison reflected the gender sensibilities that Dickinson had encouraged in her, announcing that "it is so mean that we are only allowed there on that day, as though we were only dolls to help their enjoyment when they pleased to want us." And anticipating Dickinson's upcoming lecture, Garrison declared that "[i]t makes me so happy when a woman does something grand and noble. The act is so fine a plea for woman's rights."[23] It is unlikely that her brief visit produced such ideas where there heretofore had been none, but the example of Dickinson's public activism probably expanded Garrison's thinking about woman's proper place. Like Lillie Atkinson, Fanny Garrison seems to have measured her own life as a politically engaged young woman according to the impressive yardstick presented by Anna Dickinson.

During her first trip to New England, Dickinson was befriended by the Chace family in Rhode Island, and particularly Lillie Chace, who was roughly five years younger than the orator. Lillie Chace also became a regular correspondent, providing detailed commentary on state politics and national abolitionism. Chace also shared the belief that Dickinson's success served as a gender beacon. "I am very glad of thy success," she wrote "both because I love thee, and because I am a *woman*, and as much I thank thee from the bottom of my heart for the great work thee is doing for *us*, while laboring for the country, and the Liberty of the black man." And she, too, found that Dickinson's success forced her to look inward, openly wondering if the had the "necessary 'brass'" to be a public speaker like her friend while announcing that "I want to *succeed* in whatever path of life I choose." But for the time being she was content to live vicariously through Dickinson's public successes. In this she was hardly alone. One afternoon, while writing a letter to Dickinson from her boarding school, Chace was interrupted by a roommate who sent Dickinson her love, adding that "'I dont ever expect to lecture myself, but I *feel*.'"[24]

The year after the war ended, a nineteen-year-old Lillie Chace sent Dickinson a particularly long, reflective letter. "I sometimes think you were the first girl I ever really loved," she mused, and "I am thankful I may yet see thee again 'face to face,' and in thy presence feel how true it is that womanhood and womanhood's glory and charm are inherent in her nature, not the forced growth of her hot-house seclusion." Chace went on to admit that she lacked the power "to break the bonds that hold me," and thus she—and women like her—depended on the strength of powerful advocates like Anna Dickinson.[25] There are certainly similarities between this letter and Dickinson's earlier correspondence with Lillie Atkinson and Fanny Garrison. Each young woman came from a highly political, abolitionist household and saw in Dickinson an ideological kindred spirit as well as a powerfully charismatic, slightly older woman. Enduring bonds were built in brief private moments together, and kindled through regular correspondence. In each case, Dickinson came to represent an example of what women could accomplish in public, while also seeming to have achieved the unachievable.

Numerous other women recalled similar closeness with Dickinson, often developed in nights sharing a bed together. Hartford's Isabella Beecher Hooker's niece, Lilly Gillette, first met Dickinson during a Christmas visit to Nook Farm in 1863. The following February, Lilly urged her to stay at her family's home during an upcoming visit to

Cincinnati. "When you come you will sleep with me, & when you sleep with me we will have a splendid talk," she promised. Shortly after Appomattox, Lilly — who had married Charles Dudley Warner's brother — wrote her old friend from Nook Farm, urging Dickinson to visit Hartford while the Hookers were out of town and "won't gobble her up." "We'll sleep together & I promise not to make you talk all night," Lilly vowed.[26]

In other cases the affection for Dickinson seemed shared between married spouses. Louise and Walter Brackett had a distinctive relationship with Dickinson, marked by an extraordinary, bantering correspondence. "When you again write do write some *love* to me," Lou demanded in May 1863, "dont waste it all on the *men*, I can appreciate it better than they can, believe me I can." Two weeks later she asked: "How do you live without seeing Lou? Ah! I know, with your lovers, numerous as they are." Lou closed her next letter, a chatty note about how much General Ben Butler wanted to meet Dickinson, by adding a postscript: "How I want to see you visibly — and tangibly before me so that I can *touch you*." As Dickinson's next trip to Boston grew imminent, Lou's enthusiasm for her friend grew. "I scarce can wait to see you," she wrote. "[T]he very thought of seeing your genial and magnetic face once more — makes my heart leap with pleasure — do you love me the same? Has no vile woman torn your heart from me? I fear *no man*." She went on to provide an update on Butler's interests in her young friend and on the more promising prospects from one of Butler's young colonels who apparently had expressed a serious interest in kissing Dickinson, an interest that Lou would gladly have accepted herself "if Walter was willing." The following March, Lou reported that Walter was so taken with Dickinson that he had declared his plan "to make love to you when you came to Boston again. You wont let him darling will you?" she asked. "[Y]ou are mine and belong to me, until you get married — say it is true?" The irrepressible Lou revealed that she had "an irresistible desire all through this letter to make love to you in down right earnest" but instead opted to weave a complex tale about a visit from a soldier on furlough — probably James Beecher — who had asked Walter for permission to kiss Lou, although in truth he really hoped to kiss Dickinson. She had been happy to accept the kiss, and promised that "when I next meet you — and God speed the time — I'll give you a 'Beecher kiss.' "[27]

It is hard to know what to make of this lively correspondence. Certainly both Lou and Walter were very fond of Dickinson, a fondness that continued well into the postwar years. Lou, like Dickinson's various younger friends, spoke tenderly of kisses and physical intimacies, insisting that she merited a special role in her friend's life, at least until the young orator took a husband. Perhaps the most interesting aspect of Lou's letters was her clear presumption that no man could truly replace her in Dickinson's affections, even while she assumed that Anna would eventually select a male lover.

Fanny and George Ames, of Newcastle, Delaware, developed a similar joint relationship with Anna Dickinson. In May 1864 Fanny addressed an affectionate letter to "My Dear Beasty," assuring Dickinson that her husband — "The Dominic" — was perfectly pleased that she and Anna had spent a week together eating oranges and "pet[ting]" and that "all the tenderness shown his wife by the dear little lady of Locust St only makes him love her more." A month later Fanny admitted that "I want to write you a love-letter, especially after that formidable sheet from the Dominic to tell you firstly how much I love you."[28] Most of Dickinson's relationship with the Ameses remains undocumented, but these two letters suggest another couple who had a special bond with Dickinson built on only limited contact together.

As a young woman Anna Dickinson traveled in a world that presumed that she would eventually settle down with a man, while in the meantime it appears that during the Civil War her deepest personal — and physical — intimacies were with other women. For women and men in the mid-nineteenth century, intense homosocial friendships were not uncommon and certainly not understood as evidence of sexual preference, a term that itself would have had made little sense to Dickinson and her friends. Nonetheless, as she journeyed from town to town, and home to home, Dickinson probably had greater opportunities to develop deep bonds with women and young girls — often established in late nights sharing a bed together — than she had with the multitude of boys and men who crossed her path and tried their hand as suitors within the more rigid confines of heterosexual gender interactions.[29]

Dickinson's wartime correspondence are thick with references, generally in jest, about young men who were smitten with her. For a time, Wendell Garrison — Fanny's brother — seemed to be the object of her affections.[30] Dickinson also developed a romantic relationship with Judge Joseph P. Allyn, a Connecticut politician, or at least the judge had that impression. For several months in the spring of 1863 Allyn sent Dickinson long, lovesick letters, making references to stolen moment sharing cherries during one of her visits to Nook Farm. But Dickinson lost interest or perhaps never shared the judge's ardor. At the end of July Allyn's tone changed dramatically. "God spare you from the pain you have inflicted on me these last few days and in those cruel lines," he wrote in answer to one letter. "I love you as I never loved woman before else it be the dead only sister that sleeps in yonder cemetery."[31] This brokenhearted letter speaks to the effect that the twenty-year-old Dickinson had on the poor judge, but although there are occasional references to Allyn in other letters to Dickinson, there is no indication that she reciprocated his passion.[32]

Dickinson had a more serious attachment to Pittsburgh's Elias Irish. This relationship developed during her December 1864 visit and grew when she returned to Pittsburgh shortly after the war, and the two spent time together hiking and picking blackberries. But once again the relationship evolved into one of unrequited love. One remark in an August 1865 letter seems particularly telling. In that note Irish commented on how "wondrous strange" it was that they had grown so close "on paper," but claimed that if the prickly Dickinson were in Pittsburgh with him she "shouldst' not have one pleasant word — not one — not if they were as plenty as black berries on the mountain slopes of Fayette Springs." Irish, it appears, had hoped for loving words but instead received the same sort of biting sarcasm that had made Dickinson such a celebrated speaker. Several months later he sent Dickinson a sixteen-page missive, representing several hundred pages of discarded drafts, in which he admitted that he had "gone 'clean daft' about" his "matchless black-haired Gipsey" and recalled listening as "my silver tongued enchantress builded castles in the air, and beguiled, enthralled my fancy, enthralled my heart, my soul and fancy, through many a golden hour." But, alas, these were — he acknowledged — the words of "despised love," not to be reciprocated. This story ended tragically when Irish died of tuberculosis in December 1866, leaving Dickinson feeling both sad and perhaps remorseful about her failure to accept Elias's love.[33]

Elias Irish and Joseph Allyn were in most senses quite different men, who shared a deep attachment to — even an obsession with — Anna Dickinson. Their letters to Dickinson both chastize her for her sharp tongue and perhaps for her refusal, or inability, to utter the words that they hoped to hear. Both men wrote most fondly of sweet moments with Dickinson, sharing fruit — cherries with Allyn and mountain blackberries with Irish. Although each was certainly infatuated with Dickinson, and for a time at least she felt a fondness for each suitor, we are left to wonder how well either knew her during their short visits, particularly as compared with her numerous female correspondents.

Dickinson never married, although for decades after the war the press persisted in linking her name with various public figures, including Whitelaw Reid, Ben Butler, and Senator William Allison. Other men who never met Dickinson developed strong emotional attachments based solely on her public appearances. Thomas Seville, of Elmira, New York, penned a lengthy poem praising the "woman who stands brighter than her sex." Chicago's W. M. Boucher was so struck by a Dickinson lecture that he was moved to write, declaring that "My soul longs for a companion whom I can respect for her goodness & wisdom & whose body & spirit I can love with an absorbing emotion," adding that since Dickinson was single, he wondered if she would "permit a correspondence with the view of becoming acquaintances." Six months later an E. M. Bruce of Middleton, Connecticut, penned a two-page poem dedicated to Anna, including these memorable lines: "Oh noble girl! Oh peerless queen! The world hath never known, What struggles woman's heart hath seen, What trials undergone." The following year Cincinnati's R. P. Minier proposed marriage by mail.[34]

Women periodically wrote simply to thank Dickinson for representing their gender so proudly. "*Good bless you* Anna Dickinson," one Massachusetts woman wrote, and "thank you for every word you said [and] . . . for the good your lecture did for me personally."[35] Shortly after the war, Harriette Keyser, a twenty-five year old New York schoolteacher who lived alone with her father, heard Anna speak. "I am trying to educate myself," she explained in a long autobiographical letter, "and when God calls me to any work, I shall step out of the ranks, if need be, and obey His call." Although Keyser insisted that she did not need Dickinson's words to point her in the right direction, she acknowledged that they did "encourage and strengthen" her. This letter suggests the multilayered responses that Dickinson elicited from her peers. Her words and deeds inspired both friends and strangers to action, but ironically Dickinson's refusal to bow to contemporary gender constraints also seemed to prompt some women to rationalize why they were not living out their larger dreams. Another correspondent—the mother of eight daughters—was so moved by a Dickinson lecture on prostitution that she vowed to "rescue" two prostitutes by hiring them as servants, explaining that she only had to figure out how to do so without her husband learning of their background. Other women wrote seeking advice on how to launch a career in public speaking or in other ways follow Dickinson into the public arena.[36]

Various strangers, generally men, sent Dickinson unsolicited words of advice. After Pennsylvania Quaker Amos Gilbert heard her speak in January 1861, he wrote Dickinson a long, grandfatherly letter praising the young orator for her political stances while worrying that all the love and admiration heaped upon her would threaten her own "self respect and self approval." The following month a correspondent volunteered that Dickinson lacked proper schooling "in the sternest order of reason" and thus she had learned the lower art of pandering to an audience. Such uneducated techniques, he insisted, would eventually be her undoing. By taking on "great and intricate questions requiring *time, genius* and a *masculine calibre*" she was setting herself up as a "target for the laughter and pity of all truely educated citizens," he warned. Albany's Henry

Homes generally praised Dickinson, but he found her language sometimes unladylike for mixed company, citing phrases such as " 'making to
eat dirt' " or " 'a filthy sheet' " as particularly inappropriate.[37]

These three men — all strangers — had different perspectives on Dickinson's early excursions into the public arena, but they shared a fundamental conviction that they had some insights that their age and gender
afforded them. Whatever the source of her public success, in her private
life Anna was barraged with words of advice from all manner of self-
proclaimed experts, both friends and strangers. In fact, Dickinson's political mentors included some of America's most accomplished politicians, journalists, and reformers. This elite company led Dickinson's
most virulent critics — particularly those who were offended by the very
notion of a woman entering the public arena — to conclude that she was
merely parroting the ideas of familiar radical minds. But even a cursory
glance at her voluminous correspondence demonstrates that Dickinson's
advisors were hardly of one mind, and none controlled hers.

Dickinson found a long series of advisors as soon as she left home.
Garrison sent her charmingly detailed advice on travel arrangements in
1862. Later that year Bostonian Samuel May Jr. wrote offering suggestions about how she should spend her summer, including advice on
sleep, exercise, conversation, and the right sort of books to read. That
winter, May was pleased to pass Dickinson on to the hands of the other
advisors and mentors who would try their hand at controlling her actions and shaping her career.[38] As she became more involved in partisan
politics, Dickinson often turned to Philadelphia judge William D. Kelley. Following her April 1863 address at New York's Cooper Institute,
the Republican congressman congratulated Dickinson for "illustrat[ing]
the folly of that prejudice that excludes women from any sphere of
usefulness." Still, Kelley seemed to see Dickinson as a precocious
daughter rather than a political equal, routinely addressing her as "dear
daughter" or "dear child" and occasionally signing his letters with
"papa." Their friendship grew strained when Kelley served as an intermediary in arranging Dickinson's January 1864 appearance in Washington, only to have his protégée balk at some of the preliminary plans,
leaving him frustrated that she no longer accepted his fatherly guidance
without question.[39]

The events surrounding the 1864 campaign illuminated the relationship between Dickinson and her various mentors. With the war drag-
ging on, and no clear end in sight, President Lincoln faced a strong
threat from the Democrats — who nominated General George McClellan —
and a series of challenges from radicals in his own party. Dickinson was
personally dissatisfied with Lincoln's policies, particularly his moderate
stance toward postwar reconstruction, but she was unwilling to damage

the Union cause by abandoning the president and unhappy about the prospect of sitting out the campaign. In the first months of the year Dickinson grew increasingly hostile to the president, backing off from her January endorsement of his renomination and abusing Lincoln from the stump, but she also steered clear of a radical movement — led by her friend Kansas senator Samuel Pomeroy — to draft Treasury secretary Salmon P. Chase and a subsequent effort to nominate General John C. Frémont at a late May convention in Cleveland. For Dickinson, these months in 1864 were full of conversations and correspondence about national politics. The fatherly Judge Kelley was deeply distressed with her attacks on Lincoln (and particularly her sarcastic accounts of a meeting with Lincoln that Kelley had arranged). At the other end of the Republican spectrum, Senator Pomeroy sent her a copy of his notorious "circular" supporting Chase for president and unsuccessfully tried to entice her into the movement. Republican journalist Whitelaw Reid shared Dickinson's unhappiness with the president but was equally unimpressed with the strategies of the party's insurgents and disturbed that Dickinson — whom he had recently befriended — was tempted by their appeals. "It can do no good now for you to get tangled in the stripes of personal politics, & it may do much harm," he counseled in early April.[40]

The push for Frémont posed a particular dilemma for Dickinson because her idol Wendell Phillips was at the center of the movement while most of the other leading abolitionists, including Garrison, saw Frémont's candidacy as an unacceptable compromise with the Democrats. Susan B. Anthony, who had grown increasingly fond of the young Dickinson, wrote in early July surveying the political terrain and wondered what had become of "the good old doctrine 'of two evils choose neither,'" adding that "it is only safe to speak & act the truth — & to profess confidence in Lincoln would be a lie in me." The purest strategy, Anthony concluded, would be to continue espousing the radical cause without bowing to political expediency. Anthony did her best to persuade Dickinson to "keep close to the 'still small voice' that has thus far safely led you on." A few weeks later Theodore Tilton, the editor of *The Independent*, sent Dickinson an eight-page letter devoted largely to politics and her political conundrum. Tilton, too, was highly critical of Lincoln but declared that, given the president's popularity and Frémont's shortcomings, "you have no other choice but Lincoln." Tilton urged Dickinson to use her skills to rouse popular patriotism, "teaching the masses a nobler idea of Liberty." In the months until the election, and particularly after Lincoln was renominated in Baltimore, more and more of Dickinson's advisors weighed in with their opinions. Radical Republican B. F. Prescott acknowledged that the president left much to be desired, but expressed his hope that Dickinson would not be blinded by her hatred of Lincoln and abandon the party. Lillie Chace wrote that she was thoroughly engrossed in electoral politics, but could not see her way clear to support Lincoln.[41]

Finally, in September Dickinson issued a formal statement called "The Duty of the Hour" in Tilton's *The Independent*. The content of this widely discussed public letter is a valuable window into Dickinson's thinking. The mere fact that she saw fit to make such a statement and that the public gave it such attention demonstrates her highly unusual status, even among political women. In "The Duty for the Hour," Dickinson acknowledged that she would have preferred a different candidate and declared that "I shall not work for Abraham Lincoln; I shall work for the salvation of my country's life" by campaigning for the Republican ticket. Tilton assured Dickinson that the letter had been well received, at least within his political circle. But Lillie Chace was less pleased, suggesting that having failed to raise the Republican Party up to her own level Dickinson had opted to sink down to their's. The always ironic Reid sent a congratulatory note from Cincinnati, but noted that he would only "vote for Mr Lincoln, if at all, very much as he has swallowed pills." True to her word, Dickinson campaigned more enthusiastically *against* the Democrats than she campaigned for the administration, and in fact she rarely spoke of Abraham Lincoln at all.[42]

Dickinson's correspondence in 1864, like that of the previous three years, shows how her public utterances were consistently cast within various private contexts. Personally charismatic and politically formidable, Dickinson attracted an assortment of willing advisors among close friends, professional acquaintances, and interested strangers. And every indication is that she actively solicited such advice from a wide circle of Republicans of various stripes. Meanwhile, Dickinson also weighed complex career considerations: What decisions would best enable her to build upon her fame while also continuing to be her family's burden-bearer? The accumulated weight of this diversity of voices pushed Dickinson in various directions, lending further support to the argument that she was not a mere pawn of specific older advisors. In fact, although Dickinson's words and actions often pleased her most ardent supporters, she repeatedly demonstrated an independent spirit driven by her own conclusions rather than the agendas of others.

Anna Dickinson's public and private worlds converged around the emerging trappings of her fame. As she became a household name, friends and strangers sought souvenirs of Dickinson's celebrity, illustrating the nature of renown in the North during the Civil War era. Even before she had made her splash in Boston, cartes de visite featuring young Dickinson were already finding their way into albums across the country. In March, a Quaker woman wrote from Iowa, thanking Dickinson for her picture and asking the young orator for two more inscribed photographs for friends. A few months later Joseph Ricketson sent a gushing letter, celebrating her "womanly and sympathetic appeal" and thanking her for the photograph that she had sent. Fanny Garrison's brother Frank was thrilled that Dickinson had mailed him a carte de visite and wondered if she had seen her likeness in the latest *Frank Leslie's Illustrated*. And, in a fascinating — and galling — combination of paternalism and admiration, New York editor Oliver Johnson wrote to Dickinson shortly after the war asking for an autograph for a friend, adding that he had never made such a request before "so pray be a good girl, and comply promptly."[43]

Closer to home, Dickinson's fame gradually crept into her family relationships. Dickinson's sister and mother carefully collected newspaper clippings, periodically exchanging commentary on particularly glowing or harsh reports. Susan relished the stream of visitors who dropped by their Locust Street home, and on one occasion she was pleased to report that she and her mother were met with "remarkable affability" from several social acquaintances who were especially impressed with Anna's fame. Even Lillie Chace became swept up in her friend's celebrity. In September 1863 she wrote asking for a picture to show off to friends. A few months later Chace reported that she had recently met an attractive young man — "a true blue abolitionist" — and wanted Dickinson to send several autographs, for both the young man and his sisters.[44] We can only imagine how this sort of request reshaped the relationship between these two young women who, in other circumstances, had interacted as peers.

Strangers who had seen Dickinson speak felt a special bond with her that was the true mark of celebrity. Shortly after the war Emma Fisher, of Roxbury, Massachusetts, sent a long letter suggesting the power of these passions. Earlier in the summer she had written asking Dickinson for an autograph and a lock of hair. Dickinson had sent along her signature but deflected the more personal request with the explanation that her hair had recently been shorn and she had no locks to spare. Several months later Fisher was writing back to point out that she had recently seen Dickinson lecture once again and was pleased to discover that the orator's hair had grown long enough to spare a lock or two. Fisher went on to explain that when she had first heard Dickinson speak — on working women — it had moved her to new resolutions, promising herself that she would follow Dickinson's example in helping others. She hoped to make a ring from the lock of hair to serve as a reminder of that evening's commitments, adding that "there is nothing in the world I so covet as your love and friendship but though we shall probably never meet, I earnest pray that Heaven may give you friends true and sincere."[45] Once again a woman who had never met Dickinson had developed a special attachment to her public persona, prompting a note and a highly personal request.

How might all this attention have affected Anna Dickinson? How might she have internalized the accumulated weight of family pressures, political influence, public celebrity, and a seemingly endless string of private passions and infatuations? What was the true connection between that famous public speaker portrayed by Elizabeth Cady Stanton and the charismatic young woman who seemed to touch all who met her? It is hard to imagine that all the adoration would not have had some impact on Dickinson's own sense of herself. And in fact some who met her during the war worried that Dickinson was falling prey to her own celebrity. Following Dickinson's first trip to Boston, Samuel May and Lillie Chace's mother, Elizabeth, shared their concerns for Dickinson's future. "It must be a great trial, and even danger," wrote May, "to so young a person, to be the object of so much interest, to receive so much applause, and to possess so great and happy a talent for holding and swaying the minds of large audiences."[46] As early as November 1862 Dickinson's mother, religiously conservative and personally savvy, wrote her wandering daughter a brief note: "[B]eware my dear child of being carried away by the voice of adulation. Remember under all and every circumstance, thee has an immortal soul to be saved or lost, and a frail tenement of clay, which must sometime return to its native element the earth."[47] In the years to come Mrs. Dickinson continued to worry about her daughter's physical and spiritual health, but — as we have seen — those maternal concerns were periodically muddied by her hopes that her youngest child would continue to earn enough money to maintain the Dickinson's Philadelphia household.

We know much less about Dickinson's own private thoughts than we know about the praise that she received on a daily basis. One letter to her friend James Beecher, written a month before the Battle of Gettysburg, does offer a fascinating window into the mind of the twenty-year-old abolitionist. "Dear Friend," she wrote:

I am tired, & — low be it spoken — cross. — I get nothing done, — all sort of people come to me on all sorts of trivial business, — visits of curiosity, flattery — what now? — letters pour in upon me, till I cry out in despair, remembering they are to be read & *answered* — meantime my work, actual work — study, thought, preparation, suffers — and so the other day — when the carrier had called, & Sue (that is my sister) came up with divers ominous looking missives, I cried out — "Heaven preserve us, — no more letters," . . . People tell me I have done thus & so, — give me great meetings, run after,—flatter, praise, caress me,—ah well!—then beg my heart not to be spoiled—There is too great a need of work,—too terrible danger,— too absolute necessity for all the labor of every head, & hand, & heart—to leave place for any selfish or personal failing. And when one thinks of great hearts, & noble souls, the brave men,—fighting, suffering, dying for the cause,—the greatest cause, the dearest cause that ever stood at stake,— what an inspiration to work.[48]

How we choose to read this revealing letter will say much about how we understand the woman they called America's Joan of Arc. It is evident that Dickinson felt a powerful impulse to work for the Union cause. Although a political partisan, she saw herself foremost as a patriot doing her part to support the armies in the field. But are these also the words of a young woman with an overblown sense of her own importance? Had the deluge of praise from close friends and perfect strangers gone to her head? It is certainly true that Dickinson was quite aware of her own popularity, but her comments to Beecher suggest that she recognized the dangers of empty flattery. Moreover, the attention that Dickinson received really confirmed her importance to the war effort. The letter reveals emotional exhaustion, but less from the work itself than from the trappings of fame. But perhaps Dickinson protested too much. The letter also hints that by 1863 the taste of fame had entered her marrow, not crowding out the higher ideals but shaping her daily personal life. In short, at twenty years of age Anna Dickinson was really doing important patriotic work, but she was also becoming used to her public celebrity—and influence—to a degree that might one day yield frustrated disappointment.

Anna Dickinson's wartime experiences, as reflected in her extensive correspondence, fits into several different narratives. This essentially private evidence provides a different perspective on how Civil War America—or at least Northern society—dealt with, and responded to, a highly unusual public woman. Predictably, some portion of her correspondents viewed Dickinson in the context of her gender and age, and sought to advise and control her accordingly, even while encouraging her in her transgressive life as an itinerant female orator. For others, Dickinson stood as a charismatic icon. Her example clearly had a shaping effect on a host of young women, both those she befriended and those who merely watched from afar. For these women Dickinson presented an alternative model for civilian women in the public arena, one that was quite different from the Sanitary Commission volunteers and female nurses on the one hand, and the celebrated spies and crossdressing female soldiers on the other. We might also place Dickinson into another home-front narrative, stressing that she—like so many other wartime civilians — was forced into economic adjustments in the midst of the conflict. Although driven by her political passions, Dickinson was also acting as a material provider for her sister and widowed mother. (Of course, in this case the war did not create the financial need — Dickinson's father had died more than a decade earlier — but the politics of the conflict did create a window of opportunity.) Moreover, while her specific wartime actions were quite distinctive, Dickinson impulse to engage in a useful form of "war work" was very much in keeping with many of her peers on the home front.[49]

Dickinson's wartime experiences are obviously also a crucial early component of her own life's narrative. Her postwar history is beyond the scope of this essay, but a few observations are in order. After Appomattox, Dickinson remained in the public sphere, pursuing a variety of reform agendas while continuing to support herself, her mother, and her sister. Immediately following the war she toured the country as a highly successful lyceum speaker, and when lecture fees began to dry up, she tried her hand as a playwright, actress, and author.[50] Although perhaps best known for her lecture on Joan of Arc, Dickinson's postwar lectures commonly tackled political themes, often focusing on the economic and political status of women. Despite brief returns to the stump in 1872 — campaigning for Liberal Republican Horace Greeley — and 1888, Dickinson never recaptured the partisan political voice she enjoyed during the war years.

In her quarter century of celebrity Dickinson also found herself embroiled in a string of bitter legal disputes and public disagreements involving — among others — critics, editors, politicians, and people in the theater. Along the way, Dickinson suffered through private rifts with numerous friends and allies, including Susan B. Anthony, Whitelaw Reid, Fanny Davenport, and Ben Butler. Dickinson's relationship with Anthony, twenty-two years her senior, was particularly complex. In the immediate postwar years they developed a closeness which combined both political passion and some level of physical intimacy.[51] Anthony took personal delight in the younger woman's company, but the two parted company, apparently because Dickinson — although consistently in favor of woman suffrage — refused to accept a prominent leadership role in the movement and in fact endorsed the exclusion of women from the Fifteenth Amendment, which extended suffrage to African American men.[52]

Anna Dickinson's public career ended sadly, but with characteristic flare. In 1891, with her sister's health failing and her behavior seemingly growing erratic, Susan Dickinson arranged to have Anna committed into a state asylum for the insane. This began a final, intricate chapter that would last for most of the decade and remain something of a puzzle a century later. Dickinson won her freedom with the aid of a team of lawyers and a sympathetic doctor, and then launched a series of celebrated lawsuits against the people responsible for her commitment and, later, against four New York newspapers that had reported that she was insane.[53] After achieving some measure of vindication, Dickinson retired to a life out of the public eye, eventually dying in Goshen, New York, at age eighty-nine.

How much might Dickinson's wartime celebrity have shaped her life in the quarter century to come? Like many soldiers and civilians who rose to fame during the Civil War, Dickinson's popularity endured into the postwar years, enabling her to craft a successful public career while also providing her with numerous opportunities to weigh in on the political issues of the day. But one could also write the narrative as one of frustrated ambitions. For a woman with an essentially political orientation, it must have been discouraging to be relegated to the lyceum circuit and the stage while men were directly shaping public policy. And having achieved such success — and praise — in her early twenties, Dickinson was ill prepared for the negative reviews and financial failures that accompanied some of her later efforts. In that sense, her wartime fame left Dickinson with a more difficult postwar road in that even her substantial postwar successes and public influence never quite matched her earlier accomplishments. But regardless of the challenges that lay ahead of her, at the close of the Civil War Anna Dickinson was widely recognized for her contributions to the war effort and to the Republican Party. And — for dozens of friends, hundreds of acquaintances, and thousands of anonymous admirers — Dickinson's wartime career served as evidence of what women could, given the opportunity, achieve in the public arena.

Notes

1. James Parton et al., *Eminent Women of the Age; Being Narratives of The Lives and Deeds of the Most Prominent Women of the Present Generation*, (Hartford, Conn., 1869). Stanton's essay on Dickinson is on pp. 479–512.

2. Parton et al., *Eminent Women of the Age*, 486. The only published biography of Dickinson is Giraud Chester, *Embattled Maiden: The Life of Anna Dickinson* (New York, 1951). James Harvey Young, who also wrote a dissertation on Dickinson's wartime career, authored a more scholarly Dickinson biography that has never been published. I am indebted to Dr. Young for permission to inspect both this manuscript ("Anna Elizabeth Dickinson") and his notes in the James Harvey Young Papers, Special Collections, Emory University, Atlanta, Georgia (hereafter JHY Papers). For my own brief overview of "Anna E. Dickinson's Civil War," see *The Human Tradition in the Civil War and Reconstruction*, ed. Steven E. Woodworth (Wilmington, Del., 2000), 93–110.

3. *Chicago Tribune*, November 12, 1863.

4. Parton et al., *Eminent Women of the Age*, 500, 505, 512.

5. Glenna Matthews, *The Rise of Public Woman: Woman's Place in the United States, 1630–1970* (New York, 1992), 108–19; Mary P. Ryan, "Gender and Public Access: Women's Politics in Nineteenth-Century America," in *Habermas and the Public Sphere*, ed. Craig Calhoun (Cambridge, Mass., 1992), 259–88. See also Elizabeth R. Varon, "Tippecanoe and the Ladies, Too: White Women and Party Politics in Antebellum Virginia," *Journal of American History* (September 1995): 494–521; Varon, *We Mean to Be Counted: White Women and Politics in Antebellum Virginia* (Chapel Hill, 1998); Rebecca Edwards, *Angels in the Machinery: Gender in American Party Politics from the Civil War to the Progressive Era* (New York, 1997), 12–38.

6. J. Matthew Gallman, "Anna Dickinson, America's Joan of Arc: Public Discourse and Gendered Rhetoric during the Civil War" (unpublished essay, 1999).

7. Gallman, "Anna Dickinson, America's Joan of Arc." See also Joanna Russ, *How to Suppress Women's Writing* (Austin, 1983).

8. Faye E. Dudden, *Women in the American Theater: Actresses and Audiences, 1790–1870* (New Haven, 1994), 40–42.

9. On wartime *cartes de visite*, see William C. Darrah, *Cartes de Visite in Nineteenth Century America* (Gettysburg, 1981).

10. Susan Dickinson to Anna Elizabeth Dickinson, January 27, 1861, Anna Elizabeth Dickinson Papers, Library of Congress, microfilm (hereafter AED Papers). (All dates of letters will hereafter be cited in month/day/year style.)

11. Anna Elizabeth Dickinson (hereafter AED) to Susan Dickinson, 4/28/62, 5/27/62, AED Papers.

12. Susan Dickinson to AED, 12/6/62, AED Papers.

13. Susan Dickinson to AED, 7/28/63, AED Papers.

14. Susan Dickinson to AED, 12/23/63, AED Papers.

15. Mrs. Mary Dickinson to AED, 2/11/64, AED Papers.

16. AED family correspondence, AED Papers; JHY Papers, Box 5, folder 21.

17. See, for instance, AED to Susan Dickinson, 4/15/62, AED Papers.

18. AED to Susan Dickinson, 4/28/62, Susan to AED, 11/21/62, AED Papers.

19. Joseph Ricketson to AED, 11/15/62, AED Papers.

20. N. J. Burton to AED, 8/8/63, 8/10/65, AED Papers. (This file is labeled "W. J. Burton" but James Harvey Young identifies the author as Nathaniel, [JHY Papers].)

21. Sallie Austin to AED, 11/12/65, AED Papers.

22. Lillie Atkinson to AED, 9/23/[60?], 3/12/61, 6/1/63, AED Papers. (Note: some of Lillie Atkinson's letters are incorrectly filed among Lillie Chace's letters.)

23. Fanny Garrison to AED, 6/23/62, 9/14/62, 10/12/62, AED Papers.

24. Lillie Chace to AED, 2/3/63, 3/30/63, 4/17/63, 3/12/64, AED Papers.

25. Lillie Chace to AED, 12/17/66, AED Papers.

26. Lilly Gillette to AED, 2/1/64, AED Papers (this is a portion of a note filed in the letters from Isabella Beecher Hooker); Lilly G. Warner to AED, 7/17/65, 1/16/68, AED Papers.

27. Louise Brackett to AED, 5/29/63, 6/15/63, 7/11/63, 7/24/63, 3/4/64, AED Papers.

28. Fanny Ames to AED, 5/2/64, 6/13/64, AED Papers.

29. The letters to Dickinson suggesting physical intimacies with other women raise a sequence of questions. First, what was the actual nature of these actions? Second, how, if at all, should the historian categorize these activities? And third, to what extent would answers to the first two questions contribute to our understanding of the events under examination? Historians agree that nineteenth century notions of friendships, for both men and women, differed substantially from contemporary norms, rendering the rigidity of modern labels anachronistic. Dickinson's wartime letters certainly indicate that she shared unspecified physical intimacies with several women, but none suggest that Dickinson — or her correspondents — understood their actions as being atypical, or secret, or calling into question a heterosexual future. Both her male and female friends apparently assumed that Dickinson would eventually marry a man. In modern terms Dickinson might have defined herself — either during the war years or later in life — as a bisexual, but I would argue that her actual sexual preference was less crucial than popular perception in shaping wartime responses to her. For the classic discussion of nineteenth-century female friendships among middle-class Northern white women, see Carroll Smith-Rosenberg, "The Female World of Love and Ritual: Relations between Women in Nineteenth-Century America," *Signs* 1 (Autumn 1975): 1–30. For a recent discussion of female culture among white Southern women, see Joan E. Cashin, ed., *Our Common Affairs; Texts from Women in the Old South* (Baltimore, 1996). This collection of documents includes various examples of homosocial relationships comparable to those reflected in the Dickinson letters (see pp. 91–96). The letters of African Americans Rebecca Primus and Addie Brown, edited by Farah Jasmine Griffin, illustrate a more explicitly erotic romantic relationship between two nineteenth-century women (*Beloved Sisters and Loving Friends: Letters from Rebecca Primus of Royal Oak, Maryland, and Addie Brown of Hartford, Connecticut, 1854–1968* [(New York, 1999)]). In her book *Surpassing the Love of Men: Romantic Friendship and Love between Women from the Renaissance to the Present* (New York, 1998) and in several other volumes, Lillian Faderman has established herself as leader in the pursuit of a "*usable past* for contemporary women who call themselves 'lesbian'" (p. 20). Although she casts her net more broadly than many of her colleagues, Faderman's work represents a valuable survey of attitudes and actions.

30. AED to Susan Dickinson, 4/28/62; Fanny Garrison to AED, 6/23/62; Susan Dickinson to AED, 11/21/62, AED Papers.

31. Joseph Allyn to AED, 7/21/63, AED Papers.

32. Louise Brackett to AED, 7/11/63, 7/21/63; Susan Dickinson to AED, 1/8/63, 8/13/63, AED Papers.

33. Elias Irish to AED, 8/20/65, 1/21/66, AED Papers.

34. Thomas Seville to AED, 6/12/63; W. M. Boucher [?] to AED, 4/6/64; E. M. Bruce to AED, 10/20/64; R. P. Minier [?] to AED, 11/27/65, AED Papers.

35. Emma F. Foster to AED, 4/15/65, AED Papers.

36. Harriette A. Keyser to AED, 2/20/66; Charlotte Garrique to AED, 11/1/65, AED Papers.

37. Amos Gilbert to AED, 1/7/61; Anonymous to AED, 2/27/61; Henry Homes to AED, 11/28/63, AED Papers.

38. William Lloyd Garrison to AED, 3/16/62, 3/22/62, 3/27/62, 3/30/62; Samuel May Jr. to AED, 6/19/62, 1/13/63, AED Papers.

39. William D. Kelley to AED, various letters (quote from 4/22/63), AED Papers.

40. Samuel Pomeroy to AED, various letters; Whitelaw Reid to AED, 4/3/64, AED Papers.

41. Susan B. Anthony to AED, 7/1/64; Theodore Tilton to AED, 7/13/64; B. F. Prescott to AED, 9/4/64, 10/2/62; Lillie Chace to AED, 8/21/64, AED Papers.

42. *The Independent,* September 8, 1864; Theodore Tilton to AED, 10/4/64; Lillie Chace to AED, 9/19/64; Whitelaw Reid to AED, 9/11/64, AED Papers.

43. Ruth Duzdeely [?] to AED, 3/29/62; Joseph Ricketson to AED, 6/24/62; Frank Garrison to AED, 9/12/62; Oliver Johnson to AED, 7/6/65, AED Papers. On fame, see Leo Braudy, *The Frenzy of Renown: Fame and Its History* (New York 1997), 491–514.

44. Lillie Chace to AED, 9/14/63, 3/12/64, AED Papers.

45. Emma Fisher to AED, 10/15/65, AED Papers.

46. Samuel May Jr. to Elizabeth Buffum Chace, 4/17/62, quoted in Lillie B. Chace Wyman and Arthur Crawford Wyman, *Elizabeth Buffum Chace, 1806–1899,* 2 vol. (Boston, 1914), 1:236.

47. Mary Dickinson to AED, 11/28/62, AED Papers. This note is written at the end of a letter from Samuel Dickinson to AED.

48. AED to James Beecher, 6/2/63, Schlesinger Library, Cambridge, Massachusetts.

49. Jeanie Attie, *Patriotic Toil: Northern Women and the American Civil War* (Ithaca, 1998).

50. On the nineteenth-century theater, see Dudden, *Women in the American Theater.*

51. See Lillian Faderman, *To Believe in Women: What Lesbians Have Done for America—A History* (Boston, 1999), 25–27. As Faderman notes, the Anthony-Dickinson correspondence has an erotic air, but the available evidence does not fully illuminate the nature of their relationship.

52. Young, "Anna Elizabeth Dickinson," chap. 7. See also Jean V. Matthews, *Women's Struggle for Equality, The First Phase, 1828–1876* (Chicago, 1997); and Barbara Goldsmith, *Other Powers: The Age of Suffrage, Spiritualism, and the Scandalous Victoria Woodhull* (New York, 1998).

53. The trial reports and court testimony provide contradictory evidence, supporting the notion that Dickinson might have been—at the time of her commitment—quite ill, while also leaving open the possibility that she was indeed badly treated by her sister and the other defendants.

Chapter 8

We Are Coming, Father Abraham — Eventually: The Problem of Northern Nationalism in the Pennsylvania Recruiting Drives of 1862

WILLIAM BLAIR

✤ DURING the summer of 1862, the state of Pennsylvania behaved like a problem child. Throughout the Union the mood of citizens had sustained a terrible blow. With the success of Union soldiers in the western theater and the opening of the Peninsula campaign, the Northern public had believed the war was all but over. The situation changed dramatically during the seven days of fighting around Richmond, with the Confederate army pinning its Northern enemy to the James River. Instead of having victory within reach, the Northern war effort required additional troops merely to continue the campaigning. A call for volunteers in July failed to draw enough soldiers, necessitating a second call by the president in August that threatened the use of a draft if the results fell short of quotas. The state of Pennsylvania caused some of the greatest concern among Washington bureaucrats who thought the state acted less than expeditiously. By mid-August, Republican governor Andrew Gregg Curtin had lost credibility with military authorities, who increasingly saw him as an obstacle to organizing regiments. On several occasions, the War Department sent adjutant generals into the state to push recruits to the front. The last of those men noted after arriving in Philadelphia in late August that "my presence in this city was absolutely necessary. As it is I find great difficulty in sending forward the troops. Had I attended to the excuses offered I doubt whether a regiment would have been ready for several days to come."[1]

These events present something of a paradox. A governor universally lauded in the literature of the war as a supporter of the administration had lost the trust of military leaders in Washington, who considered him more of a hindrance than a help in organizing soldiers. On the other hand, the state did as well as most others in meeting its quota under the two calls for troops during the summer of 1862. Throughout the war Pennsylvania ranked with New York and Ohio in the number of soldiers sent to the military. With such a track record, Curtin can hardly be considered a politician who impeded sending men to the national cause. Nevertheless, how do we make sense of the behavior exhibited by him and by Pennsylvanians during the recruiting drives of 1862? Did the state resist the calls? Was Curtin part of the problem, either as an incompetent or reluctant leader? Was dissent at the bottom of the reactions of the civilians and their governor? Or should we see what happened in 1862 as symbolic of something else entirely?

The answers to these questions require an understanding of the mid-nineteenth-century community and how Curtin wrestled with not only the problems of a deeply flawed system of raising soldiers but also deeply held social values within his constituency. The recruiting drives of 1862 highlight the importance that communities assigned to certain occupations and to the need for public welfare, and how these ideals affected not only who should join the military but also the terms under which a volunteer should enter the service. In the public's mind, some occupations were more eligible than others for recruiting fodder, with a person's class and political position contributing to these sentiments. The public, however, expected government or local leaders — especially rich Republicans — to compensate men for their military labors through bounties that would help care for families. Although the militia drive contained the beginnings of even greater political conflict to come, this kind of resistance was not the only factor behind Pennsylvania's problematic behavior. Politics provided friction within the Keystone State that created caution within Curtin, but the blame for a slow response lies also with the system itself and with the commonly held expectations of the nineteenth-century public.[2]

This moment of the war also reveals the contested nature of national identity in the North. David Potter long ago observed that historians typically fail to question the content of Northern national identity because it won.[3] Yet the kind of behavior that caused struggles in the recruiting drives of 1862 paralleled that seen in the South several months earlier when the Confederacy instituted conscription. The nature of loyalty and disloyalty was being redefined in this period. Songs such as "We Are Coming, Father Abraham" underscored the need for the volunteer spirit. Northerners always had equated patriotism with volunteering for the military; however, this time of conflict saw a shift toward suspecting men who remained at home as potentially disloyal. This had not always been the case. Because of the American tradition of small, volunteer armies, wars had never demanded mobilization on so extensive a scale, which meant that patriotism was not always determined solely by military service. Support for a cause could come in other ways. Besides, with the community as the primary loyalty in the nineteenth century, citizens in certain areas could bear no stigma by staying home, provided they acted in accordance with the values of their neighbors. Although Northerners did not deploy the rhetoric of state rights as prominently as their Southern brethren, the civilians and the governor of the Keystone State acted very similar to their counterparts in the Confederacy. Localism was alive and thriving in the Union.

I

On July 2, 1862 — a day after the Seven Days' Battles ended — Lincoln called for 300,000 troops to serve for three years or the duration of the conflict rather than the twelve- or nine-month options of prior enlistment drives. Within a week or two of the call, it became clear that civilians throughout the North responded less than enthusiastically. The reason most often cited for this among historians has been the growing weariness with war. A year of conflict had educated the public about combat's grimmer side. While this reason contains some truth, it does not tell the whole story. Other issues contributed. Political partisanship, for one thing, was on the rise. Democrats had grown disgruntled with the centralizing tendencies of government and the increasing outcry to turn the war into one against slavery. The system itself was fraught with inefficiencies that would try the patience of the most enthusiastic persons. Also, the change in the government toward recruiting men for three years instead of one struck the public as wrong and unnecessary, especially considering the problems that communities had in caring for the men's families to protect the domestic economy.[4]

Curtin faced real problems maintaining support for the Lincoln administration within Pennsylvania, despite the state's endorsement of the president in 1860. Lincoln had carried the Keystone State by 60,000 votes over all other opponents combined, winning majorities in fifty-three of the state's sixty-five counties. This led to a comfortable Republican majority within the State legislature as well. Yet this performance looked better than it was. The Republican Party remained a nascent institution that arguably gathered more supporters for economic concerns than for antislavery sentiments. But in the 1860 election, the second largest party was an entity called the Fusion Ticket, which united the divided resources of the Democrats. The ticket allowed supporters of both Stephen Douglas and John C. Breckinridge, the Southern Rights Democrat who advocated a Constitutional guarantee for slavery, to cast a vote for the democracy in general with the promise that electors would put the ballots behind whichever candidate had the best chance to win. The ticket amassed an impressive 38 percent of the votes. The strength of Democratic opposition became even more apparent in the 1862 state elections, which reversed the power in the legislature from a Republican to a Democratic majority. The governor himself survived a reelection campaign in 1863 over a state supreme court justice who had gone on record as opposing the draft as unconstitutional.

As great of a concern for the governor was the opposition within his own party. He faced a serious rival in fellow Republican Simon Cameron, who served as the first secretary of war under Lincoln. The difficulties between the two had deep political roots. Curtin grew up in Bellefonte as the son of a prosperous iron manufacturer who owned a 30,000–acre operation in the heart of the state. The young man broke from the family business to pursue a law career but then became immersed in politics as a Whig. He campaigned for Henry Clay, Zachary Taylor, and Winfield Scott. For his assistance in the 1854 gubernatorial campaign, Curtin won the post of secretary of the commonwealth. He and Cameron—then an antislavery Democrat—butted heads the following year as both ran for the U.S. Senate. Cameron won this post, but Curtin took the governor's office in 1860 as a moderate Republican who campaigned on business concerns but remained quiet on slavery. In the meantime, Cameron also had joined the Republican Party. The two men despised each other and formed factions that would try to undercut their rival whenever the situation presented itself.

In the early stages of the conflict, the Democratic Party in Pennsylvania remained supportive of the recruitment efforts. This support for the recruitment drive came, in part, because Major General George McClellan, a well-known Democrat and leader of the Army of the Potomac, repeatedly told the administration that he only needed more troops to bring the war to an end. The Union general remained true to democratic principles of limited war and respect for the Constitution, even if that meant protecting Southern slavery. If the man who would become one of icons for the conservative cause said that he needed more troops to quell the rebellion, then it must be so. Supporting the recruiting drive would help the general and, by extension, lead to triumph of the Union. "Facts, which are stubborn things," noted the *Pittsburgh Post*, "prove that our army should be largely increased." Success was delayed, according to this editor, because the enemy could amass a larger force against McClellan, "perhaps outnumbering his forces three to one." The editor concluded: "What we have to do we must do quickly, and for this we must have more men."[5]

This support, however, was conditional as the democracy increasingly viewed the Republican administration as trying to circumvent the Constitution. Democrats in the Keystone State were picking their slate for the fall elections around the time that Lincoln issued his first call for

300,000 men. As the party's officials assembled at Harrisburg on July 4, the convention adopted twelve resolutions that stressed support for the war, but only if the primary objectives remained preservation of the Union and of the Constitution. The resolutions urged the administration not to free slaves and to reduce government spending. They declared that the Union was a government of white men: African Americans were not entitled to political or social equality. Representatives of the party also decried extremism and opposed sectional interests of any kind. Here they aimed at the radicals who pushed for emancipation of slaves, higher taxes, and stronger measures to punish white Southerners. Finally, the Democratic resolutions opposed the waiving of habeas corpus, stressing that Lincoln had all the power that he needed in the Constitution.[6]

Democratic editors and other party leaders employed racial phobia to mobilize followers behind the notion of a conspiracy within the Republican administration. They typically targeted in this rhetoric the working class in general and the Irish in particular, especially by laying out scenarios of what would happen as fugitive slaves fled from the South. They proclaimed that white laborers would see their wages drop by at least ten cents per day.[7] But they also created the specter of what black men might do in communities with white men away at war. One man wrote the secretary of the commonwealth: "There are 45 Negroes at the Union Water Works and 50 are at the big dam in Elwood and they said that they would wait till the white men would all go to war [then] they would have their fun with the white women. Now I want you to write as soon as you get this if we shall leave them go or if we may shoot them." On October 9, the editor of the *Easton Argus* asked, "How would you like to have a gang of forty or fifty niggers coming to your house, demanding food, or threatening to burn down your barns and houses?"[8]

One other political aspect created suspicion among Democrats. Both sides realized that putting men into the army affected the balance of party power in communities. The ability of soldiers to vote away from home remained ambiguous at this time, a problem not completely rectified until a change in the state constitution for the 1864 election. Where Democrats held a majority, party leaders viewed efforts at recruitment as a means for the Republicans who controlled the Congress to sweep the home front clean of the opposition.

There was some basis for this concern. A party functionary from Uniontown, in the southwest corner of the state, was alarmed in September when it became apparent that a draft might not occur. This would be disastrous, he wrote Curtin, because more than three quarters of the men volunteering from Fayette County had been Republican. A draft could even the balance of power by forcing more Democrats into the army. Without conscription, he believed, the Republican Party could become a minority in the Legislature. A Pittsburgh Republican put it even more bluntly. "*We must have a draft or we are lost.* Nothing short of it can prevent an utter and entire defeat of our party in October."[9] When Democrats won a large share of the elections in the fall, Republicans placed some of the blame on mobilization for the military. In the central part of the state, a Boalsburg man wrote Simon Cameron: "The cause of the elections going Democratic is the Republicans are away fighting the war and the Army did not vote this year."[10]

In addition to political opposition, Curtin had to pay attention to concerns of Pennsylvanians that crossed party lines. These issues grouped themselves into two large categories: (1) the public's attitudes on military service, which included length of service and which occupations should enter first, and (2) the need for bounties as a form of social welfare.

Nineteenth-century attitudes toward the military differed from sentiments that prevail today. Civilians, who then held a militia/volunteer mind-set, expected to meet a relatively finite military emergency and then disband to become civilians once again. They did not expect that soldiers should serve for long tenures. More to the point, communities had few social networks established to absorb long-term losses to the neighborhood economy. Besides, in 1862 they still suspected that the war could not take as long as it did. Even though the South proved to be a stubborn foe, many civilians could not envision the conflict lasting much beyond another year if the Union would only gear up its considerable might. They understood that the North enjoyed considerable advantages in manpower and manufacturing. Even in 1862 it seemed inconceivable that the South could overcome these deficits, if the Union's leaders only would deploy and manage these resources.

Americans in the nineteenth century felt a much more powerful loyalty to their local communities than many people do today. This orientation meant that they hoped that soldiers would serve as close to home as possible, with community defense a paramount concern. It was not unusual for persons from within regions to ask to form units of home guards for local defense as a substitute for organizing regiments in the national service. This local orientation also meant that the men favored forming new regiments over replenishing old ones. Enlisted men could organize new units with friends and relatives. They voted for company and regimental commanders, giving them the chance to serve under familiar men, typically leaders in the community. Upper-class males who fancied themselves as officer material had a greater chance to win commissions if they formed a new command rather than one in the field.

The bias toward new regiments ran contrary to the desires of the federal government, which hoped to stimulate the greatest interest in replenishing the established units. Finally, localism would place communities into competition with each other as they openly enticed recruits from other communities to diminish the impact on their own neighborhoods.

But there is one more element that historians either overlook or stress too little when accounting for the behavior of the recruiting drives of 1862: the related issues of how mobilization affected the local economy and the families of soldiers. This early in the war, civilians did not expect men to enter the service if it stood in the way of the natural flow of labor for the agricultural seasons, and especially if it meant creating hardship for families. The first persons who should go into the service, according to the sensibilities of the time, were men who did not match the profile of the good citizen in a free-labor society, or a person who had not gained independence through owning productive property. Young men without wives or who had not yet established themselves in an occupation were considered the most eligible to answer the call of war. Many of these had enlisted in 1861 with the first wave of volunteers.

Next, community sentiments favored taking agricultural laborers, unskilled workers in towns, or the shiftless in general. Store clerks and other lesser-ranked professionals stood one step higher on the hierarchy of occupations, but they achieved this status more because of the presumption that they did not make natural soldiers: after all, these townsfolk neither hunted as much nor rode as well as good country folk. Highest on the ladder of the social value of labor stood both farmers essential to their operations and mechanics or artisans who supported war-related industries. Whenever civilians complained about the shirkers who remained in a region, they typically cited either young men unattached to family or property (also known as loiterers), or young men from prosperous families who did not work. Both groups contradicted the underlying assumptions of a free-labor society that valued industry and independence.

One could argue that these attitudes describe the orientation of a Republican middle class more than, say, Democrats from the working class. And there were signs of class biases in the attitudes about which class of individuals would make the best soldiers or would have the least impact on a community's social economy. Republicans were stereotyped in the Democratic press as propertied people who had the resources to stay out of military service. From the working-class perspective, these propertied men should pay for others to go to war if they would not go themselves. The *Harrisburg Patriot and Union* noted, for example: "[W]e should like to see some of those rich gentlemen who are averse to fighting themselves, shell out for the benefit of those who will go in if the proper inducements are held out." The editor betrayed the worldview of a perfect free laborer, however, when he proclaimed that one benefit of the draft might be "to see our street corners cleaned out" of the shiftless element in society.[11] Work was among the factors helping determine a male civilian's worth.

While class differences existed, we cannot push them too far because many persons — regardless of politics or class perspective — remained in perfect agreement on a number of issues. Few civilians believed that a man should forsake his principal duty to family or personal economics in favor of nation. Republican and Democratic newspapers, as well as communications with the governor, contained remarkable consensus on this point. Civilians also saw no problem with even agricultural laborers, or the most vulnerable persons, withholding their services from the government — as long as those men still worked or were needed for the local economy. The *Harrisburg Patriot and Union*, for instance, noted: "Until the grain is safely housed no recruiting will meet with much success in this State. We are in the midst of harvest, and the demand for labor was never greater." When the government announced in August its intentions to draft civilians if the quotas were not met, Curtin's mail filled with comments from irate persons who warned about the impact on families and on the economy. A Cumberland County farmer noted that one neighbor "has had two hands and they have both left and went to the army. Now if he whare to be drafted how would [the] crop be put out?" Holding attitudes similar to those that resulted in a planter exemption in the South, this man believed that farms with only one man on them should allow an exemption for that person.[12] Another individual from Wellsboro in north-central Pennsylvania noted that four companies were forming in the area "but to fill them now is more than we can do for they are made up of farmers & they are now busy haying & their grain is fast ripening & they refuse to go now unless it be a strict order so to do."[13]

Very few people, not even good Republican editors, seemed upset by this phenomenon or looked upon the decision to put crops ahead of Union as anything other than natural and just. Most individuals recognized that the men who had entered service in the first year of war probably had done so out of the highest sense of patriotism. While some used military service as the benchmark for proving loyalty, it was not yet a universal equation. No one charged the men of 1862 who put farming ahead of country with disloyalty; nor did they accuse these people of pursuing crass materialism at the expense of the national cause. Civilians at times did worry about such a thing in a society that stressed material pursuit. Early in the year, *Harper's Weekly* fretted about the "National Morality" as it observed: "A commercial nation is always in danger of losing its liberties, because it is willing to sell them for peace and high profits." But in this case the column focused on the contracts for military supplies for its commentary on national greed.[14] Farmers and their agricultural laborers received special dispensation.

A possible reason for the lack of concern was that most persons expected the rush to the colors to increase once the harvesting season ended. Leading journals believed that the flow of transient labor would increase then, making more civilians available for military duty. The recruiting drives hit the city of Philadelphia, for example, when it had very few unemployed persons available. Most had gravitated to the countryside to serve as agricultural workers. In the fall, workers typically flowed back into the city to eke out an existence until the labor demand picked up in the countryside once again. In the meantime, plenty of work was available and wages were high. In Philadelphia, the conditions sent men to the military, according to one observer, who were "mostly store clerks, who have left good situations at their country's call."[15] But civilians expected that the men who would become loiterers in cities over the winter would choose the security of military service over the possibility of privation.

Civilians did not label the men who remained at home shirkers at this point because most understood that without adequate provisions to care for families that communities would have to assume this obligation for volunteers. Although some of this sentiment might be self-serving to avoid higher costs to localities, there existed a genuine concern for the men and for the impact on families without the main providers. Plus, they believed, it was just the right thing to do. As a notice in the *United States Service Magazine* during the war affirmed: "When wages are high, and demand for labor exceeds the supply, temptations beyond the normal pay of a soldier must be offered to induce men to undertake a soldier's life with its perils and hardships. They must also be assured that those who may be dependent upon them shall not suffer in their absence."[16]

Communities already had experienced the high cost of caring for the destitute families of soldiers. Philadelphia provides an example. Beginning in May 1861 a Volunteer Relief Fund had been established to care for 145 families of soldiers. Women drew on this support every two weeks, taking home between one and three dollars weekly. By July 1862, the community had expended roughly $685,000 on this relief effort, and the number of families supported had grown to 7,583. Roughly half of the expenditures came in the seven months between January and July 1862. The high had come in the first week of January, with 11,697 families on the relief rolls.[17] When Lincoln called for troops, the cost had grown so much that the city had tried to trim the roster by limiting aid to wives of soldiers instead of maintaining all dependents, such as sisters or mothers. This created friction among those used to drawing the support. When one woman was denied relief money, she yelled at the clerk that she "hoped the arms would fall from the hands of the soldiers and that they would all turn traitor to the Union."[18]

Consequently, the bounties that historians so often decry as an irritant or a stigma that enervated the recruiting effort were looked upon in the beginning as not only essential to helping the cause but also as the social obligation of the community. Without the existence of an extensive, coordinated relief effort — either statewide or nationally — the burden for charity fell upon communities. Civilians would pay the cost of recruitment in one way or another — if not in the form of a bounty that could help a man's family, then through relief efforts paid for through local donations or taxes. Additionally, bounties circumvented the notion that donations came as charity. The fees served as contractual obligations for men's services, or compensation for the nation's laborers.

II

The new recruiting drive ran contrary to civilian concerns, causing Curtin to defy the national government. It did not take long for the governor to clash with the War Department: the first disputes occurred over having to recruit individuals for three years. Curtin was not the only governor to protest this term. Within a week after Lincoln's call for troops, the governors of Maine, New Jersey, and Massachusetts joined the chorus to reduce the tenure to three or six months. This was unacceptable to Secretary of War Edwin Stanton and flew in the face of military wisdom. Curtin, however, went a great deal further than urging a change in the rules. On July 21, the governor took matters into his own hands in authorizing the state to raise men for nine months in new units and twelve months in old ones. If not outright illegal, the policy directly contradicted the stated wishes of the War Department.

In taking this action, Curtin responded to urgings that came from throughout the state from a variety of civilians, even Republican newspapers. The *Philadelphia Inquirer* consistently expressed the need for enlistment terms of one year. From various portions of the state, individuals also made it known that service for three years was not acceptable and that the longer tenure diminished the response from the state. One man wrote, "It is a most serious undertaking, besides a trial for his friends, that a young man who has grown up among the blessings of peace and competence and who has never felt anything other than parental restraint, to enlist as a soldier for three years." This was not, in this person's mind, an example of unpatriotic behavior. Rather, this civilian justified the attitude based on the contractual right to enter into a labor agreement. "Part of the contract justly belongs to the soldier," he maintained, adding, "If my services to my government for one year at a time are worth anything, it shall have them. If it demands them for no less a term than three years, I claim the right to decline. The policy of enlisting for three years is good, but confining enlistments to a term of three years excludes a worthy class."[19]

While Curtin's action pleased his state, it created consternation among some governors and presented the War Department with a problem that eventually required intervention from Lincoln. Governors E. D. Morgan of New York and Richard Yates of Illinois expressed their outrage at Curtin's action and their desire that the drive for three-year men should continue. Curtin went on blithely raising regiments to suit his state's needs, while focusing primarily on forming new units rather than replenishing old ones — again contrary to national priorities but in synch with local desires. Publicly, the governor received a mild slap on the wrists from the War Department. An official in charge of recruiting, C. P. Buckingham, sent an open letter indicating that it was inexpedient to raise troops for anything other than three years, but he recognized that the government could do nothing to stop a governor from calling out troops for state service. The key was whether the government would accept these short-term units as national recruits who fulfilled the quotas of the state. For the moment, Buckingham said, the national government would accept these regiments — but only because of the emergency.

Lincoln himself had encouraged this decision, but not because he wanted to. Two days after Curtin announced his policy, the president sent a note to Stanton about this situation. "It is a question whether we should accept the troops under the call of Gov. Curtin for 9 months men & 12 months men," he observed, adding, "I understand you say it rests with me under the law— Perhaps it does; but I do not wish to decide it without your concurrence.— what say you? If we do not take these after what has happened, we shall fail perhaps to get any on other terms from Pennsylvania."[20] Lincoln's statements suggest the tensions behind the scenes between the chief executive and his department head. The governor's action obviously had troubled Stanton because it allowed Pennsylvania a privilege denied to other states. Clearly, the secretary of war did not believe he had Lincoln on his side in forcing Curtin to comply and tried to shift the responsibility — and thus the heat from other governors — to the president for the preferential treatment of Pennsylvania. Lincoln sought a consensus on the decision from his department head, but it is not known whether he received it from Stanton.

The War Department underscored that the troops would be accepted, but only as a last resort. On July 25, Adjutant General Lorenzo Thomas conceded that authorities would accept the regiments of nine- and twelve-months' men from Pennsylvania. But he added that because the governor of Pennsylvania had adopted the policy "without previous consultation or direction of the President or the War Dept., & having been made it was deemed by the President & by the War Department better to accept such troops as were offered under that call," that the government would not pay the men in these units the complete federal bounty. The men could qualify for the twenty-five dollars paid for mustering in, but they would not receive the additional seventy-five dollars upon mustering out.[21] This was a hollow gesture that did not change the amount of money that men received at the more crucial point — when entering military service. The state continued to recruit troops in this manner until the new drive in August, when the federal government allowed the organization of soldiers for nine months.

Despite this exception for Pennsylvania, recruiting progressed slowly as civilians waited to see the kind of bounties that would be offered. The possibilities expanded nearly exponentially as towns and states adopted a variety of payment plans to encourage enlistments. Men waited not necessarily because of a lack of patriotism but because they hoped to secure as much money as possible to protect their families. Actions by the governor of New York ironically had an adverse affect on recruiting. The Empire State first offered recruits an additional $25 for enlisting and then, within a few more days, raised the ante to $50. Added to the federal bounty of $25 and the one month's pay given in advance, the total amounted to $83 for enlisting, versus $38 in Pennsylvania. Throughout the counties along the northern tier of the state, men crossed the border to secure the higher bounties. An attorney from Montrose told the governor that it was hard to get men, "when stepping over the line into New York State they can get in addition to all we can offer, the fifty dollars which Gov Morgan has taken the responsibility of offering to all volunteers." From Tioga County, a county commissioner noted that the local government attempted to stop the hemorrhaging by setting up its own bounty. He had estimated that the county lost at least one hundred men who left to enlist in adjoining counties in New York State. These men and others urged Governor Curtin to call a special session of the Legislature to enact bounties.[22]

Faced with a precarious political situation, Curtin steered around the issue. He would not assume responsibility for bounties because he claimed he had no authority to spend money in this manner. He refused to call an emergency session of the legislature, saying that there was no time to do so, and that "Delay may be fatal." A letter from a constituent provides a more plausible reason behind the governor's stand. Thomas E. Cochran of York, who served as auditor general of the state, indicated to the governor that he had "grave objections" to calling the legislature into special session. He cited the expense of the bounty and the delay that would result from politicians dickering over the issue. But he especially feared "the *political* effect of such a call." He explained: "Once in session, the subjects and duration of its legislation are within its own control." This could have given Democratic politicians a vehicle to cause more harm than good. Instead, he suggested that Curtin establish a state fund into which county commissioners, municipal corporations, and private individuals could donate money to use for state bounties.[23]

Pennsylvania never adopted a state bounty in 1862, forcing on communities the responsibility for raising and distributing money to spark recruitments. They used two principle means: contributions from community leaders (whether through corporations or as individuals) and municipal resources raised through taxes. The first method fulfilled the class notions expressed earlier that the more prosperous people had an obligation to serve as proper stewards, if not by serving directly then by making it possible for others to go to war. Philadelphia's elite established a volunteer bounty fund, to which the Pennsylvania Railroad pledged $50,000. The Reading Railroad kicked in another $25,000. By September 1862 this organization had collected $460,000. Meanwhile, the city's elected officials followed the more typical course by establishing a municipal fund, to which they pledged $500,000. Philadelphians also established a division of labor, with the Citizens Bounty Fund dispersing funds to men joining new regiments and the municipal fund going to those replenishing old units. Further complicating the issue was how to reward men who signed up for different lengths of service. The city established three different bounties based on tenure of service: $20 for nine-months' service, $30 for twelve-months', and $50 for three-years' or the duration of the war.

Of course this did not end all competition. Curtin's policy exacerbated the friction between communities, especially ones located near more prosperous towns and cities. Bucks County near Philadelphia provides an example. Because the City of Brotherly Love had the resources and financial leaders who could act relatively quickly in establishing bounties, this put pressure on areas that needed more time to build their war chests. Bucks County reported difficulties in raising recruits, with an official there noting: "Owing to the tardiness of our county authorities in offering bounties a large number of our citizens have gone to

Phila. & recruited in Regts making up there."[24] Additionally, individual regiments often promised bonus money raised by a rich officer, community leaders, or other benefactor. This had at least two repercussions. In a large city like Philadelphia, the additional bounties actually slowed the organization of regiments by putting a number of different units into competition for recruits. At one point, as many as eleven regiments tried to attract new soldiers, while none had enough to go into the field. Secondly, smaller communities often felt the competitive pressure from their bigger, richer cousins. The leaders of some units opened branch offices in other towns and counties to see if they could find more bodies. A man in Lewistown complained to the state's adjutant general that a recruiting office for a brigade had opened "offering almost fabulous bounties, as well as offices."[25]

Although Pennsylvanians benefited from shorter terms for military service, a variety of bounties had sprung up, giving men an array of choices for both compensation and terms of service. At any given moment, men could opt for nine months, twelve months, and three years, with a variety of bounty packages. Plus, they could join new regiments or replenish established ones. The choices extended beyond the community — men could shop for a locality that offered more competitive rates than their hometowns, although most probably stayed within their environs. Instead of speeding up the process, the mechanism for raising the troops — and the local attitudes of the men themselves — lengthened it.

III

On August 4, 1862, the federal government laid plans for the draft that never happened nationally. Troops had responded to the president's call of early July, but too slowly. Stanton issued an order for 300,000 additional soldiers to be enlisted for nine months under the president's authority to call out the state militia. This had been made possible only several weeks earlier through legislation enacted on July 17 that enabled the president to call out militia for longer duration than ninety days. If these additional 300,000 troops failed to materialize by August 15, states would have to draft men to fill the quotas for the new muster.

The news jolted the North into more frenetic recruiting activity, while also escalating confusion, anxiety, and discontent. Although respectable numbers of recruits eventually answered both calls of the summer of 1862, the experience demonstrated that the system needed greater federal supervision. Additionally, the preparation for a draft through August and September signaled a subtle but important shift in community attitudes about the civilian men who ignored the recruiting drive. As resistance grew toward conscription, Republicans increasingly branded such activity as disloyal. Support for a man's right to ensure the security of his family similarly diminished from the Republican press.

On paper a draft sounded fairly simple, but in practice the second call for troops created numerous logistical and bureaucratic problems. First came the concern of how to mesh the earlier recruiting with the new call. Governors and others from around the country flooded the War Department with requests for clarification of how recruits in the pipeline might affect both new and old quotas. At the same time, state and local officials struggled with putting the draft mechanism into place. It took much more effort than anyone could have imagined. The governor had to appoint officials to enroll eligible persons, others to administer the lottery, and physicians to screen recruits. Regulations were not even written when the federal government announced its intentions. The first rules came out five days after the order, and some communities did not receive specific instructions on the procedures for the enrollment until August 23. State and national governments had to cooperate in supplying the soldiers with arms, food, shelter, and pay. States had the responsibility for supplying troops without the authority to set terms or handle issues of pay and supply. The federal government, meanwhile, dictated the terms and handled the final organization of the soldiers but had no control over furnishing the troops. The arrangement had forged a marriage of partners with irreconcilable differences.

Curtin objected less to a draft than to being forced to administer it. If the War Department directed recruitment, it would deflect criticism from the governor toward the national administration. When that shift in responsibility did not occur, he and others throughout the state raised a host of questions. They sounded a bit like fallen acolytes trying to trap the parish priest in theological inconsistencies, but their concerns — and the confusion — were genuine. Did Pennsylvania have to raise troops by congressional districts or could they organize by towns and counties? What if a particular town already had fulfilled its quota of three-year men? Should the townsfolk be subject to a further quota even though they had proved themselves to be good patriots? And what should be done with the men in the pipeline? Some had signed up but were waiting until regiments filled before being accepted by the government. What happened to them if they were not organized by August 15? Also, could minors enlist? If so, what kind of permission did they need — verbal or written? Finally, how about foreigners who were not yet citizens? Could they count against a state's quota?

The responses by federal authorities showed that they cared less about these issues than getting men to the front. War Department officials only wanted the manpower, no matter how it came. To most of these questions, the government answered affirmatively or told state authorities to rule on it themselves. This meant the state could accept minors and apportion quotas to communities as it pleased, as long as it hit the targeted quota overall. On one area, however, federal and state officials agreed: African Americans would not be part of the recruitment efforts. The militia act of July 17 had allowed the government to go ahead and enlist black men in the army, but the War Department rejected this choice and very few of the governors indicated any desire to recruit African Americans.

But the government did have to exert some direction to the recruitment drive. To clarify the issue of quotas between first and second calls, the War Department ultimately set up a formula by which authorities counted a recruit who enlisted for three years as worth four nine-months' men. Effectively, this meant that Lincoln and his advisers did not actually target 600,000 men for the recruiting drives but hoped to gain the equivalent of 375,000 men enlisting for three years. The men already in the pipeline were to be accepted until August 22. After that time, anyone entering new regiments would receive no bounties or advance pay from the United States (local bounties still applied), but volunteers filling old regiments could earn both until September 1.[26]

On August 9, Stanton issued orders that clarified the procedures. Each county would have a commissioner and an enrolling officer appointed by the governor. Enrollment officers would go door-to-door through communities to prepare lists of men eligible for the draft. Communities needed this kind of census work to account for the men who had left for war already, as well as identify who was eligible. The draft pool would consist of all males from eighteen to forty-five. This posed a problem for Pennsylvania because state law stipulated age twenty, and not eighteen, as the minimum for service. Certain persons would be exempt because of occupation — the usual public officials and civilians deemed necessary for the public good. Names of draftees would be placed in a container from which a blindfolded designee would draw the names of conscripts. The first draft was to be held on August 15, although it quickly became apparent that this was unreasonable. September 3 became the next date.[27] Other than these guidelines, the department gave the state wide latitude in how it filled the quotas. Governors could decide most of the issues surrounding implementation. Of course, this opened a whole new level of patronage to state officials. Governors appointed the assessors to prepare rosters of military-aged males within particular regions, as well as commissioners of the draft and physicians. States also collaborated in naming provost marshals who would police against desertion or other disturbances against the draft.

Instead of taking this on himself, Curtin opted to let local leaders select their men, reserving the right for a final veto. Once again, he wanted to assume a low profile that would not give political opponents an easy target. This kind of decentralized decision-making was excruciatingly slow. From the federal perspective, it could appear as if Curtin were deliberately hampering the selection process. It is possible that he was, but there was enough confusion and enough political issues at stake to warrant caution on his part. When this approach failed to produce results, Curtin attempted to coordinate these efforts better by appointing near the end of August his friend and Republican crony Alexander K. McClure—a newspaperman from Chambersburg—to direct the draft in the state. McClure paid particular attention to giving the appointments the appearance of nonpartisanship.[28]

Curtin deserved the vexation of the War Department for exerting little control over the raising of regiments throughout August. He allowed anyone who wanted to organize one to go right ahead. This created greater competition for recruits, ignored the needs of the veteran regiments, and meant that soldiers who might have been at the front were waiting in camps instead of being expedited into regiments. For example, at one point the state had two thousand soldiers in camp. This number could have formed two full regiments, but the men were distributed over four units, each of which competed for soldiers. None of them had enough men individually to be turned over to the federal government. At one point in August, eleven colonels in Philadelphia vied for recruits without any of the regiments being full. Enough soldiers existed to form several regiments. Instead of consolidating them, Curtin ignored the situation, despite urging by the War Department.[29]

Curtin had a more legitimate defense when it came to supplies. Recruitment of any sort created stress on the army's supply system. The military had improved in this capacity since the first year of war; however, the system still creaked under the strain. Governors throughout the Union complained about having troops at hand but no arms to give them or, most often, tents for shelter. At times, pay was handled ineptly. Some states covered the shortfall or sent the men on without weapons so they could be armed in the field.

Worse, agents of the War Department seemed ill informed and ill suited for administering the system. Their sheer incompetence could block recruitment momentum. Governor John Andrew of Massachusetts, for example, was a staunch Radical Republican who supported the war effort to the utmost. Yet even he had problems with the national government. Andrew could not get a quartermaster mustered in because a particular regiment had not organized. But he could not get a regiment organized because he had no way to acquire stores or to set the men up in camp. Just before the Battle of Second Bull Run he noted to Stanton: "If I were capable of discouragement I should be almost discouraged by the obstacles which block my efforts at every turn. If the whole recruitment, transportation, and equipment were left to the State, as last year, we should be a month ahead of our present position."[30]

Curtin was no John Andrew. Instead of overcoming obstacles, he made the most of them. He complained about a lack of weapons for his soldiers, claiming that the Constitution prevented him from sending troops outside of the state without arms. He reminded the War Department that the state had few weapons on hand because the government wanted to limit competition for the purchasing of arms. When urged by the department to bend, he refused to consolidate the recruits into regiments. Doing so potentially would have angered the elites who wanted to lead their own regiments — and raised bounties for this privilege — or disappointed the men who hoped to be with familiar persons. Even the president could not persuade the governor to act more urgently. Lincoln typically did not intervene in the military traffic of the War Department unless he could not help himself. On August 12 he implored Curtin: "It is very important for some regiments to arrive here at once." As usual with the governor of an important state, Lincoln took a politic approach in allowing the blame to fall on the federal bureaucracy. "What lack you from us?" he asked Curtin, adding, "What can we do to expedite matters?" The governor firmly maintained that he could not move his men until the federal government came through with arms.[31]

The secretary of war, presumably backed by Lincoln, did not accept this excuse. Department officials had investigated the supply situation and, while discovering a shortage of tents and some other goods, believed that the arms situation was in fairly good shape. General-in-Chief Henry Wager Halleck believed that Curtin had access to thirty thousand weapons and that the governor refused to issue them. Even if he did not have that number of arms, officials predicted that a shipment of fifteen thousand muskets was due any day. The War Department began to divert personnel into the state to ferret out what was going on and see if troops could get to the front. Because western Pennsylvania had responded well, federal authorities concentrated their efforts at Camp Curtin near Harrisburg and the city of Philadelphia.

The department had dispatched Brigadier General William Scott Ketchum to inspect Pennsylvania, then New York, but detained the officer in the Keystone State because authorities no longer trusted the governor. On August 13, General-in-Chief Halleck ordered Ketchum to muster into U.S. service all available men, whether armed or not. He point blank told Ketchum to take control of the men and disregard any orders from Curtin. Not content with those measures, Halleck the same day dispatched still another adjutant general to assess the situation, Major General John Wool. When Halleck told Ketchum about the pending visit, he reiterated that the general should take "the most summary measures" to muster in troops. Within a day, Ketchum had organized and sent two regiments out of the state.[32]

When Wool arrived in Harrisburg on August 15, he added more evidence that the state handled recruitment ineptly. Wool reported that weapons—contrary to the governor's position—were available to the troops. "If any delay occurs," he observed, "it must be attributed to the State officer in not appointing officers." In addition to the two regiments Ketchum had sent forward, another one was leaving from Lancaster and two more from Harrisburg. That brought the total to five regiments that suddenly could move with different people in charge. Wool then went to Philadelphia, where he found the eleven different regiments competing for troops and indicated they should consolidate. Despite these reports, Curtin continued to say that he needed arms and refused to reorganize the regiments. Instead, the governor pushed back the date for a draft, asked the government for soldiers to police the home front, and wondered whether he could enlist men into ethnic Irish and German units, further fragmenting the recruiting effort. Exasperated by the situation, the governor told the War Department that he thought he could move more troops into the field, then wondered: "If I make suggestions as in my judgment would produce that result, is it probable they would be adopted?" No reply came, but the answer probably was "no."[33]

A third visit from the War Department, in the form of Lorenzo Thomas in late August, makes the case stronger that the governor exerted little energy in pushing forward volunteers, although it does suggest that he had some basis for complaining about a lack of arms. Thomas arrived in Harrisburg on August 28 and then pressed on to Philadelphia when he made the indictment with which this article opened—that excuses, and not actual deficiencies, prevented men from being sent to the front. Thomas on September 1 reported that two armed regiments had gone; three more regiments were expected to leave by the following day. The latter units did not have weapons yet, lending some credence to Curtin's interpretation of supply. But the War Department showed itself willing to arm regiments from different arsenals if shortages occurred. Also, Thomas had managed to send two armed regiments to the front almost immediately, underscoring that Pennsylvania's recruiting effort lacked both energy and good coordination.[34] It was not good business for the governor to break up the forming of regiments and consolidate them into different arrangements.

We can attribute part of Curtin's caution to signs of increasing resistance to the recruitment of soldiers, especially through conscription.

Supporters of the administration likely increased anxiety at the capital with rumors of persons promising violent opposition to a draft. Undoubtedly, civilians inflated this concern based on a small number of incidents and murmuring of the opposition. South-central, south-western, and northeastern Pennsylvania provided the most concern. Republicans feared people they referred to as "Breckenridge men," or supporters of the Southern Rights Democrat who ran for president from Kentucky in 1860. Along the southern tier the numbers may have been small, but the opposition to the draft seemed to be on the rise. In Bedford County a man claimed that twenty to forty persons met in one township to conspire against the draft, "that a loyal man had been urged to join them that arms &c. were being prepared to resist the authorities." In Uniontown, men called "disunionists" reportedly declared "this is a black Republican & Abolition War, and any who volunteer are damned fools." In the same relative area, a man in Mount Pleasant caused uproar by pinning the U.S. flag to his shirt tail and parading through the streets "armed to the teeth and bidding defiance to the loyal People of the place." In Lancaster County, a correspondent reported a league forming numbering 130 persons determined to resist the draft.[35] The most known, and studied, resistance broke out across the coal region in northeastern Pennsylvania, although recent scholarship has characterized this resistance as part of labor unrest rather than antiwar sentiment.[36]

While historians today have the luxury of distinguishing and categorizing the dissent that awakened in the fall of 1862, the civilians living through this time could not. Even small monsters can feel larger in the darkness. Supporters of the administration began to define as treasonous the men who stayed at home and openly proclaimed their opposition to the draft. Blame for resistance most often fell on Democratic regions, especially those containing significant concentrations of Irish immigrants. Class assumptions affected the portrayal of disloyalty. Middle-class notions of respectability worked against some persons. Letters to the governor depicted the traitors as men who hung around barrooms in boarding houses and spread treasonous talk. Two men from Philadelphia informed the governor that regional newspapers fed the poison by advocating resistance to the draft. "While we as loyal patriotic men are straining every nerve to raise funds and men in order to help you get your quota up here — are we to be so grossly insulted by a traitor in the shape of a Democratic Editor of a treasonable County Sheet[?] . . . The patriotic men *all over the State as here in Phila* call upon you as Gov. of this great Commonwealth to *crush out promptly* every means which have a tendency towards the retarding of enlistments." Another person from Philadelphia, David Evans, had just returned from Easton and Bethlehem, where he had seen "Breckenridge men almost openly offering large Bounties to men to stay at home, against our Bounty inviting them to go."[37] Disloyalty was being equated not necessarily with men who stayed at home but with civilians who did not help the cause by raising funds or encouraging recruitment.

Wide-scale, violent resistance failed to materialize in Pennsylvania, but the threat had a telling effect on the governor that spread to the Lincoln administration. Federal soldiers were sent into the state to secure the coal regions and help the process of enlistment. Curtin, like most governors, kept pushing back the draft because of these problems. He hoped to buy time to let volunteering take its course and fill the quotas without resorting to conscription.

Ultimately, the militia draft never happened quite as planned. As one governor after another protested the short time-frame and dealt with the political fallout, they also pushed back the deadline for a draft. The War Department never punished any state for this and, in fact, kept extending the draft until it finally disappeared altogether. Some communities conducted lotteries to select conscripts, but enforcement of the drawing was uneven. Although the two calls of July and August never achieved the 600,000 men requested, they accounted for 421,465 men for three years (well above the 334,000 quota) and another 87,588 men in nine-month regiments. Pennsylvania never quite fulfilled its targets, falling short on the first call by more than 14,000 (45,321 minus 30,891) and the second call by 13,000 (45,321 minus 32,215). The recruiting effort had succeeded but not necessarily as the planners had intended. The government raised more three-year men than Lincoln's original call of July 2, which was its top priority. And it received additional nine-month regiments, some of which would distinguish themselves in the months ahead.[38] Perhaps most significantly, all learned that future conscription efforts required a different system entirely — one that would necessitate much tighter federal direction.

IV

The actions of the governor and the civilians of his state reveal patterns in the content of American national identity in the nineteenth century. Based on the overall performance of Curtin and Pennsylvania throughout four years of horrific struggle, one could hardly characterize either the person or the population as disloyal; however, the state did contain vigorous dissent that influenced how the governor attacked recruitment. It caused him to decide arbitrarily to cut the term of military service in July and to employ a softer hand in organizing soldiers into regiments. Community values, shared by persons across class and political lines, dictated some of the measures possible for raising soldiers in the Keystone State in 1862. These included shorter military service than three years, the need for bounties to protect families, the desire to form new regiments with familiar men from the same community, and the hope to remain home if performing work acknowledged as valuable for either family or neighborhood. The public attitudes that shaped these policies mirrored those of Confederate civilians who had experienced the prior April the encroachment of the nation-state in the form of the first national draft in American history.

Unlike Southerners, the most disaffected persons in the Union increasingly found expression through political channels, with the Democrat Party becoming the opposition to the administration. Similarly, Republicans began to look upon men who stayed out of the war — especially unattached males or certain immigrants — as disloyal. Those who remained home at the end of the recruitment drive could be stigmatized by Republicans as disloyal men, especially if they had no apparent means of support and/or hung around the local taverns. But even if a person sought work, he could be branded as suspect in his loyalties. A man from central Pennsylvania wrote the governor in September, "In my country's troubles I have given all my sons . . . and am entirely left alone to do the farming, and hardly a man can be hired as all the young able bodied men from these parts are gone to war except some few semi-loyal."[39] This quotation suggests that other factors than one's usefulness to the home front started entering into the picture of how to assess the loyalty of a civilian.

Northern identities were not more "national" than their Southern cousins' — at least not consistently so, and especially if one defines nationalism as recognition of the nation-state as the supreme or primary loyalty. Instead, a person's imagined community in nineteenth-century America led through a hierarchy that began with the family, then the neighborhood, fanning out to embrace church, sewing circle, tavern, township, county, state, and then Union or Confederacy. The locality did not serve the interest of the nation, but the nation-state had to represent, protect, and nurture the interests of the locality.

This created a situation ripe for dissenting views of what the larger entity should be. The United States, after all, represented a fairly young club in which the members still argued about the rules and procedures. A definition of nationalism remained ambiguous under a loose federal system. Even in the case of more mature nation-states, disagreement over the character and goals of the people — indeed even over which of "the people" should be considered citizens — are typical. National identities rarely exist as unanimous, uncontested terrain. In fact, "the nation" gains a portion of its life from some form of opposition — either from within through "disloyal" elements (immigrants, Catholics, and so on) or from without through the "other" (Rebels, Yankees, or other threats). Northerners in 1862 underwent a process in which they debated, through their actions and through their politics, what national service should mean. Staying home might be acceptable as long as one helped the Union war effort, rather than proclaimed one's desire to block recruitment or the efforts of enrollment officers. The exigencies of war raised the stakes on the meaning of that conflict as Northerners hardened in their attitudes to accept the emancipation of slaves as an additional aim of the war.

If we use Pennsylvania's behavior during the recruiting drives of 1862 as a foil with the South, we can appreciate the problems of evaluating the viability of Confederate identity. States within the Confederacy — especially North Carolina and Georgia — have been branded as having suspect national identity partly because of the actions of their governors to contest conscription. North Carolina's Zebulon Vance and Georgia's Joseph E. Brown led some of the loudest and longest opposition to centralized measures, typified by conscription. Vance earned the reputation of a defender of the common folk who tried to keep at bay the more harmful consolidation of power in what he often saw as a biased government under Jefferson Davis.

It is tempting to think of Curtin as the North's Zebulon Vance. On the surface, they share similarities. Both came from Whig backgrounds. Like Curtin, Vance supported the national entity, mobilizing an incredible number of men to military service. Like Vance, Curtin's biggest collisions with the federal government came over mobilization. Additionally, both men led states extremely divided by factionalism. North Carolina featured the only openly two-party political battles in the Confederacy, which deliberately had shunned the formation of national parties. Vance held off a growing peace movement. Curtin presided over a fractured state with a democratic opposition that gained significantly at the polls in 1862 and threatened to unseat him in 1863. Both men served key roles at governors' conferences that pledged continued support to their respective governments and war efforts. They also enjoyed popularity as men who represented the enlisted man, with Curtin earning the designation "the Soldier's Friend" for his relief efforts for the troops.

Upon greater inspection, though, the comparison wears thin. Curtin never opposed the government with the same stridency or consistency. He shared the political party of his president, as well as the chief executive's moderate views. He also failed to employ the political ideology of state rights — or any political ideology for that matter — as the means of explaining his actions. In fact, Curtin would not have viewed himself as opposing the government in any way, while Vance assumed the posture of combatting Jefferson Davis. Curtin's intransigence needs to be teased from the record, which leaves a difficult trail marked more by quiet resistance and bureaucratic frustration than outspoken defiance. Additionally, Vance may have enjoyed a more solid political base — or had greater political savvy — than his Northern counterpart. Vance won his reelection in 1864 with the support of roughly 80 percent of the electorate. In 1863, Curtin survived his election by a 15,000-vote margin out of 500,000 votes cast.[40] Yet scholars do not characterize Pennsylvanians as having imperfect nationalism, while they have cast doubt on the loyalties — or at least the national will — of North Carolinians.

So, while Curtin was an obstacle to recruiting, it remains to be decided whether he deliberately slowed the raising of troops. The answer is both yes and no: that he believed the federal measures would not work with the peculiar situation in Pennsylvania. Curtin undoubtedly believed that he acted in the best interests of the country — that the national government did not understand the tensions within the Keystone State that had to be handled with great care. When he arbitrarily cut the tenure for enlistments to nine months, he figured that having tens of thousands of nine-month soldiers on hand was better than fielding fewer regiments of three-year soldiers. He also was somewhat naïve when it came to military affairs. During the Antietam campaign of September 1862, the governor rode into Maryland and tried to have the federal government allow him to amass an army of 30,000 men, whom he would lead in a defense of his state even if he had to advance beyond its borders. He clearly did not understand military needs from a national perspective.

While a certain amount of administrative incompetence on his part contributed to the situation, he did not push troops out of mustering camps and into federal service in 1862 primarily because of his understanding of the problems at home. He would not call the legislature into emergency session to appropriate state bounties or seize control of the recruitment effort, begging the national government to take the lead instead and pushing the appointment of agents onto local leaders. These stands were taken to deflect public anger from state officials, while letting local or national officials take the blame for resentment of recruitment. Curtin clearly paid more attention to the needs of home than the demands of the Union to protect his wing of the Republican party. Yet he justified this course as the one that would best serve the Union by gaining the most troops possible under the circumstances. In the short run, his actions prevented soldiers from getting to the front more quickly, costing him credibility with the War Department. In the long run, he mobilized a significant portion of the state's population to serve the war effort. The governor consequently acted as a political leader out to protect his turf; however, he did so as a man in harmony with the social values of local communities and the imperfect nationalism of his nineteenth-century constituency.

Notes

1. *The War of the Rebellion: A Compilation of the Official Records of the Union and Confederate Armies* (Washington, D.C., 1880–1901), ser. 3, vol. 2:497 (hereafter cited as *OR*).

2. Scholars of the Civil War home front attribute resistance to mobilization to several dynamics: political fighting, class conflict, and centralization of government. For a sampling of the literature, see Frank L. Klement, *The Copperheads in the Middle West* (Chicago, 1960); Arnold M. Shankman, *The Pennsylvania Antiwar Movement* (Cranberry, N.J., 1980); Grace Palladino, *Another Civil War: Labor, Capital, and the State in the Anthracite Regions of Pennsylvania, 1840–68* (Urbana, Ill., 1990); Iver Bernstein, *The New York City Draft Riots: Their Significance for American Society and Politics in the Age of the Civil War* (New York, 1990); Jörg Nagler, "Loyalty and Dissent: The Home Front in the American Civil War," in *On the Road to Total War: The American Civil War and the German Wars of Unification, 1861–1871*, eds. Stig Förster and Jörg Nagler (Cambridge, 1997), 239–356.

3. David M. Potter, "The Historian's Use of Nationalism and Vice Versa," in *The South and the Sectional Conflict* (Baton Rouge, 1968), 34–83.

4. James W. Geary, *We Need Men: The Union Draft in the Civil War* (DeKalb, Ill., 1991), 107.

5. *The Pittsburgh Post*, July 2, 1862. See also Shankman, *Pennsylvania Antiwar Movement*, 87.

6. *The Pittsburgh Post*, July 7, 1862.

7. Wage figures from *Trenton True American*, quoted in *The Pittsburgh Post*, July 4, 1862.

8. Quoted in Shankman, *The Pennsylvania Antiwar Movement*, 99.

9. S. Fuller to Governor Curtin, September 4, 1862, and J. W. Blanchard to A. K. McClure, September 3, 1862, both in Office of Adjutant General, General Correspondence, Record Group 19, Pennsylvania Historical and Museum Commission, box 16 (hereafter OAG-PHMC).

10. James S. Brisbin to Simon Cameron, October 25, 1862, Cameron Papers, Library of Congress, microfilm, reel 8.

11. *Harrisburg Patriot and Union*, July 16, 1862.

12. *Harrisburg Patriot and Union*, July 14, 1862; John Schenck to "Sir," September 8, 1862, OAG-PHMC, box 16.

13. R. W. Jackson to A. G. Russell, August 5, 1862, OAG-PHMC, box 15.

14. *Harper's Weekly*, March 1, 1862.

15. *Philadelphia Inquirer*, August 1, 1862. See the same newspaper on August 16 for comments about the ebb and flow of labor between town and coun-

try. For a similar view, consult Ed Scull to A. L. Russell, August 3, 1862, OAG-PHMC, box 15.

16. Quoted in James W. Geary, "Civil War Conscription in the North: A Historiographical Review," *Civil War History*, 32, no. 3 (1986): 214.

17. J. Matthew Gallman, *Mastering Wartime: A Social History of Philadelphia during the Civil War* (Cambridge, 1990), 17–19; *Philadelphia Inquirer*, July 25, July 26, August 9, 1862.

18. *Philadelphia Inquirer*, July 5, 1862.

19. *Philadelphia Inquirer*, July 19, 1862; John Hamilton to A. G. Curtin, July 23, 1862, OAG-PHMC, box 15.

20. Abraham Lincoln to the secretary of war, July 23, 1862, OAG-PHMC, box 15.

21. *OR*, ser. 3, vol. 2:253, 255; Lorenzo Thomas to Captain W. B. Lane, July 25, 1862, OAG-PHMC, box 15.

22. W. and W. H. Jessup to Governor A. G. Curtin, July 22, and Robert Simpson to Andrew G. Curtin, July 30, 1862, both in OAG-PHMC, box 15.

23. Thomas E. Cochran to Hon. A. G. Curtin, July 20, 1862, OAG-PHMC, box 15.

24. John Ely to A. L. Russell, August 10, 1862, OAG-PHMC, box 15.

25. John Levan to A. L. Russell, August 15, 1862, OAG-PHMC, box 15.

26. General Orders No. 108, War Department, August 16, 1862, in OAG-PHMC, box 15.

27. *OR*, ser. 3, vol 2:333–35; Geary, *We Need Men*, 34–35.

28. Alexander K. McClure, *Old Time Notes of Pennsylvania*, 2 vols. (Philadephia, 1905), 1:543–34.

29. *OR*, ser. 3, vol. 2:422.

30. *OR*, ser. 3, vol. 2:474, 479–80.

31. *OR*, ser. 3, vol. 2:366–68.

32. *OR*, ser. 3, vol. 2:345, 379–80, 386, 394.

33. *OR*, ser. 3, vol. 2:394, 422.

34. *OR*, ser. 3, vol. 2:497.

35. R. D. Barclay to A. G. Curtin, August 28, 1862, John Collins to A. L. Russell, August 8, 1862, and Joseph Lippencott and others to A. G. Curtin, August 7, 1862, OAG-PHMC, box 15; W. H. Kindig to Gov. A. G. Curtin, September 2, 1862, OAG-PHMC, box 16.

36. Palladino, *Another Civil War*. For a different view of draft resistance, see Mark E. Neely Jr., *The Fate of Liberty: Abraham Lincoln and Civil Liberties* (New York, 1991), 57–58.

37. D. C. A. Clarke and A. H. Fuller to A. G. Curtin, August 2, 1862, OAG-PHMC, box 15.

38. *OR*, ser. 3, vol. 4:1264–65.

39. Joseph Baker to Governor Curtin, September 2, 1862, OAG-PHMC, box 16.

40. Philip S. Klein and Ari Hoogenboom, *A History of Pennsylvania*, 2nd ed. (University Park, Pa., 1980), 356–58; Alexander K. McClure, *Abraham Lincoln and Men of War-Times* (Philadelphia, 1892), 261–66.

Fig. 1. The silence of defeat. *Cathedral of St. John and St. Finbar, Charleston, S.C. Photograph of the Federal Navy and seaborne expeditions against the Atlantic Coast of the Confederacy, 1863–1865. Courtesy of Prints and Photographs Division, Library of Congress.*

Fig. 2. Sea-Island School, No. 1, St. Helena Island, established in April 1862. This was one of the first schools in which Northern female teachers taught former slaves in the occupied Confederacy. The illustration appeared on a broadside published by the Pennsylvania Freedmen's Relief Association after the war. *Courtesy of the American Memory Collection, Library of Congress.*

MARRIAGE OF A COLORED SOLDIER AT VICKSBURG BY CHAPLAIN WARREN OF THE FREEDMEN'S BUREAU.

Fig. 3. Freedpeople in the Natchez District called wedding ceremonies performed by army officers, like this ceremony in the summer of 1866, getting married "under the flag." Harper's Weekly, *30 June 1866.*

Fig. 4. Images of home, which meant so much to soldiers in the Fredericksburg campaign in 1863. Harper's Weekly, 3 January 1866.

Fig. 5. Virginia farmer John Dull, with daughter Cornelia and wife Jane, ca. 1861. After John was killed in the Confederate service near Petersburg on March 25, 1865, Jane never remarried. *Courtesy of Special Collections, Leyburn Library, Washington and Lee University.*

FRANCHISE.

And Not This Man?"

August 5, 1865

Fig. 6. Thomas Nast's image of a wounded veteran captures the sense of accomplishment and anticipation among black U.S. army veterans at the war's end.

Fig. 7. This *carte de visite* of Anna Dickinson — one of many photographs of Dickinson in circulation during the war era — was distributed by Wilson Brothers of Hartford, Connecticut. *Courtesy of Matthew Gallman.*

Fig. 8. Andrew Curtin, governor of Pennsylvania, who worried Federal authorities with what appeared to be delaying tactics in the mobilization drive of 1862. *From William H. Egle,* An Illustrated History of the Commonwealth of Pennsylvania *(Harrisburg, Pa., 1878).*

Fig. 9. Residence of Abraham and Elizabeth Brian, taken in 1863. The farm of these free blacks was located on the northern end of Cemetery Ridge near the apex of Pickett's Charge. *Courtesy of Prints and Photographs Division, Library of Congress.*

READS THE PAPERS.

Our Friend, Mr. JONES, who is deeply interested in the condition of the country, takes all the Papers, and reads them thoroughly. The following Dispatches puzzle him somewhat:

The Cabinet have issued the orders for the Evacuation of Fort Sumter.—*Herald.*

It is at last decided that Fort Sumter shall be reinforced.—*Times.*

Orders were sent off last evening to Reinforce Major ANDERSON at all costs.—*Tribune.*

It is believed that Major ANDERSON Evacuated Fort Sumter by order of the Government last evening.—*World.*

Fig. 10. A reader overwhelmed by the news, in terms of content and sheer volume of information. Harper's Weekly, *13 April 1861. Courtesy of Hargrett Rare Book and Manuscript Library, University of Georgia Libraries.*

City Hall and Fire Department, Canal Dover, Ohio.

Fig. 11. Public square in Dover, Ohio, where two deserters humiliated a provost marshal in 1865. *Courtesy of Tuscarawas County (Ohio) Historical Society.*

Fig. 12. Mary Surratt, who was executed in 1865 for allegedly taking part in the plot to kill President Lincoln. *Courtesy of James O. Hall Collection, Surratt House Museum, Clinton, Maryland.*

Fig. 13. The 1864 Maryland State Fair for U.S. Soldier Relief in Baltimore attracted children from throughout the state. *Courtesy of Museum and Library of Maryland History, Maryland Historical Society.*

Fig. 14. Andrew Evans of Ohio. *From* The History of Brown County, Ohio *(Chicago, 1883), Ohio Historical Society.*

Fig. 15. Union father, divided sons: John J. Crittenden (upper left), George B. Crittenden (above), who fought for the Confederate States of America, and Thomas L. Crittenden (left), who fought for the United States of America. *Courtesy of the Filson Historical Society.*

Chapter 9

Living on the Fault Line: African American Civilians and the Gettysburg Campaign

MARGARET S. CREIGHTON

✦ IF WE IMAGINE the Battle of Gettysburg today, it is likely the National Military Park that we picture: wide green fields, rock walls, wooded slopes, and boulder-topped hills. The monuments, too, come to mind — hundreds of them — marking the first three days of July in 1863, and their moments of bloodletting and valor. It is easy to miss, both in memory and on the site itself, another construction. This one is a small white farmhouse at the northern end of Cemetery Ridge. It sits close by the legendary High Water Mark, that point where Confederate soldiers under Generals Pickett and Pettigrew charged the center of the Union line on the afternoon of the third of July, and failed. General Robert E. Lee had brought his army into Pennsylvania hoping to shatter Federal troops, demoralize Union leadership and Northern people, enlist foreign support for the Confederacy, and end the war on his terms. But he was defeated at Gettysburg, and the High Water Mark became known not only as the climax of the Confederate invasion but, rightly or wrongly, as the turning point of the Civil War.[1] Some of the land at this high point, where the Confederate cause is considered to have been lost, belonged to the small house in question.

These days, the High Water Mark and the fields over which the charge was made get plenty of public attention. But the small white house has a battle story, too: its African American inhabitants were both casualties and survivors of the invasion of 1863. The account of their experiences, along with those of other black residents in south central Pennsylvania, not only deepens the meaning of this contested farmland but also challenges standard notions about the battle's moral and physical dimensions. Furthermore, as long as Gettysburg serves as a magnet for the American public, where millions come to learn about "American" values, it is a story of consequence.

The Battle of Gettysburg, as everybody knows, was fought by tens of thousands of soldiers. But it took its toll on civilians as well. Walk down some of the borough streets, negotiate some of its alleys, drive out towards Seminary Ridge and you can still see the signs of violence — bullet holes outlined in white on the brick, shells stuck into walls. It is hard to imagine these spaces as fighting spaces, but soldiers were killed and captured here in the early summer of 1863, and houses, with their inhabitants, stood between enemy armies. "Why do you come to town to have a fight?" a white Gettysburg woman asked soldiers on the first of July 1863. "There are some old fields out there." Thinking back on these comments twenty-four years later, she wondered at her naivete. "So little conception," she wrote, "had some of us of a battlefield."[2]

"So little conception" indeed. Over a century later, Civil War battles still tend to be viewed as isolated events, carried on by soldiers in segregated green-space, apart from civilians. And while in the nineteenth century the words "battle" and "field" were often hyphenated, or not even linked at all, now they are insistently joined, telling us where war is supposed to happen. Many of today's social historians continue to compartmentalize the coverage of war. While acknowledging the war's wide geography, they tend to avoid scrutinizing battles and leave combat and military campaigns to military "specialists."[3] In Gettysburg, though, it is easy to argue for an expanded view of things, since the tumultuous fight that took place at the beginning of July 1863 was so obviously uncontained. Confederate soldiers occupied the borough for two and a half days, fought major engagements in the town and its environs, and commandeered houses and farms in the surrounding countryside. On a broader scale, the Confederate invasion cut a huge swath of fear through southern Pennsylvania, implicating civilians at every step of the way.

In recent years a number of writers and historians have drawn on witness accounts to consider the civilian presence in the Gettysburg's battle, although few in book-length treatment. Examination of women's experiences has been particularly slight. And all of these publications have had a hard time countering the popular image of the battle put forth by the best-selling author Michael Shaara in *The Killer Angels*. Published in 1974, Shaara's Pulitzer Prize–winning book defined Gettysburg's battle for millions of late-twentieth-century readers. In Shaara's historical fiction, soldiers have Pennsylvania mostly to themselves, for "the civilians have fled and houses are dark," and within the borough of Gettysburg itself, there are only "white faces at windows, a fluttering of curtains." Shaara also dismisses the black population, although he briefly introduces a wounded African to his narrative. This man is a cringing individual, who seems to the white soldiers who find him to be brutish and uncomprehending. "What could this man know of borders and states' rights and the Constitution and Dred Scott?" one of Shaara's heroes asks. "What did he know of the war?"[4]

The African Americans who suffered the brunt of General Lee's invasion in 1863 probably knew as much about borders and states' rights and slavery as anybody. Some of them had grown up enslaved, and been manumitted or had escaped from bondage. Some had grown up free, but knew how tentative freedom was when the Mason-Dixon line was only a short distance away, and kidnappers were on the prowl. And many of them worked for abolitionist organizations or served on the Underground Railroad, supporting the lifeline to liberty.[5] All of them knew what was at stake when General Lee's army crossed the Potomac.

Researchers have not entirely neglected the history of black civilians in the Gettysburg area,[6] but few scholars have focused on these African Americans during the Confederate invasion. Their experiences are not easily recovered, but neither are they impossible to delineate. This essay draws on the memoirs, diaries, and reminiscences of white Pennsylvanians who had the time and resources to be interviewed or to print up their own battle accounts, and who occasionally acknowledge the people they called the "darkies." It depends, too, on soldiers' accounts, which include occasional references to black civilians. It also relies on period newspapers — Democrat, Republican, black-edited and white-edited, local and national, and on pension records or damage claims stored with the National Archives. Finally, it draws on AME church records kept privately, and on histories taken orally. The African American community in Gettysburg has remained remarkably intact since the nineteenth century, and stories of life during the period of the Civil War have been passed down through three and four generations.

In 1863, Gettysburg, Pennsylvania, was an enterprising borough of approximately 2,400 persons. Most of its residents labored for others and farmed, or worked at trades and in small factories. A minority served in such professions as teaching, publishing, or the law. The borough drew some distinction from the fact that it served as the county seat, boasted a theological seminary and a college, and had a sizable carriage industry. Historians, particularly military historians, are also quick to point out that Gettysburg had a singular topographic feature, one that had developed incrementally since its founding in 1786: it served as the intersection of ten roads.[7]

It was along several of these roads that word traveled in June 1863 that the Confederate army was moving north. The news, however, was not told so much as seen and felt. White Gettysburg residents witnessed waves of farmers move through the town to the north and east, urging on herds of horses and cattle, driving teams and hauling wagons full of goods. They watched as storekeepers hurriedly took produce off the shelves and hid it, and saw bankers mailing money and records away. And they listened at night—could not sleep in fact—to the noise of black women, men, and children as they hurried each other on, less concerned about livestock and livelihoods than freedom.[8]

Some of the African Americans on the move those days were passing through Gettysburg from the south and west. They were, said one white observer, "God-forsaken looking people," who traveled on foot, bowed down with massive bundles of quilts, clothing, and cooking items. Some herded a single sheep or cow, and a few wheeled their possessions in handcarts. Other black families gathering to evacuate were local. Gettysburg had what one woman called a "goodly number" of black residents. Census records put the African American population in the borough and its environs at two to three hundred, and anecdotal estimates were even higher.[9]

The hurried evacuation of the black population through the borough elicited varied responses from white observers. Some felt real pity for the "poor" folk who passed by. Others found the general consternation more entertaining than sad. One young woman commented that it was "amusing to behold the conduct of the colored people of the town," and she offered, as evidence, the dialect she overheard from a worried mother: "Fo'de Lod's sake, you chillen, cum right long quick! If dem Rebs dun kotch you, dey tear you all up." A few white witnesses also wondered whether the fugitives had real cause for alarm. "They believed," said one woman, "that if they fell into [Confederate] hands, annihilation was sure." Another woman viewed them as "perfectly bewildered." She was not sure, she said, "how much cause they had for their fears, but it was a terrible reality to them."[10] There were indeed false rumors drifting north in the summer of 1863, and there was a surfeit of confusion in southern Pennsylvania. And reality did have a way of shifting for whites and people of color. But if there was one irrefutable truth, it was the one that sent black families stumbling and running on dusty roads with their belongings: one ridge away from Gettysburg to the west, soldiers from the South were kidnapping African Americans.

General Lee had staged his invasion of the North by moving his army behind the shield of the Blue Ridge Mountains in early June. Confederate cavalry units, General Albert Jenkins leading the way, had crossed the state line into south central Pennsylvania by the middle of the month. On Monday morning on the fifteen of June, a young white woman in Chambersburg, Rachel Cormany, witnessed signs of the Confederate advance. She saw black women and men flying through town, claiming the enemy was "on their heels." The fugitives were moving so fast that Cormany noticed that their hats had come off, that people had lost their coats, and that the wind was peeling off the covers of their wagons. One woman in flight, astride her horse, was "going what she could."[11]

It was late that night when the threat materialized. Just before midnight, Chambersburg residents heard a hard pounding of hooves and went to their windows. Confederate cavalrymen were there, hammering through town by the hundreds. They were "hard looking" soldiers, with matted hair down to their shoulders, beards down to their waists, and hats garish with feathers and plumes. Their officers stopped, demanded the "mayaw of this town," and then threatened to burn the place if he did not appear. When someone shot off a gun, they claimed that they would turn Chambersburg into a waste of ashes if anybody fired again. There were about fifteen hundred of them, the vanguard of an army of thousands.[12]

Rachel Cormany, who was at home with her young daughter, went to bed after the cavalry first passed through. Soon after she woke up the following morning, she looked out to see the fears of the fugitives suddenly realized: soldiers were hunting down black women and children. "We . . . slept soundly until 5 in the morning," she recalled:

> All seemed quiet yet. We almost came to the conclusion that the rebs had left again leaving only a small guard who took things quite leasurely. Soon however they became more active. Were hunting up the contrabands & driving them off by droves. O! How it grated on our hearts to have to sit quietly & look at such brutal deeds — I saw no men among the contrabands — all women & children. Some of the colored people who were raised here were taken along — I sat on the front step as they were driven by just like we would drive cattle. Some laughed & seemed not to care — but nearly all hung their heads. One woman was pleading . . . with her driver for her children — but all the sympathy she received from him was a rough "March along" — at which she would quicken her pace again. It is a query what they want with those little babies — whole families were taken.[13]

The cavalry hunt in the houses and barns of Chambersburg went on that day and the next — for men's clothing and food and horses and hay and oats, and for more people. One resident saw the horsemen hunting in the fields, "scouring" the wheat for signs of humans, running them down. "The cavalrymen," he noted, "rode in search of their prey, and many were caught — some after a desperate chase and being fired at." The shooting did not stop there, as Confederate soldiers drove families through town at gunpoint, repeatedly firing at them.[14]

On the seventeenth of June, when the Confederate cavalry left Chambersburg, they took with them scores of kidnapped African Americans. One witness estimated thirty to forty people were taken; another counted fifty, and a third, five times that many. Some of the youngest captives were strapped on the backs of horses, mounted close to their kidnappers. Others were put in wagons. And some men were secured in a time-honored method. According to one newspaper reporter, the male captives were "bound with ropes." Another journalist concurred that "the stronger and more refractory ones were tied together, making somewhat of an extemporized coffle-gang."[15]

Chambersburg was not the only town to feel the brutality. Other border towns in Pennsylvania — McConnellsburg, Mercersburg, Greencastle — also suffered the early thrust of the invasion, and the stories of white observers were the same: stolen people driven through town with animals and goods. Horsemen from the South carried their human booty with them — with their "sad countenances" — as they ferreted through farms and houses. They came into neighborhoods, shouted, brandished weapons, made speeches and threats, searched, and left. Then they came back again. The horsemen did their work in the middle of the night and, flagrantly, in sunlight. If you were dark-skinned, no time of day was safe. One woman in Mercersburg — "poor old Eliza, and her little boy" — hid out in the grain fields during the day, and crept in at night to get something to eat. Such desperate measures may have saved Eliza, but it did little for her daughter, Jane, "who with her two children, were captured and taken back to Virginia."[16]

The terror went on for days, as the raiding parties cleaned out the southern tier of central Pennsylvania, rode back below the Mason-Dixon line, and then went north for more. One Confederate cavalryman in Jenkins's Brigade described the routine in his diary. On the sixteenth of June, he noted, "Boys capturing negroes and horses." On the seventeenth, he rode until midnight, back into Maryland. On the twentieth he was back in the North, for more "plunder." In some neighborhoods, this kind of marauding kept up as long as Lee was in Pennsylvania. A pastor from Mercersburg, Pennsylvania, described the repeated atrocities as a macabre carousel, with the Confederate horsemen passing and repassing with horses, cattle, and "our colored persons with them, to be sold into slavery." One day, he said, they came and abducted "a dozen colored persons, mostly contrabands, women and children." Later on, a group of men took "6 or 7 of our free people of color."[17] Another witness was likewise certain that the soldiers did not distinguish between the freeborn and the formerly enslaved. "They claimed all these negroes as Virginia slaves," he reported, "but I was positively assured that two or three were born and raised in this neighborhood. One, Sam Brooks, split many a cord of wood for me."[18]

In the eyes of some of these white observers, the hunt for African Americans represented humanity at its very worst. The young mother in Chambersburg found that "it grated on our hearts to have to sit quietly & look at such brutal deeds." It was, said the minister in Mercersburg, "the worst spectacle I ever saw in this war" and "a most pitiful sight, sufficient to settle the slavery question for every humane mind." Another man found the kidnapping "revolting," and a reporter from Lancaster, Pennsylvania, told his readers that "this high-handed and brutal outrage" would have "made your very heart ache."[19]

Above all, these white Pennsylvania residents could not understand why enemy depredation extended to noncombatant women and children. To some extent they expected Confederate raiding in general. The taking of horses and cattle and the pillaging of houses was an unfortunate but inescapable consequence of war. One Pennsylvania man listened sympathetically to a Confederate officer as he rationalized the conduct of his troops: "You have only a little taste of what you have done to our people in the South," commented the soldier. "Your army destroyed all the fences, burnt towns, turned poor women out of house and home, broke pianos, furniture, old family pictures, and committed every act of vandalism. I thank God that the hour has come when this war will be fought out on Pennsylvania soil." And the listener concurred: "If this charge is true, I must confess we deserve punishment in the North." Another Pennsylvanian agreed that the taking of horses, cattle, and other things was "within the rules of war."[20]

But these residents recoiled at the taking of families and the way that their towns had become the site of slave hunts, and, worst of all, that free people—people they had known forever—were abducted. They protested that what they were witnessing was shocking in a country like America—purportedly civilized and Christian. They also argued that the "carrying away of free negroes" decisively undermined Confederate assertions that the war was not about sustaining slavery. "This feature of the war," said one Pennsylvania witness, "indicated the object for which it was waged, to establish a government founded upon human slavery."[21]

White Pennsylvanians occasionally did more than condemn or report the taking of black civilians; they tried to intercede. In Chambersburg, one woman walked to the courthouse to save "Mag," who was "free born." The Confederate officer in charge said "he could do nothing." The woman then watched as Mag was marched away. Others had more luck. A resident named Jacob Hoke used a friend who "had influence with Jenkins" to bring about the release of two captives. In Greencastle, on the sixteenth of June, a group of civilians, some armed with revolvers, surrounded Confederate wagons en route to Virginia with thirty to forty women and children. The local citizens cut the horses loose, seized the Confederate guards and the chaplain accompanying the abductees, and released the African Americans. When the chaplain demanded twenty-five thousand dollars for lost "property," several residents demurred, insisted that they did not work in the slave trade, and prepared themselves for the burning of their town. Accounts disagree as to whether or not the Confederates set fire to the town and whether or not they recaptured black civilians.[22]

Witnesses do tell us that the majority of African Americans taken were women and children. Men were not given a reprieve in these raids; most were simply not at home. Just as many white civilian men had evacuated as the enemy approached, black men had left as well, and likely for the same reasons—to help hide livestock or to avoid capture. As one witness explained, these men had mistakenly assumed that they, not their families, would be targets of Confederate brutality. They had departed "thinking the women & children would not be disturbed." Some African American men were not present in Chambersburg in 1863 for another reason as well. They were away from home fighting for the Union in South Carolina. As soldiers in the Massachusetts Fifty-Fourth Infantry, they were one month away from assailing Fort Wagner, outside of Charleston harbor. Certainly they could not have imagined that their families in Pennsylvania would be fighting Confederates just as they were, but without weapons.[23]

The observers who detailed the preponderance of black women and children among the captives in 1863 were silent on the subject that had to have weighed heavily on women's minds: sexual assault. Many white Pennsylvania women anticipated an invasion of male soldiers with panic and dread. "We girls," wrote one Gettysburg woman, "pictured the most outlandish things which would be done. Children and women went about wringing their hands, alternately bemoaning our impending fate & praying for deliverance." A teenaged girl wondered what soldiers would do, saying it "was a fearful question to my young mind." One Confederate soldier remembered how he had stopped at a house early in the invasion and almost the first question he was asked, by "a girl of eighteen or twenty," was whether "our men would molest the women."[24]

What more, we must ask, did black women fear? And after some of them had encountered Confederate soldiers and been carried away from their homes, what did they endure? A number of historians have contended that sexual assault perpetrated by Civil War soldiers upon civilians has long been underidentified, and they have compiled significant evidence of abuse. Their evidence reveals that soldiers in both armies occasionally subjected both white and black women to sexual assault, including rape, and that soldiers targeted African American women in particular. Given the fact that black women were held against their will by Southern invaders in 1863, it would be extraordinary indeed if rape and other sexual violence did not play a part in their horrifying ordeals.[25]

For their part, soldiers from the South left a slim record of these forays into Pennsylvania. One surviving letter suggests that the men engaged in seizing black civilians may have had no uniform attitude toward the kidnapping. Written by a Confederate officer named William Christian to his family, and found on the Gettysburg battlefield, the letter describes the man's misgivings about taking black residents. "We took a lot of negroes yesterday," Christian wrote from Greenwood, Pennsylvania, en route to Gettysburg on the twenty-eighth of June. "I was offered my choice, but as I could not get them back home I would not take them. In fact, my humanity revolted at taking the poor devils away from their homes. They were so scared that I turned them all loose." Christian, who had been trained as a physician in Philadelphia, served as colonel of a Virginia infantry regiment.[26]

Witness reports suggest, however, that few of the Confederate soldiers engaged in abductions shared Christian's sensibilities. These accounts describe brash cruelty on the part of the marauders. In Chambersburg, a soldier abruptly ignored a mother who pleaded for her children. "All the sympathy she received from him," described the observer, "was a rough 'March along' — at which she would quicken her pace again." In another town, a white resident asked a soldier guarding wagons filled with captured [and free] black Americans how he could participate in such despicable acts. "Do you not feel bad and mean in such an occupation?" the Pennsylvanian asked. The soldier replied that "he felt very comfortable." A judge in the same town asked one of the invaders if "they took free negroes." "Yes," he replied, "and we will take you, too, if you do not shut up!"[27]

The seizing of African American families, including small children, was carried out at all levels of authority. Some of the men rampaging through towns used the simple supremacy of power — their fast horses, their guns, and their ruthless bearing. They described themselves as independent bands of horsemen who came north from Virginia and Maryland, and they used the Confederate invasion as an opportunity to terrorize and pillage. They did their work in the shadow of the Confederate army, and served only themselves. "These guerillas are far worse than the regular army," claimed one of the Mercersburg residents. He reported that one of these men bragged, "We are independent, and come and go where and when we please."[28]

Detached bands of "official" Confederate cavalry, off on their own, also abducted people. Some did so directly under the eye of the Confederate cavalry commander General Albert G. Jenkins, who had brought a glittering resume to his work in the invasion: he was a former congressman, a graduate of a Pennsylvania college, and an alumnus of Harvard Law School. Authorization for kidnapping went even higher. General James Longstreet, who commanded one of Lee's corps and was his right-hand man, instructed General James Pickett, who was in Chambersburg, to carry with him "captured contrabands" on the way to Gettysburg. And Longstreet himself was carrying out something of a tradition. When Stonewall Jackson defeated Federal troops at Harper's Ferry in the fall of 1862, during the Antietam campaign, he ordered the seizure of hundreds of "contrabands." Whether the Confederate army was more careful about differentiating runaway slaves from free people in Harper's Ferry in 1862 than they were in Pennsylvania in 1863, we do not know. It is not necessarily a relevant distinction. As one historian has pointed out, "slave-catching," whether directed at free or formerly enslaved people, was "in no way a military activity."[29]

The question of whether Union or Confederate armies bore the responsibility for extending the parameters of war to noncombatants was an absorbing matter at the time. During the invasion of 1863, particularly in lulls between battles or raids, Confederate officers and white civilians frequently discussed—often dispassionately—the conduct of the war and the comportment of the armies.[30] The issue of responsibility in the case of black kidnapping may also be a compelling topic for Americans today, especially for those who seek to honor the Confederate high-command at Gettysburg and for those who are aggrieved by such recognition. As important as the matter of responsibility may be, though, it threatens to draw attention away—again—from the African Americans who bore the brunt of the assault. These civilians may have cared something about who had the final say in this sad matter, but more than anything else they cared about staying ahead of hunters and getting out with their freedom and their families intact. Consider the story of a white teacher, who met refugees en route to Harrisburg, Pennsylvania, and discovered among them a man he knew. The fugitive was covered with dust and "very nearly dead" with exhaustion—he had travelled north forty miles from his home. He told the teacher that what he feared most was "de Rebels kotchin us an' takin' our chill'en fum us an' sellin em to de drivahs an' we wud nevah see dem ag'in."[31]

The bottom line for black families during the Confederate invasion was the matter of freedom. It was their bottom line for the war, too. They did not need to debate the war's meaning. The issue of whether slavery was or was not the heartbeat of the rebellion, or whether racial hatred infused the conduct of the war, was not something discussible, the way it was with white people. Not only was genial conversation between black and white enemies proscribed, but these African Americans were living—and fleeing—witnesses to the way race and slavery mattered.

The news of human hunting expanded and rippled beyond these first epicenters of terror, and in the last weeks of June 1863, waves of families moved out of south central Pennsylvania. They were up before daylight, some of them avoiding the roads and threading themselves through the protective cover of meadows and grainfields. Others braved the turnpikes, sending up clouds of dust as they wheeled, drove, and pushed on foot. They did not know if they could ever go back, and they took everything that mattered. In one family of eleven children, all but the baby was "loaded to full capacity" with a featherbed, quilts, skillets, ham, bread, a Bible, and a framed picture of Abraham Lincoln. Some people were too old to go, but they fled anyway. An observer saw "poor people completely worn out, carrying their families on their backs." One woman carried her two children from the Cumberland Valley all the way to Philadelphia, alternating who had to walk, who got lifted. Her shoes were worn away. Sick people went. One man traveled with smallpox. A fatally ill girl evacuated, too, and then lay dying—but free—in a Harrisburg church.[32]

Some of these African Americans took flight the way that fugitives from slavery had always traveled—by using the routes of the Underground Railroad. The refugees heading towards Harrisburg told the white teacher who met them on the road that they had been advised to use South Mountain to get to the Susquehanna River, standard practice for the Underground. They had been told "to keep yo 'ise wide open to dat big mounting on de lef' han' side all de way to de ribber." Many free blacks, of course, had no question about the way—they had been sheltering escapees and pointing them in this direction for decades, probably never imagining that they, too, would be getting up before dawn, hiding under the height of corn stalks, and working their way from one safe house to the next.[33]

White travelers to the borderland of central Pennsylvania reported that by the last days of June 1863 there was scarcely a "negro left" in the area. A newspaper correspondent measured the evacuation by the services that seemed to be missing. There were no cooks left in kitchens, no barbers to be seen. "At Mechanicsburg yesterday we made a dinner of peanuts," he noted, "the hotel proprietor declaring that his assistants had vanished. At York the same story was told, and at Carlisle there was no variation."[34]

Many of the refugees pushed east across the state to the sanctuary of Philadelphia, where ministers mobilized congregations, neighborhoods opened their meeting houses, and residents offered the shelter of their homes. Many of those on the run, though, sought refuge across the Susquehanna River in Harrisburg, the state capital. Nearly two thousand people congregated in the city's parks, took shelter in churches, and crowded into the courthouse. The governor offered homeless families rations of meat and crackers. Safety on the road and in the city, however, was a relative thing. One witness remarked that African Americans found "no shelter from white citizens." Another claimed that Union soldiers were given to scaring fugitives as they passed by on the way into the city. In Harrisburg itself, some soldiers and residents commiserated with the congregating refugees, but others were openly hostile. "If they stay at home," warned one Harrisburg newspaper, "they are in danger of capture; if they go away, they find an unfriendly world with which to deal. . . . It would be better for the contraband to stay where he is at all hazards, than run the gauntlet of the prejudice, the downright hatred . . . which he finds at his every step northward."[35]

White residents of the borough of Gettysburg had wondered, as they watched the frantic traffic through their streets in late June, whether or not refugees had reason for their fears. The very real horror that had entered Pennsylvania with Confederate soldiers ended their speculation. Black residents, of course, had not had the privilege of second guessing. And the terror that they knew was not only the fear of being stolen south, but was the deep concern that this was only the beginning—that if the Confederates were successful, who knew what dark age might ensue. A New York newspaper put the meaning of a Confederate victory succinctly to its African American audience: "Our life, our liberty, our country, our religious privileges, our family, OUR ALL is at stake."[36]

The crisis in Pennsylvania shifted from cavalry and infantry incursions to an impending battle by the end of June 1863, when the Army of the Potomac moved into Pennsylvania to counter the invaders. As the conflict began to assume a specific location, Gettysburg residents felt their concern deepen into alarm. Then when Confederate cavalry actually came shouting and shooting into the borough on the twenty-sixth of June—with infantry close behind—and when enemy soldiers seemed close to a convergence, many white people—men with horses, town officials, worried families—moved out. African Americans continued to evacuate, some slowly and deliberately, packing and shipping their belongings on trains. Some left suddenly. One day late in the month, the AME bishop attended the quarterly meeting in the borough. He spoke, wrote one attendant, "kindly and courageously." Later, the congregation sang, joining together in "The Year of Jubilee Has Come." But then word of enemy soldiers came and the news worked its way through the church. Almost as an act of magic, the singing stopped, and "in a moment bishop and people had disappeared."[37]

When white people pictured the evacuation of southern Pennsylvania by African Americans, they not only wondered if the fear they saw was fully justified, but they frequently used animal imagery to describe the blind panic of fugitives. The evacuees were like "a small flock of sheep," or they fled north like "buffalo before a prairie fire." They were driven by their captors "just like we would drive cattle," and they were "fleeing about like deer." Their language suggests their disgust at the brutality they witnessed, and their sympathy with families who were treated inhumanly. At the same time it indicates how removed these observers were from the individual men, women, and children under pursuit.[38]

It is possible to put faces on some of the African Americans leaving Gettysburg, and to recognize them as more than mass victims of Confederate terror. They were a diverse group. Some were poor folk who fled with every possession on their backs. Others were individuals of property and standing who had succeeded in the harsh world of the border country, and who, when Confederates came north, stood to lose a lot more than their liberty. Some of the local population tried to get as far away from Southern soldiers as they could. Others found that they could not leave, and some men were fighters who sought to stand up to the invaders, defiant and resolute.

For a man named Owen Robinson, slavery was no imaginary evil — it was a flesh-and-blood memory of when he was young and owned. Robinson was emancipated by his owner in 1817, and moved from Maryland to Pennsylvania. During his nearly half century of freedom, he had become a popular figure in Gettysburg. He was a "confectioner" and a magnet for children and adults with his ice cream and oyster stand. Early in the 1840s he had helped push for "progress" in the black community by launching a temperance society against the evils of "spirtus licuours." And his church did not forsake those who remained in bondage. It collected funds for a "slaves reffuge" to do what it could to "give liberty to our brethren."[39]

Owen Robinson stood to lose his business when Confederates threatened Pennsylvania, but he did not want to take chances. When rumors had circulated about Confederate troops on the move earlier in the war, he had taken his family, abandoned his restaurant, and moved out of the way. The news in June 1863 was the most sinister yet. Owen Robinson kept his manumission papers — they said that this light-complected African American, five feet seven inches tall, with a scar in his right eyebrow, had been legally emancipated. But it is likely this man had heard the stories coming over the ridge to the west. He had no doubt been told that a manumission paper was not a credential these Southern soldiers cared about. Owen Robinson once again gathered together his large family. He gave his pigs to white friends to care for, left his business to good or bad fortune, and got away.[40]

Abraham Brian had had some hard times — his first wife died, then his second, and then he was arrested for fathering a child outside of marriage. But by the time the Civil War began, Brian, in his late fifties, had put all that behind him. He married his third wife, Elizabeth, and by dint of hard work and savvy he had purchased a piece of the American Dream. He owned a farm with twelve acres just south of the borough, rented out a small house to a poorer black couple, and had more property in town. Even though he could not write, and neither could his wife, he made sure his children were educated, and sent them a mile south to a neighborhood school. In the spring of 1863 the Brians turned their backs to rising rumors, tilled their soil, planted wheat and barley, and put in a vegetable garden. But they weren't going to be farming long, that summer. Part of the problem was the location, on the west side of a place called Cemetery Hill. It may have been a decent site for growing crops and raising a family, but, as soldiers would discover on the third of July, it was also good ground for fighting. Abraham Brian and his family had left Gettysburg by the time the battle began, but their fences would serve in Union breastworks, their vegetables and wheat would feed Union men, and their small, white, story-and-a half house would sit right inside the bloody whirlwind, give soldiers shelter, and withstand shot and shell. Over a century later, it would still be there.[41]

Mag Palm was the Brians' tenant, renting a small white house — more like a shack, really — at the west end of the farm on the Emmitsburg Road. Mag Palm was a big woman, dark-skinned and tall. She was well known in town, partly because of what happened three years before the war started. She had been finishing up a day's work doing laundry for a white family in Gettysburg, when her employer and two other men lured her into an alley and tried to wrestle her into a wagon. The plan, it seemed, was to sell her in slave country. But Palm was a strong woman, muscled from years of hard work, and she fought back and broke free. Her life had taken new turns since that frightening night, and now, in 1863, she lived with a man named Alf Palm, and had a young daughter named Josephine. But the worries about kidnapping would not go away. And what was coming that June would not be two or three local men she could fight herself, and because she was a strong woman, prevail. This was an army, seventy-thousand strong. It was said that Mag Palm kept a rifle nearby, and carried it sometimes, too, and that she kept her eyes out for signs of strangers on the ridge to the west.[42]

Mag Palm was a survivor, who knew when to fight back and when to pack up and go. Randolph Johnston wanted to meet the Confederate army face-to-face, in combat. Twenty-two years old in 1863, Johnston had grown up in Gettysburg and seen his family struggle for respectability within the black community. His father, Upton Johnston, a laborer, had won half the battle—he owned property in town. But the older man had been a tough case for the AME church—he had been caught drinking, and been accused of adultery. Randolph Johnston, on the other hand, occasionally neglected his classes at church, but was never so derelict in his religious studies that he could not later become a "Minister of the Gospel." He was also educated and enterprising, and when the war began, he focused on helping black men fight, achieving what the local paper called "military notoriety" and becoming captain of a "colored company." In June 1863, with new calls for black volunteers and with an invasion underway, he quickly rallied fifty men and began drilling. He ignored white public opinion that railed against the idea of armed African Americans. One Harrisburg newspaper, for instance, claimed that giving black men guns was not only "impolitic and unwise," but likely to "bring upon us terrible calamities." "We have every kindly consideration for the negroes in their proper places," an editor had written, "but cannot consent to have them under any circumstances, placed upon an equality with white men, whether in civil or military capacity." Johnston's company, however, did not have the opportunity to prove the paper wrong, at least that summer. When the men offered their services to the United States they were told to wait. Pennsylvania would ultimately train African Americans for service in the Federal army, but the first recruits entered camp near Philadelphia on the twenty-sixth of June, the day Confederate cavalry rode into Gettysburg.[43]

Randolph Johnston and other members of his local militia company vanish from the historical record when it comes to the battle of Gettysburg itself. But other men like him were involved in the defense of the state. In Harrisburg, in late June, two companies of African Americans, including refugees from the borderland, were armed and equipped to help defend the capital. But, once again, they were prohibited from active duty. The same prejudice that had kept black men out of the army for so long surfaced in Harrisburg at the point of the invasion, and black men who were armed, drilled, and willing to fight, instead worked on entrenchments. Even then they had to keep an eye out for harassment. Union soldiers stationed at Harrisburg sometimes taunted black men who had congregated at the capital, and worse. One newspaper reported that a "fugitive slave" who had worked on the fortifications was shot in the chest, "unprovoked." Another was "rounded up and forced to work and then beaten when he resisted."[44]

Most African American men in Pennsylvania were denied the opportunity to face the Confederates with weapons, but not all. One company of black emergency militia confronted invading soldiers, and their efforts, considered one of the first military engagements in the war by men of color, is still an overlooked aspect of the Gettysburg campaign. The site of the action was the Columbia-Wrightsville bridge, a span over a mile and a quarter long, twenty-five miles southeast of Harrisburg. Before word had come of the Army of the Potomac's move north from Virginia, Confederate commanders had envisioned the possibility of taking Harrisburg from the east and the south. The bridge over the Susquehanna River was key. Emergency Pennsylvania militia, including around one hundred African American men brought in from Columbia, Pennsylvania, helped hold the bridge against twenty-five hundred seasoned Confederate troops, including artillery, until the bridge could be destroyed. "The negros," commented the officer in command of the militia, "did nobly." His report had even more to say. "When the fight commenced," he explained, the black company "took their guns and stood up to their work bravely. They fell back only when ordered to do so."[45]

When the experience of African Americans has been discussed at all in the history of the Gettysburg campaign, it has centered around the terrifying ordeals of kidnapping. Such emphasis rightfully underscores the menacing threat of the Confederate invasion. But there were also men like the Columbia volunteers, who not only were willing to bear arms for freedom, but had the opportunity to do so.

The different histories of Owen Robinson, Mag Palm, the Brian family, and Randolph Johnston point to the many dimensions of black civilian experience during the Gettysburg episode of the Civil War. Their experiences were marked by fight along with flight. Some of them were fugitives from modest success as well as destitution, and when Southern invaders entered the state, they stood to lose farms and businesses as well as their houses. For all their differences, however, these people faced an enemy in common. The invasion was a great equalizer for black families in southern Pennsylvania, underscoring for all of them the fragility of freedom and their shared and ongoing struggle.

By the time the battle began on the first of July, most African Americans had evacuated the borough of Gettysburg. But not all of them left. According to a white woman in Gettysburg who witnessed the three-day conflict, some black residents "were obliged to stay at home." What, we wonder, were the circumstances that kept people of color in town, when all the intelligence coming north spoke of impending terror? Perhaps a family wanted to protect its property, its livestock, or its hard-earned home. More likely, it seems, people did not leave because they could not. This was the case, apparently, with a man known as Jack, who was "bow-legged." When Jack imagined the velocity and power of enemy soldiers on horses, and compared it with his own hampered running, he was too doubtful. According to a white man who knew him, Jack "didn't have any confidence in his ability to outrun the raiders," and he was forced to stay.[46]

White friends and employers may have convinced African American residents to stay by promising protection. One Gettysburg woman told a widow and her daughter to come to their house; she had a loft over her kitchen, and once she had taken the ladder away, she said, "they would be safe." The black women climbed into the loft when Confederate General Early's soldiers came through and commandeered the town for the night. Another white family, four miles north of town, led its two black servants to a crawl space underneath a porch. They replaced the stones around the porch, and hung some sacks over the wall to hide the hole, "so it wouldn't look as if it had been disturbed."[47]

The decision to stay—especially when it involved an employer—was not necessarily freely made. Like so much in life, part of what determined whether or not a person could be safe or secure depended on wealth and means. Those families who appear as leaders in the Gettysburg AME church, who were men and women of property, tended to be those who were able to make the hard decision to leave behind their homes, their farms, and their businesses. It was a difficult and unhappy decision, but it was theirs to make. Others may have felt torn. Their employers in town were often white families, who needed and wanted their help—especially in this emergency—and who did not feel equally threatened. They could "offer" their workers safety and job security at the same time. In the end, though, some black women and men decided that faith in white protection, loyalty to their white friends and employers, and the security of their jobs were not as strong as the refuge of a black community away from the border and a better chance at freedom. The widow and her daughter who spent one night in a white neighbor's loft could not bear the fear of discovery. They had had such little rest that they left the next day, the daughter confessing that "she couldn't be paid to put in such another night, that she heard soldiers walking around all night—that they surely knew who was on that loft." Surely, too, the mother and daughter must have wondered how far soldiers could push white residents before they would be forced to give hidden people away.[48]

Fannie Buehler discovered the limits of loyalty. Like other white residents of Gettysburg, Buehler had counted on black workers to carry her through the crisis. She had credibility, too, among the black community. She occasionally attended the AME church, and she described her husband as an active, "black Republican" — Lincoln's sort of man. When it seemed clear that a Confederate invasion was imminent, and that her husband would need to evacuate, Fannie Buehler tried to hold on to her domestic help. But they had other intentions. One of her employees left in early June "from fear of being captured." But the other, Buehler recalled, "I thought I had captured, for she promised to stand by me, and I promised to protect her, yet when she saw the Rebels she fled I know not whither, as I never saw her afterwards." Some of these black workers, therefore, faced two sorts of capture — one by armed Confederate hunters, and the other by families they had known intimately but whose pleas and needs and promises ultimately paled against their own chance for freedom.[49]

Fannie Buehler could not persuade the African American girls who worked for her to stay. Other employers convinced, or coerced, or "captured" more successfully. A white farmer who employed a black laborer named "Isaac" had become tired of evacuating Gettysburg with every report of a raid. At the end of June 1863, he was warned yet again of an invading enemy, but he decided to stay this time, and to have his black employee remain with him. "We won't run no more," he said to Isaac. Isaac stayed. So did a twenty-year-old woman who worked as a "servantmaid" for a white woman with two small children. And at the Globe Hotel, black help was kept on. Even as the first units of the Confederate army came into town on the twenty-sixth of June, even after an army band in the town square began playing "Dixie" and other "enemy" airs, and even as men in gray combed the streets, black employees at the hotel worked into the night to hide hams, sugar, and potatoes and to dig a trench in the hotel garden to bury whiskey, brandy, and gin.[50]

So on the first of July, when soldiers of both armies converged on Gettysburg and began to bloody each other in earnest, some African American residents were still around. The lucky ones — though luck was a relative term those days — became invisible. They blended in with the woods and hillsides, and tried to hide where no one, not even a set of predatory soldiers, would think of looking. One of them went up to a church belfry. Another, during the heat of the fight on the first day, went down into a cellar, and discovered she was the only dark-skinned person there. She secreted herself in a deep corner. Jack, the bowlegged man who could not run far or fast, found a haystack, and, having crawled beneath the fetid weight, stayed motionless and hungry for days. A man who knew him said he "almost starved."[51]

While a few men and women thus sought to blend into the Gettysburg landscape, others tried to avoid notice with another ploy. They drew perhaps on hard years of experience in slave country, where they had deceived overseers or owners. Instead of rendering themselves invisible, they made themselves undesirable. They were, according to one white woman who witnessed the deceit, "at the shortest notice suddenly transformed into limping, halting, and apparently worthless specimens of humanity."[52]

Not every black woman, man, or child in Gettysburg at the beginning of July was able to hide or to dissemble, however. "Captured" by white families, all that some people could do was to live moment-to-moment and pray. It would not be easy. Confederate soldiers occupied Gettysburg on the first of July, and swept into their purview all the buildings and farms in the borough and to the north and west. They battled mostly near the two ridges of town, but they camped and marauded well beyond, knocking fiercely on kitchen doors to demand food, taking livestock and orchard fruit, breaking fences for firewood, and poking around, everywhere.

The man named Isaac knew the double-edged agony of doing an employer's bidding while doing his best to save himself. Charged with hiding seven horses plus a wagon loaded with provisions and grain, he had found an old road in the woods. He remained sequestered throughout the battle, through artillery roars that seemed to him like "continuous thunder" and as the countryside around him became "full of black smoke." His angst, and his "fearin' and tremblin'" were palpable. "We didn't have no feelin'" he said later, "for shuttin' our eyes."[53]

The work asked of some black women during the Battle of Gettysburg brought them almost face-to-face with the enemy. In the Confederate-occupied areas of Gettysburg, military officers not infrequently offered protection from pillage in exchange for cooked food. Women, including black women, were vital to this negotiation, in which property in and around the borough was probably spared damage. But the cost for African Americans — in anxiety alone — was high. The two "servants" who were hidden beneath a porch and blocked in with stones were asked to come out at regular intervals and cook for Confederate soldiers. Jacob Taughenbaugh remembered that his family posted a guard, and when soldiers were seen, the servants would be hidden under the porch. But as soon as they left, "those colored people had plenty to do, cooking." His mother sometimes fed thirteen soldiers at one meal, and he attributed Confederate forbearance to the cooking. "No wonder," he said, "the men were good to us."[54]

The young "servantmaid" came even closer to disclosure. With her employer's family, she ran from house to house within battle lines, avoiding shells and soldiers both. In one house, she was so close to the shooting she could hear the action of guns: "We were inside the Rebel lines," she recalled, "and the soldiers were all the time running in and out of the house. You'd hear 'em load their guns — clicky-click, and push 'em out the windows and fire. We didn't know what they was goin' to do with us." Later on, she, too, was called on to cook for a sick Confederate officer, after a white resident had secured a promise of protection. Her fear of Confederate abduction was then compounded by complete fatigue. "We stayed up all night doin' nothin' but cook and bake for the Rebels," she recalled. "By morning we were pretty near dead."[55]

For some black residents of Gettysburg, working to the point of exhaustion, hiding in trepidation, and taking flight from captors were the least of their problems. Some people were caught. On July first, Confederate soldiers battled over fields, walls, and railroad cuts, made sudden appearances from the north and east, routed Federal troops and sent them retreating towards Cemetery Hill. But a few soldiers, it seems, had more on their minds than warfare against armed men, and began to round up and take African Americans.

The "servantmaid" came close to being taken. Fleeing from house to house with her widowed employer and two children, moving as the battle wavered and surrounded her, the young woman crossed a field to find herself at a house swarming with Confederate soldiers. They stopped her, and turned to the white woman who was with her: "Hey, what you doin' with her? She's got to go along with us." But her employer stood her ground. "You don't know what you're talkin' about," she retorted, and kept her maid with her. The imperious mother was certainly aware of the double standard of army conduct. While her black nursemaid was looked at as seizable "contraband," she could stand up to a soldier with less risk of assault or arrest because she was a genteel white woman, pleading for her "family." The Confederate high command had exhorted its invading soldiers to treat [white] Pennsylvania women with some respect. This may have been a case in point.[56]

Some African Americans in Gettysburg may have had no intercessors. A white boy in town named Albertus McCreary claimed that on the first of July, he saw "a number of colored people" corralled together, and marched away from the borough. They passed by his house, "crying and moaning" and he could see his family's washerwoman among them. She called out to him, "Good-by; we are going back into slavery." But "Old Liz" escaped. Just in front of the Lutheran Church in Gettysburg, she took advantage of the chaos and the crowds of soldiers and civilians, and bolted. She went into the church, climbed up to the belfry, and, in a situation sadly familiar, she waited the battle-days out, hungry and thirsty. The weekend after the battle ended she found the McCreary family and gave them the good news: "Thank God," she said, "I's alive yet."[57]

These few witnesses leave us with more questions than answers. Were seizures in Gettysburg itself widespread or isolated events? Does the paucity of witnesses suggest that there was little to observe, or does it simply reflect the confusion and tumult of the battle? Even where there is a plethora of evidence, from the areas west of the borough, uncertainties remain. Where were captives sent, what did they undergo, and for how long? We know enough from scraps of information, from passing references in reports, and from poignant queries, that some people taken from Pennsylvania were lost to their families and kept south until after the war ended.[58] But the true tale of black civilians rounded up during the Gettysburg campaign, the full story of children strapped on horses, men tied in coffles, girls and women carried captive through the countryside—may be forever gone.

The people most likely to tell us what happened had many reasons not to relate their experiences. In Gettysburg itself, some black residents could not pick up the pieces of their lives for a long time. Abraham and Elizabeth Brian suffered serious battle damage to their house, their fields, their orchard, and their fences. Nearby, an African American widow named Sophia Devan could not live in her house for a year. The small shack Mag Palm had inhabited with her family was demolished by gunfire. But even if African Americans in Gettysburg had had the time or resources to write battle tales, or even if they had attracted the interest of the press, it is unclear that this unhappy affair is a story they would have wanted to tell. In 1866, men of the town, including Randolph Johnston and Owen Robinson, organized a society for mutual support and care called the Sons of Good Will. The society purchased land for a cemetery for black residents, looked after its members and worked on programs to secure social justice. It also honored black Union war veterans, and celebrated Emancipation Day every January. The Sons of Good Will clearly wanted to recognize moments of strength and promise, not episodes of suffering. And into the twenty-first century, the black community in Gettysburg—many descended from Civil War–era families—would continue to focus, in its stories of the war and in its ritual celebrations, not on the many moments of struggle and pain, but on the proud work of its veterans and on history from freedom onward.[59]

The story of assault and kidnapping in the Gettysburg campaign was also a story that many white participants in the campaign—witnesses, soldiers, newspaper editors—chose to bypass. The few accounts that do describe the events do so cursorily. Albertus McCreary, who diligently recorded the ordeal of "Old Liz," wished that he could detail her story, but it was "more than I can undertake." Another woman who reported the plight of the "colored people" explained that "if time permitted we might insert some curious scenes which occurred among them." And the young mother in Chambersburg who recorded the kidnapping of black civilians there regretted that "I cannot describe all the scenes."[60]

It was not, of course, simply a matter of time or space constraints. White memoirs focused on white ordeals and courage because that is what seemed to matter most, and, since many white women and children remained alone in town during the battle, their accounts are indeed replete with gallant action. White writers — both in 1863 and decades later — may also have slighted black suffering because they honestly wanted to commend Confederates for their restraint in Pennsylvania. The Gettysburg editor who in 1863 referred to Confederate soldiers as "Gen. Lee's army of kidnappers and horse thieves" offered an uncommon judgment. More typical was the opinion of a newspaper correspondent who described Confederate deportment in Chambersburg. He commented that Confederate soldiers had "behaved themselves very well," and noted that citizens and private property had generally been "respected and left inviolate." He admitted that "contrabands were taken, and free blacks; no distinction whatever was made in favor of any who were born free, either in the North or South; all were hurried away with all the horses and cattle that could be mustered in the neighborhood." But all in all he wanted to say that "we have had some exciting scenes, but nothing critical; no burning this time, and no real trouble."[61]

Such breezy dismissal of black experience may be rooted in the blinding prejudice that rendered the ordeals of people of color invisible or unimportant to many whites. It is not surprising, in fact, that the white citizens who left the most powerful and detailed accounts of abductions tended to be committed Christians who strongly believed that slavery was a sin. Disregard for the ordeals of African Americans may also stem from the genuine relief that many white Pennsylvania residents felt when the invaders did not do as much damage as they anticipated. By and large, white women remained physically unhurt, and most white homes and businesses, even if looted, stood intact and unburned. (Those residents who had time to record and publish their experiences may also have been those who suffered least.) Then, too, when Confederate officers engaged white residents in curbside chats, and permitted free speech and heartfelt but civil differences of opinion, and when the invaders even partook in occasional flirtations with Pennsylvania girls, many white residents had to say that, all things considered, the Confederates had been gentlemanly in Pennsylvania.[62]

Many citizen accounts of the Gettysburg campaign were also written towards the end of the nineteenth century, when some of the harshest memories of the invading army had softened, and when the white North and South had entered a period of reconciliation and reunion. The tendency to gloss over hard sectional differences, already visible during the war, increased. Civilian reminiscences, soldier memoirs, and military histories all tended to emphasize Confederate and Union soldiers' shared courage and manly valor, and downplayed ideological differences and moral conflicts. The ugly story of slavery, including its manifestation in the conduct of the war, was often sidestepped.[63]

The racially segregated history of the Gettysburg campaign that emerged in the late 1800s paralleled ongoing social divisions in Gettysburg itself. The borough's ritual recognition of the battle, in Memorial Day exercises, was distinctly segregated in the nineteenth century. And, as the battlefield became an even more popular national attraction, many businesses within the borough bid for the white Southern tourist dollar, creating a comfortable setting for some visitors but helping to foster a harder, segregated world for resident African Americans. In the 1920s the battlefield was the site of Ku Klux Klan gatherings. By the middle of the twentieth century, the borough was residentially, civically, and socially segregated. Newspapers printed white recollections of battle days with some regularity, but, with some exceptions, rarely solicited local black history.[64]

There is time, of course, for the story of African American civilians in the Gettysburg campaign to be broadly told. The contemporary black community in Gettysburg has been increasingly involved in preserving oral and written history, and in calling attention to a long-overlooked black past. The National Park Service, which runs the National Military Park, has preserved Abraham Brian's house and recently put up a wayside exhibit that describes Brian's family, his farm, and his efforts to rebuild his life after the battle. The park's interpretive plaque, however, does not tell us why Brian, his wife, and his children evacuated his home, and visitors can only assume that this family and other African Americans left Gettysburg simply because fighting came too close.

An inclusive history of the Gettysburg campaign will unveil the Brian family house for the important landmark that it is. Unlike the stone statues and brass plaques on Cemetery Hill that honor brave sacrifice and martial boldness, Abraham Brian's house narrates a different tale of temerity. Visitors to Gettysburg can see his story in the fields he once planted but could not harvest, and in the mile his children walked to get the education he never had. They can see the road he probably took, too, to save himself and his family from the threat of kidnapping and slavery in 1863. And even though it is hard to say that his house was a high water mark in any military sense, visitors should know that it commemorates a battle — a momentous battle — of a different kind.

Notes

The author thanks the following individuals in Gettysburg for their help in researching this essay: Gabor Boritt, Catherine Carter, Elwood Christ, Matt Gallman, Charles Glatfelter, Kathy Harrison, Betty Myers, Margaret Nutter, Jean Odom, Winona Peterson, Walter Powell, Tim Smith, Rogers Smith, Elisha Wansel. Elsewhere, the author thanks Patrick Bowmaster, Joan Cashin, Michael Fellman, Gary Gallagher, Amy Kinsel, John Mohr, Michael Parrish, John Patterson.

1. Edwin B. Coddington, *The Gettysburg Campaign: A Study in Command* (reprint; New York, 1997), 3–7; William A. Frassanito, *Early Photography at Gettysburg* (Gettysburg, 1995), 238–40.

2. Jennie Croll [attrib.], "Days of Dread: A Woman's Story of Her Life on a Battle-Field," *Philadelphia Weekly Press*, 16 November 1887.

3. "The Battle Field near Gettysburg," *Christian Recorder*, 18 July 1863; *New York Times*, 4 July 1863; *Philadelphia Weekly Press*, 16 November 1887; Linda Grant De Pauw, *Battle Cries and Lullabies: Women in War From Prehistory to the Present* (Norman, Okla., 1998), esp. chap. 6; George Rable, "Missing in Action": Women of the Confederacy," in *Divided Houses: Gender and the Civil War*, ed. Catherine Clinton and Nina Silber (New York, 1992), 145–46.

4. Michael Shaara, *The Killer Angels* (New York, 1974), xxi, 36, 170–71. On civilians, see Robert L. Bloom, "'We Never Expected a Battle': The Civilians at Gettysburg, 1863," *Pennsylvania History* 55 (October 1988): 161–200; Gerald R. Bennett, *Days of "Uncertainty and Dread": The Ordeal Endured by the Citizens at Gettysburg*, (Littlestown, Pa., 1994); Timothy H. Smith, "'These Were Days of Horror': The Story of the Gettysburg Civilians," in *Unsung Heroes of Gettysburg: Programs of the Fifth Annual Gettysburg Seminar* (Gettysburg, 1996), 81–89; Frassanito, *Early Photography at Gettysburg*; J. Matthew Gallman with Susan Baker, "Gettysburg's Gettysburg: What the Battle Did to the Borough," in *The Gettysburg Nobody Knows*, ed. Gabor S. Boritt (New York, 1997). On women, see E. F. Conklin, *Women at Gettysburg* (Gettysburg, 1993); Cindy L. Small, *The Jennie Wade Story: A True and Complete Account of the Only Civilian Killed During the Battle of Gettysburg* (Gettysburg, 1991).

5. Charles L. Blockson, *The Underground Railroad in Pennsylvania* (Jacksonville, N.C., 1981); Julie Winch, "Philadelphia and the Other Underground Railroad," *Pennsylvania Magazine of History and Biography* 3 (1987): 3–4; Margaret S. Creighton, *The Colors of Courage: Gettysburg's Lost Battles* (New York, forthcoming), chap. 3.

6. See Peter Vermilyea, "'We Did Not Know Where Our Colored Friends Had Gone': The Effect of the Confederate Invasion of Pennsylvania on Gettysburg's African American Community," unpublished college research paper, 25 April 1994, Adams County Historical Society, Gettysburg, Pa. (hereafter ACHS); Harry Bradshaw Matthews, "Whence They Came: The Families of

United States Colored Troops in Gettysburg, Pennsylvania, 1815–1871," 1991, ACHS; Betty Myers, Transcripts of Historical Lectures, ACHS.

7. Bennett, *Days of "Uncertainty and Dread"*, 1–3; Frassanito, *Early Photography at Gettysburg*, 2–3.

8. John Charles Wills, "Reminiscences of the Three Days Battle of Gettysburg at the "Globe Hotel,'" c. 1915, TS, ACHS; C.M.W. Foster, "The Story of the Battle by a Citizen Whose Home Was Pierced by Flying Shells," 29 June 1904, *Gettysburg Compiler*; Sarah Sites Rodgers, ed., *The Ties of the Past: The Gettysburg Diaries of Salome Myers Stewart 1854–1922* (Gettysburg, 1996), 145, 160.

9. Clifton Johnson, *Battleground Adventures* (Boston, 1915), 193; "Negroes in 1860 Cumberland Township," and "Gettysburg 1860 Census," compilations at Gettyburg National Military Park (hereafter GNMP), Historian's Office (file 796); Rodgers, *Ties of the Past*, 160; Foster, "Story of the Battle."

10. Observations of the refugees include Johnson, *Battleground Adventures*, 193; Tillie [Pierce] Alleman, *At Gettysburg, or What a Girl Saw and Heard of the Battle* (New York, 1889; reprint, Baltimore, 1994), 19–20; Rodgers, *Ties of the Past*, 160.

11. James C. Mohr, ed., *The Cormany Diaries: A Northern Family in the Civil War* (Pittsburgh, 1982), 328–29.

12. Mohr, *Cormany Diaries*, 329; W. P. Conrad and Ted Alexander, *When War Passed This Way* (Shippensburg, Pa., 1982), 131–32; Jacob Hoke, *The Great Invasion of 1863 or General Lee in Pennsylvania* (reprint, Gettysburg, 1992, 99–102. The appearance of Jenkins's Cavalry apparently contrasted sharply with the look of more neatly trimmed Confederate cavalry units, such as those associated with Jeb Stuart.

13. Mohr, *Cormany Diaries*, 329–30.

14. Hoke, *The Great Invasion*, 107–8; "From Chambersburg," *Lancaster Daily Evening Express*, 20 June 1863.

15. Conrad and Alexander, *When War Passed This Way*, 135; "The Chambersburg Telegrams," in *New York Herald*, 19 June 1863; *Philadelphia Inquirer*, 19 June 1863; *Franklin Repository*, 8 July 1863, quoted in Alan T. Nolan, *Lee Considered: General Robert E. Lee and Civil War History* (Chapel Hill, 1991), 17.

16. *Gettysburg Compiler*, 29 June 1863; Philip Schaff, "The Gettysburg Week," *Scribner's Magazine* 16 (July 1894) 25.

17. Isaac V. Reynolds (Co. A, 16th Va. Cavalry) to his wife, 9 August 1863, at www.rhobard.com/russell/letters/reynolds.html; Conrad and Alexander, *When War Passed This Way*, 137; Schaff, "Gettysburg Week," 26–29; J. D. Edmiston Turner, ed., "Diary of Rev. Thomas Creigh, 19 June–1 July 1863," paper read before the Kittochtinny (Pa.) Historical Society, 29 February 1940, http://jefferson.village.virginia.edu/vshadow2/KHS/creigh.html.

18. Schaff, "Gettysburg Week," 24. See also Coddington, *The Gettysburg Campaign*, 161.

19. Mohr, *Cormany Diaries*, 330; Schaff, "Gettysburg Week," 24; Hoke, *The Great Invasion*, 107; "From Chambersburg," *Lancaster Daily Evening Express*, 20 June 1863.

20. Schaff, "Gettysburg Week," 25; Hoke, *The Great Invasion*, 111.

21. Schaff, "Gettysburg Week," 26; Hoke, *The Great Invasion*, 111, 108.

22. Jemima Cree to her husband, c. June 15–17 1863, in "Jenkin's Raid: A Personal Account," *Centennial of the Civil War* (Chambersburg, 1963). Hoke, *The Great Invasion*, 108; Conrad and Alexander, *When War Passed This Way*, 135–136; "From Chambersburg," *Lancaster Daily Evening Express*, 20 June 1863; "The Raid in the Valley," *Lancaster Daily Evening Express*, 24 June 1863.

23. Mohr, *Cormany Diaries*, 330; Luis F. Emilio, *A Brave Black Regiment: History of the Fifty-Fourth Regiment of Massachusetts Volunteer Infantry, 1863–1865* (Boston, 1891), 339–92.

24. Rodgers, *Ties of the Past*, 162; Alleman, *At Gettysburg*, 22; Edwin B. Coddington, "Prelude to Gettysburg: The Confederates Plunder Pennsylvania," *Pennsylvania History* 30 (1963): 129.

25. See Ervin L. Jordan Jr., "Sleeping with the Enemy: Sex, Black Women, and the Civil War," *Western Journal of Black Studies* 18 (1994): 57–58; Darlene Clark Hine and Kathleen Thompson, *A Shining Thread of Hope: The History of Black Women in America* (New York, 1998), 170–71; De Pauw, *Battle Cries*, 165; Joan E. Cashin, "Into the Trackless Wilderness: The Refugee Experience in the Civil War," in *A Woman's War: Southern Women, Civil War and the Confederate Legacy*, ed. Edward D. C. Campbell, Jr. and Kym S. Rice (Richmond, 1996), 47–48. An enumeration of sexual assaults carried out by Union and Confederate soldiers, based largely on official military reports, can be found at the website http://hometown.aol.com/cwrapes.

26. *Pittsburgh Evening Chronicle*, 28 July 1863. Special thanks to Tim Smith for information on Col. Christian and on Confederate abductions in general.

27. Mohr, *Cormany Diaries*, 330; Schaff, "Gettysburg Week," 25–26.

28. Schaff, "Gettysburg Week," 25.

29. Conrad and Alexander, *When War Passed This Way*, 133; Coddington, *The Gettysburg Campaign*, 161; Gary W. Gallagher, ed., *The Antietam Campaign* (Chapel Hill, 1999), 14; Nolan, *Lee Considered*, 17.

30. See, for example, Schaff, "Gettysburg Week," 25; and Rodgers, *Ties of the Past*, 161 (26 June 1863).

31. "War Story by Prof. Harry," *Gettysburg Compiler*, 28 June 1911.

32. "Twas Fifty Years Ago," *Harrisburg Telegraph*, 14 June 1913; Jane Dice Stone, ed., "Diary of William Heyser," *Kittochtinny (Pa.) Historical Society Papers* 16 (1978): 54–88, also at http://jefferson.village.virginia.edu/vshadow/diary.html; (*N.Y.*) *Anglo-African*, 4 July 1863; *Harrisburg Patriot and Union*, 16 June 1863, 1 July 1863.

33. "War Story by Prof. Harry"; on the Underground Railroad in Adams County, see G. Craig Caba, ed., *Episodes of Gettysburg and the Underground Railroad as Witnessed and Recorded by Professor J. Howard Wert* (Gettysburg, 1998).

34. *Philadelphia Inquirer*, 30 June 1863, quoted in James Elton Johnson, "A History of Camp William Penn and Its Black Troops in the Civil War, 1863–1865," (Ph.D. diss., University of Pennsylvania, 1999), 39.

35. (*N.Y.*) *Anglo-African*, 4 July 1863; *Harrisburg Patriot and Union* 16, 25

June 1863, 1 July 1863; "War Story by Prof. Harry"; *Harrisburg Patriot and Union*, 19 June 1863.

36. (*N.Y.*) *Anglo-African*, 20 June 1863.

37. David A. Murdoch, ed., "Catherine Mary White Foster's Eyewitness Account of the Battle of Gettysburg, with Background on the Foster Family Union Soldiers," *Adams County History* 1 (1995): 49.

38. Johnson, *Battleground Adventures*, 193; "War Story by Prof. Harry"; *Harrisburg Patriot and Union*, 25 June 1863; Mohr, *Cormany Diaries*, 16 June 1863; Schaff, "Gettysburg Week," 25.

39. *Gettysburg Star and Sentinel*, 15 August 1900; Records of the AME Zion Church, 1840–1870, private collection; *Pennsylvania Freeman*, 10 February 1841.

40. Charles M. McCurdy, *Gettysburg: A Memoir* (Pittsburgh, 1929), 19.

41. Marcella Sherfy, "The Brien [*sic*] Farm and Family," *Report*, June 1972, GNMP; Memorandum of Senior Historian, 8 August 1995, GNMP; Adams County Court records, Quarter Session G, 1836–1866, August sessions, 1855.

42. Brian files, GNMP; Census of Adams County, 1860, ACHS; *Gettysburg Compiler*, 15 February 1858, 26 April 1858; *Gettysburg Star and Sentinel*, 27 October 1896; *Gettysburg Compiler*, 27 October 1896; David Schick to Elsie Singmaster Lewars, 24 April 1952, ACHS. The legendary Mag Palm appears in Elsie Singmaster, *A Boy at Gettysburg* (New York, 1924), 94; and in Gettysburg oral history: interviews with author, Catherine Carter, Jean Odom, 1997.

43. (*Gettysburg*) *Star and Banner*, 11 June 1863; Frassanito, *Early Photography at Gettysburg*, 110; Johnston Pension Records, National Archives (hereafter NA), Gettysburg AME Zion records, private collection; *Harrisburg Patriot and Union*, 2 July 1863; Johnson, "History of Camp William Penn," 43.

44. *Harrisburg Patriot and Union*, 2 July 1863; *Harrisburg Daily Telegraph*, 13 July 1863.

45. Hoke, *The Great Invasion*, 185–90; Johnson, "A History of Camp William Penn," 36–38 (quotations); Coddington, *The Gettysburg Campaign*, 169–70.

46. Rodgers, *Ties of the Past*, 160; Johnson, *Battleground Adventures*, 192–93.

47. Mary Warren Fastnacht, "Memories of the Battle of Gettysburg, Year 1863" (York, Pa., 1928), 3; T. W. Herbert, "In Occupied Pennsylvania," *Georgia Review* (Summer 1950): 104–5.

48. Fastnacht, "Memories of the Battle," 3; diary of Rev. Creigh, 26 June 1863.

49. Fannie J. Buehler, *Recollections of the Rebel Invasion and One Woman's Experience during the Battle of Gettysburg* (Gettysburg, 1900; reprint, Hershey, Pa., n.d.) 11.

50. Johnson, *Battleground Adventures*, 183–84; 189; Wills, "Reminiscences of the Three Days Battle," 11.

51. Johnson, *Battleground Adventures*, 192–93; Albertus McCreary, "Gettysburg: A Boy's Experience of the Battle," *McClure's Magazine* 33 (July 1909): 250.

52. Rodgers, *Ties of the Past*, 160.

53. Johnson, in *Battleground Adventures*, 183–84.

54. Herbert, "In Occupied Pennsylvania," 104–5.

55. Johnson, in *Battleground Adventures*, 188–90.

56. Ibid., 189; Sarah B. King, "Battle Days in 1863," *Gettysburg Compiler*, 4 July 1906; "Mrs.Thorn's War Story," *Gettysburg Times*, 2 July 1938.

57. McCreary, "A Boy's Experience," 243–53 (quotation on 250).

58. See, for example, the request made to the Freedman's Bureau in 1865 to help reunite three children taken from Pennsylvania in 1863 with their mother in William S. McFeely, *Yankee Stepfather: General O. O. Howard and the Freedmen* (New Haven, 1968), 203.

59. Sherfy report, GNMP, 5; Memorandum of Senior Historian, 8 August 1995, Brian files, GNMP; Sophia Devan damage claims, NA; records of the Sons of Good Will, 1866, private collections; interviews with author, Betty Myers, Rogers Smith, Elisha Wansel, Walter Powell, Jean Odom, Catherine Carter, Margaret Nutter, 1997–2000.

60. McCreary, "A Boy's Experience," 250; Foster, "Story of the Battle"; Mohr, *Cormany Diaries*, 330.

61. *Gettysburg Star and Banner*, 6 August 1863, 25 June 1863. See also "The Chambersburg Telegrams,"in *New York Herald*, 19 June 1863, and the *Gettysburg Compiler*, 29 June 1863 (from the *McConnellsburg* [Pa.] *Democrat*).

62. Schaff, "Gettysburg Week," 22–23 ; Herbert, "In Occupied Pennsylvania," 108; Buehler, "Recollections," 12; "A Woman's Story," *Gettysburg Star and Sentinel*, 25 September 1888; Annie Young to "My dear Mina," 17 July 1863, in Catherine Merrill, *The Soldier of Indiana in the War for the Union* (Indianapolis, 1866), 119–20, file copy in ACHS.

63. See David W. Blight, "'What Will Peace among the Whites Bring?': Reunion and Race in the Struggle Over the Memory of the Civil War in American Culture," *Massachusetts Review* 34 (Autumn 1993): 400–405; Nina Silber, *The Romance of Reunion: Northerners and the South, 1865–1900* (Chapel Hill, 1993), 124–43; Amy J. Kinsel, "'From These Honored Dead': Gettysburg in American Culture, 1863–1938" (Ph.D. diss., Cornell University, 1992). While the story of African Americans was slighted in the history of Gettysburg and its battle, there were notable exceptions, including the fictional histories of Elsie Singmaster, the oral history work of Clifton Johnson, and the writing of the prolific local historian J. Howard Wert.

64. John S. Patterson, "A Patriotic Landscape: Gettysburg, 1863–1913," *Prospects* 7 (1982): 325–26; Joan Vannorsdall and Roxy Bream, "The Ku Klux Klan," May 1968 , unpublished research paper, ACHS; *Gettysburg Star and Sentinel*, 2 June 1928; Donald H. Becker, "Trends in Negro Segregation in Gettysburg from 1900 to 1953" (master's thesis, University of Maryland, 1953), available at Abdel Ross Wentz Library of the Lutheran Theological Seminary, Gettysburg.

Chapter 10

Cannonballs and Books: Reading and the Disruption of Social Ties on the New England Home Front

RONALD J. ZBORAY AND MARY SARACINO ZBORAY

✦ AFTER eight-year-old James Cabot of Boston requested a "cannon-ball or a Secession dollar" in an 1862 letter to his father Samuel, a U.S. Army surgeon in Virginia, the boy's brother received a book, the more traditional antebellum-era present for children. Although the dutiful son replied with a thank-you note—"I am very much obliged to you for getting me that book"—he prefaced his gratitude with an eager plea for any Confederate stamps the father might find. His fascination for the paraphernalia of combat persisted despite his father's recent written exhortation: "I wish my little boys all of them could be here that they might learn what a horrible business war is, & that they might never want to have their country engaged in it."[1] The boys were too young to have understood fully the dire consequences of the Civil War and their father's repugnance to it, but they nonetheless sensed that it had affected most facets of everyday life, including literary gift exchange. Like many of their contemporaries in 1862, they coveted war relics over reading materials, cannonballs over books. In the face of a war that took their father far away from them and limited their communications to an irregular correspondence stretching over four hundred miles from Boston to the battlefront, books seemed to the boys irrelevant compared to emblems of the distant struggle.

However far removed spatially from New England the war was, it became almost omnipresent culturally, so much so that it changed the very nature of literary experience. To civilians on the home front there, wartime social disruption often registered, sometimes most keenly, through literary encounters of various sorts—from reading and study-ing to gift giving and book borrowing.[2] This is not surprising since, during the three decades before the outbreak of war, books and reading had become a key component of everyday life in the region and vital to the maintenance of social ties among friends, kin, and neighbors.[3] But with the outbreak of hostilities, representations of war in print, through correspondence, or by word of mouth infiltrated civilians' mundane experience in an essential way: literary encounters that had been largely locally oriented and socially motivated before the war were now redirected outward toward national affairs and propelled by more abstract political concerns. Literary sociability faded before patriotic duty.[4]

Although the social and the literary were ultimately destined to part ways regardless of the war, due to the worldwide emergence and valorization of solitary and atomized reading practices later in the century, the war foreshadowed the separation.[5] During the war, the literate New Englander began to divide his or her literary self into distinct modes of consciousness: one in solitary pursuit of self-edification through literature during leisure time; another devoted to formalized, institutional study; and yet another assuming the role of the literary patriot who identified with an often anonymous, indeed, abstract society of Unionists caught up in the furor of war. Of course, each New Englander may have experienced all modes in varying degrees and emphasized any of them, depending upon the available amount of leisure time, the quality of educational background, and the vicissitudes of political affiliation. Still, no matter how New Englanders focused or diffused their literary attentions, they could not elude the constraints that the war had imposed upon the social production of literary meaning.

For firsthand evidence of these changes, this essay draws upon about 430 manuscript letters and volumes of diaries authored by a diverse set of New Englanders who both wrote copiously about their literary experiences during the war and who left similar writings among the 4,800 items we consulted for a book-length project on the antebellum years. With the earlier years providing a baseline from which to assay the war's impact upon literary experience, we first briefly outline the social significance of literary culture then as these informants experienced the processes of producing, disseminating, and receiving literature—that is to say, as they wrote and compiled literature, exchanged literary gifts and read out loud, or responded emotionally and intellectually to texts. We will then note the ways in which the war placed stress upon the patterns of prior literary experience and how New Englanders either tried to adapt or even to overthrow their customary practices in the face of new and often disruptive circumstances. Because so little has been written on the ordinary white civilian's "inner civil war," this exploration of the play of ideas and their context offers to contribute to a greater understanding of what the conflict was about beyond traditional accounts of leaders and combatants. Because black Northerners experienced literacy differently, their perspective is not discussed in this article, although we explore this important topic elsewhere. Thus, we will highlight throughout "the thoughts and feelings of those who lived through the upheaval and reflected on its meaning," especially as they grappled with a deluge of war-related news.[6]

Literary Experience, 1830–1861

Throughout the three decades before the Civil War, ordinary New Englanders used published and manuscript literature in an instrumental fashion—to facilitate social relationships with family members, friends, neighbors, and acquaintances.[7] The everyday production, dissemination, and reception of reading materials was seldom accomplished for self-edification alone. Amateur production outside the publishing marketplace—including diaries, letters, scrapbooks, and commonplace books replete with transcribed quotations, newspaper clippings, excerpts from books, or critiques of texts—was geared toward a local, intimate group of readers and listeners who could appreciate the literary references. People, of course, would commonly write to one another about the books and periodicals they had been reading, but this did not mean they were merely passive literary consumers. Inspired by favorite authors such as William Cowper, Lord Byron, Charles Lamb, and Henry Wadsworth Longfellow, New England correspondents and diarists also fashioned their own poetry, songs, compositions, essays, and other pieces that were either read before classrooms, local lyceums, or during social calls, or given away as "literary gifts" for holidays and birthdays. Even the most seemingly "private" of these literary productions, like diaries, seldom remained entirely in the writer's hands, but, rather, usually circulated among family or other social groups. Nor was most professionally authored literature seen as a closely guarded personal possession, for that matter. If they could, New Englanders made virtually all their literary experiences into social ones.

They did this by often herculean efforts at sharing reading materials. Dissemination of literature to those near at hand or afar by paging items, mailing letters and periodicals, and packaging books for express delivery occupied much of New Englanders' leisure time. While she was still being courted by a string of beaus in 1839, Hannah Jackson, the future mother of the Cabot boys, knew that the art of disseminating literature was as essential as entertaining for middle-class housewifery: "When I can fold, seal & direct a letter, pack the 'Annual Register,'" she explained to her sister Sarah, "I shall think I know how to please a somewhat particular gentleman." Even among poorer folk, mailing local newspapers was a familiar activity. J. Edwin Harris, a Saco, Maine, mill operative, frequently sent and received newspapers from his sisters and friends before he joined the Union army in 1861. Periodicals were chock-full of reading matter, cheaper to send than a letter, and functioned in much the same manner—a clear sign that all was well.[8] Gift giving in all its forms, from holiday exchange to charity donation to *gratis* tract distribution, was, like newspaper mailing, both a forum for distributing literature as well as a means for social bonding, for the transaction was usually done during social calls or other face-to-face encounters. Receivers of literary gifts usually valued them more for the sake of the donor than their monetary worth. Neighbors and friends who temporarily entrusted their books to lenders, a common practice because circulating libraries were still too few and far between, also cemented social bonds over literary exchange and shared reading.

Of all these voluntary forms of dissemination, reading out loud was the most prevalent and the most sociable. For example, in his detailed diary covering most years between 1839 and 1861, Daniel Child, a Boston clerk, records that he read to his household (wife, children, and older sister) on at least half the 1,078 occasions he took up a book during leisure hours. Oral performances of texts in the home oiled the wheels of domestic labor. In this era before the sewing machine became a common household item, many women habitually listened to oral reading, often poetry or short literary pieces from periodicals, while they stitched or knit garments. For example, in describing her and her mother's daily routine in 1841, Persis Sibley, a native of Freedom, Maine, entered in her diary: "[E]ve[nin]gs we do plain sewing while they [father and brother] read or read while they listen."[9] Ordinary people's countless other oral performances—including parlor theatricals and Sunday Bible-readings—reached a receptive audience of hearers. Dissemination in all of its forms, from oral reading to mailing papers, was probably the most social of literary activities, for it always involved an act of communication in which literature provided the glue for a human bond.

Reception of literature through listening or reading was a primary way that New Englanders absorbed and formulated ideas within a social setting. Such socialization started early: literacy was almost always first acquired in the home from domestic instructors who taught children to read, listen, and respond to texts before formal education began. Schooling was invariably supplemented by home-based training, for not only was reading a routine domestic activity that children emulated, autodidacticism through home study was pursued as well. Once literate, New Englanders often read and studied an enormously wide variety of literature. This can be seen in the Taunton, Massachusetts, social library charge-records for the period from 6 May 1856 to 3 March 1859, which show a total of 280 borrowers, who left 14,560 charges distributed over 1,428 titles—an average of just over ten charges per title. Most of the titles patrons charged in common were magazines, but even the most often charged of these, *Harpers'*, accounts for only slightly over 2 percent of all charges. The book title charged out most often was Maria Edgeworth's multivolume *Works*, with but two-thirds of a percent, while the most frequently charged book by an American author was Washington Irving's life of George Washington, with just over half a percent.[10] Evidence in antebellum diaries and letters accords with such systematic materials as charge ledgers; in well over 50,000 literary encounters recorded in the antebellum diaries and letters we consulted, very few titles other than the Bible, some classics such as *Pilgrim's Progress*, and rare best-sellers like *Uncle Tom's Cabin* are mentioned more than once. Moreover, despite a good deal of scholarly speculation to the contrary, titles or genres fail to correlate with gender, partly because of the proclivity of mixed-gender group reading.[11] Women, including several discussed below, as much as men, craved the "political excitement" stirred by partisan editorials, and both sexes attended to news of a more personal, often of what they called a "shocking" nature, such as accidents, shipwrecks, and obituaries of loved ones. Besides hungering after a varied diet of novels, histories, biography, religious texts, belles lettres, science, geography, and news, antebellum New Englanders found ingenious ways to integrate reading with other work and leisure routines, such as housework and childcare (women peeked at books while nursing or cooking), calling on neighbors, traveling, farming, and sailing. Such alliances of reading to other activities necessitated reading in piecemeal fashion, and often without a serious purpose—a style then dubbed "desultory." Decrying these patterns while habitually falling into them, readers conversely highly valued study when that could be achieved due to a lack of competition from nonliterary duties.

Modern historians can be thankful that so many diarists and letter writers in antebellum New England went far beyond merely recording their literary encounters to providing, in many cases, in-depth reflections and ruminations upon the material they read or heard. They scribbled their emotional reactions to startling news, but they might in the next entry engage in finely analytical criticism of characters, plot, tone, argument, and ideas. Readers at times personalized published texts by replacing fictive characters with real ones or imaginatively inserting themselves or people within their social networks into plots or lines of poetry. Discussions based upon response to commonly received texts filled many sociable hours New Englanders spent in family circles, with social callers, at reading clubs and other societies, or even in writing to correspondents. Of course, these discussions, epistolary or otherwise, depended to a certain degree upon building a consensus in order to remain convivial, especially where political news or religious controversy was concerned. Republican partisan Elizabeth Cabot of Boston faithfully devoted from 1854 to 1861 a portion of most letters addressed to her like-minded sister Ellen Twisleton in England to discussing political news and other texts about which the two seldom managed to disagree. Because even privatized reading was a social act by virtue of prior and later discussion of what was read, and because books and periodicals became imbued with social meaning through gift giving and lending, the material object, if not the text itself, came to embody social relationships. As such, the "social imprint" upon the book—the often long genealogy of previous readers or owners—was as valued as the precious artifact itself. For antebellum New Englanders, simply to read was to be social.

Though the overall stability of this pattern of literary experience persists over the thirty-year period before the war, it is important to know if what happens to literary experience in the Civil War is a continuation of earlier trends or a departure from them. Was the social nature of literary experience in decline anyway, without the war? The clear answer is no; if anything, the patterns we just described were not weakening but strengthening as the war approached. This can be seen in several areas. Nearly all New Englanders—even religious conservatives who had always left fewer and less extensive literary testimonies than liberals—spent more time writing about their encounters with literature, especially secular material. And they were reading ever more widely and diversely, too. Traditionally, the middle and upper classes with more leisure and money to spend on books also wrote more about their varied literary encounters than the working classes, who, due to the rapid growth of lending institutions and the increasing availability of cheaper editions, nonetheless left more articulate records toward the end of the era than they did earlier. As part of the multiplying variety of reading on the market, a periodical boom in the decade before the war was expressed in almost every informant's diaries and letters through more references to this type of literature and more thoughtful responses to it, yet with little corresponding increase in discussion of the news that may have appeared in these vehicles. In short, the vast majority of New Englanders were more literary in their social relations in 1861 than they were in 1830, and they more frequently used literature instrumentally in them.

Against these trends were two technological innovations occurring just before the war that hinted at later developments through their impact on specific practices, while leaving the overall cultural pattern in place. One of these was the rapid distribution in the late 1850s through the middle class of noisy home sewing machines that weakened the long-standing link between needlework and oral reading. The other was the movement, with the advent of cheaper forms of photographic reproductions in the immediate prewar period, to replace literary albums and commonplace books as personal mementoes of family and friends with photo albums. The latter shift was eventually so sweeping that one commentator at the end of the century called those nonpictorial memory books "well nigh gone" by the time he wrote.[12] Before the war both innovations were limited in their impact and their social distribution. Indeed, certain populations of New England — specifically, the poorest rural laborers — remained virtually unaffected by these or even the overall antebellum trend toward the social intensification of literary experience.

Literary Experience during the Civil War

The Civil War erupted as literary experience in New England was so much evolving in accord with religious, social, and economic change in the region that it would seem destined to continue for decades more. The outbreak of war had little to do with initiating some countertrends, such as mechanized sewing, which probably would have been "worked around" with the advent of quieter machines, allowing for the reestablishment of simultaneous oral reading. The war, however, accelerated some changes, while igniting new trends and initiating short-term practices, notably the macabre collecting of literary war relics or infatuation with the news. More importantly, the war strained the long-established alliance between sociabilities and literature, such that New Englanders either struggled to maintain old ways in the face of turbulence or changed in accordance with it. In short, the war was a watershed in New Englanders' relationship to literature.

We turn now to exploring the ways that several New Englanders experienced literary production, dissemination, and reception during the war. Besides the Cabot boys, Hannah Cabot, Persis Black née Sibley, J. Edwin Harris, Daniel Child, and Elizabeth Cabot, whom we have already met, we will introduce several others: Seth Arnold, a Congregational minister from Westminster, Vermont; Charles Cobb, a poor farmer, musician, and sometime factory worker from Woodstock, Vermont; Ellen Morse of Scotland and Bristol, Connecticut, the wife of an army chaplain; Caroline Curtis, a lawyer's wife from Winchester, Massachusetts; the Browne family of Salem, Massachusetts, whose husband and father oversaw Union controlled plantations in South Carolina; Lilly Dana, a Cambridge schoolgirl; Ellen Wright, who was enrolled at Mrs. Sedgwick's academy in Lenox, Massachusetts; and three Providence citizens: Zachariah Allen, a semiretired industrialist; Christopher Keith, an irregularly employed, disabled accountant; and Abby Stimson, a housewife. As an individual each person has something unique to contribute to a composite profile of New Englanders' experiences with books and reading on the home front. All nevertheless felt the effects of war upon long-established literary practices, for the conflict penetrated virtually all aspects of social life. For those with family or friends in the war, separation made an obvious impact upon everyday human intercourse and family rituals, as evidenced by the absent chair at reading sessions and the increased hours spent at writing desks preparing correspondence to distant loved ones. For those who had no intimate relations at the front, or who were opposed to the war, the social impact was felt from the start, as they witnessed public leave-takings, one of which Persis Black, an antiwar Maine Democrat writing shortly after the firing on Fort Sumter, described as "young men from the best families . . . going to actual war" amidst "*men* shedding tears." Thereafter, constant "war talk," regular telegraphic dispatches and printed news, omnipresent wounded battle veterans and families in mourning for the fallen, endless classroom lessons and political sermons, frequent public lectures and speeches, and, of course, countless public flag raisings, sanitary fairs, or other benefits locally sponsored for the cause — all these ineluctably drew anyone and everyone into a social setting dominated by the spirit of war. Black, for one, found herself less likely to socialize. After an 1862 town "war meeting" to drum up enlistments drew out most of her neighbors, she admitted, "I did not go of course" and added, "There is no need of my going anywhere."[13] Indeed, she became something of a hermit, avoiding her Universalist ladies' circle and even Sunday services.

Persis Black, who was once a very social person and eloquent diarist, saw her life — and, consequently, the pages of her once highly literary journal — shadowed by war. After the war started, she virtually stopped writing about social life and also her reading, a trend that had begun, but had not yet characterized her journal by the late fifties. What little appeared concerned her childrens' academic reading, complaints about political sermons, and scattered and terse reports of war news that paled in comparison to her antebellum news accounts. "The war is terrible, but I cannot write of it," she penned with anguish in July 1863. "It is history & will be written by others."[14] Between 1861 and 1865 she did not transcribe an original poem into her diary, nor did she any longer grace it with clippings of printed verse, quotations from favorite authors, or creative allusions to literary texts that enhanced mundane events.

Like Black, most of the home-front diarists and correspondents presented here increasingly refrained from literary adornment of their writings about everyday events. War, and its close companion death, were simply the most important facts of life, and most thoughts about literature serviced those ends. Indeed, for many civilians writing to their diaries or other people on the home front, all matters besides war reportage became trivial space fillers. "I am amused at the ridiculous manner in which I mix up home incidents with news of great public interest," abolitionist Sarah Browne chided herself after years of integrating public and private matters in her writings. Elizabeth Cabot in a typically well-crafted 1862 letter apologized for "writ[ing] nonsense," explaining "as 'we are on the eve of great events' there is no news," while her previously loquacious husband, on another occasion, felt he had "nothing particular to write" due to a "wholesome want of news." Few people seemed cognizant of these drifts away from traditional substance. One exception was sixteen-year-old schoolgirl Lilly Dana, who noted how the war coincided in her dairy with the cessation of literary reflections upon her own life: "Then, I used to tell what we had for dinner, my quarrels with the girls, & such sorts of things & in the midst of it all, would generally have a Bible verse."[15] Evidently, most New Englanders, confident of a quick end to the war, dismissed their early stylistic changes as but temporary adaptations.

As the war years wore on, exigent deviations from prewar practices of literary production became inevitably habitual and permanent. Once-prolific diarists began to truncate their entries severely to mere lists of titles of books read, if any at all, wrote sporadically with large gaps, or simply abandoned journalizing altogether. Letter writing, by contrast, became more copious, especially, if not surprisingly, between friends and families of soldiers. Interest in commonplace and extract book production was being displaced by nonliterary compiling, such as keeping those aforementioned photo albums, which began to arrive in even outlying areas. "Photograph books are all the fashion now," Persis Black could confirm in 1862 from tiny Paris Hill. The craze was rather sudden, related as it was to recently developed methods of photo duplication, leaving some people confused as to "how to put them into the book," or even what to include. And they did not always replicate literary albums as records of the written sentiments of loved ones. While Salem teenager Nellie Browne patriotically "placed Col. Beecher's photograph in our book," her little brother Eddie wanted his book to be "filled up with 'notorious' characters," that is, infamous Southern leaders. But some social uses remained, albeit put to new purposes. Ellen Morse kept a personal picture album for her husband Frank, Army chaplain for the Thirty-Seventh Regiment of Massachusetts Volunteers, and sent it to him on the front where he inserted photos of men from camp. The literary fell away from other collecting practices in which it once held sway. As postage stamps increasingly became the international mode for mail transactions, making books of stamps from all over the world amused children once limited to scrapbooks of news-clippings and engravings. During the war, collectors such as Lilly Dana, who had amassed 233 numismatic items by June 1862, traded with correspondents or asked family members in the South for Confederate stamps.[16] These fashionable books of nonliterary items threatened to subvert dwindling literary production all the more.

For those who kept on writing, literary production was often inflected by the amateur's equivalent of what Edmund Wilson, referring mostly to professional writers, called "patriotic gore." Biblical quotations, for example, were strategically placed in diaries to annotate transcribed war news. " '[V]erily, verily I say unto you they shall have their reward,' " Sarah Browne quoted Matthew 6:1–3 to her diary upon reading on 5 February 1864 "that the servants of the rebel Jeff Davis have run away & that his house has been set on fire." Christopher Keith, uninterested in national politics and guarded about his partisan affiliation in the 1850s, uncharacteristically inscribed a patriotic poem about the war at the back of his diary: "Our countrys' [sic] woes demand a sadder verse, / No time have we her sorrows to rehearse." Antebellum diaries that once featured penned eulogies to the deceased now frequently memorialized kinsmen — even anonymous ones — who died in battle. At times, Abby Stimson's diary read like an obituary column of Providence men she may have hardly known, while her neighbor, Keith, commemorated Daniel Webster's son killed at the Second Battle of Bull Run. For dissenters, the encroachment of war into the experience of writing was as painful. At Mrs. Sedgwick's academy, abolitionist disunionist Ellen Wright squirmed at patriotic writing assignments, like one in May 1861 on "the Benefits of War." "My ideas upon that point are exceedingly limited," she sneered, "but they will stretch, in big writing." By contrast, previously published New England Unionist writers of modest repute, such as Caroline A. Mason, dutifully channeled their talents into wartime production for an even greater, more eager, but anonymous public of Unionists and abolitionists who sometimes stepped forward to make themselves known through a fan letter. For example, after reading one of her poems presenting a scene of home life reminiscent of his own family, one soldier declared, "Such lines as yours carry with them many a blessing as they are read by the exiled soldiers — self exiled as many of us are, away from home, kindred & friends." To the lonely soldier, the poem was akin to a warm letter filled with family news.[17]

Not surprisingly, New England noncombatants who, while away from home near battle fronts, cherished hearing about everyday family life and fancying nothing had changed, asked their correspondents to write about their literary reading among other details of home life — and not their concerns about the war. "What have you been doing these

many days? What have you been reading?" Albert Gallatin Browne
asked his daughters Alice and Nellie in January 1864 from Beaufort,
South Carolina, while serving there as a United States Treasury official;
"I now wonder if there is such a thing as time to read or ever was or
ever will be for me?" Writing from Virginia on nearly the same day to
his wife in Bristol, Connecticut, Chaplain Frank Morse echoed Browne's
query: "Are you devoting much time to reading? You better make a
selection of some choice books for a winter evening pastime." Despite
changes in her everyday life Ellen Morse had previously revealed to
him, she and other women painted, as faithfully as they could, comforting vignettes of literary life continuing in the old way. "If you could just
step into the parsonage you would find Mary, and myself sitting by the
table in the kitchen," she wrote shortly after Frank left home in September 1862. "Mary has her sewing. I have the Atlas in my lap that you
always used." Frank, in turn, longed for "a social interview" at home,
with folks "eating nuts and apples, reading the news &c." Alice Browne
reassured her father of his much missed place in the family literary circle, as she wrote in November 1863: "I glance almost instinctively at
the large rocking-chair, as if I must see you there with books and newspapers." The efforts of these correspondents to produce letters, as much
as every other day in the case of Ellen Morse, while ever striking a
cheerful tone, led them to walk a tightrope between therapeutic remembrance to prop morale and sincere disclosure to maintain intimate
relations.[18]

With the increase in letter writing came an increase in dissemination
activity through delivery systems. Not only did home-front writers mail
more correspondence and newspapers than before, they also stuffed
their envelopes with clippings and other literary scraps of a patriotic
nature and directed bundles bearing imprints through the ever mounting number of express companies. While New Englanders had stayed in
touch with distant family members and friends by sending all these literary items throughout the antebellum era, home-front distribution to
those in the South took on an even greater sense of urgency. Varied
reading matter was often in short supply for Union armies; combatants
had to rely upon what was available through tract societies, scavenging,
borrowing, and a few limited army libraries. Newspapers were especially craved, but once-familiar and treasured papers were not readily
available. Furthermore, newspapers from home carried with them local
news about townsfolk as well as the personal "imprint" of the sender.[19]

Because senders knew how eagerly their missives and bundles were
anticipated not only by the receiver but also secondary readers, they
feared misdirection. Accordingly, some civilians kept track. Daniel
Child, for one, maintained a careful record of letters or bundles he sent

to or received from his son Frank, one of the New England Guards sent to New Bern, North Carolina. Ellen Morse, who visited the post office every day to send or receive letters, pursued unacknowledged receipts with worried queries, fraught with responsibility not only to Frank but to the succession of men, especially "those in the hospital," into whose hands they fell after he had finished reading the shipment. Hannah Cabot felt the same for her surgeon husband, but went further to place him second in line of responsibility: "I shall send you several papers constantly for yr patients as well as yrself," she promised her husband, just after complaining to him about all her lost mail.[20] Personalized communications in these and many other cases became selfless patriotic acts.

Patriotism also engulfed many forms of *gratis* literary dissemination, especially that effected through charitable donations. Congregational minister Seth Arnold, for example, on various occasions sent the freedpeople a barrel of dry goods including books and donated money "for Sailor's and Soldiers reading" and to the Christian Commission and Sanitary Commission. The latter, to which several of our home-front informants contributed their goods, energies, and ticket money, was only disparaged by Caroline Curtis, a Democratic lawyer's wife, who in 1864 objected to the uncouth manner of one male agent who "scented the house with tobacco, & carried off a pile of novels & magazines for the soldiers at Readville." Generally, enthusiasts welcomed the chance to give away reading materials, and even Persis Black seemed eager to join in with her village "awakened to the call" to donate "books, pamphlets, newspapers" along with other items to a local district committee, after she heard an 1861 sermon on "Charity & benevolence."[21]

While charity grew in importance, occasional literary gift giving declined. One reason was that New Englanders showed their support by economizing on luxury goods, and books were relative luxuries. Another reason was that photo albums supplanted other books as gifts at holiday season, a time when both blank books and fancy "gift annuals" had in decades past sufficed. Oddly enough, none of the informants considered here recorded giving away a book to a departing soldier as a memento—an act that would seem to be a natural evolution from the antebellum era's practice of presenting literary gifts, symbolizing the meaningful relationship between donor and receiver, to sojourners before departure. Perhaps the pain of parting was too great to record any such transactions that took place. Some soldiers did ask their kin back home to send their own or other books; within the antebellum pattern of literary experience, these could be as redolent of social meaning as a recently presented gift, in fact, probably more so, for literary objects acquired deeper associations with time.[22] This suggests that the lack of recorded wartime literary gift exchange corresponded to the virtual disappearance of the practice itself, not just the recording of it. Given the deep social meaning that traditionally adhered to literary gifts, it comes as a surprise that war relics sent home, such as confiscated "sesech books" — titles like *The Ornithology of Carolina*, and Julius Caesar's *Commentaries* — once owned by Confederates, were prized at all, even as trophies or for their monetary value, something that would have repulsed New Englanders during the antebellum years.[23] That such relics were acceptable is but another sign of the severance on the home front of the antebellum nexus between social and literary experience and the appropriation of the two by patriotism.

Like gift giving, the activity of lending privately owned books slowed down, although social callers often carried newspapers, clippings, letters, and photographs with them to show to the host. "Dick's is nearly reduced to its primitive condition, by frequent handling," Ellen Wright admitted after passing around a photograph too often. Elizabeth Cabot once fashioned herself into a walking lending library when she sported a published piece of war-related correspondence on her clothing. "I have gone about a good deal with the letter pinned on the front of my dress," she wrote to her sister Ellen, "& when I meet those who deserved it have allowed them to read it."[24] One could in this way become a billboard for the Cause.

Reading out loud, a highly social form of dissemination because it depended upon face-to-face interaction, continued during the war, but not as evidently as before. During the 1850s, Asa Black, for example, routinely read to his wife Persis, who recorded lengthy records of some sessions; by 1861 she instead usually heard public sermons, or sabbath school lessons from her youngster. This once voracious oral reader admitted in November 1862 that she had "not even the privilege of reading a single volume for the past year." A similar pattern was followed by J. Edwin Harris, who formerly read aloud to boardinghouse mates, but seldom if ever did so after he returned from the battlefront in 1863. In several other accounts, reading aloud was highlighted as a way of entertaining children or soothing the ill, rather than as an adult recreation. Caroline Curtis's 12 July 1863 entry was typical of her Civil War diary, but not of her earlier journals, which recounted proportionally more mature listeners: "Went to church — in the afternoon, reading to the children & trying to keep them happy & quiet." Group reading probably waned due to the intrusion of "war talk" about the news or other intelligence from the battlefield into home-based sociabilities. "Do you remember how Captain Ames read to us from the New York papers, and what long war talks we would have?" Nellie Browne asked her correspondent Sarah Howard in November 1862.[25]

Certainly, there is abundant evidence that oral renderings of the news, and also telegraphs and letters from the front occupied hours of adult reading and listening. Letters were not only "loaned" to other people to read, they were read aloud. On one Sunday in December 1862, for example, a letter from Frank Child on the front was read out loud in Boston parlors not less than three times. Given that personal correspondence often relayed information of value to other people, passing it on was being only responsible. "[A]fter the battle I hope that you will send a telegraph about all our friends, if possible," Hannah Cabot begged her husband, just before the start of the Peninsular Campaign. "This waiting with a drawn sword over our heads is perhaps as trying to the friends here as it is to the soldiers themselves." Because a precedent of letting others see or listen to letters had been set in the antebellum period, it followed that some writers, who during the war often emoted more openly than before, rightly assumed and feared a public airing of even intimate letters. "I am all the time thinking every word I write that others are going to hear it read," Frank Morse confessed to his wife in October 1862. "Yet I suppose you cannot avoid it. Dont read all. Tell them it is private." Ellen, who indeed could not avoid it and read aloud his letters to her grandmother and a fellow parsonage dweller, retorted, "What made you think that every one saw your letters? . . . I hardly ever read all you write to any one." Unlike Ellen Morse, Sarah Browne, whose letters from Albert were also public property, scolded her husband, who wrote too openly about his loneliness and loss of faith in the Bible and in mankind's goodness. "When you write again," she advised him in January 1863, "leave all comment on characters unholy[;] touch only what is good." In response to a later letter filled with *"mental doubts"* which she read aloud, she offered, "[W]rite it on a sheet to *me* and marked 'private.' "[26] With family and friends hanging on every word from the front, letters had a more profound impact upon the reading public than ever before.

Perhaps because reading aloud and listening had suddenly become so pressing, doing so while engaged in other activities, especially sewing or knitting, was less likely to happen during the war years than before. On the one hand, reader/listeners wanted to fix upon important letters, dispatches, and news without distraction. On the other hand, devoted concentration necessary for rapid home-production of clothing and socks for soldiers in the first months of the war discouraged women from reading or listening while performing important handiwork. "All the ladies are still sewing their fingers off," Elizabeth Cabot told her sister Ellen in June 1861, with no mention of a reader to entertain them, and later noted that "in Boston every woman you meet has her knitting visible." While these women apparently gave their undivided attention to "patriotic toil," one student at Mrs. Sedgwick's Academy in Lenox tried to do both—even if it meant studying and knitting—a rare alliance of activities even in decades earlier. A fellow student marveled that the knitter "is now rabid on the sock subject, & keeps losing her place in her lessons to pick up her stitches." At the academy these students probably volunteered to sew hospital shirts and hem towels from fabric purchased by their schoolmarm for them, instead of the personal items they had traditionally manufactured while listening to Sedgwick read aloud during her usual 4 P.M. reading hour. After the Sanitary Commission coordinated women's efforts, the remaining vestiges of sewing and reading together for patriotic ends evidently vanished altogether, and the women considered in this essay instead raised money for the organization, staged commission-sponsored tableaux, attended fairs, packed barrels, or sorted clothes and bandages at a local station.[27]

Other factors besides the war were at work to desocialize reading. Increasingly available home sewing machines not only took the sociability out of reading, but out of sewing as well, especially insofar as they cut back on social calling. "My sewing machine . . . does not allow me one moments time to step into the neighbors," Persis Black recorded in May 1862.[28] Unfeasible to cart off to the neighbors like a sewing basket, difficult to crank with a book in hand, and impossible to silence so as to hear a reader over the noise, the machine began to alter the fundamental antebellum New England domestic routine of sewing and reading. Black and other women still performed handiwork, though, for machines could not embroider, knit, cut patterns, pin, or do fancy work. Nevertheless, women read and listened much less while sewing during the war because the combined forces of mechanization and war-oriented reading eroded the old reading-sewing alliance while diminishing the role of the oral reader as a social agent.

The encroachment of war-related literature upon everyday consciousness cannot be overestimated. Most evidently it registered as an obsession with newspapers that began as war approached, reached a crescendo in the first months of fighting in 1861, and nearly replaced all other forms of reading—let alone writing—throughout the conflict. This becomes striking because antebellum readers, whether male or female, often neglected to write about newspaper reading, it being a desultory rather than purposeful form of reading and thus deemed not worthy of record. In stark contrast, by 1861 newspaper reading had become full of import. "Nearly two months have passed away since I have opened this Journal to record the passing events," Zachariah Allen wrote in July 1861. "Much of the leisure time I have is taken up in reading the daily news of the Rebellion." Women, too, honed their political acumen more assiduously than ever by focusing on the news. The once promiscuous reader Persis Black admitted in June 1862, "The extent of my reading is the daily newspaper." The first book she picked up after April 1861 seemed like a challenge: "I am reading 'Les Miserables' & it is a large work for me who never reads anything, but the daily paper." In July 1861 Ellen Wright griped that "[t]he papers are seized, & read, with avidity. Mine is a day old, before I see it." Likewise, Sarah Browne could declare by February 1862, "My time is fully occupied in reading the accounts of our glorious victories." For some diarists, like Charles Cobb, who once fancied novels above other types of literature, his accounts of newspapers were the only evidence of any reading during the war years.[29] Conversely, only one of our diarists, J. Edwin Harris, a Union army veteran and, curiously, a prodigious reader, rarely mentioned a piece of war news while at home. Harris wrote as he did just prior to enlistment, in terse entries of titles read but little else about his everyday life — showing a consciousness already divided between his literary life and everyday political events around him.

For the majority who did capture their newspaper engagements, most kept a simple, sketchy, timeline of war events that clustered around a few key periods: the firing on Fort Sumter in April 1861; Lincoln's replacement of General George McClellan with John Pope and the latter's campaign from 11 July through August 1862; the string of events in July 1863 that included the Battle of Gettysburg, the Siege of Vicksburg, and the draft riots; and, of course, the war's conclusion in April 1865 and the subsequent assassination of Lincoln. These and other less prominent events were recorded both as a way of giving ephemeral newsprint more permanent form and to act as a reference guide for coordinating and evaluating often contradictory intelligence. Of course, record keepers were likely to record what was relevant to their embattled loved ones. Daniel Child, for example, wrote more war news in 1863, especially about North Carolina, while his son was stationed there. Similarly, Persis Black worried for her townsmen in the 1862 Peninsular Campaign: "Yorktown evacuated & other battles won — but we have not particulars as to our Maine soldiers." Most of all, newspaper readers kept track of the war's unfolding events to participate in the ongoing related discussions that had come to eclipse all other social communications. In the midst of keeping close accounts from 13 through 19 April 1861, Caroline Curtis wrote, referring to the start of hostilities, "Sallie came out to spend the day — but one thing to talk or think about." Daniel Child spent 2 January 1863 gathering opinion on the final printed copy of the Emancipation Proclamation: "I have talked with no one today who objected to the measure, or the terms." In a similar vein, Elizabeth Cabot reported that "Of final defeat no one ever speaks, one hears less of the War's being over in six months, certainly, but who ever believes that kind of talk[?]" Observers also referred to a general "excitement," a term traditionally used to describe the ill effect of widely circulated political or tragic news. "Continued public excitement having been caused by the threatened intervention of foreign nations in the rebellion," Zachariah Allen pronounced on 1 September 1862. While New Englanders like Allen may be referring to the immediate excitement around them, they could also, as if omniscient, allude to all Unionists. "The country is electrified by an official announcement that *Richmond* was taken at 8.15 this A.M.," Abby Stimson announced to her diary on 3 April 1865.[30] That these record keepers were not always as clear as Stimson about distinguishing local and national excitement further testifies to their melding of everyday social affairs with more abstract political developments.

News readers, of course, responded to events as individuals with ideas of their own or in highly personal, often emotional ways, but such responses were formulated with a keen awareness of the "many rumors" and "exaggerations & contradictions" circulating by word-of-mouth, telegraph reports, or the newspapers, as well as government attempts to censor the news through every form. "It is said to night, or rather I read it on a telegraph Board, that Fort Sumpter [*sic*] had surrendered," a skeptical Christopher Keith of Providence confided to his diary on 8 November 1863. "It may be entirely incorrect, but so I read." In response to the unreliability of news, readers armed themselves with a self-protective shield of apprehension. As Ellen Wright explained in May 1861, "[T]here is no fun in getting enthusiastic over despatches, which are contradicted the next minute." Elizabeth Cabot resigned herself: "We don't dare to believe anything the newspapers say until they have said it at least a dozen times."[31] No wonder there was such a communal pooling together of information from varied sources, such as letters, telegrams, and gossip during social calls.

Notwithstanding the disclaimers, newspaper readers, often deeply affected, responded with emotion and analytical commentary upon what they read. On reading Abraham Lincoln's Second Inaugural Address, Sarah Browne despaired, "I am much disappointed at finding it unmistakably conservative." Many readers expressed their hopes for an end to the fighting. After reading of Jubal Early's July 1864 Confederate raid into Maryland, Christopher Keith began a lengthy synopsis of two days of reading, ending on the hopeful note: "Next Spring, I am sure will see this war closed, whether we conquer the South or not." "The war continues, but it has assumed a different look to me within the last few days," Charles Cobb wrote on 24 February 1862 between engagements as a traveling fiddler, "a look of caving on the part of the South, especially in Tennessee, but perhaps it is no such thing." Others placated their fears by locating national affairs within an international context. "With the progress of liberty to the Serfs of Russia, emancipation in the West Indies, freedom to Italy, and the general advance of liberal principles throughout the world, there is no reason for despondency, although Providence 'gives vice to bloom its little hour,'" Zachariah Allen concluded after reading about the Battle of Fredericksburg. As they did when assessing public excitement, readers often blurred the line between their own opinions and the nation's mood, an unusual response in the antebellum era. Elizabeth Cabot, for example, used the collective "we" and the personal "I" almost interchangeably in her response to the distressing news reports released during the summer of 1862. "We are expecting every hour to hear of a great battle," she wrote to her brother-in-law while at her summer home in Beverly; "if we fail again . . . , I believe it will only be the signal for fresh efforts." Then, she slipped into the first person plural: "More & more we realise that we are struggling for our national existence & that we *must* succeed at whatever cost."[32] Although she had been an astute political commentator since the early 1850s, Cabot had never before so clearly identified herself with the nation.

Epistolary discussions of reading matter were often filled with apprehension not only of the news, but of striking an ever-tenuous consensus of opinion. Antebellum letter writers who shared opinions of books usually tried to agree, if only cursorily; the war, in contrast, challenged cordiality and threatened communications between those with dissimilar alliances. Elizabeth Cabot, for one, censored her own discussions of England's stance in regard to the Confederacy in letters to her sister Ellen, who was married to English politico Edward Twisleton. The couple in England equivocated about the North's pursuit of the war, which led the American sister to make her case. "I can't help hoping that you will find something to love & honor & sympathise with, in the position the North holds now," she wrote in May 1861; "for it is no matter of dollars & cents that holds us together, but a common love of law & liberty & a courage that is founded on obedience to the noblest motives & not on any sordid calculations." Whether or not this convinced the couple, they capitulated, of which Cabot observed, "[W]e are a close company again."[33] Epistolary war talk resumed until Ellen died in July 1862; Cabot seldom wrote with such astuteness to subsequent correspondents.

For those on the front, cordial literary discussions — even about extrapolitical matters — were invited, often urged upon folks back home. Such correspondence attempted to mirror face-to-face chats over commonly read materials or hours once spent in reading together, but to do this correspondents had to coordinate reading. Some New Englanders sent each other items or transcriptions of poetry to read or indicated what to read. In the hopes of addressing her husband's wavering zeal, Sarah Browne directed his attention in November 1863 to an eyewitness report in the *Salem Register* about inhumane Confederate prison conditions that she promised "will make your heart sick." In case he missed the point, she asked, "Will it not give courage to the *faintest* heart, to know facts such as these?" Other correspondents tried not only to read the same thing, but at the exact same time. "You say you have commenced reading the bible in course," Frank Morse wrote to his wife Ellen on 9 January 1864. "Can we not arrange it so that we can both read the same portion each day? I would suggest that we read three chapters per day commencing with the old testament. That will make the 28th 29th and 30th chapters of Gen.[esis] the lesson for tomorrow." The two kept up their sessions, despite problems with synchronization, until at least 17 April 1864. "Where are you reading now in the Bible?" Frank asked Ellen who had evidently set her own pace. "My chapter to-night is the 12th of Hebrews."[34]

Simulated reading circles that attempted to replicate old ways were mirrored in epistolary parenting and instruction carried on from afar. Through letters, children on the home front indirectly benefited from their embattled fathers' guidance and mothers were reassured by spousal input. After Ellen Morse conceived during Frank's 1863 furlough, he took up the book *Ministering Children* and other relevant pieces, and, after the birth, pointed Ellen to periodical articles, such as one "on the government of children," while reminding her "That matter is now entirely with you." Inspired by a similar realization, Samuel Cabot enjoined his sons to "do your lessons & dont give your mother too much trouble in helping you." More than Cabot, Albert Browne tenaciously clung to his role as father and teacher. "His dear little son is growing up without the care and oversight of his father," he apologized in a December 1863 letter. "Let father see how you have improved in knowledge and goodness, write to him and tell him what you have read, and what you think of your reading," he implored in a February 1864 letter and quoted from Noah Webster's Bible (Proverbs 8:1) — "'Hear instruction, and be wise, and refuse it not.'" After adding more transcribed citations, Albert queried, as if in the classroom: "There is a good book which I sometimes read which contains the substance of the above sentences, what book is it? . . . [R]ead it often." Eddie wrote back, "The verses that you quoted are from the Bible," and answered five other questions that Albert fielded. Besides his quiz answers, Eddie also submitted hand-drawn maps and a personal journal for his father's judgment. His mother and sister wrote excellent progress reports. "Eddie has been reading by himself, twenty three pages of the Arabian Nights,"

Sarah Browne averred on 29 February 1864. "He will be as great a reader as is brother Albert." The child's eagerness was driven in part by a competition with freed boys that Albert had fueled as he observed, on one 1863 occasion, that they were "real good scholars—can read, spell, & cypher altho they have been in school but a year." In a December 1863 letter about an African American servant boy in whom he took special interest, he boasted: "[P]oor Silas gets the word as near as he is able, but he is real smart & will soon know as much as most white boys."[35]

Under the drastic circumstances of dislocation effected by the war, subtle querying and inducements to study that marked antebellum letters gave way to strident goading and shrill competitiveness. The steady habits, disciplined comportment, and lonely hours spent mastering lessons that characterized study were difficult enough for children distracted by the war. Even twenty-year-old Ellen Wright explained that getting "the news from the telegraph office" was agitating: "I can tell you it didn't make it any easier to study!"[36] As the domestic authority figures in their life put studious reading on hold for newspaper scanning or the occasional retreat into leisurely perusal of books, students could perhaps sense their singular—indeed, isolated—experiences as readers in the domestic social setting. For study, leisurely reading, and war-related reading had taken on distinctive meanings—and the latter reading now had come to predominate over the other forms.

Conclusion

The alliance between everyday social intercourse and literature that New Englanders had crafted during the antebellum period was threatened during the Civil War years when both social and literary experiences were channeled into the Union cause. Because so many local and public forms of sociability were touched by the war, New Englanders on the home front who remained both social and literary usually took on the role of "literary patriot"—one whose everyday production, dissemination, and reception of reading material related in some way to the war. Like Unionists, dissenters were unavoidably drawn into the practices associated with literary patriotism. For both dissident and advocate alike, productive activity, such as diary keeping and both letter and essay writing, bore traces of the war both in terms of content and purpose, while dissemination of literature, especially to loved ones dislocated by the war, took on a sense of urgency. As reception of literature became virtually synonymous with engaging war news and responding to it in writing, "war talks," or epistolary discourse, reading non-war-related materials took on more trifling significance as a leisurely, self-edifying pursuit invested with little social value. Even study, disconnected as it was from the concerns of war, seemed ever more removed from the affairs of everyday life.

Because the war consumed literary experience and transformed it to serve patriotic ends, it lost an element of its once disinterested purpose — the maintenance of social ties for their own sake. Literature instead had become instrumental to warfare, like cannonballs or rifles. Otherwise, it was dysfunctional to the cause, distracting to its devoted pursuit, and, ultimately, relegated to secondary importance — sequestered into a space of its own, where in time it came to serve individual rather than social ends. "Where are the peacemakers?" Persis Black wondered as her neighbors marched off to war in April 1861.[37] She could just as well have been searching for her literary companions, who likewise seemed to vanish with peacetime, perhaps forever. New Englanders like Black, who attempted to reconstruct their literary lives socially after the war, found it was impossible to repair that delicate chain that had once so intimately linked human relations and literary meaning.

Notes

Thanks go to the National Endowment for the Humanities for a 1998–1999 Fellowship for University Teachers as well as matching support from Georgia State University for funding fifteen months of leave time, 1998–1999. We also owe gratitude to the Schlesinger Library for dual Honorary Visiting Fellowships awarded during the same period. During that time we pulled together our research, wrote the bulk of our book manuscript on antebellum literary experience, and began research on this article. The final phase of writing this article was underwritten by a Summer 2000 Research Support Grant from Georgia State University's College of Arts and Science, via the Department of History.

1. James Cabot to Samuel Cabot Jr., 29 Apr. 1862; Arthur Cabot to Samuel Cabot Jr., 9 May 1862; Samuel Cabot Jr. to James Cabot, 3 Apr. [1862?], Almy Family Papers, Schlesinger Library, Radcliffe Institute, Harvard University (hereafter SL).

2. On home-front disruptions, see Nina Silber and Mary Beth Sievens, "Introduction," in *Yankee Correspondence: Civil War Letters between New England Soldiers and the Homefront*, ed. idem (Charlottesville, 1996), 1–24.

3. Anne C. Rose, *Victorian America and the Civil War* (Cambridge, 1992), 123–24; Ronald J. Zboray and Mary Saracino Zboray, "Books, Reading, and the World of Goods in Antebellum New England," *American Quarterly* 48 (Dec. 1996): 587–622; idem, "'Have You Read . . . ?': Real Readers and Their Responses in Antebellum Boston and Its Region," *Nineteenth-Century Literature* 52 (Sept. 1997): 139–70.

4. Most accounts of reading focus on military life: Bell Irvin Wiley, *The Life of Billy Yank: The Common Soldier of the Union* (Indianapolis, 1952), 153–57; David Kaser, *Books and Libraries in Camp and Battle: The Civil War Experi-*

ence (Westport, Conn., 1984); and James M. McPherson, "'Spend Much Time in Reading the Daily Papers': The Press and Army Morale in the Civil War," *Atlanta History* 42 (1998): 7–18. Cf. Louise L. Stevenson, *The Victorian Homefront: American Thought and Culture, 1860–1880* (New York, 1991), chaps. 1 and 2.

5. Roger Chartier, ed., *The Culture of Print: Power and the Uses of Print in Early Modern Europe*, trans. Lydia G. Cochrane (Princeton, 1989); Guglielmo Cavallo and Roger Chartier, eds., *A History of Reading in the West*, trans. Lydia G. Cochrane (Amherst, 1999); Janice Radway, *Reading the Romance: Women, Patriarchy, and Popular Literature* (Chapel Hill, 1984); Elizabeth Long, "Textual Interpretation as Collective Action," in *The Ethnography of Reading*, ed. Jonathan Boyarin (Berkeley, 1993), 180–211.

6. George M. Fredrickson, *The Inner Civil War: Northern Intellectuals and the Crisis of the Union* (New York, 1965), vii; Rose, *Victorian America and the Civil War*; Stevenson, *Victorian Homefront*; Randall C. Jimerson, *The Private Civil War: Popular Thought during the Sectional Conflict* (Baton Rouge, 1988); Edmund Wilson, *Patriotic Gore: Studies in the Literature of the American Civil War* (New York, 1962).

7. Zboray and Zboray, "Books, Reading, and the World of Goods"; idem, "'Have You Read . . . ?'"; idem, "Reading and Everyday Life in Antebellum Boston: The Diary of Daniel F. and Mary D. Child," *Libraries and Culture* 32 (Summer 1997): 285–323; idem, "Political News and Female Readership in Antebellum Boston and Its Region," *Journalism History* 22 (1996): 2–14; idem, "Transcendentalism in Print: Production, Dissemination, and Common Reception," in *Transient and Permanent: The Transcendentalist Movement and Its Contexts*, ed. Charles Capper and Conrad Edick Wright (Boston, 1999), 310–81; and our book manuscript "Everyday Ideas: Socio-Literary Experience among Antebellum New Englanders."

8. Hannah Lowell Jackson to Sarah (Jackson) Russell, 6 June 1839, typed transcript, Almy Family Papers, SL; *The Annual Register; or, A View of the History and Politics of the Year*, 25 vols. (London, 1839–1863); J. Edwin Harris, Journal, 14 June, 1 Sept., and 8 Oct. 1856, Joshua Edwin Harris Papers, Collections of Maine Historical Society (hereafter MeHS).

9. Zboray and Zboray, "Reading and Everyday Life in Antebellum Boston," 291, table 2; Persis Sibley Andrews Black, 30 Nov. 1841, Diary, MeHS.

10. Taunton Social Library, "Record of Books Circulated May 7, 1856–March 3, 1859," Old Colony Historical Society, Taunton, Massachusetts.

11. Ronald J. Zboray, *A Fictive People: Antebellum Economic Development and the American Reading Public* (New York, 1993), chap. 11.

12. James Davie Butler, *Commonplace Books; Why and How Kept: A Lecture; With Suggestions on Object and Method in Reading* (Hartford, 1887), 11.

13. Persis Sibley Andrews Black, Diary, 28 Apr. 1861 and 7 Sept. 1862, Dabney Family Papers, Massachusetts Historical Society (hereafter MHS).

14. Black, Diary, 12 July 1863, Dabney Family Papers, MHS.

15. Sarah Smith (Cox) Browne, Diary, 3 May 1862, Browne Family Papers, SL; Elizabeth Cabot to Ellen Twisleton and Mary Parkman, 7 Apr. 1862; Elizabeth Cabot to Mary Parkman, 30 Mar. 1862, Cabot Family Papers, SL; Lilly Dana, Diary, 11 July 1862, Dana Family Papers, SL.

16. Persis Sibley Andrews Black, Diary, 17 Aug. 1862, Dabney Family Papers, MHS; Ellen Wright to Martha Coffin Wright, 24 June 1861, Garrison Family Papers, Sophia Smith Collection, Smith College (hereafter SSC); Sarah Ellen Browne to Albert Gallatin Browne, 30 Jan. 1864, Sarah Ellen Browne Papers, SL; Sarah Smith (Cox) Browne to Albert Gallatin Browne, 4 Jan. 1864, Browne Family Papers, SL; Frank C. Morse to Ellen J. Morse, 2 Apr. 1864, 25 Mar. 1864, and 28 Mar. 1864, Frank C. Morse Papers, MHS; Lilly Dana, Diary, 17 and 20 June 1862, Dana Family Papers, SL; Alfred J. Bacon and Catharine E. Bacon to Lilly Dana, 20 Oct. 1862; Alfred J. Bacon to Lilly Dana, 29 Sept. 1864 and 10 July 1865, Dana Family Papers, SL; Arthur Cabot to Samuel Cabot Jr., 9 May 1862, Almy Family Papers, SL; Edward Cox Browne to Albert Gallatin Browne, 23 Oct. 1863, Browne Family Papers, SL; Keith F. Davis, "'A Terrible Distinctness': Photography of the Civil War Era," in *Photography in Nineteenth-Century America*, ed. Martha A. Sandweiss (Fort Worth, 1991), 130–79; Alan Trachtenberg, *Reading American Photographs: Images as History, Mathew Brady to Walker Evans* (New York, 1989), 82–89.

17. Wilson, *Patriotic Gore*; Sarah Smith (Cox) Browne, Diary, 5 Feb. 1864, Browne Family Papers, SL; Christopher T. Keith, Diary, 16 July 1862, at back of vol. 2, Miscellaneous Manuscripts Collection, Rhode Island Historical Society (hereafter RIHS); Abby Clark Stimson, Diary, 21 July 1861, 9 and 13 Oct. 1861, 13 Dec. 1862, 22 Feb. 1864, Diman Family Papers, Manuscripts Collection, RIHS; Keith, Diary, 2 Sept. 1862; Ellen Wright to Lucy McKim, 2 May 1861; Ellen Wright to Martha Coffin Wright, 27 May 1861, Garrison Family Papers, SSC; H. B. Howe to [Caroline Atherton Mason], 22 Mar. 1863, Briggs Family Papers, SL; Caroline Atherton Mason, "The Soldier's Dream of Home" and "The Response," *National Anti-Slavery Standard* 23 (14 Feb. 1863): [4].

18. Albert Gallatin Browne to Sarah Ellen Browne and Alice Browne, [17?] Jan. 1864, Browne Family Papers, SL; Frank C. Morse to Ellen J. Morse, 6 Jan. 1864, Ellen J. Morse to Frank C. Morse, 25 Oct. 1862 and 7 Oct. 1862, Frank C. Morse to Ellen J. Morse, 7 Jan. 1864, Frank C. Morse Papers, MHS; Alice Browne to Albert Gallatin Browne, [undated] Nov. 1863, Browne Family Papers, SL; Ellen J. Morse to Frank C. Morse, 28 Sept. 1862, Frank C. Morse Papers, MHS.

19. Silber and Sievens, *Yankee Correspondence*, 2. Hannah Cabot to Samuel Cabot Jr., 29 Apr. 1862, 12 Apr. 1863, Almy Family Papers, SL; Elizabeth Cabot to Ellen Twisleton, 17 June [1861]; Elizabeth Cabot to Mary Parkman, 19 Oct. 1863, Cabot Family Papers, SL; Ellen Wright to [Frank Wright?], fragment [ca. Sept. 1861], Garrison Family Papers, SSC. McPherson, "'Spend Much Time in Reading'"; Kaser, *Books and Libraries*, 78, 26–29.

20. Daniel F. Child, Diary, 2 Nov. 1862; 1 and 28 Dec. 1862; 7, 19, and 25 Jan. 1863, Daniel Franklin Child Papers, MHS; Ellen J. Morse to Frank C. Morse, 7 Oct. 1862 and Frank C. Morse to Ellen J. Morse, 15 Nov. 1862, Frank C. Morse Papers, MHS; Hannah Cabot to Samuel Cabot Jr., 2 May 1862, Almy Family Papers, SL.

21. Seth Shaler Arnold, Diary, 11 Aug. 1862, 27 Apr. 1863, 3 Mar. 1864, 9 Feb. 1864, typed transcript, Vermont Historical Society (hereafter VHS); Lilly Dana, Diary, 4 Aug. 1862, Dana Family Papers, SL; Elizabeth Cabot to Mary Parkman, 20 Dec. 1863, Cabot Family Papers, SL; Alice Browne to Albert Gal-

latin Browne, Nov. 1863, and Sarah Smith (Cox) Browne to Albert Gallatin Browne, [undated] 1863, Browne Family Papers, SL; Caroline Gardiner Curtis, Diary, 19 Oct. 1864, Cary Family Papers III, MHS; Jeanie Attie, *Patriotic Toil: Northern Women and the American Civil War* (Ithaca, 1998), esp. chap. 4; Persis Sibley Andrews Black, Diary, 27 Oct. 1861, Dabney Family Papers, MHS.

22. Frank C. Morse to Ellen J. Morse, 26 Aug. 1862 and 15 Oct. 1864, Frank C. Morse Papers, MHS; Sarah Smith (Cox) Browne to Albert Gallatin Browne, 13 Oct. 1863, Browne Family Papers, SL.

23. Sarah Smith (Cox) Browne, Diary, 3 Oct. 1864, Albert Gallatin Browne to Sarah Smith (Cox) Browne, 4 May 1865, and Albert Gallatin Browne to Edward Cox Browne, 14 Feb. 1865, Browne Family Papers, SL.

24. Ellen Wright to Beverly Chase, 29 May 1861, Garrison Family Papers, SSC; Elizabeth Cabot to Ellen Twisleton, 11 Nov. 1861, Cabot Family Papers, SL.

25. Persis Sibley Andrews Black, Diary, 18 July 1852, MeHS; idem, Diary, 16 Nov. 1862, Dabney Family Papers, MHS; J. Edwin Harris, Journal, 20, 24, and 31 Jan. and 3 Feb. 1858, Joshua Edwin Harris Papers, MeHS; Caroline Gardiner Curtis, Diary, 12 July 1863, Cary Family Papers III, MHS; Sarah Ellen Browne to Sarah B. Howard, 20 Nov. 1862, Browne Family Papers, SL.

26. Daniel F. Child, Diary, 28 Dec. 1862, Daniel Franklin Child Papers, MHS; Hannah Cabot to Samuel Cabot Jr., 21 Apr. 1862 in 20 Apr. 1862, Almy Family Papers, SL; Frank C. Morse to Ellen J. Morse, 12 Oct. 1862 and Ellen J. Morse to Frank C. Morse, 20 Oct. 1862, Frank C. Morse Papers, MHS; Sarah Smith (Cox) Browne to Albert Gallatin Browne, 12 Jan. 1863 and 30 Dec. 1864, Browne Family Papers, SL.

27. Elizabeth Cabot to Ellen Twisleton and "Millsey," 3 June 1861; Elizabeth Cabot to Ellen Twisleton, 14 Oct. 1861, Cabot Family Papers, SL; Attie, *Patriotic Toil*; Ellen Wright to Martha Coffin Wright, 20 June 1861, 20 July 1861, 31 July 1861, and 21 Sept. 1861, Garrison Family Papers, SSC; Seth Shaler Arnold, Diary, 25 Dec. 1863 and 5 June 1863, VHS; Sarah Smith (Cox) Browne to Albert Gallatin Browne, [undated] 1863, Browne Family Papers, SL; Elizabeth Cabot to Mary Parkman, 20 Dec. 1863, Cabot Family Papers, SL; Caroline Gardiner Curtis, Diary, 17 June 1864, Cary Family Papers III, MHS; Lilly Dana, Diary, 4 Aug. 1862, Dana Family Papers, SL; Curtis, Diary, 21 June 1864.

28. Persis Sibley Andrews Black, Diary, 25 May 1862, Dabney Family Papers, MHS. On machine ownership, see Caroline Gardiner Curtis, Diary, 29 Apr. 1859, Cary Family Papers III, MHS; Sarah Smith (Cox) Browne, Diary, 10 Jan. 1862, Browne Family Papers, SL; Elizabeth Cabot to Ellen Twisleton, 3 Nov. [1861?], Cabot Family Papers, SL; Daniel F. Child and Mary D. Child, Diary, 13 May 1857, Daniel Franklin Child Papers, MHS.

29. Zachariah Allen, Diary, 15 and 22 July 1861, Zachariah Allen Papers, Manuscripts Collection, RIHS; Kathleen L. Endres, "The Women's Press in the Civil War: A Portrait of Patriotism, Propaganda, and Prodding," *Civil War History* 30 (1984): 31–53; Persis Sibley Andrews Black, Diary, 22 June 1862 and 6 Sept. 1863, Dabney Family Papers, MHS; Ellen Wright to Martha Coffin Wright, 25 July 1861, Garrison Family Papers, SSC; Sarah Smith (Cox) Browne, Diary, 20 Feb. 1862, Browne Family Papers, SL; Charles M. Cobb, Journal, 18 Oct. 1861, 24 Feb. 1862, 19 Aug. 1862, and 9 Nov. 1862, transcript, VHS.

30. Persis Sibley Andrews Black, Diary, 11 May 1862, Dabney Family Papers, MHS; Caroline Gardiner Curtis, Diary, 17 Apr. 1861, Cary Family Papers III, MHS; Daniel F. Child, Diary, 2 Jan. 1863, Daniel Franklin Child Papers, MHS; Elizabeth Cabot to Mary Parkman, 16 Aug. 1862, Cabot Family Papers, SL; Zachariah Allen, Diary, 1 Sept. 1862, Zachariah Allen Papers, Manuscripts Collection, RIHS; Abby Clark Stimson, Diary, 3 Apr. 1865, Diman Family Papers, Manuscripts Collection, RIHS.

31. Caroline Gardiner Curtis, Diary, 23 Apr. 1861, Cary Family Papers III, MHS; Elizabeth Cabot to Ellen Twisleton, 29 July 1862, Cabot Family Papers, SL; Richard B. Kielbowicz, "The Telegraph, Censorship, and Politics at the Outset of the Civil War," *Civil War History* 40 (1994): 95–118; Christopher T. Keith, Diary, 8 Nov. 1863, Miscellaneous Manuscripts Collection, RIHS; Ellen Wright to Martha Coffin Wright, [undated] May 1861, Garrison Family Papers, SSC; Elizabeth Cabot to Ellen Twisleton, 24 June [1861], Cabot Family Papers, SL.

32. Sarah Smith (Cox) Browne, Diary, 12 Apr. 1865, Browne Family Papers, SL; Christopher T. Keith, Diary, 8 July 1864, Miscellaneous Manuscripts Collection, RIHS; Charles M. Cobb, Journal, 24 Feb. 1862, transcript, VHS; Zachariah Allen, Diary, 11 Dec. 1862, Zachariah Allen Papers, Manuscripts Collection, RIHS; Elizabeth Cabot to Edward Twisleton, 19 Aug. 1862, Cabot Family Papers, SL.

33. Elizabeth Cabot to Ellen Twisleton, 5 and 26 May 1861, Cabot Family Papers, SL; James M. McPherson, *Battle Cry of Freedom: The Civil War Era* (New York, 1988), 549–53.

34. Sarah Smith (Cox) Browne to Albert Gallatin Browne, 15 Nov. 1863, Browne Family Papers, SL; Frank C. Morse to Ellen J. Morse, 17 Apr. 1864 and 9 Jan. 1864, Frank C. Morse Papers, MHS.

35. Frank C. Morse, Diary, 17 Jan. 1863, Frank C. Morse to Ellen J. Morse, 10 July 1864 and 1 Jan. 1865, Frank C. Morse Papers, MHS; Maria Louisa Charlesworth, *Ministering Children: A Tale Dedicated to Childhood* (New York, 1855); Samuel Cabot Jr. to James Cabot, 3 Apr. [1862?], Almy Family Papers, SL; Albert Gallatin Browne to Edward Cox Browne, 3 Dec. 1863 and 19 Feb. 1864, Edward Cox Browne to Albert Gallatin Browne, 28 Feb. 1864 (see also for maps); Albert Gallatin Browne to Alice Browne, 10 Oct. 1864 and Sarah Smith (Cox) Browne to Albert Gallatin Browne, 11 Dec. 1864, for exchange of journals; Sarah Smith (Cox) Browne to Albert Gallatin Browne, 29 Feb. 1864; see also Sarah Smith (Cox) Browne to Albert Gallatin Browne, 12 Jan. 1863, 11 Dec. 1864, 20 Jan. 1864, 15 Feb. 1864; Albert Gallatin Browne to Edward Cox Browne, 30 and 31 Oct. 1863, and [undated] Dec. 1863 — all in Browne Family Papers, SL.

36. Ellen Wright to Martha Coffin Wright, 27 May 1861, Garrison Family Papers, SSC.

37. Persis Sibley Andrews Black, 28 Apr. 1861, Diary, Dabney Family Papers, MHS.

Chapter 11

Deserters, Civilians, and Draft Resistance in the North

JOAN E. CASHIN

➨ JOHN AND JACOB GIFFEN of Ohio were bound and determined not to serve in the United States Army during the Civil War, and they did not serve, something they managed with surprising ease. Their ancestors migrated to the American colonies from Scotland in the 1770s and 1780s, and by the time the Giffen clan settled in central Ohio in the antebellum era, the family consisted of well-to-do Presbyterian farmers with relatives in Pennsylvania and Virginia. In 1850 Joseph Giffen was raising his boys on a farm in Belmont County, his wife apparently deceased. When the war started, Jacob was eighteen and John, twenty, but they did not volunteer in 1861 or 1862, and in 1863, when the federal draft was instituted, they served briefly before fleeing the service, Jacob heading west and moving from place to place, first to Minnesota, then Iowa, and then Nebraska. He believed that the draft infringed outrageously on his own "liberty" and ridiculed the emancipation of African Americans, and he did not want to have any contact with free blacks. His older brother John fled northward to Ontario, where he planned to teach school while continuing his medical studies. John compared the draft and the bounty system to slavery, and he rejoiced when he learned of President Lincoln's death in 1865. Calling it "great news," he hoped that Secretary of State William Seward had also been murdered. Keenly interested in pursuing his medical career, he did not want to waste any time in the United States military, "war or no war."

What is just as startling, their father Joseph Giffen seemed to be unembarrassed by their conduct, and he did everything he could to assist them. He sent money to his sons and did not try to conceal their whereabouts from residents in Belmont County. In turn Jacob routinely sent his best wishes to the Ohio kinfolk, and John conducted business by mail from his Canadian residence, renting his house to a neighbor and arranging for his father to pay another neighbor for medical books sent to him by a local doctor. John also obtained copies of the Belmont newspaper and corresponded with at least two friends back home, but no one turned the brothers in to the authorities. Fiercely opposed to the war to the end of the conflict, the Giffens could not have avoided service without their father's help and the assistance, and indifference, of their civilian neighbors at home.[1]

The Giffens and their friends had a lot of company in the North, for thousands of men avoided military service, and, as we shall see, many civilians helped them. In fact, most deserters would not have been able to hide from the authorities without some assistance from white civilians, male and female. This article focuses on those civilians and the white men from the free states who were eligible to serve in the United States Army and deserted, and it is based upon government records, newspapers, private correspondence, diaries, and memoirs. (Black troops were not allowed to enlist until 1862, and their military experience is distinctive in many ways.) Thus far no scholar has discussed the experiences of these civilians, and historians have done little research on draft avoidance in the North since Ella Lonn's book on desertion in 1928, still the most comprehensive work on the subject. Lonn points out that desertion was widespread in the Union, worse than in the Confederacy, and she explains the phenomenon with a long list of factors, including pacifism; sympathy with the other side; military defeat; delay in paying troops; lax discipline by officers; war weariness; the poor caliber of recruits, especially, she believes, among foreigners; bounty-jumping; and last but not least, encouragement by civilians. Reflecting the cultural assumptions of the 1920s, she emphasizes the shared racial background of white soldiers in both armies, but neglects racism as a cause of desertion, and although she admits that desertion revealed grave divisions in the North, she denies that there was a *"deserter-country"* in the Union as there was in the Confederacy, places where deserters and their sympathizers challenged government authority and disrupted social relations. Historians have debated whether the Northern draft was fair to men of all social classes, whether most draft evaders were immigrants, or whether Lincoln should have suspended the writ of habeas corpus and arrested civilians for opposing the war, but most scholars emphasize the unanimity of federal soldiers in the ranks and the strong support they received from civilians at home.[2]

The story is messier than that, however, and it suggests that commitment to the Union cause was tenuous at best among some white Northerners. Many of these soldiers and civilians were the products of a decentralized, small-town, rural society where the bonds of family and community were still powerful and beliefs in white supremacy were taken for granted, and just as community expectations could encourage men to enlist, they could encourage men to avoid military service. These values were deeply embedded in the region's culture and were not manufactured by the Democratic Party, the Democratic newspapers, or secret societies such as the Knights of the Golden Circle. Much of civilian draft resistance was organic and unpredictable, and therefore uncontrollable, for many people distrusted government authority and opposed racial equality long before the war started. These civilians proved willing to use cunning, guile, verbal abuse, humiliation, and, if they deemed it necessary, violence to thwart the military. In their hostility to the draft, they resembled citizens in other Western cultures, such as the Frenchmen who resisted the draft in the Napoleonic era because it threatened the family and the local economy. As one scholar remarks, the draft could become the "ultimate contest of wills," with individual men, their families, and their communities arrayed on one side and the national government on the other.[3]

First of all, we must clear up some long-standing confusion about the numbers. U.S. Provost Marshal General James Fry estimated the number of Northern deserters at two hundred thousand for the years 1863 to 1865, including approximately fifteen thousand in Canada; approximately five thousand in the trans-Mississippi West; maybe a thousand more in Europe and elsewhere abroad; and the rest in hiding in the North. These are the figures for *deserters*, it bears pointing out, not for *desertions*, which would number far more than two hundred thousand since some men deserted more than once. About eighty thousand deserters were captured, most of them in the United States, leaving approximately one hundred thousand deserters inside the Union. But Fry's reports were riddled with inconsistencies, and he admitted that no one knew how many deserters were arrested before he became provost marshal in 1863, and, even worse, that many records were missing for 1863, 1864, and 1865. Fry also acknowledged that the extant documents were not accurate and omitted an unknown number of deserters. Local records bear this out, for among a sample of twenty-five Ohio deserters compiled during research for this article, only five appear in the state's "Roll of Deserters," purportedly a full list. This tiny sample cannot prove anything in and of itself, but it is safe to say that the figure of two hundred thousand, which is only an estimate for the second half of the war, undercounts the actual number of deserters. Furthermore, at least thirteen thousand civilians were arrested during the war for a variety of reasons, yet government records fail to give the number arrested for helping deserters, so that figure too will never be known. But if only one civilian assisted one deserter one time, then at least one hundred thousand people helped men avoid military service.[4]

The federal draft presided over by James Fry began an unprecedented intervention in the lives of ordinary people in the North, and it was the first draft in the region's history. Although one historian argues that the system worked so badly that it qualifies as only a "semi-draft," it eventually reached into every hamlet. When the shooting started in 1861, the Lincoln Administration relied on a volunteer army, but by early 1863, many soldiers had died on the battlefield and enlistments were flagging. The President signed the Enrollment Act on March 3, 1863, which established, or attempted to establish, the principle that men had an obligation to serve. The bill created 185 districts based upon Congressional districts, where draft boards compiled a list of eligible men by sending officers through the community door-to-door, and provost marshals were appointed to head the enrollment boards, apprehend deserters, and arrest anyone who resisted the draft. Each district had to meet a quota, and after the names were chosen in a public drawing, men had ten days to report. The draft allowed hardship exemptions for men who were the only means of support for their families, and draftees could purchase a substitute for several hundred dollars, or, before the option was dropped in 1864, they could pay a commutation fee. As the draft went forward after 1863, some communities had to hire brokers to hunt more men or offer ever-increasing bounties to attract soldiers. But many men fled before the draft board obtained their names, or after the drawing, or right after they put on the uniform, while others served weeks, months, or years before deserting.[5]

My research on deserters leads to a somewhat different set of motives than those Ella Lonn emphasizes, motives that were both more primal and quite common among soldiers in other wars. Men who had already enlisted and then left the service did so for the elemental reasons that prompted men in other conflicts to desert, with fear, hunger, and combat fatigue leading the way. An American veteran of the Second World War discerned that many soldiers tried to avoid danger in battle, and the Civil War had its share of cowards who were designated as such by the public and the military. During the Battle of Shiloh in 1862, Northern troops hid in the forests from raw fright, and some drowned in a river nearby as they tried to escape. Even in the Union army, not every man was well fed, such as New Yorker Reuben Wickham, who had no strong political views about the war and deserted from picket duty because he was hungry. Other men experienced combat fatigue, a state of loneliness, exhaustion, and disorientation first identified by a Union surgeon during the Civil War. Such a condition probably afflicted the Ohio soldier who deserted several times because he missed his family acutely and had a chronic case of "the *blues*."[6]

Northerners who avoided service during the war had other motives, which are typical of soldiers in other conflicts. Abraham Lincoln once remarked that he could not punish a "simple-minded" soldier who deserted without trying to punish the "agitator" who persuaded him to do it, and many white Northerners agreed that men who evaded service were unintelligent, ignorant, easily swayed by other people, possessed of bad character or criminal tendencies, opinions that persisted through both World Wars and into the Vietnam era. Frank Wilkeson, a young man who ran away to join the Union army, encountered a bloodcurdling gang of bounty-jumpers who mocked earnest patriots like himself and fled the service at the first opportunity. There were undoubtedly other rough characters in the deserters' ranks, since so many men deserted — although, it must be added, convicted felons were exempted from the draft.[7]

Some deserters were foreigners, as many Americans liked to believe. James Fry himself claimed that most deserters were probably foreigners from large cities, but New York state, which had the nation's largest port and highest number of immigrants, had a desertion rate of eighty-nine per one thousand, lower than Kansas (117), New Hampshire (112), and California (101). Despite these numbers, native-born Americans assumed that most deserters were Irishmen or Germans, although they also suspected the French, the Dutch, the English, and the Poles as disloyal. Certainly many Union deserters hailed from other countries, but draft avoidance proved to be such a widespread occurrence that the stereotype began to fade before the war ended. As the *Columbus Gazette* pointed out in 1864, many immigrants remained loyal to the Union, and many whites from the rural, small-town North deserted, men with names like Jones and Williams whose families had been in this country long before 1861.[8]

Deserters in the Civil War had yet another motive, common in many societies, and that was loyalty to the family and community above all else. Many men proved to be susceptible to pleas from relatives that it was better not to enlist, or if they had enlisted, to come home. Other soldiers understood this pattern very well, one officer confiding that another man in his unit was so homesick that he might desert to see his family. A journalist noted that it was hard for young men to leave the embrace of family and friends, while another reporter, much less sympathetic, argued that men evaded service only because of the diabolical persuasions of civilians at home. Throughout the war, kinfolk, including fathers, did urge soldiers to quit the service. One New Englander, increasingly disillusioned by what he saw as the lack of patriotism in the North, advised his son to come home somehow, some way, and whatever happened, to look out for himself. Some men needed no convincing. One soldier informed his family that he was coming back whether or not he got a furlough. Home obligations prompted men to desert right up to the last weeks of the war, for one man left his unit in March 1865 so he could care for his ailing wife.[9]

Mothers had a unique ability to influence their sons, or so many Northerners assumed. One shopkeeper's son avoided military service so he could care for his aging parents, especially his mother, and he thought it would "kill" her if he joined up. Charles Keever, alias Charles Miller, explained that he deserted after two months in the service when he learned that his mother was ill. An Illinois civilian claimed that his neighbor "almost forced" her son to desert, and he drew up a petition asking that she be punished instead of her misguided offspring. Some matrons did have their own political opinions of the war, such as the mother who convinced her son to desert after the Emancipation Proclamation, which, she believed, had transformed the struggle into a wicked, "hellish" war. Now it was his Christian duty, she informed him, to leave the army. Susan B. Greene of New Hampshire initially told her son William not to desert because he might be shot, but she was horrified by the war's carnage and began to blame both the North and South for starting the conflict. She then urged her son to "frame up a good story" and come home, and despite the counsel of other family members who told him to stay in the army, William deserted in 1862, partly because of his mother's coaxing.[10]

Furthermore, some men deserted and became bounty-jumpers to give money to their families, just as men did in other wars, not merely out of greed. By 1862, it was clear to soldiers and civilians that families might suffer because the army paid troops irregularly and local charities could not support all the needy. The pragmatic, apolitical correspondence of many whites reveals the central importance of money as family members debated which action a man should take. Private William J. Smith wanted to desert because he disliked his officers, but his parents advised him to remain so he would not forfeit his pay. The Smiths, who were so poor that they had to borrow ink from a schoolteacher to write a letter, asked their son to send them any old clothes he might find around camp, and they wanted him to collect a bounty because they needed the money to buy a hog. William's sister Mary suggested that he come home anyway so they could discuss how he could make the most money, either by reenlisting for a bounty, serving as a substitute, or, if their father was drafted, by deserting and adopting the older man's identity. About the larger issues of patriotism, Union, or Emancipation, the Smiths had nothing to say.[11]

Men in uniform sometimes urged relatives to avoid military service, also for economic reasons. Implicit in their comments is the assumption that individual families should not have to contribute more than one soldier to the war, or no soldiers at all if the family's welfare might be put at risk. After two of Corporal Wallace Hoyt's brothers deserted, the corporal demanded that his father not volunteer for the service, exclaiming that he would never forgive him for it, and told him to evade the draft if he were conscripted. Other officers unabashedly told their relatives not to enlist. Assistant Surgeon Townsend Heaton, who sent money home to his parents, conjured his brother not to volunteer because it would leave their parents in a "bad fix." Some officers admitted to the most tentative commitment to the war, and an indifference to the greater issues involved, which they communicated to their relatives. Assistant Surgeon W. S. Newton was dismissed with twelve other men for desertion in 1864, and when he was reinstated, he did not know whether he felt "glad or sorry."[12]

Yet other men deserted because of their inability to adjust to the regimentation of military life, a universal motive among deserters in modern wars, and those difficulties became obvious soon after Northern soldiers arrived at camp. Some men could barely tolerate hauling logs, because that was menial labor, or scrubbing, sweeping, and making beds, because that was women's work, while others could not endure the forced confinement. Soldiers forged passes to escape, even as others blithely departed at personal whim. One man was arrested after he left camp to go hunting, and two other soldiers were found loitering at a railroad station, because, they explained, they felt like going on a "spree." A journalist believed that men left the service over trifles when they got "miffed" about something, but that missed the point entirely, for the ability to do as one pleased lay at the core of being a white man in the antebellum North.[13]

The typical farmer or shopkeeper was used to hard work but also to being his own boss, coming and going much of the time as he wished. One officer remarked that Illinois soldiers possessed a keen sense of personal independence, which he attributed to their frontier heritage, but most contemporaries believed this feisty independence characteristic of all Yankees. The average white Northerner thought he was "as good as any other person," a veteran recalled, and the typical soldier had a difficult time subordinating himself to military authority. As a captain dryly remarked, some men were "not disposed" to follow orders. Even Provost Marshal James Fry admitted that it was hard for men who behaved according to "their own ideas and wishes" to accept military discipline—at the start of the war, he insisted, after which they settled down. Yet many soldiers were never disposed to accept discipline, and some did not hesitate to act on their beliefs. Some two hundred men deserted a cavalry battalion when they discovered they would not be allowed to serve as a general's bodyguard; believing that their "rights" had been violated, they all went home. After another group of soldiers were imprisoned for misconduct at Camp Chase in 1862, some comrades fired on the guardhouse to liberate them, and during the mayhem, other privates changed sides and fired on their own officers. Eventually order was restored, but a few weeks later a party or parties unknown burned the guardhouse down.[14]

What was specific to this war, and most thought-provoking given the fact that Emancipation became an official part of the war effort on January 1, 1863, was that so many white Northerners compared the draft to slavery. Civilians and soldiers both used the analogy repeatedly, declaring that the draft was a form of bondage appropriate for the "old world," overlooking the fact that genuine bondage had existed in the New World for three centuries, or decried it as an attempt to "enslave the white man." Others compared military life to slavery, Susan B. Greene calling it "bondage" before and after her son deserted the Union army. The physical punishments of deserters outraged some civilians, because, as a journalist cried, it was a "gross outrage" to flog a "*white man*," a "free citizen of a free Republic," and comparable to what happened to a slave. This was nothing compared to the arbitrary violence that African Americans experienced under slavery, but the overwrought language reveals how little many white Northerners knew about the institution, and it underscores the widespread racialized assumption that the government should not put any restraints on the freedoms enjoyed by white men.[15]

In light of these views, it is not surprising that many deserters opposed Emancipation, and, in fact, that some men deserted in order to protest the Proclamation after it was announced in September 1862. From southern Illinois, a Unionist perceived that some men deserted in a highly emotional state, barely able to contain their fury at the Proclamation. One deserter objected vociferously to what he called the new "Abolition War," an opinion that his Indiana relatives shared when they took him in, and others quit the service to protest what they called "an unholy war and nigger war." Some deserters planned to take their opinions into the political sphere, such as the men who promised to give the abolitionists "fits" when they got home. Nor did the passage of time alter the opinions of many of these men. William B. Greene, who deserted in 1862, still opposed Lincoln's effort to free the slaves two years later. Despite a generation of activity by the abolitionist movement, racial prejudice pervaded much of white Northern society and much of the Union army.[16]

Regardless of their motives for quitting the service, many soldiers did not seem to be deterred by the penalties handed out to deserters. Article 20 of the U.S. Military Code provided for a range of punishments, including shaving the head, branding the letter "D" on the body, wearing a ball and chain, flogging, or execution, to be determined at a court-martial. Some men, to be sure, were intimidated by what they witnessed. After a Pennsylvanian saw a deserter have his head shaved and a "D" branded on his hip, he concluded that desertion might be a bad idea. Executions, which increased in the Union army after 1863, could also make an impression. Soldiers had to form a hollow square as mournful music played and their former comrades were led into place, some composed, some terrified, and others defiant; after the deserters were allowed a last moment with clergymen, a squad of soldiers fired, as some men died instantly while others had to be shot more than once, their bodies then dumped into coffins and buried on the spot. Officers as a group tended to want more executions to set an example, yet only 141 deserters were executed among the approximately eighty thousand arrested during the war, and President Lincoln pardoned hundreds of deserters who had been condemned to death. In any case, many soldiers intent on deserting would not be put off. A veteran from the Army of the Potomac remarked that a man who had decided to desert would go, regardless of the consequences.[17]

When Union deserters left the army, very few changed sides to fight for the Confederacy. Even if they opposed Emancipation, most of them hated military life, missed their families, and longed for the personal freedom they enjoyed before the war. Some decided that it was safer to hide out in the wilderness, and a provost marshal in Illinois lamented that "thousands" escaped to the far West. One such miscreant, John Taylor, fled St. Louis in 1864 with several kinsmen and fellow soldiers for Nebraska, where he traveled around for months before writing to his family, fearful that his location might be discovered, but he, like Jacob Giffen, was protected by people at home who did not report him. Taylor came to enjoy living in the West, calling it the true land of "liberty." David Viars bolted from the service in 1864, boasting that "I give them the slip," and after he found a job driving mules to California for a hundred dollars, he invited his brother to desert and join him in the West. Provost marshals working in the trans-Mississippi states expressed frustration at their inability to capture these men. In California an officer related that the state's vast size and rootless population, plus the indifference of many civilians to his efforts, made his job especially difficult.[18]

Other men chose like John Giffen to head northward into Canada since it was neutral territory, being part of the British Empire until 1867, and its long border was impossible for either government to patrol adequately. Some men fled there immediately, while others such as John Muir went to Canada as a last resort; the famous naturalist left Wisconsin for the northern border as the draft closed in on him in 1864. Many deserters crossed from Detroit into Ontario and fled to Windsor and Amherstburg and then walked the docks, finding employment as manual laborers, or fanned out into the countryside to work on farms. Union officers occasionally made illegal raids into Canada to capture deserters, for which Secretary William Seward had to apologize to the British government, but these men were almost impossible to catch. Much of the Northern press derided these draft avoiders as "skedaddlers," and some journalists were contemptuous of their alleged working-class origins, calling them "white trash." Regardless of their class backgrounds, they continued to arrive in the far north into the last months of the war, and some of them received assistance from American civilians until the very end.[19]

But the majority of deserters simply returned to live in their home communities in the North. Repeatedly their comrades said that deserters had gone home, and there, surrounded by relatives, friends, acquaintances, and neighbors, many of them lived for months or even years without being arrested. Clinton Wasson deserted his regiment in the winter of 1862 and went back to Cincinnati, where he lived with his family until a provost marshal found him the following spring. Another deserter slipped away from Washington, D.C., and lived in his native Pennsylvania for almost two years before he was caught. Two deserters managed to hide for a "long" time in Licking County, Ohio, working for sympathetic friends, before they were captured in 1864. Soldiers found eight deserters in Washington, Indiana, in 1862, all of them residents who could rely on the fact that local folk would protect them. In southern Illinois, one pro-Union civilian complained that deserters were "very plenty here, very bold," going about their daily lives unimpeded.[20]

Numerous civilians did prove willing to help men avoid military service. Provost Marshal James Fry admitted that people resisted the draft in every enrollment district, and whether the newspapers described such civilians as freedom-loving individualists or nefarious traitors, the press agreed that there were many of them. Their motives mirrored those of deserters — loyalty to family and community, opposition to the draft and Emancipation — and they continued to act on them, even after March 1863 when the government made it a crime punishable by fines and imprisonment to persuade a soldier to desert, harbor him, give him employment, or aid him after he deserted. When men deserted, civilian assistance began at the very start of the enterprise, as railroad employees, hack drivers, and merchants sold or gave clothing to soldiers that they might shed their uniforms and pass as civilians. Many others sheltered deserters, and like civilians in other wars, they were probably more likely to assist people they knew. William B. Greene lived with kinfolk in Wisconsin, where he assumed his brother's name and remained free for almost a year before he was arrested. One man allowed a draft evader of his acquaintance to stay in his house in Indiana until he was caught, and after another deserter returned home to New Berlin, Pennsylvania, his neighbors gave him a place to hide. Civilians even wrote to would-be deserters in the army to assure them that other soldiers had escaped the service without incident and no one could capture them at home.[21]

Many civilians simply kept quiet and looked the other way when deserters appeared, which allowed thousands of them to live in communities across the North. These civilians were either opposed to the war effort, indifferent to it, completely absorbed in their own affairs, or perhaps too intimidated to contact the authorities. The federal government's reward for apprehending deserters was not much of an incentive, since the amount was reduced from thirty dollars to five in 1861, and after it was raised to thirty dollars in 1863, the voucher system used for payments was inefficient. Whatever their motives, the silence of many civilians allowed deserters to resume their old occupations in their own communities using their real names. For example, one deserter calmly operated a grocery store in Hamilton, Ohio, before he was caught, and another went home to New Vienna, Ohio, where he not only ran a business but began pestering a serviceman's wife to pay a debt, much to the consternation of the man in the field. When strange men of draft age surfaced in the community, many civilians said nothing, perhaps because they needed workers. George Hullinger deserted his Illinois regiment and fled to Ohio, where he worked as a coal miner for two years before being discovered in 1865. John T. Davis deserted from the 45th Ohio Infantry and took a job clerking in a store in Wheeling; after being arrested, he escaped wearing handcuffs but managed to get all the way to Philadelphia, where he worked at a hotel under a pseudonym before he was caught again, arrested again, and escaped again. Other deserters decided it was prudent to adopt false names, such as James Kingery, who called himself James Kingsay, or George Prescott, who used a more original alias, Samuel Baufer.[22]

Many civilians knew of the hideouts that deserters set up in the countryside, and again they kept silent. In the Calumet marshes in Illinois, two men concealed themselves for "some time" trapping and selling frogs to area residents, and near Wabash, Indiana, a gang lived in the woods for several months before they were discovered and arrested. In rural Wisconsin, a deserters' band made camp in the ice-bound woods for the winter and waited for the spring thaw so they could take ship to Canada. Other men, who can only be remarked upon for their audacity, congregated near military camps and prisons, such as the group who was "pro[w]ling about" Delaware County, Ohio, in 1863 despite the proximity of Camp Chase a few miles away. Sometimes civilians became so disenchanted with the war effort, or so opposed to the draft, that they elected to join these outlaw gangs. In Litchfield County, Connecticut, a gang of deserters and their civilian friends gathered in the mountains, causing "great excitement" in the area.[23]

As this example illustrates, many Northern civilians turned out to be not merely indifferent but openly hostile to the federal draft. From New England to the Pacific Coast, provost marshals complained of uncooperative, hostile civilians, whether it concerned official attempts to get an accurate count of men who were eligible for service or to arrest deserters on the run. The animosity could take the form of verbal abuse, the "loud-mouthed, swaggering opposition" that a provost marshal reported as he tried to appoint his deputies in southern Illinois. Some civilians kept watch for draft officers, in one community blowing a horn to alert their neighbors that troops had arrived. Officers encountered other gestures of hostility, as did the enrollment officer who awoke one morning in 1863 to find his carriage broken into pieces, his harness cut, and his personal belongings destroyed. No one was arrested for the crime, and he left the area without retrieving the deserter. In Noble County, Ohio, some white residents "did all in their power to interfere" with a squad of American troops who rode in to arrest deserters, refusing to provide them with information or sell them any food.[24]

Civilian resistance easily crossed over into violence, which intensified in many places after the federal draft opened in 1863. Most of this resistance was ad hoc, personal, and spontaneous, like mob violence in the antebellum North, and it went far beyond the miniature "wars" reported in a few counties. Throughout the North, white civilians repeatedly threatened the lives of enrollment officers, assaulted them, and drove them out of town.[25] They fired on provost marshals in Sandusky County, Ohio; Wyandot County, Ohio; Coshocton County, Ohio; Delphi, Indiana; Waverly, Indiana; Morgan County, Indiana; and New Berlin, Pennsylvania.[26] Groups estimated to contain ten men, thirty men, or fifty men banded together and took up arms to protect local deserters.[27] In Fayette, Clark, Coles, Morgan, and Fulton Counties in Illinois, in Coshocton County, Ohio, and in Dubuque County, Iowa, men on both sides died in skirmishes between U.S. army troops, deserters, and civilians. The Chicago Tribune estimated in 1863 that there were five hundred communities in Illinois and Indiana where men could not be apprehended without military force, and even if the figure is exaggerated, clearly there was a great deal of small-scale violent resistance in addition to the famous draft riot in New York City in July of that year.[28]

Inevitably some provost marshals died in the line of duty—in the North, not on Confederate battlefields. A random survey of forty Midwestern newspapers, including both Republican and Democratic journals, shows that at least four officers were killed in 1863, at least two in

1864, and at least one in 1865. The number of employees of the Provost Marshal Bureau killed in the North is estimated at thirty-eight, which does not include troops sent to quell unrest in local communities, so we will never know the exact figure. Civilians were sometimes responsible for the deaths, such as the Iowan who deliberately led two marshals into a deadly ambush, while on other occasions deserters were responsible. John B. Cook's murder resembled an assassination, for two deserters shot this provost marshal at his home in Cambridge, Ohio, as he stepped into his backyard one evening in March 1865.[29]

The war and the draft polarized the Northern civilian population so deeply that some white people began to turn on each other. Civilians captured or identified approximately a third of the deserters who were caught, which only inflamed the political animosities in many communities. By 1863 fistfights, shoving matches, and shouting matches between civilians became routine, usually breaking out when the provost marshal appeared, and threats of bodily harm and the destruction of property became commonplace. Residents of North Salem, Indiana, threatened violence against their pro-Union neighbors, some of whom were afraid to leave their homes, while in Galion, Ohio, an anti-Union mob threatened to torch the house of every Republican in town. In Jay County, Indiana, whites promised to burn the town of Portland and wreak vengeance on all "Union men" if local deserters were forced back into the service. Civilians in Saline County, Illinois, who were opposed to the Emancipation Proclamation threatened their neighbors and publicly called for the county to secede from the United States.[30]

Saline County did not leave the Union, but many of the personal threats were carried out, beginning a cycle of attack and retaliation that left citizens fearing each other, and what is most striking about it is the boldness of the anti-Union side, since this was the United States, after all, not the Confederacy. In Noble County, Ohio, whites drove loyal families out of their homes and assaulted several men, including one who was dragged from his horse and threatened with a hanging and another, a disabled man, who was beaten up. In some places, nothing was sacred: a group of deserters-cum-civilians burned two churches in Crawford County, Ohio, presumably because pro-Union residents worshipped in them. Some civilians lost their lives, although once again the exact number is unknown. When a "rescue" of deserters took place in Anna, Illinois, a local man who arrested them was killed in the melee. The violence continued until April 1865, when, for instance, civilians in Woodsfield, Ohio, fired on each other after two men tried to arrest a deserter, who escaped.[31]

Women also took part in draft resistance, which may serve as one more indication of how deep the resistance went. According to conventional gender roles in the antebellum North, white women were supposed to devote themselves to the family, and now some of them took that value to its ultimate conclusion, deciding that the draft threatened the family's welfare. All over the region, they began to abuse officers of the law, publicly advocate defiance of the law, and give succor to men defying the law. Women hurled "epithets" at provost marshals and declared to their neighbors, as Elizabeth Millican did, that all deserters should escape the authorities. Asserting that she would "say what she pleases," Millican, a resident of Illinois, added that Lincoln had perverted the war for the Union into a war for Emancipation. Northern women actively helped men resist the draft, such as the wife who brought her husband a suit of civilian clothes so he could desert, and after men got away, soldiers assumed that the wives knew where they were hiding. Many of them did know. Near Chambersburg, Pennsylvania, women alerted men of the provost marshal's approach and helped them conceal themselves in the mountains. With the assistance of his wife, one deserter dressed in female attire and managed to pass as a woman for several weeks, residing quietly in rural Ohio before he was discovered and sent to the front.[32]

Women also engaged in petty physical assaults and more deadly resistance, and some were arrested. In Ohio, women threw eggs and other "missiles" at a deputy provost marshal, and they were arrested along with three men who fired on the officer. In Indiana, a crowd of women pelted an enrollment officer with eggs, whereupon they were arrested, and in other incidents, women threatened officers with farming tools, poured hot water on them, or pulled them by the hair. Sometimes they acted in concert with men. In Pennsylvania, several hundred women and men poured into the Lancaster courthouse as the draft was in progress and assaulted the staff, the women using knives and kitchen implements, but when the mayor assembled troops, the entire crowd dispersed. Women were also inevitably drawn in to the internecine violence in Northern communities. When a riot broke out on draft day in Galion, Ohio, and a man drew a pistol on his neighbor, the neighbor's wife "knocked it out of his hands." In a few cases, women picked up guns to protect their menfolk, such as the two women in Scott County, Illinois, who fired on soldiers arriving to arrest their father and brother. Eventually some female civilians died as provost marshals pursued their men. In March 1865, a corporal accidentally killed Gertrude Hancock on a Philadelphia street when he fired into a crowd while chasing a deserter.[33]

So it seems that there was a *deserter-country* in parts of the North, contrary to Ella Lonn's assertion. The most extreme form of draft resistance — open, sustained, violence directed at military officers — was concentrated in southern Illinois, which was easily as unstable as eastern

Tennessee, and spread out in a checkerboard pattern through Pennsylvania, West Virginia, Ohio, Indiana, and Iowa, with pockets of resistance scattered through New England and the trans-Mississippi West. In some of these places, the legal and political system completely broke down. A band of about a dozen guerillas, most of them deserters, "governed" the Devil's Neck neighborhood in Illinois until their capture in January 1865, and in other communities in the southern half of the state, deserters and civilians took over businesses and public offices, from which they bullied their Unionist neighbors and destroyed their property. In Greencastle, Pennsylvania, a group of thirty-five deserters put up such determined resistance that the provost marshal had to request additional troops to arrest them, the gang being "too strong" to deal with on his own. In parts of West Virginia, civilians and deserters from both armies waged a war of all upon all, as partisan bands attacked each other, preyed upon the local population, and raided into neighboring states.[34]

But we must remember that open, sustained, violent action is only one kind of draft resistance, keeping in mind the high mobility of the deserter population throughout the North. In the broadest meaning of the phrase, all of the Northern states constituted "*deserter-country,*" since at least a hundred thousand deserters were in hiding there, living at home, lurking in the woods or the mountains, or roaming from place to place, and many thousands of civilians stood ready to assist them, even at the risk of their own well-being. Every state in the Union contained deserters and noncombatants who helped them avoid service, and their presence altered the fabric of daily life everywhere in ways that scholars are only beginning to explore, if only because loyal civilians could never be entirely sure that one or more of their relatives, friends, and neighbors might be assisting or harboring deserters.

Throughout the war, the federal government's efforts to deter civilian resistance did not seem to make much of a difference. The national press listed the names of men executed for desertion and provided detailed coverage of the events, and on a few occasions, authorities allowed civilians to witness the executions. Several public events were specifically designed to intimidate civilians and draft evaders both, among them the widely reported "Rogue's March" through Indianapolis in 1864, when bounty jumpers were tied together and marched through the streets wearing placards, but that did not seem to have the desired impact either. Throughout the North, civilians were arrested, charged, and tried in military commissions and by the civil courts — which some provost marshals thought was a mistake — and they were sometimes convicted, fined, and even imprisoned, but the civil courts could be lenient and many cases were dismissed for lack of evidence.

The majority of civilian-resisters were probably never even arrested. Viewed from this perspective, President Lincoln's concern about a "fire in the rear" was realistic, and his suspension of the writ of habeas corpus was warranted. If his policy can be faulted, it should not be for doing too much. His Administration ran headlong into a segment of the white Northern people that could not be persuaded to support the causes of Union and Emancipation.[35]

Their indifference to the war effort lasted to the final weeks of the conflict, as an extraordinary incident in eastern Ohio demonstrates. In February 1865, deserters made a mock arrest of a provost marshal and humiliated him before hundreds of white civilians, and no one stopped them. Two men known only as DeLaney and Cunningham appeared in Tuscarawas County that month, and although they were evidently not natives of the county, they admitted to everyone that they were deserters and dared the authorities to arrest them. When a deputy provost marshal was dispatched to apprehend them dead or alive, the deserters cornered him in a local hotel and after taking his weapons and his money, put hand-cuffs, hobbles, and chains on him, plunked him in a wagon, and then drove around the county for two days, "exhibiting" him, as a newspaper described it, as if he were a captured horse-thief. Then they hauled the officer to the town of Canal Dover (now called Dover), Ohio, and exhibited him again to the public while DeLaney sang songs before a large crowd, requiring the marshal to keep time by clinking his chains together. At last the deserters dropped him off at another hotel, much to the crowd's "amusement," and the pair disappeared. Two weeks later, DeLaney was arrested, but Cunningham remained at large. The acquiescence of so many civilians in this two-day spectacle suggests that many still thought the draft was not legitimate, perhaps the equivalent of theft, and that they were indifferent at best to the war's larger aims or the great Union victory in the offing.[36]

When the mighty conflict concluded at last in April 1865, some of the men in hiding in the American West, in Canada, or abroad decided to stay where they were. Jacob Giffen resided in the west for some years, while the fate of his brother John, who wanted to come home, is unclear. Many were already at home of course, and thousands of them simply resumed working in their shops and farms, and in the summer and fall of 1865, thousands of deserters began to return. The indifference of some deserters, even those who were arrested, did not fade with the Union's triumph. At Fort McHenry, one such defiant personality awaited his fate, a "reckless dare-devil" who was unashamed of his record of desertion and bounty-jumping and remained in boisterous good humor on the eve of his court-martial. When Jacob Morgan's unit mutinied and tried to desert, he landed in prison at Fort Leavenworth in the summer of 1865, but that did not dampen his spirits. The charges against him could not be proved, he cheerfully told a friend, and when he was released he planned to settle in Kansas, a "slashing fine country." Some deserters continued to be unembarrassed for decades, candidly stating their blemished service records in the veterans' census of 1890. In Jackson County, Ohio, the aptly named Slick Romer announced to the census-taker that he "ran away before [the] war ended."[37]

Over the long term, there was no reckoning in the North on the issue of draft evasion. In March 1865, the federal government threatened to strip all deserters of citizenship if they did not return to the service in sixty days, but offered a pardon to men who came back to serve the remainder of their terms. Some veterans thought the pardon was too generous, but only about two thousand men took up the offer, so the government relented and asked deserters to forfeit their back pay, and that was it. This lenient treatment infuriated many veterans, especially provost marshals, one of whom suggested that the government should arrest them all, while another advocated their execution without any exceptions, arguing that human nature required grim measures in time of war. A congressman urged Secretary of War Edwin Stanton to arrest deserters as they filtered across the Canadian border into New York, but the government did nothing. There were no mass arrests, no mass punishments, and no mass executions, perhaps a tacit acknowledgment that thousands of people were involved in draft resistance and prosecution of all the offenders would be impossible. By the 1880s, deserters could get pensions if they managed to produce some documentation, such as letters from friends stating that they had reenlisted, and after 1895, there were no time limits on efforts to expunge service records, and thousands of private bills passed the United States Congress exonerating deserters or alleged deserters.[38]

Just as the government forgave, the white Northern public forgot. If I can summarize the always-complex, always-conflicted process by which a people choose how to remember a historical event, the public decided to remember the most inspiring version of the war story and forget the inglorious fact that thousands of men deserted and many civilians assisted them. None other than Provost Marshal James Fry proclaimed in 1866 that the draft had created "closer ties" and "mutual confidence" between the government and the people, ignoring much of the evidence in his own reports. In the years to come, deserters wrote few memoirs, and the many veterans who composed books emphasized the Northern public's united support for the war, even if their own accounts suggest otherwise. Writing at the end of the nineteenth century, Lincoln's secretaries John Nicholay and John Hay neatly expressed this consensus when they declared that the "lion of the North" became aroused with the shelling at Fort Sumter, and the population threw itself into the war effort, civilians and soldiers alike, with equal enthusiasm. It is probably more realistic to see white Northerners as similar to their counterparts in other western societies at war, no better and no worse. Much like Frenchmen in the Napoleonic era, these Americans clung tenaciously to values that predated the war, beliefs more durable than the appeal of public duty: loyalty to the family, the community, the white race, and the self.[39]

Notes

I wish to thank Joseph Glatthaar, Reid Mitchell, and Nate Rosenstein for their insightful comments on this article.

1. [no author], *Belmont County History* (Belmont Co., Ohio, 1988), 118–20; Joseph Giffen, dwelling 586, Belmont Co., Ohio, Federal Census of 1850; John M. Giffen to father, 20 Feb. 1865, Jacob R. Giffen to Joseph Giffen, 20 Mar. 1865, John M. Giffen and Eleanor H. Giffen to father, 18 Apr. 1865, Giffen Papers, Ohio Historical Society (hereafter OHS).

2. Ella Lonn, *Desertion during the Civil War* (New York, 1928), v, vi, 127–42, 223, and passim; Eugene C. Murdock, *One Million Men: The Civil War Draft in the North* (Madison, Wisc., 1971); idem, *Patriotism Limited, 1862–1863: The Civil War Draft and the Bounty System* (Kent, Ohio, 1967); Peter Levine, "Draft Evasion in the North during the Civil War, 1863–1865," *Journal of American History* 67 (March 1981): 816–34; Iver Bernstein, *The New York City Draft Riots: Their Significance for American Society and Politics in the Age of the Civil War* (New York, 1990); James W. Geary, *We Need Men: The Union Draft in the Civil War* (DeKalb, 1991); Grace Palladino, *Another Civil War: Labor, Capital, and the State in the Anthracite Regions of Pennsylvania, 1840–1868* (Baton Rouge, 1988); Bob Sterling, "Discouragement, Weariness, and War Politics: Desertions from Illinois Regiments during the Civil War," *Illinois Historical Journal* 82 (Winter 1989): 239–62; Mark E. Neely Jr., *The Fate of Liberty: Abraham Lincoln and Civil Liberties* (New York, 1991); Gerald F. Linderman, *Embattled Courage: The Experience of Combat in the American Civil War* (New York, 1987); Randall C. Jimerson, *The Private Civil War: Popular Thought during the Sectional Conflict* (Baton Rouge, 1988); Philip Shaw Paludan, *"A People's Contest": The Union and the Civil War, 1861–1865* (New York, 1988); Earl J. Hess, *The Union Soldier in Battle: Enduring the Ordeal of Combat* (Lawrence, Kans., 1997); James M. McPherson, *For Cause and Comrade: Why Men Fought in the Civil War* (New York, 1997). Reid Mitchell (*Civil War Soldiers* [New York, 1988], 41–43, 168–73) discusses desertion but focuses on the South.

3. John Mack Faragher, *Sugar Creek: Life on the Illinois Prairie* (New Haven, 1986); David R. Roediger, *The Wages of Whiteness: Race and the Making of the American Working Class* (New York, 1991); Judith Lee Hallock, "The Role of the Community in Civil War Desertion," *Civil War History* 29 (June 1983): 134; Frank L. Klement, *Dark Lanterns: Secret Political Societies,*

Conspiracies, and Treason Trials in the Civil War (Baton Rouge, 1984); Alan Forrest, *Conscripts and Deserters: The Army and French Society during the Revolution and Empire* (New York, 1989), 5–8, 62–64, 68, 75; Isser Woloch, "Napoleonic Conscription," *Past and Present* 111 (May 1986): 101.

4. *The War of the Rebellion: A Compilation of the Official Records of the Union and Confederate Armies* (Washington, D.C., 1900) (hereafter OR), ser. 3, vol. 5, 109, 677, 752, cf. 757; Robin W. Winks, *Canada and the United States: The Civil War Years* (Montreal, 1971), 202; Linderman, *Embattled Courage*, 176; Geary, *We Need Men*, 14–15, 66, 73, 82; Murdock, *Patriotism Limited*, 8, 44, 51; OR, ser. 3, vol. 5, 677, 752; cf. p. 757; Roll of Deserters from Ohio Regiments, 1861–1865, Adjutant General's Office, Civil War Personnel Records, Miscellaneous Records, OHS; Neely, *Fate of Liberty*, 27, 55, 60–61, 113–14, 130. Geary (*We Need Men*, 15) estimates the number of deserters at 116,000 for 1863–1865.

5. Geary, *We Need Men*, 12–15, 66, 73, 76, 168, 172; Murdock, *Patriotism Limited*, 8, 44, 51; idem, *One Million Men*, x–xi, 4–10, 92, 160–61; 335 (quote); OR, ser. 3, vol. 5, 751–52; Robert Keating, *Carnival of Blood: The Civil War Ordeal of the Seventh New York Heavy Artillery* (Baltimore, 1998), 6, 23, 59, 81.

6. S.L.A. Marshall, *Men against Fire: The Problem of Battle Command in Future War* (Washington, D.C., and New York, 1947), 50–58, 148–50, 179–82; no title, *Delaware Democratic Standard*, 19 Mar. 1863, p. 3; Lew Wallace, *An Autobiography*, 2 vols. (New York, 1906), 2:505; Reuben Wickham to his wife, 4 Jan. 1865, copy in author's possession, gift from Kristen Fuller; Peter G. Bourne, *Men, Stress, and Vietnam* (Boston, 1970), 9; Diary of Frank S. Hardy, 8 Oct. 1862, OHS.

7. *The Collected Works of Abraham Lincoln*, 9 vols., ed. Roy P. Basler, Marion Dolores Pratt, and Lloyd A. Dunlap (New Brunswick, 1953), 6:266; "Skedaddlers to Canada," *Ashland Times*, 2 Apr. 1863, p. 1; "Deserters and Why They Desert," *Cleveland Morning Leader*, 27 Oct. 1863, p. 2; "A Farmer Murdered by a Deserter for Money," *St. Clairsville Gazette*, 5 Mar. 1863, p. 1; Albert M. Cook to his father, 8 Sept. 1863, Albert M. Cook Papers, Special Collections, Syracuse University; Richard Holmes, *Acts of War: The Behavior of Men in Battle* (New York, 1985), 85–86; Frank Wilkeson, *Recollections of a Private Soldier in the Army of the Potomac* (New York, 1887), 1–21; Murdock, *One Million Men*, 80.

8. OR, ser. 3, vol. 5, 668–69; "Riot in the Third Ward," *Chicago Tribune*, 26 June 1863, p. 4; "Escaped," *Coshocton Democrat*, 6 Jan. 1864, p. 2; "The Copperhead War in Holmes County," *Ashland Times*, 25 June 1863, p. 2; "Deserters Caught," *Cleveland Morning Leader*, 5 Jan. 1863, p. 3; "A Draft Skedaddler," *Cleveland Morning Leader*, 1 Oct. 1864, p. 2, no title, *Circleville Democrat*, 27 Jan. 1865, p. 2; "Aliens and the Draft," *Columbus Gazette*, 29 Jan. 1864, p. 3; "Reported Deserted," *Daily Sandusky Commercial Register*, 16 May 1864, p. 3.

9. Edward A. Shils and Morris Janowitz, "Cohesion and Disintegration in the Wehrmacht in World War II," *Public Opinion Quarterly* 12 (Summer 1948): 286n9, 288, 289–90; Annette Tapert, ed., *The Brother's War: Civil War Letters*

to *Their Loved Ones from the Blue and Gray* (New York, 1988), 101; no title, *Delaware Democratic Standard*, 4 June 1863, p. 3; "Deserters and Why They Desert," *Cleveland Morning Leader*, 27 Oct. 1863, p. 2; Walter Gresham to General Noble, 25 Mar. 1863, Adjutant General of Indiana, 53rd Indiana Volunteers Infantry Correspondence, Roll 54, Indiana State Archives, Commission on Public Records (hereafter ISA-CPR); "Desertions from the Army," *Chicago Tribune*, 16 Feb. 1863, p. 1; Jeffrey D. Marshall, ed., *A War of the People: Vermont Civil War Letters*, foreword by Edwin C. Bearss (Hanover, N.H., 1999), 255; F. A. Kidwell to his wife, 28 Dec. 1864, Frank A. Kidwell Letters, Civil War Collection, West Virginia Archives (hereafter WVA); "General Court-Martial," *Daily Ohio State Journal*, 1 Mar. 1865, p. 3.

10. W. B. Mitchell Jr., to Cyrus Mitchell, 3 Aug. 1862, William B. Mitchell Papers, OHS; "General Court Martial," *Daily Ohio State Journal*, 21 Feb. 1865, p. 3; C. R. Bourdett to Jacob Ammen, 11 May 1863, Jacob Ammen Papers, OHS; "Desertions from the Army," *Chicago Tribune*, 16 Feb. 1863, p. 1; *Letters from a Sharpshooter: The Civil War Letters of Private William B. Greene, Col G 2nd United States Sharpshooters (Berdan's)* [sic] *Army of the Potomac, 1861–1865*, trans. William H. Hastings (Belleville, Wisc., 1993), 26, 42, 48–50, 52, 54, 67, 163n.

11. Geary, *We Need Men*, 44–45; Randall and Nancy Smith to William J. Smith, 17 Dec. 1862, 18 Dec. 1862, Mary A. Smith to "Dear Brother," 30 Nov. 1862, William J. Smith Letters, OHS.

12. Wallace B. Hoyt to "Dear Folks at Home," 3 Dec. 1863, Wallace B. Hoyt to his sister, 28 Mar. and 31 Mar. 1864, Wallace B. Hoyt Papers, OHS; Townsend Heaton to Jack Heaton, 10 Sept. 1862, 11 Oct. 1862, 11 Feb. 1863, Townsend P. Heaton Papers, OHS; W. S. Newton to his wife, 4 Aug. 1864, Civil War Letters of William S. Newton, OHS.

13. H. H. Guiteau to "Sister," 15 Dec. 1862, Hultberg Family Papers, WVA; John H. Brinton, *Personal Memoirs of John H. Brinton, Major and Surgeon U.S.V., 1861–1865* (New York, 1914), 43; Diary of Samuel C. Jones, Oct. 26–28, 1863, Civil War Collection, WVA; George W. Morehead Diary, 11 Jan. 1864, Civil War Collection, WVA; "General Court Martial," *Daily Ohio State Journal*, 1 Mar. 1865, p. 3; "Take Warning, Boys," *Delaware Democratic Standard*, 2 Apr. 1863, p. 2.

14. McPherson, *For Cause and Comrade*, 47; Brinton, *Personal Memoirs*, 45; Theodore Gerrish, *Army Life: A Private's Reminiscences of the Civil War*, with an introduction by Josiah H. Drummond (reprint, Baltimore, 1995), 45–46; "Recommendation for Dishonorable Discharge," Cuyahoga County, notation by Capt. J. Ensworth, 30 Sept. 1863, Ohio State Archives, ser. 20, Box 52, 661, OHS; OR, Ser. 3, vol. 5, 678; Thomas D. Willis to his parents, 28 Dec. 1862, Thomas D. Willis Typescripts, Schoff Civil War Collection, Clements Library, University of Michigan (hereafter CL-UM); Diary of Frank S. Hardy, 31 Oct. 1862, 21 Nov. 1862, OHS.

15. Holmes, *Acts of War*, 81; "Counseling Copperheads to Resistance," *Ashland Times*, 2 April 1863, p. 2; James E. Moses to Jacob Ammen, 24 Apr. 1863, Jacob Ammen Papers, OHS; Hastings, *Letters from a Sharpshooter*, 52, 174; "Whipping a Deserter," *St. Clairsville Gazette*, 20 Aug. 1863, p. 1.

16. Mary Logan, *Reminiscences of the Civil War and Reconstruction*, ed. and with an introduction by George Worthington Adams (Carbondale, 1970), 79–80; "The Execution of Reuben Stout," *Bucyrus Weekly Journal*, 6 Nov. 1863, p. 1; James E. Moses to Jacob Ammen, 24 Apr. 1863, Jacob Ammen Papers, OHS; Tapert, *The Brother's War*, 117; Hastings, *Letters from a Sharpshooter*, 252.

17. Lonn, *Desertion*, 57–58, 165, 180–82; Tapert, *The Brother's War*, 127–28; Gerrish, *Army Life*, 123–28; "Execution of Three Deserters in Indiana," *The Spirit of Democracy* (Woodsfield, Ohio), 25 Jan. 1865, p. 2; Jacob Dolson Cox, *Military Reminiscences of the Civil War*, vol. 1, *April 1861–November 1863* (New York, 1900), 149–52; John L. Perley to Jenny Perley, 19 Apr. 1864, John L. Perley Papers, Schoff Civil War Collection, CL-UM; Roy Morris Jr., *Ambrose Bierce: Alone in Bad Company* (New York, 1995), 53; OR, ser. 1, vol. 36, 653, 912; Sterling, "Discouragement, Weariness, and War Politics," 253; Lonn, *Desertion*, 170; John D. Billings, *Hardtack and Coffee: The Unwritten Story of Army Life*, introduction by William L. Shea (Lincoln, 1993), 157, 161, 163.

18. Lonn, *Desertion*, 192–93; Historical Report of the Provost Marshal's Office, State of Illinois, 9 Aug. 1865, by James Oakes, p. 99, M 1163, Roll 1, National Archives (hereafter NA); John Taylor to "Dear and respected friends," 25 July 1864, John Taylor to "Martha," 4 Sept. n. d. [1864], Winn-Cook Papers, Filson Historical Society (hereafter FHS); David Viars to his brother, 28 [sic] Feb. 1864, Viars Family Papers, FHS; Historical Report of the Provost Marshal's Office, Northern District, California, 1 June 1865, by M. H. Parks, pp. 1, 4, M 1163, Roll 1, NA.

19. Lonn, *Desertion*, 201; "A Deserter as is a Deserter [sic]," *Daily Sandusky Commercial Register*, 14 March 1864, p. 1; Roderick Frazier Nash, *The Rights of Nature: A History of Environmental Ethics* (Madison, Wisc., 1989), 39; "Troubles of the Skedaddlers," *Chicago Tribune*, 4 Apr. 1863, p. 2; Winks, *Canada and the United States*, 203, 200; "Skedaddlers to Canada," *Ashland Times*, 2 Apr. 1863, p. 1; "Drafting Commenced," *Jackson Standard*, 19 Jan. 1865, p. 3; "Astounding Frauds on Government," *New York Times*, 8 Feb. 1865, p. 8. I thank Stanley Engerman for the reference on John Muir.

20. Lonn, *Desertion*, 192, 203–4; Diary of Samuel C. Jones, 6 Dec. 1862, 29 Aug. 1863, Civil War Collection, WVA; "A Warning to Deserters," *Bucyrus Weekly Journal*, 24 Apr. 1863, p. 2; Private David A. Russell, Roll of Soldier Prisoners, Deserts &c, 10 May 1865, no. 17, Records of the U.S. Army Continental Commands, RG 393, NA; "Capture of Deserters," *Daily Ohio State Journal*, 11 Jan. 1864, p. 2; J. W. Burton to O. P. Morton, 1 May 1862, Oliver P. Morton Papers, ISA-CPR; A. Babcock to Jacob Ammen, 23 Apr. 1863, Jacob Ammen Papers, OHS.

21. OR, ser. 3, vol. 5, 602, 676; no title, *Delaware Democratic Standard*, 9 Apr. 1863, p. 3; "A Sure Case," *Daily Ohio State Journal*, 2 Jan. 1865, p. 2; "Arrest for Assisting Soldiers to Desert," *Daily Ohio Statesmen*, 9 Jan. 1865, p. 3; Peter Goldman and Tony Fuller, *Charlie Company: What Vietnam Did to Us* (New York, 1983), 213–220; Hastings, *Letters from a Sharpshooter*, 163–70; "Arrest of a Deserter," *Madison County Democrat*, 19 Jan. 1865, p. 3; "Cop-

perhead Riot in New Berlin, Union County, Pa.," *Belmont Chronicle*, 14 May 1863, p. 1; T. W. Barrett to General Noble, 7 Feb. 1863, Adjutant General of Indiana, 69th IVI Correspondence, Roll 71, ISA-CPR.

22. "Deserter Arrested," *Xenia Sentinel*, 6 Jan. 1865, p. 1; OR, ser. 3, vol. 5, 676–77, 752–54; "After Deserters in the Vallandigham District," *Dayton Weekly Journal*, 10 Feb. 1863, p. 2; Diary of Cyrus Hussey, 1 June 1863, University of Toledo, Ward M. Canaday Center; "Deserter," *Daily Zanesville Courier*, 16 Jan. 1865, p. 3; "A Deserter as is a Deserter" [*sic*] *Daily Sandusky Commercial Register*, 17 Mar. 1864, p. 2; Federal Census of 1890, Veterans' Census, GR 612, Bundle 133, Roll 68, Lawrence Co., Ohio, Ironton Post Office, n. p.; "General Court Martial," *Daily Ohio State Journal*, 2 Mar. 1865, p. 3.

23. "Arrest of Deserters at Calumet," *Chicago Tribune*, 27 June 1863, p. 4; Historical Report of the Provost Marshal's Office, 11th District, Indiana, 10 May 1865, by C. Cowgill, p. 16, M 1163, Roll 1, NA; Kerry A. Trask, *Fire Within: A Civil War Narrative from Wisconsin* (Kent, Ohio, 1995), 24, 231–34, 264; no title, *Delaware Democratic Standard*, 19 Mar. 1863, p. 3; "Resisting the Draft," *Chicago Tribune*, 20 June 1863, p. 1.

24. Historical Report of the Provost Marshal's Office, State of Vermont, 11 July 1865, by William Austine, p. 5, M 1163, Roll 5, NA; "Egyptian Correspondence," *Chicago Tribune*, 30 June 1863, p. 2; "Deserter Arrested," *Hancock Jeffersonian*, 13 Jan. 1865, p. 3; "Resisters of Enrollment Arrested," *Lima Gazette*, 10 June 1863, p. 2; no title, *Delaware Democratic Standard*, 8 Jan. 1863, p. 2; "The Rebellion in Noble Co.," *Bucyrus Weekly Journal*, 27 Mar. 1863, p. 1.

25. David Grimsted, *American Mobbing, 1828–1861: Toward Civil War* (New York, 1998), 3–82, 181–245; "The Holmes County Rebellion," *Ashland Union*, 23 July 1863, p. 3; "No Mercy for Them," *Chicago Tribune*, 31 March 1863, p. 2; "Resistance to the Draft in Indiana," *Chicago Tribune*, 11 June 1863, p. 1; "Resisting an Enrolling Officer," *Bucyrus Weekly Journal*, 19 June 1863, p. 3; "Butternut Mob in Stark County," *Cleveland Morning Leader*, 13 Feb. 1864, p. 4.

26. "Guerillas in Sandusky County," *Ashland Times*, 11 June 1863, p. 3; no title, *Cleveland Morning Leader*, 6 Oct. 1863, p. 1; "Arrest for Resisting U.S. Officers," *Cleveland Morning Leader*, 19 Feb. 1864, p. 4; "Murder near Delphi, Indiana," *Belmont Chronicle*, 26 Mar. 1863, p. 4; "From Indianapolis," *Clinton Republican*, 6 Feb. 1863, p. 2; "A Speck of War in Indiana," *Lima Gazette*, 4 Feb. 1863, p. 2; "Copperhead Riot in New Berlin, Union Co., Pa.," *Belmont Chronicle*, 14 May 1863, p. 1.

27. "United States Officer Killed at South Pass," *Chicago Tribune*, 8 Aug. 1863, p. 2; "From Noble County," *Ashtabula Weekly Telegraph*, 11 Apr. 1863, p. 1; "The Rebellion in Noble Co.," *Bucyrus Weekly Journal*, 27 Mar. 1862, p. 1; "From Indianapolis," *Clinton Republican*, 6 Feb. 1863, p. 2.

28. Historical Report of the Provost Marshal's Office, State of Illinois, 9 Aug. 1865, by James Oakes, p. 86, M 1163, Roll 1, NA; "Fatal Encounter," *The Coshocton Democrat*, 2 Sept. 1863, p. 2; Hubert H. Wubben, *Civil War Iowa and the Copperhead Movement* (Ames, 1980), 127; "No Mercy for Them," *Chicago Tribune*, 31 Mar. 1863, p. 2.

29. "Murder near Delphi," *Belmont Chronicle*, 26 Mar. 1863, p. 4; "Resistance to the Draft in Indiana," *Chicago Tribune*, 11 June 1863, p. 1; "The Draft in Indiana," *Chicago Tribune*, 19 June 1863, p. 1; "United States Officer Killed At South Pass," *Chicago Tribune*, 8 Aug. 1863, p. 2; "U.S. Marshalls Murdered in Iowa," *Delaware Gazette*, 28 Oct. 1864, p. 1; "Murdered," *Scioto Gazette*, 14 Mar. 1865, p. 2; Geary, *We Need Men*, 73; Murdock, *One Million Men*, 12, 93, 46; OR, ser. 3, vol. 5, 912; "Murdered," *Daily Zanesville Courier*, 6 Mar. 1865, p. 3; no title, *Ironton Register*, 16 March 1865, p. 2.

30. OR, ser. 3, vol. 5, 755; H. B. McCollum to Richard Yates, 9 May 1863, Jacob Ammen Papers, OHS; "After Deserters in the Vallandigham District," *Dayton Weekly Journal*, 10 Feb. 1863, p. 2; J. S. Woodward to O. P. Morton, 20 Mar. 1863, Oliver P. Morton Papers, ISA-CPR; Mary Smith to "Dear Brother," 13 Oct. 1862, William J. Smith, OHS; "Copperhead Developments in Indiana," *Chicago Tribune*, 11 June 1863, p. 3; John H. Stucker to Richard Yates, 12 Mar. 1863, Richard Yates Correspondence, Illinois State Archives.

31. OR, ser. 1, vol. 43, pt. 2, 88; "The Rebellion in Noble Co.," *Bucyrus Weekly Journal*, 27 Mar. 1863, p. 1; "Additional about the Crawford County Expedition," *Bucyrus Weekly Journal*, 12 June 1863, p. 3; Jacob Ammen to S. R. Curtis, 18 Apr. 1863, Jacob Ammen Papers, OHS; "Affray in Jackson Township," *Spirit of Democracy*, 5 Apr. 1865, p. 3.

32. Historical Report of the Provost Marshal's Office, 4th District, Ohio, 23 May 1865, by A. C. Veuel, p. 4, M 1163, Roll 4, NA; Hannah Thorne to Jacob Ammen, 23 May 1863, Jacob Ammen Papers, OHS; Billings, *Hardtack and Coffee*, 161; Juniper Waters [sic] to his wife, 12 Apr. 1862, Watters-Curtis Family Papers, FHS; Historical Reports of the Provost Marshal's Office, 16th District, Pennsylvania, by George Eyster, n. p., M 1163, Roll 5, NA; "A Deserter Picked Up," *Daily Sandusky Commercial Register*, 29 Apr. 1864, p. 2.

33. "Assaulting a Deputy Provost Marshall," *Cleveland Morning Leader*, 4 Oct. 1864, p. 4; "The Draft in Indiana," *Chicago Tribune*, 19 June 1863, p. 1; Murdock, *One Million Men*, 48; G. R. Tredway, *Democratic Opposition to the Lincoln Administration in Indiana* (n. p., 1973), 10; "The Draft in Pennsylvania — A Mob of Women at Lancaster," *Chicago Tribune*, 23 July 1863, p. 1; Mary Smith to William J. Smith, 13 Oct. 1862, William J. Smith Papers, OHS; George R. Clarke to W. P. [sic] Ammen, 28 Nov. 1863, Jacob Ammen Papers, OHS; "Philadelphia Letter," *Savannah Daily Herald*, 6 Apr. 1865, p. 3.

34. "Illinois Guerillas Captured," *Cincinnati Daily Times*, 2 Jan. 1865, p. 2; Logan, *Reminiscences*, 80; W. B. Taylor to George A. Flagg, 10 July 1862, George A. Flagg Correspondence, Civil War Collection, WVA; Roy Bird Cook, *Lewis County in the Civil War 1861–1865* (Charleston, W. Va., 1924), 104–11); OR, ser. 1, vol. 43, 314; General Orders, No. 23, Brig. Gen. Stevenson, Headquarters Military District of Harper's Ferry, 17 Nov. 1864, Civil War Collection, Ms. 79–18, ser. 2.11, Box 2, WVA.

35. "From the Army of the Potomac — Execution of Deserters," *New York Times*, 10 Jan. 1865, p. 5; OR, ser. 1, vol. 29, 102–3; "Shooting a Deserter," *Chicago Tribune*, 20 May 1863, p. 3; no title, *Daily Zanesville Courier*, 7 Feb. 1865, p. 2; "Bounty Jumpers' Dress Parade," *Delaware Gazette*, 25 Nov. 1864, p. 2; "Parade of Bounty Jumpers," *Daily Zanesville Courier*, 15 Feb. 1865, p. 2;

Neely, *Fate of Liberty*, 35–36, 65, 161, 180; Historical Report of the Provost Marshal's Office, 2nd District, Iowa, Davenport, 15 May 1865, by Henry Egbert, pp. 9–10, M 1163, Roll 2, NA; James M. McPherson, *Battle Cry of Freedom: The Civil War Era* (New York, 1988), 591.

36. "Two Deserters Arrest a Provost Marshall," *Weekly Steubenville Herald*, 1 Mar. 1865, p. 3.

37. John Giffen to Joseph Giffen, 25 Apr. 1865, Giffen Papers, OHS; Lonn, *Desertion*, 207; Historical Report of the Provost Marshal, 2nd District, Michigan, 10 June 1865, by R. C. Dennison, p. 11, M 1163, Roll 3, NA; Leeland Hathaway Recollections, 43–46, Southern Historical Collection, University of North Carolina-Chapel Hill; Robert J. Knotts Jr., and Robert E. Stevens, *Calhoun County in the Civil War* (Parsons, W. Va., 1982), 24–25; Federal Census of 1890, Veterans' Census, GR 612, Bundle 133, Roll 68, Jackson Co., Ohio, Oak Hill Post Office, n. p.

38. Geary, *We Need Men*, 165; Billings, *Hardtack and Coffee*, 162; OR, ser. 3, vol. 5, 109; Historical Report of the Provost Marshal's Office, 2nd District of Michigan, 10 June 1865, by R. C. Denison, pp. 11–12, M 1163, Roll 3, NA; Historical Report of the Provost Marshal's Office, State of Illinois, Springfield, 9 Aug. 1865, by James Oakes, pp 76–77, M 1163, Roll 1, NA; Murdock, *Patriotism Unlimited*, 52–53; Lonn, *Deserters*, 207, 215–18.

39. John Bodnar, *Remaking America: Public Memory, Commemoration, and Patriotism in the Twentieth Century* (Princeton, 1992); OR, ser. 3, vol. 5, 601; Brinton, *Personal Memoirs*, 15; John Nicholay and John Hay, *Abraham Lincoln: A History* (New York, 1886 and 1899), 4:85; Forrest, *Conscripts and Deserters*, 75, 144–45, 237.

Chapter 12

Mary Surratt and the Plot
to Assassinate Abraham Lincoln

ELIZABETH D. LEONARD

> There is an immense force at work on the conspir-
> acy and the track of the conspirators. When the
> time comes for revelations, such startling facts will
> be revealed as will make the people shudder.
> — *New York Times*, April 26, 1865

✦ ON APRIL 14, 1865, John Wilkes Booth murdered Abraham Lincoln as the president, celebrating the end of the nation's long, bloody
Civil War, quietly enjoyed a performance of "Our American Cousin" at
Ford's Theater in Washington, D.C. For the next several weeks, anxious
and angry Americans trained their attention on the federal government's
investigation of the murder, its arrests of dozens of civilians suspected of
conspiring with Booth, the trial and conviction of eight of those sus-
pects, and the execution of four of them. On July 8, like so many newspapers across the North and South, the *Philadelphia Inquirer* published
details of what its Washington correspondent called the "last scene of
the terrible tragedy of the 14th of April." The writer noted with palpable satisfaction that on the previous day, "the ringleaders in the mur-
derous plot to assassinate the heads of the Government, and throw the
land into anarchy and confusion, paid the penalty of their crime upon
the gallows." Even as four of the eight civilians convicted of conspiracy
(Samuel Arnold, Samuel A. Mudd, Michael O'Laughlin, and Edward
Spangler) remained in their cells awaiting word of their own futures,
shortly after 1 P.M. on July 7, the others were marched to a scaffold on
the grounds of Washington's Old Arsenal Penitentiary (located at what
is now Fort Lesley McNair) to meet their deaths.[1]

Two hours earlier, soldiers on special duty had tested the gallows
traps with three one hundred-pound weights and had readied the ropes
for their gruesome task. Around noon General Winfield Scott Hancock,
in command of the Union's armed forces in the federal capital, had
ordered the special provost marshal assigned to the prison, General

John F. Hartranft, to get ready. At about 1:15 P.M. the condemned, their guards, and their spiritual advisers moved slowly through the prison door, across the courtyard, and up the thirteen steps to the gallows platform. There each of the prisoners underwent final preparations: pinioning of the arms and tying of the legs, placing of the heavy rope around the neck and a hood over the head. Seconds later, either General Hartranft or Captain Christian Rath, the official executioner, gave the signal by clapping his hands, and the drops were allowed to fall. In that moment a hushed crowd of over a thousand people, including ticket-bearing spectators, soldiers on guard duty, officers, government officials, and friends and family of the prisoners witnessed a remarkable hanging.[2]

What made it remarkable was the fact that along with George A. Atzerodt, David E. Herold, and Lewis Thornton Powell (better known by the alias, Lewis Paine), a middle-aged woman named Mary Elizabeth Surratt also ascended the steps, becoming the federal government's first female victim of capital punishment. Many people at the time expected Mary Surratt's life to be spared and her sentence to be converted. Indeed, General Hancock himself had stationed mounted soldiers at regular intervals between the White House and the prison grounds in anticipation of the need to relay a last-minute presidential pardon. That pardon never came, however, and when Mary Surratt died by the hangman's noose in the early afternoon of July 7, 1865, her death made a macabre bit of American history.

Mary Surratt was born Mary Elizabeth Jenkins in 1823 on a tobacco farm in the area that is now known as Clinton, Maryland, to Elizabeth Anne (Webster) and Archibald Jenkins. Elizabeth and Archibald were simple folk whose families had farmed in and around Prince George's County at least since the early nineteenth century. When she was two, Mary's father died, leaving her mother to manage the family's estate (including at least eleven slaves) and to raise Mary and her two brothers alone. As a property-owning widow of thirty when Archibald died, Elizabeth Jenkins should have been able to remarry, but for whatever reason, she did not do so. Nevertheless, over the next decade she handled her family and financial affairs sufficiently well on her own to enroll Mary, at age twelve, in a private girls' boarding school in Alexandria, Virginia. Despite the fact that Elizabeth herself was an Episcopalian and her late husband had also been Protestant, the Academy for Young Ladies in Alexandria was Catholic, and during her four years there Mary Jenkins traveled new and exciting paths both intellectually and spiritually. Among other things she adopted the Catholic religion for herself, assuming the confirmation name of Maria Eugenia, possibly to honor one of her teachers whose name was Eugenia. Mary remained an extremely devout and active Catholic for the duration of her life.[3]

Shortly after her return to Prince George's County, Mary Jenkins met John Harrison Surratt, a man ten years her senior whose ancestors had been among the early settlers of the region in the late 1600s. Although he agreed to convert to Catholicism (a requirement for marrying in the Catholic Church), John Surratt was not particularly morally upstanding, having already fathered at least one child out of wedlock. Unfortunately for his future wife, John Surratt's character only became increasingly dissolute as time passed. Probably as yet unaware of her suitor's character flaws, and perhaps also because no better offer was forthcoming, seventeen-year-old Mary decided to marry John Surratt, and they were wed at a church in Washington, D.C., in the late summer of 1840. Mary quickly began to bear children: Isaac in 1841, Elisabeth Susanna ("Anna") in 1843, and John Jr. in 1844.[4]

Mary and John Surratt's marriage was not a particularly happy one, nor was their life easy. Like their families before them, Mary and John were, fundamentally, farmers. Initially, they lived in the District of Columbia, but when their house there burned in 1852, John Surratt purchased some land back in Prince George's County where the couple continued farming tobacco with the help of a few slaves. Although John Surratt was a mediocre businessman at best, by 1854, with Mary's help, he had augmented their farmlands with a tavern and a gristmill. He had also become the first postmaster of the newly established "Surrattsville" post office, transforming the Surratt family and its operations into the economic core of the small community that had arisen around it. At the same time, however, John Surratt proved to be the greatest threat to his own and his family's stability and survival. Mary Surratt, however, was stalwart, and indeed, her religious faith held her in good stead through many difficult times, though it could not relieve her suffering entirely. In January 1855 she penned an anguished letter to her priest and confidant, Father Joseph M. Finotti, in which she complained that John Sr. was "drunk on evry occation and . . . more and more dis-agreeable evry day." Clearly Mary Surratt was growing tired of her husband's dissipation, and with good reason: by 1857, through debt and misadventure, John Surratt had reduced the family's holdings in Maryland significantly. By the summer of 1862, he was dead, leaving Mary, their nineteen-year-old daughter Anna, and their eighteen-year-old son John "in desperate straits," son Isaac having left home the year before for a job as a pony express rider in Mexico.[5]

Perhaps modeling herself on her widowed mother, Mary Surratt did not remarry. She struggled on in Surrattsville for two more years, trying to hold the family, the farm, and the business together, and managing the slaves, some of whom — like their counterparts across the South — probably began to escape almost immediately in the absence of the "master." Even while John Sr. was alive, Mary Surratt — also like her mother — had sought superior educations for her children, sending Anna to a Catholic girls' school, and John Jr. to St. Charles's College, a Catholic seminary in Howard County, Maryland, where he studied for the priesthood. John Jr. was not particularly successful at the seminary, and he dropped out and returned to Surrattsville shortly after his father died, his sister having returned home some time earlier. Although John Jr. showed early signs of becoming as intemperate and irresponsible as his father, Mary Surratt was grateful no doubt for these two children's presence with her; she was grateful as well for the regular business at the tavern, which had become a wartime waystation for Confederate operatives and couriers traveling between the federal capital and the South.

By the summer of 1864, however, Mary Surratt was weary to the bone and frustrated by the clamoring of creditors: one after another her late husband's shady business deals, unpaid loans, and debts challenged her very best management skills. She decided to settle up affairs as best she could in Surrattsville, among other things selling or renting various remaining properties and leaving the house and tavern in the charge of a former Washington police officer named John Lloyd. With what personal and financial resources remained, Mary Surratt banked the family's future on an investment John Sr. had made over a decade before: a small, debt-free house in Washington. It was this house just a few blocks from Ford's Theater, transformed into a boardinghouse, that in April 1865 became the focus of the federal government's investigation into the conspiracy to assassinate Lincoln, resulting in Mary Surratt's execution.[6]

What exactly can we learn about Mary Surratt's connection to the plot to murder Abraham Lincoln? Needless to say, there has been steady and often heated debate on this question virtually since the assassination itself. A few pieces of the answer, however, are indisputable. In 1865, Mary Surratt was many things: long-suffering widow, businesswoman, Catholic devotee, and matron of a staunchly pro-Southern family whose opinions she probably shared. Although Maryland was a contested border state, the civilians of Prince George's County were generally fiercely Southern in their orientation: in the election of 1860, the county's anti-Lincoln sentiment was revealed by the fact that the Republican candidate received only a single vote, and that one did not come from a Surratt. Mary Surratt was also a mother, and specifically the mother of John Surratt Jr., who in his years since leaving St. Charles College had come to be known widely for his deep Confederate sympathies and his regular activities as a Confederate agent involved in smuggling information and contraband all along the route from Richmond to

Washington and points further north. John Jr. was much more than an "operative," however: his participation in a pre-assassination conspiracy to abduct Lincoln, carry him south, and hold him hostage for the release of any number of Confederate prisoners of war is a matter of uncontested legal and historical record.[7]

Directly or indirectly, therefore, Mary Surratt was linked to the plot to kill Lincoln by virtue of her pro-Confederate regional identity and her relationship with her staunchly pro-Southern son. Equally incontrovertible is the fact that the Washington property she owned, inhabited, and managed as a boardinghouse (then no. 541, now no. 604 H Street NW and refitted as an unremarkable Chinese restaurant named "Go Lo's") served on and off in the late winter and spring of 1864–65 much as the Surrattsville tavern had done, as a meeting place for Confederate operatives like her son. And not only random Confederate agents visited the boardinghouse; so, too, did John Wilkes Booth, who was initially brought there by John Jr., whom he seems to have met in the midwinter of 1864–65. Moreover, Booth was not the only player in the assassination plot to pass through the H Street house on at least one occasion: George Atzerodt, for example, stayed for at least one night in February 1865; and Lewis Powell/Paine spent three or four nights there in February and March 1865, on one occasion using the alias "Wood."[8]

Some of the circumstantial evidence introduced against Mary Surratt at the conspiracy trial, which lasted from May 9 to June 30, 1865, also raises serious suspicion about her possible complicity in the planning of Lincoln's murder. We know from this evidence that Mary Surratt did, for example, have an independent personal connection with Booth himself. Although Booth's primary association was clearly with John Jr., nevertheless Mary Surratt was described by several witnesses as having welcomed the charming Booth's visits to the boardinghouse and having conversed with him privately on occasion. We also know that during the week prior to the assassination Mary Surratt traveled down to Surrattsville twice (once on the eleventh and once on the fourteenth of April) in the company of Louis Weichmann, a favorite boarder who was also a close family friend and former schoolmate of John Jr. from the seminary. (Weichmann, who was employed as a clerk in the office of the Union army's Commissary General of Prisons, had been living at the H Street house since November 1, 1864.) Although Mary Surratt made these trips ostensibly to address some financial complications relating to her remaining property holdings in Maryland, there are features of the trips that did (and do) merit attention, including the fact that on the eleventh, Weichmann and Mary Surratt made their trip in a buggy hired with money given to Weichmann by Booth specifically for that purpose; and on the fourteenth — the day of the assassination — Mary Surratt brought with her to the Surrattsville house, at Booth's request, a paper-wrapped package that later turned out to contain a set of field glasses, although it is unclear whether or not she was aware of the package's contents at the time.[9]

Other irrefutable circumstantial evidence involves the visit to the boardinghouse of Lewis Powell/Paine, in disguise as a common laborer and carrying a pickaxe, just as the Washington, D.C., metropolitan police were in the process of arresting all of the boardinghouse residents late on the night of April 17. Paine, who had almost succeeded, on the fourteenth, in assassinating Secretary of State William H. Seward, appeared that night for reasons that are not entirely clear. What weighed most heavily against Mary Surratt at the trial, however, was her claim that she did not recognize her former boarder. According to Major H. W. Smith, in charge of the officers who occupied the boardinghouse that night, Mary Surratt adamantly denied having ever met Paine before. "I asked her," Smith testified, "'Do you know this man and did you hire him to come and dig a gutter for you?' She answered, raising her right hand, 'Before God, sir, I do not know this man, and have never seen him, and I did not hire him to dig a gutter for me.'" Witnesses for the defense insisted that Mary Surratt's eyesight had deteriorated so dramatically in recent years that her inability — in poor light, and under great stress — to recognize Paine in disguise was entirely plausible. Nevertheless, the prosecution interpreted Mary Surratt's denial as an attempt to cover for Paine and thus as clear evidence of her complicity with him.[10]

Of the eight witnesses called to testify against her, two supplied the most incriminating evidence: Louis Weichmann, erstwhile school friend of John Jr. and now a boarder beloved by Mary Surratt like a son; and the former police officer now responsible for the Surratts' Maryland properties, John Lloyd. Notably, the prosecution called both men to present their testimony on May 13 (Weichmann was recalled briefly on the eighteenth), only four days after the trial began and only the second day of hearing witnesses. As such, Lloyd's and Weichmann's testimony against Mary Surratt helped to set the tone for the entire trial, in which the cases of all eight alleged conspirators were considered simultaneously — an unusual but not unheard of practice for such trials. Although he insisted under cross-examination that he had always known Mary Surratt to behave in a manner both morally "exemplary" and "lady-like in every particular," Weichmann's testimony was essential in linking her to Booth, to various additional supporters and agents of the Confederacy, and to the other prisoners at the bar; in placing her in Surrattsville on April 11 and April 14; and in generating grave suspicions about her true motivations for making those visits.[11]

John Lloyd offered different but equally crucial testimony when he claimed that on April 11, Mary Surratt had not only transacted financial business in the Surrattsville area, but had as well inquired of him specifically about the "shooting irons," by which he assumed that she meant the two carbines that John Jr., David Herold, and George Atzerodt had stashed at the Surratt house some five or six weeks earlier. Lloyd indicated that on the eleventh Mary Surratt had suggested that the guns "would be wanted soon," and then on the fourteenth, just before she handed him the package containing Booth's field glasses, she "told me to have those shooting-irons ready that night, [as] there would be some parties who would call for them." The Surratt house and tavern was in fact the first stop along the escape route Booth and Herold took on the night of the fourteenth, and when they arrived Herold asked for the weapons. Lloyd's testimony positioned Mary Surratt as an accomplice with clear foreknowledge about the murder of the president.[12]

There is no question that Mary Surratt's ownership of the boarding-house, her relationship to John Jr., and the damaging circumstantial evidence given at the conspiracy trial, must be taken seriously. Needless to say, it seems patently absurd to imagine that Mary Surratt was entirely oblivious to the treasonous activities going on under her roof, and to insist on her complete and utter ignorance would be to disregard her obvious intelligence and capability as an individual. However, it is also eminently clear that the case against Mary Surratt was (and is) hardly open and shut. For one thing, in every possible circumstance and context Mary Surratt maintained her innocence of the charges against her.

Despite being "hammered mercilessly by interrogators" during the investigation, Mary Surratt's story remained consistent. She emphasized the greater significance (and the secretiveness) of her son's association with Booth over her own, although she disagreed with the characterization of her son as a Confederate spy. She denied John Lloyd's assertion that she had warned him to ready the "shooting-irons." She admitted bringing Booth's wrapped package to Surrattsville on the fourteenth of April, but she insisted that she had not known what was in it. She admitted having briefly given lodging at the boardinghouse, at one time or another, to both Atzerodt and Paine, yet she argued that they had been no more than boarders in her eyes, and also that when Paine returned on the night of the seventeenth she had truly failed to recognize him due to her poor eyesight. Finally, she acknowledged having met Herold once or twice, but denied ever having encountered Mudd, Spangler, O'Laughlin, or Arnold. Not surprisingly, perhaps, the prosecution attributed the consistency of Mary Surratt's self-defense not to honesty, but to her "cleverness," her "nerves of steel," and her "consecration to the Confederate cause." As in the past, Mary Surratt's strong religious faith was a major source of consolation during this period.[13]

According to common practice at the time in courts both martial and civil, none of the alleged conspirators was given the opportunity to speak at the trial, but had she been allowed to do so, Mary Surratt undoubtedly would have continued in the courtroom to assert her blamelessness in the face of the charges brought against her. Perhaps even more significant for a woman of her religious convictions, however, is the fact that Mary Surratt maintained her innocence right up to the moment of her final interview with her priest. According to at least one historian, when she received her final communion on July 7 from Father Jacob Walter, Mary Surratt announced her innocence before him and several others. One wonders whether, short of being a sociopath, Mary Surratt, with over thirty years of unwavering piety and religious devotion behind her, could have dared to lie so brazenly to a man of the cloth in the final moments of her life.[14]

Moreover, she was not alone in proclaiming her innocence, even to the end. Even as he awaited his own execution on the gallows, none other than Lewis Powell/Paine explicitly disavowed any connection between Mary Surratt and the assassination plot. Throughout the trial, others had risen to her defense as well. Indeed, between May 25 and June 13, Mary Surratt's attorneys called twenty-seven witnesses on her behalf, versus the eight original witnesses called by the prosecution to testify against her. Importantly, several of these defense witnesses offered strong testimony challenging the credibility of both John Lloyd and Louis Weichmann. On May 25, for example, George Cottingham, who had been involved in the arrest of various suspicious persons after the assassination, cast doubt on the quality of Lloyd's testimony by citing self-implicating remarks Lloyd had made shortly after being apprehended. Probably more damning, on May 30 the bartender at the Surrattsville tavern raised doubts about the believability of anything whatsoever that Lloyd claimed to "recall" about Mary Surratt's visit on the afternoon of April 14, particularly her warning about the "shooting-irons," noting that Lloyd had been "pretty tight" from alcohol that afternoon. On June 13, Lloyd's own sister-in-law, Emma Offutt, described him as having been "very much in liquor, more so than I have ever seen him in my life" on the afternoon of the assassination. With respect to Weichmann: during the defense testimony Augustus "Spencer" Howell—himself a Confederate blockade runner who had visited the boardinghouse on at least one occasion—stated that, despite his appointment as a U.S. government clerk, Weichmann was known in the Surrattsville area for having intense Southern sympathies. By implication, then, Weichmann had chosen to smear the reputation of Mary

Surratt in order to protect his own. Other witnesses, including Rachel Semus, a black servant at the boardinghouse, testified to Mary Surratt's faulty eyesight, and her impeccable moral character. As early as May 16, the Lewiston, Maine, *Daily Evening Journal* described Mary Surratt as "the arch criminal among those before the Commission," and on June 3, before the testimony was even complete, *Harper's Weekly* was reporting that Mary Surratt "not only harbored the principal criminals, but took a prominent part in the whole conspiracy." Nevertheless, in point of fact, the evidence against her was far from conclusive.[15]

This being the case, how then can we account for Mary Surratt's summary conviction and speedy execution? The question becomes even more striking when one considers the Victorian cultural milieu in which the events took place, a milieu characterized by strong notions about gender roles among middle-class and elite whites, the expectations associated with those roles, and the sorts of behaviors men and women should display, not least of all in relation to one another. Chivalry was not yet dead in 1865, although as in all wars the Civil War had compromised standing assumptions about gender in some degree, stretching and even perforating the boundaries between the sexes. But certainly in many ways the Victorian gender scheme remained substantially intact even in 1865, and as noted, despite the turmoil of war the federal government had still, to date, only exacted its ultimate punishment against men. In this particular cultural context, then, how does one explain the government's readiness to execute this particular woman, Mary Surratt?[16]

One explanation, of course, is simply that she was found guilty of such a heinous deed — conspiracy to assassinate the president! — that her sex was deemed irrelevant, and she was given the punishment such a criminal deserved, regardless of sex. As we have already seen, the opinion of the popular press at the time certainly tended in this direction. Indeed, with respect to her "guilt," when he published his *History of the United States Secret Service* in 1867, Lafayette Baker (chief of the National Detective Police at the time of the assassination and intimately involved in the conspiracy investigation) went so far as to contend that, in the end, Mary Surratt had actually "fessed up" to her part in the conspiracy during one of the many visits to her cell that he claimed to have made. It is of course possible that Baker was telling the truth. However, his legendary ego combined with the evidence of Mary Surratt's sustained proclamation of her own innocence provokes considerable doubt. At the same time, press coverage from the time of the assassination through the execution clearly indicates that the bulk of public opinion considered her guilty as charged.[17]

Nevertheless, we have also seen that during the trial and even while her body was still warm in the ground there were those who strove vigorously to vindicate Mary Surratt, not the least significant of whom was Benn Pitman, the "official" recorder, editor, and publisher of the trial testimony. "That Mrs. Mary Surratt was entirely innocent of any prior knowledge of, or participation in those crimes," argued Pitman after her death, "is in my mind beyond question. . . . [S]he was wholly innocent of the crime for which she was hanged."[18] So why was Mary Surratt convicted and executed if there was sufficient evidence in her favor to persuade even the official court reporter that she was not guilty? Was she simply so skillfully framed by others that the judges were virtually without a choice but to condemn her? And if so, who implicated her, and why?

Surely if one pursues this explanation at all, one has to consider John Lloyd, who testified under oath that Mary Surratt had told him to prepare the "shooting irons," the carbines that he had been storing for weeks before the assassination and that Booth and Herold called for as they fled the capital on April 14. More important: what of Louis Weichmann? Did he in fact shine the spotlight on Mary Surratt in order to turn attention away from his own connection to a number of the accused conspirators? Weichmann, after all, had lived at the boarding-house for months, was very close friends with John Surratt Jr., had himself been known to socialize with and even borrow money from Booth, was acquainted with several of the others among the accused, and so forth.[19] Did these men (and possibly others) frame Mary Surratt in order to deflect attention from their own complicity in the conspiracy? It would seem to me indefensible on the basis of the evidence to argue for the existence of such a carefully orchestrated scheme, meticulously coordinated by a group of individuals whose own participation in the assassination conspiracy was in question. Having said this, however, it must also be recognized that, wittingly or not, from the outset of the trial Weichmann's and Lloyd's testimony dug a hole for Mary Surratt from which it ultimately proved impossible for her legal counsel to extricate her.

For what it is worth, Weichmann at least suffered long and miserably for his role in the trial. "From the day I gave testimony against the miscreants who robbed Mr. Lincoln of his life," he later wrote, "I have been subjected on the part of certain people to an infamous persecution." Although he sounds a bit petulant, it is nevertheless true that from July 7, 1865, until his death in 1902, Weichmann committed a substantial amount of time, on a regular basis, to defending his testimony against those who challenged it from a variety of quarters. Indeed, just ten days after the execution the *Philadelphia Inquirer* printed Weichmann's response to some recently published attacks. "Much has been said and much has been written," he argued, "about Mrs. Surratt's innocence. . . . That a woman so kind, so compassionate, so generous and religious, should have been cognizant of plots to capture or assassinate the President, is hardly to be believed. Yet it is strangely true." Until he died, Weichmann struggled to defend himself from charges of having betrayed another to save his own skin, completing — in the year before his death — his own extensive compendium of information and analysis of the assassination, the trial in 1865, the trial of John Surratt Jr. in 1867, and related documents, which he entitled, significantly, *A True History of the Assassination of Abraham Lincoln and of the Conspiracy of 1865.* Curiously, Weichmann did not follow through with publication of his "true history," which finally appeared as a book only in 1975.[20]

But returning to the question of why the federal government was so ready to convict and execute a woman whose guilt in the conspiracy was less than fully proven: one is hard pressed to avoid the conclusion that Mary Surratt's religious faith must have played some role in sealing her fate. For Mary Surratt was a Catholic in a nation (and a courtroom) dominated by Protestants and as such, although her religious convictions were a source of tremendous strength to her, in the minds of many observers they served only to increase the likelihood of her culpability. Anti-Catholic sentiment, after all, reached its apex in America at mid-century, a consequence of — among other things — the recent flood of Catholic immigrants from Ireland and also Germany; the expansion of a nativistic, Protestant-led temperance movement whose members were appalled by what they crudely considered to be Catholic indifference to — perhaps even celebration of — alcohol abuse; and enduring questions about the implications for their loyalty to the U.S. Constitution of immigrant (and American) Catholics' allegiance to a foreign pope, especially in light of the polity's disintegration into civil war. Such concerns were prevalent among mid-nineteenth-century Protestant Americans, and for many, the term "Catholic" automatically provoked a range of fears. Indeed, on May 5, 1865, the *Philadelphia Inquirer* reported ominously — and inaccurately — that not only Mary Surratt, but indeed *all* of the prisoners were "by education . . . Catholic," as if the reading public would immediately understand the dangerous implications of such a detail.[21]

Certainly Mary Surratt's Catholic faith amplified the hostility of many, in the public and within the courtroom, to her case. But it can by no means be considered the primary reason for her condemnation. Indeed, the trial testimony itself includes little material relating to her specific religious affiliation, although numerous *favorable* comments are made about the depths of her faith. Moreover, it must be recalled that the judges convicted all eight of the accused regardless of their religious affiliations, which were diverse and in some cases unidentifiable. Additionally, although he was convicted of involvement in the assassination conspiracy, the only other devout Catholic among the defendants, Dr. Samuel Mudd—the civilian who set Booth's broken leg when Booth and Herold reached his home, south of Surrattsville, during their escape—was not sentenced to die. And it should not be forgotten that Louis Weichmann, whose testimony was so important in convicting Mary Surratt, was himself a Catholic and a former seminarian. In sum, I would argue that when the judges considered Mary Surratt's case, her Catholicism did not work in her favor. But in and of itself her Catholicism also did not decide the case against her.[22]

What other factors were at play in Mary Surratt's conviction and execution, besides a damaging cluster of circumstantial evidence linking her to the assassination conspiracy, besides Weichmann's (and Lloyd's) ruinous testimony, and besides a dominant cultural milieu characterized by virulent anti-Catholic sentiment? Some have argued that the answer lies in the very nature of the trial itself and the way it was conducted. For by the decision of the Secretary of War Edwin M. Stanton, in consultation with other federal government officials, Mary Surratt and the other seven alleged conspirators—although they were civilians—were tried together in a military rather than a civil court, which means that both the prosecutors (Chief Prosecutor Joseph Holt and his assistants, Colonel John A. Bingham and General Henry L. Burnett) and the nine men selected to adjudicate the defendants' guilt or innocence (Generals David Hunter, Thomas M. Harris, Charles H. Tompkins, David R. Clendinin, Lewis Wallace, Albion P. Howe, Augustus V. Kautz, Robert S. Foster, and James A. Ekin) were government men and officers of the Union army. As such, one might presume that they experienced grave difficulty offering an impartial verdict in this particular case and even maintaining basic constitutional standards of due process for civilian defendants.

Indeed, several students of the trial have noted that as defendants in a military court, where at least some of the rules and presumptions were different from those in civil court, the alleged conspirators enjoyed virtually no constitutionally guaranteed civil rights: once accused, they were jailed without grand jury indictment; they were only informed of the charges against them when they first appeared in court; legal counsel was not provided to them until after the trial opened; defendants were unable to consult with their lawyers during the trial; witnesses in the trial faced the judges and prosecutors at all times, even during cross-examination; and so forth. In short, the argument goes, the military setting ensured a presumption of guilt and a speedy trial with no jury and no possibility of appeal, perhaps, as some have gone so far as to suggest, because this is exactly the outcome that key figures in the federal government — among them the secretary of war, Edwin Stanton, considered ruthless by many — sought from April 14 on.[23]

As it turns out, questions were raised during the trial itself and even immediately after by Reverdy Johnson, by defense attorney Thomas Ewing Jr. — incidentally, also a Catholic — and by outside observers of the proceedings regarding the propriety of the decision about the trial's setting. It has also been argued with considerable merit, however, that a military setting was absolutely appropriate, even for civilians. After all, the war had not yet ended officially when the assassination occurred, despite the April 9 surrender of General Robert E. Lee. Moreover, Washington, D.C., was essentially an armed military camp on April 14, 1865. Furthermore, as commander in chief of the United States's armed forces, Abraham Lincoln was not just a civil figure but also a military one and, as such, treating his murder as a military crime was entirely proper. From another angle, however, it is also true that John Surratt Jr.'s 1867 trial, which was conducted in civil court, resulted in a failure to convict, which some have suggested indicates that the format of the trial made all the difference in the world.[24]

What gets lost in this debate, as at least one historian has pointed out, is the degree of bitterness that characterized the context in which the assassination occurred, acrimony so severe in the North and especially in Washington, D.C., that anything but a guilty verdict and the death sentence were supremely unlikely in July 1865, regardless of the trial's military setting. Not only were Northerners resentful of the war itself and the terrible cost it had exacted on the nation, but their wrath was magnified many times over by the sense of betrayal the timing of the assassination produced, just as it seemed that peace and a return to some golden ideal of national union had become possible. On April 16 the New York Times characterized the popular response to Lincoln's murder as something previously unseen in America: "The heart of this nation was stirred yesterday as it has never been stirred before. The news of the assassination of Abraham Lincoln carried with it a sensation of horror and agony which no other event in our history has ever excited." Two days later, the Times reported an ominous mood in Richmond: "Peace, magnanimity, hope and joy . . . have already given place . . . to hatred, distrust, despair, fierce antagonism, and thirst for vengeance that will require the most cautious handling to keep within the bounds even of prudence."[25]

The assassination provoked not only anger but also violence, perpetrated in many cases by individuals legally armed and prepared to exact retribution. On April 20 the New York Times specifically urged police restraint in the assassination's wake.[26] For many, notions of retribution encompassed more than just those individuals foolish enough to express publicly their satisfaction with the assassination; for some, any imagined conspirators in the crime, and not just the eight civilians who faced trial, merited the severest possible punishment. As such, it is probably wrongheaded to imagine that the Northern public — let alone the members of Lincoln's cabinet and a group of Union army officers sitting in judgment — could have come to any other conclusions in the spring and early summer of 1865 than that Mary Surratt and her co-conspirators were guilty and at least some of them deserved the death penalty.[27]

If the military nature of the trial in fact made little difference in terms of its outcome, where else can we turn for additional explanations for Mary Surratt's summary conviction and execution? According to some scholars, our eyes must turn at least in some measure toward her younger son. And what of him? It is beyond the scope of this essay to delve into the details of the investigation into John Jr.'s involvement in the assassination conspiracy, or to consider in any depth his separate trial in 1867 in which a hung jury, considering a poorly conceived formal charge against him, ensured his release. What is relevant here is that the question of his guilt or innocence in the conspiracy loomed large at the 1865 trial, but John Jr. himself was physically absent, having slipped out of Washington sometime between the failed kidnap attempt in March and the assassination in April. Is it possible, as has been posited, that in the white emotional heat of the moment and with the much more heavily implicated Surratt — John Jr. — unavailable for punishment, Mary Surratt's conviction and execution reflected her status as a symbolic stand-in for her son?[28]

There is some appeal in this theory, yet the point is equally well taken that if Mary Surratt's execution was meant to be symbolic of the execution of John Jr., then her conviction was equally likely to have been meant to serve as bait to bring him back to the United States to stand trial himself. And if this is the case, then surely the actual carrying out of her sentence should have been delayed until word could reach John Jr., who is known to have been hiding in Canada at this time. Instead, the hanging could hardly have occurred more quickly. The commission's findings were announced on July 5, at which point the construction of the scaffold began immediately, and the condemned were executed on the seventh. Given the dispatch with which these events followed upon one another, it is certainly hard to imagine that Mary Surratt's conviction was meant to lure her son to justice. After all, he would have had insufficient time to learn of the final developments in the case and to respond appropriately.[29]

We can with relative confidence set aside the theory that Mary Surratt's conviction and execution derived from her being cast as a substitute for her son at the trial, or as a lure to draw him out of hiding. But the foregoing discussion also recalls a significant detail about the ultimate fate Mary Surratt suffered, namely, that her conviction in the conspiracy case did not necessarily have to result in her execution. As already noted, a great many people in July 1865 anticipated that Mary Surratt's life would be spared by a presidential pardon. And as it turns out, the matter of a pardon *was* discussed — intensely, in fact — in the wake of the conviction and over the short period of time leading up to her hanging.

Of course we can never know the full details of what went on behind closed doors as the military judges sought to reach their conclusions at the end of June 1865. However, it seems that at least five of the nine were much more inclined to find Mary Surratt guilty of conspiracy than they were to execute her, and in the end went along with the others only on the condition that the judges collectively recommend to President Andrew Johnson that he demonstrate mercy in her particular case and convert her sentence to life imprisonment, on the basis of her sex and her age. Clearly Johnson did not heed the judges' recommendation, and there is much debate about *why* he did not.[30] But in much the same way that the military setting of the trial is probably moot, one could ask, does it matter precisely how the judges' clemency request (and the simultaneous and infinitely more impassioned requests of Mary Surratt's anguished supporters, including her daughter Anna) came to be set aside? Is it not safe to assume that the mood of the nation undermined the potential efficacy of such a plea? Indeed, according to the *Boston Traveler*, Johnson admitted as much in an 1869 interview when questioned whether anything would have inclined him to pardon Mary Surratt in 1865: "'I don't think I would,' he replied in his bluff way. 'She didn't do the shooting, but she was an accessory to it which is all the same.'"[31]

Can we accept the idea that Johnson, Holt, Stanton, the government prosecutors, and the judges in charge of Mary Surratt's fate truly were incapable of being persuaded to err on the side of forgiveness, in light of the inconclusive nature of the evidence against her, and the prevailing notions of gender which underlay the federal government wartime tradition of going lightly on female criminals? In point of fact, herein lies the final piece of our puzzle: Mary Surratt's sex was in fact the final (and a profoundly significant) factor tipping the balance against her. For I would argue that, within the inflamed circumstances of post-assassination Washington, D.C., and in the wake of a brutal civil war in which countless Confederate women had engaged in treasonable activities against the United States — many of them actually taking advantage of dominant notions of gender to shield themselves from harsh punishment—Mary Surratt's sex failed to offer any sort of buffer against her conviction, and was instead in large part responsible for it.

Now to say that up until July 1865 dominant notions of gender and chivalry had served to protect "troublesome" women from harsh punishments is not to suggest that these same women were *legally* immune. Even before the end of the Civil War, the idea that women should be answerable "to the law as well as to men" for their crimes—particularly crimes of treason—was not new. Certainly English common law, much of which had been successfully transferred to England's North American colonies in the seventeenth century, included longstanding traditions of coverture that essentially absolved women of legal responsibility by dissolving their status as legal entities at the moment they married. But even under coverture, widows such as Mary Surratt were legal individuals in virtually every way. Moreover, already by the 1830s state legislatures had begun to challenge coverture itself, laying preliminary foundations for the establishment of full legal status for all women, married, widowed, or single. Although such changes were far from complete in 1865, they were nevertheless well underway. Notably for Mary Surratt's case, General Orders No. 100 ("Instructions for the Government of Armies of the United States in the Field"), issued on April 24, 1863, by none other than Edwin Stanton, had already made it clear that in wartime at least, sex would not be permitted to serve as a determining factor in the punishment of criminal behavior. Wrote Stanton: "The law of war, like the criminal law regarding other offenses, makes no difference on account of the differences of the sexes, concerning the spy, the war-traitor, or the war rebels."[32]

Secretary of War Stanton's General Orders No. 100 articulated an unequivocal government position on the question of the punishment to be meted out to women who committed war crimes, and he explicitly cited the death penalty as an option. However, it is also clear that although federal law *permitted* the ultimate punishment for women convicted of war crimes, prior to July 1865 the federal government had "failed" on every occasion to administer it, and I would argue that many in the North had grown weary of this pattern.[33] Most significant for our purposes, of course, is the evidence that those who were fed up with Confederate women's betrayal of the Union included Stanton, Holt, and Johnson, and the nine military commissioners deciding Mary Surratt's case, many of whom had undoubtedly dealt with civilian women's espionage and resistance activities first hand and on a regular basis while serving as Union army officers in the field. In short, it seems entirely plausible that in a context already charged with vengeful passions, these men collectively took evidence that was hardly conclusive in and of itself, consciously or unconsciously added to it the burden of countless women's wartime treason, and allowed the sum to serve as justification for sending Mary Surratt up the gallows steps along with three men whose involvement in the assassination conspiracy was far more certain. The time had come, these men must have felt, to cast aside tolerance and finally set an example to those of the "fairer sex" who had forgotten their place.

We should note here that, in the course of the trial, Mary Surratt's sex (and Victorian notions about proper female behavior) consistently drew special attention. Certainly in their final argument in defense of Mary Surratt, her lawyers closed with a lengthy reminder of their client's sex, and all the qualities (including inviolable piety) that good Victorians would have associated with it. "[W]ho will believe . . . ," the defense attorneys pleaded,

> that a woman born and bred in respectability and competence — a Christian mother . . . whose unfailing attention to the most sacred duties of life has won for her the name of "a proper Christian matron;" . . . who will believe that she could so suddenly and so fully have learned the intricate arts of sin? . . . A strong but guileless-hearted woman, her maternal solicitude would have been the first denouncer, even abrupt betrayer, of a plotted crime in which one companion of her son could have been implicated, had cognizance of such reached her. Her days would have been agonized and her nights sleepless, till she might have exposed and counteracted that spirit of defiant hate which watched its moment of vantage to wreak an immortal wrong — till she might have sought the intercession and absolution of the Church, her refuge, in behalf of those she loved.[34]

Throughout the trial, Mary Surratt's sex drew special attention from those who sought to trade on dominant notions of womanhood in her behalf.

But throughout the trial, too, there was clear evidence of a breakdown in this sort of thinking, and an upsurge in a very different kind of thinking indeed. One explanation is that this change in attitude reflected the resistance of key figures to Mary Surratt's involvement in business and politics (managing her own financial affairs after the death of John Sr., trying to sell land, associating with Confederate spies and smugglers, and so forth). I would argue that this theory understates the case a bit: that what was really at play was a generalized frustration with scores of "she-rebels" who had thrown their weight behind the Confederate cause and had been insufficiently punished for it.[35]

To some extent, this idea is not a new one. Over a century ago one of her staunchest defenders, David M. DeWitt, gave passing attention to the idea that Mary Surratt was, by her conviction and execution, "to be made an example and a warning to the women of the South, who . . .

had 'unsexed' themselves by cherishing and cheering fathers, brothers, husbands and sons on the tented field." Again, however, to put it this way is to avoid coming to grips with the true nature of so many pro-Confederate women's behavior during the war. For although some women in the South (and in pro-Southern areas in border states such as Maryland) were actually pro-Union, and others who initially supported the Cause became quite ambivalent over time, a vast number of Southern and border-state women nevertheless functioned consistently and throughout the war not only as cheerleaders but also as actors on behalf of the Confederacy, in traitorous and even violent ways. Given this, it is probably closer to the mark to suggest that Mary Surratt exemplifed to many observers some archetypical "she-rebel" who should be made, at last, to pay for her crime.[36] Put another way, it seems to me that Mary Surratt became the supreme representative of what many in the North — the popular press, Holt, Johnson, Stanton — deemed to be the worst perversion of proper womanhood that the South had produced during the war. And the time had come, in their eyes, to put a halt to Northern tolerance of such monstrosities.

Perhaps nothing supports this theory more clearly than the vehemence with which those who opposed Mary Surratt in the spring and early summer of 1865 stated their case against her, in contrast with the actual evidence that was available for measuring the degree of her guilt. Significant, too, is the language they used to describe her, which unequivocally lifted Mary Surratt out of the sweet sphere of proper Victorian womanhood and dropped her into the menacing and mysterious realm of womanhood gone astray. As early as May 10, the *Philadelphia Inquirer* offered a description of Mary Surratt, as "large in form; very stout; [with] a keen grey eye; a resolute look; rather ugly . . . a perfect virago." The *Inquirer* augmented its description of Mary Surratt on May 11, adding that she was "the female fiend incarnate . . . the 'mater familias' of these criminals." Such descriptions persisted in the popular press right up until her death: on July 7, the date of her execution, the *New York Times* described Mary Surratt as, "a large woman of the Amazonian style . . . square built, her hands masculine, her face full, her eyes dark gray and lifeless, her hair not decidedly dark, and her complexion swarthy." A day later, the *Times* commented on her "cold eye, that would quail at no scene of torture"; her "close, short mouth, whence no word of sympathy would pass"; her "firm chin, indicative of fixedness of resolve"; and her "square, solid figure, whose proportions were never disfigured by remorse or marred by loss of sleep."[37] If the popular press in the North saw Mary Surratt in such a light, is it reasonable to assume that Stanton, Johnson, Holt, and the judges could possibly have seen her otherwise? Surely photographs of Mary Surratt from the period tend to contradict such harsh physical descriptions, in the same way that the shaky quality of the evidence against her contradicts the notion that she could possibly have been the central figure in the conspiracy. But it is nevertheless abundantly clear that the predominant image of Mary Surratt in the wake of Lincoln's assassination was as a woman who had betrayed not only the Union, but proper womanhood generally, and therefore deserved the harshest possible punishment.

Is this the same as saying that she became a symbol of all the other women of the Confederacy who throughout the war had engaged in treasonable behavior, similarly transgressing conventional notions of Victorian womanhood? I would argue that it is. Indeed, as early as May 4, even before the conspiracy trial had begun, one writer for the *Philadelphia Inquirer* suggested that Mary Surratt was cut from the same cloth as countless other female traitors against the United States. This writer compared Mary Surratt explicitly to the two most notorious female spies of the Confederacy, both of whom had been imprisoned for their crimes against the federal government but subsequently had been released. Mary Surratt, the reporter claimed, "is a large, masculine, self-possessed female, mistress of her house, and as lithe a rebel as Belle Boyd or Mrs. Greensborough [Greenhow]. She has not the flippantry and menace of the first, nor the social power of the second, but the Rebellion has no fitter agent."[38]

This *Inquirer* writer considered Mary Surratt essentially a co-conspirator with Boyd and Greenhow, even more so, perhaps, than with John Wilkes Booth. The author of another piece in the *Inquirer*, published on the day of her death, impressed upon readers the symbolism of her execution as a lesson to her Confederate sisters in crime. Nothing more than misplaced "sentiment," the author wrote, had protected "bad" women in the past. The female sex, he continued, "has too long been allowed to shield female offenders from punishment, thus to encourage the women of fiendish hearts to believe that there was no crime which they could not commit with impunity." As an example, he pointed directly to the war from which the nation was just emerging, and specifically to the female enemies — fierce she-devils and "wild inciters of rebellion" — of the United States. This writer ennumerated such women's offenses: spitting at Union officers, bedecking themselves with "jewelry" made from the bones of the Union dead, plotting against the Union and murdering its defenders. Such women, he insisted, had "been transformed by their passions into fiends, and in the long catalogue of the woes of the South the hands of female plotters and assassins have been busy." Moreover, he insisted, Mary Surratt was precisely such a woman, a "Jezebel" who had played not some relatively minor supporting role, but rather a central one as nothing less than the "mind," the "ruling spirit," the "counsellor and guide" of the conspiracy against Lincoln. To have spared Mary Surratt, the author went on, would have been a grave mistake for the nation, a concession to "mawkish sentimentality." Instead, he argued, not only did her punishment fit her crime, but her execution provided an example for others: "[L]et the remembrance be cherished hereafter," he concluded, "as a warning that women are answerable to the law as well as to men."[39]

One could argue, of course, that the foregoing was merely the opinion of one solitary observer of the events unfolding in the federal capital in the late spring and early summer of 1865. But was it? By no means. Indeed, none other than President Andrew Johnson and Chief Prosecutor Joseph Holt, at least, are on record as agreeing with this fundamental position. In response to an interviewer's question in 1884, almost two decades after the trial, Holt indicated that his own certainty about Mary Surratt's guilt and the justice of her execution had not faded. "I think," he told his interviewer, "that she was the master spirit among them all. She was a woman of unusual nerve, and also of unusual intelligence. . . . Booth himself was inferior to her in purpose." Moreover, Holt recalled, during the brief time that the issue of clemency was still under discussion, Johnson had made clear his view that "the time had about come when women who conspire to assassinate the president and rulers of their country should take the responsibility like men for their acts. He said that an example was needed." Some years later, General R. D. Mussey, who had been President Johnson's private secretary at the time of the trial, confirmed Holt's memory, describing a scene shortly before the execution in which Johnson, upon emerging from a conference room where he had been discussing the conspiracy trial and Mary Surratt's fate, commented that in his mind, "her sex did not make her any the less guilty," and indeed, that "there had not been women enough hanged in this war." The military commission's conviction of Mary Surratt provided Johnson with a perfect opportunity to lay the foundation for a new tradition.[40]

Notes

The opinions expressed and the conclusions drawn in this essay are my own. Nevertheless, I am indebted to Joan Cashin for her thorough and incisive comments on earlier drafts of this essay, and to James O. Hall for so generously giving of his time, insights, and unsurpassed knowledge of the Mary Surratt story. I am also grateful to Laurie Verge, Joan Chaconas, and the rest of the kind and helpful staff of the Surratt House and Museum in Clinton, Maryland, and to my Colby colleagues for their helpful responses to a presentation I gave based on this same work; to Colby's Social Sciences Division Grants Committee for approving a research grant (no. 01.2204) to help fund this project; and to Colby alumni Harriet S. and George C. Wiswell Jr., for providing me with a permanent research grant, from which I also drew to complete this essay.

1. *Philadelphia Inquirer*, July 8, 1865; *New York Times*, July 8, 1865; *Harper's Weekly*, July 22, 1865. Arnold, Mudd, and O'Laughlin each received sentences of life imprisonment, Spangler, a sentence of six years (Francis X. Busch, *Enemies of the State* [Indianapolis, 1954], 72). O'Laughlin died during a disease outbreak at the Florida prison where all four were incarcerated. In February 1869 outgoing president Andrew Johnson pardoned the other three without officially exonerating them (Thomas Bland Keys, "Were the Lincoln Conspirators Dealt Justice?" [*Lincoln Herald* 80 (1978): 40, 44].

2. *Philadelphia Inquirer*, July 7, 1865, July 8, 1865; *New York Times*, July 7, 1865; Busch, *Enemies of the State*, 74; Curtis Carroll Davis, "In Pursuit of Booth Once More: A New Claimant Heard From," *Maryland Historical Magazine* 79 (Fall 1984), 223; Otto Eisenschiml, *Why Was Lincoln Murdered?* (New York 1937), 179–80; Janice E. Schuetz, *The Logic of Women on Trial: Case Studies of Popular American Trials* (Carbondale, 1994), 36; Elizabeth Steger Trindal, *Mary Surratt: An American Tragedy* (Gretna, La., 1996), 223, 226.

3. James O. Hall, "The Story of Mrs. Mary Surratt: A Lecture Delivered before the Docents of the Surratt House," Mary Surratt files, Surratt House and Museum, Clinton, Maryland (hereafter SHM); Trindal, *Mary Surratt*, 13–17; Busch, *Enemies of the State*, 16.

4. Hall, "The Story of Mary Surratt," 5–6; Trindal, *Mary Surratt*, 19–20.

5. Hall, "The Story of Mary Surratt," 6–9; Busch, *Enemies of the State*, 16–18; Trindal, *Mary Surratt*, 35–65; Joseph George Jr., "'A True Childe of Sorrow': Two Letters of Mary E. Surratt," *Maryland Historical Magazine* 80 (Winter 1985): 403.

6. Hall, "The Story of Mary Surratt," 9–10; Busch, *Enemies of the State*, 17–18; Trindal, *Mary Surratt*, 62–80.

7. Hall, "The Story of Mary Surratt," 14, 16.

8. Busch, *Enemies of the State*, 19–20; Trindal, *Mary Surratt*, 91, 98–99; Schuetz, *The Logic of Women on Trial*, 37.

9. Benn Pitman, *The Assassination of President Lincoln and the Trial of the Conspirators* (New York, 1954), 113–14; Hall, "The Story of Mary Surratt," 16; Schuetz, *The Logic of Women on Trial*, 54; Trindal, *Mary Surratt*, 69, 116–17; Busch, *Enemies of the State*, 20–21.

10. Schuetz, *The Logic of Women on Trial*, 55; Busch, *Enemies of the State*, 24; Eisenschiml, *Why Was Lincoln Murdered?*, 273; Pitman, *The Assassination of President Lincoln*, 121–22, 127, 131, 132, 133, 138.

11. Pitman, *The Assassination of President Lincoln*, 113–20; Schuetz, *The Logic of Women on Trial*, 54; Trindal, *Mary Surratt*, 116–17; Busch, *Enemies of the State*, 20–21; Eisenschiml, *Why Was Lincoln Murdered?*, 274; Joseph George Jr., "Nature's First Law: Louis J. Weichmann and Mrs. Surratt," *Civil War History* 28 (1982): 101–27; Joseph George Jr., "'The Days Are Yet Dark': L. J. Weichmann's Life after the Lincoln Conspiracy Trial," *Records of the American Catholic Historical Society of Philadelphia* 95 (1984): 67–81; Thomas R. Turner, "Did Weichmann Turn State's Evidence to Save Himself? A

Critique of *A True History of the Assassination of Abraham Lincoln,*" *Lincoln Herald* 81 (1979): 265–67. For more on Weichmann's role in the trial and his life, see Louis J. Weichmann, *A True History of the Assassination of Abraham Lincoln and the Conspiracy of 1865* (New York, 1975).

12. Pitman, *The Assassination of President Lincoln*, 85–86. See also Lloyd's original affidavit, dated April 22, 1865, in Record Group 153, Records of the Office of the Judge Advocate General (Army), "Investigation and Trial Papers Relating to the Assassination of President Lincoln," M-599, reel 2, National Archives (hereafter NA).

13. Statement of Mrs. Mary E. Surratt, April 28, 1865, in the "Investigation and Trial Papers Relating to the Assassination of President Lincoln," M-599, reel 6, NA; Busch, *Enemies of the State*, 27–28, 64; Schuetz, *The Logic of Women on Trial*, 37; Trindal, *Mary Surratt*, 220; Eisenschiml, *Why Was Lincoln Murdered?*, 272. The official charges against the defendants can be found in *The War of the Rebellion: The Official Records of the Union and Confederate Armies* (Washington, D.C., 1881–1902), ser. 2, vol. 8, 696–98 (this series cited hereafter as *OR*.)

14. Alfred Isacsson, "The Case of Jacob Walter," *Lincoln Herald* 89 (1987): 24.

15. Trindal, *Mary Surratt*, 209; Pitman, *The Assassination of President Lincoln*, 124–38; *Lewiston (Maine) Daily Evening Journal*, May 16, 1865; *Harper's Weekly*, June 3, 1865.

16. Two works that deal specifically with Victorian ideals and the experience of white Southern women during the Civil War are George Rable's *Civil Wars: Women and the Crisis of Southern Nationalism* (Urbana, 1989), and Drew Gilpin Faust's *Mothers of Invention: Women of the Slaveholding South in the American Civil War* (Chapel Hill, 1996).

17. *New York Times*, July 13, 1865; Lafayette C. Baker, *History of the United States Secret Service* (Philadelphia, 1867), 563; Thomas Reed Turner, "Public Opinion: The Assassination of Abraham Lincoln, the Trial of the Conspirators and the Trial of John H. Surratt" (Ph. D. diss., Boston University, 1971), 235. See also John Brennan to Joseph George Jr., September 22, 1988, in the Mary Surratt files, SHM.

18. Turner, "Public Opinion," 235, 240; Ralph Borreson, *When Lincoln Died* (New York, 1965), 201.

19. Busch, *Enemies of the State*, 87–88; Trindal, *Mary Surratt*, 121; George, "Nature's First Law," 101–27; Eisenschiml, *Why Was Lincoln Murdered?*, 279, 290–92.

20. Weichmann, *A True History*, 4–5; George, "'The Days Are Yet Dark,'" 67–69; *Philadelphia Inquirer*, July 17, 1865. Among Weichmann's most notable defenders was the chief prosecutor and judge advocate general in the conspiracy trial, Joseph Holt, whose behavior during the trial has also been questioned; see Joseph George Jr., "Subornation of Perjury at the Lincoln Conspiracy Trial? Joseph Holt, Robert Purdy, and the Lon Letter," *Civil War History* 38 (1992): 232–41.

21. William Hanchett, *The Lincoln Murder Conspiracies* (Urbana, 1983), 90–124; *Philadelphia Inquirer*, May 5, 1865; Turner, "Public Opinion," 334. Joseph George, Jr., "The Trial of Mrs. Surratt: John P. Brophy's Rare Pamph-

let," *Lincoln Herald* 98 (1991): 17–22; Alfred Isaccson, "The Case of Jacob Walter," Lincoln Herald 89 (1987): 21–24; Mark A. Noll, "The Bible and Slavery," in *Religion and the American Civil War* ed. Randall M. Miller, Harry S. Stout, and Charles Reagan Wilson, (New York, 1998), 54; Randall M. Miller, "Catholic Religion, Irish Ethnicity, and the Civil War," in ibid., 261–96; David Brion Davis, "Some Themes of Counter-Subversion: An Analysis of Anti-Masonic, Anti-Catholic, and Anti-Mormon Literature," *Mississippi Valley Historical Review* 47 (September 1960): 205–24.

22. Pitman, *The Assassination of President Lincoln*, 124–43, passim; Lorie Ann Porter, "Not So Strange Bedfellows: Thomas Ewing II and the Defense of Samuel Mudd," *Lincoln Herald* 90 (1988): 91–101.

23. Schuetz, *The Logic of Women on Trial*, 44, 46; Busch, *Enemies of the State*, 14, 30, 37, 65.

24. Hall, "The Story of Mary Surratt," 22; Turner, "Public Opinion," 191; Pitman, *The Assassination of President Lincoln*, 251–67; *New York Times*, May 11, 1865, and May 13, 1865; Thomas Reed Turner, "What Type of Trial? A Civil versus a Military Trial for the Lincoln Assassination Conspirators," *Papers of the Abraham Lincoln Association* 4 (1982): 29–52.

25. *New York Times*, April 23, 1865.

26. *New York Times*, April 20, 1865.

27. *New York Times*, April 20, 1865; Turner, "Public Opinion," 10, 12, 27; Pitman, *The Assassination of President Lincoln*, 24–41; William A. Tidwell, *Come Retribution: The Confederate Secret Service and the Assassination of Lincoln* (New York, 1988).

28. David M. DeWitt, *The Judicial Murder of Mary E. Surratt* (Baltimore, 1895; reprint, St. Clair Shores, Mich., 1970), 257; Schuetz, *The Logic of Women on Trial*, 36. On the case of John Surratt Jr., see, among others, *The Trial of John H. Surratt in the Criminal Court for the District of Columbia* (Washington, D. C., 1867); and Weichmann, *A True History*.

29. Eisenschiml, *Why Was Lincoln Murdered?*, 295; Mike Kauffman, "Fort Leslie McNair and the Lincoln Conspirators," *Lincoln Herald* 80 (1978): 181; Hanchett, *The Lincoln Murder Conspiracies*, 115.

30. See, among other things, Joseph Holt, "Vindication of Hon. Joseph Holt" (Washington, D. C., 1873).

31. Turner, "Public Opinion," 249, 255; typescript of an undated clipping from the *Boston Traveler*, from a bound scrapbook belonging to G. A. Townsend in the Library of Congress, in the Mary Surratt files, SHM. See also Trindal, *Mary Surratt*, 201–3; Busch, *Enemies of the State*, 72.

32. *OR*, ser. 3, vol. 2, 157–59.

33. See Elizabeth D. Leonard, *All the Daring of the Soldier: Women of the Civil War Armies* (New York, 1999), 280. The same was true, not surprisingly, for the Confederate government's response to Northern women found guilty of betraying the Southern cause.

34. Schuetz, *The Logic of Women on Trial*, 58–59; Pitman, *The Assassination of President Lincoln*, 298.

35. Schuetz, *The Logic of Women on Trial*, 38; Reid Mitchell, *The Vacant Chair* (New York, 1993), 89–113.

36. According to DeWitt, Mary Surratt's execution represented "the foulest blot on the history of the United States of America" (DeWitt, *The Judicial Murder of Mary E. Surratt*, 106, 257). Thomas Reed Turner, "Public Opinion on the Assassination of Abraham Lincoln," *Lincoln Herald* 2 (1976): 69.

37. *Philadelphia Inquirer*, May 10, 1865, May 11, 1865; *New York Times*, July 7, 1865, July 8, 1865.

38. *Philadelphia Inquirer*, May 4, 1865. See Leonard, *All the Daring of the Soldier*, chap. 1, for the stories of Greenhow and Boyd.

39. *Philadelphia Inquirer*, July 8, 1865.

40. *Philadelphia Inquirer*, July 8, 1865; *Joseph* (Oreg. *Wallowa Chieftain*, May 15, 1884; Horatio King, "Judge Holt and the Lincoln Conspirators," *Century Magazine* 39 (April 1890): 956.

PART THREE ❧ *The Border Regions*

Chapter 13

On the Border: White Children and the Politics of War in Maryland

PETER W. BARDAGLIO

✤ HISTORIANS in recent years have explored the ideological aware
ness of Civil War soldiers, challenging the older view that they cared
little about political and constitutional questions. Many of the combatants, according to this new scholarship, were very conscious of the issues at stake and interested in them. Whether fighting to preserve the
Union created by the founders of the republic or fighting for freedom
from what they considered to be a tyrannical and intrusive central government, these soldiers knew what they were struggling for.[1]

What about the children of the Civil War? Historians have just begun
to examine the extent to which boys and girls in the North and South
knew what this conflict was all about and whether they felt they had a
stake in the outcome. These new studies explore how children participated in the struggle, not just as victims or spectators but as political
actors who joined in the mobilization of the home fronts and who fought
in the military. This pathbreaking work, however, has paid little attention to the distinctive experience of youngsters in the border states.[2]

The following essay will investigate how the fractious character of
public life in wartime Maryland shaped the experiences of boys and
girls who lived in divided families and communities. In particular, it will
examine how white children, mostly from literate middle- and upper-
class families, responded to the question of loyalty to the Union.

As a border state, Maryland experienced unique pressures during the
Civil War era. Most Northern states took up the cause of Unionism
with enthusiasm. But ambiguity characterized the border states, and
their citizens debated and ultimately fought out issues of loyalty. Slave
states like Maryland, Missouri, and Kentucky felt the secession crisis
and the outbreak of war with particular force. Sharing a stake in the
peculiar institution with seceding states in the South, but possessing industrial and commercial interests that linked them to the North, the
border states dreaded the prospect of a civil war being fought on their
soil. What was the best course to take?[3]

The perilous choices of loyalty that confronted white Marylanders focused attention on the constitutional and political issues at the heart of the secession crisis and the war that followed. Children experienced the fluidity and intensity of the fierce debates as well as adults, and we need to better understand how these youngsters connected to and participated in these disputes.[4] Families, especially parents, played an important role in shaping the political attitudes and behavior of these boys and girls, but this does not mean that children were politicized against their wills. On the contrary, many youngsters in Maryland demonstrated a striking eagerness to enter the political fray and act on their convictions in ways that ranged from the trivial to the profound. Their lived experience contradicted the sentimental ideal of childhood as protected and dependent, an ideal that dominated middle-class culture in the United States by the mid-nineteenth century.[5]

Freud was undoubtedly right to stress the decisive impact of childhood on an individual's sexual development, but these early years also have a critical influence on one's political outlook and behavior. Conflict has an especially strong impact on the political socialization of children. Because youngsters tend to view issues in dualistic terms, when they live in what one scholar calls "contested regimes," they tend to see their own group as "all good" and the opposition as "all bad." Growing up in a world of conflict leads both boys and girls to believe that conflict is normal and acceptable, and thus creates the conditions for its reproduction.[6] How did white children who lived in a border state split by political polarization respond to the debates over secession and war? To what extent did the political struggles of these years perpetuate themselves as these youngsters came of age and took on positions of leadership?

The tumultuous political events of the mid-nineteenth century exposed and exacerbated fault lines in Maryland that lay just below the surface. Secession and the formation of the Confederacy compelled this mid-Atlantic society as well as Kentucky and Missouri to recognize that there was no more room for compromise on the pressing questions of the day, such as slavery, that they had worked so hard to finesse. While many politicians tried to cling to a fast disappearing Unionist center, secessionist slaveholders, slaves, and other residents of the border states took up increasingly polarized positions, obliterating any middle ground. In Maryland mob violence led federal troops to occupy Baltimore and Annapolis and to take control of the railroads. Political debate after 1861 became increasingly shrill as Unionists accused Democrats of treason and Democrats attacked Unionists for trampling on their constitutional liberties. By May 1862, Marylanders had joined regiments in the opposing armies and had faced each other in combat.[7]

Caught in a tightening vise between North and South when the war broke out, white elites reacted with resentment and anger, sensing that they had lost control of their destiny. As Allen Bowie Davis of Montgomery County wrote his fifteen-year-old son at school on April 16, 1861, "Our beloved Country is now involved in Civil War — the most horrible of all national contests, and God only knows where it will end." Portraying Marylanders as "innocent victims of the wicked and insane slavery agitation between the North and the South," Davis lamented what he perceived to be the state's dilemma: "We have not provoked the contest and cannot rightfully be made parties to it — but I fear we cannot escape its consequences." Urging his son to avoid embroilment in the conflict, Davis pleaded with him not "to become too much excited upon the subject so as to lett [*sic*] it interfere with your studies and the advantages you *now* have."[8] Of course, by issuing such a caution Davis recognized the potential that his son might become — in fact, probably would become — caught up in the political controversies erupting throughout the state.

That Davis had good reason to worry about the possibility of his son becoming politically entangled in the debate over Maryland's relationship to the Union became clear three days later when the Sixth Massachusetts Volunteer Regiment sought to pass through Baltimore on its way to defend Washington. A crowd attacked the soldiers, who opened fire, and in the riot that followed four soldiers and at least a dozen civilians died in the first bloodshed of the Civil War. Mob violence was nothing new in Baltimore; throughout the 1850s young gang members who called themselves Plug Uglies, Rip Raps, and Butt Enders indulged in hard drinking and attacks on political rivals at polling places. Although such conflict between the Know-Nothings and German and Irish immigrants had become a staple of the urban scene, never before had the violence involved federal troops. Besides the sixteen deaths that April, many more were wounded before the confrontation ended.[9] Among the rioters, at least initially, was another fifteen-year-old boy, Ernest Wardwell.

Wardwell recalled years later how the war transformed his life. On the streets the morning of April 19 newsboys hawked their papers, shouting " 'all about the Yankee invaders' who were coming to pillage our city." According to Wardwell, as he walked to school, "Everybody seemed full of patriotic fire, and warlike sentiment ran high. Knots of men, some of them carrying guns and pistols, hurried through the streets, and gave rent to loud expressions of vengeance against the 'Northern Scum.' " Wardwell and his schoolmates worked themselves into such a fevered state of excitement in the classrooms that the principal dismissed the students and ordered them to proceed home immediately.

Despite this command, Wardwell and his friend Henry Cook took matters into their own hands; leaving the school, they raced off to investigate the crowd gathering at the President Street depot. Arriving on the scene, Wardwell admitted that "at first I was paralyzed with fear, but only momentarily as I caught the frenzy and became as noisy as the others." Although his father was from Massachusetts, Wardwell had grown up in Maryland, spending much of his childhood in the mountains of the western part of the state before being sent to school in Baltimore. He and Cook became part of a mob that chased the soldiers through the city "like a vociferous army of howling wolves." Impressed by the restrained response of the Sixth Massachusetts in the face of the violent crowd, however, and perhaps feeling the influence of his father's political heritage, Wardwell underwent a change of heart. Grabbing a fallen soldier's rifle, he fell in with the ranks of the Union army making their way to Camden Station, where he joined the troops boarding a train for Washington. "I could in reality no longer claim to be a schoolboy," Wardwell observed, "for I was armed with a gun and had been in a battle in which I had espoused both sides, and was now travelling at railroad speed to defend the National Capitol."[10]

Each of the two armies had recruitment policies that prohibited boys from joining and fighting. At the start of the war, for example, the Union stipulated that a recruit had to be at least eighteen years old. But a tall and older looking fifteen-year-old like Wardwell could easily pass in the rush to form a unit, bluffing his way past the recruiting sergeant.[11] Rash as his behavior may have seemed, Wardwell was not simply fulfilling a childhood dream to enter the military. Although obviously attracted by the pomp and circumstance of martial rituals, his experience in the Baltimore riot convinced him of the necessity of fighting on the Union side. Determined to overcome any objections to his enlistment on account of his age, Wardwell insisted, "If I was not old enough to march in the ranks I would begin as a 'drummer boy' — but soldier of some kind I would be, and that too for the 'star spangled flag' and the preservation of the Union." Wardwell completed his three-month enlistment with the Sixth Massachusetts and then signed on with the Twenty-Sixth Massachusetts, reaching the rank of captain by the end of the war in 1865.[12]

Although other boys besides Wardwell signed up with the Northern army, pro-Confederate sentiment remained widespread among Baltimore youth during the early years of the war. As the spring of 1861 unfolded into summer, the federal government tightened its control over Maryland in general and Baltimore in particular. Union soldiers set up camp in Patterson Park and along the railroads into the city. Other military preparations in the city included strengthening the defenses at

Fort McHenry as well as digging fortifications and installing cannon on Federal Hill. The Federals also seized weapons and ammunition destined for the Confederacy, prohibited meetings of men carrying arms without proper permission, and banned the display of secessionist flags and banners.[13]

The activities of pro-Confederate youngsters, who stepped up their harassment of Union soldiers and other demonstrations of their political loyalties, attracted the attention of authorities in Baltimore. On June 26, the day before General Nathaniel P. Banks declared martial law in the city, Dr. Samuel Harrison noted in his diary that secessionist parents had been encouraging their children to taunt the Northern troops; he "strongly suspect [ed]" that this constant show of disrespect, among other signs of continuing support for the Confederacy, would lead to a government crackdown.[14]

Of course, Harrison was right. The imposition of martial law in Baltimore, however, did not stop parents and their children — both girls and boys — from taking to the streets and voicing their pro-Confederate sympathies. Traveling through Baltimore at the beginning of July, William H. Russell, a British journalist, observed that displays of dissent could be viewed throughout the city despite the vigorous show of arms by the Union forces. "At the corners of the streets strong guards of soldiers were posted," Russell wrote, "and patrols moved up and down the thoroughfares." The police appointed by the federal authorities, in particular, waged "a small war" against women and children who exhibited "much ingenuity in expressing their animosity to the Stars and Stripes." According to Russell, for example, not only the girls but also their dolls were dressed in the Confederate colors, and women wore ribbons and bows to match.[15]

Under the circumstances, it is not surprising that the Fourth of July celebrations in Baltimore that year were muted. As the *Baltimore Republican* put it, "Instead of the happy smiling faces, we have been accustomed to meet at every step, heretofore upon this memorable day, gloom and sadness was depicted upon almost every countenance." Although the civilians left the city streets nearly deserted, the newspaper informed its readers that a contingent of about seventy or eighty boys "clad in red shirts and caps," bearing a crepe-paper Confederate flag, paraded into a Union encampment at Beecham's Hill. According to the *Republican*, "The little fellows marched around and about the camp with impunity, giving free expression to their preference for 'Jeff.' "[16] The newspaper account may well have reflected a more general ambivalence on the part of adults in Baltimore to such actions by children. The condescension implicit in the term "little fellows" seemed to suggest that their political demonstration should not be taken seriously. The editors, however, obviously took the protest seriously enough to report on it. Why not ignore the matter entirely if these children could have no political impact whatsoever?

Like the Confederate soldiers they sought to emulate, the Baltimore youths who marched on Beecham's Hill expressed their conviction that the war involved a struggle between liberty and tyranny. Harrison, for one, dismissed the political actions of children and women alike, arguing that they were "not considered responsible" for their behavior.[17] By the end of the summer, however, the political agitation of these two groups had become such a source of irritation to authorities in Baltimore that General John A. Dix, Banks's replacement, not only prohibited the display of the Confederate flag, but also banned women and children from wearing red and white ribbons or flowers, symbols of the Confederacy.[18] On September 4, Dix reported to General George B. McClellan that his campaign against public expressions of support for the Confederacy had been successful. "No secession flag has to the knowledge of police been exhibited in Baltimore for many weeks, except a small paper flag displayed by a child from an upper window," he wrote McClellan, assuring him that even in this case the offensive object was immediately confiscated. Outraged by these latest actions, Harrison declared that "no sensible man can defend this petty tyranny."[19]

On the Unionist side, parents, teachers, and other adults actively tried to politicize children, enlisting them in the effort to win the minds and hearts of other Marylanders. A number of boys and girls, for example, participated in flag presentations to federal troops. These rituals occurred frequently in 1861 as Unionist women organized patriotic activities in the city that included children.[20] On September 28, thirty-four "young misses," all dressed in white and decked out in red, white, and blue sashes, participated in such a ceremony, representing the number of states in the Union before the Civil War. Also present were thirty-four boys outfitted in Zouave costumes.[21] The nationalist symbolism adopted by these young Marylanders could hardly have been more blatant.

Children also took part in one of Baltimore's most dramatic displays of Unionist loyalty: the 1864 Maryland State Fair for U.S. Soldier Relief. Organized by women primarily from the Baltimore area, the fair sought to raise funds for the U.S. Sanitary and the U.S. Christian Commissions, the two most prominent national relief organizations for the Northern armed forces. Other cities such as Chicago, Boston, New York, and Philadelphia successfully mounted similar events. These cities, however, did not have to produce a fair in the midst of a population divided into Unionist and Confederate factions.

The memory of the 1861 riot was still raw, and the female organizers of the Baltimore Sanitary Fair, as it was commonly known, were intent on using the occasion not only to solicit donations but also to bolster the city's image by giving Unionists in the state an opportunity to express their patriotism. On the eve of the third anniversary of the April 19 violence, and in the middle of an election year, President Lincoln came to Baltimore to speak at the fair's opening. His presence had particular symbolic significance for Maryland Unionists, sending as it did a strong message about his confidence in the city's national loyalty.[22]

Among the many exhibits at the Maryland Institute, site of the fair, was the Children's Table. This display, which involved the sale of children's clothing as well as dolls and toys, raised over $700. According to the fair's privately printed souvenir newspaper, *The New Era*, residents of Plymouth, Massachusetts, provided many of the toys for the Children's Table, a much appreciated gesture of reconciliation in light of the attack on the Sixth Massachusetts during the 1861 riot. Youngsters from the Baltimore area helped out at the exhibit, gaining recognition from the fair's newspaper for their work. "The children have been untiring in their efforts," declared *The New Era*, adding that "the success of the table has been greatly owing to them."[23]

Besides assisting at the Children's Table, boys and girls exhibited drawings in the hall outside the fee-for-admission fine arts gallery on the third floor of the Maryland Institute. On April 29, seven hundred children attended the fair, accompanied by twelve of their teachers. As an expression of their patriotism, about sixty of the pupils came dressed in West Point uniforms. The Unionist demonstration made a vivid impression on those who witnessed it. "It was a glorious sight to see these little ones lending a helping hand to the Union cause," commented *The New Era*. If Lincoln had been present for this display, he surely would have thought of his own sons Tad and Willie, who paraded around the White House trying to issue orders to the guards.[24]

Working alongside their mothers, grandmothers, aunts, and older sisters, children who participated in the Baltimore Sanitary Fair must have derived a genuine sense of satisfaction from their contributions to the fundraising event. Attendance at the fair was undoubtedly a welcome change of pace for youngsters in Civil War Baltimore. The anxiety about fathers and brothers who had gone off to fight, the daily sight of ambulances packed with wounded soldiers making their way through the streets, the stress of living in an inflationary wartime economy: these were troubles that could be temporarily forgotten amidst the bustle and entertainment of the fair.[25] The event, in short, offered Baltimore children a way to enjoy themselves and contribute to the Unionist effort at the same time.

As the example of the Sanitary Fair demonstrates, women as well as men played a significant role in the politicization of children. Although prohibited from voting or holding office, women participated in the politics of the Civil War, attending rallies, circulating petitions, joining voluntary associations, writing letters, and engaging in other activities to express their views.[26] Their actions, whether they were parents, teachers, or neighbors, had a deep impact on the growing political consciousness of the children around them. Lizette Woodworth Reese, whose family moved to Baltimore towards the end of the war, recalled years later the stories that two of her teachers told her when she was a high school student in the city. One of them, an instructor in mathematics, had refused to take a required loyalty oath during the war and had been barred from teaching in the city schools. Military authorities had arrested another teacher, according to Reese, "for using high-spirited language — officially treasonable — to a Union soldier whom she considered impertinent." "With what awe I looked upon these women!" Reese exclaimed, seeing in them models of strong-minded individuals who insisted on holding their own opinions and speaking their minds.[27]

The correspondence between Madge Preston and her thirteen-year-old daughter May reveals another way in which women shaped the political outlook of children. The Prestons, a well-off Baltimore family, divided their time between a townhouse in the city and a farm southeast of Towsontown. When Madge and her husband William decided in 1862 to send May to St. Joseph's Academy in Emmitsburg, the mother and daughter began a correspondence that continued for the next five years. Besides news from home, Madge's letters included discussions of the latest political controversies and the progress of the war. The Prestons supported the Confederate cause, and Madge's account of events plainly reflected this viewpoint. Angered by the federal crackdown on political dissent in Maryland, she attacked "the tyranny of the present government." When a squad of Union cavalry came through the Prestons' Baltimore County property looking for draftees who refused to report for duty, Madge wrote May a detailed account of her efforts to provide the soldiers with as little helpful information as possible. "Is it not shameful that the quiet of one's home should be thus disturbed," she asked, "and men in the peaceful pursuit of their daily avocations ruthlessly carried off to fight the battles of a cause in which they have no sympathy and indeed are altogether opposed to?" Madge put a Confederate flag in one of the packages she sent off to school, a symbol of the shared political sentiments that bound mother and daughter together during this uneasy time. In contrast to the outspoken tone of her letters, however, Madge warned May to "be cautious in the use" she made of the flag and advised her not to "let it be the cause of unpleasantness between you and any of your young companions, or of disobedience and punishment between you and your teachers."[28]

By and large, the Civil War did not dramatically alter the Prestons' daily routine. Certainly, they had to endure the squeeze of wartime inflation and the scarcity of goods, but these difficulties constituted the bulk of the hardships they faced. Other Maryland families, less fortunate, found themselves directly in the path of combat. For the children caught between opposing military forces, the sense of uncertainty and vulnerability created enormous anxiety. Lizette Reese, whose teachers made such an impression on her when she moved to Baltimore, lived out on York Road north of the city for most of the war. She retained stark memories of the times when she and her younger sisters were so frightened that they did not want to go to bed at night. "Down the pike-road was quartered a company of blue-coated soldiers, within sound of a call from our front gate," she remembered. Further up the highway were the Confederate raiders who regularly dashed down to harass the Union troops and then melted away into the surrounding countryside. As Reese put it, "Between the blue forces and the gray we were ground between two millstones of terror."[29]

The descent of troops on a town or village could inflict fear and hardship enough, but children in a border state like Maryland had to deal with the added burden of mixed allegiances among their neighbors and relatives. The stress and confusion that girls and boys experienced as they tried to sort out their place in this treacherous political landscape could be psychologically and emotionally draining. One false step and disaster could result. Reese's experiences of growing up in a politically divided community illustrated the predicaments that faced many Maryland children during these years. "Neighbor looked askance at neighbor," she recounted. "Politics, which had been fearlessly public, became an entirely private affair, to be discussed behind drawn curtains and well-locked doors." The young girl's parents hid a portrait of General Beauregard in a walnut wardrobe, and her cousin made small, red and white flags to be pinned on women's underwear. The caution was well advised, as her family learned the hard way. Reese's grandfather, a fervent supporter of states' rights and secession, became the target of an arrest warrant for his outspoken views. The Union soldiers who set out to find him, however, ended up at the wrong house, that of a son-in-law who was, in Reese's words, "an obstinate abolitionist." When he assured the troops that the suspected father-in-law had a son in the Union army, which was true, they left without a prisoner.[30]

Like their urban counterparts, youngsters in the Maryland countryside found effective ways to declare their political sympathies. When General Stonewall Jackson led his men through the western part of the state in September 1862, they met a very mixed response from the local populace, who displayed both Confederate and Union colors. As the

Southern troops passed through Middletown, "two very pretty girls" rushed up to Jackson's men wearing red, white, and blue ribbons in their hair and carrying Union flags. According to one of Jackson's staff officers, Henry Kyd Douglas, the girls laughed and "waved their colors defiantly in the face of the general. He bowed and lifted his cap and with a quiet smile said to his staff, 'We evidently have no friends in this town.'"[31] When Confederate cavalry rode into Hagerstown just before the Battle of Gettysburg in July 1863, they encountered a similar reaction from one of the children. "A little boy stood at the corner waving a U.S. Flag while the confederates were there," noted Joseph H. Coit, an Episcopal clergyman.[32] Such bold and even dangerous gestures revealed the extent to which the war in Maryland politicized even its youngest residents by 1863.

Thirteen-year-old Margaret Mehring also experienced a surge of Unionism when the Confederate army marched through Maryland. Mehring, who attended a boarding school at a church in New Windsor, kept a diary during the days leading up to and including the battle at Gettysburg, which erupted on July 1, just across the Pennsylvania border. Although the diary may have been a school assignment, it allowed Mehring to exercise at least some control over her situation by providing her with a way to express her opinions about the momentous military and political events taking place.

The girl's writings reveal the apprehension she felt as news of the approaching Confederate troops reached the small town in north-central Maryland. On June 15, hearing that the Southern forces were near Frederick, Mehring sounded the first note of anxiety. "I do not want to be away from *home* when the rebels are in Maryland," she wrote. Noticeably relieved four days later when it became apparent that the invading soldiers were confining themselves to stealing horses as they made their way through the state, Mehring recovered her caustic sense of humor, a resource that she frequently drew upon to keep her wits about her. She observed that horse theft was "a piece of art which they [the Confederates] appear to be very near perfect in and one that I think is a pretty occupation for the much bosted Souther Chivelry to be engaged in but then I suppose that they entertain the very good *idea that exercise is necessary to health.*"[33]

The presence of the Confederate army in Maryland and Pennsylvania dispelled whatever doubts Mehring might have had about the Unionist cause. Reacting to a rumor on June 23 that fifty thousand "Rebels" had arrived at Gettysburg, she announced, "I hope they will meet a warm reception from Pensylvania in the shape of balls for *taking the trouble and liberty of calling on them without an invitation.*" In contrast, when the Union cavalry rode into New Windsor a week later, Mehring welcomed the troops with open arms. "They were dressed very nicely and rode handsome horses," she recalled. "It was a beautiful sight, for the moon shone so brilliantly that one could almost imagine it was day and the horseman riding six and eight abrest with their sords clatering while cheer after cheer rent the air." Clearly relieved at the arrival of Union soldiers, the teenaged girl insisted that the feeling was mutual: "They all said that they never felt happier than when they set foot on Maryland soil."

By the time the Battle of Gettysburg actually began, Mehring had grown used to the constant reports that "the rebels are coming." In her words, such rumors had "almost ceasded to cause an extr pulsation of the heart." Almost casually, she remarked, "We heard the cannon booming very distinctly last night and it is supposed that there is a battle going on between Littlestown and Gettysburg." There was one aspect of war, however, that Mehring could not get accustomed to: the killing. "There was another soldier buried in the Presbyterian graveyard beside of the first one," she wrote on July 6, shortly after the Gettysburg conflagration had ended and Lee's army had been forced to retreat back across the Potomac River. "It seemed hard to see him buried among strangers an by strange hands no friend to follow him to the grave or weep over his untimely end." Expressing the feelings of many Marylanders in the summer of 1863, both adults and children, Mehring cried out, in the words of a popular song, "*Oh when will this cruel war be over.*" Many children in the nineteenth century witnessed the deaths of family members in the home, but the mass slaughter of these years had a deep emotional impact on Mehring and other youngsters.[34]

The Civil War in Maryland disrupted not only Mehring's school but also institutions of learning throughout the state. Scrambling to adjust to the rapidly shifting conditions, those schools that could not meet the challenge were forced to close their doors. Although economic and military factors proved most critical, political dynamics also affected their operation as they became battlegrounds for clashing opinions among students, teachers, administrators, and parents. Political differences between young Unionists and secessionists at St. Anthony's Orphanage in Baltimore sparked constant quarrels and scuffles at recess. The sisters at St. Joseph's Academy, the Catholic girls' school that May Preston attended, banned the singing of political songs in an attempt to preserve order among the students.[35]

Perhaps the most remarkable example of how the politics of war disrupted Maryland schools can be found at the College of St. James, an Episcopal preparatory school for teenaged boys near Hagerstown. A series of stunning incidents took place there during the war that ultimately split the community beyond repair. During the public declamation exercises in January 1861, several of the students gave speeches in support of the Union, leading Rev. John B. Kerfoot, the head of the school, to issue a ban on discussions of "any political topics" in their essays and orations. The highly charged climate at St. James, which attracted many students from Southern states, also convinced the rector to postpone a series of fund-raising trips. Kerfoot, who opposed secession, remarked to his close friend William G. Harrison that he decided to remain on campus because "[a]ny day's news might stir the young blood bitterly."[36]

Despite attempts to clamp down on political expression at St. James, the headstrong boys continued to make their views known, engaging in what clearly constituted acts of civil disobedience. In April 1862, Kerfoot read a series of prayers at Sunday service composed by Bishop William R. Whittingham in accordance with President Lincoln's proclamation for a day of thanksgiving. About twenty students "rose and left the chapel in a body" before the rector had finished. Distressed by the protest, Kerfoot asked the bishop not to require such prayers in the future. When Lincoln declared a National Fast Day the following April, the rector sought to avoid another incident at St. James. He announced that those boys "who had 'conscientious' scruples about attending chapel on that day, might remain away and spend their time, if they so preferred, in the study of Latin, Greek and mathematics."[37] Kerfoot's gesture reflected his recognition that the students had become deeply immersed in Civil War politics and that their feelings had to be respected.

The invasion of Confederate troops in the days leading up to the Battle of Gettysburg in July 1863 marked a turning point in the life of St. James. During the first invasion of Maryland in September 1862, students had not arrived on campus yet. As bloody as it was, the Battle of Antietam had little impact on the school beyond postponing the opening from September 24 to November 12.[38] In 1863, however, the school was in session and the effect of Confederate soldiers passing through the grounds of St. James was electrifying. A cavalry unit dashed across the campus just after tea on June 15 and, according to one of the teachers, "[t]he boys rushed to meet them—cheering and waving their hats." Until now, the students had confined the expression of their political beliefs to words and acts of protest. The arrival of Southern troops, however, inspired a more radical response among those who supported secession; next morning eight of the boys went off to join the Confederates. "We felt then," Kerfoot said, "that the crisis was on us." Determined to put a stop to the efforts at enlistment, in his words, the rector "plainly, strongly, reproved" in the chapel that same morning those who had cheered the appearance of the cavalry and those who had left the school to join them. Most of the boys who ran off returned to the school within a few days, but the damage had been done: the military conflict was no longer a distant, abstract event. The war created a rupture in the community that could never be patched up, despite Kerfoot's contention in a letter to Bishop Whittingham that "[w]ork went on *pretty* well; *no disorder*." During General Jubal Early's raid in the following summer, the Confederates arrested Kerfoot and Joseph Coit, one of the instructors at St. James, in retaliation for the capture of Rev. Hunter Boyd of Winchester, Virginia, by Union troops. Kerfoot's arrest and the increasing financial difficulties of the school led to its closing in September 1864.[39]

The struggle between the North and South, then, marked a crucial baptism by fire for Maryland children. The hothouse atmosphere of wartime politics fueled antagonisms in the state that had a profound influence on the white boys and girls within its borders, and their political activities reflected and reinforced the deep rifts that developed. Secessionist youths marched in gangs around Baltimore, displaying their pro-Confederate sympathies and hurling insults at Union troops. Other children participated in Unionist causes such as soldier relief and flag presentations, throwing their support behind a very different set of political beliefs. Some teenagers, like Frank Wardwell and the boys at St. James, took up arms and joined the military struggle. Of those youngsters who lived through the war, few remained unaffected by the experience.

What lessons did children who grew up in Maryland during the 1860s learn as a result of their participation in the politics of war? To what extent did the political polarization of these years extend past the war's end? The story of Henry White suggests one possibility. White was three years old when his father died in 1853. The boy spent much of his childhood at Hampton, a plantation estate outside of Baltimore where his mother's family, the Ridgelys, had lived since the 1780s. According to White, intense arguments constantly erupted at Hampton about secession and the war. As he observed, "[H]ardly a day passed that I did not hear one or more such discussions, during which the parties thereto frequently lost their tempers, and ended, some of them, by not speaking to each other." Friends of his grandparents would come to Hampton and "describe the Southern Army as though they were all a band of saints; mostly on their knees at prayer when they were not fighting." Others would tell White a very different story: "[T]he Northern Army were the patriots, and the Southerners were drunkards, and young aristocrats, who for want of something better to do, took to fighting."[40]

Feelings ran high not just among neighbors but among White's family. His grandmother Ridgely believed so fervently in the Confederacy that she would not let his mother attend the wedding of old friends because of their Northern sympathies. The stress of the war, White contended, had led to a stroke that took his grandmother's life in 1867. The political conflicts of these years left White, who went on to a distinguished career as a diplomat under five American presidents, with "painful recollections" and "a horror of war in general throughout my life." "It brings out all that is worst in human nature, causes friends of a lifetime to become enemies, to be suspicious of each other's patriotism," he contended. "I have never been able to see its advantages from any point of view." White's experience of living on the border during the Civil War, in short, underscored for him the importance of compromise, of finding a middle way. Indeed, his commitment to this approach brought him to the Paris Conference at the end of World War I, where he participated in one of the greatest negotiations of modern times.[41]

We have no way of knowing for certain how many Marylanders in White's generation shared his faith in what a leading historian of the state calls the "middle temperament."[42] If the findings of contemporary political sociologists can serve as a guide, a significant number of youngsters in the border state probably adopted a dualistic view of the world during the Civil War, one that sharply divided the political terrain between supporters and enemies and that demonstrated little tolerance for the legitimacy of opposing opinions. For these children, borders meant a line drawn in the sand rather than a place to meet and engage in a productive exchange of views. The extent to which this vision of politics persisted after the war, however, is open to question.

Certainly, politics remained contentious as Republican Unionists and Democrats debated issues such as Reconstruction policies, registration procedures and requirements for voting, black civil and political rights, and public education. African Americans in Baltimore and in southern Maryland voted in large numbers for the party of Lincoln. Although in the northern and western counties white Republicans continued to support the cause of civil rights for blacks, racial fears and memories of the war in other parts of the state compelled the majority of white Maryland voters to back the Democratic party. Especially during close political contests Democrats resorted to race-baiting to secure victory. Fraud and violence marked the election of 1875 in Baltimore, where observers reported widespread ballot stuffing, shooting incidents, and near riots. Police arrested 209 people that day, divided about equally between whites and blacks.[43]

Besides political and racial conflict, industrial strife marked the postwar years. The Great Railway Strike of 1877, which began at Camden Junction outside Baltimore and quickly spread along the rail lines of the Baltimore and Ohio, resulted in a week of violence in the city until federal troops marched in to reestablish order. The bloody confrontation of labor and management during this insurrection must have reminded many citizens of the divisions that had split them into two camps during the Civil War. Democratic Governor John Lee Carroll, who invited the federal troops in to quell the labor protests, insisted that the workers' actions threatened "subversion of all government" and, if left unchecked, would have led to "national insurrection."[44]

Following the turmoil of the Reconstruction era that culminated with the 1877 strike, white Marylanders moved to heal old wounds in the body politic. In the wake of the chaos that they had witnessed growing up, the predominant impulse of those who took over political leadership after Reconstruction was to establish stability and order in the state, not to perpetuate conflict. This new harmony came at a high cost, leading to both a segregated society and "a segregated historical memory." By the 1880s, however, national reconciliation among whites was well under way and "a culture of healing and unity" had emerged.[45] The Maryland legislature in 1888 contributed to the effort at reconciliation with two measures recognizing the sacrifices of soldiers on both sides of the Civil War: it handed over a former federal arsenal to a group that planned to transform the building and grounds into a home for elderly Confederate veterans, and it approved funding for Union monuments at Gettysburg. "The suspicions, the bitterness, the animosities necessarily engendered by a protracted Civil War," proclaimed Colonel James C. Mullikin at one of the dedication ceremonies that October, "have departed our state never to return."[46]

The product of wishful thinking more than careful observation, Mullikin's remarks about the end of sectional bitterness reflected the desire of Maryland whites to put the conflicts of the past behind them. For the generation that had come of age during the war itself, though, doing so was no easy matter. Henry White, in his urgent need to pursue a career dedicated to negotiation and diplomacy, embodied the extent to which the violence and political hostilities of these years in Maryland had left an indelible mark on his generation. However different the paths they followed after the Confederate surrender at Appomattox, White and the other children of the Civil War always measured their lives by the standard of what they experienced during this searing event.

Notes

I want to express my appreciation to Robert Schoeberlein of the Maryland Historical Society, who proved a patient and accomplished guide to the society's library and archives as well as to the complexities of Maryland's experience in the Civil War. I would also like to thank Jean Baker for her careful critique of an early version of this paper and Jane Turner Censer for her astute comments at the annual meeting of the Organization of American Historians in Chicago in March 1996, where I first presented my findings. A fellowship at the National Humanities Center during the academic year 1999–2000, supported by the Jessie Ball duPoint Fund, allowed me to carry out further research and to expand and revise the essay. Finally, I am grateful to James Marten and Joan Cashin, whose thoughtful readings of the revamped paper improved it even further.

1. Recent studies of Civil War soldiers include Gerald F. Linderman, *Embattled Courage: The Experience of Combat in the American Civil War* (New York, 1987); Reid Mitchell, *Civil War Soldiers: Their Expectations and Their Experiences* (New York, 1988); Reid Mitchell, *The Vacant Chair: The Northern Soldier Leaves Home* (New York, 1993); James McPherson, *What They Fought For, 1861–1865* (Baton Rouge, 1994); James M. McPherson, *For Cause and Comrade: Why Men Fought in the Civil War* (New York, 1997); Earl J. Hess, *The Union Soldier in Battle: Enduring the Ordeal of Combat* (Lawrence, Kans., 1997); Joseph Allan Frank, *With Ballot and Bayonet: The Political Socialization of American Civil War Soldiers* (Athens, Ga., 1998). For older views, see Bell Irvin Wiley, *The Life of Johnny Reb: The Common Soldier of the Confederacy* (Indianapolis, 1943; reprint, Baton Rouge, 1970); Bell Irvin Wiley, *The Life of Billy Yank: The Common Soldier of the Union* (Indianapolis, 1952; reprint, Baton Rouge, 1971).

2. Important studies of children's lives during the Civil War include James Marten, *The Children's Civil War* (Chapel Hill, 1998); Emmy E. Werner, *Reluctant Witnesses: Children's Voices from the Civil War* (Boulder, Colo., 1998); Peter W. Bardaglio, "The Children of Jubilee: African-American Childhood in Wartime," in *Divided Houses: Gender and the Civil War*, ed. Catherine Clinton and Nina Silber (New York, 1992), 213–29; Elizabeth Daniels, "The Children of Gettysburg," *American Heritage* 40 (May–June 1989): 97–107. Marten has also published a valuable collection of material from children's magazines published during the Civil War: *Lessons of War: The Civil War in Children's Magazines* (Wilmington, Del., 1999).

3. Phillip Shaw Paludan, *"A People's Contest": The Union and the Civil War, 1861–1865*, 2nd ed. (Lawrence, Kans., 1996), 25–26.

4. Elliott West, *Growing Up with the Country: Childhood on the Far Western Frontier* (Albuquerque, 1989) has inspired the recent effort among scholars to understand how children have exercised historical agency in the American past. Following West's lead, Marten (*Children's Civil War*, 5) insists that children in the American Civil War should be viewed "not merely as appendages to their parents' experiences" but as individuals who participated in and helped to shape the history of their time.

5. Hugh Cunningham, *Children and Childhood in Western Society since 1500* (London, 1995), 74–78. Review essays on the history of childhood and children include Hugh Cunningham, "Histories of Childhood," *American Historical Review* 103 (October 1998): 1195–1208; Joseph M. Hawes and N. Ray Hiner, "Looking for Waldo: Reflections on the History of Children and Childhood in the Postmodern Era," unpublished paper delivered at the History of Childhood Conference, Washington, D.C., August 2000.

6. Robert Coles, *The Political Life of Children* (Boston, 1987); and Richard M. Merelman, "The Role of Conflict in Children's Political Learning," in *Political Socialization, Citizenship in Education, and Democracy*, ed. Orit Ichivlov (New York, 1990), 52–53, 57–58. According to social psychologists and political scientists, the experiences of girls and boys between six and thirteen shape their political values for the rest of their lives. By the age of ten, the political perceptions of most children have developed to the point that they discern disagreements over issues and, in many cases, begin to adopt their own positions on these issues. Besides the studies by Coles and Merleman, significant studies of political socialization among children include Fred I. Greenstein, *Children and Politics*, rev. ed. (New Haven, 1969); David Easton and Jack Dennis, *Children in the Political System: Origins of Political Legitimacy* (New York, 1969); Norman Adler and Charles Harrington, eds., *The Learning of Political Behavior* (Glenview, Ill., 1970); R. W. Connell, *The Child's Construction of Politics* (Melbourne, 1971).

7. Barbara Jeanne Fields, *Slavery and Freedom on the Middle Ground: Maryland during the Nineteenth Century* (New Haven, 1985), 90–98; Jean H. Baker, *The Politics of Continuity: Maryland Political Parties from 1858 to 1870* (Baltimore, 1973), 47–63; Robert J. Brugger, *Maryland: A Middle Temperament, 1634–1980* (Baltimore, 1988), 284–87.

8. Allen Bowie Davis to W. Wilkins Davis, April 16, 1861, Allen Bowie Davis Letters, MS. 1511, Maryland Historical Society, Baltimore, Maryland (hereafter MHS). On the age of the Davis boy, see Hester Davis to W. Wilkins Davis, March 30, 1864, Allen Bowie Davis Letters, MS. 1511, MHS.

9. For recent accounts of the Baltimore riot, see Frank Towers, "'A Vociferous Army of Howling Wolves: Baltimore's Civil War Riot of April 19, 1861,'" *Maryland Historian* 23 (Fall/Winter 1992): 1–27; Brugger, *Maryland*, 274–76; and Fields, *Slavery and Freedom*, 93–94. On political violence before the Civil War, see ibid., 45–47; Jean Baker, *Ambivalent Americans: The Know-Nothing Party in Maryland* (Baltimore, 1977), 121–22.

10. Frank Towers, ed., "A Military Waif: A Sidelight on the Baltimore Riot of 19 April 1861," *Maryland Historical Magazine* 89 (Winter 1994): 429–30, 435.

11. Jim Murphy, *The Boys' War: Confederate and Union Soldiers Talk about the Civil War* (New York, 1990), 8; Werner, *Reluctant Witnesses*, 8. As James Marten points out, getting an accurate estimate of underage boys in the Union and Confederate armies is difficult. Murphy and Werner both claim that between 10 and 20 percent of all soldiers in the North and South were underage when they signed up, but neither cites any sources for this statistic. Bell Wiley's sampling of 11,000 Confederate soldiers suggests that about 5 percent were under eighteen. See Marten, *Children's Civil War*, 244n6; Murphy, *Boys' War*, 2; Werner, *Reluctant Witnesses*, 9; and Wiley, *Life of Johnny Reb*, 331.

12. Towers, "A Military Waif," 428, 437–38.

13. Brugger, *Maryland*, 279; Harold R. Manakee, *Maryland in the Civil War* (Baltimore, 1961), 50–55.

14. Harrison Journal, June 26, 1861, MHS.

15. William H. Russell, *My Diary North and South* (Boston, 1863), 376.

16. *Baltimore Republican*, July 5, 1861, 2.

17. McPherson, *What They Fought For*, 9–25; and Harrison Journal, June 16, 1861, MHS.

18. Manakee, *Maryland in the Civil War*, 55; Brugger, *Maryland*, 280.

19. Dix to McClellan, September 4, 1861, *The War of the Rebellion: A Compilation of the Official Records of the Union and Confederate Armies* (Washington, D.C., 1880–1901), ser. 2, vol. 1, 591; Harrison Journal, September 16, 1861 MHS.

20. Robert W. Schoeberlein, "A Fair to Remember: Maryland Women in Aid of the Union," *Maryland Historical Magazine* 90 (Winter 1995): 470.

21. *Baltimore American*, September 28, 1861.

22. Schoberlein, "A Fair to Remember," 471, 474–76, 479–80; Brugger, *Maryland*, 290–91; Marten, *Children's Civil War*, 19–20, 180–83.

23. *The New Era*, April 25, 1864.

24. *The New Era*, April 28, 1864, April 29, 1864; James Marten, "Tad and Willie Go to War: Northern Children and the Fight for the Union" (paper delivered at the annual meeting of the Southern Historical Association, Birmingham, Ala., November 1998).

25. Judith A. Bailey and Robert I. Cottom, eds., *After Chancellorsville: Letters from the Heart; The Civil War Letters of Private Walter G. Dunn and Emma Randolph* (Baltimore, 1998); Richard Ray Duncan, "The Social and Economic Impact of the Civil War on Maryland," (Ph.D. diss., Ohio State University, 1963), 70–71; Suzanne Ellery Greene Chapelle et. al., *Maryland: A History of Its People* (Baltimore, 1986), 167.

26. Mary P. Ryan, *Women in Public: Between Banners and Ballots, 1825–1880* (Baltimore, 1990), 141–52; George C. Rable, *Civil Wars: Women and the Crisis of Southern Nationalism* (Urbana, 1989), 39–49, 144–51; Drew Gilpin Faust, *Mothers of Invention: Women of the Slaveholding South in the American Civil War* (Chapel Hill, 1996), 10–12, 193–94, 210–14; Elizabeth R. Varon, *We Mean to Be Counted: White Women and Politics in Antebellum Virginia* (Chapel Hill, 1998), 137–77.

27. Lizette Woodworth Reese, *A Victorian Village: Reminiscences of Other Days* (New York, 1929), 83. The Baltimore city council in August 1862 required a loyalty oath of all city officials, employees, and teachers (see Brugger, *Maryland*, 293).

28. Virginia Walcott Beauchamp, "Research Notes and Maryland Miscellany: Madge Preston's Private War," *Maryland Historical Magazine* 82 (Spring 1987): 69; Virginia Walcott Beauchamp, ed., *A Private War: Letters and Diaries of Madge Preston, 1862–1867* (New Brunswick, N.J., 1987), 15, 26, 48. For other examples, see 23, 35.

29. Beauchamp, *A Private War*, xxxii; Reese, *A Victorian Village*, 68.

30. Reese, *A Victorian Village*, 69–71.

31. Quoted in Brugger, *Maryland*, 295.

32. James McLachlan, ed., "The Civil War Diary of Joseph H. Coit," *Maryland Historical Magazine* 60 (September 1965): 259.

33. Margaret Mehring Diary, June 15, June 18, 1863, MHS.

34. Mehring Diary, June 30, July 2, July 6, 1863, MHS; Werner, *Reluctant Witnesses*, 151–52.

35. Richard R. Duncan, "The Impact of the Civil War on Education in Maryland," *Maryland Historical Magazine* 61 (March 1966): 37–52; Marten, *Children's Civil War*, 153; Beauchamp, *A Private War*, 75.

36. Hall Harrison, *The Life of the Right Reverend John Barrett Kerfoot*, 2 vols. (New York, 1886), 1:199–200.

37. Ibid., 1:227–28, 259.

38. Ibid., 1:233–35, 239; Duncan, "Impact of the Civil War," 38.

39. McLachlan, "Civil War Diary," 249–51; Harrison, *Kerfoot*, 1:260, 292–301.

40. Allen Nevins, *Henry White: Thirty Years of American Diplomacy* (New York, 1930), 3–4; "Reminiscences of Henry White," 23, 30, file 2920.002, Hampton National Historic Site, Towson, Maryland. Many thanks to Kent Lancaster for bringing Nevins's book and White's unpublished memoirs to my attention.

41. "Reminiscences of Henry White," 30, 26, 29; Nevins, *Henry White*, 2.

42. Brugger, *Maryland*, x.

43. Baker, *Politics of Continuity*, 164, 173, 181–82, 184; Brugger, *Maryland*, 387; Margaret Law Callcott, *The Negro in Maryland Politics, 1870–1912* (Baltimore, 1969), 44–45.

44. Clifton K. Yearly, "The Baltimore and Ohio Strike of 1877," *Maryland Historical Magazine* 51 (September 1956): 188–211; Fields, *Slavery and Freedom*, 194–200 (Carroll quoted on 194). The Maryland Unionist organization adopted the name and principles of the national Republican Party in April 1867 (see Baker, *Politics of Continuity*, 177).

45. David W. Blight, "'What Will Peace Among Whites Bring?': Reunion and Race in the Struggle Over the Memory of the Civil War in American Culture," *Massachusetts Review* 34 (Autumn 1993): 406; and Nina Silber, *The Romance of Reunion: Northerners and the South, 1865–1900* (Chapel Hill, 1993), 95. Marten makes the point about the search for order among Americans who grew up during the struggle between North and South in *Children's Civil War*, 239–40.

46. Mullikin, quoted in Brugger, *Maryland*, 393.

Chapter 14

Duty, Country, Race, and Party:
The Evans Family of Ohio

JOSEPH T. GLATTHAAR

✦ SINCE ancient times, people have acknowledged the transforming nature of warfare. Through it, nations have risen and fallen. Leaders have emerged while others have failed. Peoples have secured freedom by it; some have become enslaved from it. The demands of war have consumed millions upon millions of lives, devastated whole economies, and destroyed untold amounts of property. Yet from its ashes have emerged wondrous things. During the course of war, ordinary people have performed extraordinary deeds, while those upon whom so much was expected have faltered. By ripping apart society and its taboos, war has offered fresh insights and ideas to the observant and opened new avenues for exploration and endeavor. Individuals who have participated in war have had a rare opportunity to learn much about themselves, about the essence of humankind, and to gain great confidence in their own abilities. From this fresh perspective, war may enable its participants to reassess personal and societal priorities and to formulate a new vision of the way life ought to be, thereby influencing civilians and life back home. For all its brutality and destructiveness, war has also forced changes in individuals, both in uniform and at home, for the betterment of themselves and society.

For generation and after generation, most Northern whites, like their Southern counterparts, merely accepted notions of African American inferiority. From father and mother to son and daughter, they passed down prejudices as they would family values. No one questioned them; it was simply the way life was. As new information or stories that corroborated their stereotypes emerged, they absorbed them. With conflicting evidence, they simply dismissed it as misleading, unrepresentative, or false. In short, Northerners clung to racism tenaciously.

While the work of antebellum abolitionists and the tensions from sectional conflicts helped to thaw some people's prejudices or soften racial beliefs, it took the cataclysmic nature of civil war to compel substantial portions of the Northern populace to undertake a major reevaluation of their attitudes toward African Americans. And with many others, it needed even more than that.

In the case of Sam Evans and his father, Andrew, from Brown County in southern Ohio, that challenge to longstanding racism required more than the Civil War. Despite the presence of such eminent activists as John Rankin, Ohio was hardly a hotbed of abolitionist sentiment, and many whites did not welcome fugitive slaves in their midst or advocate racial equality. The inhabitants from the southern part of the state, the Evanses among them, lived a short distance from the Ohio River and Kentucky. Many of them retained commercial or familial ties to slave states, and quite a number, such as Andrew's father, who came to Ohio from Kentucky, had direct connections to slavery. Frequently, racial views were particularly virulent, reflecting the influence of nearby slave holders.[1]

In order to shake family bigotry, the Evanses also relied on the strength of a son's desire for independence and the power of a father's love for his children to break prejudice's stranglehold. Sam's enlistment in the Union army enabled him to detach from his fatherly yoke. In time, that military service wrought changes in Sam's attitudes, especially toward African Americans. As Sam's standing among fellow soldiers rose, and word of his reputation filtered back home, Sam's opinions began to influence his father more and more. Andrew could either defend and advance the positions that Sam and, to a lesser extent, his brothers had adopted, or disavow beliefs on which his son Sam had staked his life. Forced to choose between a lifetime of prejudices and his love for a fine son, Andrew Evans not only absorbed his son's preachings but by the end of the war surpassed them, advocating even more progressive racial views than Sam.

What makes the case of the Evans family so special is not simply that there was a change in racial attitudes. That happened in varying degrees within tens of thousands of households in the North. What is novel about the Evans family is our ability to document that evolution every step of the way. The hundreds of surviving letters reveal a frank dialogue between father and son, one that provides us with a close look at the transformations that some white Northerners underwent during the war.

The Evans family's history in Ohio began in 1800, when Andrew's father, a blacksmith by trade, migrated from Blue Lick, Kentucky. He purchased 535 acres of land just north of the Ohio River, around what is now Huntington, near Aberdeen. The following year, he brought his family to settle there. Over the years, Andrew's father and siblings cleared off the oaks, walnuts, ashes, and other timber to build a home and prepare fields for cultivation. Here Andrew Evans was born in

1807, the eighth of eleven children. By the time Andrew's father passed away, in 1858, he had built the first smith shop and had erected a flour mill on the fork of a creek.

Andrew learned his father's craft, but over time he abandoned it to his eldest son in favor of farming. A bright, capable man with good business sense, Andrew had amassed quite a little fortune prior to the Civil War. By 1860, he owned $10,000 worth of real property and $1,000 of personal wealth, ranking him the thirteenth richest of 315 households in the township. In 1833, he married a religious woman from a fine local family, Mary Hiett, and together they had eleven children. Like his father, Andrew took on all the duties that the local community thrust upon him. Since 1850, for twelve consecutive years, he occupied the post of justice of the peace.

After his death, someone described him as "a man of strong conviction," who never hesitated to express his views in public. Although he exhibited little interest in organized religion before the war, Andrew possessed a singularly clear sense of right and wrong. Complete confidence in his opinions, along with his duties as a justice of the peace, earned him the nickname "the Squire" among his children and their friends.[2]

Sam Evans was the eldest of eleven children of Andrew and Mary Evans. Born in 1834 and reared on the family land, Sam apprenticed under his father as a blacksmith at age thirteen, thus succeeding as the fifth generation of Evanses who entered the trade. A tall, slender man with dark complexion and brown hair, Sam eventually took over his father's smithing practice. Not long before the Civil War, he built a house on his father's land, about a half mile from the family home. A bright fellow like his father, Sam had little schooling but developed excellent academic skills. For a few years, he even taught school part-time. In 1858, before his grandfather's death, Sam purchased the flour mill, and he continued to work on the family farm whenever his father and siblings needed him. By the time of the war, Sam had become a popular and respected member of the community and a reliable source for blacksmith work and milling. He had yet to hold political office.

Within a week of the firing on Fort Sumter, Sam turned twenty-seven years of age. Every evidence indicates that he had always been a dutiful son. He took on the family trade, and picked up his grandfather's milling. While two younger brothers and a sister married and left home, Sam stayed behind to assist his parents, brothers, and sisters. He remained single; at the time of the Civil War, he courted a woman named Callie Campbell, without any commitment to marriage.[3]

In 1860, Brown County boasted nearly 30,000 residents. Although twenty-two counties in Ohio had more inhabitants, only five had more

African Americans. With the slave state of Kentucky just across the Ohio River, the sizeable black population surprised no one. Nor did it shock locals that the town of Ripley, a headquarters for the underground railroad efforts of abolitionist John Rankin, boasted the largest number of blacks in the county. Where the Evanses lived, in Aberdeen and Huntington townships, there were only three black residents, all female, out of almost three thousand inhabitants.[4]

Most people in Brown County derived their living from the soil. More than half the county's acreage was improved for farming, as locals produced wheat, corn, tobacco, and oats, or raised cows, swine, and sheep. Among the nonfarming trades, Sam had fallen into two of the most lucrative. Mill work was the largest manufacturing pursuit in the county, and smithing was fifth on the list.[5]

Politically, the areas around Aberdeen and Huntington were Democratic strongholds, and Andrew counted himself among those ranks. Andrew Jackson originally drew him to the party banner, and for decades afterward, he considered himself a Jacksonian Democratic. Even though the antislavery activist Rankin had presided over his marriage, Andrew had no regard for abolitionism or the Republican Party. Like most Northerners, he bore strong prejudices against people of African descent and expressed no interest in checking slavery's expansion into the territories. In 1860, he supported "the Little Giant," Stephen A. Douglas, for president.[6]

Sam, too, endorsed the Democratic candidates. Abolitionism had little sway over him, and during the 1860 campaign, Sam had chided his Republican friends, calling one of them a "Negroamus" and other jibes. A racial conservative like his father, he advocated Douglas's candidacy, although for some reason he failed to vote in the election.[7]

After Confederates fired on Fort Sumter, the Evanses rallied behind the Union. None of them responded to the initial call, but in late 1861, when state officials formed the 70th Ohio Volunteer Infantry, twenty-one-year-old John Evans received his father's blessing to join the regiment. Nine days after the unit was mustered into service, it marched to nearby Ripley, where troops organized and drilled and locals, including the Evanses, could visit John.[8]

Just before the regiment left Ohio for Paducah, Kentucky, and then destinations unknown, John came home on leave. When it was time to return, Sam took a wagon and a team of horses to run him back to his unit. A few days later, a friend brought the wagon and horses to the Evans household. In a carefully hatched scheme, Sam had run off to the army.[9]

Word of Sam's enlistment stunned the Evans household. His father brooded over Sam's action. His mother cried. His girlfriend Callie "was the most completely beaten I ever saw her," described his brother Will. "She wept bitterly." In almost twenty-eight years of life, this was Sam's first great act of rebellion. And he did so without telling anyone for one simple reason: His father would object.[10]

Not only had Sam's enlistment affected everyone emotionally, it disrupted the Evans family's dynamics. The order of birth and the ability and willingness to fulfill family obligations influenced each son's relationship with his father and the rest of the family. As the eldest, Sam played the role of the dutiful son. When he picked up the hammer and anvil and lived on his father's land, Sam met his father's primary objectives, securing adult help and obtaining a successor in the family businesses. It also opened the door of opportunities to his brothers. Before the war, brother Abraham had gone off to medical school in Cincinnati, and brother Will had married and moved to Indiana. And after war broke out, John enlisted with his father's support. They could do so only because Sam remained behind to help his father care for the family.

But for Sam, by staying at home he continued under his father's control. He lived on family land and took over the blacksmith and the mill business. He adopted his father's political views, became a valued member of the community, and did everything a parent could ask of a son. Prior to this fateful decision, Sam's sole form of revolt had been to join the Presbyterian Church, where his mother attended — hardly a grave misstep.[11]

Once Sam joined the army, he altered family relations in two important ways. For the first time in his life, he broke free from his father's yoke. While brothers Abe and Will had already gained their independence, and John had struck out for it by his own enlistment, Sam had never secured it for himself. All these years, economic ties and family obligations kept him under his father's parental roof.

Sam's act also disrupted the role of his male siblings. With Sam no longer available to help on the farm and carry on all those duties that the eldest son had performed, others would have to take up the slack. That burden fell largely on his fifth brother, Amos, who was just coming of age.[12]

From Kentucky, Sam explained his reasons for joining. There were no abolitionist sentiments, no harsh denunciations against secessionists or fiery words of patriotism. He felt a sense of obligation to go. At home, he was not helping his country in its time of crisis. Since he would eventually volunteer, and John had already joined the 70th Ohio, it made good sense in Sam's mind to enter with his brother. He did not "'advertise'" his enlistment because he thought it would stir up a ruckus at home. In a veiled admission that he knew how his father would react, Sam admitted, "If I had told the folks at home not many of them would have been willing."[13]

The same day that Sam justified his behavior to his family, he began to exhibit symptoms of an illness that had spread throughout the camp: fever, aches, and finally the telltale red blotches. Sam had caught the measles. He spent several weeks in a hospital under a physician's care. Then, after the regiment shipped out for Tennessee, they moved him and a friend into a bawdy house, where a kindly "old darky" woman, as Sam described her, nursed them back to fitness.[14]

For three weeks, the patriarchal Andrew Evans had stifled his resentment over his son's enlistment. With Sam ill, he could not restrain himself. Surely Sam's history of checkered health should have convinced him not to "take so rash a step" as enlisting in the army, his father scolded. The government had plenty of recruits; it did not need Sam Evans. He accused Sam of acting "under the impulse of the moment." The soldiers in uniform, the fife and drum had swayed him into a hasty decision, his father suspected. Now, he had fallen ill, and rather than be an aid to the cause, he was a burden to his government.[15]

His father had used Sam's illness as a means to challenge his son's stride toward independence. But it did not take long for that effort to play out. Four days after he blasted Sam, measles broke out in the Evans household, and his father ended up caring for his wife and children. No doubt, had Sam been home, he would have come down with a case as well. More importantly, a few weeks later, the Battle of Shiloh took place, with both Evans boys involved.[16]

By early April, Sam felt well enough to return to his regiment, which he located near the south bank of the Tennessee River, by a place called Pittsburg Landing. The 70th Ohio was in the Fourth Brigade in Brig. Gen. William Tecumseh Sherman's Division and under the overall command of Maj. Gen. Ulysses S. Grant. When Sam found it, the regiment occupied an advanced position facing south, in the center of Sherman's forces. The left of the 70th Ohio extended to Shiloh Church, the landmark for which the battle was named.[17]

On April 4, the Confederate cavalry surprised some pickets from the 70th Ohio, well in advance of the main line, and captured seven privates and a lieutenant. The following day was silent, but early on Sunday, April 6, the Rebels struck with a fury. As men in the 70th were cooking breakfast, the crack of musketry in their front and to the left along the picket line alerted them to the enemy's approach. The Ohioans quickly formed and advanced several hundred yards across a field and into a woods, where they organized for battle. They opened fire on the attacking Rebels, and when the enemy threatened to get around the left flank of the 70th, the regimental commander ordered the line refused, or bent back, to prevent anyone from getting behind the troops. The untested Ohio soldiers "did great execution among the enemy," according to their colonel, and drove the Confederates back into a hollow.[18]

For nearly two hours, the men of the 70th held their ground, until about a half mile to the west a large Confederate column began slicing in behind them. Around that time, Rebel artillery batteries to the front hurled shot and shell into their ranks. Without adequate support and threats to the front and flank, the Ohioans retreated through their camp and occupied a position about eighty yards beyond it. The Confederates, in hot pursuit, entered the old camp and, according to John Evans, "took what suited them and threw the rest out in the rain."[19]

It was here that Sam most likely killed his first Rebel. From about seventy or eighty yards off, lying down, he spotted three Confederates poking around a tent. He saw one pull back the flap and stick his head inside. At that moment, Sam fired. Two days later, he examined the tent and discovered a body there, in roughly the same position with a bullet hole about eight inches below the arm pit, right where Sam aimed.[20]

Not long afterward, the Confederates began turning the Union left again. The Ohioans on the extreme end of the line, Sam among them, refused their position once more by "leg wheel" to guard their flank. It did no good. In short order, Confederates began to press around them, and the colonel ordered another retreat. But amid the thunderous roar of musketry and cannon, Sam did not hear the command. He remained lying on the ground, firing at the enemy, while his comrades fell back. As Sam shot at some Confederates, several advanced undetected to within fifty yards of him. Immediately after Sam discharged his weapon, one of them fired and nearly struck Sam. Both men rushed to reload. Sam admitted in his haste he spilled some powder, but he rammed down his round quicker than the Rebel. When the man peeked his head around the edge of a tree, Sam was ready for him. He fired, and the Confederate dropped to the ground. A later examination proved that Sam had shot him in the temple.[21]

Once Sam realized that everyone had abandoned him, he fell back and reunited with his regiment. In the utter chaos, units got mixed up, and the 70th Ohio eventually joined with two other brigades from Sherman's division. Twice more that day, the Confederates drove them back, and in both instances, the 70th retired intact. By nightfall, the 70th Ohio had suffered significant losses, but it still had some fight left in it.

After a night of drenching rain, the Union army opened April 7 on the offensive. With reinforcements arriving late the previous day, Grant now had superior numbers, which he exploited effectively. The 70th Ohio attacked and helped to regain the camp of Maj. Gen. John A. McClernand's Division, expending all its ammunition in the process. By the time these men had replenished their supply, the Confederates had fallen back beyond the range of pursuit. The two-day battle of Shiloh had ended, with almost 24,000 casualties between the two sides. The

70th Ohio had sustained nine men killed, fifty-seven wounded, and eleven missing.[22]

Both Evans men emerged from combat almost unscathed, despite some harrowing moments. A musket ball cut John's blouse at the shoulder, and a buck shot passed through his sleeve without hitting him. Sam was not quite so lucky. A ball struck his cartridge box and "mashed it all in." A buck shot went through his hat, and a grape shot deflected off a tree and hit him in the neck, briefly knocking him unconscious. Sam described the injury initially as a large bruise. Not until eighteen months later did he relate its true nature. "I was shot slightly," he belatedly admitted. The lead projectile creased his neck, leaving a scar that "shows very plain." The injury, however, he waved off with a touch of bravado as inconsequential, claiming, "A little wound does not amount to a hill of beans."[23]

In fact, Sam was reluctant to communicate much about his first fight. In a letter that John wrote three days after the fight, Sam added a postscript that he had "seen the elephant" and that "[w]e have had something like hardships to stand — for a few days." Not until a month later, after prodding from his father, did Sam reveal a bit about his combat experience. Even then, he described two Rebels whom he had shot, but the rest of the letter was vague enough to suggest that he may have shot others.[24]

It fell to John and others to tout Sam's martial talents. A couple of days after the battle, John wrote home, "Sam has better pluck than I. He is truly a brave man." Fellow soldiers, too, could not mistake Sam's coolness under fire and unusual marksmanship. They must have seen Sam lying alone and firing calmly and accurately after his buddies fell back. Tales in letters or from soldiers who returned home on sick or wounded furlough proclaimed Sam's courage in combat throughout the local community. His brother John, at home just weeks after Shiloh trying to recuperating from typhoid fever, regaled the family with stories of their experiences, particularly Sam's composure in combat. Another soldier from the regiment, Bill West, visited the Evans family and spoke in glowing terms of Sam. "He passes a higher eulogy on you as a *Soldier & man* than you would ask any man to do," his father summarized. "You are his first choice." Within two months of the battle, his family had received enough independent corroboration for his brother Amos to assert that "there is not private soldier in the whole army" who "commands greater Respect or greater praise than yourself."[25]

When he finally did address his combat experiences, even Sam admitted that he handled himself well. In responding to his father's questions, Sam revealed that "I felt like shooting every fella I could see, fore I think my hair raised a little and I felt like I could shoot every secesh in the land and feel good over it." Neither bounding cannon balls, his own wound, the harrowing shriek of the Rebel yell, nor someone else's blood splattering on his face unnerved him. "Not boasting or anything of the kind," he hesitantly confessed, "I think I am a better soldier than I thought I was." Clearly, he was. Sam discovered that he possessed the character to execute well amid the horrors of combat. And everyone around him noticed that ability, too. When the 70th Ohio formed a fifty-man team of sharpshooters, Sam was the first person selected.[26]

Back home, the glowing reports of his combat performance gave Sam new standing with his father. His father would never admit he was wrong, but he accepted Sam's decision to volunteer as a correct one, and he took great pride in his son's martial accomplishments. Sam's achievements, moreover, boosted family morale at a moment of great disappointment. Back in Huntington, about the same time as the battle, Andrew Evans lost a vote for reelection as justice of the peace. Even though his friends blamed the defeat on skillful use of whiskey, lying, and unfairness on the part of his opponent, the rejection stung this proud man. Once word of Sam's bravery reached home, Andrew Evans could hold his head a bit higher as he travelled through the community.[27]

Nor did Sam's success stop on the battlefield. He proved to be almost as good in camp and on the march as he was in combat. Despite the debilitating effects of the measles, Sam fulfilled his duties and endured all the hardships. He devoured the rock-hard crackers and fatty pork without complaint, and then commented to his father that army fare was not so bad once a soldier got used to it. "Shirks" dropped out on the march one July day; he was one of nine in the company to keep up. When his shoes wore out and his feet bled, Sam refused to use that as an excuse to get out of duty. Others in his regiment endured the same problem, and if they could still keep up, so could he.[28]

All the while, he preserved an upbeat attitude. "Some of the boys are nearly always grumbling," he reported home, "but I like it very well, rather better than I thought I would." Instead of venting his frustrations, he converted them into amusement. In a witty reference to the secretive, anti-immigrant American or Know-Nothing Party, Sam counseled his father, "If you want to find a Knownothingism in its purity, just come into the army and you can find it from a col[onel] down to a private. If on a march you ask, 'where are you going' The answer is 'I don't know.'"[29]

Throughout that spring and summer, Sam's excellent conduct distinguished him as a soldier and provided a stark contrast with others in the community. When a handful of Confederate guerrillas raided in northern Kentucky, Brown County residents panicked. After much fuss, local militiamen assembled and from across the Ohio River they exchanged about thirty shots with the guerrillas. Most did their duty, noted Sam's brother Amos, but "some were Scared so they did not know anything," and "it is reported one man Shit down his leg."[30]

While Sam fulfilled his obligations as a soldier, people at home dodged military service. In August, local officials performed physical examinations for draft eligibility. Andrew Evans took great pride in the fact that he had three sons in the army — Will had enlisted in the 89th Ohio Infantry three months after Sam — and a fourth one who tried to volunteer but was rejected for health reasons. At the same time, so many men in the community went to great lengths to avoid military service. "It would surprise you to see the amount of disease and affliction now prevailing here," he alerted Sam. "None are reached by the epidemic except those between the ages of 18 & 45."[31]

As Sam's stock rose in the army and at home, the Squire began to accord him a newfound degree of respect. No longer did they communicate like a patriarch and his minion. Their discussions of war, politics, family matters, and events at home resembled those of two adults who esteemed each other.

And from his elevated status, Sam also assumed a more powerful role in the family, one his father accepted without apparent resistance. That October, when the draft selected Amos Evans for military service, the young man immediately turned to his brother Sam. Those who supported the war stigmatized conscripted men as lacking either patriotism or courage. Personally humiliated, Amos predicted to Sam, "It does not hurt me as it will the folks at home." Sam responded to his father in a carefully crafted letter, one that hit on all the right themes. He expressed outrage over the unfairness of the draft. While three Evans men had volunteered, some families had no one in uniform. Sam reminded his father that they had persuaded Amos not to enter the service but to stay home and help care for the farm and the family, a role Sam had performed for many years. Amos, Sam elaborated, was the best son his father had, and no doubt he would make a fine soldier. "Since it is so," he reconciled, "we will have to make the best we can of it." As it turned out, Amos failed the physical examination and was released from his obligation, but Sam's part in coping with the family crisis demonstrated his willingness to assume a greater role in the family, especially with his father.[32]

In military and political affairs, father and son fed off each other. Sam provided his father with a better understanding of army needs. He described the rampages of an invading army, the plundering and the hardships. In return, the Squire relayed political news and insights. Throughout the fall, his father preserved his attachments to the Democratic Party. He sharply criticized people of the *"Political Abolition faith!"*

and crowed, "We set them on their asses very nicely in the Ohio election this fall." As a War Democrat, he sneered at what he termed "the *bogus* Union, Republican party," for acting as though its members had a monopoly in loyalty to the nation. With sons in the military, he supported anything that aided the cause.[33]

During the late fall and winter months of 1862–63, Sam demonstrated his value to the army by taking on all sorts of peripheral duties. He, too, would do anything that advanced the cause, as long as he had the skills to accomplish the task. When his division lacked bread, he ran a mill and ground corn for everyone. With his mechanical background, he helped to fix train engines for the army. Another time, he built coffins for his deceased comrades. For a few months in the winter, the peacetime blacksmith repaired weapons. He even did some work for General Sherman. In his company, Sam gained the nickname "the doctor" because he took care of younger privates. He emphasized eating and sleeping well and regular exercise to preserve health. As he explained, "[I]t's much safer to keep health than to gain it when lost."[34]

Of all the outside duties to which Sam was assigned, though, the work that changed the course of his life was supervising labor parties composed of former slaves. Since early in the war, slaves had begun to flee to Union lines. By May 1861, the Federal army announced a policy of keeping those who had been employed on Rebel military projects, declaring them contraband of war and subject to seizure, but returning the rest. Although Congress ratified that approach two months later, it soon broke down. Some Union officers refused to return anyone to slavery; others resented the idea of helping Rebels or those who tolerated secession in any way. Slaves, too, fled in ever increasing numbers, and with family members in tow. Steadily, they forced a larger and larger opening, until the army announced that it would no longer assist in the retrieval of slaves.[35]

As these slaves entered Union lines, the army employed them in all sorts of capacities, particularly as military laborers, cooks, and nurses. During the summer of 1862, Sam first began to oversee runaways in the construction of Fort Pickering in Memphis. The job gave him additional pay, and he did not have to work himself, just oversee the labor of others. His brother John, back home trying to recuperate, teased him about his "new trade (of driving contrabands)." He wondered, "Are you a good hand to sling the knot?," a reference to masters whipping slaves. "I would like to see you at it," John quipped. Sam was not dissuaded from the task.[36]

Whether his lengthy exposure to African American work details, or his military travels through Kentucky, Tennessee, and Mississippi, or both, affected him, it is unclear. But when Abraham Lincoln issued his Emancipation Proclamation on September 22, 1862, to take effect January 1, 1863, Sam Evans endorsed it enthusiastically. To his father, the Ohio private explained that this was not a Republican or Democratic concept. All who supported the war should embrace it. "My doctrine has been any thing to weaken the enemy," Sam averred. "This same negro has been the means of sustainance to the Rebles in the way of building fortifications[,] furnishing supplies &c!&c!![etc.]." Within the 70th Ohio, he professed such strong support that his comrades chose him to chair a committee that drafted a resolution to Lincoln, endorsing the Proclamation and applauding the idea of black military service. "Resolved, That we believe it should be the policy of the Government to employ blacks in whatever manner they can be made most serviceable to the United States army," it read, "whether it be to handle the spade or shoulder the musket."[37]

Just a few weeks after the regiment adopted and forwarded the resolutions, Sam dropped a bombshell on his family: He had been nominated for a lieutenant's commission in a new black regiment, and he planned to accept it. Before the war, Sam had borne strong prejudices against people of African descent. And while the record of his views on the morality of slavery is vague, his enthusiasitic support for Stephen Douglas over Lincoln placed him in a minority among Northerners, indicating at best he had little interest in ending the peculiar institution or checking its expansion. Family and friends could interpret his endorsement of emancipation and black military service as an extension of his views on an effective prosecution of the war. But none of them would have predicted he would agree to command black soldiers.[38]

When Lincoln decided to issue the Emancipation Proclamation, he also determined to enlist blacks as soldiers. For political reasons, he waited until the Union won its next major battlefield victory, in September 1862, before he publicly embraced emancipation as a wartime policy. But he did not delay his plans for black enlistment. That summer, he allowed three black regiments from Louisiana to enter federal service, and a few weeks later he authorized abolitionist Thomas Wentworth Higginson to raise a black regiment in South Carolina. The following spring, Lincoln sent Adjutant General Lorenzo Thomas to the Mississippi Valley, announcing the administration's policy of recruiting blacks and encouraging competent white soldiers to act as their officers. By the time Sam Evans heard Thomas's plea, it was too late. He had already accepted an assignment to command black soldiers a week earlier.[39]

Sam first broached the subject with his family casually, in a letter to his brother John. He mentioned that the division would provide officers for a new black regiment, and men from the 70th would officer one company. He intimated nothing about an appointment. Within a few days, however, he had decided to take on the new position. When he did notify the family of his plans, Sam explained his reasoning first to his brother Amos. Sam thought Amos would support him in any decision he made and could act as family intermediary.[40]

Although his relationship with his father had changed during the war, Sam did not know how far the new boundaries extended. His father respected Sam's opinions as an experienced soldier, and he had come to appreciate Sam both for his leadership as the eldest sibling and as an individual of good character and judgment. But throwing in with black soldiers was an entirely different matter. Into a household that professed black inferiority — in fact, into a household that wanted nothing to do with people of African descent — Sam had injected the race issue. To his father, Sam simply alerted him that he had been nominated for a commission in a new black regiment and he let his name go forward. "Give me your opinion about the matter in which I am engaged," Sam requested disingenuously. "I would rather have consulted you on the subject but time would not admit it."[41]

In explanation to his father and others, Sam mentioned several factors that influenced his decision to consider and then accept an appointment as second lieutenant in the 1st West Tennessee Infantry, African Descent. Officers in his regiment nominated him, which Sam viewed as an honor. A second lieutenant received $100 per month pay, compared to $13 as a private, plus the prestige associated with holding a commission. The 70th Ohio had recently undergone some turbulence. A number of officers whom Sam liked had resigned, and Sam had not been chosen as a replacement. Most likely, his chances for promotion in the 70th Ohio were hurt by not being a member of the original regiment and also by his extensive detached service. He expressed no hostility or frustration with the choices for promotion, but for the foreseeable future, there would be no opportunities for advancement. And all along, Sam had believed that as a soldier, he should do whatever best advanced the cause. He thought he "could do as much good," perhaps more so, with black troops.[42]

For his father, Sam also included in his justification some subtle racial barbs, to convince his father he had not converted to an abolitionist. He annnounced that it was the president's intention to make "the Negro Self *sustaining*." Blacks would be organized into military units and would receive the same clothing and arms as white soldiers. To allay any fears his father might have, Sam explained that they would be treated as prisoners of war, whenever captured.

While he did not go so far as to assert that he would prefer a black man die in battle than a white Union soldier, he did admit, "My doctrine is that a Negro is no better than a white man and will do as well to receive Reble bullets and would be likely to save the life of some white men." By 1863, Federal armies had more runaway slaves in their lines than they could use. They could employ them more advantageously as soldiers. "It seems to be the policy of the President to take all the Slaves from their masters as a means of harrassing their facilities for propagating subsistence thus causing them to sue for peace," Sam noted. In a concession, he doubted they would fight as well as "*some*" of the white regiments, but good officers "may succeed in making them of some benefit to the Government."[43]

Initial opinions from home were mixed. Sam's mother communicated nothing. His eleven-year-old sister Ann told him, "I would not like to have Command over them." Not surprisingly, Amos provided the most encouragement. He applauded the policy of enlisting blacks, and with good intentions lied to his brother, "We all fully Endorse proceedings [and] leave you to consult your own conscience for advice."[44]

But four days after Amos conveyed family support, his father imparted his opinion "*Very reluctantly.*" He considered commanding black soldiers a "degraded position" and assured his son, "I would rather clean out s — — t houses at ten cents pr day, than to take your position with its pay." His father was proud to say that Sam had earned "an enviable reputation" as a soldier. "*Alas what a step!*" He insisted that they "deeply regret that it is taken." Stung and embarrassed by the decision, he grumbled churlishly, "never mind us, we will soon be out of the way." Despite all the hazards in war, they had expected to see Sam again some day. Now that he had joined a black regiment, his father believed the additional risks were so great that "we are in doubt."[45]

If Sam thought his own arguments or Amos's words would soften his father's position, he was soon disabused of that notion. "We hear that you have enlisted in the Nigger services for five years," the Squire blasted a week later. "If such is a fact, your stomach has become quite strong compared with its condition whilst you were at home." In words dripping with sarcasm, he called service with blacks "fancy business, compared to that of staying with common white men 'Sic transit Gloria,['] etc. [glory is fleeting]."

Most cutting of all, though, were his father's remarks on politics, in which once again he took a swipe at Sam. "I *cant* vote for an *Abolitionist*, nor for a Reb sympathiser," his father pronounced. Since Sam had openly supported the Emancipation Proclamation, he surely did not mistake the connection: If Sam were a candidate for political office, his father would not vote for him. Worse, his father indicated little difference between abolitionists and Peace Democrats. Both were extreme positions, and neither merited his support.[46]

Andrew Evans had pushed way too far. Perhaps in the prewar days, he could lord it over his eldest son. By mid-1863, however, Sam had emerged from his father's shadow. He had met and in many cases surpassed the most rigorous standards of manhood. He was an experienced soldier, one who had exhibited courage under fire, and he had handled all the hardships and rigors that military life could mete out. From Sam's perspective, he had proven himself as a man of character and deserved much more respect from his father than he had received.

Sam's reply measured just the right combination of firmness and outrage. He alerted his father that he could not discuss the matter before the decision because of time constraints. He had no desire to hide his actions, at least "Such things as you have the right to know." With his independence established, Sam launched his own counterattack. " 'So willing to accept a degraded position!' " the veteran rebutted. "The fact is you have never marched so far with a heavy load and sore feet as I, and have never noticed so plainly the privileges of a commissioned officer's." He believed it was not a "degraded position," insisting he would much rather have his job than the one his father preferred.

After hammering back at his father's arguments forcefully, Sam eased up. He absolved his father of any culpability for the decision, admitting, "If I have done wrong it is not your fault, but mine and will be held accountable to God." With a final flourish, Sam drew on his strength of character and self-confidence to challenge the old patriarch in a final, restrained way. "Although you have rated me *very* low," he disputed, "*I* think you are mistaken." He was glad his father had not cut him off, and he would continue to write home.[47]

Even before Sam's reply reached him, Andrew Evans realized he had reacted excessively, and he began to backpedal. He wrote Sam that he had no objection to black troops, and he "would rather have them shot than white men, nay more, I would rather have the race extinguished than to lose a single Co[mpany] of white soldiers, but I had rather let their friends lead them than do it myself." His greatest fear was that Sam had increased the chance he might lose his life. He also wondered what four white men — a captain, two lieutenants, and a first sergeant — could do if they mutinied. He signed the letter, "Love by your father."[48]

Sam understood all too well what his own motives were and why his father objected. To his brother Amos, a young man from a different generation who did not bear the same racial misconceptions as his father, Sam could explain more bluntly. He thought he had made a "pretty good soldier" in the 70th; now, duty called him to a post "where I could do more good" by helping to convert a group who could assist the army directly on the battlefield. He insisted that his political views had not changed since before the war. That, of course, was incorrect. The war had opened Sam's eyes to an entirely new vista, providing opportunities to prove his worth that were unavailable in peacetime and exposing him every day to an odious institution. His very words marked that change. He had concluded that "the Negro is no better than a white man and has just as good a right to fight for his freedom and government." Somebody had to command them. "Shall I require, as a necessity someone to do what I would not myself condescend to do?" he asked. "No, I could not do that." He was convinced that his father's true resistance stemmed from embarrassment within the community over Sam's decision.[49]

For all his rigidity and patriarchal notions, Andrew Evans was not blinded for long. Everyone in the community knew Sam Evans as a good and honorable man, and they knew Sam would do anything to further the war effort. In time, the Squire would learn that no one held Sam's service with blacks against him or his family.

More importantly, personal tragedy and other events forced Andrew to reevaluate his priorities and to shift his support behind his son Sam. Early in 1862, Sam's brother Abraham had died at home. In May 1863, just a few weeks after Sam decided to accept the commission, the Squire's mother passed away, followed two weeks later by Sam's brother John, who died of a pulmonary ailment he contracted in the service of his country. Among his adult male children, that left Sam and Will, both in the army, and Amos, whose impaired health kept him at home. Grief over these losses reminded Andrew of the fragility of human existence and drew him nearer emotionally to his surviving children. In that light, his worries that Sam would incur increased risks as an officer of black soldiers is understandable.[50]

Combining with those personal losses to ease the Squire's objections was the rise of peace advocates in the Democratic Party. Andrew Evans had been a lifelong Democrat. Like his political hero Andrew Jackson, he believed in the Union, and he supported the war from the outset. But by mid-1863 the Peace Democrats, who professed an agenda to end the war as soon as possible by letting the Southern states go their separate way, appeared to be gaining control of the Ohio Democratic Party. Just weeks before Sam accepted the commission, his father had distilled the Peace Democrats into their basic components: "The constituent parts of such, (agreeably to my analysis,) are one part Coward, one 'Southern sympathizer,['] 2 of Calf & 4 Shitass." Sam took only minor exception to his father's assessment. "I should arrange the constituent parts a little different," he elucidated. "1 part Coward, 1 S[outhern] Sympathizer, 2 Calf. The combination of these parts would produce your last, is my analysis."[51]

Strangely enough, in the face of growing attacks by Peace Democrats,

Andrew's traditional paternal role of family protector triggered a shift to a more open-minded view of Sam's service with blacks. Not only did the peace platform undermine his own philosophy, it would transform John's death into a senseless loss and it might unnecessarily jeopardize the lives of Will and Sam. Both privately and publicly, Andrew had to stand up for the cause and the efforts of his sons — even if one of them commanded black soldiers — and he did so with unbridled vehemence. His defense restored and strengthened the common ground with Sam.

When Andrew was chosen as a delegate to the state Democratic Convention in 1863, he refused to go for fear that a leading peace advocate, Clement C. Vallandigham, would receive the nomination for governor of Ohio. Andrew wanted no part in a process that selected a candidate like him. After Vallandigham received the nomination, Sam's father was disgusted. He accepted a nomination to the state Union Convention, a fusion of Republicans and War Democrats, and worked vigorously for Vallandigham's opponent, John Brough.[52]

Then, in August of that same year, Andrew dropped a bombshell on his son. "I have been Conscripted!" he announced, as Union Party candidate for state representative. Hoping to strengthen the Brough ticket in Brown County, locals nominated him without his consent. The Squire preferred not to run, but since his sons volunteered to risk their lives, he saw no way he could refuse to help at home. He ran on his reputation in the community and his support for the war. No one claimed opposition to his candidacy because Sam commanded black troops, and doubtless Sam won him a few ballots. In the November election, the soldiers' vote gave him a 150- to 200-vote majority. "I am therefore the Soldiers Representative," his father proclaimed once the results were released, "and will be pleased to represent them faithfully."[53]

Meanwhile, the new second lieutenant began recruiting and training his men. He led mounted raiding parties that confiscated weapons, horses, mules, and slaves; all the able-bodied males he inducted for military service. In three days, he had enrolled thirty-one, and less than a week later, Sam had gathered seventy, enough for a company. In short order, the government swore them into service for three years and provided uniforms, rifled muskets, and a full complement of accoutrements.[54]

All told, Sam derived great satisfaction from his new assignment. He worked with them dilligently, teaching the basics of soldiering and drill. "They learn the school of a soldier much readier than I anticipated," he commented with pleasure. Very few of them enlisted and then deserted, he noticed, a strong indicator of their commitment to armed service. Like white units, the biggest problem was disease. Measles, followed by smallpox, roared through their ranks, discouraging the sick and frightening those who waited to contract the illness.[55]

By mid-August, they had their first exchange of fire with the enemy. Guerrilla bands tested their picket line, particularly at night. Sam's company demonstrated unusual vigilance, and the second lieutenant was pleased. "I believe we have fighting stock," he proudly boasted to his father. Over the next two years, the men in the 1st West Tennessee Infantry, African Descent, renamed the 59th United States Colored Infantry in March 1864, devoted more time to battling guerrillas and coping with smuggling by Southern civilians than anything else.[56]

As an officer, Sam felt compelled to defend them against injustice. Although he did not join the fight for equal pay, he did demand equal treatment for prisoners of war, white as well as black, Union as well as Confederate. "I am of the opinion," he expressed to his father, "if the government employ black men to fight they aught to have some protection." It galled him that the Union army treated Rebel guerrillas as prisoners of war while enemy partisans shot the Federals they caught.[57]

Sam did not fear mutiny by his black soldiers, as many others did. He purchased his first a revolver in the wake of the Fort Pillow Massacre of black soldiers by Confederate Maj. Gen. Nathan Bedford Forrest's command, some eleven months after he joined the regiment. While others took furloughs, he stayed with the troops, drilling them and overseeing their day-to-day routine. His regimental commanders rewarded his efforts by securing his promotion to first lieutenant in November 1863. For the remainder of the war, when a company lacked an officer, they shifted Sam temporarily to command it.[58]

And throughout it all, as his father's coldness to service with blacks thawed, he could even joke with the Squire about it. Already dark complected, a photograph Sam had taken after his promotion to first lieutenant in late 1863 darkened him farther. "A light colored one could not be expected [with] the Regiment I am in," he quipped.[59]

Family members expressed trepidation about Sam going into combat with black soldiers. They worried about how his African Americans would respond and how the Confederates would treat him, should he ever fall into their hands. Sam had no such concerns, crediting his Christian faith with providing him the strength to perform his duty well and to handle the horrors of combat. "If a man is a true Christian," he explained, "he can be but a brave man." To his mind, "Bravery is not recklessness. It does not mean that a man should walk up to the cannons mouth disarmed and peep into the muzzle while the enemy is standing with a lited match at the touch-hole." The true essence of courage he derived from the knowledge that the only thing a man should fear is God. "We should meet danger in the full consciousness of its presence — calmly, steadily, unfalteringly." A brave man, Sam believed, was a person of character, someone who was "high-minded and really honorable" and lived in accordance with Christian values. "A man with the assurance in his own breast that God has forgiven him is not afraid to die."[60]

During its wartime service, the 59th U.S. Colored Infantry skirmished frequently with guerrillas, but it participated in only two battles. At Brice's Cross Roads (also called Guntown), Confederates under Forrest routed a Union command. At the time, Sam suffered from a severe foot infection and remained in camp.[61]

One month later, a Federal command of 14,000, almost twice as large as the one at Brice's Crossroads, under a new commander and including a game but injured Sam Evans repulsed a Confederate attack by Forrest and others at Tupelo, Mississippi. Sam's company helped repel a Rebel advance on the Union wagon train on July 13, inflicting a dozen or so casualties. The next day, they skirmished periodically with the enemy and launched a successful counterattack at night. Sam emerged with a slight scratch on the side of his head from a ball. It removed a chunk of hair above his right ear but "did not enter the hide."[62]

In combat or in camp, on the march or in garrison, skirmishing guerrillas or assisting refugees, issuing commands to black soldiers or receiving them from ranking white officers, the experiences of war helped Sam to clarify his views on the great issues of the day. "The cause in which we are engaged," Sam elucidated to his father after more than a year and a half of service, "is the cause of constitution and law, of civilization and freedom of man and God." Admit to the right of secession, he argued, and one might as well acknowledge the power to abrogate the results of a free election and set that once-mighty and prosperous country on the course of anarchy and despotism.

For Sam, the war placed the incompatibility of freedom and slavery in sharp relief. While he had entered the army to restore the Union and preserve freedom as it existed in 1860, he came to the realization that those goals were not enough. Just as secession endangered freedom, so true liberty could not coexist with slavery. Wartime exposure and occurrences had convinced him that he must work to broaden the ranks of the free to include blacks. No longer could he sing the praises and bask in the joys of freedom while people of Africans descent were held in bondage. He must fight, and so should fellow Northern patriots and lovers of liberty. "*Better settle it at whatever cost and settle it forever*," he believed. Certainly the price was high, particularly the loss of human beings, but freedom never came cheaply, not for the Pilgrims and other colonists, not for the Revolutionary generation, and not for them. "In this view," he determined, "war is most horrible, but human *rights are worth more* than *human life*." He could see no way around it. Everyone in the Northern states who could serve in the military should do so, and all others ought to support them in every way they can. Anyone who opposed the war he branded a traitor.[63]

When Sam's first cousin Jane Evans announced her opposition to both Lincoln and the war in late summer 1864, the first lieutenant blasted her. Jane despised the war, the pain and suffering it had inflicted on the North, and the changes it wrought on the status of blacks. She declared her hatred of the draft and did not want Sam's youngest brother, Laban, to have to fight for and perhaps be buried alongside a Negro. After simmering for several weeks, Sam carefully drafted his rebuke. He accused Jane of "treasonous language" for her hostility toward Lincoln and the war, calling her a Rebel and friend to Confederate President Jefferson Davis. "It would be more honorable," he assured her, "to be burried by the side of 'a' brave 'Negro' who fell fighting for the *glorious old banner* than to be burried by the side of some *cowardly Cur* (in human form) who died for fear he would be drafted and who had proven himself *recreant* to the *Boon* of Liberty consecrated by the Blood of our Forefathers."[64]

Back at home, Andrew Evans had come around to espouse similar opinions. As a father with two sons still in the service, and as a citizen with deep devotion to his country, Andrew endorsed anything that aided the war effort. The elder Evans loathed advocates of peace without victory, and he worked vigorously to strengthen the course of war. Like his son, the Squire supported " 'Abe' and 'Andy,' " as Sam called the Union presidential ticket of Lincoln and Andrew Johnson, and labored for Republican and Union candidates in the 1864 election. Hundreds of miles apart, they celebrated Union victories, grieved over Lincoln's assassination, and grew uneasy over the successor, Johnson.[65]

Between father and son, letter after letter on politics and the war flowed. Sam offered the perspectives of soldiers; Andrew provided the stance of the politically active who supported the war. Over time, they built an interesting cross-generational consensus, one based on their support of the war.

In the state legislature, Andrew Evans blended an unyielding endorsement of the war with a lofty brand of patriotism. When two locals who had been chosen in the draft ran off to Canada, he promised to introduce legislation in the next session to disenfranchise them in the State of Ohio. Bills to increase bounties for enlistees and for pay raises for state and county officials met with his disapproval. The Squire thought a man should fight for his country, not for money, and everyone needed to share in the burdens of war, including authorities at home. To this, Sam agreed. In a meeting among the officers in his regiment to lobby for pay raises, Sam voiced his opposition. They would only increase the public debt, he argued, and officers already made enough money if they used it wisely.[66]

In their quest for Union victory, first Sam and ultimately his father altered their views on race. Wartime experiences had converted Sam to emancipation and black military service. Despite his father's pronouncements earlier in the war, Andrew, with all the passion of a late convert, embraced those issues and sometimes exceeded his son in his enthusiasm for the political changes brought on by the war. He announced that he was "proud of the privilege" to cast his vote in the legislature in favor of the Thirteenth Amendment to the U.S. Constitution abolishing slavery. Several months later, while Sam hesitated to support proposals to grant blacks the right to vote at that time, believing the situation in the South was too unsettled for it, his father enthusiastically promoted the idea of African American suffrage. When Democrats threatened to use the black-vote issue against Republicans in the upcoming state and local elections, the Squire declared a willingness to meet the matter directly. "I had rather stand by and vote with a Loyal Black man," he proclaimed, "than a white Traitor." Such strong views on race no doubt damaged Andrew's political aspirations. He narrowly lost reelection to the Ohio House of Representatives in 1865. Nonetheless, son had changed father, and then father absorbed the lessons more thoroughly than the son.[67]

Sam remained in the army until the 59th U.S. Colored Infantry was mustered out of service at the end of January 1866. During those last eight months, he oversaw occupation duties and worked for the Freedmen's Bureau, struggling with thorny political and labor issues between Southern whites and former slaves. He grew increasingly disenchanted with President Johnson.[68]

By the time Sam returned home, almost four years to the day he left for the army, much had changed. Just before his brother John's death, Amos had written him, "I set 2 Evergreens in the front yard in memory of Doc & John knowing he must die. if I am gone when you get home (if you ever do) you will see them & think of me." He did. Amos passed away on Thanksgiving Day, 1864, and his sister Ann expired before he could make it home. Sam had lost four siblings and his grandmother. His girlfriend Callie left him for another.[69]

Home was not the only thing different. Sam, too, had changed. Physically, he had aged a tough four years and filled out thirty pounds. Fortunately, at six feet one inch tall, he could carry 175 pounds easily.[70]

The war had instilled a new confidence in him as well. Like his political and racial views, Sam's standing with his father had evolved during the war and had acted as a catalyst for his father's shift in attitudes. No longer patriarch to minion, the proud Andrew treated his adult son with newfound respect and a deeper form of fatherly love. Sam's rite of passage was complete. Andrew Evans died in 1879.

Sam lived in the community the rest of his life. He married Margaret Shelton in 1867, and the couple had eight children. He named the oldest U. S. Grant. Although Sam never accumulated the wealth of his father, he garnered his own accolades for public service, holding all sorts of local offices over the years, including justice of the peace. Service in the United States Colored Troops had never hurt his career. In fact, it gave him a new appreciation for African Americans, and it most assuredly enhanced his appreciation for what he and his Union comrades — black and white — had accomplished. He died of heart failure in 1910, a proud veteran, a Civil War pensioner, and a member of the Grand Army of the Republic.[71]

Notes

The author would like to thank Mr. Gary Arnold of the Ohio Historical Society for his assistance, and Dr. Joan Cashin for her advice and help.

1. For a better understanding of racial attitudes there, see Joan E. Cashin, "Black Families in the Old Northwest," *Journal of the Early Republic* 15 no. 3 (Fall 1995): 449–75; Leon Litwack, *North of Slavery: The Negro in the Free States, 1790–1860* (Chicago, 1961).

2. *History of Brown County, Ohio* (Chicago, 1883), Biographical Sketches, 156, 494, 496, 506; Carl N. Thompson, *Historical Collections of Brown County, Ohio* (Piqua, Ohio, 1969), 682–83; Federal Census of 1860, Brown County, Huntington Township, 295; Amos to Sam, 25 May 1862. Evans Family Papers (hereafter EFP). Copies are in the possession of the author, who would like to thank Ms. Anne Geiss.

3. *History of Brown County, Ohio*, Biographical Sketches, 156–57, 496; Thompson, *Historical Collections*, 682–83, 767–69. Compiled Military Service Record of Samuel Evans, 70th Ohio Infantry. Record Group (hereafter RG) 94, National Archives (hereafter NA). His brothers and sisters appear to have been more active in church matters than Sam was.

4. *Federal Census of 1860*, vol. 1, *Population*, 365–69, 375–76.

5. *Federal Census of 1860*, vol. 2, *Agriculture*, 112–19; vol. 3, *Manufacturing*, 442.

6. *History of Brown County*, Biographical Sketches, 156; Patricia R. Donaldson, ed., *Brown County, Ohio Marriage Records, 1818–1850* (Georgetown, Ohio, 1986), 43.

7. Jane to Affectionate Cousin [Sam], 11 Sept. 1864. Also see Sam to Miss Jane Evans, 15 Oct. 1864. Sam to Father, 15 Feb. 1863. EFP; Thompson, *Historical Collections*, 767.

8. For the unit history, see Thomas W. Connelly, *History of the Seventieth Ohio Regiment* (Cincinnati, n.d.).

9. Joseph Shelton Evans Jr., "The Evans Civil War Letters," introduction. Typescript in possession of the author.

10. Will Evans to Brother, 19 Feb. 1862. EFP.

11. For good discussions of the patriarchal family in the nineteenth century, see Steven Mintz, *A Prison of Expectations: The Family in Victorian Culture* (New York, 1983), 27–32 and E. Anthony Rotundo, *American Manhood: Transformations in Masculinity from the Revolution to the Modern Era* (New York, 1993), 25–28. Also see Stephen M. Frank, *Life with Father: Parenthood and Masculinity in the Nineteenth-Century American North* (Baltimore, 1998).

12. Amos took on most of the farm and home duties, but the blacksmith shop closed and the mill ran at odd hours. For information on birth order and its impact on relationships with siblings, see Stephen P. Bank and Michael D. Kahn, *The Sibling Bond* (New York, 1982).

13. Sam to Father, 26 Feb. 1862. EFP.

14. Sam to Father, 30 Mar. 1862. Also see Sam to Father and Mother, 16 Mar. 1862. D. B. Kimble to Sam, 11 Oct. 1862. EFP.

15. Andrew Evans to Sam, 9 Mar. 1862. EFP.

16. James J. Burke to Friend John, 13 Mar. 1862. Amos to Brother, 28 Mar. 1862. EFP.

17. For information on the 70th Ohio at Shiloh, see "After Action Reports" (hereafter AAR) of Brig. Gen. W. T. Sherman, 10 Apr. 1862. Col. Ralph P. Buckland, 9 Apr. 1862. Col. Joseph R. Cockerill, 10 Apr. 1862. *The War of the Rebellion: A Compilation of the Official Records of the Union and Confederate Armies* (Washington, D.C., 1900) (hereafter *OR*), ser. 1, vol. 10, pt. 1, 248–54 and 266–72; T. J. Lindsey, *Ohio at Shiloh: Report of the Commission* (Cincinnati, 1903), 35–36.

18. See AAR of Cockerill, 10 Apr. 1862. *OR* ser. 1, vol. 10, pt. 1, 270; George B. Davis, Leslie J. Perry, Joseph W. Kirkley, and Calvin D. Cowles, *Atlas to Accompany the Official Records of the Union and Confederate Armies* (1891–95; reprint, New York, 1978), plate 10, map 10; Connelly, *Seventieth Ohio*, 21–26.

19. J. B. Evans to Father, 10 Apr. [1862]. EFP. Also see AAR of Cockerill, 10 Apr. 1862. *OR* ser. 1, vol. 10, pt. 1, 270.

20. Sam to Father, 11 May 1862. EFP.

21. Sam to Father, 11 May 1862. EFP.

22. AAR of Cockerill, 10 Apr. 1862. Casualties List. *OR* ser. 1, vol. 10, pt. 1, 270, 104.

23. J. B. Evans to Father, 10 Apr. [1862]. Sam to Father, 2 Nov. 1863. EFP. Also see Affidavit of Samuel Evans, 15 June 1883. Pension file of Samuel Evans. RG 15, NA.

24. Sam to Squire in J. B. Evans to Father, 10 Apr. [1862]. EFP.

25. Andrew Evans to Sam, 28 Sept. 1862. Sam Evans to Father and Mother, 24 May 1862. Amos to Sam, 25 May 1862. EFP.

26. Sam to Father, 11 May 1862. Sam to Father, 1 May 1862. EFP.

27. S. H. Martin to Sam, 1 Apr. 1862. Jas. S. Burke to Sam, 8 Apr. 1862. EFP.

28. Sam to Father, 22 July, 12 June, 1 Dec. 1862. EFP. Sam's captain boasted about what a great soldier Sam was. See Sam to Father, 8 Feb. 1863.

29. Sam to Father, 12 June 1862. Sam to Father, 24 May 1862. EFP.

30. Amos to Sam, 21 Sept. 1862. EFP.

31. Andrew Evans to Sam, 31 Aug. 1862. EFP.

32. Sam to Father, 21 Oct. 1862. Amos to Sam, 13 Oct. 1862. Order of Col. Martin Crain, 14 Oct. 1862. Father to Sam, 19 Oct. 1862. Also see Sam to Father, 6 Dec. 1862, 16 Jan. 1863. Father to Sam, 8 Feb. 1863. EFP.

33. Andrew Evans to Son, 2 Nov. 1862. Also see Andrew Evans to Son, 5 Apr. 1863. EFP.

34. Sam to Father, 26 Apr., 4 Jan., 20 Jan. 1863. Amos to Brother Sam, 16 June 1862. Sam Evans to Parents, 12 Oct. 1862. EFP. Also see Special Order, No. 270. HQ, 1st Div., Dist. of W. Tenn. 9 Oct. 1862. Unbound Correspondence, 70th Ohio Volunteer Infantry, RG 94, NA; Lt. Col. D. W. C. Loudon memo, 31 Dec. 1862. Compiled Military Service Record of Samuel Evans, 70th Ohio Infantry, RG 94, NA.

35. For more information, see Joseph T. Glatthaar, Forged in Battle: The Civil War Alliance of Black Soldiers and Their White Officers (New York, 1990), 4–6; Joseph T. Glatthaar, "Black Glory," in Why the Confederacy Lost, ed. Gabor S. Boritt (New York, 1992), 140–47.

36. J. B. Evans to Brother, 11 Aug. 1862. Sam Evans to Father, 22 July 1862, 31 Oct. 1862. Sam Evans to Grandmother, 25 July 1862. EFP.

37. Sam to Father, 8 Feb. 1863. EFP; Thompson, Historical Collections, 767.

38. See Father to Sam, 22 May 1863, EFP, on Sam's opinions of blacks before he entered the service. Lt. Col. D. W. C. Loudon to Brig. Gen. W. S. Smith, 5 May 1863. Unbound Correspondence, 70th Ohio Volunteer Infantry. RG 94, NA.

39. Sam to Father, 17 May 1863. EFP. For more information on black soldiers, see Dudley T. Cornish, The Sable Arm: Negro Troops in the Union Army, 1861–1865 (New York, 1956); James McPherson, The Negro's Civil War: How American Negroes Felt and Acted during the War for the Union (New York, 1965); Glatthaar, Forged in Battle.

40. Sam to John, 3 May 1863. EFP. Sam broke the news, interestingly enough, in a letter to his brother Amos between May 3 and May 10, which has not survived.

41. Sam to Father, 10 May 1863. EFP. On May 11, Sam was assigned to recruiting duty for his company. See Special Orders, No. 118. HQ, 1st Div., 16 AC. 11 May 1863. Regimental Order and Court Martial Book, 70th Ohio Infantry. RG 94, NA.

42. See Sam to Father, 10 May 1863. Also see Sam Evans to Father, 31 Oct. 1862, 28 Jan., 21 Feb., 1 Mar. 1863. EFP; Robert Cowden, A Brief Sketch of the Organization and Services of the Fifty-Ninth Regiment of United States Colored Infantry (Dayton, Ohio, 1883), 51.

43. Sam to Father, 17 May 1863. EFP.

44. Ann Delia Evans to Brother Sam, 17 May 1863. Amos to Brother Sam, 14 May 1863. EFP.

45. Andrew Evans to Son, 18 May 1863. EFP.

46. Andrew Evans to Sam, 24 May 1863. EFP.

47. Sam to Father, 1 June 1863. EFP.

48. Andrew Evans to Son, 7 June 1863. EFP.

49. Sam to Brother Amos, 9 June 1863. EFP.

50. See Amos to Sam, 14 May, 17 June 1863. Andrew Evans to Sam, 16 May 1862, 18 May, 31 May 1863. EFP.

51. Andrew Evans to Son, 5 Apr. 1863. Sam to Father, 19 Apr., 26 Apr. 1863. EFP.

52. Andrew Evans to Sam, 13 Apr., 14 June, 27 June 1863. Sam to Father, 31 Aug. 1863. EFP.

53. Andrew Evans to Son, 16 Aug., 22 Nov. 1863. EFP. Brough won the gubernatorial election in Brown County and the state. The soldier vote in Brown County gave both Brough and Evans their majority. Andrew ran slightly ahead of the governor. See Joseph P. Smith, ed., *History of the Republican Party in Ohio* (Chicago, 1898), 1:161.

54. Sam to Father, 10 May, 17 May 1863. EFP.

55. Sam to Father, 17 May, 14 June, 22 June, 16 May, 23 Aug. 1863. EFP.

56. Sam to Father, 23 Aug., 16 Aug., 31 Aug., 15 Nov. 1863, 10 Feb., 5 May, 16 May 1864. EFP; Cowden, *Fifty-Ninth Regiment*, 51, 55.

57. Sam to Father, 27 Sept. 1863. EFP.

58. Sam to Father, 27 Sept., 1 Nov., 15 Nov. 1863, 27 Mar., 24 Apr., 16 Sept. 1864. EFP. Also see Company and Regimental Order Books, 59th U.S. Colored Infantry. RG 94, NA.

59. Sam to Father, 15 Nov. 1863. EFP.

60. Sam to Father, 22 Mar. 1863. EFP.

61. Sam to Father, 16 May, 22 May 1864. EFP. Also see AAR of Lt. Col. Robert Cowden, 24 June 1864. OR ser. 1, vol. 39, pt. 1, 903–5.

62. Sam to Father, 24 July 1864. EFP. Also see AAR of Col. Edward Bouton, 25 July 1864, AAR of Maj. James C. Foster, 24 July 1864. OR ser. 1, vol. 39, pt. 1, 300–3, 905–6.

63. Sam to Father, 13 Sept. 1863, Father to Sam, 7 May 1865. EFP.

64. Jane Evans to Affectionate Cousin, 11 Sept. 1864. Sam Evans to Miss Jane Evans, 15 Oct. 1864. EFP.

65. Sam to Father, 10 Oct. 1864, 17 Apr., 9 July, 16 Oct. 1865. Father to Son, 16 Oct. 1864, 11 Mar., 16 Apr., 23 Apr., 29 Oct. 1865. EFP.

66. Andrew Evans to Son, 9 Oct. 1864, 15 Jan. 1866. Sam to Father, 27 Jan. 1865. EFP. In 1865, the state House never took up the issue of draft dodging. See *Journal of the House of Representatives of the State of Ohio*, 56th Session, vol. 61 (Columbus, 1865).

67. Andrew Evans to Son, 5 Feb., 9 July, 15 Oct. 1865. Sam to Brother Will, 21 July 1865. EFP.

68. See Compiled Military Service Records of Lt. Samuel Evans, 59th U.S. Colored Infantry. RG 94, NA; Sam to Father, 21 July, 18 Aug., 16 Sept., 8 Oct., 16 Oct. 1865. EFP.

69. Amos to Sam, 27 May 1863. Andrew Evans to Son, 27 Nov. 1864, 28 Jan. 1866. EFP.

70. See Regimental Descriptive and Consolidated Morning Report Book, 70th Ohio Infantry. RG 94, NA; Sam to Father, 7 Jan. 1866. EFP.

71. Certificate of Death, 27 May 1910, in pension file of Sam Evans. RG 15, NA; *History of Brown County*, Biographical Sketches, 157. There are no records of his opinions on Reconstruction.

Chapter 15

Union Father, Rebel Son: Families and the Question of Civil War Loyalty

AMY E. MURRELL

✦ WHEN nineteen-year-old Henry Stone joined the Confederate army, he did not just turn against the Union, or what he called the "cursed dominion of Yankeedom." He also rebelled against his family and especially his father. Stone's parents were natives of Kentucky, but by 1861 were living in southern Indiana with Henry and his brothers. They were staunch Unionists, and at least one of Henry's four brothers volunteered for the Union army. But in August 1862 Henry, a middle child, felt drawn to fight for the Southern cause. He kept his decision secret, since he knew that his family would try to stop him, and he ran away without leaving even a note behind. He disguised himself as a poor farmer to make his way past Union pickets and arrived in Kentucky to join the cavalry of John Hunt Morgan. After a month he revealed his whereabouts to his father: "Pap, I do not regret one practical my leaving home and every day convinces me I did right," he explained, yet the personal cost of departing was not lost on him. "I can imagine how your feelings are, one son in the Northern and another in the Southern Army," he acknowledged, "But so it is. . . . Good times will come again." He signed his letter, "your rebelling son, Henry."[1]

Families such as the Stones were not supposed to divide when the Civil War came. Nineteenth-century Americans idealized the family as the bedrock of society, a private haven from the rancorous public world of politics and war. Mothers, fathers, and children found security and formed their identities within the family; it even provided a model of social relations for the society at large. But when the war came, the border between North and South cut right through families' households. As the *Columbia Missouri Statesman* observed in 1861, "Secession has broken up the dearest social relations in every community of the border slave States, turning son against father, brother against brother, daughter against mother, friend against friend."[2] Newspaper columns lamented the division of families. Few professed to understand how this basic social unit could give way to such destructive conflict.

Countless Americans witnessed the division of their households during the Civil War, but nowhere was this more pronounced than in the border states. In Tennessee, Kentucky, Virginia, Maryland, and Missouri, the slaveholding states of the upper South, decades of political conflicts had splintered the population and rendered national loyalties unpredictable. This was a region that put forth some of the most significant compromises to stave off sectional conflict in the 1850s, and where voters in 1860 supported moderate candidates over the more radical Republicans or Southern Democrats. Yet it was also where consensus was elusive once the Civil War came, as these states either seceded reluctantly after months of debate, as in the cases of Tennessee and Virginia, which eventually splintered in two, or remained in the Union despite vocal secessionist minorities. Kentucky's own governor, for example, supported efforts to establish an alternative Confederate government in his Union state, while in Missouri guerrilla warfare continually drew the state's citizens into violent confrontation. In this region where, as one Kentuckian put it, "treason & loyalty overlap," and where reluctant Confederates and latent Unionists lived side by side during the Civil War, the line between North and South fell in unexpected places, dividing friends, neighbors, and families.[3]

This essay examines the divided loyalties of fifty-two border state families who shared the specific division experienced by the Stone family: the enlistment of a son in the Confederate army despite the Union sympathies of his father. In each of these families, and in many others like them, wartime political allegiances settled along generational fault lines, creating an explosive situation that mirrored the greater conflict between the Union and the Confederacy. Why these families experienced such division is not easily answered. These families were, like so many families in the upper South, landowners who made their living by raising livestock and wheat. They generally lived in the low-lying areas rather than in the mountains, and most were slaveowners with holdings of under twenty slaves. They did not engage in the sort of large-scale plantation agriculture of the lower South, but were still fairly wealthy, educated, and prominent in their communities. In most cases their nuclear families were intact, with mothers, stepmothers, sisters, and brothers sharing their households and generally working together on the family land. Yet when war came the sons, who averaged twenty-two years of age, enthusiastically left home to volunteer for the Confederate service, while their fathers remained Union spokesmen for compromise and moderation.[4]

Fortunately these Union fathers and their rebel sons did a lot of arguing on paper during the war, explaining in vivid detail why they believed their loyalties were divided. Even though rebel sons that split from their fathers in most cases departed from brothers, sisters, or a mother too, it was the conflict between father and son that inspired the most introspection. Male kin disagreed in particular about how personal their conflict was and to what extent their national loyalties were linked to or contingent upon their personal, family loyalty. Together their letters offer a collective rumination on the interconnection of politics and family, of public and private life, in mid-century America. And out of this dialogue emerges a paradox of divided families: the same personal, family loyalties that gave way to and even fed the turmoil of war also provided the strongest basis for reconciliation. The divided border state family proved remarkably resilient even as it was most tested, and perhaps for that reason became a cultural resource for a nation also trying to come to terms with the meaning of rebellion.

The brewing rebellion of the sons became apparent to border state observers even before the fall of Fort Sumter. As early as February 1861, twenty-year-old Josie Underwood noticed that in her hometown of Bowling Green, Kentucky, "all the men . . . of any position or prominence whatever are Union men—and yet many of these men have wild reckless unthinking inexperienced sons who make so much noise about secession as to almost drown their fathers wiser council." Border state newspaper editors also took note of this family dynamic, including the *Louisville Daily Journal*, which months later declared father and son conflict an "epidemic" and began writing lengthy essays ruminating on its pervasiveness.[5]

What these observers noticed was the climax of a generational conflict that had been emerging throughout border state society in the decade prior to 1861. During the secession crisis some of the most vigorous proponents of slavery and states' rights were young men born in the 1830s and 1840s. These were men who had never known a time without sectional conflict, who had witnessed tenuous political compromises in Missouri as well as violent threats to slavery in "Bleeding Kansas" and in Harper's Ferry, Virginia. What they saw all around them was the elusiveness of a national consensus on slavery and sectionalism, and a political landscape in which division was the norm. This created a situation in which it was nearly impossible not to take a vigorous stance on the political issues of the day. These young men, while not unique in their support of slavery or Southern rights, developed a passionate enthusiasm for secession that set them apart from older generations, and, in some cases, their own fathers.[6]

Their fathers, meanwhile, were fixtures of the border state political establishment: among them were a Maryland governor, two Kentucky senators, and several congressmen. Most were either Whigs, or as the war approached, Constitutional Unionists and Democrats intent on forging compromises to stave off civil war. Their political affiliations generally reflected the ideological and geographic middle ground in which they lived, and it appears that most tried to impart that same sense of moderation to their sons. "I would caution you against imbibing all the notions put forth by your advocates for slavery," was how one such father responded in 1857 to his son's blustery anti-abolitionist rant. To make a case for his views this father sent the son what he called a "sensible tract" written by a Kentucky minister. Fathers such as this one detected their sons' radicalism early, but rather than demanding conformity outright they generally permitted an open exchange on matters of sectional politics. Their letters reveal an energetic but tolerant exchange of ideas throughout the 1850s, as the fathers apparently believed that beneath their sons' political vigor was a deeper agreement on partisan loyalty.[7]

By 1861, however, the political letters of these fathers and sons had taken on a starkly different tone. Any degree of political difference was no longer something as benign as words on a page; in wartime it could translate into opposing allegiances across a deadly battle. As war seemed imminent, fathers grew less tolerant of their son's independent political expression and began demanding a greater degree of conformity — sometimes enlisting the help of other male kin to do so. These fathers did not demand that their sons think exactly like them, but they did draw a line at allowing their sons to act on their ideas. Service in the Confederate army was unacceptable. "Do not resign under any circumstances without consultation with me," one Kentucky father demanded of his son who he feared would leave the U.S. army for the South. Other fathers struck compromises, even promising to support their sons economically if they stayed out of the Confederate service. Still others, hopeful that the war would last only a few months, made their sons promise to stay at home for a year before enlisting in the Confederacy.[8]

Union newspaper writers challenged fathers to keep their sons away from the Confederacy and to get them into the Union army. "If the young men are slow to enlist in the cause of human freedom," one Kentucky paper wrote, "let the old men step forward, and by their patriotic example shame their degenerate sons and grandsons." The mechanism of fatherly authority was in this paper's view the most effective deterrent to a young man's Confederate service. After all, it was considered a father's duty in mid-nineteenth-century America to watch over and nurture his son's political allegiances. Mothers might instill in sons a more vague sense of civic duty and consciousness, but in matters of partisanship a father's example was to be paramount. This newspaper challenged fathers to live up to those expectations, and most fathers did so when they demanded political obedience from their sons. Their sons generally complied at first with their requests but over time found their absence from the service difficult to tolerate. In the first year of the war these awkward promises set the stage for the "epidemic" that the *Louisville Daily Journal* lamented.[9]

To refrain from service in the Confederate army created a dilemma for these sons. Twenty-three-year-old Matthew Andrews of Shepherdstown, Virginia (later West Virginia), for example, promised his father, a pro-Union Episcopal minister, that he would not serve and would remain in law school in Virginia. But this became difficult when his classmates began to enlist. "My position is getting more and more embarrassing every day," Matthew wrote to his fiancee. "All the young men in the town have joined one of the three companies formed here," and they did not understand why he failed to join them. The pressures of his peers were severe, and indeed similar pressures resulted in the enlistments of many other young men in the South. Yet Matthew vowed to remain out of the service, he went on to explain, because he did not want to "offend" his father. The elder Andrews, meanwhile, took the opportunity in letters to his son to reinforce his political authority. "I am much more calm than you are, & have a much more intelligent & impartial survey of the whole question," he argued on one occasion, and suggested that Matthew would come around to share his opinions within weeks.[10]

Sons such as Matthew Andrews faced additional obstacles to obeying their fathers and remaining out of the service after the first year of the war. In 1862 and 1863 both the Union and Confederate governments passed conscription laws that made military service mandatory for men between the ages of eighteen and forty-five. This made it impossible simply to remain home — almost every young man had to enlist in the army supported by his state. For sons in the Union states of Kentucky, Maryland, and Missouri, the idea of being forcibly conscripted into the Union army became an additional inducement to act on their Confederate sympathies and leave home quickly. Henry Stone, who opened this essay, explained to his father that at home in a Union state he "was in great danger of being drafted where I could not have served," whereas now, after leaving to join the Confederate army, "I'm contented." Sons in the Confederate states of Virginia and Tennessee had the laws on their side, which, in many cases, did encourage a son's enlistment. But even in these regions some fathers stepped in to prevent the laws from affecting their sons. Matthew Andrews' Union father, for example, used his connections to preempt the laws and to find his son a job in the paymaster's office in Richmond, reasoning that a government job was less odious than having his son serve as a combatant against the Union.[11]

Other sons resorted to sneaking away from their fathers when it became too difficult to resist the pressures of their peers or the law. Twenty-year-old Ezekiel (Zeke) Clay's story was typical. In the years leading up to the war he was schooled by several prominent spokesmen of compromise and Union: his father, Brutus, was a Whig leader and member of the Kentucky legislature; his uncle, Cassius Clay, was a vigorous abolitionist; and his distant cousin, Henry Clay, was the architect of several plans to save the Union from civil war. Zeke also had a significant circle of friends his age who frequented pro-secession speeches and rallies and who encouraged him to join them. Zeke's family knew of his dalliances with secession ideas but was openly tolerant of his views, even in the first months of the war. His stepmother, Ann, kept her own Union opinions quiet even while venting to her husband that Zeke talked "like some one crazy" about secession. His father simply kept his silence while apparently remaining confident that Zeke would uphold his agreement to manage the family property while he served in the legislature.[12]

Over a period of several weeks in September 1861, however, Zeke secretly plotted his departure for the Confederate army. He approached a Confederate officer about obtaining a commission, yet denied having done so when his stepmother heard rumors about the meeting. He also set about making gun cartridges to take with him — surreptitiously working right under his stepmother's nose — but again denied his true motives by claiming to make them for his father. Then one night in September 1861, after telling his stepmother that he was going loon hunting, Zeke rode off on his mare, bringing with him the blanket from his bed, one of his father's rifles, and a small amount of clothing. He left behind this breezy note on the parlor table to explain his departure: "I leave for the army tonight. I do it for I believe I am doing right. I go of my own free will. If it turns out that I do wrong I beg forgiveness. Good bye. E."[13]

Brutus Clay, like other fathers in this position, could hardly contain his anger when he heard of his son's departure. Zeke had acted with the same hotheaded zeal as the South Carolinians that Clay and other border state Union men condemned. His son also had failed to show a moderation in politics that Clay expected of all his sons, and, more personally, had reneged on his promises to his father to remain at home. Zeke evidently preferred to follow the lead of "every scamp in the country" rather than his own father's, Brutus thundered to his wife, Ann, who sympathized. It was "disgraceful," she responded, and she vowed to find out what it was that had "induced a boy to take sides against a father." To the Clays this was no ordinary case of two individuals disagreeing about sectional politics: it was a very personal case of filial defiance.[14]

Other Union fathers shared Brutus Clay's angry reaction to the secretive departures of their rebel sons. These fathers may have given their sons latitude to develop independent political views, but few had known how seriously to take their sons' expressions of Southern loyalty, and fewer yet predicted that their worst fears of Confederate service would be realized. Union fathers therefore had difficulty knowing how to respond to their sons' actions. If they accepted a son's Confederate service as an independent act of political conscience, then they would be acknowledging the son's outright rejection of their own political views. But if they attributed the defection to reckless and defiant behavior, as Brutus Clay seemed to prefer, it would be much easier to remain secure in one's position as a father. Their son's action might remain a serious betrayal, but a much more familiar and manageable one. In this sense a son's rebellion could be seen as just another coming-of-age struggle set against the dramatic backdrop of war.[15]

Fathers of the Civil War generation were quite familiar with this kind of conflict. Little consensus existed in mid-century prescriptive literature about the ideal relationship between fathers and sons. A historic tradition of paternal authority in the household was gradually being eroded by an antebellum trend toward a less authoritarian and more affectionate model of child-rearing. This left fathers and sons caught between expectations of paternal dominance and the impulse toward companionship. Where a father's authority and a son's deference met was rarely clear, and this created what one historian has called an "inherent ambivalence" between fathers and sons. Conflicts with fathers thus became a ritual of growing up for nineteenth-century sons, and this is what Civil War fathers saw in their sons' defection to the Confederacy: a very familiar and personal challenge to their paternal authority.[16]

Newspaper observers encouraged Union fathers to view their sons' Confederate service as a deliberate act of filial defiance. In one of the first analyses of divided fathers and sons, the Union-leaning *Louisville Daily Journal* published an article entitled "Letters of a Father" in 1861 that elaborated on why the present rebellion of sons was part of a very natural stage in life. The American "political and social system" contained an inherent contradiction, the paper argued, one in which sons were required to defer to their fathers at the same time they were instilled with republican values of liberty. The most readily available expression of that liberty was in the rejection at home of "filial piety," the paper continued, and for that reason father-and-son conflicts were a natural creation of the republican system. The rebellion of sons from their fathers in wartime was simply a reflection of this greater flaw in the American "national character," but even worse, in this paper's view, was the Confederacy's exploitation of this with "specious appeals to the natural love of liberty."[17]

Indeed, the Confederacy's call for independence meshed well with personal desires for autonomy among this younger generation of men. Historians of secession have found that younger generations felt a natural affinity to the Southern cause precisely because of the desire for liberty nurtured in their own homes. Fathers, the guardians of their inheritance and future livelihood as the owners of land and family businesses, at times posed a substantial obstacle to sons in their transition to adulthood. A father who was unwilling to give up land or otherwise assist his son in building an independent life for himself left his son in a dependent position. This aroused resentment in a son and a frustration that made the Confederate rhetoric of "independence" and "liberty" all the more resonant.[18]

The rebel sons considered here had reached this uncertain juncture in their lives. The majority were unmarried and between the ages of sixteen and twenty-five — the transition period between childhood and the independence of adulthood. Twenty-year-old Zeke Clay, for example, had recently dropped out of college from lack of interest and had returned home to work his father's land. Henry Stone, who opened this essay, also worked on his family's land and had not yet settled into the legal career that would occupy him later. Census returns from 1860 show that roughly two-thirds of these rebel sons likewise resided in their fathers' households, perhaps hoping to inherit land or eventually purchase acreage of their own. Their financial prospects ranged from being in debt, to working as apprentices, to relying on their fathers to put them through school, to striking out on their own for new land in the Texas southwest. Almost without exception these young men were unsettled in their lifelong careers and were self-conscious of their continued dependence on their fathers. Service in the Confederacy — acknowledged or not — therefore allowed them to embrace the reality of liberty, both financially and emotionally. As one son wrote to his father of his service, "[Y]our boy who left you six or seven months ago a mere child has now grown to manhood." In this euphemistic declaration of independence, the son suggested that his father accept his service as a defining moment in his emergence into adulthood.[19]

Personal "liberty" may have attracted sons to the Confederacy, but few fathers were willing to go so far as to translate this into a deep ideological commitment to the Confederacy. The notion that their sons instead possessed no ideas at all and were deluded or coerced into the Confederate service was a much more popular view. After hearing of his son's departure, Brutus Clay speculated that his son had been influenced by a "scamp," while other Union fathers similarly directed their frustration toward an anonymous influence deluding their sons. One Union father complained that "older & more wicked men" had "seduced" his son into service. The *Louisville Daily Journal* likewise concluded that one Union man's son probably would not have fought for the South "had not poisonous sophistries been poured into his ears by older men who had a design to corrupt his mind and seduce him into the paths of treachery."[20]

These "older men" who rivaled fathers for the sons' attention were no anomaly of war. Commonly known as "confidence men," "tricksters," or "seducers," they were a fixture of nineteenth-century fathers' anxieties. Fathers were fearful that once a son reached the age to strike out on his own, whether to purchase his own land or to begin a new career, strangers might take advantage of him, corrupt him, and destroy his character. Nothing, in a father's view, was more threatening to a son's republican liberty than the potential deception and corruption of an unscrupulous stranger. Young men eager to make their mark on the world were susceptible to the words of designing men, and the confusion of war, in a father's view, provided an ideal opportunity for such men to do their work.[21]

Sometimes these confidence men were familiar: a cousin, uncle, or longtime family friend who "talked secesh" and encouraged sons to accompany them to secession rallies.[22] Other times they worked at a distance, as did the fire-eating secessionists of the lower South. But no one worked harder to win over their sons' attention, fathers became convinced, than Confederate cavalry leaders. These men — with reputations of being more daring and more talented than their Union counterparts — cut a dashing figure and appealed to a young man's desire for adventure. The most influential in the border region was thirty-six-year-old Confederate captain John Hunt Morgan of Kentucky. Already legendary among Southern partisans as an embodiment of "chivalry" and "bravery," Morgan and his men swept through Kentucky and Tennessee in July 1862 on a raid that resulted in the successful imprisonment of 1,200 Union soldiers — and only 95 Confederate casualties. Word of his victories drew crowds along his route to catch a glimpse of the man who would eventually become a folk hero of the Confederacy. His reputation awed young men. "You can't hurt a Morgan man," one Kentucky son boldly concluded after signing on to Morgan's cavalry. At least one hundred "sons of our best and strongest Union men" followed him, a Kentucky woman later recalled.[23]

Morgan and his men, fathers believed, took advantage of their sons' desire for adventure and preyed on their sons to become followers. "My son," as one father described his departure with Morgan, "was seduced into the Rebel service by designing men." Referred to also as "Morgan's gang," and "Morgan's guerrilla party," this band of rebel soldiers unnerved Union families. Fathers were convinced that their sons were too young and too impressionable to resist Morgan's overtures, despite the best efforts of the sons to convince them otherwise. One Kentucky son tried to reassure his family that Morgan's men were "gentlemen of the best families of Ky.," and therefore honorable comrades in battle. But few parents accepted this notion, preferring instead to believe, as one father explained, that their sons had been a "victim" of Morgan's "folly & delusion."[24]

Other such influences, fathers believed, lurked within their own homes and were of a decidedly feminine cast. Indeed, some fathers discovered that the "scamp" luring their son in the wrong direction was no stranger but was instead a son's own mother. Who else had such close contact with and influence over sons than mothers? Union fathers had good reason to suspect a mother's influence. While one Virginia father tried to keep his son from volunteering for the Confederacy, his wife undermined him with letters to the son laced with pro-secession sentiment. "What is the benefit of plunging Ben into this certain destruction," this father asked of his wife, demanding that she protect, rather than endanger, their son. Another Tennessee mother chose to remain with her rebel son in the South rather than follow her Union husband north to escape the hardships of war. This mother remained in contact with her son throughout the war and effectively condoned his behavior despite his father's ardent Union stance.[25]

These women occupied an uncomfortable position, caught between the conflicting roles of mother and wife. They were responsible for their sons' development into good, civic-minded, and patriotic individuals, according to the expectations of antebellum political culture, and many sons looked to their mothers for guidance in the sectional crisis. Yet at the same time mothers were expected to defer to their husbands on matters of public affairs. In these particular cases women emphasized the former over the latter and effectively competed with a father in influencing a son's political choices. But in other cases, the idea that a mother's influence might result in a father and son meeting on a battlefield was agonizing, and, as one mother put it, "pursued me like a ghost." Accordingly, some mothers chose to suppress even their own Confederate instincts and to seek family unity by asking that their sons uphold their fathers' patriotic legacies. "Your dear Father never took sides either way," wrote one Missouri mother to her son. "Try and follow the bright example your beloved Father has set you."[26]

Whether it was a family member or a cavalryman who deterred a son from his father's example, however, Union fathers found in these outside influences a way of explaining their familial conflict. To blame someone else's influence was to place the blame on a society that produced unscrupulous men (or women), and on the youth and inexperience of otherwise good young men. A son's Confederate service was therefore not an expression of political conscience but instead symptomatic of a separate struggle over a father's own paternal authority. In this way fathers could define their conflict with their sons as something personal, and perhaps, more familiar and manageable.

This reading of the sons' behavior would seem to explain the common defection of the younger generation to the South, but to listen to the sons themselves is to hear an entirely different perspective on their Confederate service. They repeatedly and adamantly denied that their action was in any way a deliberate act of defiance against their father. As Henry Stone exclaimed when he heard of his father's anger over his rebellion: "Father, when you look over my career in the past eighteen months, do you feel that I am a traitor? Have I not done my duty, and have I not followed your teachings of right? Do you feel that I'm unworthy to be your son? God forbid!" While condemning what he called the "despotism" that his father supported, Stone still rejected the notion that he might be "unworthy" as a son. If anything, he believed his action to be entirely consistent with his father's teachings by following the dictates of his conscience.[27]

Clearly a son would have every reason to deny a personally motivated rebellion against his father. But in his denial was a very real conflict between fathers and sons, a disagreement over the relationship between family and political loyalties. Where fathers saw the two as intertwined — politics as a mere reflection of their personal relationship — sons argued that the two were entirely separate. "I am a secessionist, but that shall not conflict with a duty I owe my father — that of being respectful, and kind," Virginian William Thomson explained to his father in February 1861. Thomson drew a sharp distinction between being a secessionist and being a son, or between acting politically and acting personally. Dividing his loyalties in this way allowed Thomson and other sons to view their Confederate service quite differently — and more innocently — than their fathers did.[28]

Sons accordingly described their enlistment as a pure act of political conscience. Zeke Clay seemed to know his father would attribute his departure to youthful rebellion when he assured him in his departing note that "I do it for I believe I am doing right." "I know I'm right," wrote another son, but exactly how influential this sense of political "right" was in mobilizing sons is hard to determine. This same question has vexed most historians who study why soldiers fought in the Civil

War, and it is likely that a combination of both ideological convictions and personal considerations motivated most soldiers. But in letters to Union fathers, these rebel sons talk as if ideology was the only consideration that guided them in war. They wrote about fighting "tyranny," "Black Republicanism," and the "despotism of Lincoln," calling on popular rhetoric to emphasize that their military service was guided only by *politics*. Their division from their fathers could be explained simply as the divergent conclusions of two rational, thoughtful men.[29]

Behind those words, however, the political first principles of the sons did not differ terribly from those of their fathers. On the most central and divisive issue of the war — slavery — Union fathers and rebel sons were, for the most part, in striking agreement. Roughly three-quarters of the fathers were slaveholders, and thus, the majority of sons grew up in households in which slavery was openly accepted and tolerated. Rebel sons therefore could associate slavery with their father's interests and could see in secession the protection of something upon which their fathers depended. Although their fathers, in contrast, may have seen in secession the "doom of slavery," as one Virginia father put it, or acknowledged its eventual collapse, the sons still could argue that wartime service supported their fathers' principles. The only question that divided them was: how could slavery be best protected, by the Union or by an independent Confederacy? Similarly, on the future of the Union, fathers and sons found common ground, as each considered how to best combat the sources of disunion. One Kentucky son explained that he decided to "oppose Abolition more than secession, for one is the cause of our national dissension, the other the effect." His father, on the other hand, felt that preserving the Union was best served by opposing secession. Such ideological congruence on the war's central issues undoubtedly encouraged rebel sons to downplay filial rebellion and to claim that their service instead realized their fathers' true ideals.[30]

The sons may have been tempted to criticize their fathers' Union stance as a betrayal of their common ideals, but if they were thus tempted they restrained themselves in their letters home. They did not hold back, however, from objecting when their fathers attempted to punish them for their Confederate service. Indeed, Union fathers considered punishment a necessary response to the personal rebellion they detected in their sons' enlistment. "Just as he has acted, he will be dealt with," was how Brutus Clay furiously explained his decision to withdraw his son's inheritance after his departure. Since Zeke had denied Brutus his authority as a father, Brutus would reciprocate by refusing what he owed in return: protection. Disinheritance was rare among divided fathers and sons, but other fathers joined Brutus Clay in refusing to send money or clothing, even when it was possible to cross the lines to do so, and in preventing their sons from visiting their homes. These and other punishments served the indirect purpose of restoring the paternal authority that Union fathers lost when their sons defied them to join the Confederacy. Zeke Clay did not take his father's declaration seriously, however. With humor, he wrote to his stepmother to ask if the disinheritance meant he could still keep his wristwatch.[31]

Other sons took punishments more seriously. A father's disapproval was devastating enough, but many sons believed that their father's punishment was unwarranted. They saw little purpose in lessons on respect or obedience when they believed they still upheld these values in their support for the South. One punishment in particular was deemed especially unfair: a father's refusal to write letters. Certainly security measures taken by the Union and Confederate governments could make it more difficult to write frequently during the war, but it is clear that some fathers deliberately chose this as a form of punishment. After all, for most fathers and sons in peacetime, letter-writing was a basic means of sustaining a relationship. The failure to write regularly had always been a basis for chastisement, and not to write at all was an act of profound significance, a severing of emotional ties. In the insecurity of wartime, when soldiers found themselves lonely and threatened with death, this could be an especially devastating punishment.[32]

One Virginia father stopped writing after finding his sons' letters "full of the lies [of] Rebel Genl. Bobby Lee." Warner Thomson, a farmer trying to maintain a living in the path of war, became fed up with his son's rebel allegiance after his own livelihood was threatened. Thomson suffered financial losses when advancing Confederate troops forced him to flee his Shenandoah Valley home temporarily in 1863, and to make matters worse, his secession neighbors — especially women — had grown increasingly hostile toward him. An outcast, Thomson found it impossible to extend pleasantries to a son who allied himself with the Confederates and opted for silence over false sentiments. His son William, an eighteen-year-old aspiring teacher and a soldier in a Tennessee regiment, recoiled at his father's silence. "Pa has ceased to think of me as his son," he cried to his stepmother, complaining that his father evidently cared more about Abraham Lincoln than his own son. This was especially traumatic for him when his brother, Jonathan, who also joined the Confederate army, was imprisoned by Union authorities. Without his father to comfort him, William became dependent on the kindness of strangers to help him cope with his brother's imprisonment. For "all intents and purposes," William concluded of his situation, "I am a lone orphan."[33]

In his father's silence William detected that he had been consigned to the most desperate position of unwanted child. He saw the worst in the absence of his father's letters, revealing the extent to which he relied on his father's affection. His reaction was yet another reflection of the inherent ambivalence, or the tension between authority and affection, that characterized antebellum families. Whereas Warner Thomson, stunned by his son's Confederate service, chose to reemphasize his parental authority, William Thomson found his father's affection increasingly necessary and important once he endured the foul weather, loneliness, and tainted meat of his life in camp. In pleading letters William accused his father of violating an obligation to extend that affection toward his children: "No one is capable of more devotion to a parent than I am," he concluded, "but in order that this feeling should have *full* force, there must be a corresponding affection on the part of the parent."[34]

Warner Thomson's silence was an inadequate measure of his true sentiments, however. He was in fact more conflicted than William believed and found it difficult to condemn his son outright, even if his cause was "entirely wrong." Warner frequently turned to his diary to wrestle with their relationship. "My natural affection for my sons & love for my country," he once wrote, "cause a struggle in my mind — it is a painful one." Warner had difficulty reconciling his son's act with his desire to maintain their family ties. "I feel as if I am committing wrong to allow an active enemy of my country to remain in my house," he wrote of the idea of allowing William to visit, but "than I am met with the feelings of affection natural to a parent — it is a trial — sore trial." His loyalty to the Union cause — as well as his own security — compelled him to react as a stern patriarch; but deep down Warner possessed more complicated feelings toward his son. He temporarily resolved this conflict by asking family members for frequent reports on his son.[35]

Warner Thomson's reliance on other family members was not unusual. When relations between fathers and sons became strained, mothers and sisters — whether they wanted to or not — typically assumed a mediating position. In the Thomson family, Warner's wife (William's stepmother), Josephine, eventually became a surrogate correspondent. William believed that Josephine's intervention was essential for saving him from permanent orphan status: "I hope you will not fail to improve it," William wrote of his relationship to his father, asking that she encourage his father to communicate with him. Some women eagerly embraced this mediating position, writing letters, sending supplies, and even making appeals to fathers on their sons' behalf. Josephine Thomson, however, seemed only to resent being used as a surrogate. "You seem to wish me to write only that you may hear from him," she complained to William on one occasion, demanding that he carve out a separate place for her in his thoughts and feelings.[36]

Fathers might have found it less painful to join their sons in separating their political and familial lives, but something else kept them from doing so. A son's Confederate service was to their fathers even more than a private crisis of filial deference: it was a potential source of public embarrassment. In a region influenced by a Southern honor culture that forced people to think about how their friends and neighbors judged them, an errant son was a black mark to the family name. This was particularly true for men of military or political prominence, who contended daily with the scrutiny of both their allies and their pronounced enemies. Mid-nineteenth-century political culture revolved around establishing the reputations and character of men who became leaders. To what extent one's private or family life should affect or shape that public reputation, however, was not settled in the popular mind. So when wartime newspapermen floated rumors about the divided political loyalties of some of the nation's most prominent families, Union fathers were placed in an awkward position.[37]

Nothing illustrated this more vividly than one episode in Kentucky. It involved John J. Crittenden, a U.S. senator famous nationally for trying to prevent the war through compromise. Crittenden was known and respected among his Whig colleagues for his integrity, eloquent speeches, and cautious political skills, frequently referred to as "noble" and as a "great statesman" in the border-state press. Yet Crittenden had not been successful in exercising these conciliatory skills within his own household, as his youngest son, Thomas, dutifully became a soldier for the Union, while his oldest son, George, joined a Confederate regiment. George had disappointed his father before, with his weakness for alcohol and his penchant for debt, but his defection to the Confederacy for the first time made George the subject of press attention. In May 1862, George D. Prentice, the Unionist editor of the *Louisville Daily Journal*, published a scathing attack on George Crittenden's Confederate career. Crittenden had joined the Union's "malignant enemies" and had become one of the "most malignant of those enemies," Prentice wrote. His "treachery" was "sad," and had brought unknowable pain to his friends in Kentucky. For this, Prentice concluded, the name Crittenden "can no more be dishonored." The *St. Louis Daily Missouri Democrat* picked up this story and went further to suggest that Crittenden's rebel son "may somewhat affect his patriotism."[38]

John Crittenden was furious at these attacks. "My son is a rebel—I defend him not," he wrote three days later in a private letter to the *Journal*'s Prentice, "but what public good can such denunciations, as that article contains, do?" What angered Crittenden most was not the article's attack on George Crittenden's decision to go South—Crittenden himself had stopped writing to George for that very reason—but its suggestion that the Crittenden family honor had been damaged as a result. In keeping with his stature as an honorable statesman Crittenden corrected Prentice's assessment of his family: "Geo. B. Crittenden, save his act of Rebellion, & the occasional habit of intemperance, is beloved by all his family as one of the *best* & noblest of their race." Even though his son was "deluded" into rebellion, and his behavior deserved condemnation, Crittenden acknowledged, his family had come to believe that George was serving his cause well and acted with "honorable" intentions. Family honor, he claimed, was not necessarily damaged by a wayward son if that son acted honorably in his new position. For this reason Crittenden pronounced the article "most cruel."[39]

Equally galling to Crittenden was Prentice's apparent belief that there was some public benefit in revealing the Crittenden family problems to his readers. He urged Prentice, in a note at the bottom of his letter, to keep this matter "private" in the future. Crittenden thus claimed for himself and his family a right to privacy that some Americans believed was inherent in the growing division of middle-class life into separate spheres of home and world. Ideally, domestic life by mid-century was to stand distinct from the disruptions of work and politics, and this, Crittenden apparently believed, afforded him a wall of protection around his private life from the prying eyes of journalists. Of course such a demarcation, as numerous historians have documented, was never as neat as promised.[40]

George Prentice continually exploited that murky distinction between public and private life. He remained vigorous in his exposes of rebel sons, once advocating the hanging of the U.S. assistant surgeon general's rebel son as a means of restoring that family's honor. His attention to family life appears on the surface to be nothing other than the zealous behavior of an extremely patriotic Union man. Indeed, Prentice was, in the words of the *Richmond Enquirer*, "one of the most decided enemies of the Southern cause," and one of Kentucky's loudest Democratic voices against secession. To police the loyalties of families was in Prentice's view to defend the interests of the Union. But even as he delved into the private lives of others, Prentice soon found himself in the same position as other Union fathers: he too was placed on the defensive regarding *his own* rebel sons, twenty-three-year-old Courtland and twenty-year-old Clarence.[41]

Months after his attack on George Crittenden, Prentice learned that the *Cincinnati Commercial*, his strongest Republican rival, published rumors that his older son, Courtland, had stolen his prized silver mounted rifle when he joined John Hunt Morgan's cavalry. The paper speculated that Prentice found his son's behavior "disgraceful." Taking a page out of John Crittenden's book, Prentice immediately fired off a note to the *Commercial*, which was subsequently published in other border-state papers, denying that his son was guilty of stealing the rifle.

He never owned such a rifle, he explained, and went on to say he was sorry to see his "lamented boy" slandered. Prentice jumped to his son's defense, his position as a protective father temporarily outweighing the demands of his own politics. Prentice was partly motivated by the fact that Courtland lay defenseless in a hospital bed, the victim of friendly fire in Augusta, Kentucky. Prentice and his wife went to visit their son days after George wrote the response and witnessed their son's eventual death. Prentice asked readers a few days later to spare his family from additional newspaper coverage. "The tears of weeping eyes," he explained, "are not for the public gaze."[42]

Observers likely would have abided by his request, given that death and mourning were widely accepted as private and solitary matters. But Prentice undermined himself with a three-column eulogy of his son that first appeared in the *Journal* and later traveled in an abridged form to newspapers across Missouri and Ohio. In "William Courtland Prentice: A Brief Sketch," Prentice publicly mused on his son's virtues. Courtland was "manly" and possessed "the strength of a young Hercules." He was constantly in search of outdoor adventures and recognized as a skilled marksman after moving to Texas in 1860. He was also a "wild" and adventurous youth, who early on had grown impatient with school discipline. This, Prentice explained, made it difficult for Courtland to resist taking up arms when his loyalties directed him toward the South during the war. Although at first Courtland remained at home in deference to his father, he became miserable, "like an imprisoned lion." Prentice went on to explain that although he sympathized with him, he believed his son would have remained at home had it not been for those ubiquitous "bad men" who were able to lure his son away. Prentice concluded that his family would remember Courtland as a "brave and noble though misguided youth."[43]

Prentice did not explain what compelled him to delve into a character study of his son in the pages of the newspaper. Perhaps he believed that such an explanation was necessary to blunt the stinging criticism of his son's service. His eulogy effectively established that Courtland's service was an aberration in an otherwise harmonious father-son relationship: Courtland had been a loyal son despite his misery, George was a watchful father, and only outside influences had pushed Courtland into the rebel army. Not unlike John Crittenden he went even further to prop up Courtland's reputation with details about his sense of adventure and manly honor. Prentice might have hoped that his essay would silence the question of his family's honor once and for all, but instead his seemingly apologetic stance toward his son's Confederate service opened the floodgates for suspicion and innuendo.[44]

In March 1863 Prentice became the target of rumors that his other rebel son, Clarence, was feeding him information about the movements of Confederate troops. The *New York Times* charged that Prentice was on his way to Europe to escape the path of rebel troops whom he had been warned were making their way into Kentucky. It accused him of withholding this information from other Union partisans and thus using his connection to the Confederacy for selfish purposes. Prentice hotly denied the accusation in a letter to the editor and condemned the paper for subjecting his family to such "malignant calumnies." Months later, a rival border state newspaperman, Unionist William G. Brownlow of Tennessee, published a withering attack on Prentice's loyalty based on the rebel service of his surviving son. "You are but one degree removed from a rebel and a traitor," Brownlow reminded him, and for that reason "your paper is no longer a Union authority." This time Prentice chose silence rather than openly respond to what undoubtedly wounded him as a proud Union man.[45]

Prentice was only one target of a greater tendency among journalists to invoke family division as a way of questioning the reputations of public men. Most common were articles written by Union partisans to evaluate the position of Confederate leaders. Typical was a March 1862 article that originated in the *New York Tribune* and circulated through the border state press reporting that Confederate president Jefferson Davis and vice president Alexander H. Stephens were "of Yankee . . . paternity." The writer traced both men's parents to the town of North Killingly, Connecticut, where each supposedly had lived until finally settling in the South. Relatives of each man still lived in the town, the article noted, including an eighty-year-old man by the last name of Stephens who made the dubious claim of being a cousin of both men. "What could more forcibly exemplify the foolishness of the rebel cry of 'mudsills,' 'pedlers,' 'slaves,' 'cowards,' 'poltroons,' against Northern Society!" exclaimed the *Louisville Daily Journal*. Family ties made it impossible to draw sharp distinctions between the two societies upon which Southerners depended. It was hypocritical, this paper therefore charged, for these Southern leaders to distance themselves from a society to which they were so intimately related.[46]

Rumors of political division in Southern leaders' families played very well into Northern critics' hands. After all, it was the veneration of lineage and kinship, so central to Southern conceptions of honor and gentility, that Confederate leaders and writers often identified to distinguish their new nation from the corrupt and degenerate Yankees. The Confederate nation was a perfected land of cavaliers, descended directly from English bloodlines both noble and pure. Yet, Northern critics charged, this revealed nothing more than a distorted genealogy. "The parents of Jeff Davis and Alex Stephens were probably no better than the average of Yankee men and women," the *Louisville Daily Journal* put it succinctly. Although the paper actually was mistaken—Davis's parents were born and raised in South Carolina, while Stephens's were from Georgia—the deeper point underlying the attack was more credible. It was a fallacy for Confederates to suggest that their family identities were as distinct as their political ones.[47]

Jefferson Davis's bloodlines continued to attract Union attention. Stories abounded of various Davis children born illegitimately and residing in different parts of the country. He was rumored to be the father of an Indian child in Wisconsin, as well as of a Minnesota boy turned "assassin." Such stories—however fictionalized—represented Davis to readers as a promiscuous man, one who actively blurred the genetic lines that supposedly existed between the North and South. A more widespread paternity rumor, however, portrayed Davis actively blurring racial lines by fathering a son with one of his slaves in Mississippi. This story, which first appeared in February 1864, reportedly originated with a *London Times* reporter who was tipped off by an anonymous source "occupying a high position in the United States." The reporter, accompanied by an officer in the Union navy, traveled to Mississippi, conducted an investigation, and declared the story confirmed by the child's mother. The story then took off, appearing in Union newspapers across the country, from the *Boston Journal* to the *St. Louis Daily Missouri Democrat*.[48]

The story changed from version to version. Sometimes it was the mother's name that was different, other times it was the circumstances of Davis's relationship with the enslaved woman that varied. But one detail was consistent in all accounts: that the son was now serving in the Union navy under the name "Purser Davis." "Jeff Davis's Son in the Federal Service," proclaimed one such story, which noted with glee the irony of the Confederate president facing his black son in battle. Another telling of the story entitled "Miscegenation by Jeff. Davis" was not so amused but made no secret of its usefulness. "This same Jeff. Davis flaunts abroad his professions of Christianity, and sneers at the Puritanical habits of New England," the *St. Louis Daily Missouri Democrat* pointed out, while "his own life is a fitting exemplification of the *Barbarism of Slavery*."[49]

Different layers of this story served different purposes. To an abolitionist it was another example of the sexual exploitation of enslaved women, as the St. Louis paper suggested. To Republicans accused by fellow Northerners of embracing interracial sex in their calls for emancipation, it was proof that Southerners themselves were the worst practitioners of miscegenation. (One such newspaper even coined the term "Davisegination.") And to patriotic Unionists the idea of a white Confederate leader sharing bloodlines with a black Union soldier again poked holes in Southern pretensions of racial and genetic purity. It did not matter whether this story was true or not, or that Davis apparently ignored it and did not publicly respond. Those who latched onto it were searching for something with which to undermine Davis's, and the Confederacy's, legitimacy as a separate nation apart from the Union. Private family histories linking Northerners and Southerners together provided a useful and popular means.[50]

Confederate lineage thus captured the Union imagination, as some of the South's most prominent families had their family trees scrutinized in the pages of Union newspapers. Most accounts centered on families in which recent generations appeared to "betray" their ancestors' national loyalty. The Lees of Virginia made frequent appearances, with articles praising Revolutionary War hero Henry "Light Horse Harry" Lee while condemning his son, Robert E. Lee. The Keys of Maryland were also noticed when it became known that Francis Scott Key's daughter was under investigation for Confederate spy activity. The Breckinridges of Kentucky, who produced a Confederate general, likewise were lamented in the pages of newspapers. Kentuckian Henry Clay, long identified with forging compromises to stave off civil war, was featured for having several grandsons who fought for the Confederacy. The Clay grandsons' service was a "sad" postscript to the storied life of that "illustrious statesman," according to the *Louisville Daily Journal*. Most troubling was the family of Thomas Jefferson. "Alas, how his descendants are divided in this war!" exclaimed the *Nashville Daily Press* before outlining how all the former president's grandsons were fighting for the Confederacy while his granddaughters sided with their Union husbands.[51]

Tracing the political lineage of these prominent families offered to Southerners an effective reminder of where they came from, and to Northerners additional ballast for their charge of Confederate treason. But indirectly this process also established a blueprint for reconciliation. Implicit in these articles, and in the greater impulse to identify the "Union" heritage in Southern families, was a sense of impermanence. Political division and alienation could hardly endure when the force of history and family ties were fully realized; Confederates and Unionists alike could not ignore their deep interconnections. Private, family life thus was centrally linked to the future of the nation. These genealogies demonstrated that there was something deep and inalienable that bound Northerners and Southerners together, something that would provide the basis of reunion.

Reluctantly or not, nearly every pair of divided fathers and sons acknowledged the pull of these personal ties at some point during the war. As we have seen, the death of his son in battle compelled George Prentice to sentimentalize their relationship; an attack on his son's honor similarly drew John Crittenden to his son's defense. Death, illness, and the loneliness of war created pressures that mediated against even the best attempts to remain estranged. A process of reconciliation thus coincided with the escalation of hostilities. The unique context of war gave the very familiar conflicts of deference and authority an urgency that forced fathers and sons to move beyond arguing in letters and to forge some sort of truce, or a working relationship, that could assuage their colliding loyalties.

Constant reminders of the deadly nature of the war sensitized rebel sons to their fathers' welfare. Isaac Noyes Smith, a native of Charleston, Virginia (later West Virginia), had not hesitated to join the 22nd Virginia Volunteers in 1861, even though his father was a prominent Union man. But by September of that year he had grown "depressed" at the fierceness of the war. It was difficult for him even to rejoice at the prospect of Confederate success. "Virginia is to be red with blood before the end," he noted in his diary, "yet my source of constant trouble is that my father will be in danger." This was at times a terrifying thought, Smith continued, for "I am here actually leading a set of men one of whose avowed objects is the arrest and judicial or lynch murder of my father." His father's welfare distracted Smith from what otherwise might have been a zealous defense of the Confederate cause.[52]

Other sons acted upon these sentiments and offered direct protection to their Union fathers. One rebel son sent $300 in Confederate scrip to his Union father in Tennessee in order to assist him in dealing with rebel merchants. Others made sure their families were protected from Confederate army raids. The *Louisville Daily Journal*, for example, took note when Robert J. Breckinridge suffered no losses after Confederate cavalryman Kirby Smith and his men raided his hometown. Smith had apparently sent Breckinridge a letter of protection ahead of time, and as a result, "not so much as a grain of corn has been taken from him." The paper noted with a hint of envy that Breckinridge was more fortunate in this regard "than many of his Union neighbors." His protection may have been made possible by his son, twenty-four-year-old William. This young man had made it clear to his father he still valued his father's welfare and was relieved to know that his father would benefit from any Confederate setbacks. "I am glad that if we are driven from Kentucky," he wrote in October 1862, "that you . . . will be benefited by our loss."[53]

Rebel sons took some solace in using their positions to protect their fathers. When Brutus J. Clay's other rebel son, Christopher, wrote home warning of that same raid in 1862, he advised his family to bury their silver and warned them that Confederate leaders were plotting to take his father "hostage." To protect his father Christopher called on a "friendly rebel" to watch over him. Christopher Clay was proud of having made these arrangements and prouder yet that no corn or other property was taken from his father during the raid. As his stepmother informed Brutus Clay: "He & E[zekiel] say that you will yet be indebted to your rebel sons for saving your property." To these sons the act of protection exhibited a personal loyalty, and filial duty, that their father had accused them earlier of abandoning. Brutus Clay cared little, however, for what meaning lurked behind their gesture. He replied to his wife that "all the protection I want from my rebel son is to shoot the rogues who come to steal."[54]

The tone of Brutus Clay's response was typical of the state of mind of other Union fathers. Although they too came to the aid of their sons, sending money and clothing in desperate times, often that assistance was accompanied by an expectation that their sons would abandon the Confederacy. A father's aid could be conditional: protection for a son offered in exchange for his deference again. Union fathers thus conceived of their own vision of reconciliation that restored their lost paternal authority, and they often succeeded. To understand why, it is important to remember that events on the battlefield worked in a Union father's favor. Confederate military weaknesses left sons demoralized and in need of material assistance, particularly after 1862. By this time in the war sons were growing increasingly ready — albeit to varying degrees — to seek their fathers' aid and accept a reunion on his terms. Fathers thus could end their conflict as they defined it at the beginning: a personal rebellion that should end with a decisive reassertion of their fatherly authority.

Fathers sometimes looked to the biblical tale of the prodigal son as a model for this conception of reconciliation. The tale offered a useful allegory, for it outlined the process by which an errant son could be welcomed back into the family fold. A son was to first recognize the error of his ways, according to this story, then repent his sins and resubmit himself to his father's protection and authority. His father could then embrace his son again and restore his own status as father. The Confederate sons' likeness to the rebellious son in scripture was not lost on this younger generation. One Kentucky son, broken and tired from fighting, declared himself "prodigal & poor" to his sisters in 1862. Newspaper and magazine editors likewise compared the increasingly desperate position of rebel sons to the prodigal son. The *Missouri Statesman* reported as early as 1861 that the Hannibal, Missouri, mayor's son had returned "prodigal like," and speculated about whether the "fatted calf" would be killed. "Return of a Prodigal Son," is how the *Louisville Daily Journal* entitled one article about a son who deserted his Tennessee regiment and returned home to his parents' embrace.[55]

The story of the prodigal son particularly resonated when more and more border state sons filled the cells of Union prisons, especially at Camp Chase in Ohio and Camp Douglass in Illinois. Prison life was notoriously grim, and some men would do anything to be released — including disavowing their Confederate service. In 1863 the *Nashville Daily Press* recognized the opportunity that this afforded Union fathers and urged "every sensible man . . . to get his son out of the rebel army." Those loyal citizens with "deluded relatives" in the Confederate service can, the paper explained, take advantage of a Lincoln Administration policy allowing prisoners to take the oath of allegiance to the Union as a favor to his friends or family. All it would take was a repentant son and a family willing to write a petition.[56]

Numbers of Kentucky fathers got their chance after a failed raid through the state in 1863 led to the arrest and imprisonment of hundreds of soldiers in John Hunt Morgan's cavalry. Many soldiers escaped along with their leader, but others heeded the urging of their families to take the oath to the Union and be released from prison. Petitions testifying to their newfound Union loyalty poured into congressional offices. In February 1864, Congressman Brutus J. Clay, painfully aware himself of the ordeal of these families, received thirty-three appeals by Union fathers in his congressional district asking for the release of their rebel sons.[57]

In their petitions these fathers typically explained their sons' service as the naiveté of youth. Their sons had been "seduced" into the service by "designing men," they wrote, but after two years of war their sons were now repentant of their errors. One man explained that his son was intoxicated when he joined the rebel army but was immediately sorry once he became sober and realized what he had done. A more typical letter was that of A. H. Calvin of Fayette County, Kentucky. His son had enlisted with John Hunt Morgan the previous year, but once imprisoned wanted to return home as quickly as he could. Calvin was at first unwilling to help his son. "I thought he had not repented enough," Calvin explained, but after receiving numerous letters from his son claiming to be sorry for fighting with the Confederacy, he became convinced that his son was ready to become a "good and Loyal citizen." Calvin promised, as did other Union fathers, that his son would be true to his word. He would make sure of it.[58]

This language of repentance suffused fathers' descriptions of their sons' behavior. "He has repented for the sins that he commited in joining the rebelion," one typical petitioner explained. Fathers listened for signs that their sons were sufficiently prepared to be prodigal. One uncle who had assumed a fatherly role in a boy's life was upset when the boy had not expressed enough willingness to apologize for his service. "Had you said in your note that you had been duped, deceived, betrayed into this rebellion, and that you repented," the uncle wrote, "I would have labored for your release." Because he had not, and because he still sided with men who threatened to kill his uncle, the uncle informed him that "you can never have my aid." This man left the boy to suffer for his sins; the boy had not yet earned forgiveness.[59]

Parents skeptical of their sons' repentance sometimes preferred prison over a parole. "I would much sooner see it then to see you in the Rebble army," one father explained to his son in 1862. This father sympathized with his son's incarceration but refused to help him because he did not trust his son to return home after being released. Other fathers chose to view imprisonment as a boon to their child's health and well-being. The *Louisville Daily Journal* argued that sons would be well cared for while in the custody of United States officials, as they would not experience the cold, hunger, and battlefield dangers that came with Confederate service. Even better, prison could serve as a deterrent to their rebellious behavior: the paper argued that by remaining in prison "they will not be guilty of the awful crime of . . . attempting to strike down the glorious flag that protected them in their cradles."[60]

Some rebel sons themselves preferred remaining in prison to returning home to their parents. Indeed, not all sons were ready to repent, or "swallow the dog," as one Tennessee soldier put it. Thomas Hall of Maryland recoiled at the idea of his father appealing to the Union government for his release. "What—you & my sister go to the Ape as supplicants in my behalf!" he exclaimed after hearing that Abraham Lincoln had been consulted about his release. "I would rather spend my days in prison than obtain liberty by such means." Ezekiel Clay likewise refused his father's arrangement for his parole when it became clear that Zeke would not be exchanged and returned to the Confederate army. Zeke wrote to his father that it was inconsistent with his "views of honor" to deny him the option of an exchange, and explained that the parole as it stood would make him a deserter from the Confederate army—a "brand of disgrace." This should not have been difficult for Brutus to understand, he continued, if he took "a father's interest in my welfare."[61]

Brutus Clay was forced to reckon with the collision between his son's individual honor and that of his family. He never followed through on his threat of disinheritance, and even indicated in a letter to his daughter that he could understand Zeke's latest request. "I would certainly not wish him to do any thing that was dishonorable," he acknowledged, but at the same time he also viewed Zeke's release as something quite honorable. The fact that the government was allowing Zeke to have his home as his prison was showing "greater defference" to him,

Brutus reasoned. More important to Brutus was the honor that would come to him when he stopped his son from taking up arms against the Union again. Zeke would have to come home on these terms — and he eventually did. Like other sons whose fathers obtained their parole, Zeke was powerless to resist his fate. When he eventually returned home, Brutus gave him land and instructed him on building a livelihood closer to the Clay family home. Zeke once again had to answer to his father, and their conflict thus ended with Brutus's reassertion of his paternal authority.[62]

Not all cases ended in such a prodigal reunion. Edmund Patterson, for example, was so angry that his Union father did not come to his aid when he was imprisoned in Ohio that he did not speak to him again until 1890. For some families it took generations to achieve some sort of reconciliation, for others it happened right away. But for almost all, the experience of war as a personal, family conflict — which to sons seemed at first more devastating than the political conflict they preferred — ironically made reconciliation possible. It gave members on both sides an incentive to sort through their differences and a means by which to forge new bonds. That means was the same uneasy territory in which fathers and sons negotiated their relationship before the war. Fathers' concerns about their sons' filial dependence remained, even as they reasserted their own authority with new vigor. And sons still sought to assert their independence, as well as their political views, even as they asked for their fathers' help. This was all familiar to fathers and sons, and though heightened by the stress of war, made reunion manageable. It also made reunion seem possible for the nation.[63]

"As it is in the family and household, so it is in the state, and between States." When the *Charleston Mercury* wrote these words in January 1863, it appealed to leaders North and South to see the intimate connection between family life and national politics. The family provided an ideal "basis of political relations," the paper suggested, one that valued personal ties over differences, affection over conflict. In the *Mercury*'s view, only this domesticated politics could bring a peaceable end to the Civil War. The nation therefore should act like a family writ large.[64]

The *Mercury* was not the only publication that turned to the family to help think about national reconciliation. The divided family — and particularly the divided father and son — became a staple of wartime and postwar short stories, novels, and newspaper essays exploring the question of reunion. This was not the first time the family provided a model for a nation. It was a popular convention in antebellum political culture, both in the United States and abroad, to talk of ideal relations among the states in generational terms. The nation was "father," or sometimes "mother," the states its "sons," and the nation of people, the "great American family." But the line between metaphor and reality blurred in a war that quite literally pitted sons against fathers, and this language — particularly its masculine overtones — took on a new resonance in popular culture. It spoke of tragedy, but it also offered meaning to the conflict. At least in the eyes of Northerners, the Union became the father — often under the leadership of "Father Abraham" — the Confederacy the rebelling or "degenerate son." The war was to bring those errant sons back into the family fold.[65]

Here again the parable of the prodigal son was resonant. On Christmas 1864, for example, *Harper's Weekly* published an allegorical illustration entitled "the return of the prodigal son," and with it an article making clear the North was willing "to welcome the rebellious children back to the family banquet." The Union was ready to reassert its fatherly authority if its sons would repent and return to the national household, this illustration suggested, and this allegory seemed apt for the divided nation. It depicted a reunion of loved ones, but not of equals: a submissive, childlike South was urged to return to the dominant, paternal North. It was imagery not unlike the trope of intersectional "marriage" described by historians of postwar reunion, in which mid-century writers cast the North as the dominant husband, the South the submissive wife. Instead of gender, though, *generations* articulated definite and unequal roles for the sections. The relationship of father and son embodied the central questions of reunion — authority and repentance — while still capturing the ambivalence that would surround the reintegration of the North and South.[66]

This language of prodigality provoked a lively dialogue on the reunion question in the border states. Former Confederates resisted its implication of repentance, while strident Unionists were vocal about its misrepresentation of the South. "It is interesting to note the difference between the Prodigal Son and these returning rebels," Tennessee's Republican governor William G. Brownlow argued in an October 1865 speech that was later published in the *Nashville Daily Press*. Criticizing members of his state legislature who he believed were too lenient on former Confederates — and who frequently quoted this parable — Brownlow noted that the prodigal son "did not secede," like the Confederates, and more significantly, sincerely repented his sins. Nothing about the Confederates, in Brownlow's view, was deserving of the prodigal label. "Do rebels, coming home, come repenting of their unparalleled crimes?" he asked. "Are they not coming back because they are whipped, and 'perish with hunger'?"[67]

Defeat and resignation should not be mistaken with repentance, Brownlow argued, but he was outnumbered in his view. Maryland's governor A. W. Bradford, who had a rebel son of his own, urged a Baltimore crowd in 1866 to "welcome back the returning prodigal." Newspapers across the border states likewise published overtures to the "returning prodigals" throughout the 1860s. In this middle region of the country, where former Confederates and Unionists had to find a way to live side by side again, this family imagery made reconciliation seem possible. Real families that split grappled with the same fundamental questions about the meaning of conflict and loyalty that also troubled leaders North and South. But just as divided fathers and sons could—however uneasily—patch up their differences on the grounds of a stronger personal bond, so too could the nation. The overriding message of this metaphoric image was clear: as a family, the nation could manage both conflict and reconciliation.[68]

Notes

I would like to thank Edward Ayers, Cindy Aron, Joan Cashin, Gary Gallagher, and Scott Taylor for their very helpful suggestions and comments on this essay.

1. Henry Stone to mother and father, February 13, December 5, 1863, Henry Stone to father, September 7, 1863, Stone Family Papers, Filson Historical Society, (hereafter FHS).

2. "What Secession Has Done," *Columbia Missouri Statesman*, October 4, 1861, 1.

3. Joseph C. Breckinridge to Robert J. Breckinridge, February 23, 1862, Breckinridge Family Papers, Library of Congress (hereafter LC). On the Civil War in the border states, see James M. McPherson, *Battle Cry of Freedom: The Civil War Era* (New York, 1988), 276–307; Edward Conrad Smith, *The Borderland in the Civil War* (New York, 1927); Daniel Crofts, *Reluctant Confederates: Upper South Unionists in the Secession Crisis* (Chapel Hill and London, 1989); Lowell H. Harrison, *The Civil War in Kentucky* (Lexington, 1975), 1–13; Michael Fellman, *Inside War: The Guerrilla Conflict in Missouri during the American Civil War* (New York, 1989); Edward L. Ayers *Valley of the Shadow: Two Communities in the American Civil War*, http://www.jefferson.village.virginia.edu/vshadow2; William W. Freehling, *The South versus the South: How Anti-Confederate Southerners Shaped the Course of the War* (New York, 2001).

4. I have found only three cases which demonstrate the reverse: fathers who sided with the Confederacy while their sons fought for the Union.

5. Diary of Johanna Louisa "Josie" Underwood, February 9, 1861, Special Collections, Kentucky Library, Western Kentucky University, Bowling Green, Kentucky (hereafter WKU); "Letters of a Father, No. 1," *Louisville Daily Journal*, September 9, 1861, 2.

6. On the generational divide, see William Barney, *The Secessionist Impulse: Alabama and Mississippi in 1860* (Princeton, 1974), 61–88; Peter S. Carmichael, "The Last Generation: Sons of Virginia Slaveholders and the Creation of Southern Identity," (Ph.D. Diss., Pennsylvania State University, 1996).

7. Samuel Halsey to Joseph J. Halsey, July 23, 1857, Morton-Halsey Family Papers, Special Collections Department, University of Virginia Library (hereafter UVA).

8. John J. Crittenden to George Crittenden, April 30, 1861, Crittenden Family Papers, FHS. See also John Cox Underwood, "Lincoln, Sumner, and Corwin: Reminiscences of Interviews with Charles Sumner, President Abraham Lincoln, and Judge Thomas Corwin," n.d., 3, WKU; Samuel Kennard to his parents, March 12, 1862, Civil War Collection, folder 181, Missouri Historical Society (hereafter MHS); letter from Adjutant General Lorenzo Thomas to Union Secretary of War Simon Cameron, as quoted in Harrison, *The Civil War in Kentucky*, 15.

9. No title, *Louisville Daily Journal*, September 19, 1862, 2. On political socialization within families, see Richard L. McCormick, *The Party Period and Public Policy: American Politics from the Age of Jackson to the Progressive Era* (New York, 1986), 164; George C. Rable, *The Confederate Republic: A Revolution against Politics* (Chapel Hill, 1994), 178; and especially, Jean H. Baker, *Affairs of Party: The Political Culture of Northern Democrats in the Mid-Nineteenth Century* (Ithaca and London, 1983), 22, 29–70.

10. Matthew Page Andrews to Anna Robinson, May 7, July 28, 1861, Charles Wesley Andrews to Matthew Page Andrews, May 27, 1861, Charles Wesley Andrews Papers, Special Collections Department, Duke University, (hereafter Duke). On the social pressures compelling men to fight, see James M. McPherson, *For Cause and Comrades: Why Men Fought in the Civil War* (New York, 1997), 88–89; E. Anthony Rotundo, "Boy Culture: Middle-Class Boyhood in Nineteenth-Century America," in *Meanings for Manhood: Constructions of Masculinity in Victorian America*, ed. Mark C. Carnes and Clyde Griffen (Chicago, 1990), 15–36.

11. Henry Stone to his father, February 13, 1863, Stone Family Papers, FHS; Letters of Matthew and Charles Andrews, Charles Wesley Andrews Papers, Duke. On conscription laws, see McPherson, *Battle Cry of Freedom*, 427–31, 492–94; Phillip Shaw Paludan, *A People's Contest: The Union and the Civil War, 1861–1865*, 2nd ed. (Lawrence, Kans., 1996), 189–90; Emory M. Thomas, *The Confederate Nation: 1861–1865* (New York, 1979), 152–55.

12. Ann Clay to Brutus J. Clay, September 19, 1861, Clay Family Papers, Margaret I. King Library, University of Kentucky (hereafter UKY).

13. Ezekiel Clay to family, September 24, 1861, Clay Family Papers, UKY.

14. Brutus Clay to Ann Clay, October 14, 1862, Ann Clay to husband Brutus, September 25, 1861, Clay Family Papers, UKY.

15. See also William Preston Johnston to Rosa, September 18, 1861, William Preston Johnston Papers, FHS.

16. On affectionate child rearing, see E. Anthony Rotundo, "American Fatherhood: A Historical Perspective," *American Behavioral Scientist* 29 (September/October 1985): 7–13; Robert E. Griswold, *Fatherhood in America: A History* (New York, 1993), 11–30; Stephen Frank, *Life with Father: Parenthood and Masculinity in the Nineteenth-Century American North* (Baltimore, 1998), 23–51; Jay Fliegelman, *Prodigals and Pilgrims: The American Revolution against Patriarchal Authority, 1750–1800* (Cambridge, 1982). On the endur-

ance of patriarchal authority, see Bertram Wyatt-Brown, *Southern Honor: Ethics and Behavior in the Old South* (New York, 1982), 117–98, quote 170; Joan E. Cashin, *A Family Venture: Men and Women on the Southern Frontier* (New York, 1991), 32–52; Joseph F. Kett, *Rites of Passage: Adolescence in America, 1790–Present* (New York, 1977), 45. Additional works on the conflicted relationship between fathers and sons include Steven Mintz, *A Prison of Expectations: The Family in Victorian Culture* (New York, 1983), 59–101; Anne C. Rose, *Victorian America and the Civil War* (Cambridge, 1992), 68–108, 166–68; Mary P. Ryan, *Cradle of the Middle Class: The Family in Oneida County, New York, 1790–1865* (New York, 1981), 32; James Oakes, *The Ruling Race: A History of American Slaveholders* (New York, 1983), 69–71.

17. "Letters of a Father, No. 1," "Letters of a Father, No. 2," *Louisville Daily Journal*, September 9, 20, 1861, 2.

18. Barney, *The Secessionist Impulse*, 61–88; Carmichael, "The Last Generation," 1–37.

19. William Sydnor Thomson to Warner Alexander Thomson, March 24, 1861, Warner Alexander Thomson to William Sydnor Thomson, March 17, 1861, William Sydnor Thomson Papers, Special Collections Department, Robert W. Woodruff Library, Emory University (hereafter Emory). See also Crittenden Family Papers, UKY; John Kemphsall Papers, Tennessee State Library and Archives (hereafter TSLA). Thirty-nine of the 52 families studied for this essay could be found in the census records, and of those 39, 31 (or 79 percent) had rebel sons living in their father's household in 1860. The fact that nearly 50 percent of these sons were also oldest children perhaps underscores just how much they depended upon their fathers to guide their futures. Indeed, sociological and psychological studies suggest that oldest children identify more closely with and are more likely to inherit family legacies than other children. Of the rest of the sons, 31 percent were middle sons, 12 percent were the youngest, and 7 percent were only children (Federal Census of 1860, Kentucky, Maryland, Missouri, Tennessee, Virginia). On birth order and parental identification among siblings, see Stephen P. Bank and Michael D. Kahn, *The Sibling Bond* (New York, 1997), 6–7, 55–56; Susan Scarf Merrell, *The Accidental Bond: The Power of Sibling Relationships* (New York, 1995), 223–30; and Lorri Glover, *All Our Relations: Blood Ties and Emotional Bonds among the Early South Carolina Gentry* (Baltimore, 2000), 28.

20. S. F. Gano to Brutus J. Clay, March 29, 1864, Clay Family Papers, UKY; no title, *Louisville Daily Journal*, October 23, 1861, 2.

21. See Karen Halttunen, *Confidence Men and Painted Women: A Study of Middle-Class Culture in America* (New Haven, 1982), 1–32.

22. William C. P. Breckinridge to Robert J. Breckinridge, July 15, 1862, W. L. Breckinridge to William C. P. Breckinridge, May 3, 1862, Breckinridge Family Papers, LC; C. L. Field to Brutus J. Clay, May 24, 1861, Clay Family Papers, UKY.

23. Diary of C. Alice Ready, March 8, 1862, Southern Historical Collection, University of North Carolina, Chapel Hill (hereafter UNC); "Errant Youth," *Louisville Daily Journal*, September 25, 1861, 3; Henry Stone to James Stone, September 3, 1863, Stone Family Papers, FHS; Christian Ashby Creek, ed., "Memoirs of Mrs. E. B. Patterson: A Perspective on Danville during the Civil

War," *The Register of the Kentucky Historical Society* (Autumn 1994): 351. This estimate of how many sons followed Morgan is taken from a combined count of the following sources: manuscript collections of Union families in which sons served with Morgan; letters written by Union fathers to their Kentucky congressmen complaining of Morgan's influence; and newspaper accounts of service in Morgan's cavalry. See the 1862 issues of the *Louisville Daily Journal* and the *Nashville Daily Press*, and the letters from fathers to Congressman Brutus J. Clay, Clay Family Papers, UKY. On Morgan's appeal, see McPherson, *Battle Cry of Freedom*, 514; James A. Ramage, *Rebel Raider: The Life of General John Hunt Morgan* (Lexington, 1986), 1–7, 65–70, 100–101.

24. Will S. Richart to Brutus J. Clay, January 22, 1864, A. H. Calvin to Brutus J. Clay, January 16, 1864, John [Leer?] to Brutus J. Clay, February 18, 1864, James Hanagan to Brutus J. Clay, March 29, 1864, Clay Family Papers, UKY; Henry Stone to his mother, January 4, 1864, Stone Family Papers, FHS. On soldiers' desire for "adventure," see McPherson, *For Cause and Comrades*, 26–28; Bell Irvin Wiley, *The Life of Johnny Reb: The Common Soldier of the Confederacy* (Baton Rouge and London, 1978), 17.

25. C. W. Andrews to Sarah Andrews, June 1, 1861, Charles Wesley Andrews Papers, Duke; Diary of Louisa Brown Pearl, TSLA.

26. Adeline L. Lawton to Alexander J. Lawton, June 8, 1861, Alexander R. Lawton Papers, UNC; Bethiah McKown to John D. McKown, April 17, June 4, 1863, John D. McKown Papers, Western Historical Manuscript Collection, University of Missouri. On the "republican mothers," see Linda Kerber, *Women of the Republic: Intellect and Ideology in Revolutionary America*, (New York, 1980), 283; Reid Mitchell, *The Vacant Chair: The Northern Soldier Leaves Home* (New York, 1993), xi–xiv, 86–87.

27. Henry Stone to father, February 5, 1864, Henry Stone to father and mother, December 5, 1863, Stone Family Papers, FHS.

28. William Thomson to Warner Thomson, February [?], 1861, William Sydnor Thomson Papers, Emory.

29. Ezekiel Clay to family, September 24, 1861, Clay Family Papers, UKY; Henry Stone to his father, December 29, 1862, July 21, 1863, Stone Family Papers, FHS; Matthew Page Andrews to Anna Robinson, March 10, 1861, Charles Wesley Andrews Family Papers, Duke; Samuel Kennard to parents, March 12, 1862, Letters of Samuel Kennard, MHS. On why soldiers fought, see Wiley, *The Life of Johnny Reb*, 15–27; Randall C. Jimerson, *The Private Civil War: Popular Thought during the Sectional Conflict* (Baton Rouge, 1988); Reid Mitchell, *Civil War Soldiers* (New York, 1988); McPherson, *For Cause and Comrades*.

30. C. W. Andrews to Matthew Page Andrews, May 21, 1861, Charles Wesley Andrews Papers, Duke; Henry Stone, "My Reasons for Evading a [Union] Draft," September 25, 1865, Stone Family Papers, FHS. Of the 39 families located in the census, 33 (or 84 percent) were included as slave owners (Federal Census for 1860 *Slave Schedules*, Kentucky, Maryland, Missouri, Tennessee, and Virginia). On proslavery Unionism, see John C. Inscoe and Gordon B. McKinney, *The Heart of Confederate Appalachia: Western North Carolina in the Civil War* (Chapel Hill, 2000), 83–104.

31. Brutus Clay to Ann Clay, October 14, 1862, Ann Clay to Brutus Clay, September 10, 1862, Clay Family Papers, UKY. See also William Sydnor Thomson Papers, Emory. On disinheritance practices among Southern planters, see Joan E. Cashin, "According to his Wish and Desire: Female Kin and Female Slaves in Planter Wills," in *Women of the American South: A Multicultural Reader*, ed. Christie Anne Farnham (New York and London, 1997), 100–104.

32. On the importance of letters to parenting, see Steven M. Stowe, *Intimacy and Power in the Old South: Ritual and the Lives of Planters* (Baltimore, 1987), 144–47; James Marten, "Fatherhood in the Confederacy: Southern Soldiers and their Children," *Journal of Southern History* 63 (May 1997): 269–92.

33. Diary of Warner Thomson, May 29, 1864, Warner Thomson to William Sydnor Thomson, December 3, 1860, William Sydnor Thomson to Josephine Thomson, July 27, 1864, William Sydnor Thomson Papers, Emory.

34. William Sydnor Thomson to Josephine Thomson, July 27, 1864, William Sydnor Thomson Papers, Emory; Wyatt-Brown, *Southern Honor*, 170.

35. Diary of Warner Alexander Thomson, February 19, 1863, William Sydnor Thomson Papers, Emory.

36. William Sydnor Thomson to Josephine Thomson, July 27, 1864, Josephine Thomson to William Sydnor Thomson, August [?], 1864, William Sydnor Thomson Papers, Emory.

37. Exactly how far the South's honor culture extended is difficult to determine, although the border-state families considered here clearly embraced its tenets. On the idea of family honor, see Rose, *Victorian America and the Civil War*, 182–83; Wyatt-Brown, *Southern Honor*, 132–33. On the intersection of private life and public reputation in antebellum America, see Norma Basch, "Marriage, Morals, and Politics in the Election of 1828," *Journal of American History* 80 (December 1993): 890–918; Jacob Katz Cogan, "The Reynolds Affair and the Politics of Character," *Journal of the Early Republic* 16 (Fall 1996): 389–417.

38. "John J. Crittenden," *Louisville Daily Journal*, March 10, 1864, 2; John J. Crittenden to George Crittenden, April 30, 1861, John J. Crittenden Letters, FHS; no title, *Louisville Daily Journal*, May 5, 1862, 3; "Mr. Crittenden's Position," *St. Louis Daily Missouri Democrat*, June 21, 1861, 3; Crofts, *Reluctant Confederates*, 17; Albert D. Kirwan, *John J. Crittenden: The Struggle for the Union* (Lexington, 1962), vii.

39. John J. Crittenden to George D. Prentice, May 8, 1862, John J. Crittenden Letters, FHS.

40. Ibid. For an overview of the literature on separate spheres, see Linda Kerber, "Separate Spheres, Female Worlds, Woman's Place: The Rhetoric of Women's History," *Journal of American History* 75 (June 1988): 9–39.

41. No title, *Louisville Daily Journal*, March 26, 1862, 2; no title, *Richmond Enquirer*, June 18, 1861, 2; James M. Prichard, "Champion of the Union: George D. Prentice and the Civil War in Kentucky," (master's thesis, Wright State University, 1988).

42. "George D. Prentice and His Son," *St. Louis Daily Missouri Democrat*, October 4, 1862, 1 (reprinted from the *Cincinnati Commercial*); "Letter from George D. Prentice," *St. Louis Daily Missouri Democrat*, October 8, 1862, 1

(reprinted from the *Cincinnati Commercial*); no title, *St. Louis Daily Missouri Democrat*, October 3, 1862, 1 (reprinted from the *Cincinnati Gazette*); "George D. Prentice in Memory of His Rebel Son," *Columbia Missouri Statesman*, December 12, 1862, 1) (printed also in the *St. Louis Daily Missouri Democrat*, October 11, 1862).

43. "William Courtland Prentice: A Brief Sketch," *Louisville Daily Journal*, October 8, 1861, 3; (reprinted as "George D. Prentice in Memory of his Rebel Son," *Columbia Missouri Statesman*, December 12, 1862, 1). On mourning as a private affair, see Halttunen, *Confidence Men and Painted Women*, 124–52.

44. For an analysis of how religious beliefs motivated other men and women to publish similar funeral narratives during the war, see Drew Gilpin Faust, "The Civil War Soldier and the Art of Dying," *Journal of Southern History* 67 (February 2001): 3–38.

45. "A Note from Geo. D. Prentice–Reply to a Slander," *Columbia Missouri Statesman*, March 27, 1863, 3 (also published in the *St. Louis Daily Missouri Democrat*, March 20, 1863); "Parson Brownlow on George D. Prentice — A Withering Expose of a Copperhead," *St. Louis Daily Missouri Democrat*, November 16, 1864, 2. Prentice's pride in his newspaper's Union influence is reflected in a remark he once made to Abraham Lincoln: "[W]ithout it [the *Journal*], Kentucky could not have been kept in the Union" (George Prentice to Abraham Lincoln, November 16, 1861, George D. Prentice Papers, UKY).

46. No title, *Louisville Daily Journal*, March 11, 1862, 2.

47. Ibid. On the southern veneration of bloodlines, see Wyatt-Brown, *Southern Honor*, 118–25; Carmichael, "The Last Generation," 128–30; William R. Taylor, *Cavalier and Yankee: The Old South and American National Character* (Cambridge, Mass., 1979), 145–76. On Davis and Stephens, see William C. Davis, *Jefferson Davis: The Man and His Hour* (New York, 1991); Thomas Edwin Schott, *Alexander H. Stephens of Georgia: A Biography* (Baton Route, 1988).

48. "One of Jeff. Davis's Children in Wisconsin," July 23, 1863, *St. Louis Daily Missouri Democrat*, 1 (reprinted from the *Oshkosh (Wisc.) Northwestern*, also published in *Frank Leslie's Illustrated Newspaper*, August 8, 1863, 311); and no title, *Louisville Daily Journal*, June 18, 1865, 3; "Jeff Davis's Son in the National Service," *Louisville Daily Journal*, February 9, 1864, 2; "Miscegenation by Jeff. Davis," *St. Louis Daily Missouri Democrat*, April 27, 1864, 5 (reprinted from the *Boston Journal*); "Jeff Davis's Son in the Federal Service," *St. Louis Daily Missouri Democrat*, February 3, 1864, 1 (reprinted from the *London Star*).

49. "Miscegenation by Jeff. Davis," *St. Louis Daily Missouri Democrat*, April 27, 1864, 5; "Jeff Davis's Son in the Federal Service," *St. Louis Daily Missouri Democrat*, February 3, 1864, 1.

50. "Davisegination," *Franklin Co., (Pa.) Repository*, June 22, 1864, 1. I have found no evidence of any public response by Davis in the border-state newspapers.

51. "Did the writing of a patriotic song entitle the writer's posterity to immunity in treason and adultery?" the *Louisville Daily Journal* asked hypothetically of Francis Scott Key (no title, August 19, 1861, 2). Of the numerous articles on

the Breckinridges, see "Is He Loyal?" *Louisville Daily Journal*, November 3, 1864, 3; "An Uncle on his Nephew," *Columbia Missouri Statesman*, August 15, 1862, 2. On the Clays, see no title, *Louisville Daily Journal*, October 26, 1863, 3. On the family of Thomas Jefferson, see "Jefferson's Descendants," *Nashville Daily Press*, November 21, 1863, 2.

52. William C. Childers, ed., "A Virginian's Dilemma: The Civil War Diary of Isaac Noyes Smith," *West Virginia History* 27 (January 1966): 184.

53. "Union Feeling at the South," *Columbia Missouri Statesman*, February 28, 1862, 3; "Dr. R. J. Breckinridge," *Louisville Daily Journal*, November 3, 1864, 3; William Breckinridge to Robert J. Breckinridge, October 27, 1862, Breckinridge Family Papers, LC.

54. Ann Clay to Brutus J. Clay, April 17, August 19, September 17, 24, 1862, Brutus J. Clay to Ann Clay, October 14, 1862, Clay Family Papers, UKY.

55. George Starling to Mary, December 22, 1862, Lewis-Starling Papers, WKU; "Return of a Prodigal Son," *Columbia Missouri Statesman*, December 13, 1861, 2; "Return of a Prodigal Son," *Louisville Daily Journal*, February 28, 1862, 4.

56. No title, *Nashville Daily Press*, August 28, 1863, 2; Col. W. Hoffman to Brig. Gen. A. Schoepf, August 4, 1863, and Col. W. Hoffman to Maj. Gen. W. S. Rosecrans, August 7, 1863, *The War of the Rebellion: A Compilation of the Official Records of the Union and Confederate Armies* (Washington, D.C., 1880–1906), ser. 2, vol. 6, 175, 186.

57. See, for example, Burgess Ecton to B. J. Clay, January 8, 1864, Clay Family Papers, UKY.

58. Will S. Richart to Brutus J. Clay, January 22, 1864, Allen Kiser to Brutus J. Clay, February 20, 1864, M. E. Glover to Abraham Lincoln, February 28, 1864, A. H. Calvin to Brutus J. Clay, January 16, 1864, Clay Family Papers, UKY.

59. M. E. Glover to Abraham Lincoln, February 28, 1864, Clay Family Papers, UKY; "Letter from a Rebel Prisoner to his Loyal Uncle — The Uncle's Reply," *St. Louis Daily Missouri Democrat*, April 18, 1862, 1.

60. Henry Whisler to his son, June 5, 1862, Camp Chase Papers, Virginia Historical Society, Richmond, Virginia; no title, *Louisville Daily Journal*, February 20, 1862, 2.

61. Memoirs of John Kempshall, 5, TSLA; Thomas Hall to his father, November 3, 1862, Thomas W. Hall Papers, Maryland Historical Society (hereafter MDHS); Ezekiel Clay to father, January 18, 24, 1865, Clay Family Papers, UKY.

62. Brutus Clay to daughter Martha Davenport, January 21, 1865, Clay Family Papers, UKY.

63. John G. Barrett, ed., *Yankee Rebel: The Civil War Journal of Edmund De Witt Patterson* (Chapel Hill, 1966), viii.

64. "Seymour and the Union," *Charleston Mercury*, January 12, 1863.

65. On family metaphors, see Anne Norton, *Alternative Americas: A Reading of Antebellum Political Culture* (Chicago, 1986), 40–41, 266–73; Jan Lewis, "The Republican Wife: Virtue and Seduction in the Early Republic," *William and Mary Quarterly* 44 (October 1987), 689–721; George Forgie, *Patricide in the House Divided: A Psychological Interpretation of Lincoln and His Age*

(New York, 1979); Mitchell, *The Vacant Chair*; Melvin Yazawa, *From Colonies to Commonwealth: Familial Ideology and the Beginnings of the American Republic* (Baltimore, 1985); Lynn Hunt, *The Family Romance of the French Revolution* (Berkeley, 1992); and Frank Costigliola, "The Nuclear Family: Tropes of Gender and Pathology in the Western Alliance," *Diplomatic History* 21 (Spring 1997): 163–83.

66. "Christmas," *Harper's Weekly*, December 31, 1864, 834. On the equation of reunion with a marriage, see Nina Silber, *Romance of Reunion: Northerners and the South, 1865–1900* (Chapel Hill, 1993), 39–65; Norton, *Alternative Americas*, 132–202, 240–76; Paul Buck, *The Road to Reunion, 1865–1900* (Boston, 1937), 196–235; Jane Turner Censer, "Reimagining the North-South Reunion: Southern Women Novelists and the Intersectional Romance, 1876–1900," *Southern Cultures* (Summer 1999): 64–91.

67. "Gov. Brownlow's Message," *Nashville Daily Press*, October 3, 1865, 2.

68. Governor A. W. Bradford, "Address," [?], 1866, Governor A. W. Bradford Papers, MDHS; "Duty of the Returning Prodigals," *Nashville Daily Press*, May 26, 1865, 2.

About the Contributors

PETER W. BARDAGLIO A Professor of History at Goucher College, he received his doctorate from Stanford University in 1987. His first book, *Reconstructing the Household: Families, Sex, and the Law in the Nineteenth-Century South* (1995) won the James Rawley Prize from the Organization of American Historians.

WILLIAM BLAIR He received his doctorate in 1995 from Pennsylvania State University, where he is now Associate Professor of History and the editor of *Civil War History*. His dissertation won the Allan Nevis Prize. He has published *Virginia's Private War: Feeding Body and Soul in the Confederacy* (1998) and coedited *A Politician Goes to War: The Civil War Letters of John White Geary* (1995).

W. FITZHUGH BRUNDAGE A Professor of History at the University of Florida, he received his doctorate in 1988 from Harvard University. He is the author of *Lynching in the New South: Georgia and Virginia* (1993), winner of the Merle Curti Award, and editor of *Under Sentence of Death: Lynching in the South* (1997).

JOAN E. CASHIN An Associate Professor of History at Ohio State University, she received her doctorate from Harvard University in 1985. She is the author of *A Family Venture: Men and Women on the Southern Frontier* (1991) and editor of *Our Common Affairs: Texts from Women in the Old South* (1996).

MARGARET S. CREIGHTON An Associate Professor at Bates College, she received her doctorate in 1985 at Boston University. She has published *Rites and Passages: The Experience of American Whaling* (1995) and coedited *Iron Men, Wooden Women: Gender and Atlantic Seafaring, 1700–1900* (1996).

J. MATTHEW GALLMAN The Henry R. Luce Professor of Civil War Studies at Gettysburg College, he received his doctorate at Brandeis University in 1986. He is the author of *Mastering Wartime: A Social History of Philadelphia during the Civil War* (1990) and *The North Fights the Civil War: The Home Front* (1994).

JOSEPH T. GLATTHAAR A Professor of History at the University of Houston, he received his doctorate at University of Wisconsin-Madison in 1983. He has published *The March to The Sea and Beyond: Sherman's Troops on the Savannah and Carolinas Campaign* (1985), which won the Bell Irvin Wiley Award; *Forged in Battle: The Civil War Alliance of Black Soldiers and Their White Officers* (1990), which won the award for best book from the American Society of Military History; and *Partners in Command: Relationships between Leaders in the Civil War* (1994).

ANTHONY E. KAYE An Assistant Professor of History at Pennsylvania State University, he received his doctorate from Columbia University in 1999. He is working on a book on slaves in Mississippi that is under contract with University of North Carolina Press.

ROBERT KENZER The William Binford Vest Professor of History at the University of Richmond, he received his doctorate in 1982 from Harvard University. He is the author of *Kinship and Neighborhood in a Southern Community: Orange County, North Carolina, 1849–1881* (1987) and *Enterprising Southerners: Black Economic Success in North Carolina, 1865–1915* (1997).

ELIZABETH D. LEONARD An Associate Professor of History at Colby College, she received her doctorate in 1992 from University of California at Riverside. She is the author of *Yankee Women: Gender Battles in the Civil War* (1994) and *All the Daring of a Soldier: Women of the Civil War Armies* (1999).

AMY E. MURRELL An Assistant Professor of History at the State University of New York-Albany, she received her doctorate in 2001 from the University of Virginia. She is completing a book on families divided by the Civil War.

GEORGE C. RABLE The Charles G. Summersell Professor of Southern History at the University of Alabama, he received his doctorate from Louisiana State University in 1978. His books include *But There Was No Peace: The Role of Violence in the Politics of Reconstruction* (1984), *Civil Wars: Women and the Crisis of Southern Nationalism* (1989), and *The Confederate Republic: A Revolution against Politics* (1994).

NINA SILBER An Associate Professor at Boston University, she received her doctorate in 1989 from University of California at Berkeley. She is the author of *The Romance of Reunion: Northerners and the South, 1865–1900* (1993) and coeditor of *Divided Houses: Gender and the Civil War* (1992).

MARK M. SMITH He received his doctorate in 1995 from the University of South Carolina, where he is now Professor of History. He is the author of *Mastered by the Clock: Time, Slavery, and Freedom in the American South* (1997) and *Debating Slavery: Economy and Society in the Antebellum American South* (1998).

MARY SARACINO ZBORAY An independent scholar, she received her master's degree in anthropology from New York University in 1980. She is the author of numerous articles on American cultural history and coauthor with Ronald Zboray of *A Handbook for the Study of Book History in the United States* (2000).

RONALD J. ZBORAY An Associate Professor of Communications at University of Pittsburgh, he received his doctorate in 1984 from New York University. He is the author of *A Fictive People: Antebellum Economic Development and the American Reading Public* (1993) and coauthor with Mary Saracino Zboray of *A Handbook for the Study of Book History in the United States* (2000).

Index

abolition, 3; and desertion from Union army, 269; and missionaries, 37–40, 202; and Republican Party, 37, 341–42, 345, 352. *See also* emancipation

African Americans: as free blacks in the North, 209–36, 294; as freedpeople in the South, 42–44, 60–84; as fugitive slaves, 211, 219, 342; as soldiers and veterans, 69, 136–56, 223–24, 343–45, 349; as voters, 326; as workers, 71–75. *See also* slavery

assassination of Abraham Lincoln, 2, 252, 262. *See also* Booth, John Wilkes; Lincoln, Abraham; Surratt, Mary

Booth, John Wilkes, 286, 290–92, 295, 297

border regions, 313–31, 332–57, 358–91

Brady, Mathew, 162

Camp Chase, 268, 380

celebrity. *See* fame

Chesnut, Mary, 26–27

children: in the border regions, 3, 313–31; in the North, 216–17, 237, 255; in the South, 41, 67, 112–35

Christmas, 101–3

culture, 3, 86–88, 119, 237–61, 327

Curtin, Andrew, 183–208

Davis, Jefferson, 62, 72–73, 205–6, 351, 376–77

death: of civilians, 347, 352; described by civilians, 244–45; by execution, 270, 286, 299; and mourning customs, 95–96, 119, 374; of soldiers, 48, 93–96, 113–30, 338, 374. *See also* religion

Democratic Party: in antebellum era, 335; and civilians, 172–73, 341–42, 352, 359, 361; and the draft, 185–88, 263–64; and Reconstruction, 326; and secession, 361, 373; in state politics, 352;

and war effort, 244, 342, 347–48. *See also* abolition; emancipation; Lincoln, Abraham; Republican Party

desertion: from the Northern army, 262–85; from the Southern army, 204, 263. *See also* draft resistance

Dickinson, Anna, 159–82

doctors, 237, 268, 286, 297. *See also* medical care

domesticity: as perceived by Northerners in the South, 38, 53; as recalled by Northern soldiers, 85–111

Donald, David Herbert, 149

Douglass, Frederick, 4, 144

draft resistance: in the North, 183–208, 252, 262–77, 351, 362; in the South, 204, 263. *See also* desertion

emancipation, 3; commemorated by blacks, 144–46; as experienced by slaves, 42–44, 60–84; as perceived by whites, 37–56, 252–53, 269, 342–45. *See also* abolition; Democratic Party; Lincoln, Abraham; Republican Party

Evans, Andrew, 333–57

Evans, Sam, 333–57

fame, 4, 161–62, 175–79, 372–73

family life, 2–3, 85; in border regions, 313–31, 333–57, 358–91; in the North, 88–92, 163–65, 215–19, 267–68, 274–75; in the South, 46–49, 67, 92–93, 112–35. *See also* fathers; gender; marriage; masculinity; mothers; women

fathers: and daughters, 90; and draft resistance, 262, 266; and rebel sons, 358–91; and Unionist sons, 333–57. *See also* family life; gender; marriage; masculinity; mothers; women

Fifteenth Amendment, 139

First World War. *See* World War I

Fort Sumter, 244, 252, 279, 334, 360
Fort Wagner, 146
Forten, Charlotte, 39, 43–44, 50, 148
Fredericksburg campaign, 85–111
Free blacks. *See* African Americans
Freedmen's Bureau, 2, 137, 352

gender: as defined by white Northerners, 38, 96, 171; in Mary Surratt's conviction, 300; roles changed by the war, 3, 294. *See also* family life; fathers; marriage; masculinity; mothers; women
generations, 383. *See also* children; family life
Gettysburg campaign, 2, 209–36, 252, 322–24
Grand Army of the Republic, 139–50, 353
Grant, Ulysses S., 66, 337
guerilla warfare, 276, 349

historiography: on children and the war, 313; on civilians, 1; on desertion, 263; on end of slavery, 60–61; on Gettysburg campaign, 210–11; on widows, 112–13
home front: Northern, 12–18, 85–111, 159–82, 183–207, 209–36, 237–51, 271–77; Southern, 12–18, 18–24, 60–84, 101, 112–35

immigrants: in antebellum era, 296, 315; and desertion, 263, 266; and disloyalty, 3–4, 205

kidnapping of free blacks, 213–28. *See also* Gettysburg campaign

Lee, Robert E., 101, 209, 211, 212, 230, 377
Lincoln, Abraham: as emancipator, 61, 65, 219; as object of assassination plot, 2, 286–309; as political figure, 172–74, 193–94, 200, 253, 262, 265, 277, 319, 361. *See also* Republican Party
looting by armies, 67, 69–70, 98–101

marriage: among civilians in the North, 222–23, 245, 275, 288; by ex-slaves, 42, 49, 71; by soldiers, 96, 112–35. *See also* family life; fathers; gender; masculinity; mothers; women
masculinity: of black Northerners, 223–24; of black Southerners, 52, 136, 148; of white Northerners, 38, 268, 352–53; of white Southerners, 379–83. *See also* family life; fathers; gender; marriage; mothers; women
medical care, 91, 94–95, 342. *See also* doctors
memory of the war, 1, 3, 61, 136–56, 230–32, 278–79
mothers, 130, 163, 216, 267, 288–89, 367. *See also* family life; fathers; gender; masculinity; women

Napoleonic wars, 264, 279
Natchez District, 60–84
nurses. *See* doctors; medical care

O'Hara, Scarlett, 113, 130

politics. *See* abolition; Davis, Jefferson; Democratic Party; emancipation; Lincoln, Abraham; Republican Party
prisoners of war, 117, 380–82

race: and gender, 35–59; and identity among whites, 268–69; and prejudice among whites, 3–4, 45, 51, 61, 230, 332–33. *See also* memory of the war; Reconstruction; segregation; slavery
reading habits: in the North, 237–61, 315
reconciliation between postwar whites, 150–51, 231, 327, 384
Reconstruction, 4, 56, 326–27
religion: and abolition, 37, 159; and death, 96, 98; and emancipation, 63, 147; of Mary Surratt, 296–97; and missionary work, 37–38; and reading, 241, 255; and soldiers, 93, 96–98, 379–80
Republican Party: and abolition, 37; and civilians, 172–73, 241–42, 342, 352,

359; and the draft, 204; and Grand
Army of the Republic, 139; and state
politics, 185–89, 192–93, 206, 326,
352. *See also* abolition; Davis, Jefferson;
Democratic Party; emancipation; Lincoln, Abraham

secession, 62, 360–68
Second World War. *See* World War II
segregation: in postwar era, 140–41, 327
sexual assault: of black women, 46–47,
50–51, 139, 216–17
slavery: end of, 12, 19–29, 35–59, 60–84,
144; free blacks kidnapped into, 209–
36. *See also* abolition; emancipation;
Lincoln, Abraham; Republican Party
sounds of war, 9–34
Southern Claims Commission, 2, 60, 75
Southern Unionists, 62, 358–91
Surratt, Mary, 2, 286–309

Thanksgiving, 49–50, 86–88
Thirteenth Amendment, 20, 55, 352
Tubman, Harriet, 148

United States Colored Troops, 70–71,
136–43, 349–53. *See also* African
Americans; slavery

veterans, 3–4, 136–56, 353

widows, 112–35, 163, 288
women: as disloyal Northerners, 274–75,
300–5, 320; as fugitive slaves, 222; as
loyal Northerners, 159–86; as readers,
243–56; as teachers, 35–59; as traders,
74; as wives, 46, 96, 367. *See also* family life; fathers; gender; masculinity;
mothers; widows
World War I, 152, 266, 326
World War II, 265, 266